CLIO AND THE POETS

MNEMOSYNE

BIBLIOTHECA CLASSICA BATAVA

COLLEGERUNT

H. PINKSTER · H.W. PLEKET · C.J. RUIJGH

D.M. SCHENKEVELD · P.H. SCHRIJVERS

S.R. SLINGS

BIBLIOTHECAE FASCICULOS EDENDOS CURAVIT

C.J. RUIJGH, KLASSIEK SEMINARIUM, OUDE TURFMARKT 129, AMSTERDAM

SUPPLEMENTUM DUCENTESIMUM VICESIMUM QUARTUM

D.S. LEVENE & D.P. NELIS (EDS.)

CLIO AND THE POETS

CLIO AND THE POETS

AUGUSTAN POETRY AND THE TRADITIONS
OF ANCIENT HISTORIOGRAPHY

EDITED BY

D.S. LEVENE AND D.P. NELIS

BRILL

LEIDEN · BOSTON · KÖLN

2002

This book is printed on acid-free paper.

Library of Congress Cataloging-in-Publication Data

The Library of Congress Cataloging-in-Publication Data is also available.

Die Deutsche Bibliothek - CIP-Einheitsaufnahme

Clio and the poets / ed. by D.S. Levene and D.P. Nelis. – Leiden ;
Boston ; Köln : Brill, 2002
   (Mnemosyne : Supplementum ; Vol. 224)
   ISBN 90–04–11782–2

ISSN   0169-8958
ISBN   90 04 11782 2

PRINTED IN THE NETHERLANDS

CONTENTS

ABBREVIATIONS

ANRW	*Aufstieg und Niedergang der römischen Welt* (1972–).
CIL	*Corpus Inscriptionum Latinarum* (1893–)
EV	F. Della Corte, *Enciclopedia Virgiliana* (1984–1991).
FGrH	F. Jacoby, *Fragmente der griechischen Historiker* (1923–).
FLP	E. Courtney, *The Fragmentary Latin Poets* (1993)
HRR	H. Peter, *Historicorum Romanorum Reliquiae*, vol. 1, 2nd ed. (1914), vol. 2 (1906).
IG	*Inscriptiones Graecae* (1873–).
ILLRP	A. Degrassi, *Inscriptiones Latinae Liberae Rei Republicae*, vol. 1, 2nd ed. (1965), 2 (1963).
ILS	H. Dessau, *Inscriptiones Latinae Selectae* (1892–1916)
LIMC	*Lexicon Iconographicum Mythologiae Classicae* (1981–)
MRR	T. S. R. Broughton. *The Magistrates of the Roman Republic* (1951–2)
OCD	S. Hornblower and A. Spawforth, *Oxford Classical Dictionary*, 3rd edition (1996).
ORF	H. Malcovati, *Oratorum Romanorum Fragmenta*, 2nd ed. (1955), 4th ed. (1967).
RE	A. Pauly, G. Wissowa, W. Kroll, *Real-Encyclopädie der klassischen Altertumswissenschaft* (1893–).
RG	P. A. Brunt and J. M. Moore, *Res Gestae Divi Augusti* (1967)
Roman Statutes	ed. M. Crawford, *Roman Statutes* (1996)
TLL	*Thesaurus Linguae Latinae* (1900–)

Otherwise, abbreviations generally follow the conventions established by Liddell and Scott, *Greek-English Lexicon*, *The Oxford Latin Dictionary* and *L'Année philologique*.

INTRODUCTION

D. S. Levene & D. P. Nelis

The original versions of the essays in this book were given at a conference with the title 'Augustan Poetry and the Traditions of Ancient Historiography', which took place at the University of Durham on 31 August–3 September 1999. The brief given to the participants was that papers should illustrate 'the ways in which Augustan poetry, in all its dense social and textual engagement, interacts with the traditions of ancient historiography'. This interaction could take a variety of forms: not only direct influences on poets by historians, but also poetic influences on historiography, and wider examinations of themes and techniques that intersect the two genres in Augustan literature.

This book covers the whole of that range. Of course, the interests of the individual scholars has led to greater emphasis being placed in some areas than in others. This is most obvious if one looks at the authors and texts concentrated on. Virgil (and especially the *Aeneid*) and Ovid (and especially the *Metamorphoses*) understandably form the most popular areas of discussion; there is much less (for example) on Tibullus. But the aim of the book overall is to present a wide-ranging general examination of authors, themes and approaches to the topic.

Likewise, the perspectives that these essays bring to the question are very different from one another, and there are significant divergences of approach. Some of them are precise examinations of relatively short texts; others are much more broadly focused. Some are rooted closely in a strong historicism; others explicitly or implicitly challenge a purely historicist methodology. Some argue for direct causal links between poetry and historiography (in either direction); others look to broader parallelisms; still others directly argue *against* significant relationships between the genres. It follows from this that the book as a whole does not and cannot present clear and unequivocal answers to the questions about the relationship between poetic and historical genres in the Augustan age. Rather it should be read as a complex and evolving contribution to a complex and evolving debate: as something that sets challenges and opens up arguments rather than decisively closing them down.

Many of the readers of this book will doubtless be looking into it in order to read particular essays in their particular area of interest, ignoring all those essays which do not appear to touch directly on their current work. That choice is of course the reader's privilege, although one may regret the structures of scholarship and study that have increasingly pushed scholars into specialisation and students into a narrow focus on particular topics. But we have edited and arranged this book in the hope that some people at least will read it through as a whole, and so engage fully with the complexity of debate and argument that it represents. The order of the essays is therefore deliberate and designed to that end: to highlight connections and bring out the developing threads of discussion and debate between the different essays. The main purpose of this introduction is to set out explicitly something of the rationale for our decisions, and so indicate one way in which this discussion and debate might be read.

C. J. Classen's essay stands first (Chapter One): it surveys the full range of Augustan poets, and so establishes the general field upon which the arguments will be fought out. The more important reason for its position is that Classen's conclusions present from the start a sceptical challenge that every other essay in the book has to meet. He argues for the actual influence of historiography on poetry being all but non-existent: that while the poets sometimes may treat historical *topics*, they do not do so in a distinctively historiographical *way*. This distinction between content and form, and its relationship to the question of genre, is in all its manifestations at the heart of the entire book, though the other essays often reach very different conclusions.

What Classen argued across the entire genre, Francis Cairns then examines for a single poem (Chapter Two). His close reading of Propertius 3.3 looks at two aspects of Propertius' presentation of past events — his lack of chronological order and his apparently anachronistic account of Ennius' *Annales* — that have puzzled commentators and led them to propose emendation. Both alleged problems, he argues, stem from a tacit assumption that poetry will in its presentation of the past mirror the approach of historiography. This, he suggests, is not so. In poetry, unlike historiography, we should not expect chronology to lie at the centre of the presentation, nor should we demand clear identification of particular individuals and events: achronicity and conflation is more the norm.

However, atemporality is sometimes found in historians too: does that have any bearing on poetic treatments? V. E. Pagán (Chapter Three) argues that it does. She compares the ecphrastic handling of the Battle of Actium on the Shield of Aeneas with Tacitus' digression on the Varus disaster in *Annals* 1.61–2: both authors address Augustan material which lies outside their strict chronological limits, and do so in ways that in some respects parallel one another. Ecphrasis and digression are ways in which poets and historians respectively introduce apparently extraneous material; and in both of these instances, the presentation is spatially orientated, and the role of the audience viewing within the work is crucial to its interpretation.

Even the achronicity of poetic time may therefore be linked to historiography; poetic achronicity in the wider narrative is examined by Andrew Feldherr in his study of *Aeneid* Book 5 (Chapter Four). He argues for the story of the boxing match in particular involving the reader in a complex of of repetitions and variation. Virgil presents Dares and Entellus in their fight drawing on accounts of earlier fights in order to govern and explain their own behaviour: through a process of selection and imitation they create for themselves models of how the narrative will proceed. The sacrifice of the bull at the end of the match then offers the readers further possibilities of interpretation, by replaying the fight once again in a ritual sphere. The ritual of sacrifice offers to the spectator a role analogous to that of a reader of past events — an historical perspective — and yet a participatory role also: and the poem's handling of the past as a whole closely mirrors this ambivalence. This all, however, also brings historiography back into the frame: for the ambivalence in reading the past finds strong parallels in the historians' handling of contentious historical events.

What is true of Virgil may also be true of Horace. Ellen O'Gorman (Chapter Five) identifies in Horace's *Odes* treatments of the past which may show awareness of historiographical approaches, but at the same time work against them by reading the past in a manner that owes little to historiography directly, but depends instead upon the assumptions of the lyric tradition. She examines the tension between the poems' 'historicist' assumptions concerning the necessary distance of the past and the way in which Horace places himself in the eternal poetic present of lyric (both elements mirrored in the work of various modern critics) — a poetic present which, she suggests, nevertheless imports historical assumptions of its own. Cynthia Damon's study of *Odes* 4.4 (Chapter Six), on the other hand, is also concerned with the potential tension between historical and generic presentations, but suggests a more direct influence of historiography: by comparing Horace with his Pindaric models she argues that he departs from those models by setting the object of praise against a long background of a family past, a past of a sort that was not available to Pindar precisely because the resources of historiography were not available to him. Even if this is a matter of content rather than form, it is still, for Damon, a content that could not exist for Horace in such a way were it not for the traditions of the historians.

Even features of writing that appeared distinctively poetic *may* therefore be argued to be related to historiography more closely than might have initially appeared: we can return to Virgil with this possibility in mind. Clifford Ando (Chapter Seven) and Marko Marinčič (Chapter Eight) both look at how Virgil models particular aspects of Roman history in his poetry. Ando examines the theme of Italian ethnicity, which had been developed by the Roman historians through the second century B.C. and the Social War: Virgil had a variety of models of ethnicity from which to select, and chose one which highlighted a continuous cultural unity of Italy stretching back to primitive times, a unity in which Rome was only one element. Marinčič takes the Arcadia theme of *Eclogue* 4 and relates it to the historical myth of Hercules and Cacus in *Aeneid* 8: Hercules in both works is set up as a paradigmatic model for Roman history as a whole. This too can be linked to historiography more directly: the story of Hercules and Cacus was simultaneously being treated by Livy. But for Livy the story was problematic, and he realised the exemplary potential of the story precisely by distancing it from 'history proper', whereas Virgil incorporates it into the eschatological pattern that he is presenting for the entire history of Rome.

From here we move to Ovid's *Metamorphoses*: three of the essays, with increasingly close focus on particular episodes, all argue in different ways that Ovid is creating his work to a specifically historiographical model. Stephen Wheeler (Chapter Nine) uses the opening lines to suggest that Ovid is recognisably setting the entire poem within an historiographic tradition. In particular, given Ovid's overall chronological structure, he argues that it is influenced above all by the methods of the genre of 'universal history' — 'universal historians' like Diodorus Siculus had the same dilemma of how to handle a multiplicity of narratives within a broad chronological framework, and met it in very similar ways. Philip Hardie (Chapter Ten) then looks at two books in particular within Ovid's narrative — 14 and 15 — and compares them to various models of *Roman* historiography. He sees Ovid's patterning and selection of episodes as in some respects resembling and drawing on Livy's handling of a history of comparable chronological scope, but one that also operates in very un-Livian ways. The ideology of the final episode is more closely derived from Augustus' own presentation of his achievement in the *Res Gestae*, but without unequivocally endorsing the picture that it represents; instead he presents a complex and fractured narrative centring on the theme of the *unus homo*, and so looks forward as much as backwards: his 'history' is as much Tacitean as Livian. Finally we come to Stratis Kyriakidis's study of one particular episode within those books (Chapter Eleven): the catalogue of the Alban kings in Book 14. Ovid, he suggests, was acquainted with the various historical accounts of these that we possess, but adapts them in order to de-heroise the history of Roman foundation; moreover, he argues that insertion of the story of Vertumnus and Pomona was deliberately to replace the violent foundation story that stood in that position in the historians with a love-myth about the *failure* of violence, and so create an alternative picture of the historical process.

From Ovid we move back once again to Virgil, and two essays which examine the interaction between epic and historiography in an area where their themes regularly overlap: that of wars and battles. Andreola Rossi (Chapter Twelve) looks at the motif of sufferings at the fall of cities, a motif which famously for Polybius was the touchstone in his argument that Phylarchus' manner was inappropriate to history. Virgil's employment of this *topos* drew on both tragedy and 'tragic history', but presented a vision that was associated particularly with the latter: the inevitable cycle of destruction and defeat. This vision is however set against an alternative historical picture of Roman destiny and preordained success; it is the tension between these, she argues, that generates much of the ambivalence of the poem. This leads very naturally into Rhiannon Ash's consideration of the handling of battle narratives in epic and historiography (Chapter Thirteen): she argues for a direct influence of Sallust's treatment of the battle of Pistoria in the *Catiline* on Virgil's handling of a battle narrative in the second half of the *Aeneid*. Virgil's battles in general, focusing on a narrow selection of leaders, owes a lot more to the traditions of Roman historiography than to Homeric battles, and one battle in Book 9 appears to draw on Sallust in particular. But Ash takes the story one stage further, and argues that Virgil's battles in *Aeneid* 9 fed back into historiography, being imitated in their turn by Tacitus.

Both Rossi and Ash thereby bring into sharper focus a different aspect of the relationship between the genres: that historiography was not simply a self-standing source from which poets might draw, but itself could depend heavily on poetic models. Ann Vasaly (Chapter Fourteen) looks at another example of such influence: the book-structure employed by Livy in his first pentad. Both within individual books and across the pentad as a whole, Livy employs large-scale structuring techniques, creating symmetrical units and patterned narratives, marking them off sometimes by formal devices, sometimes by the employment of recurrent themes. This procedure may seem very natural to us, but she argues that it is actually unparalleled in earlier historiography: it is a technique derived from the poetry book, and in particular the experimental poetry books published in the triumviral and Augustan periods.

More complex interactions between historiography and poetry are then explored by Molly Pasco-Pranger and Hans-Friedrich Mueller, both of whom take a semi-legendary episode that is treated by historians and poets and use the parallels to trace distinctive features of its development and significance. Pasco-Pranger (Chapter Fifteen) looks at the presentation of Numa in Ovid's *Fasti* and Plutarch's *Life of Numa*, and shows that both authors treat the king in terms that associate him with models of poetic creation and inspiration; she argues that the common source is likely to be Varro, who has influenced not only these two writers, but the whole idea of the poet as *vates* which became so prominent in the Augustan era: thus a key part of the Augustan poet's definition of their own role itself derived from historiographic models. Mueller (Chapter Sixteen) examines the story of the Potitii as told by Livy, Dionysius of Halicarnassus and Valerius Maximus, but also as it is hinted at in *Aeneid* 8. The story, he suggests, operates in the historians as a paradigm of the dangers of religious corruption, and it is precisely Virgil's awareness of this paradigm that provides the resonance to his own brief allusion to Potitius celebrating the rites of Hercules in primitive Rome.

We have moved a considerable way from the original discussion: the range of interactions between poetry and historiography has been argued not only to consist in overlapping content, but it may be possible to argue that the content is significantly related to historiography in a way that goes beyond merely being set in the past. The final essay, by T. P. Wiseman (Chapter Seventeen), provides a comprehensive examination of the central generic issue: whether it is possible to make clear divisions of subject matter between 'poetry' and 'historiography'. Livy, like Varro before him, appears to make a straightforward demarcation between the themes appropriate to the two genres, but in fact the criteria for making the division is harder to discern than might appear. It is not chronological, nor is it to do with the supernatural. Nor is it even to do with the claims of truth in the one genre against pleasure in the other. All of these possibilities were raised in the ancient world, but none could be accepted without considerable qualification, and an historian who sought to confine his history in these ways would be doing so more out of philosophical partisanship than because of accepted rules. That the practices of poetry and history overlapped is, for Wiseman, not merely a chance decision of particular writers: it is intrinsic to the ways in which they were commonly viewed.

According to Livy (*Praef.* 13), poetic prefaces (but not — he claims — historical ones) would appropriately end with a prayer; modern academic prefaces tend to be designed to propitiate our friends and colleagues rather than the gods. We owe a great deal of thanks to various people: to all who spoke, attended and argued at the original conference, to the University of Durham for hosting it, and to the British Academy for providing funding towards it. In the process of organizing the conference and editing and publishing the essays we likewise have been greatly indebted to a number of people: sincere thanks to Joan Booth, I. Du Quesnay, Denis Feeney, Robert Kaster, Chris Kraus, John Moles, Ruth Morello, Sylvia Simms, H. Smolenaars, to Adrian Furse for compiling the indices, and to Marcella Mulder, Michiel Klein Swormink and Gera van Bedaf of Academic Publishers Brill. And we should both like to offer a special word of thanks to Tony Woodman, whose encouragement and advice have been indispensible at every stage.

CHAPTER ONE

CLIO EXCLUSA

C. J. Classen

When elegiac poetry began to take roots in Rome, historiography had established itself and flourished for a long time in various forms as annalistic history, contemporary history, historical monograph and autobiography, and even other literary genres had taken possession of its subject matter. Poets like Ennius had presented the whole of Roman history in epic form, and orators and others had drawn on the large stock of historical examples; unfortunately the scanty fragments of early Roman oratory and early Roman poetry do not allow us to illustrate this as convincingly as one might wish to do.

The first Roman poet whom one traditionally credits with composing elegies (apart from the short poems of Q. Lutatius Catulus, Valerius Aedituus and Porcius Licinius) is Catullus.[1] While his poems show him alive to some political issues of his time and very ready to attack some contemporary politicians, he never refers to figures of the Roman past for comparison or illustration. Where he calls Caesar *cinaedus Romulus* (29.5,9), he uses the vocabulary of contemporary political invective,[2] while expressions like *Romuli nepotes* (49.1) and *Remi nepotes* (58.5) simply refer to the Romans in general, and correspondingly *opprobria Romuli Remique* presumably means no more than 'disgraces to the Romans' (28.15).

Tibullus

The first impression one gets when turning to Tibullus' elegies[3] is that he is more interested in the past. For a number of times he speaks of the earliest period of life at Rome or of human life in general.

---

[1] Cf. Mynors (1958).
[2] See Classen (1998[1962]) 33–40.
[3] Cf. Luck (1988); useful still: Smith (1913); see also Murgatroyd (1980), (1994).

As is only too well known, most of his poems deal with the present, with the experience of love and of disappointed love, or with the future, with the expectation of love. But he alludes to the past when adducing parallels from Greek myths or when presenting the hearer with a mythological figure, e.g. with Medea (1.2; Circe and Medea: 2.4), with Nisus and Pelops (1.4), Peleus and Thetis (1.5), Herophyle and Amalthea (2.5) or with Admetus and Apollo as his servant (2.3) in an elegy in which he idealizes the simple life of peasants: 'Happy those prehistoric days . . .' (*felices olim*: 2.3.29).[4] Greek history, on the other hand, plays virtually no role in Tibullus' elegies, unless one regards the Sibyls of 2.5.67–8 as part of Greek history, though some of them may not be taken to be as Greek and as historical as the Pytho of 2.3.27.

Indeed, closer examination reveals that what Tibullus has to say about the past has little to do with what we would call history, let alone with Roman history. In the third elegy of the first book he paints a picture of life under Saturnus (35–48), when Earth had not been opened up to make travel possible to distant parts. It is a description which has not a single Roman feature — *Penates* and *Lar* are mentioned before this section begins (1.3.33–34) — and it reminds one of the numerous poetic representations of the Golden Age or of the simple life as Tibullus pictures it e.g. in the first elegy of this book (with one or two Roman elements such as *Pales* and the *Lares*: 1.1.20; 36).[5] The same is to a large extent true of the tenth elegy also: The poet portrays life before the invention of iron and swords, life without war and fighting, which he contrasts with his own time, when he himself is forced to take up arms (*nunc ad bella trahor*: 13). Here the Roman colouring is due to the personal elements which the poet introduces ('were I living then': *tunc mihi vita foret*: 11, translation: G. Lee) and to the personal appeal to the family's gods, the *patrii Lares* (15), made of an old piece of wood, who protected the ancestor's home already in the past (17–18); and the past he characterizes by describing the simple forms of the cult of the *Lares*, thus giving it a Roman appearance (19–24).

The gods of the forefathers are invoked in the first elegy of the second book (*di patrii*: 17) in which Tibullus begins his account of a

---

[4] Translation by Lee (1982) 33.
[5] See Wifstrand-Schiebe (1981) esp. 54–107; on 2.3 see 108–20.

country festival (*lustratio agri*) by reminding the audience that traditional practices are being observed (*ritus ut a prisco traditus extat avo*: 2).
Later he praises these gods as masters (*magistri*: 37) for leading people
out of primitive life, teaching them to eat better food, to build houses,
to water the land and other aspects of progress, not of sophisticated
civilisation, but the knowledge and arts to meet the basic requirements of life (37–50). Here, too, Tibullus turns to the past. However,
while he sets the whole in a Roman context, he is not concerned
with Roman history; only in passing he praises Messalla (31–34)
while primarily painting a vivid picture of a feast and the happy
and relaxed atmosphere in the country in Italy. Indeed, one should
not overlook that at the end he speaks of the sound of the Phrygian
pipe that will drown the prayers (85).

The fifth elegy is devoted to Messalla's son who had been made
decemvir sacris faciundis. The poet prays to the god Apollo, recalling
the manner in which he had praised Jupiter and enumerating his
gifts and achievements (in the fashion characteristic of such prayers),
and asks him to teach the young Messalinus the meaning of the
Sibyl's oracles as she had helped Aeneas. First Tibullus gives an
account of Rome before its foundation, as it were, combining remarks
on what had not happened ('Not yet had Romulus built the walls
of the eternal city': 23) with a sketch of the simple life the peasants
led on the Palatine hill or in the area of the Velabrum (23–37). Next
he puts in the Sibyl's mouth what she prophesied to Aeneas about
his victory, his settling in Italy, his founding Lavinium and his being
worshipped like a god, futhermore about the foundation of Alba
Longa by Ascanius, about Ilia sleeping with Mars and finally about
Rome's growing power, destined to rule the world. It is a prophecy
of a very general nature which mentions only a few names from the
legendary pre-Roman period; not a single fact is alluded to from the
time after the foundation of the city. The poet ends with a picture
of a successful and fruitful year that he is praying for, a picture of
the blessed and simple life in the country which in many respects
resembles that which he had painted of the life before the city's
foundation at the beginning of the poem (cf. 79–104, especially
91–104 with 25–38).

More than once Tibullus describes the primeval age, sometimes
in general terms, sometimes adding a few Roman elements; for to
him it represents the ideal life of peace and pleasure and unrestricted
love for which he longs (see 2.3.29–30, cf. 68–80). But Roman history

in the strict sense (of recorded events) he ignores. Even in celebrating Messalla's birthday he pictures the places in West and East where he was successful (1.7.3–20) and also in Egypt (with a long excursus on Osiris and the earliest stages of civilization: 21–48), but without giving details of his victories. And then he refers to the future tasks which Messalla will have to fulfil (1.7.57–62) and to his children for whom he expresses his good wishes; yet contrary to general practice he does not say a word about Messalla's origin, his family, his nobility, his ancestors and their deeds and achievements.

Do we have to conclude that Tibullus is totally immersed in his own time, in his own world, in his love and in his pleasure, that he lacks interest in the past completely or that he is even without any feeling for the past? Or is elegy as a genre incompatible with history, and should we conclude that Tibullus chooses this genre because it leaves no room for references to history? The mythological examples prove that the elegists do not exclude the past altogether, and this is true even of Tibullus; but he takes them all from Greek mythology. However, he does not ignore the Roman past completely either. For, as we have seen, in picturing early stages in the life of mankind, he occasionally adds Roman elements, especially references to Roman religious practices (2.1.51–60; 2.5.27–32), mentioning the *Lares* and the pastoral divinity *Pales* or speaking of traditional rites (2.1.1–2, cf. 7) or of the gods who have guarded his home for generations (1.1.19–20; 1.3, 33–4; 1.10.15–28). But where he honours a contemporary like Messalla he does not follow the tradition in praising his *gens* as well, but reversing the common practice, he even sings 'Messalla, famed for triumphs over Aquitanian tribes, conqueror bringing glory to bearded ancestors' (*gentis Aquitanae celeber Messalla triumphis et magna intonsis gloria victor avis*: 2.1.33–4, text and transl.: G. Lee); or he expresses good wishes for the future: 'Messalla, may your family grow to increase your glory and stand about you in old age with honour' (*at tibi succrescat proles, quae facta parentis augeat et circa stet veneranda senem*: 1.7.55–6, translation: G. Lee). Thus he does not look to the past for glorious deeds and examples, it is the future which he hopes will bring glory to the past generations; and where he speaks of himself as giving an example, it is very much in keeping with the subject matter of his elegies, not with that of historiography: 'Delia, you and I must be Love's paradigm when we are both white-haired' (*nos, Delia, amoris exemplum cana simus uterque coma*: 1.6.85–6, transl.: G. Lee). We may summarize, then, that Tibullus deliberately excludes history from his poems, even contemporary history and even Augustus, with the only exception of Messalla; but he does not ignore Roman tradition which he presents in the form of Roman religion, cults and festivals.

Propertius

And Propertius?[6] At first sight he seems to offer a different picture: In praising Italy he addresses Rome with the words: 'Fame is not ashamed of your history' (*Famam, Roma, tuae non pudet historiae*: 3.22.20) or, as A. W. Camps translates: 'Fame glories in your history'.[7] *Historia*, in most cases in Propertius, means the story which is or the stories which are told about an individual (1.15.24; 3.20.28; 4.1.119, cf. 2.1.16) or which people tell about themselves (4.7.63–4). But in the passage just quoted *historia* is clearly something more, as the context shows: It is all that is and may be said about Rome: 'It is a land more fit for war than disposed to crime: Fame blushes not for your history, Rome. For we stand a strong nation as much through humanity as through the sword: our anger stays its hand in victory' (*armis apta magis tellus quam commoda noxae: Famam, Roma, tuae non pudet historiae. nam quantum ferro, tantum pietate potentes stamus: victrices temperat ira manus*: 3.22.19–22; transl.: G. P. Goold). This meaning, referring to a long chain of events, is supported by another passage in which Propertius exhorts the Romans about to start a campaign in the East: 'Make expiation to the Crassi and their defeat! Away, and serve Rome's history well' (*Crassos clademque piate! ite et Romanae consulite historiae*: 3.4.9–10; trans.: G. P. Goold). What does the poet mean by *Romana historia*? The numerous references to the Roman past in Propertius' poems may be most conveniently divided into three groups: the legendary era, contemporary history and the period between these two, i.e. the period roughly between the death of Romulus and the death of Caesar — a division I am borrowing from the earlier annalists.

---

[6] Cf. Rothstein (1920–4), Camps (1961), (1965), (1966), (1967), Hanslik (1979), Fedeli (1994) and (1965), (1980), (1985), Goold (1990).
[7] Camps (1966) 158 adding 'the ironical understatement (meiosis) adds a positive emphasis'.

Occasionally Propertius refers to events or achievements of the last of the periods mentioned, without actually making it the subject matter of a poem, e.g. when he alludes to the spring where Pollux watered his horse, allegedly in 494 B.C. after the battle of Lake Regillus, hardly a piece of history (3.22.26), to the destruction of Corinth in 146 B.C. (3.5.6) or to the aqueduct of Q. Marcius Rex, built in 144 B.C. (3.2.14; 22.24).[8] In the third poem of the third book, in justifying form and content of his poetry, Propertius first presents himself as having a vision on Mount Helicon (3.3.1–26), and considering possible topics for his poetry he mentions the fight between the Curatii and the Horatii, the Capitol being saved by the geese, the battles of the second Punic war and the trophies which L. Aemilius Paullus brought back home to Rome. It depends on our reading *cecinit* or *cecini* in 3.3.7 whether we assume (reading *cecinit* with Camps, Hanslik, Fedeli and Goold) that Propertius is referring to Ennius' *Annales* or (reading *cecini* with Rothstein and others, following some *deteriores*) to poems he is dreaming of writing himself.[9] At any rate, Apollo, in a traditional fashion, known from Callimachus and others,[10] turns him away from such plans, as does Calliope at the end of same poem, warning him against the singing of wars in general and of the victory of Marius and the defeat of the Teutons or of the Swabians in particular (this an event of contemporary history: 3.3.39–46).[11] In an earlier poem, addressed to Maecenas, he himself explicitly rejects such topics, adding that if Fate had given him the talent he would compose epic poetry, but not about Greek myths or history, not about the beginnings of Rome, not about the threats of Carthage or of the Cimbri, and not about Marius (2.1.17–24), but he says: 'I should tell of your Caesar's wars and policies, and after mighty Caesar you would be my second theme' (*bellaque resque tui memorarem Caesaris, et tu Caesare sub magno cura secunda fores*: 2.1.25–6, transl.: G. P. Goold).

Apart from the legendary era, clearly, it is periods of great danger which he regards as possible subjects for his poetry. Elsewhere (3.11)

---

[8] For the battle cf. Cicero *N.D.* 2.6, Livy 2.19–20; for the destruction of Corinth Polybius 39.2 and 3 (13 and 14 = 40, 7 and 8); for the *aqua Marcia* see D. Cattalini, in Steinby (1993–9) I 67–9.

[9] For further discussion of this question see Cairns, ch. 2 below.

[10] *Aet.* fr. 1.21–28, Vergil, *Ecl.* 6.3–5; later Horace, *Odes* 4.15,1–4; see also *S.* 1.10.31–5 (Quirinus).

[11] Cf. Cassius Dio 51.21.6.

we find Augustus' victories and achievements compared with the great deeds of the past, e.g. of M. Curtius and of P. Decius Mus, of Horatius Cocles and of M. Valerius Corvinus, of P. Cornelius Scipio Africanus, M. Furius Camillus and Cn. Pompeius and with the defeat of Hannibal, Syphax and Pyrrhus. Modern editors and commentators have arranged and rearranged the verses in which these Roman heroes and *imperatores* and their enemies are mentioned (59–68) without coming to generally accepted results.[12] What they agree upon is that they are all assembled here to stress that Rome need not have feared Cleopatra because the young Caesar was there to protect the city (66) and that this hero saved Rome like many others before him, perhaps even in a manner surpassing the others. For, as he summarizes, 'Leucadian Apollo will tell of a host turned in flight: one day put an end to a war of such vast array' (*Leucadius versas acies memorabit Apollo: tanti operis bellum sustulit una dies*: 69–70, transl.: G. P. Goold). The past is not presented for its own sake nor at length with details, but merely to provide a foil for Octavian's success. Similarly Propertius speaks a little earlier of Cleopatra's threat to the statues of Marius or to the freedom gained through the expulsion of Tarquinius, a threat rendered meaningless by Augustus (45–50), or he reminds the reader of Pompeius death (34–6).

The dead Marius together with the dead Jugurtha illustrates the fact that the victor is spared by death no less than the vanquished (3.5.15–16), while the dead M. Claudius Marcellus together with Caesar is referred to as having enjoyed the privilege of rising to the stars (3.18.33–4). And from the stars, the poet says in the last book, Caesar is admiring Augustus (4.6.59–60), while he lists Claudius Marcellus with Romulus and A. Cornelius Cossus as those who succeeded in personally killing an enemy and dedicated their arms as *spolia opima* (4.10). The poet describes at length how each hero killed his enemy (*ferit*: 46); for it is his intention here, in accordance with his earlier announcement ('I shall sing of rites and gods and ancient names of places': *sacra deosque canam et cognomina prisca locorum*: 4.1.69), to explain the name of the temple of Iuppiter Feretrius; and as alternative interpretation he points to the fact that the victors carried the arms of the vanquished (*seu quia victa suis umeris haec arma ferebant*: 47).

---

[12] While Rothstein leaves the order of the mss., Camps and Goold place 65–8 before 59–64, Hanslik and Fedeli 67–8 before 59–66.

Here he chooses an aetiological elegy with the explanation of the name presumably because Augustus had rebuilt the temple (or shrine) — admittedly at an unknown date before the death of Nepos.[13]

I should add that in the first elegy of the fourth book in which Propertius announces the programme I have just referred to he speaks mostly of the mythical past of Rome, except for one brief line naming Decius and Brutus ('Then came the heroism of Decius and the axes of Brutus': *hinc animi venere Deci Brutique secures*: 4.1.45; transl.: G. P. Goold) which he combines with a line on Octavian and Venus as his ancestor: 'And Venus herself bore her Caesar's arms' (*vexit et ipsa sui Caesaris arma Venus*: 46; transl.: G. P. Goold). Great men of the past are briefly praised in the funeral elegy for Cornelia (4.11) as ancestors of herself, the daughter of P. Cornelius Scipio (probably cos. suff. 35 B.C.) and Scribonia (4.11.29–30; 32; 37–40), and as ancestors of her husband, L. Aemilius Paullus Lepidus (4.11.39–40);[14] and for comparison with Cornelia the poet adduces the Vestal virgins Claudia Quinta who helped bringing the ship with Cybele to Rome in 205 B.C. (4.11.51–2) and Aemilia who also succeeded in proving her chastity (53–4).[15] The reason why Propertius paid so much attention to Cornelia and even wrote this elegy is, no doubt, that her mother Scribonia was married to Octavian. And though he divorced her after a brief period, Cornelia and her husband seem to have enjoyed the emperor's special favour; for he was chosen to be censor in 22 B.C., the year, incidentally, in which Cornelia died. Propertius uses the past also to glorify others who are connected with Octavian, e.g. Maecenas whom he addresses in the elegy 3.9: 'These decisions of yours will equal those of the great Camillus' (3.9.31–2).

Our survey so far seems to suggest that in addition to the numerous immediate references to the young Caesar or to Augustus and his victories and other achievements it is only in connection with the emperor that Propertius turns to illustrations and parallels from the legendary era or from history. However, occasionally he speaks in other contexts of the past, mostly in general terms without naming particular individuals. The line quoted above in which he assures

---

[13] See Coarelli in Steinby (1993–9) III 135–6, who suggests 32–30 B.C.
[14] On these see Syme (1986) 110–12, 246–9.
[15] Cf. Cicero *Har.* 27, Livy 29.14.12, Ovid, *Fast.* 4.305–44 (Claudia Quinta, see below) and Dionysius of Halicarnassus *AR* 2.68.3–5; Valerius Maximus 1.1.7 (Aemilia).

Tullus that Fame is not ashamed of Rome's history (3.22.20) is pre-
ceeded by general praise: 'All the (aforementioned) marvels shall give
way to the Roman land; here nature placed all that ever was (of
any value) anywhere' (*omnia Romanae cedent miracula terrae; natura hic
posuit, quidquid ubique fuit*: 17–18), and it is followed by a verse which
briefly summarizes what he considers to be the basic factors in Roman
history, as we have seen, military power and respect for others
(3.22.21–2: *ferrum* and *pietas*). For *pietas* W. A. Camps prefers the
translation 'righteousness' and adds '*pietas* embraces all conduct gov-
erned by a proper sense of obligation.'[16] It is worth noting here that
what Roman coins illustrate and emphasize till the end of the Republic
may be summarized as *virtus* and *pietas*.[17]

Once Propertius makes a door remember the old times when it
was opened for triumphs and was dedicated to Chastity (of Tarpeia
or of the patricians — depending on whether in 1.16.1–2 one accepts
Tarpeiae, the reading of the manuscripts, or prefers Phillimore's
conjecture *Patriciae*).[18] In another poem he says in the past houses
were pure till someone started decorating them with lewd paintings
while now temples (frequented in the past) are covered with weeds
and cobwebs (2.6.27–36). As in these verses the poet generalizes and
gives us an idealized picture of the past, so he generalizes in contrasting the girls of the past and the girls of his own days, e.g. in
2.25.35–6, where one cannot even be sure whether he thinks of
Greeks or Romans: 'But if the times now were, which girls of old
liked well, I should now be in your shoes' (*at si saecla forent antiquis
grata puellis, essem ego quod nunc tu*; transl.: G. P. Goold); W. A. Camps
even translates: 'but if the manners that the heroines of old approved
were still in vogue today', thus taking us back into the heroic age,
i.e. well beyond history.[19] Other comparisons or rather contrasts are
even less historical, as the poet sets girls and wives of his own time
(*puellae* and *nuptae*) against such faithful ones of Greek myths as Euadne
and Penelope (3.13.24), and they are followed by a picture of simple
life and of uninhibited love, especially as enjoyed by the young in
the country in Italy no less than in Greece (3.13.25–46). While in this
poem Propertius turns to Greek mythology and history to illustrate

---

[16] Camps (1966) 158.
[17] See Classen, (1993 [1986]) 39–61.
[18] *Tarpeiae*: Rothstein, Camps, Hanslik, Fedeli; *Patriciae*: Goold.
[19] Camps (1965) 174.

the change brought about by gold (*aurum omnes victa iam pietate colunt*: 48, cf. 51–8), in 2.32.47–8 he makes people like the old Tatius and the severe Sabines serve as examples to be confronted with Lesbia as a contemporary representative of those who disregard proper behaviour. Clearly, not even the slightest attempt is made by Propertius in his poems to use Roman history for his poetic aims, let alone to do it justice. Indeed, with regard to himself, he remarks that he has neither much inherited wealth nor famous ancestors (*cui parva domi fortuna relictast nullus et antiquo Marte triumphus avi*: 2.34.55–6), that he does not care for a woman who takes a pride in her famous ancestors (2.13.10), and at his funeral he does not expect, indeed, he does not wish a long succession of masks of ancestors (2.13.19–20). For, as he points out in his elegy on Marcellus, even noble birth could not prevent his early death (3.18.11).

Propertius speaks of Roman history, but he does not appear to be interested in the course of events, the development of the empire, the great men and their achievements or the causes for the moral decline. However, he does make use of the Roman past where it helps him to praise Octavian/Augustus or such other important contemporaries as Maecenas; but for the emperor he prefers to draw on the very distant age of Romulus or even of Aeneas. Admittedly, Propertius' fourth book has more of a Roman colouring; and by his announcement 'I shall sing of rites and gods' (*sacra deosque canam*: 4.1.69) in a couplet by some taken to be the end of the first elegy, he raises hopes and expectations. But in the following couplet he makes the astrologer warn him at once: 'Where do you rush to in your folly, to sing *vaga verba*, words with no clear direction (such as prophesies seem to be)'.[20] Thus he confines himself, in fact, in this last book to some gods, to Apollo in the sixth poem[21] and to Iuppiter Feretrius, because Augustus rebuilt his temple (4.10, see above note 13), further to Vertumnus (4.2), a virtually unknown god[22] of Etruscan origin (like Maecenas) and fourthly to the founding of the Ara Maxima by the thirsty Hercules whom he introduces as *Amphitryoniades* and pictures as in his anger forbidding girls to pray at his altar (4.9).

---

[20] At 4.1.71 I read with some *deteriores*: *quo ruis imprudens vaga dicere verba, Properti?*
[21] Camps (1965) 104 remarks, 'The central feature of this elegy is a narrative ... of the battle of Actium'.
[22] Camps (1965) 72 notes, 'We know hardly anything of Vertumnus beyond what we read in the present poem'.

This is not what one expects from the announcement *sacra deosque canam*, even less — in another aetiological poem — the story of the love-sick Tarpeia who betrayed her country (4.4).

Propertius does not lack national pride. Indeed, once he asks himself 'Why do I seek examples from the Greeks', in this case, admittedly, for mistakes or crimes (*cur exempla petam Graium*: 2.6.19–22), and he praises Italy (3.22, see also 4.1.53–4), he is concerned about Rome (3.13.59–61) and about the degeneration of her people (4.1.37–8), and he is proud of Rome and her history (3.22.20 [see above]; 3.4.10, cf. also 3.1.15) — always in elegies of the third or fourth book. But already in the first book he expects to be regarded as superior to the great poets of Rome (1.7.21–2), and such sentiments occur again in the last lines of the second book (2.34.81–94) as at the beginning of the third (3.1.1–2; cf. also 22–3) and in the first elegy of the fourth book: after speaking of Ennius and his poetry he asks Bacchus to offer him ivy leaves for a crown so that Umbria may boast of his poems, Umbria, he adds, the country of Rome's Callimachus (*Umbria Romani patria Callimachi*: 64).

Virgil and Horace

It would be tempting now to consider the other elegies of the corpus Tibullianum, the love elegies of Ovid, the lyric poems of Horace and Virgil's *Aeneid*. For the attitude towards history and the way it is used, in each case reveal important aspects of the poet's understanding of his poetry and its function, of his relation with and attitude to the literary tradition and to other poets, past and present, to his contemporaries in general and the emperor in particular, and also his religious feelings, his views of life and death.

A few remarks on Virgil, Horace and Ovid have to suffice as basis for a comparison with Tibullus and Propertius and some general considerations. In Virgil's *Eclogues*[23] there are a few allusions to contemporary poets and contemporary events such as the confiscation of land as well as to Caesar and the young Caesar Divi filius. But in pastoral poetry there is no place for history, not even for historical examples or comparisons, and the same is true of the *Georgics*,

---

[23] Cf. Mynors (1969).

though there the references to Caesar and the future emperor are more frequent, and in the praise of Italy, the *laudes Italiae* (2.136–76), Virgil illustrates the *genus acre* of the inhabitants with a few names of the past, the Decii, perhaps the Marii, the Camilli, the Scipiadae and finally Caesar, the young emperor (2.167–72). But while one has extracted philosophical, political and religious ideas (cf. e.g. 1.498) from the poem, for historical ideas one looks in vain. They are, however, most obvious in the *Aeneid*, the most 'historical' poem of the time. As we all know, one meets with allusions to the legendary period (apart from Aeneas and his time), e.g. to Romulus and some of the later kings (Numa; Ancus Marcius; Tarquinius Priscus), with the prophetic speech of Jupiter in the first book (257–96) and the description of Aeneas' shield in the eighth book, both culminating in triumphs of Augustus (1.291–6; 8.714–28), in the peace restored by him and the greatness of the Roman empire: *Romanos rerum dominos gentemque togatam* (1.282). This idea is more explicitly expressed in Anchises' account of the great men in Roman history (6.847–53); in the last lines (6.851–3) the poet interprets Rome's successful development, as he sees it, by revealing some basic principles of Roman policy, and he continues to do so in the following verses on the two Marcelli (855–86) by stressing the *pietas*, *prisca fides* and *invicta bello dextera* of the young Marcellus (878–9). Here Virgil betrays a deep understanding of Roman history and of the factors responsible for Rome's greatness and necessary for the future of the empire, though he does not write a work of historiography, and possible influence of works of history must be regarded as marginal.

Again, to characterize Horace's views in a few words is not an easy task.[24] In his early poems he mentions the young Caesar, later he addresses him, praises him, and celebrates his victories (*Epode* 9; Odes 1.37; 1.12.46–60) and, finally, he dedicates the first epistle of the second book to him. Thus the poems mirror the development of a relationship which culminates in a personal friendship. Moreover, many of the poems seem to express and support ideas and ideals similar to those of Virgil's *Aeneid*, *i.e.* that which has been regarded as 'Augustan' so that some scholars have called Horace a court-poet, a *Hofdichter* or a propagandist, whereas others, pointing to the poems which lack such sentiments or to his refusal to praise the emperor's

---

[24] Cf. Borzsák (1984), Shackleton Bailey (1985).

res gestae, regard him even as anti-Augustan.[25] I shall return to the use of these terms later. Here it suffices to say that neither group does Horace justice; for no poet true to his calling and certainly not Horace ever subordinates his poetry to political propaganda. Indeed, having been involved more directly in the civil war than Virgil and escaped its dangers, he shows his concern about Rome and her future in some early political epodes, and this he maintains throughout his life, though anxiety gives way to confidence in the young Caesar after his victories and later to trust in Augustus and his policy and measures. What matters here is not that Horace speaks of contemporary events or persons nor that he makes use of Greek mythology or Greek history, but that in addition to Aeneas, Romulus and other kings he refers to some of the great heroes of Roman history.

While in the *Satires* he refrains from illustrating his moral lessons with examples of the past[26] and mentions Cato and Sulla in a not very complimentary manner (*Satires* 1.2.31–2; see also *Odes* 3.21.11–12; *Epistles* 1.1.13–14) and Laelius, Scipio and others with little or no respect (*Satires* 2.1.16–17; 71–4, see also 2.1.65–8; further 1.6.12–18; 19–21; 41–2), in the ninth *Epode* the triumphs of Marius and Scipio serve for comparison. Later in the *Odes* Cato (2.15 with Romulus and the *veteres*), in the first book of the *Epistles* Curius Dentatus and Camillus are introduced as types representing the past (1.1.62–4 — apart from general phrases: *gens antiqua; veteres*), similarly Cato and Cethegus in the second epistle of the second book (2.2.115–18) and the Gracchi and the Mucii Scaevolae as individuals (2.2.87–9). Almost a whole ode is given to M. Atilius Regulus (3.5.13–56), and Regulus also forms a large group with the Scauri, with L. Aemilius Paulus, C. Fabricius Luscinus, M.' Curius Dentatus and M. Furius Camillus, enumerated after Romulus, Numa and others as heroes of whom the poet might sing (1.12.33–48). But it is not so much in such a passage or in the *carmen saeculare* that we notice Horace's historical awareness, it is in a phrase like *Graecia capta ferum victorem cepit et artis intulit agresti Latio* (*Epistles* 2.1.156–7) that he shows his understanding of Rome's history and the historical situation, just as a sentence like *quid leges sine moribus vanae proficiunt* (*Odes.* 3.24.35–6) reveals his understanding of his own time and its social and moral problems.

[25] See e.g. the account of Doblhofer (1992) esp. 36–41.
[26] See Classen (1998 [1993]) 171–86.

In addition one may refer to the Roman Odes (*Odes* 3.1–6) which
point to his aims and intentions: he endeavours to stress the need
for new moral standards or rather a redefinition and revival of the
moral values. This is, of course, not new, as Sallust's writings teach
us. But unlike Sallust Horace does not turn to history in order to
analyse the decline, nor does he use historiography and its patterns
as medium to address his contemporaries. In the *Satires*, he uses
examples from everyday life, later from the past; but it is individuals he mentions without placing them in their historical context, let
alone attempting to understand the course of events. Only in judging the achievements of Lucilius and in discussing the choice of
vocabulary in poetry does he show his sense of history.[27]

Ovid

Turning to Ovid[28] I shall leave aside — at least for the time being —
the problem whether he was Augustan, un-Augustan or anti-Augustan
and rather consider his attitude towards history. In the *amores* apart
from the mention of figures from the time of Aeneas and Romulus,
of a few writers and of some contemporaries, especially the young
Caesar and his victories (1.2.51–2; 3.12.15), there is only one reference to M. Furius Camillus and his conquest of Falerii (3.13.2 in
the poem in which Ovid stresses the Greek origin of the festival
there described). Similarly in the *Ars Amatoria* once only we encounter
P. Cornelius Scipio honouring Ennius who is allowed to share his
grave (3.409–10).

    And the *Fasti*? Again the earliest period from Aeneas to Romulus
and to the kings plays a considerable part either in connection with
Augustus or with the foundation of cults and temples or with both.
From later centuries there are some brief allusions to individuals or
particular events and a few longer episodes, interestingly two from
the early Republic, the death of the Fabii (2.195–242) and the threat
to the Capitol in the sixth book (6.351–94), two from the Punic wars,
the saving of the *palladium* from the burning temple of Vesta by the

---

[27] Cf. *S.* 1.10.64–72, *Ep.* 2.3.46–72 (without transposition of 45), see also 270–4.
[28] Cf. Kenney (1995), Anderson (1977), Alton, Wormell (1997); see also Bömer
(1957–8), (1969–86).

Pontifex Maximus L. Caecilius Metellus (241 B.C.), also from the sixth book (437–54), and the bringing of the statue of Cybele to Rome in the fourth book (247–92 with the Claudia episode and remarks on the cult in the temple later built by a Metellus: 293–348).[29]

Furthermore, in the first book (589–606) we find a list of *cognomina* given for outstanding military services such as *Africanus* and *Isauricus, Creticus* and *Numidicus*, not in chronological order, culminating in *Magnus* (for Pompeius) and *Maximus* for the Fabii, the greatest and yet not equal to *Augustus*, the *cognomen* which the emperor shares with Jupiter only, as the poet stresses (1.607–16). A few further remarks may help to appreciate Ovid's intention more clearly:

1) Twice he narrates episodes in which a Metellus plays a prominent part and, in addition, two Metelli are mentioned with their *cognomina*; 2) the highest position in the list of *cognomina* (*Maximus*) is given to the Fabii who are also the subject of a story in the second book; 3) the enumeration of the *cognomina* is not used by Ovid to describe at length the heroic deeds of the *imperatores* he lists — in the case of Nero Claudius Drusus he even speaks of his death (1.597) — and together they are introduced as foil for the emperor who has conquered more and is, therefore, given a more illustrious name; 4) Ovid attributes the saving of the Capitol only once to a military action (6.185–6), twice to other, not very heroic factors, to the legendary geese (1.453–4, a fact that does not prevent them from being sacrificed themselves) and to the last loaves of bread by means of which the Romans induce the enemy to withdraw (6.351–94). And he speaks of the defeat of the Fabii at the river Cremera (2.195–6) and of the death of other great men, twice of the death of the consul C. Flaminius (217 B.C.: 6.243–4; 763–8), once of the death of the consul P. Rutilius Lupus and of the former consul T. Didius on the same day the following year (6.563–8).[30] A little earlier (6.461–8) he combines a victory (of D. Iunius Brutus in Spain) with the defeat of M. Licinius Crassus Dives, also mentioned elsewhere (5.579–94) where the poet praises the emperor for retrieving the Roman standards

---

[29] On the saving of the *palladium* cf. Cicero *Scaur.* 48, Dionysius of Halicarnassus *AR* 2.66.3–6; on the temple built by Metellus see Bömer (1957–8) II 237–8 (without deciding whom Ovid means), Pensabene in Steinby (1993–9) III 206–8 (suggesting Q. Caecilius Metellus Numidicus, cos. 109 B.C.).

[30] Death of C. Flaminius, Polybius 3.82.1–84.6; of P. Rutilius Lupus, Appian *BC* 1.191–4; *MRR* II 36 uses Ovid as evidence for T. Didius' death in 89 B.C., but see on the problems involved Bömer (1957–8) II 376–7.

from the Parthians; and the victory of the dictator A. Postumius
Tubertus in 431 B.C. is referred to (6.721–4), no doubt, because he
used a quadriga with four white horses such as was granted to Caesar
in 46 B.C.[31] It should be noted also, that most of these references
to death and defeat are found in the sixth book.

Clearly, Ovid does not appear to be anxious to record great deeds
of the past when speaking of great names or of famous locations
such as the *lacus Curtius* (6.403), let alone betray an interest in the
course of history, in the causes of particular events or achievements,
in the great past or in the future of the empire. Rather he refers to
defeat, danger and crime (e.g. the *crimen regni*: 6.643), and this with
increasing frequency. And as he represents Romulus both in a positive and a negative light, as was common practice in the time of
the Republic,[32] a good many opportunities are left unused where
Augustus might have been praised; this is at least the view of Sir
Ronald Syme which, however, G. Herbert-Brown has disputed.[33] At
any rate, despite their topic the *Fasti* do not allow us to attribute to
Ovid a genuine interest in history or in Roman history, let alone in
patterns of historiography; and the same is true of the *Metamorphoses*,
though they end with Augustus' triumph (15.847–70) and the whole
is structured by a chronological order.[34]

'Augustan' Poetry

I have dealt with five poets here, all active in the so-called Augustan age
and all influenced by contemporary events, especially by C. Octavius
becoming first C. Iulius Caesar, then Imperator Caesar Divi filius
and finally Augustus; but they overlap only partly in time and write
very different kinds of poetry, displaying very different attitudes to the
past, to history and to historiography. They are all labelled 'Augustan',
and we are therefore called upon to explain the differences indicated.
For a number of reasons we tend to divide history (also history of
literature or history of art) into sections and give each period of time

---

[31] On Tubertus' triumph cf. Diodorus Siculus 12.64.1–2, Livy 4.29.2–4.
[32] See Classen (1998[1962]) 21–54.
[33] See Syme (1978) 23–36, Herbert-Brown (1994) 215–33.
[34] On the fifteenth book see Hardie ch. 10 below; on chronological order in the
Metamorphoses see Wheeler ch. 9 below.

a particular name, whether Republican or Augustan age and Tudor or Victorian age and — even less forgivable — fifth or fourth century etc. There is also a tendency to assume that all people or at least the majority or the average persons of a particular period are typical representatives of their time and share moral attitudes and political views, artistic tastes and aesthetic judgments. Furthermore, individuals are regarded as monolithic types, whether Aeneas or Romulus, Brutus or Camillus, Scipio or Cato, Sulla or Catiline, each of them being supposed to represent one particular way of life, one quality or one homogeneous group of qualities, implying certain views and attitudes as regards gods and men, state and society, politics and culture. But life is not like that, and literature even less so. There is no real art, no poetry without originality, without creativity, without deviation from the tradition; and there is no achievement without disappointment or failure, there is no guilt without some redeeming feature, without some positive aspect. As most individuals show different traits in their character, an artist may place different or even conflicting elements side by side in a work of art, an author different or even conflicting sentiments in a piece of literature, provided he chooses an appropriate form. More important, there is no reason why authors, living in the same age, may not react very differently to their time and to their contemporaries or to tradition. It is for this reason that I prefer not to use such generalizing terms as Augustan or Republican, or for that matter, anti-Augustan.

Of course, all poets, indeed all writers are conditioned by the world they live in, their social, cultural and political environment, by their education and their personal experiences, by the literary tradition and the language they write in. But authors are not helpless victims of their age; they are all free to react in a very personal, one might say creative manner, free to react to the contemporary scene, to conform or rebel, and free to change their views, to develop new attitudes, to take into account (or ignore) political changes as well as new literary tastes of the respective audiences — and ancient authors are more audience-conscious than modern writers, including modern scholars. They may, of course, also indicate that they do not care for large audiences.[35] Like all authors, poets are also free

---

[35] Cf. e.g. Horace *S.* 1.4.71–4; 10.73–91 (following Lucilius, *frr.* 588–90; 592–3; 594; 595–6 Marx = *frr.* 589–90; 594; 596; 591–3 Krenkel), see also *Ep.* 1.20.

to choose whichever genre they consider most appropriate for their
subject and the particular purpose they have in mind in presenting
their work to the public, and poets like Ennius, Horace and Ovid
demonstrate the extent of this freedom as they move from one genre
to another. And while literary genres have their laws, writers are
not imprisoned in them; on the contrary, they are free to modify or
develop them, indeed one might say they are challenged to do so,
whether in reaction to changes in the world of politics or in the
taste of the public and in aesthetic standards. And Ovid's works are
the best example to illustrate how much freedom there is within the
framework of literary genres, freedom for originality.

Thus, in trying to understand a piece of literature — as we all
know — one has to bear in mind the time at which it is written, the
genre the author chooses and the manner in which he presents his
ideas, whether in conformity with tradition or not, that is one has
to consider the particular form he selects for his topic and the stylistic means by which he endeavours to assist his audience in appre-
ciating his work or by which he tries to instruct or guide, entertain
or amuse, puzzle or alienate. I should add that in analysing works
of literature I have also found it helpful to remember which alternative an author does not use, whether he ignores it or rejects it.

History and the past were perceived in Rome and by the Romans
in very different ways. For the great *gentes* it was a family business
to preserve the memory of their ancestors. Those who started composing historical works like Fabius Pictor and the other early annalists laid special emphasis on the legendary period, the foundation of
Rome and the kings, dealt only briefly with a few outstanding personalities and victories (following defeat or serious dangers) of the
following centuries and paid more attention again to contemporary
events. Later historians tended to provide fuller accounts; but analysis
of the causes of success or decline was rare; it is found e.g. in Sallust
or Tacitus, and to a certain extent in some of Cicero's works — or
in such actual political measures as taken by Augustus who realized
the need for the revival of old standards and who succeeded in securing for himself the position to bring about the necessary legislation.

Returning to the poets we are considering here I think it is helpful briefly to remind ourselves of a few authors of the late Republic:
Cicero, a man of the world of politics, very carefully analyses the
past in his theoretical writings and emphasizes the fundamental importance of certain values and virtues also in other works, while in some

of his speeches he undermines some of these central concepts, e.g. in defending Murena or Caelius or Milo. His contemporary M. Terentius Varro, also active in the world of politics, in his satires combines criticism of the moral decline in Rome (as before him P. Cornelius Scipio Aemilianus Africanus Minor in his speeches or Lucilius in his satires) with admiration for the ideal past, and later devotes much time to the study and exposition of the Roman past, not merely of a few heroes and victories, but of most aspects of the social and cultural history of the Roman people, not least their deities, priesthoods, cults, festivals and temples.[36] Catullus, having at least marginally experienced public life, occasionally attacks contemporaries like Caesar or Mamurra, but shows no interest in the affairs of Rome, ignoring history and giving new interpretations to such concepts as *officium*, *fides* or *otium*. At the same time Sallust, having started a career in politics and given it up later, is clearly dominated by concern for Rome and her future and endeavours by means of historical analysis to show ways for general improvement, for a restoration of the essentials of public life and the traditional moral standards. This is the picture which four writers present to us who lived and wrote at the same time and who show themselves to be very different from each other — and by way of a footnote one might add Caesar who destroyed the fabric of the Republic, developed a new literary genre in his *Bellum Gallicum* and his *Bellum civile* and yet strove to imitate Romulus and some aspects of the earliest Roman tradition.[37]

And the five poets whose attitude towards tradition, history and historiography we have looked at here? They are all regarded as 'Augustan', as they all lived roughly at the same time. Moreover, they all enjoyed the same kind of education and they all, no doubt, read the poems of Ennius, the first author who structured Roman history; and yet their views and their means of expressing them differ considerably. It seems helpful, therefore, briefly to recall a few chronological facts before we start comparing their works and the features peculiar to each of them.

The young Caesar was born in 63 B.C.; he succeeded in being recognized as Caesar's heir in 44 B.C. and in defeating the last of his most powerful enemies in 31 B.C. He increased the number of

---

[36] Cf. Astbury (1985), Mirsch (1882), Cardauns (1976), Riposati (1939); there is no adequate modern edition of the *De gente populi Romani*.

[37] See Classen (1998 [1962]) 43–54.

patricians in 29 B.C. (*Res Gestae* 8.1),[38] revised the roll of the senate
in 28 B.C. (*Res Gestae* 8.2), started dedicating new temples in 29 B.C.
(*aedes* for Divus Iulius), restored eighty-two old temples in 28 B.C.
(cf. *Res Gestae* 20.4) and transferred the 'republic from his power to
the dominion of the senate and people of Rome' in 27 B.C., accepting the name of Augustus (*Res Gestae* 34.1–2). The following years
he devoted to the restoration of peace and order in the provinces,
and only after refusing the appointment as supervisor of laws and
morals (*curator legum et morum: Res Gestae* 6, 1) in 19 B.C. and 18 B.C.
he began with his legislation on bribery, luxury, marriage (and adul-
tery), unfair practices of merchants and buildings — that is in the
year after the death of Virgil and probably Tibullus and after the
publication of most of Horace's poems,[39] though he started his 'Bild-
propaganda' and probably the plans for his building programme
much earlier.[40]

Virgil was was born in 70 B.C., his *Eclogues* were published probably
about 35 B.C., the *Georgics* about 29 B.C., the *Aeneid* after 19 B.C.;
Horace was born in 65 B.C., his *Satires* were published about 35–34
and 30–29 B.C., his *Epodes* about 31 B.C., the first three books of
Odes in 23 B.C., the first book of *Epistles* in 20 B.C., the rest later.
Tibullus and Propertius were fifteen (or more) years younger than
Virgil and Horace, Ovid more than twenty.

For both Virgil and Horace the civil war brought unpleasant personal consequences, both longed for peace and the restoration of
public order and of the traditional values, and both began to express
their views long before Augustus established himself as sole ruler,
and yet they chose different genres and used history both in their
own way. Virgil, assuming the function of a Roman *vates*, praised
emperor, Rome, the Romans and their values partly through the
mirror of the legendary past with a hero who is not beyond reproach,
but human, a model to be followed, not an ideal too perfect to be
emulated. And in his epic he inserts references to history, to great
men and decisive events, but also to the gradual growth of the empire
and the factors determining this development, thus implying an understanding of the historical process; and on the basis of this he also
formulates his hopes for the future, however, without following or

---

[38] Cf. Brunt and Moore (1967) 20.
[39] See now Bleicken (1998) (with bibliography 764–92).
[40] See Zanker (1968), (1989).

adopting the patterns of Roman historiography. Horace prefers a variety of forms. In his *Satires* he criticizes contemporary society and recommends traditional or natural values as a remedy, as in his *Epodes* he combines pessimism with optimism. Only later in his *Odes* he turns to history as a store-house for examples; and in these poems, though written in traditional Greek, not Roman forms, he stresses — like Virgil — ideals and values and elaborates them, long before the emperor finds time for his legislation on these matters. I am prepared, therefore, to subscribe to a remark by G. K. Galinsky that 'The poets in particular contributed significantly to the creation of the Augustan ethos'[41] — provided one changes 'Augustan ethos' to 'ethos of the time' and provided that one takes it to refer to Virgil and Horace, not to Tibullus and Propertius, not to Ovid.

Tibullus had some experience of military service, not of public life, and like Catullus he turns away from it, away from contemporary society and its values, away from events of his time and away from history, away from the past except for Greek mythology or the unreal, idealized life in early Rome or of pre-Roman time, and for this elegy offers itself as the most suitable form. Recent scholarship has shown him to be a Hellenistic poet at Rome,[42] rightly, but also to be an Augustan poet.[43] I doubt whether he would have understood this classification (or that as anti-Augustan). Even more strictly than Catullus he kept aloof from politics in his life and in his poetry. Instead he proclaimed *Venus, semper tibi dedita servit mens mea* (1.2.99–100),[44] and for this theme, love, together with peace, golden age, country life, *otium, inertia* he chooses the elegy as the most appropriate form, indeed as the only possible form.

Propertius, also victim of the confiscation of land after the civil war, implies indirectly not to be allowed to speak on the Forum (*insanum forum*: 4.1.134) and devotes his time to live up to the ideal of a *poeta doctus*. He fills his poems with references to Greek mythology and to the legendary era of Rome; but from Roman history he takes but a few examples when praising the emperor. He claims to have considered other topics and even deals with Roman aetiology in some poems, again to extol the emperor. But his subject, too, is

---

[41] Galinsky (1996) 121.
[42] See Cairns (1979).
[43] See Solmsen (1968–82 [1962]) II 324–54.
[44] Cf. 2.5.111–14; 3.4.15; 2.6.

love, presented in Hellenistic form. Clearly, Propertius is proud of
Rome and knows Roman history, and he is aware of the possibilities it offers to anyone wanting to sing the emperor's praise. However,
by vaguely hinting at these possibilities without using them, he shows
his independence — and as his theme he chooses love, not Rome,
not Roman history, not moral values, and therefore elegy.

   These four poets and most of their works were known to Ovid
when he started writing poetry, all when he began composing the
Metamorphoses and the *Fasti*. Virgil and Horace, both critical of the
society of their time, tried to show new ways by returning to old
standards, as did the emperor — but later; Tibullus and Propertius,
also critical of the contemporary society, created their own world of
peace and love and reinterpreted values in their elegies within this
framework. Ovid, also rejecting a senatorial career, writes poetry,
and in choosing elegy opts for a personal, a-political form; and
indeed, in the *Amores* or in the *Ars Amatoria* he shows little concern
for Rome, let alone for Roman history. G. K. Galinsky recently
referred to a paper by Brooks Otis, saying that he 'aptly characterized the Art of Love as a glorification, however peculiar, of the
Augustan way of life'. In fact, in his article Otis ends by distinguishing two Ovids, 'the urbane and witty amatory elegist whose whole
career was in essential opposition to his contemporary Augustans
and Augustus himself and the sympathetic connoisseur of the master
passion as it met him in the field of legend and myth. This second
Ovid appears only occasionally in elegy; he manifests himself completely in the *Metamorphoses*.'[45]

   Indeed there are two sides to Ovid's poetry, though I would never
talk of two Ovids (as I cannot find two voices in Virgil). On the
one hand Ovid is a child of his time in that he meets the high artistic standards as regards literary technique, metrical perfection, carefully considered choice of words, no less carefully selected rhetorical
devices, in short subtlety, refinement, sophistication. But on the other
hand, as regards the choice of genre, literary convention (or invention), selection and treatment of the subject matter, he is very different
from Virgil and Horace, and in his *Metamorphoses* and *Fasti* also very
different from Tibullus and Propertius. He chooses a traditional genre,
but he uses it in a new manner: He selects elegy, but he uses it for

---

[45] Galinsky (1996) 126, Otis (1938) 188–229, quotation 229.

a didactic poem, first, admittedly, on love, in the *Ars Amatoria*, but later in the *Fasti* for a historical topic. He chooses the epic form, but instead of unfolding the story of a great hero (or a group of heroes) he presents to the reader a large number of metamorphoses, mythical, but not heroic. And where one expects to be offered — as one does in the *Fasti* — accounts of *virtus* or *pietas*, a series of victories, achievements, foundation of temples and creation of festivals, one is confronted with a mixture of some such stories and eulogies of the emperor on the one hand and on the other hand not only with occasional critical or sceptical remarks about the *officium fori* and the *labor militiae* (1.302), but with stories of or allusions to defeat or crime from history, and in addition from mythology a *causa pudenda* (1.392–440: Priapus and Lotis) or the story about Priapus and Vesta (4.319–46, introduced with the remark: *est multi fabula parva ioci*) or a *fabula plena ioci* (2.303–58: Faunus, cf. also 3.738) and from Roman legends the violation of Silvia (3.9–40) and of Lucretia (2.721–85). F. Altheim maintained that whichever topic Ovid treats, it is eroticised.[46] This is not true; in fact the number of such stories, though some are rather long, is limited, and there are many others without any erotic element. What matters is not, I think, that Ovid tells such stories, but that he inserts them into a didactic poem on the Roman calendar, and that by choosing the form of elegy he denies this topic the degree of solemnity to which it seems entitled.

Does this make him or his poetry anti-Augustan? I have indicated the problems which I see when such terms are being used. As regards Ovid it seems fair to say that he pays due respect to the emperor, but not more. He does not subject his poetry to any kind of official policy, he does not write to convey a political message — partly, perhaps, because he is aware that this has been done by Virgil and Horace. We must never forget that he writes after them, that he has their poems in front of him, just as Virgil and Horace have Lucretius and Catullus in front of them, to imitate their poems, to borrow from them or to react against them. Like them, like Virgil and Horace, like Tibullus and Propertius Ovid, too, is primarily anxious to show his skill as poet, his mastership; furthermore he wants to entertain and to please, to amuse and to surprise, not only *prodesse*, but also *delectare*, and the unexpected form for a particular subject-matter, the

---

[46] See Altheim (1951–3) II 257.

unexpected story or scene in a context, the unexpected word or phrase — this is Ovid's art, this is Ovid at his best, Ovid's very personal contribution to literature.[47] It is in accordance with this aim that he neither ignores history like Tibullus and Propertius nor uses history in the manner of Virgil and Horace, but plays not primarily with time,[48] I would say, but with history — neither following nor rejecting Augustus and his policy, but playing with, rivalling and trying to outdo the great Virgil. It is, I think, not with Augustus, but with Virgil in mind, that Ovid composes both *Metamorphoses* and *Fasti*.

Thus, while none of the poets discussed here seems to be influenced by historiography, except perhaps for details, the attitude towards history proves a helpful instrument to reveal the identity, the individuality and the particular character of each of them whom I prefer not to call Augustans, and especially of the most difficult and the most delightful, Ovid, who plays with *teneri amores*, but also with history, not frivolously, but seriously and ingeniously.[49]

---

[47] Barchiesi (1997 [1993]) 262 rightly emphasizes that the 'Romans who were Ovid's regular readers for some twenty years expected clever manipulations and surprising turns'.

[48] I should stress that I found Newlands (1995) most helpful and stimulating.

[49] See Kraus (1939) 1975–6, reprinted in: von Albrecht and Zinn (1968) 158–9 (with reference to J. Huizinga); Latacz (1994 [1979]) 569–602, who refers to Hesse's *Glasperlenspiel* and his concept of *lusus sollemnis* (600, see also 578; 589).

CHAPTER TWO

PROPERTIUS THE HISTORIAN (3.3.1–12)?

Francis Cairns

I. *Introduction*

'... *quot editores, tot Propertii*' — 'for every editor a different Propertius'.
This well-worn tag is known widely beyond the specialist world of
Propertian scholarship. But non-specialists may not be fully aware
of its context or current relevance. The words are those of John
Swinnerton Phillimore in the penultimate paragraph of the preface
to his 1901 Oxford Classical Text of Propertius. They end the sentence: *Sin autem poetae cogitationem suo cuique arbitrio resarcire licet, non
interpretari, quot editores, tot Propertii.* Phillimore was concerned that multiple emendations and unbridled transpositions (he mentions the
names of Lachmann, Housman and Postgate in this connection) were
jeopardising Propertius' text. His warnings and example may have
helped to produce that greater degree of caution and self-restraint
among interpreters of Propertius which generally prevailed up to the
1980s, when Paolo Fedeli's Teubner text of 1984 could still preserve
a prudent balance between conservation and conjecture. But by the
end of the last millennium signs had begun to manifest themselves
of a revival of excessive and unnecessary tampering with the text of
Propertius.[1] That is why this paper discusses a Propertian passage
in which a transposition and a conjecture have been proposed, both
of which can, I believe, be shown definitively to be otiose, and, more
importantly, to destroy important aspects of the poet's meaning.
The elimination of single conjectures and transpositions, or even the
revelation of basic principles of Propertian composition, will not, of

---

[1] I have in mind particularly the writings of J. L. Butrica, S. J. Heyworth (although
it should be emphasised that Heyworth (1986) 200–2 adopts a conservative position
on both the textual matters treated here), and H.-C. Günther — esp. Günther (1997).
Smyth (1970) remains, albeit unintentionally, the single most cogent warning against
the folly of wholesale emendation and transposition in Propertius.

course, miraculously safeguard the text of Propertius from impru-
dent tamperers. But even the slightest gain is a gain.

Propertius' third book starts with a cycle of three elegies, all concerned with literary matters and together constituting a 'programmatic prologue' to Book 3. In elegy 3 Propertius relates his dream
of a Callimachean poetic initiation on Mount Helicon; and his account
quickly modulates into a catalogue of some of the events from Roman
history described by Ennius in his *Annales*. The relevant text (carried
on to the end of the sentence in line 16) is:

> Visus eram molli recubans Heliconis in umbra,
>   Bellerophontei qua fluit umor equi,
> reges, Alba, tuos et regum facta tuorum,
>   tantum operis, nervis hiscere posse meis;
> parvaque iam magnis admoram fontibus ora   5
>   unde pater sitiens Ennius ante bibit,
> et cecinit Curios fratres et Horatia pila,
>   regiaque Aemilia vecta tropaea rate,   8
> victricisque moras Fabii pugnamque sinistram
>   Cannensem et versos ad pia vota deos,   10
> Hannibalemque Lares Romana sede fugantis,
>   anseris et tutum voce fuisse Iovem   12
> cum me Castalia speculans ex arbore Phoebus
>   sic ait aurata nixus ad antra lyra:
> 'quid tibi cum tali, demens, est flumine? quis te   15
>   carminis heroi tangere iussit opus?
>   (Propertius 3.3.1–16)

I dreamed that lying in the soft shade of Helicon, where flows
the fountain of Bellerophon's horse, I possessed the power to proclaim to my lyre's accompaniment Alba's kings and their deeds,
a mighty task. I had already put my puny lips to that potent
spring (whence father Ennius once thirstily drank and sang of the
Curian brothers and the spears of the Horatii, and Jupiter saved
by the cackling of geese; the victorious delays of Fabius, the calamitous battle of Cannae, gods that turned to answer pious prayers,
and Lares that drove off Hannibal from their abode in Rome,
and royal trophies transported on Aemilius' galleys), when Phoebus
observed me from the Castalian wood, and said, as he leaned
upon his golden lyre beside the cave: 'Madman, what business
have you at such a stream? Who bade you touch the task of
heroic song?'

                                        (Trans. G. Goold)

II. *Chronological Order in Propertius 3.3.7–12?*

Two 'problems' have been perceived in this passage by certain critics, and two 'solutions' have been proposed. The first alleged problem (the succinct formulations of the major recent proponent of intervention in these matters — Butrica (1983)[2] — are quoted here and later) is: 'Propertius' failure to observe historical sequence (the Gaulish attack of 387 coming after the Second Punic War) is peculiar, nor is it defended securely by supposedly parallel passages.'[3] The first 'solution', and the one adopted by Butrica (1983) 464–7 following a nineteenth-century predecessor, was to transpose lines 8 and 12 and thus to restore chronological order. This matter has, of course, been discussed intermittently since the nineteenth century;[4] and some specialists (in particular Hermann Tränkle[5] and Paolo Fedeli[6]) have justified the transmitted order of the lines by pointing to other passages of Propertius where similar breaches of chronological order in historical passages have been perceived. Some[7] of these are 3.9.49–52, 'where the death of Remus is mentioned before his youth'; 3.12.25–36, where Propertius offers a non-chronological summary of the *Odyssey*; and 3.9.37–8, where the war of the Epigonoi against Thebes precedes the (earlier) war of the 'Seven against Thebes'.

But these parallels have been mostly impugned: Butrica eliminated 3.9.49–52 — Remus' death preceding his youth — with another transposition![8] 3.12.25–36, Propertius' non-chronological *Odyssey* summary, he pronounced irrelevant because, supposedly, it summarises the wanderings of Odysseus 'without special reference to Homer'.[9] 3.9.37–8 (the second Theban war comes before the first), which was noted by Fedeli (1985) 122 in his post-Butrica defence of the transmitted

---

[2] Butrica (1996) 135–6 reasserts without additional arguments the positions of Butrica (1983).

[3] Butrica (1983) 464.

[4] For more on this transposition, cf. Butrica (1983) 466 and n. 11.

[5] Tränkle (1960) 102–3.

[6] Fedeli (1985) 122.

[7] Certain of Tränkle's (1960) parallels, i.e. Propertius 3.5.31ff., 3.22, and 4.2, do not convincingly enter this category — even if 'historical' is extended to include 'mythistorical'. Undoubtedly, however, they further illuminate the background to Propertius' practice.

[8] Butrica (1983) 464 n. 2, accepting a suggestion of Peiper.

[9] Butrica (1983) 464 n. 2.

order of Propertius 3.1.7–12,[10] has not subsequently been attacked. But it involves only a single couplet and could possibly be understood differently.[11] Butrica himself mentioned Propertius 3.9.53–6 (the triumph of Octavian and the Parthian settlement come before Pelusium and the death of Antonius) only to dismiss it, along with other chronological distortions in 3.9, on the ground that 'the themes of 3.9.49–56 are named not as parts of a continuous epic but as subjects for individual compositions and chronological order is therefore not necessary'.[12]

Of course these attacks on the Propertian parallels for achronicity could themselves be counter-attacked. To void 3.9.49–52 through yet another transposition amounts to blatant denial of the evidence; and to imagine that any later poet could summarise the wanderings of Odysseus without reference to Homer's *Odyssey* verges on the absurd. Finally the distinction between 'parts of a continuous epic' and 'subjects for individual compositions' is clearly tendentious. But such counter-attacks would still leave the argument in mid-air: parallels in Roman poetry for non-chronological order other than these Propertian examples are needed. Where, then, might illumination be found? Fedeli also pointed to Horace *Odes* 1.12.33–48:[13]

> Romulum post hos prius an quietum
> Pompili regnum memorem an superbos
> Tarquini fasces dubito an Catonis   35
>   nobile letum.
> Regulum et Scauros animaeque magnae
> prodigum Paulum superante Poeno
> gratus insigni referam camena
>   Fabriciumque.   40
> hunc et incomptis Curium capillis
> utilem bello tulit et Camillum
> saeva paupertas et avitus apto
>   cum lare fundus.

---

[10] Fedeli (1985) 122 also noted as parallel passages with historical content Horace *Odes* 1.12.37ff. and Virgil *Aeneid* 6.752–886; both are discussed below.

[11] If *nec semper proelia clade pari* (38) were interpreted as 'battles not always equal in slaughter', the line could be taken as a second reference to the war of the Epigoni, implicitly contrasting it with the war of the Seven.

[12] Butrica (1983) 464 n. 2. Further historical achronicity can be found in Propertius 3.11.29–72, to which Cairns (1983) 89 adverted, but which does not seem to have entered the controversy about Propertius 3.3.7–12. Since Propertius 3.11 also involves major interpretational problems, I reserve treatment of it for elsewhere.

[13] Fedeli (1985) 122; Tränkle (1960) 102–3 does not mention this passage.

crescit occulto velut arbor aevo   45
fama Marcelli: micat inter omnis
Iulium sidus velut inter ignis
        luna minores.

After these I doubt whether first to mention
Romulus, Pompilius' peaceful kingdom,
Tarquin's proud rods, or the famous death of
Cato the Younger.

Regulus, the Scauri, and Paulus, lavish
Of his noble spirit as Punic victim,
Gratefully I'll record with Camena's glory,
Also Fabricius.

He and Dentatus and Camillus, useful
Fighting men, unshorn and unpolished, came from
Cruel lack of means and ancestral farms with
Homesteads in keeping.

Like a tree it grows by unseen progression,
Fame of Marcellus, and among them all the
Julian star's gleam, like the moon among the
Sky's lesser fires.
                        (Trans. G. Lee, slightly modified)

This passage and several others of Horace's lyric poetry which I have
treated elsewhere in another connection[14] offer that certainty about
Propertius which eludes us if we look only at Propertian elegy. For,
while elegiacs are easy prey for transposers, stanzaic lyrics are not.

    The achronicity of *Odes* 1.12.33–48 is blatant. Romulus, Numa,
and *Tarquini fasces* (33–5) all belong to early Rome (i.e. pre-500 B.C.),
whereas the younger Cato (35) died in 46 B.C. In line 37 Regulus
(died 250 B.C.) is followed by the Scauri (M. Aemilius cos. 115 B.C.
and M. Aurelius cos. 108 B.C.); but in line 38 with L. Aemilius
Paullus (cos. 219 and 216 B.C., killed at Cannae) we are again back
in the late third century B.C. C. Fabricius Luscinus (40), victor over
Pyrrhus at Beneventum, takes us even further back to the first quarter of the third century B.C., as does his contemporary M. Curius
Dentatus (41). Finally M. Furius Camillus (42) moves us into the late
fifth and early fourth century B.C. before 'Marcellus' (46) evokes
Rome's champion against Hannibal – M. Claudius Marcellus of the

---

[14] Cf. Cairns (1983) 83–5, 88–90.

last quarter of the third century B.C. This passage therefore preserves neither chronological nor reverse-chronological order.

Further examples of Horatian achronicity are:[15]

> 1)   Nolis longa ferae bella Numantiae
>   nec durum Hannibalem nec Siculum mare
>   Poeno purpureum sanguine mollibus
>   aptari citharae modis
>   (Horace *Odes* 2.12.1–4)
>
>   Fierce Numantia's long wars, stubborn Hannibal,
>   The Sicilian sea purple with Punic blood —
>   You'd not wish for such harsh themes to be made to fit
>   The soft tones of the cithara.
>   (Trans. G. Lee)

Here Horace moves from the Numantine wars of the second century B.C. (the last of 153–133) in line 1 back to the Second Punic
War of the late third century B.C. (218–201 B.C.) in line 2, and
then further back to the naval engagements of the First Punic War
(260–241 B.C.) in lines 2–3, thus reversing chronology.

> 2)   non his iuventus orta parentibus
>   infecit aequor sanguine Punico
>   Pyrrhumque et ingentem cecidit   35
>   Antiochum Hannibalemque dirum
>   (Horace *Odes* 3.6.33–6)
>
>   Not sprung from such parents were the Roman young
>   Who dyed Sicilian waters with Punic blood
>   And smote Pyrrhus and Antiochus
>   The Mighty and devilish Hannibal.
>   (Trans. G. Lee, slightly modified)

This passage displays mild temporal dislocation: the (later) First Punic
War of 264–241 B.C. (34) precedes the earlier war with and defeat
of Pyrrhus of 280–275 B.C. (35). Similarly in lines 35–6 Antiochus
(a later enemy of Rome, 194/3–188 B.C.) comes before Hannibal,
whose war (the Second Punic War) with Rome lasted from 218 to
201 B.C. This second dislocation is masked by the fact that Hannibal
joined Antiochus in his later war against Rome.

---

[15] I shall revert to these passages below for another purpose.

3)   Altera iam teritur bellis civilibus aetas,
         suis et ipsa Roma viribus ruit.
     quam neque finitimi valuerunt perdere Marsi
         minacis aut Etrusca Porsenae manus
     aemula nec virtus Capuae nec Spartacus acer   5
         novisque rebus infidelis Allobrox,
     nec fera caerulea domuit Germania pube
         parentibusque abominatus Hannibal
                     (Horace *Epode* 16.1–8)

A second generation is ground down by civil wars,
    and Rome is falling, ruined by the might of Rome.
What Marsian neighbours never could destroy
    nor hostile armies of Etruscan Porsena,
nor Capua's ambitious courage, nor the bravery
    of Spartacus, nor false, rebellious Allobrox,
nor savage blue-eyed warriors of Germany,
    nor Hannibal, so hated by our ancestors
                     (Trans. D. West)

The order is: Social War (90–88 B.C.), Porsenna's attack on Rome
(trad. c. 508 B.C.), war with Capua (216–211 B.C.), the revolt of
Spartacus (73–71 B.C.), the revolt of the Allobroges (121 B.C.), the
invasions of the Cimbri and Teutones (105–101 B.C.) and finally the
various threats presented by Hannibal (218–183 B.C.). As in *Odes*
1.12.33–48, neither chronological nor reverse-chronological order is
present.

These Horatian passages, and also that well-known section of *Aeneid*
6 — the parade of Roman heroes (756–886) where similar temporal
distortions appear[16] — are sufficient, in my view, to establish that
Roman poets sometimes deliberately choose to summarise historical
events in non-chronological order, as they can also choose to retain
chronological order (see below). The question why poets sometimes
select non-chronological order can now be raised. The answer is
contained in a magisterial paper by A. J. Woodman,[17] who was
approaching the problem from the other end: he was asking why
Virgil does maintain chronological order in *Aeneid* 8.630–62. But his
findings also answer the question why Roman poets often do not

---

[16] In addition to the overall function of this passage's achronicity, it has precise
and definable aims in terms of Virgil's interpretation of the events he describes: cf.
Norden (1957) *ad loc.*; Cairns (1989) 60–2.
[17] Woodman (1989) 133–4 and 141 n. 7.

maintain chronological order. Drawing in part on Herkommer (1968) 117–19 Woodman observed that 'Chronological ordering was recognised as above all an historiographical technique' (135). The testimony which he quoted to this effect will bear repetition:[18]

> Cicero *De Oratore* 2.63: *rerum ratio ordinem temporum desiderat*; cf. Cicero *Ad Atticum* 1.16.1: *respondebo tibi* ὕστερον πρότερον Ὁμηρικῶς. Sallust *Historiae* 1.8: *a principio urbis*; Livy *praefatio* 1: *si a primordio urbis res populi Romani praescripserim*; Tacitus *Annales* 12.40.5: *ad temporum ordinem redeo*; Pliny *Epistulae* 1.1.1: *collegi non servato temporis ordine (neque enim historiam componebam)*; Pliny *Epistulae* 3.9.28: *succurrit quod praeterieram . . . sed quamquam praepostere reddetur. facit hoc Homerus multique illius exemplo*; Florus *praefatio* 1: *a rege Romulo in Caesarem Augustum*; Servius *Aen. praef.* (p. 5 92–6 Harvard): *hanc esse artem poeticam ut a mediis incipientes per narrationem prima reddamus . . . quod etiam Horatius sic praecepit in* Arte Poetica *. . . unde constat perite fecisse Vergilium.*

The import of Pliny's remark about *historia* and of Servius' comment is confirmed by another passage discussed by Woodman (Macrobius 5.14.11), which contrasts Virgil's achronic technique (in origin, of course, Homeric) with the practice of historians:

> item divinus ille vates res vel paulo vel multo ante transactas opportune ad narrationis suae seriem revocat ut et historicum stilum vitet, non per ordinem digerendo quae gesta sunt, nec tamen praeteritorum nobis notitiam abstrahat.

> Moreover, past events, whether they have occurred recently or long ago, are fittingly recalled and introduced into the sequence of his story by that godlike poet Homer, but they are not arranged in chronological order, for, although he is careful not to withhold from us a knowledge of the past, his aim is to avoid writing as a historian.
>
> (Trans. P. V. Davies)

And Virgil, as Woodman shows, was also fully conscious of the difference between historians and poets in this respect. He makes Aeneas begin his account of himself to Venus with:

> O dea, si *prima* repetens *ab origine* pergam
> et vacet *annalis* nostrorum audire laborum
> (Virgil *Aeneid* 1.372–3)

---

[18] A few further quotations to the same affect can be found in Herkommer (1968) 117–19.

O Goddess, if I were to start at the beginning and retrace our whole
story, and if you had time to listen to the annals of our suffering
(Trans. D. West)

and he signals his understanding of the conventions elsewhere in the
words:

> illic res Italas Romanorumque triumphos
> haud vatum ignarus venturique inscius aevi
> fecerat ignipotens, illic genus omne futurae
> stirpis ab Ascanio pugnataque *in ordine* bella.
> (Virgil *Aeneid* 8.626–9)

There the God of Fire, with his knowledge of the prophets and
of time that was to be, had laid out the story of Italy and the
triumphs of the Romans, and there in order were all the generations
that would spring from Ascanius and all the wars they would fight.
(Trans. D. West)

Another of Woodman's observations, made in the context of Virgil's
diverse practices about chronology, directs our attention to an important implication of Propertius 3.3.7–12. In discussing Horace *Ars
Poetica* 136–149:

> nec sic incipies, ut scriptor cyclicus olim:
> 'fortunam Priami cantabo et nobile bellum.'
> quid dignum tanto feret hic promissor hiatu?
> parturient montes, nascetur ridiculus mus.
> quanto rectius hic, qui nil molitur inepte: 140
> 'dic mihi, Musa, virum, captae post tempora Troiae
> qui mores hominum multorum vidit et urbes.'
> non fumum ex fulgore, sed ex fumo dare lucem
> cogitat, ut speciosa dehinc miracula promat,
> Antiphaten Scyllamque et cum Cyclope Charybdim;   145
> nec reditum Diomedis ab interitu Meleagri
> nec gemino bellum Troianum orditur ab ovo:
> semper ad eventum festinat et in medias res
> non secus ac notas auditorem rapit . . .

and don't begin in the style of the ancient cyclic poet:
'Of Priam's fate I sing and a war that's famed in story.'
What can emerge in keeping with such a cavernous promise?
The mountains will labour and bring forth a comical mouse.
How much better the poet who builds nothing at random:
'Tell, O Muse, of the man who after Troy had fallen
saw the cities of many people and their ways of life.'
His aim is not to have smoke after a flash, but light

emerging from smoke, and thus revealing his splendid marvels:
the cannibal king Antiphates, the Cyclops, Scylla, Charybdis.
He doesn't start Diomedes' return from when Meleager
died, nor the Trojan war from the egg containing Helen.
He always presses on to the outcome and hurries the reader
into the middle of things as though they were quite familiar.

(Trans. N. Rudd)

Woodman drew on Brink's earlier recognition that 'the influence of
Virgil . . . permeates the whole *Ars*',[19] to advance the following interpretation of these lines:

> . . . there can be little doubt that Horace's praise of Homer via criti-
> cism of cyclic epic should be read in the light of Virgil's composition
> and publication of the *Aeneid* . . . Virgil, by inviting his readers to see
> his poem in specifically Homeric terms, suggested a contrast between
> his own work and the 'cyclic' *Annales* of Ennius, whose claim to be a
> second Homer is revealed as inadequate by his decision to write *ab
> initio*. (133)

The correctness of this reading is amply demonstrated by *Epistles*
1.2, where Horace's ostensible discussion of Homer is manifestly also
a discussion of Virgil.[20]

Now it is precisely Ennius and his *Annales* that are the main subject of Propertius 3.3.5–12. If Virgil, by returning to Homeric practice, was implicitly criticising Ennius for having written annalistically,
it is all the more likely that Propertius was not only 'varying' on the
chronology of the *Annales* in 3.3.7–12 (as no doubt he does elsewhere) but was also 'correcting' Ennius' historical order of narration
in learned Hellenistic fashion.[21] We might go even further and hypothesise that there were discussions of, and a verdict upon, Ennius'
Annales within the circle of Maecenas in the 20s B.C.[22] Such dis-

---

[19] Brink (1971) Pref. xx.

[20] Cf. e.g. Cairns (1989) 85–9, 209.

[21] Achronicity in Augustan poetry can, of course, also be linked with the temporal distortions commonly found in hellenistic poetry and in its archaic lyric models:
cf. Cairns (1979) General Index *s.v.* temporal dislocation. But any lingering doubt
that Propertius was conscious in this elegy of the history/poetry divide should be
dispelled by Woodman (1998), pointing out *inter alia* that *tantum operis* at Propertius
3.3.4 repeats the exact words used by Livy (*praef.* 13) to describe the work which
he is undertaking.

[22] However Mr I. M. Le M. Du Quesnay points out to me that Horace *Epod.*
16.1–8, with its clear achronicity, predates the 20s B.C., as does Virgil *Ecl.* 6, which
contains both a central (albeit mythical rather than historical) section (31–81) in

cussions may even lie behind, not just Virgil's and Propertius' non-chronological passages, but also Horace's chronological distortions in the *Odes*. After all, the *Odes* were published in 23 B.C.; *Aeneid* 6, where the large-scale temporal distortions climax with Marcellus who died in 23, was read by Virgil to the imperial family in that year; and the composition of Propertius Book 3, which contains every plausible example of historical achronicity so far identified in Propertius, falls between 25 and 23–22 B.C. in the view of one authority,[23] between 25 and 20 B.C. — 'perhaps 24–21' — in the view of another.[24] We should, then, perhaps reflect that transpositions such as the one proposed in Propertius 3.3, as well as perverting the poet's text, may be destroying important evidence for literary history.

III. Cecini *or* Cecinit *in Line 7?*

The second 'problem' concerns line 8. Butrica (1983) 464 formulates it thus: 'More damaging, however, is that 8 must describe the triumph of L. Aemilius Paullus in 167, two years after the accepted date of Ennius' death.' Since (self-evidently) Ennius could not have included in his *Annales* an event which occurred two years after his own death, a number of Propertian scholars — including Butrica (1983) — have accepted the humanist emendation *cecini* in place of the transmitted *cecinit* in line 7.[25] The alteration may seem slight, but it has major consequences: it makes Propertius, and not Ennius, sing of the Curii, Horatii, and other heroes of lines 7–12.

Two principal focuses can be perceived in the various scholarly discussions of this problem. The first has been to enquire whether Propertius is really referring to the triumph of L. Aemilius Paullus in 167 B.C. or whether he is thinking instead of the victory of an earlier Aemilius — either that of another L. Aemilius Paullus over Demetrius of Pharos in 219 B.C. or the naval victory of L. Aemilius

---

which chronology is not respected and a passage in which the two Scyllas are conflated (74–7) — on conflation cf. pp. 39–44 below. Interest in these phenomena cannot therefore have been confined to the 20s B.C.

[23] Fedeli (1985) 29.

[24] Camps (1966) 1.

[25] Later also Kierdorf (1994), who gives (368–9) an account of the earlier fortunes of the conjecture *cecini*.

Regillus over King Antiochus at Myonessus in 190 B.C., both of
which were won before Ennius' death. The event of 167 B.C. was
undoubtedly the best known of the three possible referents: cf. Camps
(1966) *ad loc.* writing of the 'triumphal return of L. Aemilius <L.f.
M.n.> Paullus <RE Aemilius (114)> after his conquest of Perseus,
king of Macedon <167 B.C.>; the enormous booty and the fact that
the conqueror entered Rome by sailing up the Tiber from the sea
are dwelt on in the accounts of Livy (XLV.35) and Plutarch (*Aemilius
Paullus* <30.2–3>'.[26] The second possible referent, a 'victory of an
earlier L. Aemilius <M.f. M.n.> Paullus <RE Aemilius (118)> over
Demetrius of Pharos <219 B.C.>' (Butler and Barber (1933) *ad loc.*)
has found little favour with commentators.[27] The third, the naval
victory of L. Aemilius M.f. Regillus, <RE Aemilius (127)> over
Antiochus at Myonnesus (190 B.C.),[28] has fared better: Martina (1979)
51–6 argued with great vigour and learning that, for the political
ends of his patron M. Aemilius Lepidus, Ennius in *Annales* Book 14
magnified out of all proportion this naval victory of Regillus. Hence,
according to Martina (1979) 56–61, Propertius is referring here primarily to that victory in line 8.[29] But, without undervaluing Martina's
heroic scholarship, one inevitably reflects that, after the sensational
and well-known triumphal return of L. Aemilius Paullus in 167 B.C.
and his voyage up the Tiber from the sea with his enormous booty,
perceptions of the earlier achievements of the Aemilii must have
been diminished in Romans' consciousness of their past while the
the naval triumph of 167 B.C. will have loomed larger. It seems,
then, impossible to exclude the event of 167 B.C. from the reference of *regiaque Aemilia vecta tropaea*; and indeed, towards the end of
his discussion of this point Martina (1979) 59 veers towards the position of Shackleton Bailey (1956) 139–40, who admitted the possibility that Propertius had in mind both Regillus' victory and Paullus'
triumphal entry into the Tiber. Martina then usefully wrote: 'Ci tro-
veremmo quindi di fronte a un curioso caso di contaminazione' (59).
This approach, however, need not imply that line 8 is the result of

---

[26] Cf. also Cicero *Fin.* 5.70.
[27] Cf. Polybius 3.16, 18–19; Appian *Ill.* 8.
[28] Cf. Livy 37.30.
[29] Martina also offers a useful summary of various earlier treatments of the problem. Skutsch (1985) 552–3 rather excessively claims that Martina has "proved" that
Regillus' victory is Propertius' theme.

confusion on Propertius' part,[30] i.e. that Propertius erroneously attributed the characteristics of Paullus' famous triumph of 167 B.C. (which
Ennius could not have described) to the earlier victory of Regillus
in 190 B.C. (which Ennius doubtless did describe). Butrica (1983)
465–6 had already voiced obvious objections to this sort of solution,
when he pointed out that Propertius was a dedicated student of early
Latin poetry and that, if he had nevertheless committed a historical
blunder or confusion here, his error would surely have been cor-
rected 'at a recitation or after publication'. A subtler and more convincing path must be found if we are to preserve the MS reading
cecinit in line 7.

The second focus of the *cecinit/cecini* debate has been the question
whether Propertius asserts in 3.3 that, as a dreamer, he actually
started writing an epic poem, or whether Propertius merely claims
that he contemplated doing so in his dream. If Propertius represents
himself as an actual epic poet, then the emendation *cecini* becomes
more plausible. If Propertius does not do so, then Ennius is the only
epic poet in the elegy, which strengthens the transmitted reading
cecinit. Fedeli (1985) 123 assembled a number of arguments against
the supposition that Propertius actually composed epic in his dream
and hence against *cecini*. One particularly deadly objection was that,
in Fedeli's words, *posse* (4) and *admoram* (5) 'indichino solo il tenta-
tivo da parte di Properzio di accostarsi all'Ippocrene'. The opposite
viewpoint (i.e. that Propertius did write epic in his dream) was upheld
most recently by Kierdorf (1994),[31] with particular concentration on
lines 15–16 and 21 (*cur tua praescriptos evecta est pagina gyro<s>?*) — from
the (later) speech of Apollo to Propertius. Kierdorf claimed that there
were two standard situations in ancient *recusationes*: either the poet
contemplates or attempts writing epic (this is undeniably a commonplace); or the poet has actually begun writing epic. Kierdorf
then argued that Propertius 3.3 portrays the second situation, i.e.
Propertius is claiming to have treated (in his dream) all the epic
themes of lines 7–12. Hence, Kierdorf concluded, we must read *cecini*
in line 7.

However the two alleged parallels which Kierdorf advances to support his view that there is a second standard situation (i.e. the elegiac

---

[30] Cf. Fedeli (1985) *ad loc.*, referring to earlier scholarship.
[31] Kierdorf did not rehandle the problem of the triumph of Paullus and line 8,
although he was clearly aware of this background to the *cecinit/cecini* question.

poet has actually begun writing epic) do not stand up to scrutiny:
the first is implausible and the second is a spoof. In Virgil *Eclogue*
6.3: *cum canerem reges et proelia,* the imperfect is quite certainly (with
Della Corte (1985) *ad loc.*) conative, despite Kierdorf's denial of this —
i.e. Virgil had not actually started to write epic. Kierdorf's second
example is Ovid *Amores* 2.1.11–14:

> ausus eram, memini, caelestia dicere bella
> centimanumque Gyen — et satis oris erat —
> cum male se Tellus ulta est, ingestaque Olympo
> ardua devexum Pelion Ossa tulit.
>
> I'd dared relate Heaven's wars and hundred-handed
> Giants, I well recall — of words no lack —
> Earth's fell revenge, and, piled upon Olympus,
> High Ossa with steep Pelion on its back.
>   (Trans. A. D. Melville)

Here Ovid undoubtedly does claim to have started an epic gigan-
tomachy — although the claim is couched in such exaggerated terms
as to invite disbelief.[32] But Ovid's assertion does not involve or document a second standard situation: rather he is giving a unique extra
twist to the single standard topos — 'the poet attempts to start or
thinks about starting an epic'; Ovid enhances this topos into the
unparalleled exaggeration 'the poet has actually started an epic'. So
Kierdorf's parallels fail to convince. His lexical arguments about
admoram (5), i.e. that it implies actual drinking, and about *tangere* (16),
i.e. that it shows Propertius having made a start on an epic, are
equally unconvincing, especially since the parallels offered in the latter case are examples of *attingere*, not *tangere*. Finally, it is not clear
on what grounds Kierdorf denies that *flumine* in line 15 has the same
referent as *fontibus* in line 5; common sense demands that they be
identical.

Fedeli's second deadly argument against *cecini* was that, if the text
meant what Butrica (1983) wants it to mean, we would require after
visus eram and *admoram* not the perfect *cecini* but an imperfect.[33] Since

---

[32] Cf. McKeown (1998) 10–14 on ll. 11–16 for discussion of the reality of this
claim.
[33] Cf. in addition Häussler (1976) 319–20 (Exkurs 23) with further arguments
and references. Häussler's sound contribution seems to have escaped the notice of
later commentators on this problem, with the exception of Martina (1979) 57 n. 142.

this point does not seem to have been universally understood, it will bear expansion along lines laid down by Heyworth (1988) 200–201 and Courtney (1988) 96, referring to their predecessors.[34] In simple terms, an inverted *cum*-clause such as that of lines 13ff. is normally preceded by a main clause or clauses whose verb or verbs are either pluperfect or imperfect. This is what happens here as the sentence moves from first-person *Visus eram* (1) to first-person *admoram* (5) to the third-person inverted *cum*-clause *cum ... Phoebus/ ... ait* (13–14): 'I was dreaming and I had brought my mouth to . and then Phoebus said'. The three other clauses of lines 1–12 containing third-person verbs, i.e. *qua fluit ...* (2), *unde ... bibit* (6) and *et cecinit ...* (7ff.), do not form part of this progression; the first two are adverbial subordinate clauses, the third is a principal clause following on parenthetically from *unde ... bibit*. Hence the verbs of these clauses are as appropriate either present or perfect tense. But the emendation *cecini* would introduce an additional first-person verb. Its clause would then cease to be parenthetic and would become one of the series of clauses leading up to *cum ... ait*. But in that case its verb would have to be imperfect or pluperfect. So on syntactical grounds alone the emendation *cecini* cannot be correct.

However, given the controversial nature of this problem[35] and its major consequences for the text, it may be useful to add a new line of argumentation in the form of another principle ('conflation' or 'assimilation') which underlies some Roman poetic treatments of the past. This principle also turns out to be widely exemplified and it is often employed in association with achronicity. It can best be approached through a concrete example where both principles can be seen in action, and where, as in Propertius 3.3.8, there has been debate about which member of the same family is being featured. This is Horace *Epode* 9.23–6:

> io Triumphe, nec Iugurthino parem
> bello reportasti ducem
> neque Africanum, cui super Carthaginem   25
> virtus sepulcrum condidit.

---

[34] These works should be consulted for technical matters and bibliography.
[35] Heyworth (1986) 201 refers to Propertius' distortions of Virgil in 2.34; but parallel motives for distortions of Ennius here are hard to find.

Io Triumphe! From Jugurtha's war you did not bring
    a greater warrior home to Rome,
not even Africanus equalled him, whose valour
    made a sepulchre where Carthage once had stood.
(Trans. D. West)

Africanum (25) poses a problem analogous to that of Propertius 3.3.8:
is Horace referring to the elder Scipio who defeated Hannibal (and
whose tomb may have been celebrated)[36] or to the younger Scipio
who later destroyed Carthage?[37] Whereas, faced with the parallel
Propertian problem, some scholars have thought that Propertius might
have been confused, no-one has alleged this of Horace! So, with
Bentley, we must hypothesise that Horace was deliberately engaging
in 'conflation', here of the achievements of different members of the
same family. A breach of chronological order of the type exemplified
above can be seen too: the Jugurthine War of 111–103 B.C. is mentioned (23–4) before the Punic Wars (the second of 218–201 B.C.,
the third of 149–146 B.C.).

    This is not the only place where Horace conflates these same two
Scipios: he also does so in *Odes* 4.8.13–20:

non incisa notis marmora publicis,
per quae spiritus et vita redit bonis
post mortem ducibus, non celeres fugae   15
reiectaeque retrorsum Hannibalis minae
non incendia Karthaginis inpiae
eius qui domita nomen ab Africa
lucratus rediit clarius indicant
laudes quam Calabrae Pierides . . .   20

Neither marble engraved as public document
By which spirit and life come back again to good
Leaders after their death, nor Hannibal's swift flight
Nor the threatenings that rebounded upon himself,
Nor the fires that laid impious Carthage low
Place in clearer relief than the Calabrian Muse . . .
(Trans. G. Lee)

---

[36] Cf. Cairns (1983) 83–5, 87–8. Ennius is probably again at the root of this passage: Scipio Africanus Maior had a statue of Ennius placed on his own tomb (Pliny
Nat. 7.114).
    [37] For the problem cf. (more recently) Cavarzere (1992) *ad loc.* and Mankin (1995)
ad loc.

Here (as at *Odes* 3.6.33–6) he assimilates the second and third Punic wars too. It is amusing to note that some puzzled editors of Horace have resorted in this latter passage, not to transposition, but to excision: they cut everything between *non celeres* in 15 and *rediit* in 19! *Odes* 4.8.13–20 is an even more convincing, indeed determinant, parallel for Propertius 3.3.8 because Ennius is explicitly present here too — in *Calabrae Pierides* (20). It should also be observed that, on a literal reading of Horace's text, Ennius is again said to have celebrated an event posthumously: this time it is the destruction of Carthage by the younger Scipio in 146 B.C., some twenty-one years after his own death. The appearance of Ennius here and in Propertius 3.3 in the same context of conflations prompts speculation, unprovable and not needed for my argument, but perhaps worth recording: might Ennius have been an exponent of the 'conflation' principle exemplified in these two passages which refer to him? And might Ennius have specifically conflated Scipios? This would certainly help to explain both these and some other passages exemplifying conflation behind which the presence of Ennius might be suspected.[38]

It must be stressed, however, that 'conflation' is not just a poetic device: as applied to individuals from the same family it is part of the fundamental Roman ideology of the family, the most extreme manifestion of which is the notion that the glory of descendants somehow enhances their ancestors. An excellent example comes from one of the epitaphs of the Scipios:[39]

> virtutes generis mieis moribus accumulavi,
> progeniem genui, facta patris petiei.
> maiorum optenui laudem ut sibei me esse creatum
> laetentur; stirpem nobilitavit honor.
> (Courtney (1995) 42–3 No. 13)

---

[38] Cf. also n. 37.

[39] I am indebted to Prof. Gwyn Morgan for this reference and for discussion of the point at issue, thanks to which I would now, in contrast to Cairns (1984) 167 and 236 n. 148 regard Tacitus *Ann.* 11.21.3 as irrelevant. But Statius *Silv.* 1.4.68–9 remains a secure example (although Flavian 'special pleading' might be suspected); and Horace *Odes* 1.12.45–6 seems, albeit obliquely, to achieve the same implication via conflation. [Cicero] *Sal.* 5 and Quintilan *Inst.* 3.7.18, 21, 26 reflect similar ways of thinking. Finally, although all the examples noted above are Latin, the concept also appears at Lycophron 1226ff., but interestingly at the beginning of the controversial prophecy of the rise of Rome to world dominion. I owe this last example to Dr A. Hardie.

One wonders, of course, whether its provenance is purely fortuitous, particularly since there is a historical case of a confusion or conflation among Scipios: Cicero's contemporary Metellus Scipio wrongly claimed that a statue of Scipio Africanus Minor was that of his great-grandfather P. Scipio Nasica Serapio.[40] Cicero makes merry at the error of a *nobilis*; but it may reflect a conflatory habit of mind prevalent among Roman aristocrats and more generally. The habit will have been encouraged by the Roman tendency to pluralise, even in prose, the names of distinguished heroes of the past (e.g. *Camillos, Fabricios, Curios* at Cicero *Pro Caelio* 39).[41] More broadly such conflations/assimilations are rhetorical strategems useful for both encomiastic and psogistic ends: the latter use emerges in the assimilations of the various Punic wars (see below), which discredit Carthage doubly.

The commonness of conflation and its frequent link with achronicity have been mentioned. A brief re-examination of those same Horatian passages which served above to illustrate non-chronological order will demonstrate this.

1. *Horace* Odes *1.12.33–48*

This passage contains two conflations which have been the partly uncomprehended cause of sharp scholarly debate.[42] The first appears in the context of the kings of Rome (lines 33–5): *Romulum post hos prius an quietum/Pompili* regnum *memorem an* superbos/Tarquini fasces *dubito* . . . Here the three Tarquinii of legendary regal Rome who shared the *praenomen* Lucius are conflated: the 'proud fasces' of Tarquinius (*pace* Nisbet-Hubbard (1970) *ad loc.*) point primarily to the fifth king of Rome, L. Tarquinius Priscus, who introduced the *fasces*, originally a symbol of royal authority. However *superbos* (34) alludes to Rome's last king, L. Tarquinius Superbus, expelled from Rome and replaced by two consuls; one of them — and the third element

---

[40] *Att.* 6.1.17; cf. Shackleton Bailey (1989 [1998]).

[41] Henderson (1997), esp. Chh. 6–10 and App. 1–2 (a reference I owe to Prof. Susanna Morton Braund), studies this phenomenon — "the 'generalising' plural" — extensively in Roman verse authors, handling at some length *inter alia* Horace *Odes* 1.12 (App. 1) and Virgil *Aen.* 6.808–86 (App. 2). At times (e.g. 36 and 141 n. 48 on the Scipiones) his approach verges on that of this paper. But, where transposition and emendation in Propertius 3.3.7–12 is concerned, he would seem (143 n. 52) to favour the interventionist camp.

[42] Cf. Treloar (1969); (1972); (1973); Jocelyn (1971); (1973); Dunston (1973).

of the conflation — was his cousin L. Tarquinius Collatinus, who, although he had been a prime mover against Superbus, was himself exiled from Rome along with the rest of the *gens Tarquinia* on the motion of his consular colleague, L. Iunius Brutus. The conflation found here is more complex than usual and constitutes a multivalent comment on good and bad royal and consular authority. But the passage will have been less opaque to Horace's contemporaries than to modern scholarship. *Aeneid* 6.817–8: *vis et* Tarquinios reges *animamque* superbam/*ultoris* Bruti, fascisque *videre receptos?* incorporates all the same concepts and some of the same uncertainties; and the first consul Brutus, implicit in Horace, is explicit in Virgil. This suggests that a standard rhetorical debating point underlies both poets' lines.[43]

The second conflation is more striking if less complex: it is the laudatory assimilation of Augustus' nephew, the young Marcellus, to his distinguished ancestor of the second Punic War.

2. *Horace* Odes *2.12.1–4*

Here other conflations are implied: again, as in *Odes* 4.8.13–20 between the elder Scipio, victor over Hannibal, and the younger Scipio, not only destroyer of Carthage but conqueror of Numantia; and, as there, and in *Odes* 3.6.33–6, between two of the Punic wars.

3. *Horace* Odes *3.6.33–6*

The effect of the two temporal dislocations here (as at *Odes* 2.12.1–4 and 4.8.13–20) is in part to assimilate two (here the first two) of the Punic wars.

4. *Horace* Epode *16.6*

Horace's reference to the Allobroges here has been variously interpreted[44] — as an allusion to their war with Rome of 121 B.C., or to their promise of subsequently witheld support to Catiline in 63 B.C.,

---

[43] The Virgilian parallel passage is mentioned by Jocelyn (1971) 75 n. 63, 76 n. 71 and by Dunston (1973) 59, but its implications are not teased out, even though Fraenkel (1957) 295 n. 2 had already expounded some of them and had gone some way towards the interpretation of *Odes* 1.12.34–5 offered above.

[44] Cf. Cavarzere (1992) *ad loc.*; Mankin (1995) *ad loc.*

or to their insurrection of 61 B.C., or to the desertions of some
Allobroges from Caesar to Pompey in 48 B.C. The idea that Horace
is thinking of more than one incident can be entertained if conflation
is operating here.

IV. *Conclusions*

In Propertius 3.3 the transposition of lines 8 and 12 and the emendation of *cecinit* (7) to *cecini* are both unnecessary, because non-chronological order is one standard feature of Augustan poets' treatments
of historical events, and because conflations of historical personages
sharing the same *nomen*, and of certain historical events, are not infre-
quent in Augustan poetry. The possibility that 'historical', i.e. chronological, order and 'poetic', i.e. non-chronological, order were being
discussed in the circle of Maecenas around 23 B.C. — in connection
with Ennius' *Annales* and also with Virgil's ongoing *Aeneid* — has already
been noted. If Ennius also conflated Scipios and Punic wars, those
conflations would have been of equal interest to Maecenas' circle,
especially since Ennius' portrayal of the achievements and 'deification'
of Scipio Africanus Maior provided Augustan writers with a precedent and exemplar for their treatment of Augustus.[45] This could well
help to explain the prominence of conflations, and indeed of those
same conflations around the same time in the work of both Horace
and Propertius; and it should be observed that the conflation of the
Aemilii at Propertius 3.3.8 belongs to the same subject-area, since
Scipio Africanus Minor was by birth an Aemilius, none other than
the son of L. Aemilius L.f. M.n. Paullus, the victor of Pydna.[46]

---

[45] See now Bosworth (1999) esp. 5–6.
[46] I am grateful to Prof. A. J. Woodman for valuable advice on this paper and
to Prof. J. L. Butrica for confirming that he stands by the conclusions of Butrica
(1983).

CHAPTER THREE

ACTIUM AND TEUTOBURG:[1]
AUGUSTAN VICTORY AND DEFEAT
IN VERGIL AND TACITUS

V. E. Pagán

In the Shadow of Augustus

For all they tell of the Augustan age, Vergil and Tacitus do so indirectly. Neither author deliberately sets out to write an account of
the rise and rule of Octavian. In fact, they appear to avoid the subject scrupulously. The *Aeneid* is fundamentally the story of the mythological foundation of Rome; the *Annals* is a history of the Julio-Claudian
dynasty beginning with the accession of Tiberius in A.D. 14. Though
these authors choose to tell the history of Rome long before and
just after Augustus, it would seem the *princeps* is unavoidable, and in
a way, central to their stories. Certainly these two works are some
of the more frequently consulted sources for attitudes toward the
Augustan principate, in spite of the obvious absence of the *princeps*
in the very plots themselves. This is because Vergil and Tacitus are
able to incorporate into the *Aeneid* and the *Annals* information about
Augustus even though technically speaking his life falls outside of the
temporal termini of their narrative frameworks.

Despite the fact that the subject matter of the *Aeneid* and the *Annals*
precludes the Augustan age, two watershed events of this era are
nevertheless included in the epic and the history: the victory at
Actium in 31 B.C. and the defeat at the Teutoburg forest in A.D. 9,
forty years later. *Aeneid* Book 8 closes with the ornate and extended

---

[1] The toponym 'Teutoburg' is a shorthand for the place where Varus lost three
legions to Arminius in A.D. 9. German precedent is set by Heinrich von Kleist
who uses the noun 'Teutoburg' throughout his 1808 play, *Die Hermannsschlacht*. The
place name is unattested in ancient literature; Tacitus speaks only of the *Teutoburgiensis
saltus* (*Ann.* 1.60.3). Conclusive evidence for the location of the battle is provided
by Schlüter (1999).

description of the shield of Aeneas. Depicted are several scenes foreshadowing the history of Rome: Romulus and Remus with the she-
wolf, the rape of the Sabine women, the punishment of Mettus,
Cocles and Cloelia at the bridge, the attack of the Gauls, and Catiline
and Cato in the Underworld. At the center of it all is a grand portrayal of the battle of Actium and the triple triumph two years later
(8.671–731). Thus Vergil's Actium looks to the distant future. *Annals*
Book 1 follows the campaigns of Germanicus on the Rhine. During
his expedition against the rebellious Cherusci, he comes upon the
place where the three legions under Quintilius Varus were annihi-
lated six years before. According to Suetonius the loss of the legions
at the Teutoburg forest was one of the most severe and ignomin-
ious defeats Augustus had ever suffered.[2] In a flashback, Tacitus
lingers for two haunting paragraphs (1.61–2) on an event that took
place six years before the starting point of the *Annals*. Tacitus'
Teutoburg is a return to the recent past.

    In comparing these two episodes, my special concern is the way
Vergil and Tacitus manage to transcend the temporal frameworks
of the *Aeneid* and the *Annals* and to incorporate the Augustan victory and defeat into their narratives. The poet and the historian are
faced with the problem of how to include events which fall outside
of the temporal termini of their narratives. Two rhetorical devices
allow the authors to solve this dilemma. The poet finds a formal
resolution to the problem in ecphrasis; the historian solves it in digression. But the use of these two rhetorical devices is a symptom of
unresolved anxieties about the content of these passages, namely, the
rise of Octavian and the subsequent problem of imperial expansion.
Since ecphrasis and digression are discrete narrative units, they give
the impression that intractable political issues can be managed, and
indeed eloquently.[3] Thus these rhetorical maneuvers provide a win-
dow to the authors' method of literary production.[4] As Vergil and
Tacitus manage to narrate Augustan victory and defeat, they also
reveal the victory — as well as the defeat — of their own efforts to
do so, for in order to include these Augustan events at all, they must

---

[2] Suetonius *Aug.* 23.1: *graves ignominias cladesque duas omnino nec alibi quam in Germania
accepit, Lollianam et Varianam . . .*
[3] Cf. the observation of Putnam (1998) 163: "Only through art, and in the mind's
eye alone, can the wild actions that make up the story of Rome be tamed into
submission."
[4] Macherey (1978) 100.

divorce them, both temporally and formally, from the rest of the narrative.

These two seemingly disparate passages merit comparison for several reasons. Both are battle scenes, fulfilling — and deviating from — similar rhetorical expectations. Both passages play with time; Actium is foreshadowed on the ecphrastic shield, Teutoburg is remembered in a digressive flashback. Both battles were mythologized by contemporaries and both experienced a wide-ranging *Nachleben* in poetry and prose.[5] We can also observe the way Augustan themes are treated in discrete narrative units by authors separated by more than a century. In both passages, the authors force the reader to become a spectator, viewing the battle of Actium on the shield and gazing upon the ruins of Varus' defeat. According to Tony Woodman, such vividness, or *enargeia*, is characteristic of both poetry and historiography.[6] Finally, the comparison is also validated by Tacitus' affinity for Vergil.[7]

Casting Actium and Teutoburg

Let us proceed with a few observations on the subtle ways these two passages are set apart from the rest of the narratives in which they appear, for both authors manage to incorporate these Augustan battles into texts in which they seem to have no place. Tacitus and Vergil achieve such high degrees of *enargeia* in their depictions of Teutoburg and Actium by using digression and ecphrasis. According to Cicero, digressions are regarded as a source of pleasure and entertainment for the reader.[8] In addition to the varieties of fortune and the vicissitudes of circumstance which delight the reader,[9] ancient

---

[5] Actium in contemporary architecture and literature: Gurval (1995); Teutoburg in the ancient tradition: Pagán (1999) 308 n. 25.

[6] Woodman (1989) 140.

[7] Walker (1952) 11, (1991); Syme (1958) 357; Baxter (1972) 255; Goodyear (1981) 108–9; Tarrant (1997) 69–70.

[8] Cicero *de Orat.* 2.311: *digredi tamen ab eo quod proposueris atque agas, permovendorum animorum causa saepe utile est.* Cicero *Inv.* 1.27: *digressio aliqua extra causam aut criminationis aut similitudinis aut delectationis . . . causa interponitur.* Ecphrasis also entertains; cf. Aeneas' initial reaction to the shield: *ille deae donis et tanto **laetus** honore/expleri nequit* (*Aen.* 8.617–18).

[9] Cicero *Fam.* 5.12.4: *nihil est enim aptius ad delectationem lectoris quam temporum varietates fortunaeque vicissitudines.*

historiographers also include topographical descriptions for the purpose of entertainment.[10] No doubt pleasure is a fundamental aspect
of literature. Yet the amusement of the reader is rarely innocuous;
Horace links delight to admonition.[11] Thus the digression of the
return to Teutoburg engages the curiosity of the reader with its
depiction of the strange and the macabre, but it is also laden with
thematic overtones meant to seduce the reader into a particularly
Tacitean view of imperialism and its discontent.

The ecphrastic depiction of the battle of Actium on the shield is
arguably one of the most profound moments of foreshadowing in
Latin poetry. The shield is certainly the most extended ecphrasis in
the *Aeneid*. To the extent that it stands 'outside of' the text, ecphrasis, in the etymological sense of the word, is a paradoxical medium,
an ideal setting for competing and conflicting modes of thought.
Ecphrasis halts the narrative per se. By stopping to describe an object,
the poet ceases to advance the action of the characters. The viewer
stands still and performs no action while beholding the object described.
Yet it is easy to detect a responsion between the description and the
narrative; the imagery of the ecphrasis provides another venue for
interpreting the action of the epic. So the shield, distinctly set apart
from the poem by rhetorical cues, can be interpreted to represent
in a microcosm the ideology of the entire *Aeneid* writ large.[12] In
essence, ecphrasis betrays a tension between particular and general,
part and whole, and ultimately, individual and society. To resolve
this tension by insisting that ecphrasis is either distinct from, or integral to, the rest of the narrative denies the power of the figure and
reduces its effectiveness.[13]

Ecphrasis, like digression, does more than entertain. Digression,
like ecphrasis, is both separate from, and integral to, the rest of the
narrative. In form, Actium and Teutoburg are temporally removed
from the rest of the *Aeneid* and the *Annals*. But the content of both —
the Augustan victory and defeat — casts an inescapable shadow across
the entire poem and history in which they appear.

---

[10] Horsfall (1985) 199; Woodman (1988) 183.
[11] Horace *Ars* 343–4: *omne tulit punctum qui miscuit utile dulci,/lectorem delectando
pariterque monendo.* On pleasure, cf. Barthes (1975).
[12] So the interpretations of Hardie (1986) esp. 362–4 and Harrison (1997).
[13] See the influential essay of Fowler (1991).

In *Virgil's Epic Designs*, Michael Putnam argues that throughout the *Aeneid*, ecphrasis betrays moments of friction in the narrative.[14] It is precisely this friction which interests us. To begin with, several times Vergil calls attention to the shield's status as artifact.[15] For example, adverbial phrases locate the scenes from Roman history on the shield: *illic* (8.626, 628), *nec procul hinc* (8.635), *haud procul inde* (8.642), *hinc procul addit* (8.666), and *in medio* (8.675). Verbs of visual perception force the reader to behold the object: *aspiceres* (8.650), *cernere erat . . . videres* (8.676). Adjectives describe the fabric of the metal work: *auratis . . . argenteus* (8.655), *aurea . . . aurea* (8.659, 672), and *argento* (8.673), as does the verb *coruscant* (8.661). But these cues are absent from the depiction of Actium, as Alessandro Barchiesi notes:

> There is no mention of the artist as author of the image (no *fecerat* or *addit* or *extuderat*) and no reminder of the materiality of what is being described . . . Augustus is just himself, a maker of history and not an artist-made icon.[16]

This trope, in which the historian fades into the background allowing history to speak for itself, typifies ancient historiography.[17] By employing it here, Vergil opens the door of his epic and admits a moment of history. At this threshold we can glimpse the tension inherent in Vergil's poetic treatment of this particular historical event.

This tension is also evident in the mirroring of future and past. From the perspective of Aeneas, the events on the shield stretch out before him in the distant future. Yet for Vergil and his audience, the very same events are historical and contained in the recent past. Caught between the future and the past, the narrative action grinds to a halt. Yet at the same time, the events depicted on the shield cover hundreds of years; history accelerates at break-neck speed along a straight and narrow path. Furthermore, the shield reveals a tension between a teleological and a cyclical vision of history,[18] for linear history on its narrow path is enclosed within a circumscribed

---

[14] Putnam (1998) 14.

[15] Cf. Zetzel (1997) 201.

[16] Barchiesi (1997) 276. Contra, West (1990) 295–304 who argues that throughout the entire ecphrasis, the scenes on the shield, including Actium, were so presented as to illustrate vividly scenes which would be conceivable and effective on a metal shield; the materiality of the shield is at every point present to the reader.

[17] Barthes (1986) 131–2; White (1987) 3–10.

[18] For further discussion of this tension see Rossi ch. 12 below.

artifact. The boundaries of the shield unify its contents. As the entire
surface of the shield is covered, so the whole of Roman history, *genus
omne futurae/stirpis* (8.628–9) proceeds from foundation to Republic to
triple triumph, with no room left to spare. No part of the shield is
empty; Vulcan makes use of every available surface. Yet we know
that the events on the shield are merely a selection, and the vision
represented is fragmentary and incomplete. There is plenty of history beyond the edges of the shield.

Barchiesi characterizes ecphrasis as lending a sense of reduction,
containment, and marginalization to its contents.[19] In no way can
the contents represented on the shield spill over into the rest of the
epic action. Romulus, Remus, the Sabine women, Mettus, Cocles,
Cloelia, Catiline, Cato — none of these appear again in the action of
the epic. They have no place in the world of Aeneas who is so over-
whelmed by the 'indescribable' shield (*non enarrabile textum*, 8.625) that
he cannot even comprehend their import (*miratur rerumque ignarus imagine gaudet*, 8.730). But the ecphrastic shield bears a weighty paradox,
for the physical shield itself does appear later in the poem, when
Aeneas arrives with his allies. Standing high on the prow of the ship
he lifts the gleaming shield with his left hand, and the Trojans let
out a cry to heaven (10.261–3):

> stans celsa in puppi, clipeum cum deinde sinistra
> extulit ardentem. clamorem ad sidera tollunt
> Dardanidae e muris.

Of all the scenes on the shield, only Actium recurrs in the epic, in
the subtle repetition of the phrase *stans celsa in puppi* from line 8.680:
stans celsa in puppi, geminas cui tempora flammas. The recurrence of the
ecphrastic shield and the echo of Actium militates against its con-
finement. Thus the paradoxical nature of Vergil's representation of
Actium, and his choice of ecphrasis as the medium, is but a small
token of the contradictory reactions which Actium, the culmination
of years of civil strife, surely generated.[20]

From the fullest expression of Augustan victory we turn to the
most haunting depiction of Augustan defeat. Tacitus' description of

---

[19] Barchiesi (1997) 276.
[20] Cf. Gurval (1995) 158–9, on Horace *Epod.* 9: 'The narrative of the epode displays an intense and mixed emotional reaction to the campaign at Actium ... it is
a poet's personal and complex response to a critical and still confused situation.'

the battle of the Teutoburg forest in A.D. 9 interrupts the temporal surface of the *Annals*, which formally begin with the accession of
Tiberius. Germanicus' return to the site of the battle of the Teutoburg
forest provides an occasion for the narration of this Augustan event.
It is not unusual for a historian to backtrack in his narrative. For
example, in the four opening paragraphs of the *Annals* Book 2, Tacitus
must supply background information about Rome's relations with
Armenia prior to the reign of Tiberius, so as to make the on-going
diplomatic and military operations intelligible. Indeed, Augustus figures
prominently in 2.1–4, setting up puppet rulers. Like the return to
Teutoburg, this digression is set apart from the rest of the narrative
both rhetorically and temporally. Tacitus announces the subject succinctly, *is fuit Vonones* (2.1.2) and proceeds to explain the course of
events; the digression closes with a promise to relate the rest of the
story in its due place: *in loco reddemus* (2.4.3). Temporally the information in these chapters covers the nearly fifty years before the opening of the *Annals*, from 37 B.C., the rise of Phraates IV in Parthia,
to A.D. 11 or 12, the beginning of the reign of Vonones in Armenia.
But the return to Teutoburg is a very different type of digression
from that on the East. For one thing, the present action of Germanicus'
campaigns is conflated with an event in the past, namely, the defeat
of Varus. Furthermore, unlike the digression on Armenian affairs,
the graphic description of Teutoburg at 1.61.2–3 forces the reader
to visualize the incremental approach to the center of the battlefield:

> prima Vari castra lato ambitu et dimensis principiis trium legionum
> manus ostentabant; dein semiruto vallo, humili fossa accisae iam reliquiae
> consedisse intellegebantur. medio campi **albentia ossa,** ut fugerant,
> ut restiterant, disiecta vel aggerata. adiacebant fragmina telorum equo-
> rumque artus, simul truncis arborum **antefixa ora.** lucis propinquis
> barbarae arae, apud quas tribunos ac primorum ordinum centuriones
> mactaverant.

> Varus' first camp with broad circumference and measured headquar-
> ters was evidence of the work of three legions; thereupon from the
> half-leveled rampart and the shallow trench it was understood that
> the already diminished remnants of the legions had pitched there. In
> the middle of the plain the whitening bones were scattered or heaped
> as the men had fled or stood their ground. Lying nearby were the
> broken pieces of weapons and the limbs of horses, likewise human
> heads were nailed to the trunks of trees. In the neighboring groves
> were the barbarian altars near which they had immolated the tribunes
> and centurions of the first ranks.

The further the soldiers advance toward the center of the battlefield, the further they recede from civilization. This movement through space is syncopated with a movement through time. As the soldiers move toward the center of the battlefield, they advance toward the moment of the battle, a static moment in the past. Every step forward leads them to a point further back in time. This forward motion emphasizes their active participation in a temporal progression that usually characterizes the future.[21] But as the soldiers march forward to meet the events of the battle, time moves backward to meet the soldiers, until the massacre rises before them (1.61.4):

> et cladis eius superstites, pugnam aut vincula elapsi, referebant **hic** cecidisse legatos, **illic** raptas aquilas; primum **ubi vulnus** Varo **adactum, ubi** infelici dextera et suo ictu mortem invenerit; **quo** tribunali contionatus Arminius. . . .

> And the survivors of this disaster, having escaped battle or capture, were recounting that here the legates fell, there the eagles were taken; where the first wound inflicted Varus, where he met death with an unlucky right hand from his own blow; on which platform Arminius harangued his men. . . .

Note the preponderance of adverbs of location (*hic, illic, ubi, ubi, quo*) which, like the visual cues on the shield, call attention to space and force the reader to behold the scene. Several scholars have noted the Vergilian reminiscences in *Annals* 1.61–2. For example, Tacitus' *albentia ossa* captures Latinus' desperation at *Aeneid* 12.36. The grisly *antefixa ora* recall the inhumanity of the beast Cacus at 8.196–7. And *vulnus adactum* brings the reader back to the pathos of Mezentius upon the death of his son at 10.850. So the Vergilian diction in the return to Teutoburg points toward thematic hints of the *Aeneid*.[22]

The pause at Teutoburg to bury the dead halts the main action of the narrative. Repetition emphasizes this suspension.[23] The first

---

[21] For the relationship between time and space in Roman culture, see Bettini (1991) 113–93; for the subject's participation in the temporal process, see 131.

[22] For further verbal echoes in this passage, see Koestermann (1963) 212, Walker (1952) 72 n. 5, Soubiran (1964) who also notes similarities in metrical patterns; Woodman (1979) 147, Putnam (1989). Syme (1958) 357–8 also comments on the poetic intensity of 1.61. For thematic connections to the *Georgics*, see Pagán (1999) 305–6.

[23] Bettini (1991) 139: 'Repetition as such tends to *negate* time, certainly not to mark its progression'.

words of 1.62 (*igitur omnis qui aderat exercitus*) condense the introduction of 1.61: *igitur . . . omni qui aderat exercitu*. Nothing has transpired since the army first came upon the *Teutoburgiensis saltus* at 1.60.3 except the recreation of the battle in the mind's eye. Moreover, the episode begins and ends with Germanicus' desire to bury the dead.[24] Usually digressions are signalled in a traditional manner: 'I return to the main topic.'[25] But instead of using the customary proclamation, Tacitus leads the reader back to the present time of the narrative with the unassuming anastrophe: *igitur omnis qui aderat exercitus* (1.62.1). By narrating events which took place in the year 9 within the account of the year 15, Tacitus achieves an easy exchange between past and present, disguising the actual interruption of the temporal surface of the narrative. Having transgressed the initial temporal boundary of the *Annals*, Tacitus pilots us safely back on course to the year 15. The momentary glimpse of the Augustan defeat vanishes as quickly as it appeared, and the narrative of the *Annals* returns to the campaigns of Germanicus on the Rhine: *sed Germanicus cedentem in avia Arminium secutus* (1.63.1).

It is only fitting then, that Germanicus makes a pilgrimage to Actium. In his person defeat and victory are united, for as the adopted grand-nephew of the victor Augustus and the grandchild of the conquered Antony, he gazes upon both victory and defeat simultaneously, in language that confounds the sad emotions of his visit to Teutoburg with the joy of Actium (2.53.2):

> simul sinus Actiaca victoria inclutos et sacratas ab Augusto manubias castraque Antonii cum recordatione maiorum suorum adiit. namque ei, ut memoravi, avunculus Augustus, avus Antonius erant, magnaque illic imago tristium laetorumque.

> At the same time, in memory of his ancestors, he visited the bay famous for the Actian victory and the booty dedicated by Augustus and the camp of Antony. For Augustus was his great uncle and Antony his grandfather, as I have related, and in such circumstances the manifestation of both grim and successful events was great.

---

[24] Woodman (1979) 145.

[25] E.g., Tacitus *Ann.* 4.33.4: *sed ad inceptum redeo; Ann.* 6.22.4: *ne nunc incepto longius abierim*; Sallust *Jug.* 4.9: *nunc ad inceptum redeo; Jug.* 42.5: *quam ob rem ad inceptum redeo; Cat.* 7.7: *ni ea res longius nos ab incepto traheret*; see Fraenkel (1957) 98, Wiedemann (1979) 13–14, Woodman (1983) 162, Woodman (1988) 184.

In viewing the battlefields of both Actium and Teutoburg, Germanicus alone beholds the geographical and temporal boundaries of the legacy of his forebear; he alone beholds all the pathos that victory and defeat contain.

The Shadows of Time

We have seen how in both the ecphrasis and the digression, the authors manipulate representations of time so as to separate the events from the rest of the narrative. To understand the effects of these temporal manipulations, it is useful to turn to Bakhtin's model for time in narrative. In his seminal essay, 'Forms of Time and of the Chronotope in the Novel,' Bakhtin awakens us to the problem of representing novelistic time as open and unrestricted. He poses, but does not answer, the question of how an author can ultimately achieve freedom in a narrative in which time is always a constraining factor. Bakhtin's initial steps toward a theory of time begin with a chronological history of the novel, from antiquity to Rabelais, and the result is a crude framework for understanding the relationship between time and space.[26] Gary Morson refines Bakhtin's ideas of time, and in *Narrative and Freedom*, he constructs a theory of time built on more formal methods of argumentation than Bakhtin's loosely construed survey. Morson begins by examining the familiar trope of foreshadowing, a device which imposes order on causality. Most importantly, 'foreshadowing seems utterly to preclude the possibility of options.' It is this trope, more than any, which robs narrative of its sense of freedom. Characters have no choice, or if they do, it is merely illusory. Then, in an analysis of twentieth century novels, Morson posits the solution to this dilemma: authors use what he calls 'sideshadowing,' in which 'two or more alternative presents, the actual and the possible, are made simultaneously visible.' Sideshadowing opens up possibilities in narrative; what emerges is not one single linear narrative, but a network of possible outcomes and conclusions. Sideshadowing allows us to see *what might have been*; this is the essential ingredient of the novels of Dostoevsky and Tolstoy. Thus sideshadowing allows for a degree of freedom from the constraints of time.[27]

[26] Bakhtin (1981) 84–258.
[27] Morson (1994) 49, 118.

But such open possibilities are precisely what history denies; historians resist the temptation to narrate what might have been and instead reduce the narrative to a single strand of what indeed happened. Thus Michael Bernstein, in *Foregone Conclusions*, takes the final step in developing Bakhtin's theory of freedom and time by applying the concept of temporal shadowing to historical texts. He explores the concept of what he calls 'backshadowing':

> Backshadowing is a kind of retroactive foreshadowing in which the shared knowledge of the outcome of a series of events by narrator and listener is used to judge the participants in those events *as though they too should have known what was to come.*[28]

Foreshadowing provides knowledge of future events to the reader, but denies it to the characters; it is a trope of fiction. Sideshadowing opens up possibilities of future events to the reader; this is also a fictive move. But backshadowing assumes prior knowledge of the outcome of events and freights this knowledge with a moral judgement of the characters and their ignorance. Backshadowing is the essential characteristic of history, in which both author and reader know full well the singular outcome of events, and confident in this knowledge both despise the characters who stumble in the darkness of their ignorance toward foregone conclusions.

The concept of the shadows of time as developed by Bakhtin, Morson, and Bernstein helps us understand how the poet Vergil and the historian Tacitus manipulate time in their representations of Actium, a future event, and Teutoburg, a past event — and to what effect. Whatever the reasons Vergil and Tacitus declined to write about Augustan events directly, they were not prevented from writing about them altogether. Ecphrasis and digression resolve the problem in form; foreshadowing and flashback allow the authors to include Actium and Teutoburg in their narratives. But the interplay between past, present, and future is not without profound effect. For the manipulation of temporal 'shadows' predisposes the reader to interpret events in a particular way. Events that are foreshadowed are taken to be inevitable. Events that have already happened lead the reader to conclusions as yet unknown to the characters themselves. Bernstein's premise is to the point:

---

[28] Bernstein (1994) 16, original emphasis.

> At its extreme, foreshadowing implies a closed universe in which all
> choices have already been made, in which human free will can exist
> only in the paradoxical sense of choosing to accept or willfully — and
> vainly — rebelling against what is inevitable.[29]

This succinctly describes the effect of the history of Rome depicted
on the shield of Aeneas. The universe is indeed enclosed in the com-
pass of the shield. The choices have been made. There is no room
for what might have been. The course of events is inevitable, and
Aeneas has no choice but to accept it. And if in the end we are to
admire this hero, it is because at least he does not rebel in vain
against what is to come (8.729–31):

> talia per clipeum Volcani, dona parentis,
> miratur rerumque ignarus imagine gaudet
> attollens umero famamque et fata nepotum.

> Such scenes on the shield of Vulcan, the gift of his mother,
> does Aeneas admire, and he rejoices in the image of things
> he does not understand, lifting upon his shoulder the glory
> and the destiny of his children's children.

The linear vision of history on the shield is contrasted with the cyclical version of history in the return to Teutoburg, and both are heavily freighted with innuendo. The foreshadowing on the ecphrastic
shield precludes choice and seals the fate of Aeneas; thus the hero
appears morally superior. But the backshadowing in the digressive
Teutoburg forest grants the audience the moral high ground. Initial
judgement is passed by Tiberius (1.62.1–2):

> primum exstruendo tumulo caespitem Caesar posuit, gratissimo munere in
> defunctos et praesentibus doloris socius. quod Tiberio haud probatum . . .

> Germanicus Caesar first set up an altar by raising a burial mound, a
> most welcome duty toward the dead as he was conscious of the grief
> of those present. This was hardly acceptable to Tiberius. . . .

With the simple relative pronoun *quod* Tacitus redirects attention
from the far-off distant lands of the lower Rhine back to Rome. The
effect is stunning. It seems that Tiberius censures Germanicus' action
almost as soon as it is performed. No account is taken of the great
distance a messenger needs to traverse to inform Tiberius of the pol-

---

[29] Bernstein (1994) 2.

lution that Germanicus incurs. No account is taken of the time such a long journey requires. As quickly as Germanicus raises the burial mound, so it seems Tiberius condemns him.

Tacitus also grants the reader the opportunity to pass judgement. Shortly after the burial of the legions at Teutoburg, the general Caecina engages the Germans, and the circumstances of the massacre of Varus and his men are unwittingly recreated. Caught again in deep swamps, hampered by their baggage and unable to wield their weapons, the Romans are trapped by the Cherusci. Arminius charges, crying, "Behold Varus and his legions bound yet again by a similar fate!" It is hard to believe that this Caecina, who had just beheld the grisly sight at the Teutoburg forest, could be so foolish as to allow it to happen again. He should have known better.

By manipulating temporal elements of the narrative — by casting temporal shadows, so to speak — an author can drain events of their immediacy so that they seem either inevitable, as in the case of foreshadowing, or obvious, as with backshadowing. Thus the author creates a pact with the reader. Through an acknowledgment of the outcome of events, still unknown to the characters at the time, both author and reader can either exult (as at Actium) or scorn (as at Teutoburg) the ineffectual characters. From this omniscient vantage point, the impact of the Augustan victory and defeat is tamed. The posture is not unfamiliar. "The battle of Actium," says Ronald Syme, "was decided before it was fought."[30]

Conclusion

Ultimately the questions that Actium and Teutoburg raise are simple, even if the answers are elusive. What is the battle of Actium doing in an epic poem celebrating the mythological foundation of Rome? What is a historian, who from the start proclaims his devotion to *urbem Romam* (1.1.1) at the accession of Tiberius (1.1.3), doing in the middle of the Teutoburg forest in the time of Augustus? What is it about Actium and Teutoburg that Vergil and Tacitus could not resist? Augustus looms large over the *Aeneid* and the *Annals*, yet in these passages Vergil and Tacitus transmit neither clear-cut opposition nor

---

[30] Syme (1939) 296.

ringing endorsement, but a sense of genuine dubiety about the *princeps*, perhaps not entirely their own.[31] If we observe parallels between
the figures of Aeneas and Augustus,[32] then we must sense in the tri-
umphant Augustus the ambivalent moral actions of Aeneas at the
close of the epic. In the end, the conflation of Augustan victory and
defeat is best exemplified in the Forum, where Augustus and Tiberius,
aggrandizing themselves at the expense of their failed predecessors,
erected triumphal arches to commemorate the recovery of the Roman
standards from the far-flung defeats at Carrhae and Teutoburg.[33]
With a sleight of hand, the most humiliating losses are reversed and
transformed into monuments marking the eastern and western-most
limits of the empire in the heart of the city of Rome.

Presented with moments of extreme cultural and political crisis,
both authors rise to the occasion and respond with moments of
extreme emotional and rhetorical sophistication, but neither can
sufficiently justify the Augustan victory or defeat. Elsewhere future
events are interpreted in the *Aeneid*, for example, Anchises comments
on the parade of heroes in the Underworld. But the shield portray-
ing Actium is simply laid before Aeneas without comment and shoul-
dered without understanding. It is left for the reader to determine
its meaning. Like the shield, Teutoburg interrupts the temporal framework of the narrative. Similarly, Tacitus refrains from appending the
customary epigram, the hallmark of his sententious style;[34] the cost
of empire is left to speak for itself.

Vergil does not refrain from including references to Augustus in
his poetry, and Tacitus promises, should he live long enough, to
address the *princeps* directly.[35] But Augustan victory and defeat fall
beyond the proper scope of the *Aeneid* and the *Annals*. The difficulty

---

[31] Johnson (1973) 177: 'Each of the extant Augustan poets (along with poets not
extant and most other Augustan citizens) approved of Augustus at some times and
at some times disapproved of him.'

[32] As *Aen.* 10.261 *stans celsa in puppi*, and *Aen.* 8.680: *stans celsa in puppi* suggest;
see Binder (1971) 150–258.

[33] Evidence for the 'Actian' arch is evaluated by Gurval (1995) 39–47, who follows Nedergaard in concluding that only the Parthian arch can be attested with
certainty. Arch of Tiberius: Tacitus *Ann.* 2.41.1: *arcus propter aedem Saturni ob recepta
signa cum Varo amissa ductu Germanici, auspiciis Tiberii*; *CIL* VI 906 a–b, 1269, 31575
a, c.

[34] See Sinclair (1995).

[35] Vergil *Geo.* 3.16–48; Tacitus *Ann.* 3.24.3: *sed aliorum exitus, simul cetera illius aetatis
memorabo, si effectis, in quae tetendi, plures ad curas vitam produxero.*

is resolved in form: Vergil and Tacitus neatly package these unsettling events and their questionable outcomes in ecphrasis and digression. Yet unease with the content remains; Augustus casts an inescapable shadow over the entire endeavor. The rhetorical devices of ecphrasis and digression may defeat the modern search for definitive answers about Actium and Teutoburg in the *Aeneid* and the *Annals*, but the very production of these two remarkable texts is no small victory for poet and historian alike.[36]

---

[36] I thank David Levene and Damien Nelis for their energy and kindness in hosting the conference and the members of the audience for their constructive criticisms. Special thanks to Susanna Braund, Carole Newlands, and Richard Thomas for their comments on drafts, Albert Henrichs for the reference to Kleist, and A. Wolpert — as always.

CHAPTER FOUR

STEPPING OUT OF THE RING:
REPETITION AND SACRIFICE IN THE
BOXING MATCH IN *AENEID* 5

Andrew Feldherr

John Elsner's 1991 interpretation of the Ara Pacis,[1] exposes a tension in the representation of sacrifice that forms so important a part
of the iconography of power in Augustan Rome. How, he asks, can
a fixed and positive configuration of the historical position of Rome
and Augustus be conveyed by depicting a ritual process with the
potential to generate as much ambivalence on the part of its participants as sacrifice? Elsner's point is not so much that it can't, as
that we can't be sure that it can. Considering viewing as a process
bound up with ritual actions makes it more difficult to pronounce
about the significance of monuments in isolation from the responses
of the viewers themselves, who had the possibility of reading the
national myth inscribed in the sculptures as a closed and complete
narrative that guided the interpretation of the sacrifice they were
making, or rather of allowing the tensions of the real sacrifice to
destabilize their responses to that story. In this paper, I want to use
Vergil's treatment of the boxing match of Dares and Entellus and
the subsequent bull sacrifice to suggest that a similar contrast between
seeing things historically — by which I mean from the perspective
of those outside a closed narrative of the past — and sympatheti-
cally, from the perspective of those participating in that narrative, is
integral to the way the poem structures its readers' responses.

I have chosen to concentrate on this particular episode because
it offers one of the most explicit accounts of sacrifice within the
poem, and locates it within a complex of episodes that specifically
direct attention to the role of history and to the relationship between
the rituals of the Augustan present and of the Trojan past. Karl

---

[1] Elsner (1991).

Galinsky rightly called Book 5 an *Aeneid in parvo* because its events recapitulate the Odyssean experiences of earlier books from a perspective of comprehension and closure and at the same time look forward to the conflicts of the later books and to the foundation of Rome that lies beyond them.[2] But Galinsky's description is also true in the sense that Book 5 accentuates the poem's explicit concern with its own 'historiographic' status, that is, with the impact that the representation of the past can have on the present.[3] From both perspectives the boxing match, the central event of Anchises' funeral games, becomes a microcosm within a microcosm. It touches the temporal limits of the events of the entire poem: the exploits of the Trojan competitor Dares look back before the fall of Troy, the starting point of Aeneas' narrative, while the imagery of the episode anticipates the final combat between Aeneas and Turnus. At the same time, as I will devote the first section of my paper to demonstrating, the contest itself is embedded in contradictory stories about the past, and the questions of what earlier events it repeats, how it varies them, and how these issues are resolved by the various levels of audience who watch the fight, inform Vergil's presentation of the story.

Lest historiography seem to have sneaked into the discussion uninvited, I will anticipate my argument by outlining the two larger points I will be making about the relationship between sacrifice and the representation of the past. First, just as historians like Livy — and Augustus for that matter — exhorted their audiences to the selective replication of the past, toward an imitation that is more than just imitation, so the treatment of sacrifice within the episode hinges precisely on whether it merely repeats the violence of the contest.[4] Thus the reader's understanding of that sacrifice brings into focus the problems he or she faces in interpreting the representation of many ambiguous scenes from the Roman past — not least the final scenes of the *Aeneid* itself. In fact the audience within the episode is confronted with a similar problem of reconciling the outcome of the boxing match itself to the various traditions within which it is embedded.

---

[2] Galinsky (1968) esp. 183–5.
[3] See Feldherr (1995) esp. 259–65.
[4] For Livy, see esp. *praef.* 10; on Augustus as a producer of *exempla*, cf. his own claim in *RG* 8, and Velleius Paterculus 2.126.4.

Second, the way in which each reader will perceive this issue depends precisely on his own historical relationship to the sacrifice itself. The degree of distancing that I will argue is required to read the sacrifice as providing a resolution to the episode is correlated with the ability to see things from the perspective of the future rather than of the immediate present.

Let me begin by highlighting one of the paradoxes of the view of history exemplified by the games in *Aeneid* 5: the future will be just like the past only better. The drive toward repetition shows itself in the image of the perfect circle, of the voyage out and back, a motif that begins with the boat race and culminates in the *cursus* and *recursus* of the *lusus Troiae* (5.583), where the past comes to life again before the eyes of the spectators, and the performing youths literally complete a historical circle by reproducing the names and faces of their lost ancestors. The achievement of this epiphany depends on a combination of imitation and avoidance on the part of its participants, very like Livy's prescription for the *mala* of contemporary Rome.[5] Thus in the boat race, Mnestheus — the rememberer[6] — spurs his crew on by imitating a speech of Aeneas[7] while Sergestus fails to avoid the mistake of an earlier competitor and runs his ship on the rock. The selectivity of imitation leads to the possibility of progress. Together with circles and re-runs, the image of the arrow moving ever nearer the goal (5.525ff.) equally governs the book's structure. The ships in the boat race may all make the same double journey, but of course they don't finish in the same order.[8] And the hierarchy imposed by the finish in that and other competitions has a moral and indeed cosmological significance. Mnestheus' valor and emulation of the past receive their due, but the winner is the one who can mobilize the power of the gods.

The central relationship between progress and repetition sketched in this brief account of Book 5 perfectly conforms to David Quint's magisterial analysis of the role of narrative repetition in the poem as a whole. Quint employs Peter Brooks' distinction between repetition as something passively experienced that condemns losers to

---

[5] On repetition in Livy see esp. Kraus (1998).
[6] Williams (1960) 69.
[7] *Aen.* 5.189–93; cf. 1.198–203.
[8] See Feldherr (1995) 251–2 and Hardie (1987).

repeat the past — 'the return of' — and as a more dynamic process
in which protagonists revisit the scene of past calamities and repeat
them as victories — 'the return to'.[9] Thus the pointless amblings of
the early books of the *Aeneid*, where the aim is merely the recreation
of the doomed civilization of Troy, give way to the repetition with
a difference of the poem's later books, in which the losers play the
winners; defeat and the sacking of cities are replaced by victory and
the founding of cities.

The optimistic reading of Book 5 as a process at once repeating
and transcending the past through the selective reproduction of it
before the eyes of an audience of spectators (Trojan and Sicilian)
and of readers (for whom seeing the past in turn becomes a spur
to further imitation) has received crucial qualifications from scholars.
Michael Putnam has stressed that such moments are much easier to
achieve under the laboratory conditions of the games than in the
real events of the poem (and even here the sacrificial imagery anticipates the loss of Palinurus at the end of the book).[10] Similarly Georgia
Nugent has highlighted the emphatic selectivity of this audience
apparently *sine fine*, the deliberate exclusion of the women, who, precisely because they are left out, become unwitting agents of stasis
and mere repetition.[11] The narrative of the boxing match, though,
highlights problems implicit within the historiographic engine that
drives this progress: how do you know what to imitate, and, correspondingly, how do you differentiate progress from mere repetition?

I want to approach these issues by cataloguing the levels of repetition involved in the boxing match. First, both of the contestants
themselves view the coming fight as a repetition of an earlier battle, in particular of a battle between native and foreigner. Dares'
appearance recalls for his Trojan audience the fatal beating he gave
the Bebrycian king Butes at the funeral games for Hector (5.370–4);
Acestes spurs Entellus to compete by reminding him of his master
Eryx, who, we later learn, was himself defeated and killed by Hercules
(5.410–16). If Entellus fails to imitate him here, Eryx will be *nequiquam memoratus*, pointlessly remembered (5.392).

So too the very form of the contest involves repetition. Boxing is,
self-evidently, a paired competition that takes the form of a series

[9] Quint (1993) 53, citing Brooks (1985) 99–100.
[10] Putnam (1988) 64–104.
[11] Nugent (1992).

of repeated actions. The fighters redouble their blows (*ingeminant*), hands flash out repeatedly (*crebra*). Appropriately the very words that signify this multiplicity are themselves double in the narrative, where in general the rate of lexical repetition is strikingly high (*ingeminant*, 5.434, *ingeminans*, 5.457; *crebra*, 5.436 *creber*, 5.460; cf. also *crepitant*, 5.436 *crepitant*, 5.459; *errat*, 5.435 *pererrat*, 5.442; etc.). On a larger structural level the fight itself is doubled — twice. Entellus collapses after attempting to deliver a knock-out blow — repeating the move that was the finale for his literary forebearer Amycus in Apollonius' account.[12] After Acestes emerges to raise his friend from the ground, the fight begins again, this time though with Entellus as winner. The second repetition, the repetition of the entire fight as sacrifice, will be dealt with later.

The two contestants, in addition to bringing very different narrative prototypes to the coming battle, also demonstrate contrasting historiographic positions in the assumptions they make about the relationship between past and present. Both views differ significantly from the 'Livian view' of progress through selective imitation. The quick and confident Dares seems to lack any sense of historical vision. Like the Trojans earlier in the poem's narrative, his optimism depends on the simplistic expectation of what Quint calls bad repetition, the mere re-enacting of the past in the present. He won before; he will win again now. That his own accomplishments took place literally in the shadow of the tomb of a man who was once greatest (*maximus . . . Hector*, 5.371), and include the tale of the defeat of an opponent described as *victor* (5.372) already suggests that eternal recurrence is at very least uncertain. Indeed the history of his career conspicuously elides the decisive turning point that divides the Trojans' present from their past — the fall of Troy itself, an event that not only marks the beginning of Aeneas' own history, but, as we shall see, has an important role to play in the present narrative.[13] In Entellus' case the relationship between past and present is much more complicated. He is fully aware of the difference between present and

---

[12] For Vergil's use of Apollonius Rhodius in this scene see now Nelis (2001) 8–21.
[13] The fall of Troy was also of course frequently treated as the beginning of history itself (cf. e.g. the beginning of the chronology of Eratosthenes, *FGrH* 241 F1, and, of course, Livy 1.1). The event formed a watershed in Varro's *De gente populi romani* although it does not there demarcate the historical from the mythical period (frg. 14P, see the discussion by Wiseman ch. 17 below).

past, but seems to view the possibility of emulating past accomplishments as something ruled out by the mortal condition itself.
Indeed his pessimism has significant resonances in contemporary historiography and poetry, recalling at once the image of civic decay
embraced by Sallust and Livy, without the latter's assertions of the
therapeutic effects of *imitatio*, and Lucretius' explanation of decline
in terms of the natural exhaustion of the earth. Thus his own *vires*
effetae (5.396) recall the *tellus effeta* that leads into the complaint of the
grandis arator at the end of Lucretius' second book (2.1150). Entellus
may be described as a *heros* (5.389), as opposed to the *vir* Dares
(5.369), but that status seems only to signal the decline from god
(Eryx/Hercules) to hero to man that underlines his predicament.

The presence of alternative narrative models for the coming encounter implies a more complicated procedure than simply the choice
of the right figure to imitate in some shared tradition, and the outcome of the fight blurs the picture even more. Matters would have
been far simpler had Vergil's challengers simply offered two competing tales of victory, as for example Livy does in his most famous
encounters between Roman and other, the Gallic duels of book seven
(7.10 and 7.26). Then we would be back in the familiar Roman situation of right making might and might making right, where the
winner's narrative is shown to have been always already true.[14] Here,
though, the outcome of the boxing match reverses the expectations
created by every earlier story. Dares loses his battle against the foreigner at another set of funeral games; Entellus, unlike his master
Eryx, and despite his pessimism, wins his fight against the visiting
stranger.[15] The effect of this pattern of reversals is that both for

---

[14] See Feldherr (1998) 51–5.

[15] This pattern of variation within the narrative parallels the way that Vergil,
like Apollonius before him, confuses audience expectations about the outcome of
the fight by combining the characteristics of winners and losers in earlier epic boxing matches in his portrayal of both Dares and Entellus, a pattern now treated in
detail by Nelis (2001) 13–21. Thus, for example, Dares, like the Iliadic victor Epeios,
proclaims the challenge, but also resembles the loser of that bout, Euryalos, in that
he too can point to an earlier victory that seems to predict his triumph (*Il.* 23.679–80).
So too the defeat of a Bebrycian, together with his youth, allies Dares to the
Apollonian victor Polydeuces, who of course also wins, but his role as challenger
likens him to Amycus. The huge and chthonic Entellus, by contrast, seems obviously to be playing Amycus, and like him produces the terrifying spectacle of vicious
boxing gloves (*Arg.* 2.51–4). But the revelation of his mighty physique (*Aen.* 5.421–3)
in turn 'reveals' him as an Odysseus, whose role as a restorer of order is foreshadowed in the boxing defeat of the beggar Iros (*Od.* 18.66–74). Throughout the

Entellus to achieve his victory and for the Trojan audience to accept
it as something other than the revenge of the barbarian, both must
take on the roles of the opponents within their own story. Unlike
Mnestheus, who imitates a figure that he already resembles in race
and status, Entellus wins by playing the victorious Hercules, and
within the doubled narrative of the match itself, becomes a Dares.
The 'second round' that Entellus wins is in terms of its vocabulary
very much a repetition of the first, but here Entellus ends up as the
victor.[16]

The slippage between different roles that results from Entellus' victory is one that the poet has already prepared for by blurring the
distinctions between combatants. If Vergil changes history by having
Entellus win, he has also done so by the very fact of making Entellus
a Sicilian, for as Servius tells us, Hyginus had named Entellus among
the Trojan followers of Aeneas (Serv. *ad Aen.* 5.389). Nor is this confusion of identities only apparent to Vergil's audience. The question
of what side Entellus is on, of maintaining distinctions between Sicilian
and Trojan, becomes particularly acute when he produces the horrible gloves of Eryx crusted with blood and brains. These hideous
memorials cause revulsion and astonishment, yet the figure who wore
them, as Entellus stresses, was Aeneas' own brother (*germanus . . . tuus*,
5.412).

The treatment of these gloves at once provides the most explicit
manifestation of the loss of distinction between the opponents and
already suggests its double-edged significance. Entellus agrees to give
up Eryx' gloves if Dares will give up his Trojan *caestus* (5.420). He
calls upon Aeneas and Acestes to make the fight equal, *aequemus pug-
nam* (5.420). Just as his narrative of the contest between Hercules
and Eryx had eroded the sense of Entellus' foreignness, so the strip-
ping of arms becomes a loss of distinctive national identities.[17] But

---

passage, as Nelis describes in detail, Vergil's invocation of earlier epic models blurs
the audience's expectations of and attitude towards the combatants.

[16] The very words that describe his ultimate victory, *versat Dareta* (*Aen.* 5.460),
hint at this: Entellus at once overturns Dares, and, perhaps, applies or varies the
model of Dares, since *versare* can be used to describe how a student will adapt a
rhetorical figure (*OLD* s.v. 7) though never with a personal object.

[17] Rhiannon Ash reminds me of further evidence for how the assumption of foreign weaponry could raise the issue of preserving national identity; Caesar's argument
at Sallust *Cat.* 51.38 that the *maiores'* taking over the *arma* of the Samnites provides
a positive precedent for the importation of foreign practices and institutions.

this loss can be read two ways: On the one hand, the substitution for the monstrous and deadly arms of Eryx powerfully defines the separation between past and present: this battle will be no fatal encounter inspiring future vengeance, but a controlled contest within the context of games, resemblance with a profound difference. On the other, the removal of those gloves signifies the loss of the difference between the civilized and the foreign that might have given such a fight meaning, as it certainly did in the Apollonian encounter between Amycus and Polydeuces.[18] As is the case for Aeneas at the end of the poem, even if Dares wins he cannot win as a Trojan. So in a larger sense, if you agree that Entellus winds up playing Dares at the end of the fight, is this to be read as progress in Quint's terms of repetition with a difference, as successful *imitatio*, or rather does it imply a destabilizing equality between the combatants, a blurring of difference that makes Eryx a kinsmen of Aeneas indeed?

I have suggested so far that Vergil's narrative of the fight has set before both the audience within the poem and the reader two related problems of maintaining distinctions between pairs, first between the pair of fighters before them, and between the boxing match itself and its antecedents. The sacrificial ritual that distinctively ends Vergil's boxing match (further differentiating his 'repetition' of the scene in Apollonius)[19] recapitulates the same two issues. The ox itself becomes an explicit substitute for Dares: *hanc . . . meliorem animam pro morte Daretis/persolvo* (5.483). Seeing the ox as 'not Dares' is also crucial to negotiating the second kind of resemblance involved in sacrifice. The ox is not Dares because the boxing match is over. The boxing match is over because these are not the violent days of Eryx who would happily have added Dares' own *cerebrum* to the decorations of his *caestus*. Thus a whole set of progressions achieve glorious closure. If Apollonius connected the slaying of Amycus with the transition from lawless barbarism to Jovian order, the sacrificial difference in Vergil's text in turn civilizes his predecessor by substituting ritual for slaughter. The closure of Vergil's own narrative is also apparently absolute. The boasting and self-confidence that drove Dares to fight are presumably diminished, but at the same time there is no death

---

[18] Cf. the comments of Hunter (1993) 28–9.
[19] This variation also has the effect of transforming what had been merely a simile in Apollonius, who compares Amycus to 'a man about to fell an ox' (*Arg.* 2.91). For other transformations of image to reality in the book, see Feldherr (1995).

to avenge as there was for Entellus. Eryx, rather than having his
memory become vain, is honored as a god, summoning up the same
hierarchies of beast, man, and god also highlighted at the end of
the boat race. Finally we should also emphasize the historiographic
significance of this repetition with a difference, in light of Entellus'
early view that the essential distinction between past and present was
a mark of decline. As he saw it, the actions of the gods (i.e. Hercules)
revealed the comparative weakness of humans. Here the arrows are
reversed; human success becomes a sign of the presence of the gods.

All this progress, though, depends on seeing Dares as different
from the bull and the sacrifice as different from the boxing match,
but certain elements of Vergil's description seem to lead toward
identification rather than distinction. First, of course. is the way that
the bull is killed, not as a sacrificial victim, but as a boxing opponent. Indeed the lines that describe the trembling cow hurled lifeless to the ground suggest the image of Entellus himself collapsing
after his mistimed blow,[20] and the verb used of the fighter on that
occasion was *concidit* (5.448), which, as Hardie points out, is particularly associated with the death of the sacrificial victim.[21] Such a
confusion of sacrificant and victim not only mirrors the indistin-
guishability of the original combatants but perpetuates it: the substitute Dares is also an Entellus. Thus the substitution of the bull
for Dares, in this reading, far from marking an advance over the
shedding of human blood, in fact serves to reveal the ox in every
boxer. And far from designating the ending point of a linear progression, it returns us to the beginning of the cycle. Boxers after all,
prepare for battle by donning the hides, *terga* (5.405), of bulls. As
Kraggerud (1960) has pointed out, the name of Dares' victim, Butes,[22]

---

[20] At *Aen.* 5.431–2, Entellus is described as *tremens*, and panting hard (*vastos quatit
aeger anhelitus artus*), so too the dying bull is *tremens* (*Aen.* 5.481) and, in a different
sense, *exanimis*.

[21] Hardie (1993) 52, citing *concido OLD* s.v. 1c. The instance Hardie is discussing,
where *concidit* is used of another 'sacrificial substitute', Nisus, slipping in the blood
of an actual victim, occurs in the episode immediately preceding the boxing match
(*Aen.* 5.333).

[22] The function of the name Butes in eliding the difference between the victim
and the opponent for whom he substitutes is interesting since Butes also helps to
blur the difference between the combatants and their respective heritages. Whether
or not Vergil had any precedent for the Bebrycian Butes Dares boasts of defeating (a figure not previously attested), the name and the Apollonian context recall
a better known Butes who, far from reinforcing the opposition between savage and

the Bebrycian (cf. βέβρυχα) kinsman of Amycus (cf. μυκάομαι) conspires
to give him a certain bovine cast. And, according to the scholia to
Lycophron, 'bull' was Eryx's own nom de guerre (Tzetz. *ad Lyc.* 866).

My point in suggesting this other aspect to the bull sacrifice has
not been simply to root out disconcerting undertones in another
upbeat passage of the *Aeneid*. Rather I have wanted first to demonstrate in action the link suggested by Hardie and Bandera between
the poetics of repetition and the Girardian logic of sacrifice,[23] and
at the same time to look again at its implications for the reception
of Vergil's 'repetition' of the boxing match as a literary narrative.
Llewelyn Morgan (1998) has recently made an important but very
different attempt to use sacrificial logic to understand the representations of violence within the poem. He suggests that the analogy
between the kinds of violence frequently highlighted by 'pessimistic'
readings of the *Aeneid* and those generated by such rituals as sacrifice
and gladiatorial combats in fact served to normalize these darker
passages. If such rituals had a positive civic and religious value despite
their violence, then so perhaps can Vergil's poem. Morgan's analogy, however, can work in reverse as well: the interpretative problems that Vergil's poem raises become all the more compelling because
they are posed in terms similar to those of the actual ritual practices that were essential in defining the Roman community. Thus
rather than turning to ritual to make sense of the problems in Vergil,
we can use Vergil's text as a way of exploring how precisely the
constructive and the destructive[24] can co-exist in responses to actual
ritual practice. Nor can we simply avoid the problem by dividing
the good violence of sacrifice, where all the arrows point in the right
direction and all the right distinctions are made, from bad, com-
petitive, internecine violence. Such a potential for confusion is built
into the logic of sacrificial substitution itself, which is necessarily a
two-way street. This is revealed by Entellus' explicit demand that
the ox be recognized as a substitute for Dares: the very attempt to

---

civilized races, reminds one of the kinship between Trojan and Sicilian. This was
the Argonaut Butes who was rescued by Aphrodite after he tried to swim to the
Sirens' island and became, by her, the father of Eryx. (*Arg.* 4.912–9, Diodorus
Siculus 4.83, Hyginus *Fab.* 260).

[23] Hardie (1993) esp. 19–26 and Bandera (1981) esp. 233–4.

[24] Morgan (1998) 185–7.

impose a distinction between the two simultaneously asserts their equivalence.[25]

Does this passage, then, give us any clues about what enables an audience to perceive the positive dimension of sacrificial ritual, rather than being caught up in its violence? Obviously the essential question is how closely the audience identifies with the victim, but I think we can isolate one particularly important criterion for orienting audience response, and that is the time-relation between audience and event. I take a clue here from Morgan's demonstration that the Romans recognized the paradoxical combination of the productive and destructive in gladiatorial combat: the emperor Julian is quoted as calling such displays 'grim but necessary', σκυθρωπῶν μέν, ἀναγκαίων δὲ ὅμως.[26] The grim but necessary may have been the bread and butter of Roman socialization, but one area where this language was frequently applied was of course the historical *exemplum*, as in Livy's paradoxical 'unendurable remedies' (*praef.* 9). One of the several passages within Livy that echo this programmatic phrase comes when the consul Torquatus sentences his own son to death for fighting a duel without permission, *triste exemplum sed in posterum salubre iuventuti* (8.7.17). Torquatus' terms explicate the paradox in two particularly interesting ways: first he makes it clear that the intended audience for the *exemplum* will be the *iuventus*, that is the age class who identify themselves most strongly with the victim, and that the healthful effects will be felt *in posterum*, in the future, not among those actually watching the execution but afterwards.[27]

---

[25] Cf. Girard's (1977) 5 reflections on sacrificial substitution: 'Sacrificial substitution implies a degree of misunderstanding. Its vitality as an institution depends upon its ability to conceal the displacement on which the rite is based. It must never lose sight entirely, however, of the original object, or cease to be aware of the act of transference from that object to the surrogate victim; without that awareness no substitution can take place and the rite loses all efficacy'.

[26] Julian *Or.* 4.156b–c; see Morgan (1998) 190.

[27] The final effect of the *exemplum* will in fact not be as unanimously beneficial in the future as the *imperator*'s words predict. For all the narrator's subsequent insistence on the good that was done by such cruelty (*ea severitas profuit*, 8.8.1), his narrative also perpetuates the perspective of the *iuvenes* themselves: so great was the mourning at the young Torquatus' funeral that *Manliana imperia non in praesentia modo horrenda sed exempli etiam tristis in posterum essent*, (8.7.22), language explicitly echoing the dictator's words. Thus the narrative also perpetuates the perspective of those who identify most closely with the victim himself, providing a narratological conduit to the victim's own point of view that never allows the story to become simply *salubre*.

What I am suggesting is that if the audience can adopt a 'historical' perspective on sacrifice, seeing it as it were from the future, as though it were already over, their capacity to identify with the victim will be very much less than those immediately present, especially those, like the Trojans here, who are invited to see the victim as one of them. This imposition of historical distance relates very closely to one of the earlier points I made about the hermeneutic ambiguities of the ox-slaying: the problem of whether it is to be seen as a representation, after the fact, of an event upon which Aeneas has placed an emphatic *finis* (5.463), or as a perpetuation of a contest that is still unfinished. In this case, the two audiences that I would like to try and distinguish are the Trojans, whom Entellus directly constitutes as an audience (*haec cognoscite Teucri*, 5.474), and their descendants, the poet's own readers. There is of course no explicit description of how the Trojans reacted to the bull's death, certainly nothing to suggest that they found it repulsive, or even tasteless. But there are a couple of expressions in Vergil's account that, if they do not exactly reveal what the Trojan reaction was, at least invite an awareness of it as something potentially distinct from a later reader's. To take but one example, there is the description of the victor's exaltation, *superans animis tauroque superbus* (5.473). *Superbus* here can be taken as an unproblematic 'post-game interview' adjective — it is used in precisely the same construction of the crews in the boat race (5.268). But Don Fowler's point that *superbus* can always also have pejorative connotations, and that it functions precisely to signal the presence of alternative or 'deviant' ways of seeing, seems especially appropriate when it is used of a figure who was just said to *saevire animis acerbis* (5.462).[28]

---

[28] Fowler (1990) 47–52, esp. 51. It is also significant for my argument here that some of the more problematic uses of *superbus* in the poem involve its application to the Trojans (*Aen.* 1.21, 2.556, and 3.2). If throughout its history in the poem the word asks the reader potentially to take sides and to isolate or diagnose the perspective of the character who applies it, its use here of Entellus gains further significance. Because the issues raised by the word seem particularly connected with Troy, Entellus' adoption of it at once further signals that he is playing the role of the Trojans, and concomitantly allows readers to measure their separation from such Trojans, both because they are aware of how differently the word might sound to the partisan Trojans of the narrative, and because it emblematises those negative aspects of Troy that seem to guarantee and justify its fall.

Again, I am not claiming to excavate signs of Trojan disquiet, simply to suggest that the lines create an awareness of possible differences between the reader's reaction to the scene and that of a Trojan spectator. Indeed the Trojans themselves could have seen the event in a number of different lights, especially if they recognize, for example, that both they and Entellus are sacrificing to characters linked with Venus, Eryx, and Anchises. But if the Trojan audience have already been given clues to the affinity between themselves and the sacrificant, Vergil's audience have received an even more powerful indication that Entellus' victory really is their victory, and this indication is only available to those who know how the Trojans' own story ends. When Dares is assaulting the immobile Entellus with a flurry of blows, just before the Sicilian's fall, Vergil uses a simile with no antecedent in Homeric or Apollonian boxing matches: Dares is like a man besieging a lofty city (*celsam urbem*, 5.439). The lofty city besieged cannot help but suggest Troy itself, and the connection is made more emphatic at the moment of Entellus' own *casus*, when he is compared to a pine tree falling on Erymanthus or Ida (5.448). As Kraggerud points out, the specification of mount Ida places the tree in proximity to Troy, and indeed Aeneas had used a very similar image, an old mountain ash slowly uprooted by persistent farmers, to describe the fall of Troy in book two (2.626–31).[29] Entellus may think of his victory as a vindication of Eryx. The Trojans may or may not wish to claim him as their own. But for Vergil's readers, his own fall and resurrection is the collective history of the Trojans/Romans themselves, and the plot of the *Aeneid* as promised in the proem.

Seeing past events as finished stories, if it perhaps differentiates Vergil's audience from the audience described in the poem, does inform the perspective of at least one figure within the narrative, the Trojan leader himself. Aeneas' own reperformance of past defeats comes in the significant form of textual allusion (significant because it links Aeneas' attempt to reproduce and vary the past with the readers' own awareness of the poem as representation). As Heyne

---

[29] Kraggerud (1968) 217–18. The alternative location for the tree in the simile, Erymanthus, site of one of Hercules' great exploits, recalls the alternative narrative tradition within which the fight can be placed, that of Entellus and the Sicilians for whom the present match is a sequel to that of Eryx and Hercules. In this case, though, the reference to Erymanthus points out how Entellus has 'revised' that tradition by taking on the role of the victor.

noted long ago, the rhetorical question with which Aeneas compels
Dares to yield recalls language that had been spoken to him by
Poseidon at *Iliad* 20.332–9 when he was fighting against the might-
ier Achilles.[30] As Entellus' victorious re-enactment of Eryx's duel both
places him in the role of the god Hercules and leads to the contact
with the divine that comes through sacrifice, so Aeneas is simultaneously playing a god and revealing the workings of the divine within
the spectacle. But it is not only the Iliadic passage that is called to
mind by Aeneas' words. The hero has also been enjoined to surrender
to the will of the gods at a significant moment of defeat within
Vergil's own poem, the fall of Troy itself. The goddess Venus descends
to place an end to Aeneas' madness, by revealing to him the divine
agents at work in Troy's destruction (2.594–611). This epiphany
immediately precedes the simile of the falling ash recalled in the
description of Entellus. Thus Aeneas' own reperformance of the past
helps to signal the reader's own sense of *déjà vu*, the hindsight, which
I have suggested helps them to see the boxing match and subsequent sacrifice in a positive light, and marks Aeneas' own progress
from the mere imitation of his Greek opponents at Troy to playing
the god.

Another appeal to the audience's past experience as readers both
complements Aeneas' imposition of a happy ending on the conflict
and at the same time highlights the difference in perspective between
Aeneas, who as a character replays events that he has personally
experienced, and Vergil's reader, who of course comes after the text
itself. Most commentators pass over in silence the collocation of *infelix* and the line-end *dementia cepit.* (5.465). It occurs only here in the
Aeneid; yet Vergil uses it in a particularly significant passage of the
Eclogues: Silenus' apostrophe to Pasiphae, *a! virgo infelix, quae te dementia cepit!* (6.47; for the line-end *dementia cepit* used of the madness of
love, cf. also 2.69). That Silenus was there consoling Pasiphae for
the 'love of a snowy *iuvencus*' (6.46, cf. *Aeneid* 5.366, 477) and that
Aeneas here is said to *mulcere* Dares, as though he were himself an

---

[30] There are other suggestive echoes of the Iliadic scene here: 1) Aeneas' own
hyperawareness of the weakness of men in the face of gods, which also resembles
Entellus', recalls his speech to Achilles (cf. Ζεὺς δ' ἀρετὴν ἄνδρεσσιν ὀφέλλει τε
μινύθει τε, *Il.* 20.242). 2) So too does the specific signalling, in this case through
the processes of intertextuality, of the reciprocity of stories and the interchange-
ability of roles (*Il.* 20.246–50).

animal to stroke (5.464), create further points of contact between the two passages. The collocation of Dares and Pasiphae cannot help but make Dares even more ridiculous, and correspondingly harder to identify with seriously; yet the very consciousness of the intertext anchors the reader in the immediate present, distancing him not only from Dares but from Aeneas himself, who may be quoting what the gods have said to him before — either in this poem or the *Iliad* — but is certainly not quoting Vergil.

What I have tried to suggest through this analysis is that not only do the sacrificial overtones of accounts of violence in the *Aeneid* invite discordant responses, but that the nature of sacrificial ambiguity, depending as it does on the choice between participation and detachment, mirrors precisely the kinds of interpretative choices made by the reader of the poem as a whole as a representation of the past. As Fitzgerald's interpretation of the images on the temple doors at Cumae so brilliantly describes, every representation within the poem offers a similar choice between detached viewing — as one who comes after — and adopting the perspective of the contemporary.[31] So sacrifice here can be viewed by its immediate audience either as a representation, an image of an event that is emphatically over, whose very occurrence enforces a sense of closure, or as a repetition of that earlier event that can re-awaken the conflicts whose end it ostensibly celebrates. And the reader of Vergil's text faces the corresponding choice of seeing the immediate audience as a model for their own response or as a foil to it, in the sense that they are in a better position to achieve a historicizing distance on events. Representations of sacrifice thus at once break down the separation between present and past, and alternatively provide a secure vantage point on distant events, demarcating them as over and claiming meaning for them. An interesting approach to this second aspect of sacrifice comes from Barchiesi's recent article on the statue of Minerva on the temple walls at Carthage.[32] As Barchiesi suggests, the implications of that image change dramatically as one moves from Troy to Carthage, to the point of view of a Roman viewer, and finally to the newly established Roman colony at the site of Troy. If the story itself has a story, and changes its meanings as it is read by different audiences with

---

[31] Fitzgerald (1984), esp. 57–8.
[32] Barchiesi (1998).

different historical perspectives, perhaps sacrifice can become one of the moments when each of these points of view is articulated. It is no accident that this fundamentally ambiguous image appears on the front of a temple, which would also have provided the visual backdrop for sacrifice.

With that last point in mind, I want to end by making some suggestions about how the poem's deployment of the logic of sacrifice in this passage can be related to two of its most complex and compelling modes of signification: allusivity and ecphrasis. As Hardie has elegantly summarized, the relationship between a text and its antecedents in the tradition can be described in agonistic terms:[33] the new text surpasses the models it invokes and subordinates them to its own narrative and thematic structures. So in the boxing match the sequence of victories each combatant brings to the contest also evokes a succession of prior texts: Dares' defeat of a Bebrycian can thus be correlated with Vergil's recasting of the epic narrative that records an earlier Bebrycian boxing match, Apollonius' *Argonautica*, just as that episode in turn signals its own manipulations of the *Iliad* and the *Odyssey*.[34] As sacrifice requires the audience's continual awareness of the difference between the ritual act and the violence for which it substitutes, so the text presently unfolding before the reader endeavors to stand apart from the previous narratives it invokes. But in both cases of course such distinctions can never be absolute; the sacrificial victim can always be recognized as a stand-in for a human victim, and the 'voices' of previous texts can always make themselves heard over the one in which they are embedded. In the case of Vergil's boxing match, it is literally sacrifice that marks his overcoming of Apollonius. What in the previous poem had been merely an image — Amycus rises up like a man about to fell an ox (2.91) — becomes actual, and perhaps the movement from simile to ritual reflects an effort to give the text some purchase outside the merely literary tradition. So too from the reader's perspective the closure provided by sacrifice, which by preventing further rivalry always aims to be the

---

[33] Hardie (1993) 101–19.
[34] See again Nelis (2001) 8–21. The metaliterary aspect of the boxing match is perhaps as old as the tradition itself. Thus the Iliadic example features a contestant, Euryalos, who was victorious in the funeral games for the Theban hero Oedipus (*Il.* 23.679–80), a cross reference to another cycle of epic narrative, and it may be no coincidence that this is the fighter who loses.

end of the story, contrasts with the multiple and confusing pattern of resemblances between winners and losers that characterizes both the internal narratives of Dares and Entellus and the poet's own manipulation of preceding epic boxing matches.[35] Thus we can recognize sacrifice in the poem as an important 'trope of allusivity', a way in which the author describes the formation and reception of his own text. But more importantly, we can follow the lead of Stephen Hinds by reversing the trope and seeing how the text's and reader's struggle to impose a final meaning on the narrative approximates the dynamics of sacrificial ritual.[36]

Sacrifice also plays an important structural role in demarcating the stories within stories that emerge from the poem's great ecphrases, and here too images of sacrifice 'frame' the narrative metaphorically as well, by positioning the reader at once inside and outside the text. When, at the end of the account of her first meeting with Aeneas (1.632), the scene set in motion by the Trojan's reading of the sculptures on the temple of Juno, Vergil mentions that Dido proclaimed a sacrifice, it seems an afterthought, little more than a narrative formula designed to bring events to a close. Sacrifice even more emphatically signifies a turning away from ecphrasis — an end of absorption in the representation of the past and a resumption of the present story — at the temple of Apollo at Cumae, when the Sibyl keeps Aeneas from examining the pictures by reminding him of the necessity for sacrifice (6.37–9). Yet the sacrifice she enjoins recalls the first scene represented on the doors, so that the very gesture with which Aeneas moves beyond viewing literally puts him in the picture.[37] Zetzel's point that this sacrifice in turn predicts the rituals prescribed for the saecular games of 17 B.C.E. places the reader in a similar relationship to the *Aeneid*'s own representation:[38] the extratextual ritual that marks progress toward the future is already embedded in the past. The sacrifice that ends the next major ecphrasis, the shield of Aeneas, even more strikingly juxtaposes the perspective of one

---

[35] See above, note 15.

[36] See Hinds (1998) 5–10 on 'Tropics of Allusivity' and 10–16 on 'Reversing the Trope', cf. also Hardie (1993) 19–26, a discussion of the *Aeneid's* sacrificial ending, to which my understanding of the poem is much indebted.

[37] Fitzgerald (1984) 58, whose reading however emphasizes the differences more than the similarities between the represented sacrifice and the one performed by Aeneas.

[38] Zetzel (1989).

anchored in the present, and one absorbed in the events represented.
Here far from marking an ostensible turning away from ecphrasis,
the sacrifice forms part of the ecphrasis itself: the final scene described
on the shield portrays the sacrifice that begins the Actian triumph,
an event less than ten years old to the poem's first audience (8.715).
Does this depiction of the present provide the reader with an external point of view that helps him to interpret and organize the events
represented both on the shield and in the poem? Or rather does it
encourage a sense that this present is itself a construct of the poem
and far from clarifying its ambiguities participates in them?[39] The
way each reader answers this question will be crucial for his understanding of the poem's conclusion, which again hinges both on the
interpretation of an ecphrasis, the Danaid scene inscribed on Turnus'
baldric (12.941–6), and the response to an act that, Aeneas claims,
is really a sacrifice (12.949). The distinctive feature of this 'sacrifice'
is made clear by contrast with the sacrificial conclusion of the fight
between Dares and Entellus: just as there is no mitigating substitution, there is also no separation between sacrifice and event.[40] The
sacrifice is not the re-enactment or representation of the death of
Turnus; it *is* the death of Turnus. Again, however, an allusion to
contemporary ritual practice at first seems to encourage the reader
to adopt just the kind of historical perspective necessary to adopt a
sacrificial view of the slaying of Turnus: it has often been pointed
out that the scene depicted on the baldric of Turnus also formed
part of the iconography of the portico of the Temple of Palatine
Apollo.[41] This was also the location of both the statue of Apollo,
which formed the conclusion of the poem's last ecphrasis, and the
sacrificial altar (Prop. 2.31.7). On the one hand readers can use this
reference to contemporary experience to consolidate the work's prob-

---

[39] For a different perspective on this question see also Pagan ch. 3 above.

[40] Thus I disagree slightly with Bandera's (1981) 234 discussion of the poem's
ending. It is not so much Vergil who has portrayed Turnus as the sacrificial victim, but merely the character Aeneas. Whether we see Vergil as endorsing a process
of sacrificial logic that closes the epic with a positive evaluation of its violence or
as exposing such strategies of resolution as inevitably partial, depends on how much
we remain aware that line 949 is part of the direct speech of a participant in the
narrative.

[41] For a discussion of how the presence of this scene within the sculptural program of Augustus' temple affects interpretation of the ending of the poem, see esp.
Harrison (1998).

lematic closure:[42] just as in the account of Dares and Entellus Vergil transformed Apollonius' simile of sacrifice into real sacrifice, so too the poem as a whole achieves clarity and meaning when completed by contemporary ritual. On the other, they can read the historical iconography embedded in the present ritual through the eyes of the past, adopting the uncertain position of the figures within the narrative, in particular of the sacrificial victim Turnus.[43]

---

[42] Sauron (1991) demonstrates that the sculptural decorations of the altars in the Augustan theater of Arles specifically repeated motifs from the temple of Apollo on the Palatine, interestingly suggesting that this space provided the ideal ideological vantage point for viewing theatrical representations.

[43] I am extremely grateful to the participants at the Durham conference for their many suggestions, especially to Dr. Helen Lovatt. I would also like to thank Prof. Damien Nelis for showing me extracts from his forthcoming book. I alone am responsible for the errors that remain.

CHAPTER FIVE

ARCHAISM AND HISTORICISM IN HORACE'S *ODES*

Ellen O'Gorman

The present alone is inadequate to our desires, not least because it is
continually depleted to further enlarge the past.

David Lowenthal

'Augustan poetry is deeply rooted in its socio-political setting; it is
also deeply concerned about its place within the traditions of Greek
and Latin letters'. This was the opening sentence of the call for
papers sent out by David Levene and Damien Nelis early in 1999,
for the conference of the book 'Augustan Poetry and the Traditions
of Ancient Historiography'. This bipartite claim provoked me to write
an abstract, a paper and now an article on Horatian lyric, aimed at
exploring the implications of this simultaneous location of Augustan
poetry in 'its' time, place and literary tradition.[1] What struck me at
first about this mode of situating of poetry was its emphasis on
grounding, rooting and embedding, where a more aesthetically centred
approach, which would see the poem as an autonomous creation,
might emphasise poetry's capacity to float free and soar above the
realm of the historical. In this piece I am therefore interested in
exploring the tensions and contradictions which animate historicist
readings of poetry, particularly the contradictions of temporality, and
in considering how we might respond to rather than simply duck
the challenge which the aesthetic poses to historicism.

As a mode of criticism which insists upon the prime importance
of historical context for interpreting a text, historicism implicitly sets

[1] Conversations with Duncan Kennedy, Charles Martindale and Vanda Zajko
have, as always, inspired and informed my thoughts for this piece. I have also
benefited greatly from exchanges on historicism with Kirk Freudenburg and Bruce
Heiden. Further thoughts were provoked by discussion with the members of Horace
graduate seminar at the Ohio State University, Spring 2000: Catalin Anghelina,
Scott Keister, Amber Lunsford and Tina Wirick. Robert Fowler also kindly read
and commented on the original paper. Thanks to all of the above, and to the
organisers of the conference.

itself in opposition to other modes of interpretation which appeal to
more literary considerations, which evaluate the text in the wider
(perhaps universalising) contexts of the poetic tradition, of genre and
of formal structure. From the perspective of such an opposition, it
is hardly surprising that W. B. Stanford listed 'Historicists' among
the enemies of poetry.[2] For lovers of poetry, a historicist analysis can
be seen to exhaust the poem's meaning in the context of its original reception, leaving little room for consideration of a more timeless
aesthetic value. Yet classicists have so far resisted a turn to aesthetic
theory, and have instead concentrated on the literary tradition as a
context for evaluating text, which allows aesthetic value its place
while remaining aware of some sort of historical change. The problems with this sort of literary history are well-known: the tendency
to subordinate individual texts to a plot of development and decline,
so that the poet becomes trapped in his place in the tradition; the
danger of emptying all utterances and acts of their historical specificity and reducing them (or expanding them) to a series of timeless
tropes; and the possibility offered by the literary tradition to over-
write expanses of time and shifts of culture with a narrative of simple generic continuity.[3] The last problem is, of course, most striking
when we examine Horace's inscription of himself into the lyric canon.
    The literary tradition, then, is a historical narrative which works
against historicism. But returning to historicism, we may ask what
are its inner tensions and contradictions. Historicist readings which
situate a text in its contemporary cultural context are readings which
presuppose the entire era as a finished text. The literature itself
becomes partial, incomplete, while the reader is implicitly enjoined
to read as widely as possible in order to 'complete' the text by situating it in its 'proper' context. While this fragmentation can dimin-
ish the text, reducing it to part of a larger whole, a historicist reading
of this sort can also effect an expansion of the text into the many
facets of its culture, incorporating both political assent and dissent.[4]
This sort of totalising expansion of the text into its culture continues with the claim of historical specificity; the text is understood pri-

---

[2] Stanford (1980) 8–32.
[3] Martindale (1993).
[4] Habinek (1998) in particular seeks to explore the possibilities of a more historically engaged mode of reading, by considering literature's interventions in society.
See also Oliensis (1998) 2–3 on Horatian poems as 'speech acts'.

marily in relation to its historical context, and, moreover, the historical context is apprehended primarily through the text, with which it is practically coterminous. And yet the unreflective historicist reading claims to escape its own presuppositions; by insisting on the prime importance of historical context for interpreting a text, unreflective historicism projects its own interpretation as true for all time, and as validated by the past itself.[5] This projection of the historicist reading as eternal is precisely what historicism exposes elsewhere as temporally relative.[6]

As I remarked above, classicists have in recent years avoided more aesthetically grounded modes of criticism in favour of two modes which draw upon different facets of historicism, and which consequently can be combined. This combination of reading texts within both 'their' historical context and the literary tradition, however, creates a hybrid form of historicism, where time is alternately filled with and emptied of meaning.

We can examine this further by looking at one of the most committedly historicist readings of Horace in recent scholarship, Ian Du Quesnay's study of *Odes* 4.5.[7] This study takes the expansion of the text into the culture of its original reception to extremes; a 40 line poem is exegised in 60 pages of prose. The apparent drive of the study is to leave nothing unsaid on the subject, thereby projecting the text-plus-context as the full story to which nothing need be appended. Du Quesnay's expansion of 4.5, it should be said, preserves and elaborates some properties of the ode itself, in particular in the anxiety to make present the absent Augustus[8] and in the closural claim,

---

[5] Galinsky (1996) 237–45 represents a striking attempt to historicise poetic transcendence, with the claim that cultures such as that of fifth-century Athens and Augustan Rome occupied defining moments which 'called for an appropriate articulation' (238). The problem with this is that these 'defining moments' can from another perspective be seen to be within a modality of historical experience which defines the moment, rather than the other way around. See, for example, Kennedy (1992).

[6] My use of the qualifier 'unreflective' here attests to the higher aspirations of some historicists, for whom historicism can be, in Paul Hamilton's words, 'suspicious of its own partisanship' (1995) 3. This point was also made, in very different terms, by Prof. T. P. Wiseman during the discussion at the Durham conference.

[7] Discussion with Ian Du Quesnay at Durham informs many parts of the following paragraphs.

[8] In many respects this ode is emblematic for historians of the early Principate, not for the data it yields, but for the desires to which it gives voice. I will discuss this further below.

explicit in Horace but implicit in Du Quesnay, that the passage of
time is not going to change the story.

> dicimus integro
> sicci mane die, dicimus uvidi,
>   cum sol Oceano subest.

> We say this, thirsty, the dawn of day as yet untouched. We say
> this, drenched, when the sun goes beneath the Ocean.
>   (*Odes* 4.5.38–40)

Dicimus is the unchanging constant.

What we have here is precisely this movement between strict
adherence to and transcendence of time which I outlined earlier. In
Du Quesnay's analysis, time means everything and it means nothing, and in this alternation he stands as a representative of a well-
established critical tradition. To look closer at this alternation, I here
summarise part of the argument of Du Quesnay's reading of the
second stanza of the ode. Two pages of text (158–9) are framed by
extended quotations from Menander Rhetor in his prescriptions for
the *epibatērion* and the *klētikon*, the first of which illustrates the *topos*
of comparing one's ruler to the sun. The second stanza is thereby
read first within its generic setting. Du Quesnay continues.

> While the conventional nature of the material softens the abruptness
> of the metaphor, the contemporary resonances deepen and enrich the
> passage. Augustus had long associated himself with Apollo, and
> identification of Apollo with the sun and of the sun with the ideal
> ruler were commonplace in Hellenistic literature. Apollo had been
> prominent in the celebrations of the Ludi Saeculares in 17 B.C. and
> again in the following year with the celebration of the Ludi Quinquinnales
> on the fifteenth anniversary of Actium. In both cases the games were
> celebrated by the Quindecemviri, to which priestly college Augustus
> belonged. But the relationship of Augustus to Apollo, ever since the
> building of his temple of the Palatine (28 B.C.) was even more spe-
> cial. The Carmen Saeculare seems to identify Sol and Apollo (9–12),
> and it is to Sol that the obelisk of the Horologium will be dedicated.[9]

The conventional (generic) and the contemporary here work in harmony to promote the successful poem (and the successful reading of
the poem). But the power of time to mean, which is strongly asserted
in the quotation above — note the repeated emphasis on dates and

---

[9] Du Quesnay (1995) 158.

anniversaries — is at the same time denied by the illustrative significance accorded to Menander Rhetor, writing in the 3rd century A.D.[10] The terms on which the first mode of analysis depends — precise chronology — are implicitly at odds with the second — genre across time. Within this rhythm of time accorded and denied meaning, the very matter of time itself, the Horologium of Augustus,[11] appears like a Dali clock, signifying something more elusive than the passing of the hours.

The question of the harmony or disjunction of contexts, historical and generic, is especially pressing in the case of Horatian lyric, which could be said to be at once thoroughly modern and thoroughly archaic; thus, it exposes the discontinuities within the narrative of 'tradition', both literary and critical. How can we (or Horace, for that matter) claim in the same breath that the proper context of this lyric is Augustan Rome and the Greek lyric canon?

Denis Feeney, in his analysis of how Horace rewrote the lyric tradition, stresses discontinuity first in his emphasis on the distance in time and culture between Horace and those he claimed as his predecessors, remarking that 'Horace was as far removed from Alcman as we are from Petrarch, and as far removed from Pindar as we are from Tasso'.[12] This archaising gesture by Feeney highlights the success of Horace's self-inscription into the lyric canon. Hence, although Horace's successful literary history constructs the lyric tradition in terms of continuity, the measure of that success remains as the gulf between Horace and the other poets with whom he claims this relationship. In that respect, Horace claims Greek lyric as the proper context for his poetry, and we go along with that claim in various ways. We may highlight the temporal and cultural improprieties of this context, as Feeney has done, in order to emphasis Horace's

---

[10] Du Quesnay never states the dates of Menander, which would not be relevant to the argument in the way that the dates of Augustus' various actions are; the question of what is 'relevant', from my perspective, highlights the inherent anachronism of this aspect of scholarship.

[11] On which see Du Quesnay (1995) 139.

[12] Feeney (1993) 43. I might add that this is a good example of a more self-aware historicism, which situates the critic in his own historical context, and does not claim to hold true for all time. At the same time, this archaising gesture depends upon an equivalence of time units (see Feeney's comments on time at the end of his paper); from another viewpoint one could argue that six hundred years of European history troped as dramatic change is not necessarily equivalent to six hundred years of any other period of history.

achievement, or we could remark that the validity of this context is based on its explicit construction in Horace's poems; hence, arguably, it is not so much context as text.

But how historical is Horace's literary history? Given the *Odes'* hyper-awareness of time it is perhaps surprising that when Horace writes himself into the lyric canon he glosses over the temporal gulf between himself and his lyric peers. Yet it can be argued that lyric itself offers Horace the possibility of achieving this effect of near-simultaneity, since lyric brings to the foreground the poetic present, the now of writing or singing, from which position the poet reflects on time past and future. When Horace self-consciously speaks from the position of the present about his lyric endeavour, and situates himself in relation to his predecessors Alcaeus and Sappho, he brings those forebears into his poetic present, effectively inscribing them as near-simultaneous. The most sustained presence of the Greek lyricists is in *Odes* 2.13, of which Feeney appositely remarks 'Sappho and Alcaeus in Horace's underworld are not an evocation of a past from which Horace is irredeemably cut off, but an image of a past-in-present which he may join'.[13] These lines, then, might be read as an example of how anti-historicist the literary tradition can get. Indeed, the poetic present of lyric almost seems to offer an escape from time-bound considerations of history. But it is worth picking out some of the strands of time making up the fabric of this poetic now which appears to inscribe past under present.

The now of lyric does not, of course, stand outside the poetic tradition; when Horace speaks in the poetic present he also speaks within the tradition of previous poets speaking in the poetic present. It is the weight and influence of past time that enjoins lyric to occupy this present. In addition to this inherent traditionality of the present, we find lyric ceaselessly positioning its own present within the context of past, present and future. The exemplary Teucer in *Odes* 1.7 neatly sums these up in order:[14]

> o fortes peioraque passi
> mecum saepe viri, nunc vino pellite curas:
> cras ingens iterabimus aequor.

---

[13] Feeney (1993) 55.
[14] Nisbet and Hubbard (1970) 94: 'here Horace has recaptured the simplicity and force of archaic Greek poetry, and related it with remarkable ingenuity to a contemporary situation'.

> O brave men, you who often with me suffered worse, now drive
> care away with wine: tomorrow we shall once more journey
> over the mighty sea.

> (*Odes* 1.7.30–2)

Past, encapsulated in the participle *passi* (you who have suffered),
and the future, marked by *cras . . . iterabimus* (tomorrow we shall journey), enclose the present injunction, *nunc* and the imperative *pellite*.
The notion of repetition, implied in the use of *iterabimus*, hints at the
similarity of past and future, from which the present is differentiated.
Moreover, although the sympotic present here is defined in terms of
its expulsion (*pellite*) of past and future concerns (the *curas* standing
for both memories of *peiora* and worries about tomorrow's journey),
so that it is created as a time of respite from a succession of hardships, nevertheless the status of the present *as* a time of respite hinges
upon the existence of sequential time in past and future. Hence,
although the lyric present here seems explicitly removed from temporal succession, its explicit mention of past and future is required
in order to set up its status *as* present.[15] This relationship is most
appositely summed up by Paul Ricoeur in *Time and Narrative*, when
he states '(t)here is no present, and hence neither past nor future,
in physical time as long as some instant is not determined as 'now',
'today', hence as present'.[16] Ricoeur here turns the process around;
whereas I have emphasised the role of the past (lyric tradition) in
creating the present (poetic now), Ricoeur reminds us that the present can equally be taken as our starting point from which to construct the past, a reminder which leads us back to Horace's evocation
of his lyric predecessors within his poetic present.

We have seen how the now of lyric exists within a complex of
both accommodation and renunciation of past and future; this brings
out the full dynamic of what Feeney has called the 'past-in-present'.
Indeed, if we return to *Odes* 2.13 we can trace a distinction between
two types of present in the final stanzas of the poem, a distinction
which, we shall see, is not without its problems.

---

[15] This is replicated at the level of the poem as a whole, where the exemplum
from the mythical past is summoned up to reinforce the injunction to enjoy the
present. At the same time, however, Teucer's capacity to 'repeat' the old Salamis
in a new place is at odds with the sharp differentiation of place in the earlier lines
of the poem: cf. Nisbet and Hubbard (1970) 94.

[16] Ricoeur (1988) 108. My reflections upon temporality in poetry throughout this
paper is especially informed by De Man (1971).

> quam paene furvae regna Proserpinae
> et iudicantem vidimus Aeacum
> sedesque discriptas piorum et
>   Aeoliis fidibus querentem
> Sappho puellis de popularibus,
> et te sonantem plenius aureo,
> Alcaee, plectro dura navis,
>   dura fugae mala, dura belli!
> utrumque sacro digna silentio
> mirantur umbrae dicere; sed magis
> pugnas et exactos tyrannos
>   densum umeris bibit aure vulgus.
> quid mirum, ubi illis carminibus stupens
> demittit atras belua centiceps
> auris et intorti capillis
>   Eumenidum recreantur angues?
> quin et Prometheus et Pelopis parens
> dulci laborem decipitur sono,
> nec curat Orion leones
>   aut timidos agitare lyncas.

How nearly I saw the realms of dark Proserpina, and Aeacus delivering judgement, and the separate abodes of the just, and Sappho with Aeolian harp lamenting her native girls, and you, Alcaeus, sounding more resonantly with your golden plectrum, singing the hardships of the seafarer, the hardships of exile, the hardships of war. The shades wonder at both singers, their words deserving reverent silence; but the thickly crowded mob drinks in more avidly the sound of battles and tyrants driven forth. Why wonder, when the hundred-headed beast, soothed by these songs, droops its black ears, and the serpents entwined in the hair of the Eumenides are refreshed? Even Prometheus and the father of Pelops are beguiled from their labour by the sweet sound, nor does Orion concern himself further with chasing the lion and the nervous lynx.

(*Odes* 2.13.21–40)

The Underworld is itself a place constituted by tradition; it is traditionally represented in terms of unmediated encounters between the living and the dead. Hence initially it might be read as a spatial representation of tradition itself in its ahistorical mode. In the timeless present of the Underworld the newly-dead Horace (almost) joins with the long-dead Sappho and Alcaeus in a meeting where temporal distance has no meaning. Yet, as Ricoeur has suggested, in a world where there is no past or future the concept of present founders. The timeless present of the Underworld is constituted by an endless iteration of instants within which each denizen performs a repeated function without variation (rolling a stone up a hill, fetching water, judging sinners etc.). These instants are denied full interrelation because their unvarying repetition does not allow for any one instant to become distinguishable from any other instant. The Underworld is, in a very real sense, a time-free zone.[17] Hence we find here a present (if we may call it that) very different from the lyric present we have already seen in *Odes* 1.7, which is grounded in an idea of sequential time from which it seeks to distinguish itself.

The abstract instants which make up the present of the Underworld, then, would allow Horace to join Alcaeus and Sappho, but not within a lyric present, and therefore not in any meaningful poetic relationship. The atemporality of this present would not allow for tradition, which, as I stated at the outset, remains despite its own disclaimers a narrative of past time in temporal succession; this succession does not occur in the non-time of the Underworld. Of course, Horace does not enter this non-time, since what he recounts here is what *almost* happens: *quam* **paene** ... *vidimus*, which governs lines 21–8. But by line 26 the missed opportunity to *see* the lyric predecessor in the timeless Underworld is sidelined in favour of the opportunity, ever-present in lyric, to apostrophise, with *te ... Alcaee*. The direct, unmediated access to the lyric predecessor through apostrophe replaces the near meeting in the Underworld. More importantly, it privileges lyric as the place for a meaningful encounter of past and present, as opposed to the abstract, iterated instants which we have seen constitute the present of the Underworld.

The extent to which the poetic present is a different sort of present from these abstract instants is evident in the final stanza of the ode, where the poetry of Sappho and Alcaeus breaks into and disrupts the endless repetitions of Underworld activity. The torments of Prometheus and Tantalus alluded to by *labor* and the explicitly recounted activities of Orion are representative examples of the unvarying repetition which renders the time of the Underworld nonsequential. The poetry, however, suspends these repetitions and thereby makes one instant — the instant of listening to the poem — different from another; poetry, then, causes sequential time to break into the non-sequential time of the Underworld. This is, however,

---

[17] An allusion to Cairns (1972) 32.

paradoxical, since the activity of the two poets is itself inscribed
under the figure of unvarying repetition at the outset of the scene,
marked by the present participles: *paene . . . iudicantem vidimus Aeacum . . .
et . . . querentem Sappho . . . et te sonantem . . . Alcaee*. Like Aeacus, Sappho
and Alcaeus are engaged in timeless Underworld activity, yet their
poetry not only represents and reflects upon time[18] but effects an
intervention of time into the realm of the timeless. This has implications too for Horace's own capacity to bridge the temporal gulf
between himself and his predecessors without abandoning the temporality which makes his relationship with them a meaningful one.
His apostrophe to Alcaeus clears the temporal barrier by uniting the
two poets in the present of the utterance, but retains that present
in its precarious relation to sequential time.

The poetic present, then, for all its claims to timelessness, is historically constituted and indeed can operate as a form of history by
its capacity to subsume the past under the present. A potent symbol for the rich temporality of the poetic present is the wine so often
summoned to dispel the cares of past and future. Wine can serve
as a figure for lyric poetry (*pocula Lesbii* 1.17.21) or poetic inspiration in new forms,[19] but it also significantly serves as a reflective
instrument of time by means of its vintage. It is not simply wine
that, for instance, replaces the cares of Maecenas with his pleasure
in the present (*mitte civilis super urbe curas* 3.8.17) but wine begun, set
up, in the consulship of Tullus (*amphorae . . . institutae consule Tullo*
3.8.11–12). By appealing to the wine's special antiquity (and therefore its capacity to subsume all daily cares in the enjoyment of the
present) Horace not only has recourse to the inherently politicised
Roman calendar, but also once more emphasises the extent to which
the present is underpinned by the past and the past is inherently
also present. Ricoeur uses the term 'quasi-present' to denote 'any
remembered instant (which) may be qualified as present, along with
its own retentions and protentions'.[20] One quasi-present in 3.8, for
example, is the remembered instant of the tree falling, whose future
is the present of this ode.[21] Another quasi-present is the year of

---

[18] The content of the poems — fickleness of lovers, trials of war — entail representations of past, present and future.

[19] Cf. in particular Miller's (1994) provocative reading of the *Sabina diota* (*Odes*
1.9.8) 158–9. On the wines of forgetfulness and remembrance cf. Oliensis (1998)
148–9.

[20] Ricoeur (1988) 108.

[21] Note how the anniversary is set forward in a vow (*voveram*) in lines 6–8, so

Tullus' consulship, conjured up in order to guarantee the enjoyment of the present, and remaining as a visible trace of the past, or, as Ricoeur provocatively puts it, as 'a reflective instrument of time'. It has often been noted how the vintage of wine introduces a historical event which interacts disturbingly with the events celebrated or dispelled by the present. The wine of *Odes* 3.14 is particularly memorable in this respect since it recalls the Marsian war (*Marsi memorem duelli* 3.14.18). The mindfulness of the wine here is set against the more common quality ascribed to the drink, that of forgetfulness (cf. *oblivioso Massico* 2.7.21). The tension between wine's capacity to memorialise (by its vintage) and its tendency to obliterate memory replicates exactly the tension within the poetic present between its need to situate itself in relation to the past and its anxiety to dispel the past. One final comment on wine is worth making here: it is the patina of age which makes the wine attractive and the occasion special. If wine is a potent symbol of the past-in-present, it stands for a past which needs to retain its 'pastness', not to be subsumed into the present. One might even say that wine is a symbol of the archaic.

The archaic as symbolised by wine, then, seems to offer an aesthetic moment which stresses its presentness (the wine is enjoyed *now*) but which requires historical time to guarantee the aesthetic effect (the wine must *have* aged in order to be enjoyed now). But before we explore this further we should consider Horace's own exploration of this dynamic, where he moves precisely to separate out the aesthetic and the historical.

> vile potabis modicis Sabinum
> cantharis, Graeca quod ego ipse testa
> conditum levi, datus in theatro
>   cum tibi plausus,
> care Maecenas eques, ut paterni
> fluminis ripae simul et iocosa
> redderet laudes tibi Vaticani
>   montis imago.
> Caecubum et prelo domitam Caleno
> tu bibes uvam: mea nec Falernae
> temperant vites neque Formiani
>   pocula colles.

---

that the poem's present is the fulfilment (protention) of its quasi-present. Yet the present within which the remembering takes place is what conjures the past as quasi-present.

> You will quaff lowly Sabine wine from mediocre pots, wine
> which I myself laid down, sealed in a Greek jar, when such
> applause was given to you in the theatre, Maecenas, knight,
> dear friend, that the banks of your ancestral river and the mock-
> ing echo of the Vatican hill together returned that praise to
> you. You will drink Caecuban wine, and the grape tamed by
> the Calenian press: my goblets will not be seasoned with a
> Falernian vine or the Formian slopes.
>
> (*Odes* 1.20)

Here the wine that appears as an echo in time of the applause for
Maecenas (matching the echo in space of lines 5–8) is explicitly prefigured as *vile*; the moment of drinking is denied aesthetic value. Coun-
terbalancing this purely 'historical' tipple, at the end of the poem,
comes the wine-list of aesthetic enjoyment — Caecuban, Calenian,
Falernian and Formian — to which Maecenas, but not Horace, has
access. Nisbet and Hubbard remark that the point of this poem is
to contrast Horace's simplicity with Maecenas' luxury, but the irony
of the ode from my perspective is that it sharply differentiates the
aesthetic from the historical (the fancy wines of the final stanza are
undated). And the punchline is that it assigns the politician Maecenas
to the realm of the aesthetic, and the poet Horace to that of the
historical. Interestingly, this experiment in separating out the two
strands of experience, which are elsewhere interwoven in the representation of Horatian wine, avoids and perhaps cannot but avoid
the present. The action of drinking and enjoying (or enduring) wine
is here consigned to the future: *potabis, tu bibes*. Attempts have been
made to differentiate between or otherwise rationalise these two
futures,[22] a critical response which shows awareness that these two
acts (will) operate within different modalities of experience. But, more
importantly for my argument, this disjunction of the aesthetic and
the historical precludes the appearance of a lyric 'now'. The Horatian
experiment of *Odes* 1.20, therefore, sets up 'the archaic' as an aesthetic present deriving its enjoyment from the simultaneous acknowledgement of and separation from a historical past. To renounce the
aesthetic dimension of the wine, as Horace does in this ode, is to
consign the lyric present to a disjunctive set of futures.

This, then is one difference between what is past and what is
archaic. Horace's use of wine seems to suggest that the archaic is a

---

[22] Nisbet and Hubbard (1978) 246, 251 see the first as promissory and the second as concessive.

sign of past-in-present where the past retains its discernible antiquity, and indeed where a distance between past and present is evoked in the same moment as they are brought together. But archaism, like the past, is an effect of modality, not an intrinsic quality. As Stephen Hinds has reminded us, poets are not in themselves archaic, but are rendered archaic by subsequent generations of writers and readers.[23] And some of the reasons for reading one's predecessors as archaic are given not only by Hinds but by a number of other critics, most notably Harold Bloom. But what we encounter in a writer like Horace is the gesture of archaising one's own writing, an encounter we fulfil by archaising within our own reading of Horace. But what is this archaising for? How we respond to that question returns us to the central tensions of historicism and the place of the *Odes* in the contemporary social/political environment.

One of the ways we contextualise Horace's archaising is by linking it to the idea of restoration, which might be seen to be the dominant modality of the Augustan period. The construction of a past-in-present which remains discernibly past, a process I am calling 'archaising', is subjected to a further interpretation, where the relationship of that past to the present in which it appears is one of repetition after a time of absence, or more precisely of restoration. This form of contextualising often focuses upon the trope of the Golden Age, as it appears particularly in the *Carmen Saeculare*. As Duncan Barker has shown, however, it is overly crude to suppose a seamless transition from the Horatian Golden Age to the Augustan Golden Age, or to assume that either is inherently univocally expressed.[24] Another related mode of contextualising is to see in Horace's archaism a restoration of the Greek lyric fusion of personal with political (a sort of post-modern romanticising view of the Greek past). Feeney gives voice to this view when he remarks that 'archaic lyric offered Horace a way of recapturing (the political)'.[25] Here,

---

[23] Hinds (1998) 52–74. I suspect that there is more of a leapfrog effect in archaising than Hinds is suggesting. For example, Horace's relationship with archaic Greek lyric is, as Feeney (1993) notes, mediated through Hellenistic poetry; is archaism created by distinguishing between a more recent and a more distant past?

[24] Barker (1996); see especially 437–8, where Barker, by focussing on the shift from the Greek *genos* to the Latin *saeculum*, emphasises discontinuities in the transmission of the golden age as an idea.

[25] Feeney (1993) 45. For an opposite reading of this cf. Oswyn Murray's article in the same volume, although I am more inclined to Feeney's view than to Murray's.

rather than simply link Horatian archaism with Augustan restoration Feeney suggests that archaism is what allows Horace to speak
about his contemporary political environment. There are problems
of course with this history of politics and poetics, which is itself
inscribed under the modality of restoration, not least in its implicit
de-policitising of post-archaic poetry. Indeed, the recent restoration
of politics to our readings of the Hellenistic poets presents a powerful alternative history to this one.[26] But leaving that to one side, let
us return to consider why it is that an archaising mode of discourse
is regarded as appropriate or even essential for representing or
reflecting upon contemporary events.

   This is a question relevant for Sallust, and later Tacitus, as much
as for Horace. What happens is what Colin Burrow has characterised as an 'audible grating' of cultures and times.[27] That is, the
juxtaposition of signs within 'Augustan' poetry which retain discernible
traces of classical Greek lyric creates a further effect by evoking the
disjunction between the two, the extent to which the archaic symposium does not fit in modern Roman society, or the violence done
to Latin syntax as it is forced into Alcaic or Sapphic metres. We
frequently use metaphors of assimilation or accommodation to describe
these Horatian effects, metaphors which work to harmonise the grating sound. And they are predicated on judgements which have already
concluded that archaising is at least appropriate and possibly necessary. In an attempt to re-emphasise the improprieties of archaising, let us turn to Horace's distinctive history of the battle of Philippi.

> O saepe mecum tempus in ultimum
> deducte Bruto militiae duce,
>   quis te redonavit Quiritem
>   dis patriis Italoque caelo,
> Pompei, meorum prime sodalium?
> cum quo morantem saepe diem mero
>   fregi coronatus nitentis
>   malobathro Syrio capillos.
> tecum Philippos et celerem fugam
> sensi relicta non bene parmula,
>   cum fracta virtus, et minaces
>   turpe solum tetigere mento.
> sed me per hostis Mercurius celer
> denso paventem sustulit aere;

---

[26] Cameron (1995).
[27] Burrow (1999) 3.

te rursus in bellum resorbens
    unda fretis tulit aestuosis.
ergo obligatam redde Iovi dapem
longaque fessum militia latus
        depone sub lauru mea, nec
            parce cadis tibi destinatis.
oblivioso levia Massico
ciboria exple; funde capacibus
        unguenta de conchis. quis udo
            deproperare apio coronas
curatve myrto? quem Venus arbitrum
dicet bibendi? non ego sanius
        bacchabor Edonis: recepto
            dulce mihi furere est amico.

O you who often with me were led into extremities, when Brutus
led campaigns, who has restored you as a citizen to your ancestral gods and the Italian sky? Pompeius, with whom I often
broke up the long day with neat wine, my garlanded hair shin-
ing with Syrian ointment. With you I experienced Philippi and
headlong flight, when I unheroically left my shield behind, when
valour was shattered and the lordly ones touched their chins to
the shameful ground. But swift Mercury carried me through the
enemy and lifted me, shivering, up into the thick air; a wave
sucking you back into battle carried you through stormy straits.
And so, return to Jove the feast owed to him, and rest your
limbs, worn out from long campaigns, under my laurel, and
don't be sparing with the casks designated for you. Fill up the
light goblet with forgetful Massic; pour ointments from generous shells. Who will hasten to attend to the garlands of damp
parsley or myrtle? Whom will Venus call on as the arbiter of
drinking? I will go bacchic, as wild as an Edonian: when my
friend has been restored, it is sweet for me to go mad.

(*Odes* 2.7)

The immediate subject of this poem is restoration, Horace re-united
with an old friend, and the structure of the poem itself replicates
this, with recollections of past companionship in the first three stanzas and injunctions to celebrate in the final three stanzas framing
the central scene, where *me* in line 13 and *te* in line 15 splits the
poem in two as the companions go their separate ways. The temporal continuity of companionship, however, is emphasised over this
central rupture.[28] Given the emphasis on restoration and reunion in

---

[28] Lowrie (1997) 195–6.

the subject matter, it is appropriate that this ode is seen to express
a happy union of personal and political, Greek and Roman.[29] Indeed,
a historicising reading can easily expand the reunion of Horace and
Pompeius into an expression of or about Augustan ideologies. If we
adopt such a line, moreover, we can view the harmonising of all these
elements as a more or less brutal imposition of order, though the
question of how much the ode accedes to full harmonisation remains
an open one. The kind of history that is told in the first half of the
poem clearly relates to this question of harmony and continuity.

Although the poem is structured as an address to Pompeius, thereby
setting the poem in the present, the early part of the poem consists
of a series of reminiscences about the past that Horace shares with
his friend. The emphasis on past companionship, with the repetition
mecum . . . cum quo . . . tecum, organises the past around the person of
Pompeius. Indeed, the first three scenes of the past are not linked
in any sort of temporal order, although each scene has an internal
temporal dimension (*saepe, tempus in ultimum, morantem diem fregi* and
cum fracta virtus etc.). Past time in the first three stanzas, therefore,
appears as discontinuous flashbacks, perhaps iterated (*saepe*), but not
situated in any temporal progression. Instead, they are grouped
around the figure of the returning Pompeius.

At the same time as the past here is discontinuous, it is also implicitly configured as repetition of an even more remote past. The proper
nouns *Brutus* and *Philippi* evoke historical events which are frequently
put in relation to an archaic Brutus and the recent past of Pharsalia,
while the name of Pompeius in a civil war context is always provocative. The idea that sequential time contains a pattern of recurrence
and repetition is finally expressed in the separation stanza, when
Pompeius is pulled back into battle by the undertow. By using sea
imagery, Horace evokes not only the idea of violence, destruction,
and limited human control, but also the sense of a naturally recurring event. The wave of civil war must inevitably return to beat
upon the shores of Italy. This temporal pattern is a familiar one in
historiography; indeed it underpins claims to history's usefulness.
Here in *Odes* 2.7 it threatens to emplot the discontinuous flashbacks
of the first three stanzas, particularly since Horace's recollections are
grouped around the figure of Pompeius, whose return is the subject

---

[29] West (1998) 50–1.

of the poem. 'With you I experienced civil war. And now you're back. . . .' Restoration remains the dominant modality, but in a rather more scary form, as the return of the repressed.

Horace's recollections of the battle of Philippi, however, are primarily focused around his escape from battle. His first experience is of *Philippos et celeram fugam* at line 9, when he leaves his shield behind (but is still with Pompeius), and in the separation stanza he is carried up into the air by Mercury, leaving Pompeius behind. Both scenes are notorious borrowings from the lyric and epic traditions,[30] effectively archaising Horace's presence on or rather absence from the battlefield. This could be seen as an escape by time-travel, as Horace breaks into the sequential and recurring time of battle by engaging in activities which evoke a different order of time. These orders of time could then be symbolised by the opposing elements into which Horace and Pompeius are carried in the central stanza. Pompeius, as we have already seen, is sucked back into the waves of civil war, an image which carries with it the idea of recurrence. Horace, on the other hand, is carried up into the air (*denso aere*), in a moment which transcends the immediately recurring time patterns of war by appealing to a more extended pattern of time, that of the literary tradition.[31] If we were to take this line further, however, seeing archaism here as a way of creating a distance between the poet and the war in which he finds himself, we would end up constructing an opposition between Horace's archaising literary stance and the implicitly modernised battle itself. But Horace in effect archaises the entire battle of Philippi, not just his escape from it.[32] This is arguably achieved through Horaces' introduction of the battle narrative as focussed through his own sensory experience of it (*sensi*), an experience recalled and framed by the repeated symposia which he has shared and shares with Pompeius.[33] The effect of the sympotic frame

---

[30] Nisbet and Hubbard (1978) 107–8, 113–16.

[31] Which does not preclude recurrence — remember that *densus* can in other contexts mean 'frequent', 'recurring'. Also recall that Alcaeus threw his shield away, but eventually returned to the life of a soldier. This literary tradition, then does not preclude the possibility of repetition, even in the present. See below for recurring civil war in the final symposium.

[32] Nisbet and Hubbard (1978) see this as whimsical treatment; my reading here takes a different tack, though I think their reminder of the possible offensiveness of this account is a good one.

[33] In that respect this ode offers the reversion and expansion of *Odes* 1.7.30–2, quoted earlier in the paper.

on the recollected past is felt in the picture of Horace miming
Archilochus on and off the field, but, more than this, the lone detail
of the fallen *minaces*, represented in Homeric defeat, demonstrates
the spread of the archaic effect from Horace's field of experience to
the battlefield as a whole.

Now this could be seen as political tact; the ode is usually read
as an injunction to let the past lie, while enjoying present peace,
hence the oblivion-inducing wine at line 21. By archaising Philippi,
Horace could be allowing the civil war to exist as a quasi-present,
stripped of the potential to reawaken political disorder. The question towards the end of the ode of who sets the limits of drinking
in the celebration party (*quem Venus arbitrum dicet bibendi?*) then suggests the same answer as the first question of the poem (*quis te
redonavit. . . .?*); Octavian here, as in *Odes* 1.37, underwrites the time
of drinking and of leisure generally by taking on the responsibilities
and control of the state.[34] Yet Horace's representation of the final
drinking party is made in terms which convey the familiar madness
of civil war (*non sanius Edonis . . . furere*). These vestiges of the terms
under which the two friends drink work ironically against the oblivion inducing wine, suggesting that the drink may erase the memory
of the past, but the symposium itself causes the drinkers forgetfully
to re-enact the conflicts of the present.

More strikingly, Horace's archaising of Philippi challenges a 'straight'
historical understanding of that event. To return to the points raised
by *Odes* 1.20, we could say that it is the inter-relation of the aesthetic present with the historical past which transforms that understanding. That is, just as the historical past guarantees, is assimilated
into and yet denied by the aesthetic moment, so too does the aesthetic moment inform understanding of the past, which becomes
mediated through the enjoyment of the present. Poetry, caught up
in the thick mist of intertextuality, does not succeed in escaping from
history. Nor is the history in which it remains enmeshed itself made
up of a simple pattern of temporality.

From this position let us return to *Odes* 4.5, the starting point of
this paper, to consider what an aestheticised historicism might begin
to look like.

---

[34] Cf. Fowler (1995) 258.

Divis orte bonis, optime Romulae
custos gentis, abes iam nimium diu;
maturum reditum pollicitus patrum
     sancto concilio, redi.
lucem redde tuae, dux bone, patriae:
instar veris enim vultus ubi tuus
adfulsit populo, gratior it dies
     et soles melius nitent.
ut mater iuvenem, quem Notus invido
flatu Carpathii trans maris aequora
cunctantem spatio longius annuo
     dulci distinet a domo
votis ominibusque et precibus vocat,
curvo nec faciem litore dimovet:
sic desideriis icta fidelibus
     quaerit patria Caesarem.
tutus bos etenim rura perambulat,
nutrit rura Ceres almaque Faustitas,
pacatum volitant per mare navitae,
     culpari metuit fides,
nullis polluitur casta domus stupris,
mos et lex maculosum edomuit nefas,
laudantur simili prole puerperae,
     culpam poena premit comes.
quis Parthum paveat, quis gelidum Scythen,
quis Germania quos horrida parturit
fetus, incolumi Caesare? quis ferae
     bellum curet Hiberiae?
condit quisque diem collibus in suis,
et vitem viduas ducit ad arbores;
hinc ad vina redit laetus et alteris
     te mensis adhibet deum;
te multa prece, te prosequitur mero
defuso pateris et Laribus tuum
miscet numen, uti Graecia Castoris
     magni memor Herculis.
'longas o utinam, dux bone, ferias
praestes Hesperiae!' dicimus integro
sicci mane die, dicimus uvidi,
     cum sol Oceano subest.

Son of the blessed gods, best guardian of Romulus' race, now you are absent too long; you who promised early return to the sacred council of senate, return. Restore the light to your land, blessed leader: for when your face, just like the spring, shines on the people, the day proceeds more gracefully and the sun shines more brightly. Just as a mother calls on her son, whom

the South wind with hostile gusts keeps far away from his sweet
home, across the wastes of the Carpathian sea, delayed now for
more than a year, she calls him with prayers, omens and pleas,
nor does she divert her gaze from the curve of the shore: so
the fatherland, stricken by loyal desire, yearns for Caesar. The
cattle wander safely through the countryside, Ceres and kindly
good Fortune feed the country, sailors flit across a pacified sea,
loyalty fears to be blamed, no assault pollutes the chaste household, tradition and law have tamed ugly sin, mothers are praised
for children like their fathers, retribution accompanies and follows blame. Who will shiver at the Parthian or the cold Scythian,
or the young which bristling Germany brings forth, so long as
Caesar is safe? Who will be concerned with the war in fierce
Iberia? Each man spends his day on his own hillside, and trains
the vine around the barren trees; then he returns joyfully to his
wine and summons you as a god to the second course; you he
calls on in many a prayer, you he summons with neat wine
poured from bowls, and mingles your divinity with the Lares,
just like Greece in memory of Castor and mighty Hercules. 'O
blessed leader, may you offer long holidays to Hesperia!' We
say this, thirsty, the dawn of day as yet untouched. We say this,
drenched, when the sun goes beneath the Ocean.

                                                              (*Odes* 4.5)

I want to begin by re-emphasising the glaring absence that the ode
(and Du Quesnay's study of it) works to cover over, namely the
absence of Augustus. This poem is not merely a representation but
also an articulation of desire, and in order to explore that articulation it is necessary for Horace and for us to suspend the fulfilment
of that desire. Desire, of course, always renders its object absent. At
the same time, however, it strives towards the desired object, making it partially present by investing intermediary, fetishised objects
with the quality of what is desired. Most commonly in literary artic-
ulations of desire (especially in love poetry) these fetishes constitute
the words of the desiring subject, or the images called up by the
words. Now this is familiar enough territory for readers of, say, *Odes*
1.23, but many would ask what it has to do with Horace and
Augustus, let alone with historicism.[35]

---

[35] The work of Ancona (1994) offers illuminating insights into the workings of
temporality within certain odes of Horace, but by concentrating exclusively on the
explicitly erotic odes she avoids facing the consequences that the Horatian dynamic
of time and dominance holds for Augustus.

Yet the dynamic of desire briefly sketched here is as descriptive of the situation of the historicist as it is of the love poet's. Language as the intermediary between the desiring reader/poet and the desired object — Augustus/the presence of the past — is invested with the qualities of that desired object which must of necessity remain absent. This can be seen, for example, in Horace's filling out of the expression of desire with an extended simile, in lines 9–16, where the absence of the son, dwelt upon in lines 9–12, delays not his return but his mother's prayer. Even more than this, the extent to which language is made to stand in for (and thereby make 'present') the still-absent object of desire is strongly articulated in the concluding lines, which I emphasised at the start of this paper: *dicimus . . . dicimus* (38–40). The emphasis at the end of the poem is on speech, prayer and summoning, all of which both imply and deny the presence of Augustus. And, as I stated earlier, this desire which becomes the investment of presence in language is the desire of the modern historian of antiquity.

But the present of *dicimus* is here again mediated through the experience of drinking wine, an experience in the present which, we have seen, exists in a tension between acknowledgement and renunciation of the past. The return of each Italian rustic (including Horace) to his wine replaces the desired return of Augustus with which the poem starts: *reditum pollicitus . . . redi* (3–4)/*hinc ad vina redit* (31). And it is from the return to the time of drinking that each rustic can go on to summon Augustus in his divinity; the repeated *te* of ll. 32–3 marks the closest Augustus comes to being present in the poem, before he is replaced by the prayer and by Horace's assertion of the prayer's constancy over time. Indeed the closing words of the poem, which assert this unchanging and timeless *dicimus*, also leave us with another image of absence, the sun hidden in the west. Thus *subest* balances the opening *abes*, while Augustus' association with the sun is made in ll. 5–8. In this sense, Augustus, the sun which rises and sets, who dictates the time of drinking, both partakes of and remains outside the present of wine and prayer. More importantly for the aesthetic historican, it is through this present that he is apprehended and made partially present.

CHAPTER SIX

AB INFERIS: HISTORIOGRAPHY IN HORACE'S ODES

Cynthia Damon

Horace's lyric poetry was not an obvious candidate for discussion at a conference on Augustan poetry and the traditions of Latin historiography. Horace does mention historiography twice in his first collection of *Odes*, but only twice. And both references occur in *recusationes*, i.e., in statements about what Horace does not and will not do. In Book 4, historiography as a genre gets no mention whatsoever. And yet it is in two poems of this book, the fourth and fourteenth, that Horace's lyric project comes closest to one of the functions of historical narrative, the recording of *res gestae*. What I hope to show in the present paper is that for the task of commemorating the Alpine campaigns of Augustus's stepson Drusus in *Odes* 4.4 Horace adapts the Pindaric approach to encomium by drawing on the resources of historiography. A genre that grew up after Pindar, historiography gives Horace, I argue, the material for an authoritative encomium on military success. It also gives him an alternative to a commemorative strategy attested on Augustan monuments and rejected in the *praeteritio* of lines 18–22, where he refuses to inquire into the Amazon past of Drusus' contemporary opponents, the Vindelici. Wilfully independent though this encomiastic strategy seems in a poem on a topic recommended to him by Augustus, the poem nevertheless provides Augustus with praise perfectly suited to his aspirations.

Horace's two references to the writing of history both occur in Book 2. The first is the famous opening *Ode* of the book, where Pollio's *Historiae* on the subject of Rome's recent, troubled history are accounted a risky undertaking:

> Motum ex Metello consule civicum
> bellique causas et vitia et modos
>   ludumque Fortunae gravisque
>   principum amicitias et arma
> nondum expiatis uncta cruoribus,
> periculosae plenum opus aleae
>   tractas (1–7).

> The civic turmoil from Celer's consulship,
> War's origins, mistakes and development,
>> The play of Fortune and the fateful
>>> Friendships of principals, and their weapons
>
> Defiled with bloodshed still unatoned today,
> A dicey, indeed a dangerous, enterprise
>> Your subject.
>>>>>> (Trans G. Lee)

The poem's final stanza, which follows an evocation of the civil wars of 49–46, declares such material unfit for *ioci* and announces verses performed *leviore plectro*. In poem 2.12 the inconcinnity between historical subject matter and lyric style is again the issue, but here the rejection is Maecenas's:

> Nolis longa ferae bella Numantiae
> nec durum Hannibalem nec Siculum mare
> Poeno purpureum sanguine mollibus
>> aptari citharae modis (1–4)
>
> Fierce Numantia's long wars, stubborn Hannibal,
> The Sicilian sea purple with Punic blood —
> You'd not wish for such harsh themes to be made to fit
>> The soft tones of the cithara.
>>>>>> (Trans. G. Lee)

As are the projected *pedestres historiae* that would suit such topics:

> tuque pedestribus
> dices historiis proelia Caesaris,
> Maecenas, melius ductaque per vias
>> regum colla minacium (9–12)
>
> Besides, you will narrate better yourself in prose
> As historian, Maecenas, the many fights
> Caesar won, and describe menacing kings, their necks
>> In chains, led through the streets of Rome.
>>>>>> (Trans. G. Lee)

If these passages from Book 2 attest an awareness of contemporary historiography, they do so only to help Horace reject its subject matter for the *Odes*.

Or at least for the first collection of *Odes*. For in the fourth poem of the second collection we find the very elements that Horace rejected in 2.12: wars (*bella*, 17), the Sicilian sea (*Siculas . . . undas*, 44), and Hannibal, here not *durus* but *perfidus* (49). No mention, however, either acceptance or rejection, of historiography.

So far as one can tell from programmatic statements in *Odes* 4, in fact, the vehicles of commemoration that Horace's lyric now measures itself against are not accounts of past events couched in literary prose, not *pedestres historiae*, but physical *monumenta* both private and public. At the beginning of 4.8, for example, the *carmina* that Horace can offer Censorinus are contrasted with libations, *paterae*, bronze statues, *aera*, and tripods, the *praemia fortium Graiorum* (lines 1–4). Later in the poem Horace measures *carmina* against *tituli*, the *incisa notis marmora publicis* (13). And *tituli* recur in poem 4.14, there coupled with *memores fasti* (line 4).[1]

What makes Book 4 different from the earlier books, as everyone knows, is its flirtation with Pindar. The second poem, *Pindarum quisquis studet aemulari*, may look like a disavowal of the Pindaric style, but as in so many of Horace's disavowals (those that we glanced at from Book 2 included), so in this one Horace takes as much as he rejects. And Pindar's would seem to be a suitable voice for the more public material that Horace includes in Book 4, where, besides the military successes celebrated in the fourth and fourteenth poems, we find 4.2 and 4.5 on Augustus's return from a long absence in the Western provinces, and 4.15 on the Augustan era: *tua, Caesar, aetas*, as Horace says in line 4. This is the kind of material for which Pindar's courtier polish and choral camouflage were more appropriate than the civic and individual voice of Alcaeus so prevalent in books 1–3.[2] But Horace was not a Pindar, nor did his world have a place for a Pindar, as can be clearly seen in the third poem of Book 4, where Horace claims for himself Muse-given authority akin to that of Pindar — *quod spiro et placeo, si placeo, tuum est*, he says to Melpomene (24) — but simultaneously, and hardly incidentally, refers to the commission for the *carmen saeculare* (lines 13–15) and to his celebrity status on the streets of Rome (22 *monstror digito praetereuntium*).

---

[1] *Odes* 4.14.1–5, *quae cura patrum quaeve Quiritium/ plenis honorum muneribus tuas,/ Auguste, virtutes in aevum/ per titulos memoresque fastos/ aeternet?* Cf. also *Odes* 4.2.18–20 *pugilemve equumve/ dicit et* **centum potiore signis/munere** *donat*. Livy, too, privileges the literary: 6.1.2 *rarae per eadem tempora litterae fuere, una custodia fidelis memoriae rerum gestarum*. Festus, by contrast, aligns physical and literary *monumenta*: 123L *monimentum est... quicquid ob memoriam alicuius factum est, ut fana, porticus, scripta et carmina*.

[2] Cf. 1.32.3–5, *age, dic Latinum,/ barbite, carmen,/ Lesbio primum modulate civi*.

So I begin the investigation of what historiography contributes to Horace's encomiastic project in *Odes* 4.4 with a section on an un-Pindaric feature of Horace's most Pindaric ode.

With its 28-line long, simile-enriched, hyperbaton-enhanced opening sentence *Odes* 4.4 seems to proclaim Pindaric aspirations. The Pindaric aspects of the poem are well-documented in the scholarly literature: Pasquali and Syndikus are particularly good on the Pindaric elements of 4.4.[3] At first glance the most Pindaric feature in the whole Pindaric poem is the presence of a story about a figure from the past that redounds to the credit of the present *laudandus*; it makes sense, I suppose, that a poetic structure — the inset narrative — should cross the divide between Pindar's world and Horace's more easily than diction, metaphor, and meter do. But the link between story and *laudandus* in Horace's ode is rather different from the links in Pindar's epinicia.

Pindar's stories are connected to his *laudandi* variously. Geography yields the most connections. For victors from Aegina, for example, Pindar tells stories about the island's mythical first family, Aeacus and his descendants Peleus, Telamon, Achilles, Ajax, and Neoptolemus. For Theban athletes he tells stories about Theban-born Heracles; for Telesicrates of Cyrene a story about the city's eponymous nymph; and so on.[4] The *laudandus*'s particular experiences or circumstances can also occasion stories: Pindar gives a story about the invention of the flute for a victor in the flute competition at Delphi, for example, and for Hieron on his sickbed he offers stories about wounded Philoctetes and healer Asclepius.[5] Physical characteristics, too, can yield a sufficient connection: in *Isthmian* 4 the victor, like Heracles, is short in stature but of spirit unbreakable; in *Olympian* 4 both the *laudandus*, Psaumis of Kamarina, and the exemplary Argonaut Erginos have prematurely white hair.

More closely comparable to Horace's procedure in *Odes* 4.4 are the links based on genealogy, i.e., passages where Pindar claims that *laudandus* X is a descendant of hero Y, as in *Nemean* 5, where the victor Pytheas is 'of the same stock' as Peleus (43 ὁμόσπορον ἔθνος). But heredity-based links are in fact relatively rare: there are only a

---

[3] Pasquali (1920) 764–75, Syndikus (1972–73) *ad loc.*
[4] Aegina: *O.* 8, *N.* 3–8, *I.* 5, 6, 8; Thebes: *I.* 1 and 4 (both on Heracles); Cyrene: *P.* 9.
[5] Flute: *P.* 12; Hieron: *P.* 1 and 3.

handful of them in some 44 surviving epinician poems.[6] They are also rather circumscribed in their reach: claims of heredity in Pindar almost always link generations that are adjacent or nearly so, i.e., father and son or uncle and nephew. An example of particular relevance to *Odes* 4.4 is *Isthmian* 7, where the central story is one of relatively recent occurrence, celebrating the military glory of the victor's uncle, who died fighting for Thebes. The uncle's military and the nephew's athletic renown are easy to link in this poem because, as Pindar points out in line 24, uncle and nephew were homonymous (24 ὁμωνύμῳ; both were called Strepsiades).

The situation is quite different in *Odes* 4.4: the central figure of Horace's exemplary story predates his *laudandus* by some 200 years. That is, the tale comes not from the period of living memory, nor yet from the very distant past, but from what one might call the historical past, the period that each generation is able to construct for itself from monuments and records and earlier accounts. But before we consider what Horace gained by departing from Pindar's practice in choosing his central story, we need to look more closely at the story Horace tells.

The story comes in two (or possibly three) parts. First, there is an introduction where the poet connects, via nomenclature, C. Claudius Nero, consul of 207 B.C., with the present *laudandus*, Nero Claudius Drusus: line 37 *quid debeas, o Roma, Neronibus* echoes *Nerones* from line 28, but the later passage refers to past holders of the name, the earlier to the stepsons of Augustus. The introduction also identifies the core event of the story: *Hasdrubal devictus* (lines 38–9).

This phrase is a telegraphic, or perhaps I should say an epigraphic, reference to the battle on the Metaurus River in 207 B.C., a battle that constituted a turning point for Roman fortunes in the second Punic war. According to Suetonius, it was one of three signal services rendered to Rome by the emperor Tiberius's Claudian forbears, a victory on a par with Appius Claudius Caecus's successful opposition to an alliance with Pyrrhus and Appius Claudius Caudex's victory in the first Punic war (264 B.C.; *Tiberius* 2.1).

---

[6] Cf. *O.* 2.46–7 ὅθεν σπέρματος ἔχοντα ῥίζαν, *O.* 6.71 ἐξ οὗ πολύκλειτον καθ' Ἕλλανας γένος Ἰαμιδᾶν, *O.* 7.93 σπερμ' ἀπὸ Καλλιάνακτος, *N.* 11.33–7 τό τε Πεισάνδρου πάλαι/αἷμ' ἀπὸ Σπάρτας ... καὶ παρ' Ἰσμηνοῦ ῥοᾶν κεκραμένον/ἐκ Μελανίπποιο μάτρωος.

The historical situation was this: Claudius Nero had been engaged with Hannibal in Apulia when he intercepted Hasdrubal's message summoning Hannibal north. Nero determined to race north himself to join forces with his fellow consul, hoping to deal with Hasdrubal before the Carthaginian forces could themselves unite. The trick was to get away without Hannibal's knowledge; much of Nero's subsequent fame rested on the fact that he succeeding in deceiving old *perfidus* Hannibal himself. To make a long story — 9 chapters in Livy (27.43–51) — shorter, the Romans win, Hasdrubal finds death on the field of battle, Nero takes Hasdrubal's head back south with him and tosses it down in front of Hannibal's pickets.

The second part of the story in *Odes* 4.4 begins here; it is Hannibal's soliloquy on the inevitability of Roman victory in the war with Carthage, lines 50 and following.[7]

The third part, if there is a third part, lies in the final stanza, which some editors (including Shackleton Bailey but not Klingner) assign to the poet.[8] For the purposes of this paper, however, the speaker of the final stanza doesn't really matter, so I return to the question I left hanging a moment ago: what did Horace gain by developing a story of such relatively ancient vintage?

I noted earlier that in Pindar the claims of heredity rarely reach beyond adjacent generations. How many generations of Claudii Nerones intervene between the man who fooled Hannibal and thereby defeated Hasdrubal, and the youth, Augustus's stepson Drusus, who fledged his military career in the Alps? We can't say with certainty, but it must be on the order of six or seven.

The Claudii Nerones were, in Syme's words, 'the inferior line of the Claudii'; what he means by this is that they fall out of the consular lists for nearly two centuries.[9] The Claudius Nero of 4.4, Gaius,

---

[7] Cf. Livy 27.51.12 on Hannibal's words at the news of the Metaurus disaster: *Hannibal tanto simul publico familiarique ictus luctu adgnoscere se fortunam Carthaginis fertur dixisse.*

[8] I prefer Hannibal to have the lines. One thing Shackleton Bailey doesn't tell you in his apparatus is that the reading of the major manuscript groups for the verb in line 73 is *perficient*. And the principal exception is what Richard Tarrant (1983) 185 calls 'the mysterious Blandinius Vetustissimus,' a manuscript whose reading should probably not preempt that of the rest of the tradition, at least not without discussion. The future tense of *perficient*, together with the rather exaggerated *nil . . . non*, makes the stanza a despairing survey of Carthage's future prospects, something quite suitable in the mouth of a general who has just been beaten at his own game.

[9] Syme (1986) 55.

was consul in 207, and his cousin Tiberius was consul in 202, but thereafter there are no consulships for the family until the future emperor Tiberius's first, in 13 B.C., the year *Odes* 4 was published. (Tiberius's father's *cursus* ended with a praetorship in 42.) But despite the relative obscurity of the intervening generations in this line, the link between the Gaius Claudius Nero of the second Punic war and the present Nero Claudius Drusus is an easy one to make. In part this was a natural result of Roman naming practices. For Pindar, by contrast, the pair of Strepsiadases is an exception, albeit a highly convenient one. But the connection is also made possible by the access Romans had to their historical past, an access not readily available to contemporaries of Pindar (pre-Herodotus, pre-Hellanicus, even pre-Hecataeus as they were).[10] Annalistic histories, however fictional and even mendacious they may have been, provided the Romans with a continuous fabric of history. The Neronian thread in that fabric may vanish for six or seven generations, but when it reemerges it will be the same thread. Or, to use the metaphor that Horace applies to another member of the imperial family, Marcellus, contemporary achievements have their root in a family's past: *crescit occulto velut arbor aevo/fama Marcellis* (*Odes* 1.12.45–6).

To put it somewhat differently again, ancestral *uirtus* is a guarantee, perhaps even the best guarantee, of contemporary *virtus*: so Cicero in the passage from which I drew the title of the paper. None of his contemporary orators, he says, has stocked his memory with Rome's history. And yet this was a source from which each could obtain unimpeachable witnesses (*Brutus* 322 *ab inferis locupletissimos testis excitaret*). Witnesses of the sort that he himself summons up from the dead so memorably in the *Pro Caelio*, for example, where Appius Claudius Caecus decries the decadence of his descendant Clodia: *aliquis mihi ab inferis excitandus ex barbatis illis, non hac barbula qua ista delectatur sed illa horrida quam in statuis antiquis atque imaginibus videmus, qui obiurget mulierem et qui pro me loquatur* (*Pro Caelio* 33). The rhetorical task of *Odes* 4.4 is praise, of course, not blame, but here, too, the past provides an unimpeachable *testis* for the point Horace wants to make. The evidence of *virtus* in Gaius Claudius Nero, consul of 207, makes plausible the poet's assertions about a contemporary

---

[10] Compare the contemporary reference possible via the geographical name *Siculum mare* at *Odes* 2.12.2: 'Panegyricists of Octavian could not possibly have forgotten the historical associations of these waters' (Nisbet and Hubbard (1978) *ad loc.*). On Horace and the historical past see further Feeney (1993) 57–60.

flowering of *uirtus* on the same stock. And having the past as *testis* for the present helps the *laudator*, the praise poet, overcome his own inherent lack of *auctoritas* in Roman eyes.[11] As I said earlier, Horace was no Pindar.

Other solutions to the problem of the encomiast's *auctoritas*-deficit had been tried. Eye-witness status was one such: Ennius and Archias, to name just two, had accompanied their *laudandi* on the military campaigns that they eventually celebrated in verse. Theophanes of Miletus likewise produced eye-witness testimony in historiographical form on Pompey's Eastern campaigns. Little or nothing remains of these works, but we can see something of their rhetorical strategy in Tibullus 1.7, an elegy celebrating Messalla's triumph over the Aquitani, where Tibullus carefully establishes his title to praise Messalla:

> non sine me est tibi partus honos: Tarbella Pyrene
>   testis et Oceani litora Santonici,
> testis Arar Rhodanusque celer magnusque Garunna,
>   Carnutis et flavi caerula lympha Liger (9–12).

> Not without me was your glory gained: witness the Tarbellian
>   Pyrenees and shores of the Santonic Ocean;
> witness Saône and rapid Rhone and great Garonne
>   and Loire, blue stream of flaxen-haired Carnutes.
>   (Trans. G. Lee)

But not every *laudandus* had the foresight to include a poet or his-torian among his *comites*. And this left an opening for bids such as the *Panegyricus Messallae* and the *Laus Pisonis*, the authors of which, would-be encomiasts without eye-witness status, offer other creden-tials to fill the *auctoritas* gap, among them devotion, enthusiasm, and promises of future service.[12] These qualities serve well enough in poems that aim at securing a personal reward for the poet; the

---

[11] A point made, but not developed, by Putnam (1986) in speaking of the 'authen-ticating force of Hannibal's long monologue' (93) and in saying that the soliloquy 'praises Rome more convincingly than any open encomium from the creating "I" could' (99).

[12] Devotion: *Pan. Mess.* 191 *sum quodcumque tuum est, Laus Pis.* 259 *animus constan-tior annis,* 213 *amor.* Enthusiasm: *Pan. Mess.* 7 *est nobis voluisse satis, Laus* Pis. 251 *ani-mosa voluntas.* Promises: *Pan. Mess.* 203 *nulla mihi statuent finem te fata canendi,* 16–17 *ut tibi possim/inde alios aliosque memor componere versus, Laus Pis.* 248 *tu mihi Maecenas tereti cantabere versu.* Aim: *Pan. Mess.* 201–2 *quod tibi si versus noster . . . inerret in ore, Laus* Pis. 218–19 *dignare tuos aperire Penates,/hoc solum petimus,* 246 *vota.*

author of the *Laus Pisonis*, for example, says that all he wants is for Piso's front door to be always open for him (218–19 *hoc solum petimus*). But in 4.4 Horace is not just speaking for himself and his stance is no longer that of the individual citizen on the model of Alcaeus. So in writing *Odes* 4.4 Horace, who was nothing if not pragmatic, summoned up *ab inferis* (or better, perhaps, *ex historiis*) a *testis* who would himself win credence.

So far we have looked at how the story in Horace's victory poem differs from those of Pindar, and what he gains by basing his central story on an event from the historical record despite his earlier rejection of historical themes. We can go further, I think, and link his turn to history with his use of physical monuments as a foil for poetry in this book.

To do so let us look at a part of the poem that has troubled, indeed disgusted, many a reader. I refer to the interjection of the first-person voice at lines 18–22, where Horace mentions the axes wielded by the Vindelici and ducks the question — *quaerere distuli*, he says — of the connection between the Vindelici and the Amazons who invented the battle axe:

> videre Raetis bella sub Alpibus
> Drusum gerentem Vindelici; quibus
>   mos unde deductus per omne
>   tempus Amazonia securi
> dextras obarmet, quaerere distuli,
> nec scire fas est omnia (17–22).[13]

> So Vindelicians saw under Raetian Alps
> The warrior Drusus marching (I now postpone
>   Enquiry whence the custom came that
>   Time out of mind has equipped their right hands
> With Amazonian battle-axe, for to know
> All the answers is not fitting)
>
>   (Trans. G. Lee)

This passage is usually explained as an imitation of Pindar's *praeteritiones*. Of these there are two common types. Pindar sometimes asserts that there is too much material for the time available: in

---

[13] For *Raetis* in place of Shackleton Bailey's †Raeti† see Syndikus (1972–73) 2.327–8. On the invention of the axe see Pliny *Nat.* 7.200–1: *invenisse dicunt... Penthesileam Amazonem securim.*

Nemean 4, for example, the hurrying hours (34 ὧραι . . . ἐπειγόμεναι) keep him from telling the whole tale. Similarly, in *Isthmian* 1 he is stopped from telling everything (60 πάντα δ᾽ ἐξειπεῖν) by the brief measure of his song (61–2 βραχὺ μέτρον ἔχων/ὕμνος). The μαρκότεραι ἀοιδάι of *Olympian* 13.41–2 and the poet's lack of leisure in *Pythian* 8 (29 εἰμὶ δ᾽ ἄσχολος ἀναθέμεν πᾶσαν μακραγορίαν) fall into the same category. Elsewhere he protests the story's content. Thus his blushes on the subject of fratricide in *Nemean* 5 (14–16 αἰδέομαι μέγα εἰπεῖν . . . στάσομαι), his exhortation in *Olympian* 9 (35–36 ἀπό μοι λόγον/τοῦτον, στόμα, ῥίψον), and the halt he calls in *Pythian* 2 lest he embark on an invidious tale (52–3 ἐμὲ δὲ χρέων/φεύγειν δάκος ἀδινὸν κακα-γοριᾶν).

The supposed Pindaric model for Horace's lines has not protected them from assessments such as "the harshest, queerest, most pre-posterous digression in the world" (this is Macaulay's) and this rather longer description of Ralph Johnson's: "It is . . . as though a contes-tant in a ski-jump had taken the run with full speed and full con-trol, had executed the start of his jump with utter power and grace, only to somersault of set purpose and without warning so as to plum-met ignominiously headfirst into the snows."[14] At first glance, at least, nobody thinks this *praeteritio* good.[15]

For my purposes it is enough to say that it is not Pindaric. The gnomic statement of line 22, *nec scire fas est omnia*, comes close to Pindar's style in form, but to my mind Horace's *praeteritio* as a whole is utterly different from those just paraphrased.[16] In both Pindaric types the poet knows more than he tells. Where time was short, another occasion will yield more of the story. The myths centered on the Aeacidae, for example, are spread over some 10 odes for vic-tors from Aegina. And the 'scandalous' content of the second set is presumably circulating in authors other than Pindar. Horace's lines, by contrast, announce a deficiency of knowledge (and a refusal to pursue it).

---

[14] Macaulay quoted at Fraenkel (1957) 429 note 3. He continues, 'But there are several things in Pindar very like it.' Johnson (1969) 172. Other assessments: Putnam (1986) 88 'an evidently pedantic search into an obscure piece of aetiology.' White (1993) 129 'Horace's most egregious rendering of Pindar's manner.' See also Pasquali (1920) 774–5, Wilkinson (1951) 109.

[15] Johnson (1969) is perhaps its most enthusiastic spokesman. But one may won-der whether 'ironic' (172), 'clever' (177), and 'a small but pleasant joke' (180) are descriptions to which Horace would have aspired for it.

[16] Its content, however, is not paralleled in what we have of Pindar.

For Horace's *aporia* Fraenkel adduced parallels from ethnographic writing. From Tacitus's *Germania*, for example (46.4 *cetera iam fabulosa . . . quod ego ut incompertum in medio relinquam*) and from the ethnographic digressions in Sallust's *Bellum Jugurthinum* (17.2 *sed quae loca et nationes . . . item solitudines minus frequentata sunt, de iis haud facile compertum narraverim*) and Tacitus' *Agricola* (10.7 *naturam Oceani atque aestus neque quaerere huius operis est ac multi rettulere*). These passages, however, express the difficulty of obtaining reliable information, not the refusal to know that is Horace's pose. Indeed at *Agricola* 11.1 Tacitus makes up for the lack of historical data with historical reasoning: he doesn't know whether the peoples of Britain are indigenous or immigrant, but he notes that the variety of physical types on the island yields an argument for immigration, since the Scots, like the Germans, have red hair and large limbs, etc.[17] This is all very different from Horace's *quaerere distuli*.

In connection with the *praeteritio* Fraenkel also supplied a reference to Tibullus 1.7, a poem that, as we have already seen, has much in common with 4.4. He points to the zetema posed, but not answered, in lines 23–4 *Nile pater, quanam possim te dicere causa/ aut quibus in terris occuluisse caput?* In Fraenkel's view this was one of the 'silly pedantries of certain panegyrists' that Horace's parenthesis parodies.[18] But here again his *comparandum* doesn't quite hit the mark, for Tibullus's lines, despite their aura of empty learning, are quite functional. The zetema about the sources of the Nile is the fifth of five unanswered questions. The series constitutes a catalog of Messalla's Eastern destinations: first Cilicia (lines 13–16), then Palestine and Tyre (lines 17–20), then Egypt (lines 21–6). In other words, Tibullus's questions are not designed to get information but rather to give it. The final question, however unanswerable, leads directly into the *mythos*, a mythical *mythos* in the Pindaric manner, with Osiris as its subject. This is precisely the kind of story that Horace refuses to tell in 4.4.

Others, including Ralph Johnson, have seen in Horace's digression a Callimachean refraction of Pindar, comparing, for example, the famous outburst in Book 3 of the *Aetia*:

---

[17] *Ceterum Britanniam qui mortales initio coluerint, indigenae an advecti, ut inter barbaros, parum compertum. habitus corporum varii, atque ex eo argumenta. namque rutilae Caledoniam habitantium comae . . .*

[18] Fraenkel (1957) 430.

"Ηρην γάρ κοτέ φασι — κύον, κύον, ἴσχεο, λαιδρέ
θυμέ, σύ γ᾽ ἀείσῃ καὶ τά περ οὐχ ὁσίη·
. . .
ἢ πολυιδρείη χαλεπὸν κακόν, ὅστις ἀκαρτεῖ
γλώσσης
                                              (fr. 75.4–5, 8–9 Pf.).

For they say that once upon a time Hera — dog, dog, refrain,
my shameless soul!
You would sing even of that which is not lawful to tell.
. . .
Surely much knowledge is a dangerous thing for him who does
not control his tongue

But here, too, the poet's pose is one of πολυιδρείη, and what is οὐχ
ὁσίη is telling, not knowing.[19]

If Horace's digression is not Pindaric, not ethnographic, not
Hellenistic (counting Tibullus as Hellenistic), what is it? Michèle
Lowrie has the right answer to this, in my view: she takes Horace's
quaerere distuli as a *recusatio*. In her view, the digression 'divulges local
information of the sort that would make for a colourful and detailed
history, had he chosen to give one.'[20] He doesn't so choose, of course,
and moves on to a different kind of history, the story of the aftermath of the battle on the Metaurus river. Now a *recusatio* is something we are not at all surprised to find in a poem that responds,
according to Suetonius, at least, to a request from Augustus (*Vita
Horati*): *scripta quidem eius usque adeo probavit mansuraque perpetua opinatus
est, ut non modo saeculare carmen conponendum iniunxerit, sed et Vindelicam
victoriam Tiberii Drusique privignorum suorum.* But why Amazons? And
why was the passed-over Amazon story a suitable foil for the story

---

[19] Johnson (1969) 174. Cf. Callimachus *Cer.* 17 μὴ μὴ ταῦτα λέγωμες ἃ δάκρυον
ἄγαγε Δηοῖ. On similar passsages from Apollonius Rhodius (*Arg.* 4.984–85, 4.1511)
see Tarrant (1998).
[20] Lowrie (1997) 329. Reckford (1960) 24 and White (1993) 129 both observe
that axes and Amazons characterize Drusus' opponents as worrysome, barbarous,
and badly in need of conquest or civilization. (On this and other functions of
Amazons see Dowden (1997).) This is true enough — Strabo and Cassius Dio comment on the barbarism of tribes in this area at this time, Cassius Dio citing the
crucifixion of Roman citizens (54.20.4), both authors the execution of male cap-
tives, male infants, and unborn males as well (54.22.2, Strabo 4.6.8) — but it does
not account for the fact that Horace prepares the way for a story he then refuses
to tell. Cf. Johnson (1969) 172 'If the archeological information was essential to his
epinician, ought he not to have spent more time in the library before he sat down
to his desk? If it was not essential after all, why any mention of it?'

that Horace does end up telling? To answer these questions we need to look briefly at some objects and texts that exemplify or describe a contemporary mode of representing conquests.

Personifications of defeated cities, kingdoms, and tribes featured in representations of victories both Greek (Classical and Hellenistic) and Roman.[21] The reign of Augustus yielded an abundance of work including such personifications, some of it alluded to by contemporary poets. They appear on the shield of Aeneas, for example:

> incedunt victae longo ordine gentes,
> quam variae linguis, habitu tam vestis et armis.
> hic Nomadum genus et discinctos Mulciber Afros,
> hic Lelegas Carasque sagittiferosque Gelonos
> finxerat
>
> > (*Aeneid* 8.722–6)

> While the defeated nations walked in long procession in all their different costumes and in all their different armour, speaking all the tongues of the earth. Here Mulciber, the God of Fire, had moulded the nomads and the Africans with their streaming robes; here too the Lelegeians and Carians of Asia and the Gelonians from Scythia with their arrows.
>
> > (Trans. D. West)

And likewise in Ovid's *Fasti: prospicit (sc. Mars) in foribus diuersae tela figurae/ armaque terrarum milite uicta suo* (5.561–2).

The Virgil passage prompted in Servius a reference to the Augustan *porticus ad Nationes*, a lost monument whose sculptural program is quoted in the surviving portico of the temple of Aphrodite Prometor (i.e., Venus Genetrix) in Aphrodisias.[22] Some of the sculpted representations of the 50 or so conquered peoples originally represented in the Aphrodisias portico can still be seen; here, as in the poets' descriptions, armament is one of the identifying elements.[23] Combining sculptural and epigraphic information from the portico we know the names of 16 peoples depicted there. Among them were the Trumpilini, an Alpine tribe that was the object of a campaign in 16 B.C., and

---

[21] See Bienkowski (1900), Kuttner (1995) 69–93, Ostrowski (1996).

[22] Servius on *Aen.* 8.721 *porticum enim Augustus fecerat in qua simulacra omnium gentium conlocaverat: quae porticus appellabatur: 'ad Nationes.'* On the monument see Smith (1988).

[23] The best preserved representation, that of the Piroustae, wears a helmet and carries a round shield. See Smith (1988) plate I.

the Raeti, one of the tribes faced by both Tiberius and Drusus in
15 B.C., i.e., in the campaigns celebrated in *Odes* 4.4 and 4.14.[24]
We do not know whether the Vindelici, too, were represented in
the portico.

When in our poem Horace characterizes the Vindelici that Drusus
fought beneath the Raetian Alps by their Amazonian axe (20 *Amazonia
securi*), he is thus alluding to a familiar and current mode of representing the defeated in monuments glorifying the victor.[25] The mode
is well exemplified by the object pictured in plates I–II, found in
ancient Moguntiacum but now in the British Museum, an object
that connects Amazons, victories and Nerones in a fashion curiously
reminiscent of *Odes* 4.4.

The plates show two scenes from the sheath of the so-called 'sword
of Tiberius'. Plate I reproduces the tableau from the lip of the sheath:
it is an audience scene with a Jupiter-like *princeps* receiving a stat-
uette of Victoria from a man in military garb. The cult statue of
Mars Ultor looks on. The *princeps* rests his left arm on a shield bearing the inscription FELICITAS TIBERI. Standing behind him is a
full-size Nike holding another shield, this one labeled VIC AUG,
i.e., VICTORIA AUGUSTI. At the tip (Plate II) is an axe-wielding
Amazon.

This combination of scenes has yielded several explanations. The
one that makes the best sense of the Amazon considers the sheath
a commemoration of the victory of Tiberius over the axe-wielding
Vindelici in 15 B.C., i.e., a physical counterpart to our poem (though
with the emphasis more strongly on Tiberius than on his younger
brother Drusus).[26] In this view Augustus sits on the *sella* and receives
the Victoria from Tiberius, while the Amazon represents the defeated
nation. Another view puts Tiberius on the *sella*, makes Germanicus
the victor and has the Amazon represent Germania or a generic
barbarian foe.[27] Not being an art historian I am in no position to

[24] For these two tribes the inscriptions, but not the statues, survive (see Smith
(1988) Plate IX). Historical sources on the campaigns include Velleius Paterculus.
2.39.3, 2.95.2, Suetonius *Tib.* 9.1, *Aug.* 21.1, Livy *Per.* 138.
[25] Axes are well represented in the iconography of Amazons, as can be seen
among the 819 images of Amazons in *LIMC*.
[26] This is the view of Walker and Burnett (1981) and others. For bibliography
see Decker and Selzer (1976).
[27] Espoused by Gagé (1930 and 1932), Zanker (1988), and Kuttner (1995). I am
grateful to Clifford Ando for these and other references to the work of Jean Gagé.

decide between these two views, but it hardly matters. All I really want to do is show that what Horace rejected, namely, an Amazon-aetiology for the Vindelician axes, was just the sort of story that might underlie an Augustan monument, a physical monument, that is, of the tribe conquered in 15 B.C. (There is, in fact, an Augustan victory monument featuring Amazons, a round monumental statue-base from Nicopolis on which is depicted an Amazonomachy alluding, presumably, to the victory at Actium.)[28] In lines 18–22 of 4.4, then, Horace seems to be turning away from a standard type of victory narrative, and this in a poem suggested, apparently, by Augustus.

He has got the rest of the poem to make up for his uncooperative behavior. So now it is time to ask just what *Odes* 4.4 does for Augustus.

One of the pervasive political themes in Book 4 of the *Odes* is the assent, indeed the enthusiasm of the populace of Rome and the peoples of the empire for Augustus. The enthusiasm not only of contemporaries, but also of future generations — the last word of the book is *canemus*, after all. But Augustus's ambitions reached further: he wanted the past on his side as well. Two well-known commemorative efforts of the Augustan period, one a physical monument, the other an event, will illustrate this point briefly.

The first is another Augustan sculptural showpiece, the double portico of the Forum Augustum with its 'Hall of Fame' collection of statues of past Romans. In the hemicycle at the head of the left portico Augustus put the Iulii and the kings of Alba Longa, centered on a representation of Aeneas with Anchises and Ascanius. In the right hemicycle, and perhaps along both porticoes, were displayed statues of men who had made the empire great, *ex minimo maximum.*[29] The centerpiece on the right side was Rome's founder, Romulus, carrying the *spolia opima*. The statues themselves do not

---

[28] See Bol (1998) 145–6, with plate 151e. 'Die in den Bildern impliziten Vorstellungen wären am Ort des Geschehens als Anspielung auf den Kampf gegen die 'Amazone Kleopatra' ohne weiteres nachzuvollziehen. Bezeichnenderweise sind die gegen die Amazonen antretenden Krieger, die ansonsten in den von der griechischen Kunst übernommenen Kampfszenen agieren, nicht mit den dort üblichen Rundschilden, sondern mit dem langen eckigen *scutum* der Römer ausgestattet'.

[29] Suetonius *Aug.* 31.5 *proximum a dis immortalibus honorem memoriae ducum praestitit, qui imperium Romanum p. R. ex minimo maximum reddidissent. itaque et opera cuiusque manentibus titulis restituit et statuas omnium triumphali effigie in utraque fori sui porticu dedicavit, professus et edicto: commentum id se, ut ad illorum vitam velut ad exemplar et ipse, dum viveret, et insequentium aetatium principes exigerentur a civibus.*

survive in more than tiny fragments, but some of the *tituli* do. In date the *summi viri* (or at least the 19 of them we know the names of) range from A. Postumius Regillensis, named for the battle of Lake Regillus in 496 B.C. through Appius Claudius Caecus (censor in 312 B.C.) to the Drusus of our poem, who was memorialized in the right-hand portico after his death in 9 B.C. Suetonius also records Augustus's statement about the purpose of the statues: he wanted his fellow citizens to measure himself and his successors against the examples set by the *summi viri*. The standard of achievement set by the past was to be maintained in the present and commended to the future.[30]

Much the same goal is evident in the funeral procession Augustus designed for himself: "And after these (i.e., after the portraits of Augustus himself) the masks of his ancestors came in procession, and those of his other relatives who had died, . . . and then the masks of the other Romans who had excelled in some way, beginning with Romulus himself."[31] The *imagines* that escorted Augustus on his journey to the pyre are the men Augustus adopted, so to speak, as his ancestors, and they were the men who had "excelled in some way."[32]

Drusus did not live to succeed Augustus or to inherit the burden of his acquired ancestors,[33] but in *Odes* 4.4 Horace takes his measure against a man, C. Claudius Nero, who might well have qualified as a *summus vir*.[34] To put it another way, in *Odes* 4.4 Horace gives the imperial family the vote of the past. As *testis* to C. Claudius Nero's success Hannibal sheds a reflected light of glory on Nero's descendant Drusus, and through Drusus on Augustus, whose *fausta*

---

[30] At *Fast.* 1.591–608, for example, in the discussion of the meaning of the name 'Augustus', Ovid obliges with a series of comparisons introduced by the general statement 591–2 *perlege dispositas generosa per atria ceras;/contigerunt nulli nomina tanta uiro.*

[31] Cassius Dio 56.34, H. Flower's translation.

[32] Cf. Flower (1996) 234 'He effectively appropriated the ancestors of other families to enhance his own position as a leader who was exceptional beyond the achievements of his own generation and his family's.' For discussion of the presence of the *imagines* from other families in the imperial funerals of Augustus' reign (Marcellus, Agrippa, Octavia, Drusus, Gaius, Lucius, and Augustus himself) see Flower (1996) 232–46.

[33] At his funeral, however, the *imagines* of the Iulii were present alongside those of the Claudii, despite the fact that Drusus was never a member of the Julian family (Tacitus *Ann.* 3.5.1).

[34] We do not know whether Nero was among the masks at Augustus's funeral, or among the statues in his Forum.

penetralia and *paternus animus* (4.4.25–9) so shaped the young Nerones that the conquered Vindelici perceived him through them (25 *sensere*).[35]

The comparison is three-fold. First, the opponents of the younger and the older Claudius are both given four-footed analogues. In the contemporary part of the poem the poet likens the Vindelici to a *caprea* about to fall victim to the young Drusus-lion (16 *dente nouo peritura*).[36] In the second, historical, part of the poem Hannibal himself likens his Carthaginians to deer, *cervi*, who voluntarily, foolishly (and ultimately, fatally), pursue their ravening Roman pursuers, the *lupi rapaces*, led by the earlier Claudius. The opponents are again similar in their wide-ranging destructiveness, the Vindelici being *diu lateque victrices catervae* (23–4), Hannibal the equivalent of a forest fire or storm wind at sea (42–4). And finally, the Claudii are both credited with cleverness. Drusus's *consilia* stopped the Vindelician rampage (23–4 *catervae consiliis iuvenis repressae*); his ancestor's cleverness — highlighted by Livy[37] — is either attested by Hannibal (if Hannibal gets the last stanza) or implicit in the poet's generalization about Claudian accomplishments (if the poet gets the last stanza). Whatever decision one makes about the text and punctuation of that stanza, it is clear that Drusus's *consilia* are the contemporary manifestation of Claudian *curae sagaces*.

Hasdrubal devictus: that could be recorded on a *tabula dealbata* or depicted in stone. It was, in fact, inscribed in the calendar, on the 23rd of June, as Ovid's *Fasti* tells us: *et cecidit telis Hasdrubal ipse suis* (6.770). The victory also received architectural commemoration in the form of a temple to Iuventas that was vowed by Claudius Nero's consular partner in victory, Livius Salinator (Livy 36.36.6). This temple burned in 16 B.C.; according to Dio, the fire occurred on the night before Augustus left for Gaul and set in motion the campaign eventually celebrated in *Odes* 4.4 (54.19.7). The temple was restored by Augustus, as he tells us in his *Res Gestae* (19.2). Contemporary victories, too, had their *tituli*, *monumenta*, and *memores fasti*. But for a monument that embraces past and present, that gives value to the

---

[35] Lowrie (1997) 328 'The Nerones substitute for Augustus as objects of praise, but the praise nevertheless returns to him.'

[36] Putnam (1986) 87–8.

[37] 27.43.7 *consilia*, 27.45.2 *consilium in speciem audacius re ipsa tutius*, 27.46.8 *consilium suum*, 27.47.6 *Hannibalem elusum*.

present by showing that it is of a piece with the past, you need a poem.[38] And that is what Horace offers Augustus.

What historiography and the historical tradition it preserves offers young Drusus's encomiast, then, is a fabric of *res Romanae* in which the Neronian thread is both long and at times brightly colored, and an ancestor whose achievements both guarantee and provide a measure for Drusus's conquest. Even with an axe, an Amazon cannot compete.[39]

---

[38] Reckford (1960) 25 'His feeling for the meaningfulness of the past is Pindaric; it also owes much to Virgil's epic, published two years before.'

[39] Subsequent to the Durham conference I presented this paper at the Boston University Roman Studies Conference (April 2000). I gained much from its discussion on both occasions and I am grateful to both audiences and especially to the conference organizers David Levene and Damien Nelis in Durham, and Pat Johnson in Boston. My thanks also go to Michèle Lowrie, whose comments improved this paper.

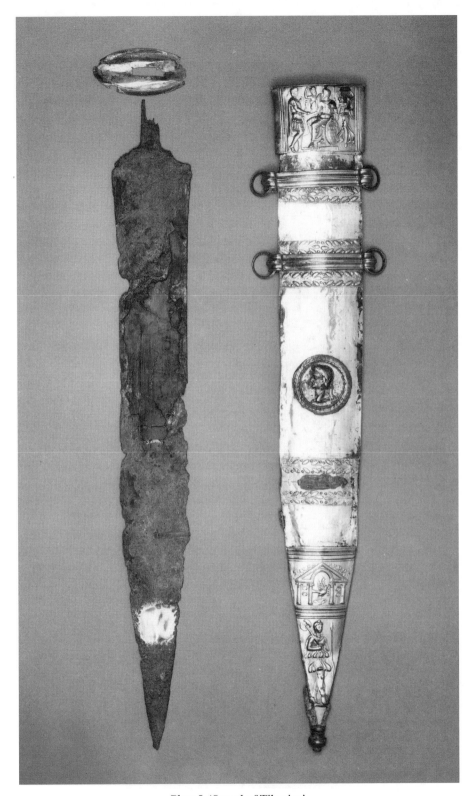

Plate I. 'Sword of Tiberius'

Plate II. Audience scene from the 'Sword of Tiberius' (top); Amazon from the tip of the 'Sword of Tiberius' (bottom)

CHAPTER SEVEN

VERGIL'S ITALY: ETHNOGRAPHY AND POLITICS IN FIRST-CENTURY ROME

Clifford Ando

At the end of the Roman Republic, in the aftermath of the Social War, all Italians were Romans, but not all Romans were Italians. To anyone but a Classicist, this assertion would seem paradoxical, because precisely the opposite situation obtains today, when national states subsume individual polities just as loyalty toward the national state takes precedence over loyalty to the city of one's birth. This assertion may also reveal a profound conceptual problem within Roman thought, though the nature of the problem was quite different for Romans than for us. Like many others in the ancient world, the Romans regarded the city as the pre-eminent paradigm of the political collectivity; it was, therefore, not obvious what sort of entity a united Italy would be.[1] Certainly neither Greek nor Latin had a term to designate such a vast community. Nor was it obvious what could unite the population of Italy: certainly not language, nor custom, at least not in the conditions that obtained at the start of the first century, nor even Roman citizenship, at least as it was traditionally conceived. The challenge that Romans and Italians faced, then, was to develop a conceptual framework for a united Italy that could surmount these obstacles.[2] In the late Republic and early empire individuals put forward different solutions to this problem, and this essay explores those advanced by Cicero, Augustus, and Vergil.

If Romans did not locate the crux of this paradox where we do now, wherein lay the problem for them? To answer this question, we must begin with the terms Roman and Italian. Strictly speaking, only citizens of Rome were Roman. What is more, Romans tended

---

[1] Ando (1999) considers Greek attempts to understand the political collectivity of the empire.

[2] Cf. Feldherr (1997) 138–41.

to associate citizenship with ancestral *origo*: your *patria* was generally the city whence your family sprang, and there you held citizenship.[3] The self-declared identity of Aulus Postumius Albinus succinctly concretizes this understanding: *nam sum homo Romanus, natus in Latio.*[4] Romans also found it very difficult to conceive of citizenship as an honor, apart from the privileges and obligations that it entailed: one could earn a lower sort of citizenship that came with obligations and no privileges, but not the other way around. Romans consequently had no equivalent for Hellenistic ἰσοπολιτεία; political rights in some far-off polity were, through sheer impracticality, regarded and explicitly labeled as equivalent, as though not intended to be exercised. Thus, for example, those who regard *hospitium publicum* as a status that brought 'all the private rights and privileges of Roman citizenship' without 'its burdens and obligations' seem, to me at least, to have misunderstood its import.[5] *Hospitium publicum* was explicitly not a form of citizenship and was, on the contrary, ideologically distinct from it.[6] Consider, for example, Cicero's defense of Lucius Cornelius Balbus: it does not matter for us today, as it did not matter for Cicero, whether Balbus might, as a matter of law, hold citizenship in Gades and Rome simultaneously.[7] Before the jury Cicero emphasized not that Balbus had conformed to any existing statute, but rather that he had formally renounced his status as a *Gaditanus* once he moved his domicile to Rome: Cicero insisted that Balbus now dealt with his former countrymen through pacts of *hospitium*, precisely because *hospitium* did not imply shared patriotic sentiment.

If 'Roman' was, at some level, a legal term with very circumscribed application but with complex ideological associations whose implications we must still untangle, 'Italy' and 'Italian' were, until the first century B.C., as fluid as Roman was precise.[8] Italy had purely geographic significance: it was a peninsula that housed populations diverse in origin, language, and customs.[9] Roman legislation

---

[3] Thomas (1996) passim, but esp. 61–8, 97–102. Cf. Syme (1979–91) vol. 6, 106, 165–66, distinguishing between Hadrian's *origo* and birthplace.
[4] *HRR* fr. 1 = Aulus Gellius 11.8.3.
[5] E.g. Cornell (1995) 321.
[6] So, rightly, Brunt (1987) 515–16.
[7] See *Balb.* 28–30, 42–3, and *Caec.* 100, and cf. Brunt (1982), Rawson (1985a) 44–6, Errington (1988) 153. Contra, Sherwin-White (1973) 302–4.
[8] Klingner (1965) 11–33.
[9] The diversity of Italy in the second and first centuries B.C.: Tarpin (1998), Torelli (1995) 1–15, Crawford (1996), David (1996), Torelli (1999).

prior to the Social War tended to use the phrase *terra Italia*, which denoted land on the Italian peninsula inhabited by Romans. This, for example, is the practice followed in the *lex agraria* of 111.[10] Italy could also designate the Italian peninsula as a whole. Livy, summarizing a *senatus consultum* concerning the survivors of Cannae, wrote that none of those men could return *in Italiam* so long as the enemy was *in terra Italia*.[11] The usage in Livy might otherwise be suspect, but it harmonizes with that of the elder Cato who, in his speech on the Achaeans in 151, began a sentence 'And when Hannibal was ravaging and harrying *terram Italiam* . . .'[12] We do not, alas, know how that sentence ended: that clause and that clause alone worked itself into the lexicographical tradition for its usage of *vexo* and was in this form cited by Gellius, Donatus, and Macrobius.

Even as a geographic term, moreover, the meaning of *Italia* evolved over time. Strabo, for example, reminded his readers that the boundary between Cisalpine Gaul and the 'rest of Italy' had once been designated by the Aesis but was later marked by the Rubicon.[13] Strabo himself regarded the division between Cisalpine Gaul and Italy as political, and *Italia* as the natural designation for all land below the Alps. Nor was Strabo alone in this belief. Cicero, too, occasionally labeled Cisalpine Gaul a part of Italy, whenever inclusive language served his cause. Thus, on the first of January, 43, when Cicero delivered his third Philippic and sought to create a unanimous opposition to Antony, he cited the example of *provincia Gallia*, 'the flower of Italy and bulwark of empire', which had thrown its support behind the *maiestas* of the Roman people.[14]

This development in the signification of *Italia* remained a topic for inquiry in the fourth century A.D., and knowledge of it proved useful in the vindication of details in Vergil's *Aeneid*. By that time, *Italia* had long designated all land below the Alps, and so Vergil's assertion that Aeneas was the first to come from Troy to Italy seemed flatly to contradict the story of Antenor as related by Venus later in the first book. The anonymous author of the *libellus* on the origin

---

[10] *Lex Agraria* (*Roman Statutes* no. 2), e.g. ll. 1, 21, and 50. Cf. Brunt (1988) 113–14.
[11] Livy 25.7.4.
[12] *ORF* 8.48.187: *cumque Hannibal terram Italiam laceraret atque vexaret*. . .; cited by Aulus Gellius 2.6.7, Servius on *Ecl.* 6.76, and Macrobius 6.7.10.
[13] Strabo 5.1.11.
[14] *Phil.* 3.13.

of the Roman people transmitted with the history of Aurelius Victor placed the onus of his explanation on the meaning of *primus*: comparing Vergil's usage elsewhere, he argued that *primus* at *Aeneid* 1.1 must have the meaning *princeps*, designating priority in significance and not in time.[15] Servius, on the other hand, offered three explanations, all of which depend ultimately on the limits of *Italia*. Servius himself preferred merely to argue that Vergil wrote in a fashion most appropriate to the usage of his day, when Italy ended at the Rubicon: Antenor did not, therefore, reach Italy, but rather Cisalpine Gaul. When, afterwards, the borders of Italy were moved to the Alps, it was the innovation that created the error.[16] Servius has, of course, confused the chronology of Italy's evolving boundaries, an error that we can easily forgive.[17]

Finally, there is no evidence that Romans aspired to unite Italy politically, or to view it as a natural, ethnic unity, prior, perhaps, to Livius Drusus, and certainly not before the Gracchi.[18] Two authors sometimes thought to have advocated such a programme, Cato and Quintus Lutatius Catulus, cannot, on extant evidence, be shown to have done so.[19] Cato in his *Origines* did not argue, indeed, could not have argued for any necessary unity among those peoples whose origins he related. In addition to cities in Italy proper, he investigated the Ligurians and Cisalpine Gauls, both of whom had only recently been conquered. And the inclusion of notable facts about Spain and North Africa in his later books suggests that Cato established the geographic limits of his inquiry purely by reference to the limits then reached by Roman arms.[20] Likewise, the *Communis historia* of Quintus

---

[15] *Origo gentis Romanae* 1.5–6.

[16] Servius on *Aen.* 1.1–2; cf. also on *Aen.* 1.13.

[17] On the boundaries of Italy see T. J. Cornell in *OCD*[3] s.v. Italy.

[18] *De viris illustribus* 58.8 depicts P. Scipio Aemilianus denouncing the supporters of Gracchus for their 'non-Italian' origins: *ob res gestas superbus Gracchum iure caesum videri respondit; obstrepente populo: 'taceant', inquit, 'quibus Italia noverca, non mater est'*. For some general remarks on this problem in Roman-Italian relations, see Brunt (1988) 131–2.

[19] Brunt (1988) 117 misunderstands Dionysius of Halicarnassus, *A.R.* 1.11.1 when he represents him as saying that Sempronius Tuditanus and many others traced 'the origins of every Italian people'. Dionysius merely numbers Sempronius Tuditanus among the most learned Roman historians and then asserts that he and others agreed with Cato regarding the origins of the 'Aborigines'.

[20] See *HRR* frr. 31–44, 78, 80, 96, and 97. See Astin (1978) 212–29. Purcell (1990) 19 continues cautiously to view Cato as an Italian nationalist, but seems to misunderstand the import of Cato's investigations of Gaul.

Lutatius Catulus did not purport to narrate the history of a *communis patria*, despite the widespread later use of that term. In spite of his woefully inadequate collection of the fragments of that work, Hermann Peter understood perfectly the aims of its author: Catulus aspired to write a universal history in Latin. *Communis historia* was his translation of the Greek term κοινὴ ἱστορία, which Polybius, Dionysius and Diodorus all used to describe their genre.[21] Catulus was therefore the intellectual forebear of Cornelius Nepos and Pomponius Atticus, and not a proto-Italian nationalist.

Peter Brunt has suggested that Cato chose to downplay the wars that Rome fought with Italians and to emphasize instead those in which Romans and Italians fought side by side.[22] This is at least possible. It is, however, certainly true that the cooperation of Italians and Romans in the conquest of the Mediterranean drew attention to the differential proceeds they derived from that shared project. The Social War thus took place because most of the inhabitants of the Italian peninsula desired to be full participants in the Roman state.[23] They insisted on the absolute inequality of *civitas sine suffragio* and all other legal statuses within the traditional hierarchy of Roman diplomatic relations: they recognized only a dichotomy of ruler and ruled. Although this formulation finds its clearest expression in the narrative of Appian, we can nevertheless recognize it in Latin authors from Cicero to Velleius.[24] Above all, it reveals that the opponents of Rome in the Social War achieved their sense of unity through that opposition. They selected Corfinum, the metropolis of the Paeligni, as Strabo designates it, as their capital; and they established a government explicitly parallel and opposed to that of Rome, and called their state Italica.[25] Italy and Italian therefore became a political unity and an ethnic category for the first time in 90 B.C., and they were defined in the first instance by their exclusion of Rome.[26]

---

[21] Peter, *HRR* cclxvii.

[22] See Brunt (1988) 117.

[23] Brunt (1988) 105 and 111; David (1996) 146–51.

[24] Appian *BC* 1.34.152; Cicero *Phil.* 12.27; Velleius Paterculus 2.15.2.

[25] Strabo 5.4.2; Diodorus Siculus 37.2.3–4; Velleius Paterculus 2.16.4. On Italian coinage see Brunt (1988) 111–12.

[26] We cannot know what, if any, purpose the term 'Italian' served in political rhetoric in the years immediately prior to the war: without any useful fragments of the speeches of Livius Drusus, we are simply at a loss. There are a very limited number of second-century inscriptions on which Italians designated themselves *Italici*

The Roman victory in that war raised as many problems as it solved. I highlight two of special significance. First, the vast extension of the franchise created a state unlike any other in the ancient world up to that time. Neither traditional vocabulary nor traditional conceptual categories could comprehend the new entity that the peace settlement had created. Even four centuries later, when intellectuals had grown accustomed to such economies of scale, Servius lacked the terminology to describe the no-longer familiar phenomenon of the colony: these, he argued, were groups of men who by unanimous consent settled in a fortified location; their inhabitants had a *res publica* by *consensus* of the *civitas*.[27] What Servius attempted to describe was the purely Roman attempt to create colonies whose inhabitants retained their status as participants in the *res publica* of Rome. He could not use 'metropolis' because Rome lacked the category and the word: Romans simply did not believe that colonists could esteem their colony as their *patria* above the claims of Rome itself.[28]

The second problem created by the resolution of the Social War was as follows. Roman linguistic practice, like the iconography of Roman triumphal art, described wars in which there were winners and losers. But how could Romans describe a war in which, to adopt the phrasing of Velleius, the fate of the Italians had been as cruel as their cause was just, and whose outcome granted to the losers all that they had sought in the first place? It had been, after all, Italian arms that so empowered Rome that it felt entitled to despise men of the same race and blood as though they were foreigners and aliens.[29] More to the point, how could one celebrate a victory, or describe a war, if doing so would revisit a long-standing and bitter

and not members of their individual communities (*ILLRP* 320 and 343), but this usage becomes quite common only after 90. To these inscriptions compare *ILS* 23, again from the second century, when Popilius Laenas referred *fugiteivos Italicorum* whom he sought and captured. His diction was not friendly. Cf. Brunt (1988) 117.

[27] Servius on *Aen.* 1.12.

[28] *Metropolis* enters Latin through transliteration and appears only in inscriptions from Asia Minor. Compare the diction of Velleius Paterculus 2.7.7: *in legibus Gracchi inter perniciosissima numerarim, quod extra Italiam colonias posuit. id maiores, cum viderent tanto potentiorem Tyro Carthaginem, Massiliam Phocaea, Syracusas Corintho, Cyzicum ac Byzantium Mileto, genitali solo, diligenter vitaverant et civis Romanos ad censendum ex provinciis in Italiam revocaverant.* Cf. Cicero *Agr.* 2.87.

[29] Velleius 2.15.2: *quorum ut fortuna atrox, ita causa fuit iustissima: petebant enim civitatem, cuius imperium armis tuebantur: per omnis annos atque omnia bella duplici numero se militum equitumque fungi neque in eius civitate ius recipi, quae per eos in id ipsum pervenisset fastigium, per quod homines eiusdem et gentis et sanguinis ut externos alienosque fastidire posset.*

injustice at the heart of a new and fragile community? Provincials in Africa, Asia, and Spain later found ways to celebrate their participation in the empire by manipulating the iconography of Roman triumphal art in *local* monuments, but their situation cannot be compared with that prevailing in Italy without considerable qualification.[30] Artists and orators at Rome required a name and a category for this conflict that they could use within a Roman context.

Normally Romans named wars after their opponents, after the people or the king against whom they fought. This war presented them with several options: *bellum Italicum*, perhaps the most obvious choice insofar as it utilized the name by which the enemy had designated itself; *bellum Asculanum*, after the city in which the war started; or *bellum Paelignum*, after the tribe whose capitol had served as the capitol for the federation. It is clear that no absolute consensus emerged, but the ideological import of the choice was obvious: the name would single out one group as hostile to the aims and aspirations of Rome. The name they chose more often than any other was *bellum Marsicum*.[31] Romans thus avoided a designation that would embody and recall the bitterness of the war itself, but they did so by creating a scapegoat. The Marsi and the Samnites had been particularly stubborn during the war itself, the Marsi boasting that no Roman had ever triumphed for a war in which the Marsi had not fought. Yet this choice, which was one the Romans had to make even if they didn't like their options, had profound consequences in the decades that followed.

Let me digress for a moment on this issue of naming. Although this designation allowed Romans to identify the Marsi as their true *hostes* in the war, and to celebrate the deeds of their generals against a proper foe,[32] in more reflective moments they acknowledged that the war was not strictly analogous to a war with a foreign race. Nor was it, significantly, a civil war: the Italians had not been citizens when they took up arms. They therefore developed the term 'social war', which was for decades *not* the name of this war, but the label for one type of war, namely, for *bella cum sociis*.[33] What is more,

---

[30] On provincial celebrations of their membership in the empire, see Ando (2000).
[31] See Strabo 5.4.2.
[32] E.g. *Man.* 28.
[33] See *Agr.* 2.90: *multa postea **bella gesta cum regibus**, Philippo, Antiocho, Persa, Pseudo-philippo, Aristonico, Mithridate et ceteris, multa praeterea bella gravia, Carthaginiense, Corinthium, Numantinum; multae in hac re publica **seditiones domesticae**, quas praetermitto, **bella***

although they use slightly different labels, Cicero in the first century B.C. and Ampelius in the fourth century A.D. each recognized that the war fought between 90 and 88 was qualitatively different from the wars by which Rome had conquered Italy in the fifth and fourth centuries, and different again from the civil wars that were yet to come.[34] By the middle of the first century A.D., the elder Pliny seems to use 'Social War' for the particular rather than the genre,[35] and certainly by the fourth century Ampelius must designate the Social War as one example of a *bellum internum* precisely because his age recognized *bellum sociale* as the proper name for the wars of 90–88.

In the generation born immediately after the war, two patterns emerged for understanding the nature of the community that now existed on the Italian peninsula. The first I call the Vergilian, because I believe Vergil to have been its most eloquent exponent, although I will deal with Vergil's presentation of this position later. For now I concentrate on his intellectual predecessor, Cornelius Nepos. The second pattern I call the Ciceronian, to which I shall presently turn.

I have suggested that modern attempts to view Cato's *Origines* as a political tract advocating Italian unity are misguided. The first extant author to read his text in that fashion was, however, not our contemporary, but one of Cicero's, Cornelius Nepos. For Nepos, in spite of Cato's inclusion of details about Gaul, Africa and Spain, insisted that Cato described in his second and third books 'the origin of every Italian community'.[36] And Nepos offered the general verdict on Cato that it would not be easy to find any matter concerning Greek or Italian affairs of which he was unaware.[37] The first use of 'Italian' to refer to the cities of Italy could be a purely geographical reference. But the deliberate contrast between 'Greek and Italian' rather than 'Greek and Roman' *may* be a deliberate attempt

---

cum sociis, *Fregellanum, Marsicum; quibus omnibus domesticis externisque bellis Capua non modo non obfuit, sed opportunissimam se nobis praebuit et ad bellum instruendum et ad exercitus ornandos et tectis ac sedibus suis recipiendos.* See also *Phil.* 12.27: *memini colloquia et cum acerrimis hostibus et cum gravissime dissidentibus civibus* . . . [recalling conversations between Pompeius and Vettius Scato, the *dux Marsorum*]. *erat in illo colloquio aequitas; nullus timor, ulla suberat suspicio, mediocre etiam odium. non enim ut eriperent nobis socii civitatem, sed ut in eam reciperentur petebant.*

[34] See Ampelius 40.1, on *civilia bella*, and 41.1, on the *quattuor genera bellorum*: *gentile, internum, servile*, and *civile*.
[35] Pliny *Nat.* 3.70.
[36] Nepos *Ca.* 3.3.
[37] Nepos *Ca.* 3.2.

to assert the existence of a unitary Italian culture that subsumed that
of Rome. This reading of Nepos suggests that we place greater political emphasis on the dedication to Nepos in Catullus 1: I suspect
that was intended to signify a degree of ethnic as well as intellectual
affinity, a nod from one Gallic Italian to another, acknowledging the
latter's devotion to a specifically Italian culture.[38]

If we turn now to Cicero, we find a very different model and
very different justification for the unification of Italy.[39] I concentrate
on two issues: first, on Cicero's reason for rejecting the path blazed
by Cornelius Nepos and, second, on the model he put forward in
its place. To that end I turn first to his second speech against the
agrarian law proposed by the tribune P. Servilius Rullus. Rullus had
proposed a remarkable programme in which the state would dis-
tribute public land, including lands that the state would buy for this
purpose, and, in the process, found colonies throughout Italy and
the provinces. When Cicero challenged him on the dangers of founding colonies abroad, Rullus retreated and restricted his proposal to
Italy. 'Now there's a restricted territory', exclaimed Cicero, with
potent sarcasm.[40] The details of the legislation need not trouble us
here.[41] Cicero objected to the legislation on several grounds, not least
because he believed that colonies had become anachronistic. Our
ancestors, he argued, had established colonies against the suspicion
of danger, so that a colony was not so much a town of Italy but a
fortress of the empire.[42] Now that all of Italy was filled with citizens

---

[38] Catullus 1.5–6: *unus Italorum/omne aevum . . . explicare*. '*Romanorum*' would not, of
course, have suited the metre. But *Italorum* has 'by nature', as Servius might say
(cf. on *Aen.* 6.779), a short first syllable. This is the first occurrence of '*Italia*' with
a long 'i' in extant Latin. But it seems pointless to argue that Catullus could only
have altered his diction by changing this one word, and that the lack of a reasonable alternative left him no choice whatsoever. On intellectual affinities between
Nepos and Catullus see Wiseman (1979) 154–74, Habinek (1998) 94–7.

[39] Of course, Cicero adjusted his rhetoric to his audience: just as he spoke
differently before the Senate and the people, so he could be more inclusive or more
Romanocentric, depending on time and circumstance. Both early and late in his
career — *Catil.* 2.24 and *Phil.* 7.22–3), for example — he explicitly assuaged the fears
of the Roman populace that the Italian communities, which were filled with their
fellow-citizens, would not break ranks and join Catiline or Antony, respectively.

[40] *Agr.* 2.56: '*definio*' *inquit*, '*Italiam*'. *satis certa regio*.

[41] For the legal details see Jonkers (1963).

[42] *Agr.* 2.73: *quo in genere sicut in ceteris rei publicae partibus est operae pretium diligen-
tiam maiorum recordari, qui colonias sic idoneis in locis contra suspicionem periculi collocarunt,
ut esse non oppida Italiae sed propugnacula imperii viderentur.*

and no longer needed supervision, the use of colonies there could only be intended to station troops and clients near Rome.[43] Rullus also proposed, so Cicero insisted, to include the *ager Campanus* in his plan and, above all, to establish a colony at Capua.

Why was this so dangerous? Cicero reminded his audience of past attempts to found colonies at Capua. While other Roman colonies made no attempt to establish themselves as self-sufficient polities and were therefore content with *duumviri* as their only magistrates, the colonists at Capua had insisted on naming their magistrates 'praetors', to whom they gave lictors and *fasces*.[44] The object of Rullus and his allies, claimed Cicero, was not to establish a colony for the people of Rome; it was to establish another Rome in opposition to this one, 'the *communis patria* of us all'.[45]

What is more, it was irrelevant that Rullus might not have complete control over those selected to colonize Capua. 'For men's *mores* do not derive naturally from their race and parentage, but they derive from those things that nature itself supplies for our subsistence, from the air we breathe and the food we eat'.[46] Thus the Carthaginians were liars and cheats not because that was inherent in their racial composition, but rather because of the nature of the land on which they settled. The Ligurians, likewise, owed their hardy rusticity to the poverty of their soil. So too the beauty, health, and bounty of Campania engendered in its inhabitants that well-known Campanian arrogance. Cicero has grounded his objection to the

---

[43] *Agr.* 2.86.

[44] *Agr.* 2.93: *nam et ipse qui deduxit, et qui magistratum Capuae illo creante ceperunt, et qui aliquam partem illius deductionis, honoris, muneris attigerunt, omnis acerbissimas impiorum poenas pertulerunt. et quoniam M. Bruti atque illius temporis feci mentionem, commemorabo id quod egomet vidi, cum venissem Capuam colonia iam deducto L. Considio et Sex. Saltio, quem ad modum ipsi loquebantur, 'praetoribus', ut intellegatis quantam locus ipse adferat superbiam, quae paucis diebus quibus illo colonia deducta est perspici atque intellegi potuit. Nam primum, id quod dixi, cum ceteris in coloniis IIviri appellentur, hi se praetores appellari volebant. quibus primus annus hanc cupiditatem attulisset, nonne arbitramini paucis annis fuisse consulum nomen appetituros? deinde anteibant lictores non cum bacillis, sed, ut hic praetoribus urbanis anteeunt, cum fascibus bini. erant hostiae maiores in foro constitutae, quae ab his praetoribus de tribunali, sicut a nobis consulibus, de consili sententiae probatae ad praeconem et ad tibicinem immolabantur.*

[45] *Agr.* 2.86: *tunc illud vexillum Campanae coloniae vehementer huic imperio timendum Capuam a xviris inferetur, tunc contra hanc Romam, communem patriam omnium nostrum, illa altera Roma quaeretur.* Cf. *Phil.* 12.7: *an vos acerrimam illam et fortissimam populi Romani libertatis recuperandae cupiditatem non imminutam ac debilitatam putatis legatione pacis audita? quid municipia censetis? quid colonias? quid cunctam Italiam? . . . quem ad modum nostrum hoc consilium Capua probabit, quae temporibus his Roma altera est?*

[46] *Agr.* 2.95.

agrarian law very precisely in the racial diversity of Italy, and he has argued his case using the commonplace association in ancient thought of climate and culture. This correlation, so common in ethnographic writing, had received scientific support from Eratosthenes, and would shortly find a wider audience at Rome through the writings of Alexander of Ephesus, although most Roman readers probably read the theories of those men through the Latin adaptations of their works by Varro of Atax.[47] Cicero obviously did not argue that Italians could not unite, but they could not, on this model, do so through a shared ethnicity or even through inherently shared *mores*. The geography of Italy demanded diversity.

More than a decade and a half after formulating this rejection of Italy as an ethnic unity, Cicero turned to the construction of an alternative. In the books *De legibus* he undertook to provide a constitution for the ideal state that he had described in his *De re publica* some years before. In the conversation that opens the second book, Cicero referred to the land in which he, Quintus, and Atticus walked as his *patria*, which elicited a question from Atticus: 'Have you then two *patriae*? Or is our *communis patria* the only one? Unless, that is, you think that Cato's fatherland was not Rome, but Tusculum?' To which Cicero responded: 'Absolutely I think that both he and all other municipal men have two *patriae*: one by birth, and one by citizenship . . . Thus we consider as our *patria* both the place where we were born, and that place by which we are adopted. But that *patria* must be preeminent in our affection, in which the name of the *res publica* signifies the common citizenship of us all. For her it is our duty to die; to her we ought to give our entire selves, and on her altar we ought to place and to dedicate, as it were, all that we possess'.[48]

Cicero has alleged that political loyalties need not stand in conflict with each other. Although the next sentence has been badly mutilated in the exemplar for the Leiden corpus, it seems clear that Cicero concluded this section by urging that loyalty to the *communis patria* must take precedence over loyalty to any other political collectivity. In the hierarchy of allegiances outlined by Cicero, loyalty

---

[47] In his *Ephemeris* and *Chorographia*: see *FLP* frr. 13–14 and 16–17. For a survey of Roman geography and ethnography, see Rawson (1985b) 250–66. Thomas (1982) should be consulted with caution. For the influence of Posidonius on ethnographic theory at Rome, see Norden (1959). On Cicero see Vasaly (1993) 131–55.
[48] *Leg.* 2.5.

toward Rome occupies a superordinate position: its laws and its culture provide the normative fabric that will, to borrow the phrase of
Rutilius Namatianus, 'create from distinct and separate nations a single fatherland'.[49]

Cicero has here crafted a completely different basis for Italian
unity, namely, shared citizenship in the Roman state. In turning
away from ethnicity or culture, he has chosen to expand the traditional
parameters of *civitas* and *patria*. He has thus crafted a new paradox,
which immediately drew the attention of Atticus. This model, which
resonates so well with modern discourses on the nature of patriotism,
does not, and perhaps cannot, address the lived realities of this new
Roman state: how was an ancient democracy to function on such a
scale? How could the rituals of a Mediterranean city-state be expanded,
iterated, and adapted to include so many citizens who would never
see their preeminent *patria*? Asking these questions should not lessen
our appreciation for Cicero's profound achievement in privileging a
legal abstraction as the basis for a larger community.[50] Furthermore,
at a purely emotive level the Ciceronian model held an obvious
appeal for those born and bred in the *municipia* of Italy, for it allowed
them to boast of their *patriae natales*, even as they participated in,
and contributed to, the development of a shared, Roman culture.[51]

Before I turn to Vergil, I want to discuss the views of his contemporary and patron, the emperor Augustus. For his actions, and
especially his diction, lie at the heart of all that happened in his age.
In the late 30's, as Octavian's relations with Antony soured, each
dynast sought to bind his soldiers and his subjects to himself with
solemn oaths of personal fidelity. In the summer of 32, following the
publication in Italy of Antony's will, a tide of support for Octavian —

---

[49] Rutilius Namatianus *De reditu suo* 1.63.

[50] Cicero often invoked the loyalty of all Italy in the speeches after his return,
but he has almost always made it clear that he invokes Italy as the home of the
populus Romanus: see, for example, *Dom.* 90: *illa fuit pulchritudo populi Romani, illa forma
quam in campo vidisti tum cum etiam tibi contra senatus totiusque Italiae auctoritatem et studium
dicendi potestas fuit*. See also *Dom.* 26 and 82 and *Red. Sen.* 25 and 39. Observe, too,
how Rome is privileged in descriptions of Italy, which has but one *urbs* and a single
res publica (*Red. Pop.* 4): *quae species Italiae, quae celebritas oppidorum, quae forma regionum,
qui agri, quae fruges, quae pulchritudo urbis, quae humanitas civium, quae rei publicae dignitas,
quae vestra maiestas!* It is on this basis that later Cicero can refer to *tanta consensione
Italiae* (*Red. Pop.* 18).

[51] On the contours of Roman patriotism see the useful preliminary study of
Bonjour (1975).

or, at least, revulsion at his opponent — swept the regions of the West. City after city gathered to swear the oath of loyalty. Augustus recalled this show of support in a famous chapter of his *Res Gestae*: '*Tota Italia* of its own free will swore allegiance to me and demanded me as its leader for the war in which I was victorious at Actium; the Gallic and Spanish provinces, Africa, Sicily, and Sardinia swore the same oath of allegiance'.[52]

When Ronald Syme sought to describe the gradual and ultimately overwhelming flood of support for Octavian that swept Italy and the Roman aristocracy starting late in 33, he paused briefly to consider this use of *tota Italia* and suggested that the invocation of Italy had precedents earlier in the century. But the vast majority of his parallels are not, in fact, strictly analogous: almost all of them refer to a combination of Italians and Romans or Latins and allies, or to Italians defined as those who were *not* citizens of Rome.[53] What Augustus referred to in 2 B.C. or in 13 A.D. or whenever he drafted this text, was the unanimous support of all the citizens of Rome then resident in Italy. Why not say precisely that? Why not, in fact, when writing thirty years later, simply claim the support of all of Rome? Whatever Octavian's options, the absence of Rome and presence of Italy in this list suggests, if no more than that, the possibility that Rome and Roman could be subsumed within the larger categories 'Italy' and 'Italian'.

The year 32 had been fraught with worry, and with promise. Octavian needed to unify the West as never before. But if *tota Italia* had expressed something of the revolutionary atmosphere of that moment, the moment itself was short-lived. For by the end of his life Augustus had returned to a purely Romanocentric perspective. Among the documents he left with the Vestal Virgins was a set of instructions for Tiberius and the Roman populace. Among other things, he cautioned them 'especially that they should not free too many slaves, lest they fill the city with an indiscriminate mob, and that they not enroll a great many to citizenship, in order that there be a substantial distinction between themselves and their subjects'.[54] Gone for good was the inclusive rhetoric of the triumvir struggling for his life.

---

[52] *RG* 25.2.
[53] Syme (1939) 285–6.
[54] Cassius Dio 56.33.1–3.

We should not be surprised to find Vergil preoccupied with precisely the problem of Italian unity, on the one hand, and with relations between Rome and Italy on the other. As Kate Toll has stressed,
Vergil was not born an Italian and may not have been a Roman,
either. Rather, those two identities came to him and to his native
land separately, over a period of decades, and Vergil would thus
have 'conducted his own reconsideration and scrutiny of them'.[55] We
would thus be remiss if we did not read his poetry as a contribution to an on-going discourse about the nature of the community
that then existed on the Italian peninsula. The import and thrust of
Vergil's message for and about Italy emerges with particular clarity
if we reflect for but a moment on the contemporaneous works of
Horace, for Horace refused to subscribe to *tota Italia*. For example,
in the 30's, in *Epode* 16, Horace lamented that internal strife could
destroy a city that no one else could, neither the Marsi nor the
Etruscan bands of Porsena, neither Capua nor Spartacus, neither
Gauls nor Hannibal. This list, in joining these names in opposition
to Rome, can only have reminded readers of the bitter struggles that
issued in their present condition.

In his works of the 20's Horace singled out the Marsi three more
times. In *Ode* 3.5 Horace lamented that Marsian and Apulian soldiers then lived with foreign wives in Parthia, forgetful of the toga,
of Vesta, of Jupiter and of Rome herself. Porphyrio understood the
passage perfectly: 'Since Horace was commemorating the greatness
of the deeds of Augustus, he railed against those who fought under
Crassus and, having forgotten Roman virtue, settled among the
Parthians and bore the shame of captivity with equanimity'.[56] Why
should Horace not lament at the suffering of soldiers betrayed by
their commander's incompetence? Perhaps, once again, because he
has selected some Italians to be non-Romans. If so, why not the
Marsi, who then so often bore the full weight of responsibility for
the Social War? The Marsi certainly serve that function in *Ode* 3.14,
however convivial its mode,[57] and may do so again in *Ode* 1.2, where

---

[55] Toll (1991) 3–4, (1997) 34–6, and, rather more distant in its topic and conclusions, Horsfall (1976).
[56] Porphyrio at *Odes* 3.5.6–8.
[57] *Odes* 3.14.14–20.

Horace refers to the civil wars as directly continuous with the strife of the early 80's.[58]

What, then, of Vergil and Italy? Let me turn first to the *Georgics*. I happily follow Richard Thomas and David Ross in their under- standing of the ethnographic model that underlies the presentation

---

[58] See *Odes* 1.2.29–40:

> cui dabit partis scelus expiandi
> *Iuppiter? tandem venias precamur*
> *nube candentis umeros amictus,*
>   *augur Apollo;*
> *sive tu mavis, Erycina ridens,*
> *quam Iocus circum volat et Cupido;*
> *sive neglectum genus et nepotes*
>   *respicis auctor,*
> *heu nimis longo satiete ludo,*
> *quem iuvat clamor galeaeque leves*
> *acer et Marsi peditis cruentum*
>   *vultus in hostem;*

Nisbet and Hubbard (1970) on 40 argue that *hostem* cannot designate Romans, but in civil war anything is possible, and Mars fights on both sides: see Cicero *Fam.* 6.4.1 (*nam cum **omnis belli Mars communis** et cum semper incerti exitus proeliorum sunt, tum hoc tempore ita magnae utrimque copiae, ita paratae ad depugnandum esse dicuntur ut, utercumeque vicerit, non sit mirum futurum*), Vergil *Geo.* .509–14 (*hinc movet Euphrates, illinc Germania bellum; /vicinae ruptis inter se legibus urbes/ arma ferunt; **saevit toto Mars impius orbe**, /ut cum carceribus sese effudere quadrigae, /addunt in spatia, et frustra retinacula tendens / fertur equis auriga neque audit currus habenas*), Vergil *Aen.* 10.755–7, and Servius on *Ecl.* 4.13 (citing *Geo.* 1.510–11). The politically-charged diction in Propertius 1.22.3–5 can scarcely be explained, let alone appreciated, but it participates in, indeed, is only intelligible within a contemporary debate on the nature of Rome, Italy, and the nature of *patriae: si Perusina tibi patriae sunt nota sepulcra, Italiae duris funera temporibus, cum Romana suos egit discordia cives.* . . . It is, of course, true that *hostis* almost never designates Romans, but then civil wars were hardly "natural": see Cicero *Fam.* 1.9.15, on Clodius (*monumentum vero senatus hostili nomine et cruentis inustum litteris esse passi sunt*), Horace *Ep.* 1.18.62 (among boys re-enacting Actium some must act *hostili more*), Livy 1.59.4 (the rape of Lucretia turns Tarquinius into an enemy), Livy 6.3.6, 9 (viewed from the Etruscans perspective, the Romans are *hostes*); Lucan 1.203 (Caesar addresses his *patria* about Pompey: *ille erit, ille nocens, qui me tibi fecerit hostem*), 1.374–8 (Laelius speaks to Caesar: *per signa decem felicia castris/ perque tuos iuro quocumque ex hoste triumphos: /pectore si fratris gladium iuguloque parentis/ condere me iubeas plenaeque in viscera partu/ coniugis, invita peragam tamen omnia dextra . . .*), 1.622 (Arruns takes the auspices, but the liver is divided against itself: *cernit tabe iecur madidum, venasque minaces hostili de parte videt*), and Tacitus *Hist.* 2.66.1 (Roman legions *sparsae per Italiam et victoribus permixtae hostilia loquebantur . . .*) and 2.87.2 (Vitellian legionaries act in Italy *ut hostile solum vastabantur*). For further uses of *hostis* to refer to both sides in the civil war, see Lucan 2.283, 395, and 440, and cf. 3.625 (from the sea-fight between *gemini fratres*). On Horace's identity-politics see Sirago (1958), Bonjour (1975) 193–6; on Horace and Italy see Habinek (1998) 88–102.

of Italy's climate in the first book of the *Georgics*.[59] But I diverge from their readings of the *laudes Italiae* in Book 2. I argued earlier that Cicero used precisely this scientific model to argue for the necessity of Italian diversity. Vergil emphatically does otherwise. When he compares vines elsewhere with 'our' vines, Servius understood that he meant 'Italian' vines.[60] And when Vergil concluded this catalogue with the assertion that the *patriae* of plants are diverse, Servius understood that Vergil labeled all of Italy a single *patria*.[61] But Vergil was doing far more than labeling Italy a single region with a single climate: he was insisting on the unity of the Italian people, completely reversing the arguments of Cicero. And in a few lines he turned his back on Horace, too. For at the close of the *laudes Italiae* Vergil listed the peoples who had made Italy great: the Marsi, the Samnites, Liburians and Volscians, the Decii, Marii, Camilli and Scipiones.[62] If the concluding set of names listed the great families who distinguished an unnamed *populus Romanus*, Vergil has joined them seamlessly with the peoples of Italy, and together they constitute the people not of Rome, but of Italy.[63]

Vergil was working on the *Georgics* during Octavian's build-up to Actium, and it is tempting to see Vergil participating in, and attempting to elevate, the spirit of unity that ennobled that otherwise disgraceful civil war. I have suggested that Octavian soon abandoned his inclusive, Italian rhetoric for a purely Roman point of view. Vergil, I think, did not. He signaled his allegiance to Italy throughout the *Aeneid*, and not simply in his laments against the horrors of civil war. He did so rather obviously in his descriptions of Actium on the shield, and in that context, given Octavian's rhetoric at that time, Vergil's diction comes as no surprise.[64] But he did so elsewhere in ways more subtle, by taking stands that both fascinated and puzzled his ancient readers.

---

[59] Thomas (1982). See also Ross (1987) 42–3 and 115–28, Thomas (1988) 7–9, 107–12, 131, 179–80.

[60] *Geo.* 2.83–108, and cf. Servius on *Geo.* 2.89.

[61] Servius on *Geo.* 2.116.

[62] I must confess a certain *aporia* before the last line of the *laudes: Ascraeumque cano Romana per oppida carmen* (*Geo.* 2.176). Is Vergil asserting an identity between Italy and *oppida Romana*? Is he using *Romana* merely as a contrast with the Callimachean reference in *Ascraeum*? The latter seems improbable, if, indeed, 'Rome' and 'Italy' were as politicized as I have suggested.

[63] *Geo.* 2.167–72. See also below, on *Geo.* 2.532–5.

[64] *Aen.* 8.624–9, and esp. 8.678.

These readers quite obviously prized their erudition regarding the early history of the Italian peninsula. A startling number of the historical narratives of the fourth century attempt to describe the history of Italy prior to Aeneas or else prior to the foundation of the Republic. But these narratives all possessed a certain inevitability: the history of Italy, as it were, ended when the history of Rome began. Even for the elder Pliny, whose geography fourth-century readers knew well, the tribes *ex antiquo Latio* had perished without a trace.[65] Vergil's insistence at *Aeneid* 1.6 that his poem narrated the origin of the *genus Latinum* therefore required explanation. Servius called attention to Vergil's diction, and he based his explanation for it on the curse of Dido in Book 4 and the prayer of Juno in Book 12. Dido had asked that Aeneas and his descendants live under an unjust peace, and Juno wanted the name 'Trojan' to disappear.[66] Aeneas had therefore abandoned common practice, in which the victor imposes his name, language, and customs on the loser,[67] and surrendered his right to obliterate the Latin name. Instead, he chose to reconcile the Latins to his rule by taking their name.[68]

But Servius did not, I think, feel altogether comfortable with this explanation, nor was he capable of articulating why that was so. Thus when Vergil inserted in the prayer of Juno in Book 12 the wish, 'Let Rome's children be powerful through Italian virtue', Vergil suggested, as he did at the close of the *laudes Italiae* and again at the end of *Georgics* 2, that Rome and Italy were an inseparable unity and that Roman *virtus* was not a native characteristic, but was ultimately derivative from a greater Italian set of *mores*.[69] Thus, rather

---

[65] Pliny *Nat.* 3.70.

[66] See *Aen.* 4.618 and 12.819–28. On the reconciliation between Jupiter and Juno in 12, its import in the *Aeneid* and in Augustan political discourse, see West (1998) and Gottlieb (1998).

[67] Servius on *Aen.* 4.618.

[68] Servius on *Aen.* 1.6.

[69] Cf. *Aen.* 8.271–2 (on the *Ara Maxima*), 8.825 on the Salii, 8.313 (labeling Evander *Romanae conditor arcis*), and 8.337–9 (on the *Ara Carmentalis*), even 8.541–5 (on Evander's *penates*). The continuity of religious practices from Evander's Rome to the Augustan age in itself argues for the priority of Italian roots in latter-day Roman institutions. One could make a similar argument about the necessity, often expressed, for Aeneas and his Trojans to shed their Trojan heritage: *they* must assimilate to native Italian customs, and not the other way around. But cf. *Aen.* 7.641–4, the beginning of the catalogue (*Pandite nunc Helicona, deae, cantusque movete, / qui bello exciti reges, quae quemque secutae / complerint campos acies, quibus Itala iam tum / flouerit terra alma viris, quibus arserit armis . . .*). 'Italian' here seems to include everyone but the Trojans and their allies.

casually, Servius attributes the joy and diction of Aeneas and his
comrades at their first sight of Italy (. . . *humilemque videmus Italiam.
Italiam primus conclamat Achates, Italiam laeto socii clamore salutant*) to
Vergil's desire either to indicate the *naturam provinciae*, or to express
a more abstract truth about physics.[70] This was also the boast of
Numanus in his invective in Book 9: some god or madness had sent
the Trojans to Italy, which was home to a singular *durum genus*.[71]
Servius glossed that phrase with the explanation, 'The *disciplina* and
lifestyle (*vita*) of Italy is praised, which Cato in his *Origines* and Varro
in his book on the *gens* of the Roman people recorded'.[72] Of course
Servius recognized that Juno's wish expressed something controversial, but its import in Augustan discourse on Italian ethnicity was
lost to him. He wrote, '[Juno] seems to say this: if it is fated that
Rome's origin descend from the Trojans, let the Trojans take the
name of the Italians, so that the Romans might seem descendants
not of the Trojans, but of the Italians'.[73] But Vergil had not been
arguing simply about nomenclature, and *that* Servius would not, or
could not, recognize.

Servius could not understand Vergil's intent because the fate of
Italy as a political ideal had been decided four centuries before. The
Ciceronian model had prevailed. When Ovid in *Amores* 3.15, for
example, celebrated a canon of Roman poets identified by their
patriae naturae, he participated in the Ciceronian system.[74] It helped,
of course, that the difficulties aroused by the functioning of the
Roman democracy were effectively removed with the foundation of
the Principate. And the Principate helped in other ways, by creating opportunities for individuals to express their loyalties to Rome
through an empire-wide cult whose necessity needed no justification.
And as a conceptual problem, the place of Rome in Italy fell away
before the greater scale of a Roman empire. The full consequences
of its scale could be realized only after Actium, when the tremen-
dous conquests of the revolutionary age had to be integrated into
mental constructs of the *imperium Romanum*.[75] It helped, too, that few

---

[70] Vergil *Aen.* 3.521–4 and Servius on *Aen.* 523.
[71] Cf. *Aeneid* 6.756–62.
[72] Servius on *Aen.* 9.600.
[73] Servius on *Aen.* 12.827.
[74] *Am.* 3.15.7: *Mantua Vergilio gaudet, Verona Catullo.* He doesn't identify poets' *patriae*
in either *T.* 4.10 or *Ep.* 4.16.
[75] On this problem and the representations of the world it produced, see Nicolet
(1991) and Ando (2000) 277–335.

had anything personal at stake in this issue. Velleius Paterculus alone of his generation, and almost alone in extant Latin literature, felt with tragic horror the justice of both sides in the Social War.[76] It was thus still possible for Velleius to use *tota Italia* to refer to all Italians in opposition to Romans, while Pliny, but a few years later, could identify *urbs Roma* as but one of the glories of *Italia*, because Italy existed for him only as a geographic entity, one without political significance.[77]

This is not to say that relations between Rome and Italy ceased to be a topic of inquiry altogether. In the early fifth century, Macrobius in his *Saturnalia* crafted an astonishing explanation for the Roman conquest of Italy.[78] He began a discourse on the secret names of cities. He, like virtually every other antiquarian from the age of

---

[76] Velleius Paterculus 2.15–27. But cf. Ovid *Am.* 3.15.8–10: *Paelignae dicar gloriae gentis ego,/quam sua libertas ad honesta coegerat arma,/cum timuit socias anxia Roma manus.*

The diction of Livy at times suggests an adherence to the Vergilian model: see 1.23.1–2 (*haec nuntiant domum Albani. et bellum utrimque summa ope parabatur, civili simillimum bello, prope inter parentes natosque, Troianum utramque prolem, cum Lavinium ab Troia, ab Lavinio Alba, ab Albanorum stirpe regum oriundi Romani essent. eventus tamen belli minus miserabilem dimicationem fecit, quod nec acie certatum est et tectis modo dirutis alterius urbis duo populi in unum confusi sunt*) and esp. 1.40.2, where Livy's diction argues for the existence of an *Italica stirps: tum Anci filii duo etsi antea semper pro indignissimo habuerant se patrio regno tutoris fraude pulsos, regnare Romae advenam non modo vicinae sed ne Italicae quidem stirpis, tum impensius iis indignitas crescere si ne ab Tarquinio quidem ad se rediret regnum, sed praeceps inde porro ad servitia caderet. . . .* But cf. Feldherr (1997), who develops a rather different portrait of 'the Ciceronian model of patriotism'.

[77] Velleius Paterculus 2.2.2: *P. Mucio Scaevola L. Calpurnio consulibus abhinc annos centum sexaginta duos descivit a bonis, pollicitusque toti Italiae civitatem, simul etiam promulgatis agrariis legibus, omnibus statim concupiscentibus, summa imis miscuit et in praeruptum atque anceps periculum adduxit rem publicam.* See also 2.15.1: *mors Drusi iam pridem tumescens bellum excitavit Italicum; quippe L. Caesare et P. Rutilio consulibus, abhinc annos CXX, universa Italia cum id malum ab Asculanis ortum esset (quippe Servilium praetorem Fonteiumque legatum occiderant) ac deinde a Marsis exceptum in omnes penetrasset regiones, arma adversus Romanos cepit.* Cf. Pliny *Nat.* 3.39–40, describing *Italia: nec ignoro ingrati ac segnis animi existimari posse merito si obiter atque in transcursu ad hunc modum dicatur* **terra omnium terrarum alumna eadem et parens,** *numine deum electa quae caelum ipsum clarius faceret, sparsa congregaret imperia ritusque molliret et tot populorum discordes ferasque linguas sermonis commercio contraheret ad colloquia et humanitatem homini daret, breviterque una cunctarum gentium in toto orbe* **patria** *fieret.* Contrast the practice of Propertius in 3.22, where all of Italy is named *Romana terra* (3.22.17).

[78] Macrobius *Sat.* 3.9. For an earlier, aggrandizing statement about Rome's relations with Italian gods, see Tacitus *Ann.* 3.71.1: *incessit dein religio, quonam in templo locandum foret donum, quod pro valetudine Augustae equites Romani voverant equestri Fortunae: nam etsi delubra eius deae multa in urbe, nullum tamen tali cognomento erat. repertum est aedem esse apud Antium, quae sic nuncuparetur, cunctasque caerimonias Italicis in oppidis templaque et numinum effigies iuris atque imperii Romani esse. ita donum apud Antium statuitur.* Romans developed rather late quite sophisticated theological justifications for their empire, a topic that deserves careful study.

Augustus to the end of the empire, knew that 'Rome' was not the real name of the city founded by Romulus. Its real name, he insisted, was its Latin name, though what he intended by that we cannot recover. But this investigation brought him to the topic of tutelary deities and the prayers for *evocatio* and *devotio*: the former summons forth the gods of a city so that they will cease to protect it; the latter does the same and condemns the population to complete annihilation. Macrobius compiled a list of the cities which Rome had devoted to destruction. But he and the men of his age all must have recognized the possibility that Rome could have summoned the gods of all her opponents to her side. Although, sadly, neither Servius nor Macrobius commented directly on *Aeneid* 8.715, 'Augustus fulfilled an immortal vow to the Italian gods', perhaps for them the line required no explication. The gods of Italy were now Roman gods, resident at Rome, serving beneath a Roman commander against their foreign foes.[79]

[79] My thanks to audiences at Durham, Florida International University, the University of Illinois, and the University of Southern California, as well as to Ruth Abbey, Karen Dang, Sabine MacCormack, and Pete O'Neill.

CHAPTER EIGHT

ROMAN ARCHAEOLOGY IN VERGIL'S ARCADIA
(VERGIL *ECLOGUE* 4; *AENEID* 8; LIVY 1.7)

Marko Marinčič

Arcadia was 'discovered', according to Bruno Snell, in 42 or 41 B.C. by Vergil who transformed the Polybian land of singing shepherds into a spiritual landscape.[1] The idea of subsuming the manifold aspects of Vergil's originality under a Greek toponym is largely motivated by the fact that Arcadia did not play any particular role in Greek bucolic poetry. But since there are no indications whatsoever that Vergil idealized Arcadia in the manner of the Renaissance poets, Richard Jenkyns is probably correct in arguing for a much later date and for Sannazaro as the inventor.[2]

This, however, scarcely accounts for the motive of Vergil's introducing Arcadia into his pastoral poetry. Apart from the highly speculative attempts to provide the bucolic Arcadia of Thyrsis and Corydon with a Greek background,[3] there remain two possible solutions that, in my view, deserve serious consideration. Vergil obviously had a fondness for Arcadia as the homeland of Pan,[4] additionally, his choice might have been suggested by the legend of the Arcadian settlers on the site of the future Rome,[5] especially since this legend explained

---

[1] Snell (1953).

[2] Jenkyns (1989).

[3] According to the hypothesis put forward by Wilamowitz (1906) 111 n. 1, there was a mention of Arcadia as the cradle of bucolic poetry in the integral version of Theon's *Prolegomena* to Theocritus; see also Bickel (1951) 308. The vigorous scholarly controversy surrounding the relationship between Vergil *Ecl.* 7.4 (*Arcades ambo*) and the epigram of Erucius, *Anth. Pal.* 6.96.2, has led to no compelling conclusion; see Jachmann (1952) 171–2. For the view that Arcadia played a major role in post-Theocritean Greek bucolic poetry see McLennan (1976), who adduces further examples from Hellenistic epigrammatic poetry.

[4] See E. A. Schmidt (1972) 172–85.

[5] See Christ, Schmidt, Stählin (1920) 183 n. 9, Dahlmann (1948) 348–53, Bickel (1951) 308–14. For the prehistory of the 'Roman Arcadianism' see Bayet (1920).

the cult of the Lupercal as an importation of the Arcadian cult of Pan Lykaios.[6]

The first occurrence of Arcadia is in the Fourth *Eclogue*, the only poem in the collection of overtly political character, together with *Saturnia regna*. In what follows, I will suggest that the mention of Arcadia, instead of transporting the reader into a fanciful spiritual landscape, actually implies an identification of the poet's hope with the pseudo-historical ideal of a Roman 'historical myth' well known to the Roman audience.

The Fourth *Eclogue* engages in a profound intertextual dialogue about programmatic issues, Roman history and contemporary politics, and we are very fortunate to possess some if its main literary models. It has long been recognized that the *puer* of the Eclogue most closely recalls the Hercules of Theocritus *Idylls* 24 (*Heracliscus*) and 17 (*Encomium to Ptolemy*).[7] More particularly, the cosmic process coinciding with the evolution of the *puer* is designed so as to mirror single stages of the life of Hercules. The final phase of this process is the phase of *pacatus orbis*, corresponding to the final achievement of Hercules as *soter* and *pacator mundi*.[8] The second phase, the phase of the *iuuenis* with Argo and Achilles, corresponds to the heroic phase of Hercules (Hercules actually took part in the Argonautic expedition).

An account of Hercules' early career would normally begin with the episode which forms the main action of Theocritus' bucolic *Heracliscus*: the *wunderkind* reveals his true nature by strangling Juno's twin snakes in his cradle; so it should not come as a surprise that in the *Eclogue* the extinction of the snake, *occidet serpens* (24), is expected to take place during the period immediately following the child's birth.

In Theocritus' *Heracliscus*, the strangling of the snakes is commented upon by a prophecy of Tiresias, a prophecy including a paradisiacal picture of *Tierfrieden*:

> γαμβρὸς δ᾽ ἀθανάτων κεκλήσεται, οἳ τάδ᾽ ἐπῶρσαν
> κνώδαλα φωλεύοντα βρέφος διαδηλήσασθαι.
> ἔσται δὴ τοῦτ᾽ ἆμαρ ὁπηνίκα νεβρὸν ἐν εὐνᾷ
> καρχαρόδων σίνεσθαι ἰδὼν λύκος οὐκ ἐθελήσει.
> (24.84–7)

---

[6] At the same time, it associated the Palatine with Pallantium (Varro *L.* 5.53; Dionysius of Halicarnassus *A.R.* 1.31.4); cf. Ogilvie (1970) 52.
[7] See Kukula (1911) 64–74, Bollack (1967) 313–7, V. Schmidt (1972) 80–2, Clausen (1994) 123–4.
[8] See Kukula (1911) 64–5.

Even if lines 86–7 are interpolated,[9] Vergil definitely could read them in his text of Theocritus.[10] He certainly had Theocritus in mind when designing his 'messianic' prophecy (*nec metuent armenta leones . . . occidet serpens*).[11] (Which does not, of course, preclude the influence of either a Sibylline prophecy, or an Oriental prophetic text, or both.)[12] Consistent with his strategy of transforming a mythic hero into an abstract eschatological pattern (the bucolic mode being the main vehicle of transformation), he replaced the first deed of Hercules by the abstract ('Oriental'?) motif of the death of the snake which encapsulates the allegorical essence of the victories of Hercules as ἀλεξίκακος, warder-off of evil.

Although Theocritus is probably not referring to the myth of the Golden Age,[13] the prophecy of Tiresias with its bucolic transcendence seemed very appropriate to be used as a model for a poem in which a child prodigy initiates a new 'bucolic' golden age. The references to the Myth of the Ages are usually viewed in the context of Vergil's polemic against Catullus 64.[14] Catullus' nostalgia for a heroic age suggestive of both golden and iron ages has been described in terms of irony;[15] at any rate, the prophetic song of the Fates celebrating the bloody deeds of Achilles is hardly nostalgic. Vergil seems to reply to Catullus' heroic age and to the 'Sallustian' pessimism of his epilogue by a proto-Augustan prophecy of a genuine golden age, which is introduced by the birth of a child much different from the Catullan Achilles, a child who will bring peace to the whole world. Although the *puer* too has to go through a new heroic age with a new Argo and a new Achilles, this time the heroic age is only a transitional period, and there is no ambiguity about Achilles: he is an unequivocally negative character, perhaps even an opponent of the *puer*.

---

[9] Gow (1952) *ad loc.*

[10] See V. Schmidt (1972) 65.

[11] Kukula (1911) 64, n. 2, Bollack (1967) 313, E. A. Schmidt (1972) 168–9, V. Schmidt (1972) 64–5. The lion who substitutes the Theocritean wolf perhaps hints at the upmost deed of Hercules, his victory over the Nemean lion.

[12] Cf. *Orac. Sib.* 3.791–5, Isaiah 11:8–9.

[13] See Gatz (1967) 171.

[14] Cf. Anderson (1928) 47–8, Putnam (1970) 136–65, Winsor Leach (1971) 172–5, V. Schmidt (1972) 39–54, G. Williams (1974) 45, Du Quesnay (1977) 68–75, E. A. Schmidt (1985) 84–5, van Sickle (1992) 37–64, Arnold (1994) 149–51.

[15] Cf. Putnam (1961), Kinsey (1965), Curran (1969), Bramble (1970), Konstan (1977).

Hence, the mythic identity of the child as Hercules can be considered as an aspect of the anti-Catullan polemic.[16] Catullus repeatedly alludes to the tragic circumstances of Thetis' marriage with a mortal,[17] and he does not omit to mention the death of his hero.[18] The *puer*, on the contrary, is a *Iouis incrementum*, he will rule the pacified earth in harmony with his father, attain immortality and marry a goddess.[19] Even if Catullus' epilogue is a piece of topical moralizing rather than an indictment of Rome's corruption,[20] Vergil replies to it as if Catullus were speaking of his own time. The three phases of the life of the *puer* are blended with an inverted account of the Catullan Myth of the Ages so as to produce an impression of the *ferrea gens* gradually giving way to the *aurea gens* as the *puer* grows up (*quo ferrea . . . desinet ac toto surget gens aurea mundo*, 8–9).

As an unidentified, abstract hypostasis of the exemplary Hercules, the *puer* is virtually identical with the cosmic process he provokes. In the Aeneid, I shall argue, the same model is applied to the whole Roman history: the actors are dissociated from the process and the exemplary Hercules is incarnated in three 'historical' heroes.

1. The first phase, the phase of Hercules who wins over the snake-like monster Cacus in Roman Arcadia, corresponds to the phase of the *puer* when the serpent died out. This is a victory at the same time representing the eschatological ἀρχή of Roman history and typifying the future victories of Aeneas and Augustus.[21]

2. The heroic phase of the *iuvenis* is remythologized in terms of a 'historical myth' of Aeneas. At *Aeneid* 6.83–97, the Sibyl prophesies a new Trojan war and a new Achilles; the *alius Achilles* is commonly identified with Turnus. Aeneas, who as a representative of the 'historical' Heroic Age actually faced Achilles, has to confront a new, Latin Achilles.

The opening lines of the *Eclogue, paulo maiora canamus . . . magnus . . . nascitur ordo*, are echoed by *Aeneid* 7.44–5: *maior rerum mihi nascitur ordo, / maius opus moveo*. This refers to the Iliadic part of the poem vis-

---

[16] Du Quesnay (1977) 72–3 makes a similar point in connection with Theocritus 17.

[17] Cf. Catullus 64.26–7, 295, 301, 322.

[18] Catullus 64.362.

[19] For a fuller argument see my forthcoming article "Der Weltaltermythos in Catulls Peleus-Epos (c. 64), der Kleine Herakles (Theokr. Id. 24) und der römische 'Messianismus' Vergils" Hermes 129 (2001).

[20] Konstan (1993) 76, modifying his own earlier view.

[21] For the 'typological' model of history in the Aeneid see Binder (1971), Gransden (1976) 14–20, Glei (1991) 26–8 and *passim*.

à-vis Aeneas' Odyssey, but also to the myths of the *Eclogue* being made 'historical': the genealogy of Latinus establishes the Age of Saturnus as a 'historical' epoch. Aeneas' arrival in Latium is set in a scenery of 'Saturnian' bucolic peace, and the Latin wars are fore-shadowed by 'the war of the herdsmen'. On a purely formal level, this can be regarded as an Alexandrian pastoral reduction;[22] how-ever, Wimmel failed to notice that Vergil reproduces the pattern of the Eclogue according to which the advent of a new Golden Age is disrupted by *altera bella*, a new Trojan war: the Paradise motif is materialized in terms of a Promised Land and the Latin war is a material replay of the Trojan war. The main action of the *Aeneid* is based on a Herculean matrix:[23] 'Herculean' labours (*labores*, 1.10) are imposed upon Aeneas by Juno, his opponent Turnus bears a strong resemblance to Cacus,[24] and Allecto is a hellish monster with snakes in her hair; as is well known, Allecto and Juno are closely modelled on Lyssa and Hera-Tyche of Euripides' Hercules.

3. Aeneas' 'Herculean' catabasis[25] functions as a frame for a cos-mic revelation of Roman future culminating in Anchises' prophecy of Augustus as a new Hercules (6.791–805: *hic vir* . . .). The phase of the *puer* as *vir* is identified as the age of Augustus. The new Saturnian era is prophesied by Anchises in terms of *aurea saecula* (6.792–4) and by Jupiter in terms of a victory over *furor impius* (1.294–6), corre-sponding to Augustus' victory over the monsters of Actium (8.698–703; cf. Cleopatra with her snakes, 696–7). Through Apollo's contribution to that victory (8.70), Apollo's own expected reign (cf. *Eclogue* 4.10: *tuus iam regnat Apollo*) becomes a historical reality. Roman history is thus seen as an organic process. The 'real time' of the *Eclogue* is only the last in a series of cycles of peace, new war and restored peace.

As for *hic vir*, it made G. Binder[26] believe that the Eclogue was an *augurium post eventum* about Octavian: the *puer* is meant to represent Augustus. But it is Hercules, not Augustus, who provides the link. As M. Labate convincingly argued, Jupiter's prophecy is, in part at least, an adaptation of the prophecy Tiresias delivers in Theocritus'

---

[22] See Wimmel (1973).

[23] Galinsky (1972a) 131–49.

[24] Buchheit (1963) 126–30, Galinsky (1966) 42–50.

[25] See Galinsky (1972a) 134–6 on Hercules as a model for Aeneas, and Lloyd-Jones (1967) for a catabasis of Hercules as a possible model for Book 6.

[26] Binder (1983), see also Glei (1991) 56.

Heracliscus.[27] Following his suggestion, one could reflect on a meta-literary aspect of the recurring Hercules theme.

In the *Eclogue* Vergil promised an 'Arcadian' panegyric to a little Roman Heracliscus who as a grown-up Hercules will pacify the whole world (*pacatum reget orbem*):

> o mihi tum longae maneat pars ultima vitae,
> spiritus et quantum sat erit tua dicere facta!
> . . .
> Pan etiam, Arcadia mecum si iudice certet,
> Pan etiam Arcadia dicat se iudice victum.
> (*Eclogue* 4.53–4, 58–9)

> Ah, if the last days of my life could only be prolonged, and breath enough remain, for me to chronicle your acts
> . . .
> If Pan himself, with Arcady for judge, were to contend with me, the great god Pan, with Arcady for judge, would own defeat.
> (Trans. E. V. Rieu)

The *Aeneid* fulfils this promise on the levels of both mythic paradigm and contemporary history; in other words, the promise is fulfilled by both 1. and 3 (see above). On the level of the Hercules paradigm, it is a material fulfilment, the victorious Hercules being incarnated in flesh and the hymn being sung by official representatives of the Roman cult: the account of the Roman victory of Hercules is followed by a hymn of the Salii. Since we are now looking from the perspective of the grown-up Hercules, the hymn of the Salii lists Juno's snakes retrospectively as his *first* exploit:

> . . . qui carmine laudes
> Herculeas et facta ferunt: ut prima novercae
> monstra manu geminosque premens eliserit anguis . . .
> (*Aeneid* 8.287–9)

> . . . hymning the praise of Hercules and his great deeds: how he seized the two snakes, the first monsters sent against him by his stepmother, and throttled them, one in each hand . . .
> (Trans. D. West)

---

[27] Labate (1987).

The final invocation, *salve, vera Iovis proles, decus addite divis* (301), is evidently meant to recall the *Eclogue: cara deum suboles, magnum Iovis incrementum* (49; cf. *teque adeo decus hoc aevi, te consule, inibit*, 11).

At least from the perspective of the *Aeneid*, the Hercules-Cacus episode looks like an emblematic fulfilment of the promise made in the *Eclogue*. *Arcadia iudex* turns out to be the audience of Hercules' victory over Cacus, a victory at the same time emblematic of Vergil's Herculean poetic labour. Along with the 'historical typology', Vergil constructs his own 'poetic history', a literary continuity with his earlier work. It may be noted that the *puer* who is identified as *hic vir . . . Augustus Caesar* in the Aeneid, is referred to as *hunc . . . iuvenem* in the *Georgics* (1.500): the prophecy is fulfilled by the composition of a tripartite opus which is based on the same biological pattern as the *Eclogue*. Only in the *Aeneid* was the pattern of the 'Life of Hercules' applied to the whole of Roman history with Hercules in Roman Arcadia, Aeneas, and Augustus as its three milestones. On the other hand, the *Eclogue* is an eminently engagé text, it is about contemporary Roman politics, and it seems highly unlikely that Vergil could have mentioned Arcadia in such a poem without being aware of its 'historical' implications.

The story of Hercules, Evander and Cacus the brigand[28] definitely came into existence before the time of Livy and Vergil; it was known as early as in the second century B.C.[29] Although the existence of the Roman toil of Hercules in itself does not provide a satisfying argument, the prophecy of Carmenta as reported by Evander in Livy (*Iove nate, Hercules, salve . . . te mihi mater, veridica interpres deum, aucturum caelestium numerum cecinit*, 1.7.10) is reminiscent not only of the song of Salii but also of the *Eclogue* which is undoubtedly earlier, and it is readily arguable that Livy and Vergil had a common model in front of them. As for the *Eclogue*, Carmentis who prophesies the apotheosis of Hercules and Rome's future greatness would have presented an ideal Roman counterpart to Theocritus' Tiresias. If Small

---

[28] Cacus never is depicted as a monster in sources anterior to or contemporary with the *Aeneid*. For a detailed examination of the traditions concerning Hercules and Cacus see Münzer (1911); Bayet (1926); Small (1982).

[29] Gnaeus Gellius (fr. 9 Peter = Solinus 1.7–10). The version of *Origo gentis Romanae* 7.6–7 refers to a certain Cassius, probably Cassius Hemina, and gives Recaranus as the true name of the hero. The common assumption is that the name derives from Geryon, but see Burkert (1979) 86 on (T)recaranus ('three-horned') and the Italic three-horned Hercules.

is right in identifying the Etruscan seer Cacu as the legendary ancestor of Cacus,[30] the theme of prophecy was an important constituent
of the myth in its earliest form. In the original version the (Etruscan)
seer Cacu would have dwelled at the top of the *scalae Caci* on the
Palatine.[31] There is no sign that such a version included a visit by
Hercules, but in Cn. Gellius' account Cacus is the one who suffers
the violation of *ius hospitii*, and a Kakios receives Hercules on the
Palatine without any hostile intent in Diodorus Siculus 4.21.[32] Later,
when Cacu was transformed into a cattle thief and assumed a negative character as κακός, Evander, the Good-man, was introduced
into the story,[33] and the prophetic character of Cacu was transferred
to Evander's mother whose original function might have been to
direct the Arcadians to their future dwellings.[34] It is not possible to
establish when the cattle possessor and subjugator of Cacus was
identified as Hercules returning from Spain with the cattle of Geryon,[35]
and we do not know whether Cacus ever received Hercules as a seer.
But if there ever existed an identification of Cacus with the seer, the
persistence of the theme of prophecy even after Cacus had become
a villain is due to the fact that there was a relevant subject for the
prophecy. If, on the other hand, Cacus never was associated with
the Etruscan seer, there is an obvious reason why the originator of
Livy's version adopted the traditional pattern of a prophecy following a heroic deed of Hercules:[36] a major motivation for inventing a
Roman toil of Hercules was evidently to endow an important Roman
cult with an aura of heroic past. In such a context, it was most natural for the prophecy of Hercules' deification to produce an appendix on Rome's future greatness.

---

[30] Small (1982).

[31] Romulus and Faunus also were associated with the Palatine in a divinatory
context; cf. Small (1982) 16–22.

[32] He still appears as a host (though a treacherous one) in Propertius (4.9.7).

[33] The choice of Evander is attributable to the etymology of his name and to
his association with the Palatine. In addition, Arcadia perhaps suggested the analogy with the story of the Infant Hermes who stole Apollo's cattle on the evening
of his birth *in Arcadia* (*h. Merc.* 18); for the points of contact between the two myths
see Small (1982) 10–12. According to one version, Evander was the son of Hermes
and a nymph (Dionysius of Halicaranassus *A.R.* 1.31.1).

[34] Dionysius of Halicaranassus *A.R.* 1.31, Vergil *Aen.* 8.335–6.

[35] According to Small (1982) 24–9, Hercules with his cattle took over a local
story based on the motif of cattle-stealing; see Fontenrose (1959) 334–46 for a extensive list of local brigands Hercules encountered on his way.

[36] Cf. Pindar *N.* 1.36–52; Theocritus 24.

In *Aeneid* 8 the prophetic Hercules hymn is attributed to the Salii, but this is an obvious anachronism: Vergil wanted to give them a role because Augustus was invoked in the Salian song.[37] The prophecy originally belonged to Evander's mother[38] who was identified by the Romans with Carmentis/Carmenta,[39] a goddess of child-birth[40] and of prophecy.[41] There is even an obscure version going back to Eratosthenes according to which Evander was the son of the Italic Sibyl,[42] and Livy introduces Carmenta as a proto-Sibyl.[43]

In both roles, the Roman prophetess of Hercules would suit the character of the *Eclogue* as a Sibylline prophecy of the birth of a Roman Hercules. A 'Roman' Hercules prophecy could provide both a model for romanizing the prophecy of Tiresias and an intertextual vehicle of polemic against Catullus. From the alienation of the present, Catullus emigrates to a mythic heroic age, only to find himself disillusioned by Achilles. Vergil replies by alluding to a Roman 'historical myth', which, through his prophetic hope, becomes realizable again as a historical epoch. When Vergil prophesies a panegyric winning the national literary award of Arcadia, Arcadia clearly stands for Rome, the Rome he is hoping for. Like the *images* of the Temple in *Georgics* 3,[44] the *song* of the Sibyl and the Fates is an emblematic promise of a future poem. The essential character of that poem is anticipated by the intertextual presence of the prophecies of Tiresias and Carmentis, and the promise is fulfilled by one or both of these prophetic models being used as models for three pivotal emblematic passages of the *Aeneid*, the prophecy of Jupiter, the prophecy of Anchises, and the hymn of the Salii.

---

[37] Cf. Macrobius 3.12.1: *Salios Herculi dedit, quos tantum Marti dicavit antiquitas.* See Bellen (1963) 29.

[38] Vergil himself credits Carmentis with a prophecy of Rome's future: *futuros/ Aeneadas magnos et nobile Pallanteum* (340–1).

[39] She was (originally?) called Nikostrate (Coelius Antipater ap. Strabo 5.230, Pausanias 8.43.2; cf. Servius on *Aen.* 8.51,336), or Themis (Plutarch *Quaest. Rom.* 56). Cf. Dionysius of Halicaranassus *A.R.* 1.31.1.

[40] Varro *Antiquitates rerum divinarum* frr. 103–4 Cardauns, Ovid *Fast.* 1.617–36.

[41] Servius on *Aen.* 8.51, Dionysius of Halicaranassus *A.R.* 1.3.1; she combines both functions in *Fasti Praenest.* and in Augustin *C.D.* 4.11 (Varro?) who refers to multiple *Carmentae* functionally identical with the Parcae (*fata nascentibus canunt*).

[42] *Sch. in Plato Phdr.* 244b.

[43] 1.7.8–9: *quam fatiloquam ante Sibyllae in Italiam adventum miratae eae gentes fuerant.*

[44] Not surprisingly, the Hercules theme (Hylas, Molorchus) plays a central role in the programmatic proem to Book 3.

From there it takes little effort to link the *puer* to Augustus. But is it necessary to assume that the child is Augustus in a pastoral disguise only because the land of Pan suggests Evander's 'Roman Arcadia'? It is a well-known feature of the highly unified Vergilian oeuvre that many ideological issues and key motifs of the *Aeneid* may be anticipated in the *Eclogues* as if the whole design of the *Aeneid* had been present in the mind of the bucolic poet. This continuity is mainly achieved retrospectively; but the case of the *Eclogue* is different: it is actually a prophecy. The continuity of theme is reinforced by an explicit promise of a poem Vergil actually fulfilled. Even so, the promise is prudently vague and it could have been fulfilled in many ways, even without Saturnus as an earthly king in Latium, Aeneas, or Augustus. The 'historical' Saturnus was probably invented by the author of the *Aeneid*,[45] and the identification of Aeneas[46] and Augustus as two historical incarnations of the *puer* was achieved *post factum*, through the prophecy of the Sibyl at the beginning of Book 6 and by the prophetic speech of Anchises at the end of the same book. The fact that the deified saviour of the herdsmen in *Eclogue* 1 is commonly identified as Octavian is a strong case in favour of Binder's suggestion,[47] but Pollio as the addressee is an even stronger case

---

[45] As argued by Wifstrand Schiebe (1997). However, since the poet expresses his hope for a historical, Roman 'golden' epoch, it seems reasonable to assume that the advent of Saturnus implies a bit more than the return of the Hesiodic Golden Race; it suggests at least the myth of Kronos in the West, if not Italy as Saturnia. The 'return' of Kronos to Rome thus entails at least an embryonic historicization of Saturnus.

[46] Merkelbach (1961) 85 identified the *Cumaeum Carmen* with the prophecy the Sibyl delivered to Aeneas, as in the *Aeneid*, Tibullus 2.5 and in their presumable common source (for a possible common source see Norden (1927) on *Aen.* 6.83–97). The intertextual presence of Aeneas in the poem cannot be ascertained, all of the relevant poetic texts (e.g., the encounter with the Sibyl in Naevius' *Bellum Punicum*) being lost or fragmentary. Lycophron's *Alexandra*, also an important model for Catullus 64, might have occurred to Vergil while prophesying a new Trojan war: not only does Aeneas have an important role in that poem, there is even a mention of the Sibyl of Cumae (1279). Even before Vergil, in the context of Aeneas' flight to Italy, the Cumaea could have been identified with the Trojan Sibyl who prophesies to Aeneas in Dionysius of Halicaranassus *A.R.* 1.55.4 and possibly in Tibullus 2.5; there is a direct parallel with Evander whose prophetic mother was identified as Carmentis when she moved to Italy. Unfortunately, we do not know whether Livy, who mentions Carmenta as the most famous prophetess *ante Sibyllae adventum*, credited this Sibyl with an Aeneas prophecy.

[47] Cameron (1995) 53ff. interpreted the *Heracliscus* as a covert panegyric for Ptolemy; but contrast the more cautious remarks by Huttner (1997) 138–40 and 284.

against, and the Dionysian attributes of the *puer* are suggestive of
Mark Antony rather than Octavian.[48] On the other hand, the very
fact that Augustus never promoted his connection with Hercules[49]
seems to imply that Horace and Vergil used Hercules as a trans-
political poetic paradigm; in spite of Mark Antony they felt feel to
use it for their own 'Augustan' purposes. Mark Antony could claim
to be a descendant of Hercules, but does this mean that Theocritus
and the whole tradition of Hellenistic ruler-panegyric suggested Mark
Antony to the Roman audience?

The Herculean *puer* is no more Mark Antony than Octavian, he
is as an exemplary hero generating a teleological model of history
and a metapoetic matrix of Vergil's poetic biography. Since the phase
of the grown-up Hercules is at the same time the phase of a future
Roman victory and of Vergil's Roman panegyric, the *Eclogue* may
be read as promising a poem using the exploits of the grown-up
Hercules as an exemplary model for a future Roman victory, and,
possibly but not necessarily, for a future Roman hero. Vergil does
not specify the exemplary exploit of Hercules, but the presence of
a Roman Hercules in Arcadia suggests to the reader the only 'Roman'
victory of Hercules as the most obvious choice.

Only a very naive reader will be ready to believe that the young
bucolic poet, who was not yet interested in grave historical subjects,
confined himself to the little Hercules and to the bucolic Arcadia,
the land of Pan and singing shepherds, because they were more suitable to his tender age (he was about 30 at the time of the *Fourth
Eclogue*). Vergil's adopting the bucolic mode is a conscious choice
(which can at the same time be natural, but not purely instinctive).
He actually says that he will grow up, sing of the 'grown-up Hercules',
and that the Arcadians will applaud. The young poet, the abstract
bucolic Hercules and the bucolic Arcadia are all waiting to find their
way into historical reality. Vergil does not know or say anything
about the future, but he does know what he hopes for and how he
would like to celebrate it: he will sing of the exploits of the Roman
Hercules as soon as he can see the pacificatory achievement of his
hero. Until then, the hero of his poem is at the same time a process
and a hero, he is a polysemous bucolic abstraction indiscriminately

---

[48] See especially Du Quesnay (1977) 58.
[49] Huttner (1997a).

including the Theocritus' Heracliscus, the Roman Hercules and, at
least as a potentiality, the yet unidentified new Roman Hercules. In
much the same way as Hercules, Rome is deliberately reduced to
Arcadia; both the Heracliscus and the Arcadian proto-Rome reflect
metaphorically the condition of the poet who is still unsure about
the outcome; at the same time, the 'subjective' landscape of Arcadia
forms the link between Hercules in Roman Arcadia and what Vergil
hopes would be a replay of that victory. Roman mythic history, then,
is projected into a bucolic Arcadia, which is not an irrelevant idyllic
dream (as opposed to historical reality), but an emblematic reduction
of Vergil's prophetic hope. Only as such Arcadia can be a place of
exaltation.

What has been said so far might lead one to the conclusion that
the Aeneid simply historicizes the *Eclogue* by actualizing the mythic
paradigm and the potentiality of a new golden age as 'Roman mythic
history' and 'Roman present'. If so, the result would be little more
than a 'civil' rendering of a typically Hellenistic pattern with a mythic
ancestor as a panegyrical model:[50] the dynastic hero becomes a proto-
founder of a city (firstly because Vergil does not want to write a *Herr-
scherpanegyrik*, secondly because Mark Antony was a direct descendant
of Hercules, but Octavian was not).

Vergil would not have been the first to use the Hercules myth as
a vehicle of 'civil panegyrism'. Livy motivates Romulus' decision to
accept Hercules' cult in its Greek form by the fact that even then
Romulus considered Hercules as his model (1.7.15). The adjective
augustus, applied to both Hercules (1.7.9–10: *formam augustiorem
humana . . . aucturum caelestium numerum*) and Romulus (1.8.3), links this
passage with the *praefatio* where the historical myths are being defended
as ennobling the origins of Rome (*miscendo humana divinis primordia
urbium augustiora faciat*) and providing exemplars for the present. If
Livy intends to call Augustus to mind,[51] *Aeneid* 1.257–96 would provide a close parallel to this passage, particularly since in Jupiter's

---

[50] Labate (1987) speaks of a conversion of 'poesia cortiggiana' into 'poesia civile'.
The conversion is even more radical in the *Eclogue* where the Life of Hercules is
transformed into an abstract historical/cosmic process, and Hercules is not (yet)
used as a panegyric model for any mythic or historical personage like Aeneas or
Augustus.
[51] Cf. Ogilvie (1970) on 7.9,10. Martin (1971, 1972) detects similar allusions to
Augustus behind Dionysus' Euhemeran version of the Hercules-Cacus story.

prophecy the conversion of the life of Hercules into a historical process establishes Romulus and Augustus as new Herculean heroes. But the prophecy also draws on Ennius' *Council of the Gods* in *Annales* 1 (frs. 51–5). Ennius was probably the first to use Hercules as a model for the deification of Romulus (frs. 110–11) and probably even of Scipio,[52] so Livy might have substituted Augustus without knowing anything of the Aeneid. Horace comes to a much similar result in his 'Ennian' (?) *Ode* 3.3 which opens with a promise of the deification of Augustus on the models of Pollux, Hercules, Bacchus, and Romulus. So it is very likely that it was Ennius who suggested the exemplary potential of Hercules to both Livy and Vergil, and since the prophecy of Jupiter in *Aeneid 1* is at the same time modelled on the *Heracliscus* and on Ennius' *Concilium Deorum*, we may assume that Ennius gave Vergil a decisive stimulus for the transformation of the *Heracliscus* into a Roman 'civil panegyric'.

In deifying Romulus on the pattern of Hercules, Ennius certainly drew on the tradition of ruler-panegyric;[53] yet Cicero, the source of the Romulus fragment, remarks that the divinity of Romulus had its roots in popular belief, and adduces Hercules as a parallel case;[54] so Ennius most probably elaborated a pre-existent popular analogy with Hercules.[55] Besides, Ennius applied the pattern of persecution by Juno and her eventual reconciliation to a period of Roman history,[56] and it can be inferred from Horace *Odes* 3.3 that he established at least an indirect analogy with the life of Hercules.[57] Ennius' audience certainly was able to appreciate the mythic parallel; it was probably recognized already by the audience of the religious spectacle of

---

[52] See Anderson (1928) 29–37.

[53] See Feeney (1984), (1991) 122–3.

[54] *Tusc.* 1.12.28: *ex hoc et nostrorum opinione 'Romulus in caelo cum diis agit aevum', ut famae adsentiens dixit Ennius, et apud Graecos indeque perlapsus ad nos et usque ad Oceanum Hercules tantus et tam praesens habetur deus.*

[55] See Anderson (1928) 30, Galinsky (1972a) 140.

[56] Servius on *Aen.* 1.281: *bello Punico secundo ut ait Ennius placata Iuno coepit favere Romanis.*

[57] The fact that Juno was reconciled with the Romans only during the Second Punic war militates against the assumption that Horace modelled his speech of Juno on Ennius' *Concilium*; cf. Buchheit (1963) 146. In spite of that, Feeney (1984); (1991) 125–127, recently argued for Ennius as a model. The fact that Romulus was deified on the model of Hercules makes it very improbable that Juno obstinately opposed his apotheosis; if, on the other hand, she did not take part in the *concilium* at all, her reconciliation with the Romans was at least *foreshadowed* by the apotheosis of Romulus on the model of Hercules.

207 B.C. when a literary hymn to Juno composed by a Greek poet
was used for the first time in the context of Roman state cult.

It is far from certain that Ennius ever mentioned or even knew
a 'Roman' Hercules episode, and it is impossible to determine to
what extent the Roman cult of Hercules was relevant to his using
Hercules as an exemplary hero, but the association existed before
Vergil: it enabled Livy to link the exemplary Hercules with Romulus
as a religious reformer and it suggested to Vergil the idea of using
the hero as an allegorical pattern of Roman history. In his *praefatio*,
Livy seems to allude particularly to the story of Hercules and Cacus
when opposing the *incorrupta rerum gestarum memoria* to the *poeticae fabulae* of the period *ante urbem conditam*.[58] But even there he evades the
fallacy of defending or questioning the historicity of such legendary
stories (*nec adfirmare nec refellere*); instead, he attributes to them an
exemplary value which can be even enhanced by their fabulous character. By attaching the Hercules-Cacus myth to the Romulus section ('because Romulus regarded Hercules as his model'), he avoids
representing it directly as a part of the early Roman history, while
at the same time he emphasises its exemplary potential not as an
abstract paradigm but as a true epic narrative. Nevertheless, it was
Vergil who actually transcended Livy's dilemma between poetic fable
and history, and he did it in a very particular way. Already in the
Eclogue, he established a subjective link between the allegorized mythical model and historical reality. In the *Aeneid*, Hercules is not straight-
forwardly re-mythologized or historicized to furnish the mythical
aition for the cult of Hercules at the Ara Maxima and the date of
the first Roman victory. The link between mythical model and historical reality remains exemplary rather than causal; the subjective
link mentioned above is replaced by an eschatological continuum
based on the allegorical Hercules as a pattern of time and on the
permanence of the cult; the Roman history can be seen as a series
of Herculean victories because the cult of Hercules perpetuates the
memory of Hercules' Roman victory. The idea was probably suggested by the prophecy of Rome's future greatness which accompanied the institution of this cult. With Carmentis in mind, Vergil
transforms the *poesia cortiggiana* of Theocritus into *poesia civile*, while

---

[58] Cf. Wiseman ch. 17 below.

at the same time he upgrades the 'bucolic eschatology' of the *Heracliscus* into an eschatological model of historical typology.

The typological model of history with Aeneas and Augustus as new Herculean heroes is essentially constructed by the respective prophecies of the Cumaean Sibyl and Anchises in Book 6. The Cumaea usurps the roles of the Homeric Tiresias (!), the various Sibyls of the Greek Aeneas myth and the Cimmerian Sibyl of Naevius' *Bellum Poenicum* (17–18 Morel),[59] but she may also be modelled on Carmentis, the Roman proto-Sibyl, who celebrated Hercules' victory over Cacus by prophesying his deification and Rome's future greatness. The very personage of the Sibyl who accompanies the new Hercules to the nether regions calls the *Eclogue* to mind. It is impossible to identify a distinctive 'Sibylline' eschatology as a common ideological basis for the *Eclogue* and for *Aeneid* 6, but it is certainly no accident that the revelation of Book 6 is contained within a Herculean catabasis, and the key passage 791–807 transcends the conventional use of Hercules as a panegyrical model[60] insofar as it reenacts the 'allegorical' Hercules of the *Eclogue*, Hercules as an eschatological pattern of Roman history. At the final point of the revelation, the future *'aurea/Saturnia saecula Augusti'* are described as a timeless *imperium Romanum* of cosmic dimensions (*iacet extra sidera tellus,/extra anni solisque vias, ubi caelifer Atlas/axem umero torquet stellis ardentibus aptum*, 6.795–7). A few lines later, the future *imperium* of Augustus is likened to Hercules' pacificatory achievement. While the obvious point of comparison lies in the over-natural extent of both 'empires', Vergil only lists one toil suitable for this purpose, with a curious tendency to confine Hercules to Peloponnesus, and, most notably, to Arcadia:

> nec vero Alcides tantum telluris obivit,
> fixerit aeripedem cervam licet, aut Erymanthi
> pacarit nemora et Lernam tremefecerit arcu
> (*Aeneid* 6.801–3)

> Hercules himself did not make his way to so many lands though his arrow pierced the hind with hooves of bronze, though he gave peace to the woods of Erymanthus and made Lerna tremble at his bow.
>
> (Trans. D. West)

---

[59] See Waszink (1948).
[60] See Norden (1899).

Although there is no direct reference to Evander's Roman Arcadia, the victory over Cacus is conspicuous by its absence.[61] At the heart of the eschatological model of Roman history lies Hercules the *soter* as an allegorical pattern of time; accordingly, Arcadia is the eschatological locale of the first, or rather archetypal Roman victory. This is the implicit (and the only possible) *tertium comparationis* between the pacifier of Arcadia and the ruler of the 'cosmic' *imperium Romanum*,[62] and even if Cacus and Evander are not explicitly mentioned, the definitive eschatologization of the Roman Hercules prophecy in Book 6 coincides with the transformation of Cacus into a snake-like infernal monster in Book 8.[63]

Therefore it would be a grave misunderstanding on Livy's part to refer to the exemplary and literary potential of the myth as an alternative to the quasi-historicity of the Vergilian Hercules. Vergil evades the alternative not only by raising gods and mythic heroes to a higher, trans-historical exemplary reality,[64] but also, most importantly, by making them fully operative within an eschatological concept of Roman history.

The development of the Vergilian Hercules from an abstract paradigm to the eschatological initiator of Roman history runs parallel to another similarly complex development taking place on the level of genre. Here, the dichotomy between Alexandrian and non-Alexandrian

---

[61] See Galinsky (1972a) 136; cf. (1972) 110: "Hercules pacifies (*pacarit*) Arcadia, an achievement for which Vergil had praised Octavian in the First *Eclogue* and which Hercules will repeat in his conquest of Cacus in the bucolic setting of proto-Rome, which is ruled by Evander, king of the Arcadians".

[62] Correspondingly, the new *Saturnia saecula*, while partially referring to the historical Saturnus of the *Aeneid*, may imply a recourse to the 'mythical' Saturnus of the *Eclogue*, to Kronos-Saturnus as the king of the Universe; cf. Dionysius of Halicaranassus *A.R.* 1.38 on the eponymous god of Italy-Saturnia as 'the giver and accomplisher of all happiness' and as 'embracing the whole universe'.

[63] Paratore (1971) clearly was wrong in believing that Livy knew *Aeneid* 8 at the time of the first pentad, and that he deliberately reduced Cacus to a mortal. Since there is no trace of the monster before the *Aeneid*, Vergil was almost certainly the first to transform the treacherous herdsman into a fire-breathing beast. Dionysius euhemerizes a version with Cacus as a robber without knowing anything of Cacus the monster, and the analogy between Cacus and Turnus can, in part at least, be attributed to the fact that as Vergil was the first to humanize Turnus, originally a chthonic deity closely connected with fire, while on the other hand he deified Cacus who, as a brother of Caca, the proto-Vesta, could easily become a son of Vulcanus; cf. Galinsky (1966) 36–7, Small (1982) 32–4.

[64] On the narrative status of the Vergilian gods see the illuminating observations by Feeney (1991) 129–87.

proves to be deficient in both its heads. If the mention of Arcadia in the Fourth *Eclogue* was rightly identified as an allusion to Evander's Roman Arcadia, the Cacus story initially suggested itself to the author of the Roman *Heracliscus* because of its essentially 'pastoral' character.[65] The inherent 'Alexandrianism' of the story, however, never came to be realized. Even in the Eclogue, the 'pastoral' Arcadia suggests a *potential* full-scale Roman toil of Hercules: in the context of a promise of a panegyric poem, both the bucolic Heracliscus and the 'pastoral' Roman toil of Hercules are *potentially* epicized. In the proem to *Georgics* 3, Vergil rejects the Alexandrian Hercules represented by the personages of Hylas[66] and Molorchus,[67] but even if the reference is to an 'anti-Callimachean' panegyric poem as a possible alternative, the actual result is far more complex. In *Aeneid* 8, Vergil uses Alexandrian formal patterns in transcending Alexandrianism. The Evander episode is remarkably Alexandrian in form. The *humilitas* of Evander's Pallanteum is emphasized by the narrative being modelled on the Eumaeus episode in *Odyssey* 14 and on the Molorchus episode of Callimachus' *Victoria Berenices*.[68] As in Callimachus, a heroic aition is contained within a realistic framework; but in Callimachus the struggle with the lion was hardly narrated at length, and it was probably mirrored in the aition of the mousetrap.[69] In Vergil, both the extensiveness of the heroic narration and the demonic character of the antagonist militate against Alexandrian aesthetic principles.[70] Vergil narrates a grand myth whose only reductional quality is that of being an eschatological beginning.

Likewise, the 'humbleness' of Evander's Arcadia is a case of Alexandrian realism being exalted into Stoic virtue. Aeneas' entering the modest dwellings of Evander is described in terms of humility: *aude, hospes, contemnere opes et te quoque dignum/finge deo, rebusque veni non asper egenis* (8.364–5). From the primitive hut of Evander, Aeneas emerges as a θεῖος ἀνήρ, the type of the Stoic Hero,[71] to repeat

---

[65] See n. 28, 33 and 62.
[66] Cf. E. A. Schmidt (1972) 289.
[67] Cf. Thomas (1983).
[68] George (1974).
[69] Livrea (1979).
[70] Wimmel (1973) 63 tried to reconcile the Cacus narration with Callimachus by referring to the propensity of the Hellenistic poets towards the supranatural: "Wenn nämlich das Heroische sich ins Übermäßige, ins Zyklopische steigert, dann bekommt es für den alexandrinischen Kunstsinn einen neuen Akzent, eine skurrile Beimischung."
[71] Gransden (1976) 29.

Hercules' Apolline victory over infernal powers. Callimachean realism is subjected to exaltation in the frame narration in much the
same way as it is 'demonized' in the inset story. Vergil transcends
the Alexandrianism of the bucolic Heracliscus and of Callimachus'
Hercules not by simply swelling the legend of Hercules and Cacus
to a full-scale epic myth, but the Hercules-Cacus myth is accorded
full narrative status as a narrative product of eschatological and moral
allegoresis. The form of the story thus corresponds to its function as
an eschatological ἀρχή of a process basically modelled on the life of
Hercules. If, then, the eschatological reality of Vergil's exemplary
Hercules eludes the simple opposition between myth and history and
between Callimachean and anti-Callimachean, it is hard to avoid
the question whether the final point of this process is conceivable as
a historical era which can be celebrated by a panegyric poem.

Though Augustus is identified as the final hypostasis of the *puer*
representing the phase of *pacatus orbis*, the promise of the *Eclogue* is
fulfilled only on the level of the Hercules paradigm by the exemplary Roman Hercules being incarnated in flesh. Whereas Hercules
finally obtains his hymn, the panegyric for Augustus once more takes
the form of a prophecy, a prophecy promising to the new Hercules
a timeless utopia of an imperium *extra anni solisque vias* on the one
hand and a mythic Arcadia on the other. On the levels of both time
and space Vergil thus reproduces a pattern of the *Eclogue*, where the
phase of *pacatum reget orbem* is first announced in political terms, as
a pacified *imperium Romanum*, only to be reduced to a fantastic *par-
adis terrestre* and extended beyond the boundaries of the human cosmos (*aspice convexo nutantem pondere mundum . . .*); the celebration of this
final phase is promised in terms of a bucolic Arcadia.

Given the link with the Fourth *Eclogue*, it would be possible to
read the passage as an implicit *recusatio*. However, even in the *Eclogue*
the bucolic mode is a means of expressing the hope for a historical
actualization of a mythical ideality. In the *Aeneid*, the 'historical' new
Golden Age is conceived as a prophetic projection of an eschatological ideality, while in its cosmic extension, the future *imperium
Romanum* is emblematized as Arcadia. It would be tautologous to say
that the panegyrical topos of a spaceless eternal imperium *extra anni
solisque vias* makes the apotheosis of Augustan Rome unrealizable in
space and time. It makes it possible as an ideality non-existent without the prophetic voice of a *vates* who now speaks through his characters like Jupiter, the Sibyl and Anchises. The objectivization of the

poet's voice thus reflects the evolution taking place on the levels of genre and subject-matter. Instead of abandoning the autonomous status of a *vates* he enjoyed in his bucolic Arcadia, Vergil raises it to a metaliterary level. By materializing the *laudes Herculis* and by prophesying the Herculean labours of Augustus he gains the full glory of his promised verse.[72]

[72] I am grateful to Karl Galinsky for many suggestions towards the improvement of this paper.

CHAPTER NINE

OVID'S METAMORPHOSES AND UNIVERSAL HISTORY

Stephen M. Wheeler

In ancient literature and literary criticism, poetry and history do not
always make strange bedfellows.[1] Even Ovid flirts with Clio. From
the very beginning of his most ambitious work, the *Metamorphoses*, he
carries on a dialogue with the traditions of ancient historiography.
After announcing his subject (1.1–2 *in nova fert animus mutatas dicere
formas/corpora*), Ovid introduces a historical dimension when he prays
to the gods to favor his undertaking (2–3 *di coeptis (nam vos mutastis
et illa)/adspirate meis*) and to guide it continuously from the beginning
of the world down to his own times (3–4 *primaque ab origine mundi/
ad mea perpetuum deducite tempora carmen*).[2] Ludwig was the first to point
out that the idea to include all time in the *Metamorphoses* derived
from the genre of universal history, which flourished toward the end
of the first century B.C.E.[3] Ludwig claimed further that Ovid based
the unity and structure of his epic on the historian's division of time
into three epochs: early (1.5–451), mythological (1.452–11.193), and
historical (11.194–15.870). Ovid's purpose, according to Ludwig, was
to do for poetry what the universal historian had done in the realm
of history: namely, to document the progress of human civilization
from chaos to the Roman empire. Ludwig's observation that the
chronological comprehensiveness of the *Metamorphoses* is indebted to

<hr />

[1] For the increasingly recognized affinities between poetry and historiography in
subject matter and rhetorical treatment see Wiseman (1979) 143–53, Woodman
(1988) 98–100, and Wiseman in ch. 17 below. Cf. also Feeney (1991) 250–64,
although he is interested in ancient criticism that differentiates the closely related
genres of epic and history.

[2] Tony Woodman (*per litteras*) points out that Ovid, as 'poetic historian', puts
into practice what Livy, the historian-who-would-be-poet, can only wish for, which
is to begin his history with a prayer to the gods. Cf. Livy *praef.* 13 *cum bonis potius
ominibus votisque et precationibus deorum dearumque, si, ut poetis, nobis quoque mos esset, liben-
tius inciperemus, ut orsis tantum operis successus prosperos darent.*

[3] Ludwig (1965) 74–86, esp. 80.

universal history has found agreement in subsequent secondary literature, but few accept his thesis that Ovid systematically implements
chronological order — the hallmark of historical writing — to structure the *Metamorphoses*.[4] More recently, Schmidt has maintained that
any comparison of the *Metamorphoses* with universal history is erro-
neous.[5] He argues that the purpose of the chronological framework
in the proem is not to structure the *Metamorphoses*, but to lend its
true subject, humanity, an air of totality. In Schmidt's view, Ovid
has no interest in history and does not think historically. His epic
is not historically structured; there are no historical epochs, no historical processes. The *Metamorphoses* is instead a timeless gallery of
human characters, whose transformations into animate and inani-
mate nature are narrative metaphors for human behavior. The question is, does Schmidt go too far in his critique of the universal
historical interpretation of the *Metamorphoses*?[6]

The purpose of this paper is to introduce new evidence support-
ing the claim that Ovid borrows the techniques of the historian and
exploits the traditions of ancient historiography to shape and direct
the response of his audience to the *Metamorphoses*. To begin with, I
demonstrate that Ovid's announcement of a chronological starting-
and end-point in the proem is a *topos* found in historical prefaces
and that the maximum expansion of his chronological coverage is
characteristic of universal history. Once the connection with universal history in the proem has been substantiated, the question arises
whether the *Metamorphoses* may be read as a universal history. If one
assumes that historical narrative consists of a succession of events in
chronological order, then the *Metamorphoses* may not always fit the
bill. However, the ordering of time in universal history has another
dimension that distinguishes it from the norm of local history: namely,
the synchronic narrative of events in different parts of the world. In
the second part of the paper, I show how the historians Polybius,
Diodorus Siculus, and Pompeius Trogus achieve a universal perspective by alternating between diachrony and synchrony in the
ordering of their narratives. In the concluding part of the paper, I

---

[4] See Galinsky (1975) 85 and Solodow (1988) 18 and 29–30; cf. Hardie (1986) 379–80.
[5] Schmidt (1991) 43ff.
[6] Cf. Hardie's review (1993a) 264: 'He throws the baby out with the bath-water in draining the poem of all historical and temporal sense'.

consider the diachronic and synchronic structures in the *Metamorphoses* that could support a reading of the poem as a universal history.

I. *Chronology and Genre*

Ludwig's observation that the chronological framework of the *Metamorphoses* is based upon universal history is, I think, correct, but not for the reasons that he gives. According to Ludwig, Ovid renews and expands upon the Hesiodic continuum of the *Theogony* and *Catalogue of Women* by bringing the mythological narrative down to his own day. Ludwig argues that Ovid's totalizing chronological framework must have been derived from universal history because there is no poetic precedent for it in the Hesiodic model of the *Theogony* and *Catalogue of Women*, which does not continue beyond the age of myths. This argument is weak because the temporal comprehensiveness of the *Metamorphoses* could easily have grown out of Roman traditions of epic poetry. For example, Ovid's wish to narrate *prima . . . ab origine mundi* (*Metamorphoses* 1.3) echoes Lucretius (cf. 5.548) and may recall the fifth book of *De Rerum Natura*, which covers the history of nature from the creation of the universe to the culmination of human civilization.[7] Ovid also has a precedent for an epic poet narrating history from earliest beginnings down to his own day in Ennius's *Annales*.[8] Finally, the *Metamorphoses* may be viewed as a super-epic that subsumes the time schemes of all previous epic cycles, which, when put together, embrace all time.[9] The chronological span of the *Metamorphoses*, although characteristic of universal history, may also be traced to sources in the epic tradition.

The question remains whether Ovid gives an explicit cue to motivate universal history as a background for the *Metamorphoses*. I think that he does, although no one to my knowledge has underscored it. Ovid's articulation of the chronological framework in the proem (*prima . . . ab origine mundi . . . ad mea . . . tempora*) follows the well-established practice of a historian who prefaces his work by defining its starting-point and end-point in chronological terms.[10] In the third chapter

---

[7] On the allusion to Lucretius, cf. Bömer (1969) *ad loc.*, Due (1974) 97, and Myers (1994) 6.

[8] Cf. Hofmann (1985) 225, Wheeler (1999) 23–4.

[9] Cf. Hardie (1993b) 13.

[10] For this *topos* in historiographical prefaces, see Herkommer (1968) 65–75, Woodman (1989) 135.

of the *Epistula ad Pompeium Geminum*, Dionysius of Halicarnassus observes that the most important task of a historian is selection of a noble and pleasing subject matter. The second task is to know from where one should begin and to what point one should proceed (*Pomp.* 3.8): γνῶναι πόθεν τε ἄρξασθαι καὶ μέχρι προελθεῖν δεῖ. The convention of defining the beginning and end of a historical work probably derives from Hellenistic historiographical theory and may be influenced by the Aristotelian doctrine of tragic unity advanced in the seventh chapter of the *Poetics* (cf. 1450b23–26).[11] In the preface to his *Antiquitates Romanae*, Dionysius follows his own precepts, when he defines the beginning- and end-point of his history (1.8.1): 'And so I begin my history from the oldest myths (ἀπὸ τῶν παλαιοτάτων μύθων) . . . and I bring the narrative down to the beginning of the first Punic war' (καταβιβάζω δὲ τὴν διήγησιν ἐπὶ τὴν ἀρχὴν τοῦ πρώτου Φοινικικοῦ πολέμου). Here one may observe that Dionysius's presentation of his chronological framework parallels Ovid's and that the verb-object combination καταβιβάζω δὲ τὴν διήγησιν is close in meaning to Ovid's *deducite . . . carmen*.[12]

An even closer parallel to Ovid's chronological framework is to be found in the preface to Diodorus Siculus's *Bibliotheca Historica* (1.3.6): 'If someone should write down according to his ability the actions of the whole cosmos that have been passed down to mem-

---

[11] On the origins of the historiographical convention of defining the beginning and end of a work, see Scheller (1911) 41–3, Burck (1934) 179, and Fornaro (1997) 193. Heath (1989) 77–81 questions the influence of Aristotlian unity on Hellenistic historiographical theory.

[12] Cf. Lucian *Rh. Pr.* 20. ὅπως δὲ καὶ τὸ πλῆθος τῶν λόγων θαυμάζωσιν, ἀπὸ τῶν Ἰλιακῶν ἀρξάμενος ἢ καὶ νὴ Δία ἀπὸ τῶν Δευκαλίωνος καὶ Πύρρας γάμων, ἢν δοκῇ, καταβίβαζε τὸν λόγον ἐπὶ τὰ νῦν καθεστῶτα. Here Lucian, tongue in cheek, advises the teacher of rhetoric to dazzle his audience with a lecture that includes a compendious universal history. Like Dionysius, Lucian uses the conventions of a historical preface (chronological framework with the verb καταβιβάζειν). In *De Saltatione*, Lucian similarly deploys the historiographical *topos* to introduce the repertoire of a pantomimist (*Salt.* 37): ἀπὸ γὰρ χάους εὐθὺς καὶ τῆς πρώτης τοῦ κόσμου γενέσεως ἀρξάμενον χρὴ αὐτὸν ἄπαντα εἰδέναι ἄχρι τῶν Κλεοπάτραν τὴν Αἰγυπτίαν. That the pantomimist should be able to dance a universal history may not be an exaggeration; cf. a second- or third-century C.E. Greek verse inscription to an unknown pantomimist buried in Rome ἱστορίας δείξας καὶ χειρσὶν ἄπαντα λαλήσας (*IG* 14.2124, Peek, *Griechische Vers-Inschriften* 742). On the inscription see Weinreich (1948) 73–7, Jones (1986) 42. Galinsky (1975) 68–9, 139, and (1996) 265–6, argues that the Lucianic passage on the dancer's repertoire shows the affinity of the *Metamorphoses* with pantomime in the Augustan age; it should be observed, however, that the parallelism of chronological framework may stem from another source to which Ovid and Lucian allude: universal history.

ory, as if of a single city, from the earliest times (ἀπὸ τῶν ἀρχαιοτάτων χρόνων) until his own times (μέχρι τῶν καθ' αὑτὸν καιρῶν) it is clear that it would be much labor, but he would compose for students the most useful work of all' [Loeb Classical Library translation of C. H. Oldfather]. Here Diodorus not only defines his framework but also commends it to his reader as useful, which is another typical prefatory strategy.[13]

To define the beginning and end of a history has the obvious function of letting the reader know what the contents of the work are and how it relates to other histories. In this respect, the chronological framework is not only a prefatory *topos*, but also a convenient way to identify a history as a whole. During the course of his history, Diodorus gives at least twenty brief descriptions of the starting- and end-points of historians who cover the events that he is narrating.[14] One Diodoran notice excites special interest. The fourth-century historian Anaximenes of Lampsacus wrote a history of Greece that began from the birth of the gods and the genesis of mankind and ended with the battle of Mantinea and the death of Epaminondas (Diodorus Siculus 15.89.3): ἀρξάμενος ἀπὸ θεογονίας καὶ ἀπὸ τοῦ πρώτου γένους τῶν ἀνθρώπων, κατέστροφε δ' εἰς τὴν ἐν Μαντινείᾳ μάχην καὶ τὴν Ἐπαμεινώνδου τελευτήν. Diodorus tells us further that Anaximenes included practically all the doings of the Greeks and barbarians in twelve books; it would therefore appear that the history had a universal conception bridging the divide between myth and history. Canonized among the ten classic Greek historians by the Alexandrians, Anaximenes provides a precedent for Diodorus. Nor is he the only example of a universal historian from the fourth century. Anaximenes's teacher Zoïlus of Amphipolis, also known as Homeromastix, composed a three-book world history, that, according to the *Suda*, covered time from the theogony to the death of Philip II (*FGrH* 71 T1): ἀπὸ θεογονίας ἕως τῆς Φιλίππου τελευτῆς. Zoïlus's history appears to have been a compendium whose purpose was to situate the Macedonian court in the context of Greek history.

The Hellenistic convention of defining a history's contents by its chronological starting-point and end-point took root in the Roman tradition of historiography. In his famous letter to L. Lucceius, Cicero

---

[13] Cf. Lucian *Hist. Conscr.* 53.
[14] Cf. Marincola (1997) 243.

exhorts the historian to write a separate monograph that covers the time from the Catilinarian conspiracy to Cicero's return from exile (*Epistulae ad Familiares* 5.12.4): *a principio . . . coniurationis* **usque ad** *reditum nostrum.* This chronological framework delimits the unity of the proposed work (5.12.4 *modicum quoddam corpus*) and contrasts it with Lucceius's continuous history concerning the Italian and civil wars (cf. 5.12.2). A chronological framework may also define where a continuator picks up and leaves off a historical narrative. A. Hirtius informs L. Cornelius Balbus in the prefatory letter to the Eighth Book of *Bellum Gallicum* that he has *also* continued Caesar's unfinished *Bellum Civile* (Hirt. *De Bello Gallico* 8 *praef.* 2): *novissimumque imperfectum* **ab** *rebus gestis Alexandriae confeci* **usque ad** *exitum non quidem civilis dissensionis, cuius finem nullum videmus, sed vitae Caesaris.* Hirtius's historical continuation 'from the Alexandrian war to the death of Caesar' does not appear to have survived; indeed, scholars doubt that he penned any of the three extant commentaries that continue Caesar's *Bellum Civile.*[15] On the topic of historical continuations, one may add that it was customary for Roman continuators to title their works with points of departure from known events. Tacitus titles or, more likely, sub-titles his history of the Julio-Claudian emperors *Ab Excessu Divi Augusti.*[16]

To return to the *topos* of defining a chronological framework in the historical preface, the first extant example in Roman historiography occurs at the beginning of Livy's *Ab Urbe Condita.*[17] In his opening sentence, Livy defines his point of departure as *a primordio urbis* (*praef.* 1), restating the title of his work. Later in the preface, he identifies his terminus as *ad haec nova* (4) and *ad haec tempora* (9).[18] This is not the only example of the prefatory *topos* in Livy's work.

[15] For discussion of Hirtius's preface to the Eighth Book of *Bellum Gallicum* and the continuations of *Bellum Civile* see Hall (1996) 411–5 and Carter (1997) xxxii–iii.

[16] On the question of the title of Tacitus's *Annales* see Goodyear (1972) 85–7. Somewhat differently, Pliny the Elder composed a thirty-one-book history entitled *A Fine Aufidii Bassi* (cf. Pliny *Nat. praef.* 20; Pliny *Ep.* 3.5.6), which defines its point of departure with reference to another historian.

[17] The fragmentary evidence for a chronological framework in Sallust's *Histories* (*a principio urbis ad bellum Persi Macedonicum* 1.8 Maurenbrecher) does not appear to refer to Sallust's own work, but to the works of other historians covering the history of Rome from the foundation to 168 B.C.E. On this disputed point see McGushin (1992) 67–8, Scanlon (1998) 198–200.

[18] A point overlooked by Herkommer (1968) 67 n. 7, who claims that it is not necessary for Livy to define his end-point because the history reaches into the present.

In the preface to Book 6, he begins by summarizing the contents of the first pentad (6.1.1): *quae **ab** condita urbe Roma **ad** captam eandem Romani . . . gessere . . . quinque libris exposui.*[19] The second pentad is distinct from the first in that it begins *ab secunda origine* (6.1.3), meaning from the refoundation of Rome by Camillus after the Gallic sack.[20]

Later examples of the prefatory *topos* by which a historian defines the contents of his work reinforce the claim that Ovid's chronological framework may be read within the tradition of historiography. Florus opens his epitome of Roman history with a concise statement of its subject matter (*praef.* 1.1): *populus Romanus **a** rege Romulo **in** Caesarem Augustum septingentos per annos tantum operum pace belloque gessit.* He closes the first book of his history with a chronological overview of what he has already narrated and a preview of what is to come in the second book (1.47.3): *posteri centum (sc. anni), quos **a** Carthaginis, Corinthi, Numantiaeque excidiis et Attali regis Asiatica hereditate **deduximus** **in** Caesarem et Pompeium secutumque hos, de quo dicemus, Augustum, ut claritate rerum bellicarum magnifici, ita domesticis cladibus miseri et erubescendi.* Here Florus uses the verb *deduximus* for the activity of narrating a history within a chronological framework (*a . . . excidiis . . . in Caesarem*); the parallel with Ovid's phraseology in the proem to the *Metamorphoses* is striking. I think it unlikely that Florus alludes to Ovid. Rather *deducere* is the proper verb for such a narrative.[21] Given Florus's usage of the verb *deducere*, one may be tempted to conclude that Ovid's use of the same verb within a chronological framework is proper to historiography.[22] If this is the case, the combination of *deducere* with

---

[19] In longer historical works, it is common for the historian to insert shorter prefaces at the beginning of books or book-groups to orient the reader; cf. Herkommer (1968) 76. On the pentadic organization of Livy's history see Luce (1977).

[20] For Livy's new beginning and the refoundation of Rome see Kraus (1994a) ad loc. and (1994b).

[21] Cf. *TLL* V.1.282.29–47.

[22] Augustine uses *deducere* when discussing Varro's *De Gente Populi Romani* and works like it that trace a series of time-periods: (Augustine *C.D.* 18.2): *erat etiam **tempore illo** regnum Sicyoniorum admodum parvum, **a quo** ille undecumque doctissimus Marcus Varro scribens de gente populi Romani, velut antiquo tempore, **exorsus est**. ab his enim Sicyoniorum regibus ad Athenienses pervenit, a quibus ad Latinos deinde Romanos . . . Sed quoniam res Graecae multo sunt nobis quam Assyriae notiores, et **per Graecos ad Latinos ac deinde ad Romanos**, qui etiam ipsi Latini sunt, **temporum seriem deduxerunt**, qui gentem populi Romani in originis eius antiquitate rimati sunt.* It is improbable that Augustine is thinking of Ovid's usage of *deducere* but rather reflects normative usage in historical contexts. Cassiodorus uses the same verb for Jerome's continuation of Eusebius's chronicle down to his own times (Cassiodorus *Inst.* 1.17.2): *chronica vero, quae sunt*

carmen perpetuum (cf. Cicero *Epistulae ad Familiares* 5.12.2 *perpetuis . . . historiis*) within a chronological framework sends a consistent signal that the *Metamorphoses* has historical pretensions. The verb *deducere* is, of course, polysemous and capable of signaling the poet's commitment to a Callimachean program, which could be viewed as antithetical to that of a historical program.[23] Such an ambiguity would not be surprising. It is well known that the *Metamorphoses* manifests a tension between its historical scheme and the erotic and aetiological stories that do not explain how the universe evolved from chaos into the Roman empire.[24]

To round out the survey of our historiographical *topos*, it is worth observing that the habit of defining a chronological framework remains a standard feature of prefaces in late antique historiography. Sulpicius Severus opens his two-book summary of universal history (from a Christian point of view) by announcing a chronological framework from the origin of the world to his own times (403 C.E.): *res **a** mundi exordio sacris litteris editas breviter constringere et cum distinctione temporum **usque ad** nostram memoriam carptim dicere aggressus sum* (*Chronica* 1.1.1). Although his title, *Chronica*, appears to indicate a chronographical work, Sulpicius is primarily concerned with summarizing the early books of the Old Testament. More ambitiously, the Christian apologist Orosius composes a universal historical summary in seven books, *Historiae Adversum Paganos*, which polemically refutes the claim that Christianity is responsible for the decline of the Roman empire. He begins the work with a tripartite chronological framework from the creation to 417 C.E., which not only alludes to Livy but also exploits the wordplay between *urbs* and *orbis* (1.1.14): *dicturus igitur **ab** orbe condito **usque ad** urbem conditam, dehinc **usque ad** Caesaris principatum nativitatemque Christi ex quo sub potestate urbis orbis mansit imperium, vel etiam **usque ad** dies nostros.* A final late antique example of the structure we have been examining can be found in the preface to Jerome's

---

*imagines historiarum brevissimaeque commemorationes temporum, scripsit Graece Eusebius; quae transtulit Hieronymus in Latinum, et **usque ad** tempora sua **deduxit** eximie.* Given the purpose and context of the *Institutiones*, it is also unlikely that Cassiodorus models the phraseology *ad tempora sua deduxit* on Ovid.

[23] On the implication of a *carmen deductum* in the words *perpetuum deducite . . . carmen* and mixed programmatic signals see Kenney (1976) 51–2; cf. Hofmann (1985) 224–6. However, Rosati (1999) 246–7 observes that the metaphor of spinning can also be appropriate for epic and narrative poetry; cf. Hardie (1993b) 63 n. 8.

[24] Well described by Burrow (1988) 99–100.

Vita Malchi, where he promises next to write a history **ab** *adventu Salvatoris* **usque ad** *nostram aetatem, id est* **ab** *apostolis* **usque ad** *huius temporis faecem* (1.1).[25] Here Jerome means to translate Eusebius's *Historia Ecclesiastica* with a continuation down to his own day. As things turned out, however, Jerome did not undertake this project; his rival Rufinus did.

The aforementioned examples of temporal frames demarcated by the prepositional structure *ab ... ad* (or *in*) in historical prefaces lead to two conclusions about the chronological framework at the beginning of the *Metamorphoses*. First, Ovid follows a well-established practice common in historiographical prefaces. Second, Ovid's chronological framework arouses the expectation of a chronologically ordered narrative, which is the mark of history rather than of poetry.[26] If there were any doubt lingering about this point, one may compare the remarks of Eustathius in Macrobius's *Saturnalia* about how Homer distinguishes his poetry from history (5.2.9): *ille vitans in poemate historicorum similitudinem, quibus lex est incipere ab initio rerum et continuam narrationem ad finem usque perducere*. The rule for historians is to begin *ab initio rerum* and to narrate continuously *ad finem*. Note too that the historian's activity, *continuam narrationem ... perducere*, is similar to what Ovid wishes the gods to do for him, *perpetuum deducite ... carmen*. The third conclusion to be drawn from Ovid's temporal framework, which is set at the chronological maximum, is that it implies a special sort of history: universal history.[27] Finally, as an addendum, it may be noted that just as histories are referred to by their chronological

---

[25] My thanks to Paul Harvey for drawing my attention to this example.

[26] Ovid's poetic enterprise could be compared with cyclic poetry, but the point would be the same. For Aristotle (*Po.* 1459a37ff.) and Horace (*Ars* 146–9) reject cyclic poetry as unpoetic and too much like history. For the ancient distinction between chronological order in historiography and chronological inversion in poetry see Brink (1971), 219–22, on Horace *Ars* 146–49; Heath (1989) 115–6; and Woodman (1989) 134–5, who argues that Vergil adopts the manner of the historian when he represents the events on the shield of Aeneas in chronological order. 'Vergil the historian' clearly furnishes an important precedent for 'Ovid the historian'.

[27] Although it lacks internal divisions, Ovid's framework is broadly comparable to the universal historical framework that Varro introduces in *De Gente Populi Romani* (*HRR* II. fr. 3 (Censorinus, *De Die Natali* 21.1): *nunc vero id intervallum temporis tractabo, quod* **historicon** *Varro adpellat. hic enim tria discrimina temporum esse tradit, primum* **ab** *hominum principio* **ad** *cataclysmum priorem, quod propter ignorantiam vocatur* **adelon**, *secundum* **a** *cataclysmo priore* **ad** *olympiadem primam, quod, quia multa in eo fabulosa referuntur,* **mythicon** *nominatur, tertium* **a** *prima olympiade* **ad** *nos, quod dicitur* **historicon**, *quia res in eo gestae veris historiis continentur.* On this question see Wiseman ch. 17 below.

frameworks, so too Ovid, in his later poetry, refers to the *Metamorphoses* by its chronological framework.[28]

Before turning to the question of whether and how the *Metamorphoses* embodies universal history, I should briefly address Feeney's somewhat different reading of the chronological framework in the proem. Feeney works from the premise that the chronological framework 'looks like a programme for a chronography'.[29] In this category he places Roman works such as Cornelius Nepos's *Chronica* or Varro's *De Gente Populi Romani*, which are rooted in the tradition of Greek chronography and can be traced back to Apollodorus and Eratosthenes.[30] According to Feeney, Ovid evokes the genre of chronography in order to ignore, refuse, and renounce official ideological constructions of time, while simultaneously building an alternative time machine that maintains a strategic uncertainty about temporal schemes.[31] Feeney masterfully evokes the chronological possibilities that Ovid does not implement, but one may question his thesis that Ovid raises the spectre of chronography at the beginning of his poem in order to deconstruct it.

I think it is unlikely that Ovid or his audience would associate the chronological framework of the *Metamorphoses* with chronography *per se*, given the historiographical precedents already cited.[32] That is, I would maintain a theoretical distinction between universal history and chronography, even if the distinction is sometimes blurred. In its purest form, chronography is something altogether different from history: it is a record or table of historical events that are precisely dated by reference to an absolute dating system of regular intervals, based on Olympiads (or lists of Olympic victors), king lists, or annual lists of office holders (priestesses of Hera, archons, or consuls).[33] Jacoby

---

[28] Cf. Ovid *Tr.* 2.559–60 *prima surgens ab origine mundi/in tua deduxi tempora, Caesar*, with the significant change from *mea* to *tua* discussed by Feeney (1999). See also Hinds (1999), who examines Ovid's allusions in the *Tristia* and *Ibis* to the chronological framework in the *Metamorphoses*.

[29] Feeney (1999) 15.

[30] Feeney (1999) 13–15. Cf. Ludwig (1965) 80, who is more concerned with universal history than chronography, although he does not make a sharp distinction between the two genres.

[31] Feeney (1999) 18–30.

[32] The following discussion develops points in Wheeler (1999) 125–6.

[33] For this definition of chronography see Mosshammer (1979) 85–6, who points out that the term may also apply to the process by which precise dates are established for persons and events not yet included in an absolute chronology.

defines chronography as one of the five sub-genres of historiography, distinct from genealogy, ethnography, history, and horography.[34] The relationship of chronography to historiography, however, is contested. Fornara, for example, disagrees with Jacoby in identifying chronography as a form of history and suggests that it be considered in a category of its own:

> The end of chronography is the arrangement of events in a mechanically sequential pattern. That pattern is determined without regard for the interrelation of events; by the same token, it condones the juxtaposition of incommensurables. The nature of chronography is to articulate disparate material by fixed intervals; history depicts the actions of men as they occur in time. The genres are connected only in their common utilization of some of the data of the past.[35]

Momigliano argues that historians and chronographers have different methodologies and that the dichotomy between the two was deeply engrained in the Greek literary tradition.[36] The crucial point is that chronography, as a science, is a specialized and technical form of inquiry that is neither the goal of history nor poetry.[37] In his letter to Lucceius, Cicero observes that what gives pleasure in reading history is not the chronological record of events (*Epistulae ad Familiares* 5.12.5 *etenim ordo ipse annalium mediocriter nos retinet quasi enumeratione fastorum*) but the narrative of an outstanding individual's changing fortunes. One would assume that Ovid's audience is similarly interested in the pleasure of a narrative about universal change rather than a set of absolute dates of when what metamorphosis occurred.

Of course, the *Metamorphoses*, like universal history, could orient itself according to chronographical works, but there is no reason to assume that it aims to exemplify such a work. Its very scope goes beyond the limits of chronography. In the first place, the origin of the world belongs to what Varro terms the obscure period of time (cf. *HRR* II, *De Gente Populi Romani* fr. 3). Moreover, much of Ovid's material precedes the Trojan war, which is generally considered the *terminus post quem* for reliable chronography. A generation earlier than

---

[34] Jacoby (1909) 87–8; cf. Marincola (1997) 2 and (1999) 286.
[35] Fornara (1983) 29.
[36] Momigliano (1977) 192.
[37] Apollodorus of Athens set his chronicle in comic trimeters in order to enhance memorization; cf. Pfeiffer (1968) 255. There is no evidence for a Latin chronicle set in verse.

Ovid, Diodorus Siculus uses the chronology of Apollodorus from the sack of Troy, but makes a point of not giving an absolute chronology for events prior to the Trojan war because he has not received a trustworthy chronographic table (παράπηγμα) of this period.[38] There is evidence, however, that chronographers attempted to give the mythic period a chronology. For example, Hellanicus of Lesbos, identified by Jacoby as the first chronographer, dates events before the Trojan war with reference to the priestesses of Argos (*FGrH* 79b).[39] In the first century C.E., Castor of Rhodes (*FGrH* 250) began his chronography from the reign of the Assyrian king Ninus and so will have dated the mythic period according to the reigns of kings. Such works, I think, are important for understanding the games that Ovid plays with time in his poem, but it is hard to believe that Ovid's masterwork aims to realize such a specialized genre.[40]

What about the claim that the chronological framework of the *Metamorphoses* evokes such works as the *Chronica* of Cornelius Nepos and Varro's *De Gente Populi Romani*? The comparison with Nepos may stand up if the *Chronica* were a form of universal history rather than the bare bones of a chronography.[41] According to Catullus, Cornelius Nepos included the whole of time (Catullus 1.6 *omne aevum*) in his work. Nepos certainly went beyond the temporal limits of his chronographic model, the *Chronica* of Apollodorus, by averring that Saturn was not a god but a mortal king of Latium (*HRR* II, *Chronica* fr. 1). There is no textual support for Feeney's claim that Nepos gives dates for Saturn's reign.[42] The evidence of Minucius Felix, *Octavius* 21.4 [or 23.9] — as well as Tertullian *Apologeticum* 4, *Ad Nationes* 2.12, and Lactantius 1.13.8 — only indicates that Nepos, like other historians

---

[38] D.S. 1.5.1; cf. 4.1.1. It is unclear whether or not Diodorus knew the chronography of Castor of Rhodes, which includes chronology before the Trojan war. If Diodorus knew Castor, he would be implicitly questioning the reliability of his chronography.

[39] Jacoby (1909) 87–8; cf. Fornara (1983) 28.

[40] In his *RE* article s.v. 'Ovid' (18.1940–41), Kraus observes that Ovid would have relied on mythological compendia to order myth chronologically. Even if one grants Ovid greater independence in the disposition of his material, he responds to the impulse of his times to systematize myth.

[41] Scholars are divided in their classification of Nepos's *Chronica*. Some consider it to be the first universal history of its kind: Woodman (1975) 286 n. 4; Wiseman (1979) 157–8. Others consider it to be more chronographical in nature: Starr (1981) 167–8.

[42] Feeney (1999) 14.

(Cassius Hemina, Diodorus, and Thallus), promulgated the euhe-merist view that Saturn was a man. Given that Nepos is chiefly dependent upon Apollodorus for Greek chronology, it is possible that he did not deal with material before the Trojan war in a chrono-graphic manner.[43] In the late fourth century C.E., Ausonius sent a copy of Nepos's *Chronica* to Sextus Petronius Probus, which he char-acterizes as fables and so suitable for the education of children (*Epistulae* 10): *apologos Titiani Nepotis chronica quasi alios apologos (nam et ipsa instar sunt fabularum) ad tuam nobilitatem tuam misi gaudens atque etiam glorians fore aliquid, quod ad institutionem tuorum sedulitatis meae studio con-feratur.*[44] If Nepos *Chronica* contained fables, it is possible that the work had a greater narrative dimension than a chronography and could have furnished a model for the chronological framework of the *Metamorphoses* as a world history.

Varro's *De Gente Populi Romani* was of undoubted importance as an intellectual background for the *Metamorphoses*, but not necessarily in its chronographic capacity. To be sure, Varro grounded his research in chronographic science, calculating the length of historical cycles and fixing the dates of important events, such as Rome's founda-tion. But to view this work as 'chronographic' is to lose sight of its historical interests. Varro's principal subject matter was legendary kings, the origins of the Roman people, and possibly also precedents in the distant past for the deification of Julius Caesar.[45] One of the objectives of *De Gente* was to rationalize myth and, in particular, to reveal how certain gods were once kings and received divine honours. Varro also treated matters such as the wanderings of Aeneas and Rome's borrowings from other peoples.[46] Would Ovid's chronological framework suggest comparison with such a work? One may observe that *prima . . . origine mundi ad mea . . . tempora* does correspond broadly to the universal historical scheme of time that Varro introduced at the beginning of *De Gente*.[47] But Varro's overview of time did not define the contents of his work; it served as a frame of reference for a history that began with the Sicyonian kings and proceeded to

[43] On Nepos' transcription of Apollodorus see Rohde (1891) 534ff.
[44] Cf. *RE* 4.1410.29–40 (Wissowa).
[45] See further Taylor (1934) 221–9.
[46] Taylor (1934) 222 and Rawson (1985) 245.
[47] For Varro's universal historical scheme see n. 27; cf. Ludwig (1965) 79 and Feeney (1999) 15.

Athenian, Latin, and Roman kings.[48] It appears improbable, then, that Ovid's chronological framework aimed to reproduce a work such as *De Gente*. Nonetheless, Varro's euhemerization of myth and rationalisation of apotheosis may have been relevant as a foil to the *Metamorphoses*.

II. *Diachrony and Synchrony in Universal History*

Ovid's announcement of a chronological framework in the proem of the *Metamorphoses* may not advertise a chronographical work, but it does raise the expectation that the poem will proceed in chronological order. Moreover, given the program to narrate *ab origine mundi ad mea tempora*, the audience may look forward to the poetic equivalent of a universal history, which trumps Ennius's poetic version of Roman history in the *Annales*. But what is universal history? This type of historiography — which is to be distinguished from monographs about contemporary history or continuous local history told from the beginning — attempts, in its strongest form, to tell the story of the world or mankind from beginning to end.[49] Yet, as is frequently pointed out, the impulse to tell everything that happened everywhere poses a narrative problem: how does one narrate events that take place at the same time in different parts of the world?[50] If Ovid embarks on a world history, presumably he faces the same challenge of representing a universal perspective. The question to be raised in the next two parts of the paper is whether the comparison to universal history is relevant or useful for an understanding and

---

[48] Varro's actual temporal coverage is attested in Augustine *C.D.* 18.2 (see n. 22 above). We also learn from Augustine (18.3) that Varro concluded the second book with the Trojan war. Peter (1902), 242, conjectures that Varro would have reached the foundation of Rome by the third book, and the fourth and final book would have dealt with the *Urgeschichte* of the Roman people.

[49] I follow the definition of the genre given by Alonso-Núñez (1990) 173 and seconded by Clarke (1999) 250. On the genre of universal history see further Burde (1974), Sacks (1981) 96–121, Fornara (1983) 42–6, Momigliano (1987), Wiseman (1987) 247–8.

[50] Momigliano (1987) 31: 'I would be making the understatement of the century if I were to say that universal history has never been a clear notion. Taken literally, the idea of universal history verges on absurdity. Who can tell everything that has happened? And who would like to listen if he were told?' On the compositional problem of universal history, cf. Clarke (1999) 249–52.

appreciation of the *Metamorphoses*. As stated at the beginning of this paper, Schmidt claims that the *Metamorphoses* is not organized historically, but, as I hope to demonstrate, this is not entirely true, if one views the poem in relation to universal history rather than local history. The critical point here, I think, is that universal history has a tendency toward spatial universality, which means that it may organize itself not only according to time but also according to space.[51]

The first extant historian to articulate a view of the genre of universal history was Polybius. Although he does not narrate all of time in the mode of Ephorus or Diodorus Siculus, Polybius claims to be a universal historian in the *Histories*, because he attempts to represent the process of history in different parts of the *oikoumene*. For this reason Polybius contends that his work is more useful than monographs or local histories (3.32.2):

> How much easier it is to possess and peruse forty books, all as it were woven together thread by thread (κατὰ μίτον ἐξυφασμένας), and thus to follow clearly events in Italy, Sicily, and Libya from the time of Pyrrhus to the capture of Carthage, and those in the rest of the world from the flight of Cleomenes of Sparta on till the battle of the Romans and Achaeans at the Isthmus, than to read or possess the works of those who treat of particular transactions [slightly modified Loeb Classical Library translation of W. R. Paton].[52]

This passage is obviously a late addition to the *Histories*; however, the metaphor of weaving is not an afterthought but a defining metaphor of Polybius's view of universal history.[53] At the beginning of his work, Polybius observes (1.3.4) that from the 140th Olympiad (220/16 B.C.E.), history became unified and the affairs of Italy and Africa became interwoven (συμπλέκεσθαι) with those of Greece and Asia, all leading to a single end. The key term for this interweaving of political and military events in time and space is *symploke*. On the one hand, the metaphor of *symploke* objectifies the intertwining strands of local events that form the subject-matter of a unified universal history; on the other, it is a metaphor for what universal historical

---

[51] On the temporal and spatial dimensions of universal history see Clarke (1999) 255–76. For time and space as the two principal criteria for the *dispositio* of history see Dionysius of Halicarnassus *Th.* 9.2; cf. Heath (1989) 85–7.

[52] κατὰ μίτον is an emendation (Ursinus). For the interpretation of κατὰ μίτον ἐξυφασμένας I follow Walbank (1957) ad loc.

[53] See Walbank (1974) 197–9; cf. Clarke (1999) 274–5.

writing does. The reader experiences profit and pleasure, according
to Polybius, 'from the weaving together and comparison of all events
in the world' (1.4.11 ἐκ μέντοι γε τῆς ἁπάντων πρὸς ἄλληλα συμπλοκῆς).

In order to represent the *symploke* or nexus of events in time and
space, Polybius organizes his history both diachronically and synchronically. On the diachronic axis, he orders his material by
Olympiads following the chronological scheme of Timaeus, whose
history he continues. Within each year, however, Polybius switches
to a synchronic survey of what happened region by region in a fixed
order: Italy, Sicily, Spain, Africa, Greece and Macedonia, Asia and
Egypt. Such a method of representing events in different parts of
the *oikoumene* is open to the criticism that it is discontinuous, for it
does not follow a sequence of events to its end, but keeps moving
from one place to the next, leaving earlier events half-finished and
embarking upon others.[54] The alternative to *symploke* is to narrate
kata genos, as Diodorus Siculus puts it (5.1.4). To narrate *kata genos*
is to divide up one's material under various cities and peoples and
to treat their chronologies separately, which allows for greater narrative continuity. This is the method of narration that Ephorus employed
in his universal history. Polybius's claim to uniqueness as a historian
is his attempt to synthesize events in different parts of the world and
thus to give insight into the process of *tyche*. However, he does not
believe that it was possible to write such a history until his own
times, when Rome came onto the stage of history (2.37.2; cf. 1.3.3–4,
1.4.1–2; 4.28). That is, before 220 C.E. there was no universal history, only local histories.

According to Polybius, then, universal history is to be distinguished
from other forms of history by its simultaneous representation of
events in different parts of the world. One might reasonably expect
a universal history to have a recognizably different narrative structure from that of a continuous history of one city or people, which
adheres to a diachronic format.[55] The Polybian approach to uni-

---

[54] Dionysius of Halicarnassus (*Pomp.* 3.13, *Th.* 9.2) levels this criticism against
Thucydides who likewise breaks up narrative continuity by covering events in different
places during the same season. Cf. Fornara (1997) 200.

[55] It should be pointed out that the interweaving of diachrony and synchrony is
not exclusive to universal history. Arguably, Polybius's method of *symploke* is already
embedded in Thucydides's history; see n. 54 above. The distinction between universal history and local history is based on the degree to which the former culti-
vates a universal perspective through synchrony.

versal history finds a successor in Diodorus Siculus, whose forty-book *Bibliotheca Historica* appeared around 30 B.C.E. However, unlike Polybius, who limited the chronology of his subject matter, Diodorus is the first historian to attempt to include all of history from the creation to the present (60 B.C.E.). In the first six books, he presents a euhemerist version of myths and legends that document culture-heroes and the progress of civilization prior to the Trojan war; he organizes this material *kata genos* because he does not possess a reliable chronological table. The following eleven books are a chronologically ordered history from the Trojan war to the death of Alexander. The final twenty-three books present all subsequent events down to Julius Caesar and the war between the Romans and the Celts. As soon as absolute dating is possible, Diodorus treats his material annalistically, but within each year he parcels out the events that took place in Greece, Sicily, Africa, and Italy. In this fashion, Diodorus follows the Polybian model of alternating between the diachrony of successive years and the synchrony of a geographical survey within each year, even though he is aware that it disrupts narrative continuity (20.43–44). For Diodorus, the organizational benefits of the alternation between diachrony and synchrony outweigh its disadvantages.

Pompeius Trogus may also shed some light on the narrative economy of universal history. His forty-four-book *Historiae Philippicae*, probably completed at the turn of the era, is a Latin representative of the genre and comes down to us primarily in an epitome by Justin of the third or fourth century.[56] Trogus's universal history began from the Assyrian king Ninus and ran down to the time of Augustus. Although Justin claims that Trogus imposed a chronological system upon his history (*praef.* 3), he gives no indication that Trogus marked off events by Olympiads or annual magistracies.[57] Trogus frequently gave the lengths of empires and regnal periods, for which he may have been indebted to Timagenes's work on kings (*FGrH* 88), but, as far as one can tell, he did not anchor his notices to an absolute date. In fact, there is only one absolute date in Justin's epitome, and it is wrong. The independence of the Parthians from Seleucus II Kallinikos is pegged to 254 B.C.E. (Just. *Epit.* 41.4.3): *primo Punico bello, L. Manlio Vulsone M. Atilio Regulo consulibus.* The only problem

---

[56] On Justin's date see Syme (1979–91) 6.358ff.
[57] Cf. Heckel (1997) 25–6; Clarke (1999) 260–1.

is that Seleucus II reigned between 246 and 226. Apparently, Trogus wanted to synchronize the independence of the Parthians with the arrival of Rome's first fleet in Africa anticipating the future rivalry of Rome and Parthia.[58] Trogus' universal history is of particular interest, because it may have been less chronologically systematic than that of Diodorus.

The underlying rationale of Trogus's history seems to have been some conception of the succession of world-empires.[59] The narrative began with the Assyrian empire and concluded with the submission of Spain to Augustus in 19 B.C.E., at which point Justin (probably not Trogus) imposed closure with the idea of the conquest of the entire world (44.5.8 *perdomito orbe*).[60] As the title *Historiae Philippicae* suggests, the main emphasis of the work did not fall on Rome but on the rise and fall of Macedonian power, i.e. Philip II, Alexander, and the Hellenistic successor kingdoms (Books 7–40). Clarke argues that Trogus was concerned with the same challenge as Diodorus of representing history in different theaters of action.[61] He solved his problem differently, by relaxing the chronological framework and leaving more room for synchronic narrative weaving and digressions.[62] Trogus recorded events in loose and relative association, frequently making a transition by an *interea, eodem tempore*, or *dum haec aguntur*.[63] He was particularly fond of synchronisms and coincidental parallels in different parts of the world.[64] However, the lack of chronological rigor in Pompeius Trogus does not mean that time was unimportant to his history. According to Seel, synchronisms functioned as bridges from one part of the world to the next and were perhaps the most important part of Trogus's artistic narrative.[65] If this analysis of Trogus is on the mark, then the impressionistic interweaving of time and geography in Ovid's *Metamorphoses* may not be so distant from universal history.

---

[58] Burde (1974) 111.

[59] Cf. Momigliano (1987) 45–6; Alonso-Núñez (1987) 62–5; Clarke (1999) 274.

[60] Trogus treats the Parthian empire in Books 41–2, but it has not been conquered by Rome. On the Parthian question see Clarke (1999) 263.

[61] Clarke (1999) 269; cf. Burde (1974), 99.

[62] As Clarke (1999) 272 observes, the chronological order from Ninus to Augustus "is completely swamped by a wealth of ethnographic, geographical, and mythological material, which is spatially motivated in so far as it is demanded by the arrival of the narrative at a new place."

[63] Cf. Burde (1974) 113 and Heckel (1997) 26.

[64] On synchronisms see Alonso-Núñez (1992) ch. IV and Clarke (1999) 267–9.

[65] Seel (1955) 54.

III. *Diachrony and Synchrony in the Metamorphoses*

The question remains in what ways the *Metamorphoses* may be read as a universal history. There are several reasons why one might resist such a reading. First of all, critics observe that the chronological framework is frequently violated and hence not an important structuring principle.[66] On the one hand, Ovid *poetically* inverts chronological order by letting characters retrospectively narrate events that occur at earlier (often indeterminate) times. On the other, he tolerates chronological contradictions in the poem's order of events. More fundamentally, Schmidt claims, in opposition to Ludwig, that there are no historical epochs in the *Metamorphoses*.[67] Feeney likewise maintains that canonical moments of demarcation and origin are missing or destabilised.[68] Finally, it is frequently pointed out that the main narrative sometimes proceeds by a synchronic connection (*interea*) rather than a diachronic one (*post hoc*), with the result that many episodes are not ordered in diachronic sequence, but happen more or less at the same time.[69]

None of the mentioned issues decisively nullifies the possibility of reading the *Metamorphoses* as a universal history. To begin with, the historical framework cannot simply be dismissed as trivial, because it continually reasserts itself as a conceit throughout the work, especially at the beginning and the end. It may therefore be better to think of the *Metamorphoses* in terms of a tension between the narrative modes of history and poetry (i.e., between chronological order and inversion), rather than to think of it as exemplifying one mode to the exclusion of the other. Furthermore, chronological inconsistencies do not point to the absence of time as an ordering principle in the *Metamorphoses*, but rather to the possibility of ordering time in different ways. As I have argued elsewhere, the reader's expectations of chronological continuity are necessary for the games that Ovid plays with time in the *Metamorphoses*.[70] As for the existence or non-existence of chronological divisions in the poem, there is enough

---

[66] See, e.g., Crump (1931) 198–200.

[67] Schmidt (1991) 43.

[68] Feeney (1999) 18–22 makes a case for Ovid's systematic exclusion of the canonical dates and events that anchor chronographies; in contrast to Schmidt, he does not draw the conclusion that the *Metamorphoses* lacks a temporal dimension. Rather, he argues (24–30) that Ovid creates his own form of time.

[69] Cf. Wilkinson (1958) 238 and Solodow (1988) 126–7.

[70] See Wheeler (1999) 117–39.

evidence to support the thesis that Ovid does mark periods of time. Finally, the claim that the *Metamorphoses* is ahistorical because many of the stories are ordered synchronically rather than diachronically assumes that history is purely diachronic, which is not the case. As we have already seen in Polybius, Diodorus, and Trogus, universal history consists of an interweaving of diachronic and synchronic or temporal and spatial elements of narrative. Ovid's alleged weak sense of time may therefore not be a result of his indifference toward history, but of a universal historical approach that seeks to represents the simultaneity of events in the world. In the remaining pages, my purpose is accordingly to take a fresh look at the evidence for temporal ordering in the *Metamorphoses* and to show that the chronological framework of the proem is not a mere starting- and end-point with no time in between. Thereafter, I present a selection of synchronized events that give the *Metamorphoses* universal historical scope. Finally, I briefly consider in what ways the *Metamorphoses* resembles Diodorus's *Bibliotheca Historica* and in what ways it challenges the assumptions of such a universal history.

What evidence is there for temporal order in the *Metamorphoses*? First, one may point to the tripartite division of the poem into stories about gods, heroes, and historical figures — a division that most readers of the *Metamorphoses* accept — which is at home in epic as well as history.[71] Following the creation of the world, Ovid summarizes the history of the human race in the Hesiodic scheme of the succession of ages or races, identified with the metals of gold, silver, bronze, and iron (*Metamorphoses* 1.89–150). The decline from the golden age begins when Jupiter succeeds his father Saturn and introduces change in the form of the four seasons (113–24). The epochal division of time into the four races/ages of mankind is a well-worn poetic topic that belongs to classical mythology rather than classical historiography.[72] Nevertheless, the 'four ages' of man fulfill the expectations of a universal history, by providing a familiar historical narrative of moral decline.

---

[71] First formulated by Crump (1931) 204 and 274–8. This tripartite division corresponds to the Greek definition of epic's subject matter reported by Diomedes in *Art. Gramm.* 3 (Keil, *Gramm. Lat.* 1.483–4); cf. Due (1974) 120. However, it also corresponds to Varro's 'historical' division of time into three periods: see n. 27 above.
[72] Cf. Momigliano (1987) 31–5.

The succession of the four ages/races of mankind leads to another epochal demarcation in the flood of Deucalion and the creation of a new race of humans from stones. Neither Schmidt nor Feeney make much of Deucalion's flood, but it is clear that this must be a recognizable historical division in the mythic period.[73] In *De Gente Populi Romani*, Varro used the flood of Deucalion to articulate the mythic period (cf. *HRR* II, fr. 5a–b, 9, 10). According to Varro, the flood of Deucalion occurs after the flood of Ogygus, during the reign of the second Athenian king Cranaos (fr. 10, *ap.* Augustine *De Civitate Dei* 18.10). Peter conjectures that Varro divided time into cycles of 440 years in which the flood of Deucalion marked the beginning of the second cycle, the Greek expedition to Troy the third, and the foundation of Rome the fourth.[74] Although Ovid does not follow Varro's chronology, he uses the flood of Deucalion as a watershed in the chronology of myth.[75]

Between Deucalion's flood and the Trojan war, the next major Varronian temporal division, Ovid orders his narrative according to different principles. One is to follow the outline of heroic genealogies.[76] Another is to follow the succession of kings, whose relative chronology chronographers had established. The tale of Io is of particular interest because Ovid represents her father Inachus as a river-god. In the chronographic tradition (*ap.* Augustine *De Civitate Dei* 18.3), Inachus was the first king of the Argives. In Book 2, Ovid indirectly offers another temporal point of reference in the reign of Cecrops (2.555), whose daughters become the subject of two episodes. Cecrops was, of course, the founder and first king of Athens. In Book 6, Ovid returns to Athens and the king is Pandion, who, in turn, is succeeded by his brother Erechtheus. In Book 7, Aegeus, son of Pandion, is king of Athens. Thus it is possible to discern the

---

[73] So Ludwig (1965) 81.

[74] Peter (1902) 242ff.; cf. also *HRR* II, xxxv. Arnobius, *Adv. nat.* 5.8, only knows the flood of Deucalion and writes of Varro: *in librorum quattuor primo, quos de gente conscriptos Romani populi dereliquit, curiosis computationibus edocet ab diluuii tempore, cuius supra fecimus mentionem* [sc. Deucalionis], *ad usque Hirti consulatum et Pansae annorum esse milia nondum duo.*

[75] Later, in the *Metamorphoses*, as Medea flies over Othrys, Ovid is reminded of the metamorphosis of Cerambus, which he dates to the time of the flood (7.355–6): *cum gravis infuso tellus foret obruta ponto,/Deucalioneas effugit inobrutus undas.* In the *Georgics*, Vergil identifies Deucalion with the point in time when nature's laws first took effect (*Geo.* 1.60–3).

[76] See Grimal (1958).

presence of chronological order in the sequence of Athenian kings. In between the notices about the kings of Athens, Ovid includes the history of Thebes. Books 3 and 4 feature the period of the foundation of Thebes and the history of the house of Cadmus.[77] In Book 6, Ovid returns to Thebes to tell the story of Niobe who is the wife of Amphion, a royal successor of Cadmus. Once again, the order of Ovid's mythic narrative follows the proper succession of kings.

At the end of Book 6, Ovid marks the beginning of a new period with the quest for the golden fleece and the first ship (6.721 *per mare non notum prima petiere carina*). This constitutes something of a chronological contradiction, because man had already learned to sail in the first book (1.132–4). However, if one reads the flood of Deucalion as the beginning of a new cycle, then it is possible to regard the *Argo* as the first ship of the second cycle of human history. In Books 7–9, the thalassocracy of Minos and the career of Hercules provide a chronological frame of reference. In book 9, Hercules ends his career while Minos grows old and his political power declines (9.439–49), illustrating the passage of time.[78]

In the final pentad of the poem, Ovid marks a new beginning with the foundation of Troy and the reign of Laomedon (11.199–204). This demarcation involves a break in chronological order and retrogression to an earlier time (hence the reappearance of Hercules), but it also marks the beginning of a new chronological sequence.[79] At the end of Book 11, an unidentified speaker gives the genealogy of Trojan royalty (11.755 *ordine perpetuo*) in which he introduces Priam as the successor of Laomedon (757–8): *Laomedonve senex Priamusque novissima Troiae/tempora sortitus*. Once again, Ovid establishes a chronological framework to orient the reader's sense of time. The phrase *novissima Troiae tempora* foreshadows the Trojan war and the fall of Troy that becomes the focus of narrative of Book 12 and 13, and so marks another clearly defined period of time.[80] Ovid looks for-

---

[77] Schmidt (1991), 45 n. 19, notes the history of Cadmus as an exception to his rule of there being no history in the *Metamorphoses*.

[78] Cf. Feeney (1999), 24, who observes that the pool of Salmacis is new early in the poem (4.284), but well known at the end of the poem (15.319). The speech of Pythagoras in Book 15 is particularly concerned with the changes wrought by the passage of time including the rise and fall of cities (15.420ff.).

[79] For a more detailed discussion of this point see Wheeler (1999) 135–9.

[80] Feeney (1999), 20, reads these lines as meaning that Troy has already fallen. The subsequent narrative of the Trojan war and fall of Troy is therefore a flashback and Ovid thereby makes the fall of Troy, which occurs in 13.404–5, 'entirely valueless as a secure foundation for the time-frame of the poem'.

ward to this phase of his universal history as early as Book 8, when he remarks that Nestor could have died during the Calydonian boar-hunt, if he had not pole-vaulted into a tree to avoid the boar's attack (8.365–6): *forsitan et Pylius citra Troiana perisset/tempora.*[81] In Book 9, Ovid likewise previews the future when Hercules hands Philoctetes the arrows that will see Troy a second time (9.232): *regnaque visuras iterum Troiana sagittas.*[82] Later, in Book 15, Pythagoras recalls that he was Euphorbus during the Trojan war (15.160–1): *ipse ego (nam memini) Troiani tempore belli/Panthoides Euphorbus eram.* The repeated references to the Trojan war and the fall of Troy throughout the *Metamorphoses* give it an epochal character, which is perfectly in keeping with historiography.[83]

Trojan times are succeeded by the migration of Aeneas to Italy. Although there is considerable temporal complexity in Ovid's little '*Aeneid*', it is clear that the events in the main narrative are chronologically subsequent to, if not motivated by, the Trojan war. Following the deification of Aeneas and the foundation of Alba Longa by his son Ascanius, the principle of chronological order becomes especially obvious as Ovid catalogues eleven Alban kings from Silvius to Proca (14.610–22), who bridge the four-hundred-year gap between Aeneas and Romulus.[84] At the end of the king-list, Ovid dates the story of Pomona to the reign of Proca (14.623 *rege sub hoc Pomona fuit*). After Pomona, Alban history is summarized, including the foundation of Rome, as a transition to Romulus's war with the Sabines and his deification.[85] In the latter scene, Mars announces to Jupiter that it is time to deify Romulus (14.808–9): *tempus adest, genitor, quoniam fundamine magno/res valet et praeside pendet ab uno.* The reign of Romulus forms a distinct period at the end Book 14, and the reign of Numa

---

[81] Later, during the Trojan war, Nestor reminds his audience that he has lived for two hundred years (*Met.* 12.187–8): '*vixi/annos bis centum; nunc tertia vivitur aetas*'. The alert reader will recognize that, according to Ovid, Nestor survived all those years thanks not to his courage but to his ability to flee.

[82] At this point in the poem, Ovid and his audience will assume that Troy has been founded, even though this will not be the case until Book 11.

[83] On the importance of the Trojan war as a point of chronological reference in Cato's *Origines* see Dionysius of Halicarnassus *AR* 1.74.2; cf. Feeney (1999) 16.

[84] Ovid's version of the king-list parallels (with some variations) Dionysius of Halicarnassus *AR* 1.71, Diodorus Siculus 7.3, Livy 1.3.6–9; cf. Vergil *Aen.* 6.756–70; Ovid *Fast.* 4.39–53. For discussion of the tradition of the Alban king-list see Bömer (1958) on *Fast.* 4.39, Ogilvie (1965) on Livy 1.3.6, Kyriakidis ch. 11 below.

[85] On the reasons for the suppression of Rome's foundation see Wheeler (2000) 111–4.

another at the beginning of Book 15. After Numa, Ovid's outline of Roman history becomes elliptical, as he leaves behind the list of kings and skips down to an unidentified point of time in the early Republic to relate the story of the legendary praetor Cipus. From there he springs to 292/1 B.C.E. to treat the translation of the cult of Aesculapius to Rome, and then to the assassination and deification of Julius Caesar in 44 B.C.E. Finally, Jupiter gives a historical summary in chronological order of the chief events in the reign of Augustus, ending with his adoption of Tiberius in 4 C.E. (15.819–37). In the final book of the *Metamorphoses*, Roman history and universal history are one in the same as the *urbs* becomes synonymous with the *orbis*.[86]

As the foregoing survey shows, the chronological structure of the *Metamorphoses* consists of more than a starting-point and end-point. The poem possesses an underlying chronological order that is based on genealogy, the succession of kings, and the sequence of events in mythology that would have been familiar from mythological handbooks and *chronica* such as that of Castor of Rhodes. It also has well-recognized points in time, such as Deucalion's flood and the Trojan war, that articulate time's progress.[87] The evidence for diachrony in the body of the poem suggests that Ovid's program to narrate a universal history in the proem is not unjustified. Some critics nevertheless dismiss the chronological framework of the poem on the grounds that it is not consistent enough (as though this were a regrettable failing on Ovid's part).[88]

One of the ways in which Ovid breaks up the chronological continuity of his narrative is to let his narrative travel through space rather than time. Like universal history, the *Metamorphoses* thus conveys a totalizing view of the world.[89] That is, instead of spinning out a series of tales in chronological order, it 'weaves in' events that take place in different parts of the world at the same time. Ovid's

---

[86] On book 15 as history see Hardie ch. 10 below.

[87] Here one may observe that Ovid includes precisely the temporal demarcations that Lucian identifies as starting-points for a universal history in *Rh. Pr.* 20 quoted in n. 12 above.

[88] Ovid knows better: *annales* were famously boring. On the tedium of chronological order see Heath (1989) 87. For praise of Ovid's chronological flexibility see Wilamowitz (1924) 1.243.

[89] For Ovid's geographic perspective in the *Metamorphoses* see Lyne (1999) 96–102; on spatial universality as a characteristic of universal history see Clarke (1999) 261–5.

transitions from one place to another are frequently based on a syn-chronism of events — a practice entirely in keeping with universal history. A few examples of synchronization will suffice to illustrate the point. In the transition between the stories of Daphne and Io in Book 1, the Ovidian narrator suggests that they took place at the same time. Io's father, Inachus, could not visit Daphne's father, Peneus, because he too had lost his daughter (1.568–87). Ovid thus switches his narrative focus from events in Thessaly to events in Argos. In Book 4, the exploits of Bacchus are synchronized with those of Perseus through the observation that both were in the sky at the same time (4.614–6 *inpositus iam caelo est alter, at alter/viperei referens spolium memorabile monstri/aera carpebat*). Later, in Book 6, Thebes mourns over the fate of Niobe, but the Athenian king Pandion can-not attend the funeral because the Thracian Tereus threatened him with war at the same time (6.412–23); so Ovid shifts the narrative from Thebes to Athens and Thrace. In Book 8, Ovid skillfully inter-weaves the narratives of Minos, Daedalus, and Theseus through syn-chronizing formulae (cf. 8.5 *interea*; 8.183 *interea*; 8.260–4 *iam . . . iam*). The transition between the stories of Byblis and Iphis in Book 9 is based on the fact that they take place at the same time in Miletus and Phaestus (9.666–8). At the beginning of Book 12, the meta-morphosis of Aesacus at Troy coincides with Paris's rape of Helen in Sparta and the launching of the Greek fleet at Aulis (12.1–10). In the final book of the poem, Ovid entertains the possibility that Numa was a student of Pythagoras (15.12–483), even though Roman historical authorities had rejected this particular synchronization of Roman and Greek history.[90] Ovid's alternation between diachronic and synchronic modes of continuation in the *Metamorphoses* has the effect of dissipating the linearity of time, but this should not dis-qualify the poem's concern with time or its universal historical pre-tensions. As we have seen, the universal histories of Diodorus and Trogus likewise sacrifice chronological order for the sake of a syn-chronic spatial perspective.

It is difficult to prove that Ovid knew the universal histories of either Diodorus or Trogus, but in the case of Diodorus there are some obvious parallels between the *Bibliotheca Historica* and the *Metamorphoses*.

---

[90] Cf. Livy 1.18.2; Cicero *Rep.* 2.27–9. For further discussion of this point see Feeney (1999) 22–4; cf. Wheeler (1999) 127–8.

In addition to their comparable chronological span, both works begin in similar ways. Ovid and Diodorus introduce their universal histories with a *diakrisis* type of cosmogony.[91] Both treat zoogony as a process of spontaneous generation from the earth. Both give a list of the kings of Alba to bridge the time between Aeneas and Romulus. Finally, Diodorus's treatment of myth concerns itself with cultural benefactors and their apotheosis, looking ahead to the apotheosis of Julius Caesar, which is mentioned several times (1.4.7; 4.19.2; 5.21.2, 25.4; 32.27.1–3). Ovid likewise devotes considerable attention to the apotheosis theme in the later books of his poem and indeed concludes with Julius Caesar's catasterism. All of these points in common may be coincidental, but they attest to overlapping areas of interest between the *Metamorphoses* and universal history.

One may conclude, then, that the *Metamorphoses* shares common ground with historiography both in its subject matter and in its arrangement. The dialogue between the *Metamorphoses* and the genre of universal history is perhaps inevitable. The universal historical tendency of epic poetry was present from Hesiod on and was valorized in the Augustan age by Vergil in his description of the idealized songs of Silenus (*Eclogues* 6.31ff.) and Clymene (*Georgics* 4.347 *aque Chaos et densos divum numerabat amores*), both of which constitute a poetic or mythological model for universal history in the tradition of the *Theogony* and *Catalogue of Women*.[92] Ovid's well-known allusion in the proem (1.4 *deducite . . . carmen*) to the *carmen deductum* exemplified by the song of Silenus (cf. *Eclogues* 6.3–5) implies the poetic affiliations of the *Metamorphoses* but at the same time suggests that a *carmen deductum* is an 'interwoven' universal history.[93] In order to compose such a poem, Hesiod was no longer a viable model and Vergil's catalogue-like descriptions of the songs of Silenus and Clymene could offer no guidance. Ennius's *Annales*, on the other hand, focused primarily on national history. The most accessible and current models for a large-scale universal history would have been historiographical. Despite the historical pretensions of the *Metamorphoses*, there remain two vital points of difference between it and the norm of universal history. First, contrary to Ludwig's reading of the *Metamorphoses* as a norma-

---

[91] Cf. Spoerri (1959) 34–8.
[92] Cf. Hardie (1986) 66–7, 83–4, Wheeler (2000) 54 n. 22.
[93] For the *carmen deductum*, see n. 23 above.

tive universal history (an interpretation introduced at the beginning of this paper) Ovid does not seek to reveal in history a deeper rationale such as divine providence that explains and justifies the rise of Roman hegemony in the Mediterranean world. As everyone by now knows, Ovid doggedly resists a teleogical account of history, emphasizing rather the randomness and improbabilities of fortune in divine and human affairs. This point of difference between the *Metamorphoses* and history entails another. The universal historian aims to offer a verisimilar and credible account of the history of the world and therefore tends to rewrite myths in a rationalizing and euhemerizing vein. Ovid moves in the opposite direction. He composes a poetic universal history that entertains the fabulous and divine dimensions of myth.[94] Even historical events in the *Metamorphoses*, such as the assassination and deification of Julius Caesar, are dressed up as supernatural phenomena manipulated by the gods. If the historian can rationalize myth, Ovid's answer is that the poet has the power to mythologize history. In the case of the *Metamorphoses*, all of history is mythologized, from beginning to end.[95]

---

[94] For this crucial difference between the ways that epic and history treat myth see Feeney (1991) 260–2.

[95] This is a revised version of the paper I gave in Durham on September 1, 1999. I would like to thank David Levene, Damien Nelis, and those members of the audience who took an interest in the paper and raised questions about it. I am also grateful to Denis Feeney, who let me see Feeney (1999) before it appeared in print, and to Paul Harvey, Jim O'Hara, and Tony Woodman for reading earlier drafts and giving helpful comments. Finally, acknowledgment is due the Alexander von Humboldt Foundation for providing generous research support while I prepared this piece for publication under the auspices of the Seminar for Classical Philology at the Free University Berlin.

CHAPTER TEN

THE HISTORIAN IN OVID. THE ROMAN HISTORY OF *METAMORPHOSES* 14–15

Philip Hardie

Ovid writes the long historical epic that Virgil self-consciously had abjured. To call this repository of mythological marvels a *historical* epic might seem to fly in the face of common sense. But the compact four-line prologue signals, among other things, that we are embarking on a historical *magnum opus*, a point that Stephen Wheeler has recently brought into sharp focus, developing Walther Ludwig's classification of the poem as one of the universal histories that enjoyed a vogue in the Augustan period.[1] Ovid's work will stretch from the beginning of the world to the poet's own times; Diodorus Siculus, following the historiographical convention of defining the starting and end points in a historical proem,[2] marks the limits of his *Bibliotheke* as (1.3.6) 'from the most ancient times ... until our own times'. Most importantly, Wheeler shows that the two words that have been the obsessive focus of interest for those scholars who see the definition of the *Metamorphoses* primarily in terms of Callimachean or non-Callimachean poetry, namely *perpetuus* and *deducere*, are firmly at home in historiographical contexts: *perpetuus* is used to define continuous histories as opposed to monographs; and *deducere* is used of leading historical narrative from one point to another. This combination, within the same lexical items, of Callimachean poetics and historiographical terminology, neatly reinforces a recent observation by Denis Feeney, that if we read Catullus' first, programmatic, poem from an Ovidian angle, it becomes clear that the *Metamorphoses* is both Catullus (it is *novus*) and Nepos (like his *Chronica* it is a work that covers *omne aevum*, the product of *doctrina* and *labor*).[3] This seemingly paradoxical

---

[1] Ludwig (1965) 78–80; Wheeler (1999) 22–4; cf. also Wheeler ch. 9 above.
[2] Herkommer (1968) 65ff., cited by Wheeler (1999) 215 n. 39.
[3] Feeney (1999) 14.

combination is already written into Catullus' first poem, for the neo-teric poet is as jealous of his *doctrina* and *labor* as is the author of the *Chronica*, and Catullus' closing wish that his trifling *libellus* should *plus uno maneat perenne saeclo*, alludes to the subject matter, *anni* and *saecla*, of Nepos' chronographical work. And, as Feeney points out, *perennis* is used by Ovid of his own pretension to immortality in the epilogue to *Metamorphoses* at 15.875. In the light of this paradoxical convergence of the projects of Catullus and Nepos one might ask if Catullus' self-deprecation about his 'trifles' did not pick up on an apologetic tone in Nepos' own preface, that might be paralleled in the diffident modesty of Livy's preface.[4]

One might be hard-pressed to find a serious engagement with his-toriographical traditions in Catullus, although a start could be made by reading poem 64 as an elliptical sketch of a *perpetuum carmen* from remote mythical times *ad mea tempora*, a universal history marked by a Sallustian pessimism, in contrast to the, at least superficial, pro-gressivism of Ovid's historical world-view in the *Metamorphoses*. With the latter might be compared very generally the progressivism of Virgil's fourth *Eclogue*, a poem which is an extended 'imitation through opposition' of Catullus 64, and which operates by reversing a Hesiodic scheme of universal history.[5] But there is no doubt of the interest shown by the Roman Alexandrian poets' hero, Callimachus, in the Greek historiographical traditions, for example in the Herodotean allusions of the *Aitia* prologue, or in the footnoting of the source for the Acontius and Cydippe story in the history of Xenomedes of Ceos. A recent Italian commentator on Callimachus notes that 'with a light virtuosity, [he] makes the whole mythical history of Ceos into a summary appendix to the narrative of the erotic adventures of the two young people'.[6] One could compare the way in which Ovid's Alban king list at *Metamorphoses* 14.609–21, completed at 772–4, a perfunctory means of leading the *perpetuum carmen* down from the death of Aeneas to the foundation of Rome, frames the leisurely erotic narrative of Vertumnus and Pomona.[7]

---

[4] Moles (1993) 140 (but noting that 'Livy's apparent diffidence is strikingly at variance with the historiographical norm'). Catullus overtly predicates of Nepos the *audacia* (1.5 *ausus es*) required of high literary endeavour: cf. Livy *Praef.* 1 *ausim*. For a combination of self-deprecation (through synkrisis with a greater endeavour) and literary *audacia* see the sphragis to the *Georgics*.

[5] On the 'history' embodied in *Ecl.* 4 see also Marinčič ch. 8 above.

[6] D'Alessio (1996) 486 n. 77.

[7] On this section see Kyriakidis ch. 11 below.

Even the semi-titular first two words of the *Metamorphoses, in nova,* can on a first reading be taken historiographically: Andrew Feldherr suggests that the words 'point forward to the overall chronological schema of his work'.[8] *in nova fert animus,* 'my spirit leads to recent things'. Compare Livy *praefatio* 4: *et legentium plerisque haud dubito quin* **primae origines** *proximaque originibus minus praebitura voluptatis sint, festinantibus* **ad haec noua** *quibus iam pridem praevalentis populi vires se ipsae conficiunt.* Feldherr raises the further point that the equivocation in the word *nova* between 'strange, miraculous' and 'recent, up to date' challenges the conventional distinction between *fabula* and *historia* (cf. Livy 1.6); this is one of the many areas where Ovid explores and tests the limits of poetic and historical authority.[9]

This essay focuses on the 'Roman history' which occupies the last 80 lines of book 14, and book 15 of the *Metamorphoses*. The fifteen books of the *Metamorphoses* match the fifteen books of the first edition of Ennius' historical epic, but of course Ovid only catches up with the material of the *Annales* in *his* thirteenth book (Aeneas' departure from Troy), and does not reach the central Roman matter of Ennius until towards the end of the fourteenth book. That book ends with the apotheosis of Romulus, as had the first book of the *Annales*. Correspondingly, both *Annales* 2 and *Metamorphoses* 15 begin with the accession and reign of Numa. But to bring the story *ad mea tempora* Ovid has not only to accelerate, but to overtake Ennius. He makes a virtue of this necessity by making his last book into a kind of microcosm of the whole of Ennius' *Annales*: the Speech of Pythagoras is a greatly expanded version of the Pythagorean Speech of Homer to Ennius in the proem of the *Annales*, while the epilogue to book 15 reworks motifs from Ennius' epitaph for himself, and possibly also elements from the passage near the beginning of *Annales* 16 which contrasted 'the transient nature of fame based on the monuments with the eternal glory which [Ennius'] poetry would bestow on his heroes'.[10] This passage formed part of the proemial material in the three-book extension to the first edition of the *Annales*, but will also have formed a retrospective reflection on the achievement of the first fifteen books of the first edition.[11] Further beginnings of a Roman

---

[8] See Feldherr (forthcoming).
[9] See Marincola (1997) 117–27 'Myth and history'; but cf. also Wiseman ch. 17 below.
[10] Skutsch (1985) 568.
[11] The passage is also alluded to in another of Ovid's models for his epilogue, Horace *Odes* 3.30.

narrative are allusively contained in the apparently very Greek, very
Callimachean story of Myscelos and the foundation of Croton at the
beginning of *Metamorphoses* 15. This is not only modelled in some
detail on the *Aeneid*'s central narrative of a city-founding exile,[12] but
the very Ennian description of nightfall at 30–1 echoes specifically
the description of sunset and sunrise preceding the auspice of Romulus
(*Ann.* 84–5, 87 Skutsch).[13]

The story of Myscelos thus supplies the foundation narrative that
had conspicuously been elided in book 14 of the *Metamorphoses*, where
both of the key founders in Roman legendary history, Aeneas and
Romulus, had passed across the stage but without extended accounts
of their founding activities. In terms of prose classifications *Metamorphoses*
15 can thus be read, allusively, as a free-standing example of an *ab
urbe condita* history of Rome. But as an exercise in miniaturization,
Metamorphoses 15 also challenges Virgilian exercises in pouring Ennian
quarts into pint-pots: firstly the two parts, taken together, of the
Speech of Anchises in Book 6 of the *Aeneid*, reaching from an allusive reworking of the proemial Dream of Homer in the *Annales* to
the latest triumphs of Roman history; and secondly the history of
Rome displayed on the Shield of Aeneas in Book 8. Viewed against
these precedents, *Metamorphoses* 15 appears as something of a hybrid:
true to the poem's overall project of a linear chronology, Book 15
has the sequential structure of the Shield of Aeneas, where, as Tony
Woodman has pointed out, the words *in ordine* (*Aen.* 8.629) signal the
historiographical affiliations of the Virgilian Shield;[14] on the other
hand the actual experience of reading *Metamorphoses* 15 is more that
of a parade of individual 'heroes', Numa, Pythagoras, Virbius, Cipus,
Aesculapius, Julius Caesar, Augustus, all in one way or another of
exemplary quality.

Metamorphoses 15 may also be compared to the Shield of Aeneas
in respect of its leap from a point in mid-Republican history, the
introduction of Aesculapius to Rome in 291 B.C., to recent history,
the death and apotheosis of Julius Caesar. The Virgilian Shield leaps
from the Gallic attack on the Capitol in 387 B.C. to the Battle of
Actium. The result in both cases is the 'hourglass effect' that Badian

---

[12] Hardie (1997) 195–6.
[13] Possibly with a further echo at 39 *o cui ius* **caeli bis sex** *fecere labores* of *Ann.* 88
cedunt **de caelo ter quattuor** *corpora sancta*: different ways of saying 'twelve' in epic.
[14] Woodman (1989) 132–4.

has noted in early Roman annalistic historians,[15] the tendency to concentrate on remote and recent Roman history, eliminating or attenuating the narrative of the intervening stretch of time. Note further how Ovid introduces his account of the apotheosis of Julius Caesar as a parallel to the introduction to Rome of the god Aesculapius; on the Shield of Aeneas the salvation of Rome from the barbarian hordes of the east at Actium is the antitype of the city's close shave with the northern barbarians in the early fourth century B.C.[16]

Peter Knox has argued that the chief literary affiliation of *Metamorphoses* 15 is with Callimachean aetiology.[17] The book is clearly engaged in dialogue with the other major work on which Ovid was working at the same time as the *Metamorphoses*, the *Fasti*, which might be described as a Roman *Aitia*. There is more than one way to understand Ovid's programme of spinning a narrative down to the first word of the *Fasti*, *tempora*: 'towards the *genre* of my *Fasti*' could be one of them. Fritz Graf has pointed out that the *Metamorphoses* is notably thin on religious and cultic aitia *until* Ovid comes down in time to Roman history.[18] But it would be wrong simply to collapse the Roman episodes of the *Metamorphoses* into an aetiological category; a long narrative poem should preserve its distance from Callimachus, and in any case one would expect that a hexameter poem that challenges both Ennius' *Annales* and Virgil's *Aeneid* would take them on on their own ground of incorporating elements of the prose historiographical traditions.

To look briefly at the use of historiography in the two earlier Latin epics: Ennius' *Annales* have a special place in Roman historiography, as the first work in Latin in either prose or verse to cover the whole span of Roman history. But Ennius will have read Fabius Pictor, and perhaps others of the Greek-language historians of Rome, and will also have consulted the public records for the appointment of magistrates.[19] In one fragment we catch Ennius not only using a prose source, but giving the allusive colour of that source, in the description of an eclipse (153 Skutsch): *Nonis Iunis soli luna obstitit et*

---

[15] Badian (1966) 11; see also Wallace-Hadrill (1987) 226 on the clustering of festivals in the *Fasti* towards the Augustan and legendary, esp. Romulan, eras.

[16] Hardie (1986) 124–5.

[17] Knox (1986) ch. 5.

[18] Graf (1988) 61–2. See also Myers (1994) ch. 3 '*Metamorphoses* 14–15: Italy and aetiological metamorphosis'.

[19] Skutsch (1986) 7.

nox, which echoes the official terminology of the *Annales Maximi*, as preserved in the report at Aulus Gellius *Noctes Atticae* 2.28.6 of Cato's refusal to mention *quod in tabula apud pontificem maximum est . . . quoties lunae aut solis lumini caligo aut quid obstiterit.*

Virgil's use of the historians is much more visible. Epic and historiographical sources are inextricably intertwined in *Aeneid* 2, as demonstrated by the difficulty in deciding the exact lines of influence that connect Virgil's, Ennius', Livy's, and the early annalists', accounts of the sacks of Troy and Alba Longa.[20] Virgil draws on the latest, as well as the earliest, documents of the Roman historiographical tradition: John Moles has pointed to his probable use of Pollio's history of the civil war in the description of the vast headless trunk of Priam (*Aeneid* 2.557–8), foreshadowing the fate of Pompey the Great,[21] and it is generally accepted that some at least of the parallels between Virgil and Livy point to the poet's use, and critique, of the historian.[22] If Ovid sets out to overgo the *Aeneid*, we might expect an *aggiornamento* in the form of allusion to prose historical texts later than those drawn on by Virgil, including the later books of Livy.

Can we then see Ovid in *Metamorphoses* 15 playing the role of a Livian kind of historian, instead of, or as well as, that of a 'Roman Callimachus', as Peter Knox would have it? At first sight the signs are not promising. A table of contents of the book runs as follows: a Greek founder of a Greek city; a meeting between a Roman king and a Greek philosopher, whose historical impossibility is the subject of an excursus in Livy (1.18.2–4), as well as in Cicero's *De re publica* (2.28–30); a very long speech by that same Greek philosopher on natural-philosophical and paradoxographical topics; the after-life in an Italian rural sanctuary of a famous character from Greek tragedy, and the inconsolable grief of a Roman queen who melts into water. By one of Ovid's most obtrusively artificial transitional procedures this transformation is linked to other examples of 'believe it or not': an Etruscan seer who starts life as a clod of earth, a spear of Romulus that suddenly sprouts leaves, and a murky Roman general who sud-

---

[20] See Austin on *Aen.* 2.486ff.; also Austin on 2.195–8 ('a postscript . . . in the historical manner'); 2.554–8 ('*hic exitus*: a formula . . . very close to the historians' manner'); Woodman (1989) on *Aen.* 8.626–62; Horsfall (1991) 45 on the use of Herodotus 4 in *Aen.* 3; 112–14 on use of Varro; (1999) on *Aen.* 7.37.
[21] Moles (1983).
[22] See esp. Woodman (1989).

denly sprouts horns. It is perhaps with some relief that, only some
250 lines from the end of the book, we come to a genuinely historical
episode, the introduction to Rome from Epidaurus in 291 B.C. of
a cult of Aesculapius, even if this historical episode is introduced by
Ovid's only invocation in the whole poem to the Muses of *poetry*,[23]
and even if we are treated to the spectacle of a snake behaving like
a rather dignified human being. Jumping in one bound virtually *ad
mea tempora* (the year of his conception, to be precise, a fact whose
significance will be drawn out below), Ovid has only time for one
further historical event, the death and apotheosis of Julius Caesar,
wrapped up in a mixture of epic divine machinery and fulsome panegyric. Notably lacking in Ovid's 'Roman history' are such things
as the wars with the other peoples of Italy, internal political conflicts,
and the great wars with external enemies.

Bronwen Wickkiser suggests one way to put back the historical
into this narrative, precisely by focussing on the element of the mar-
vellous and supernatural, which may be compared to the prodigy-
lists of the Roman annalistic tradition.[24] Another way would be to
consider the way in which a historian like Livy shapes and articu-
lates his narrative by imposing various kinds of pattern on his material, thus establishing what Chris Kraus describes as the 'system of
cross-references among characters and actions both throughout the
AVC and outside it, i.e. with other histories'.[25] I have already adverted
to the general outline of a summary Roman history in *Metamorphoses*
15; within this is there a shaping hand at work? One recurrent theme
is that of mortal crisis successfully overcome, accompanied by imagery
of rebirth or of healing. Pythagoras, the exile from his home city,
may stand almost as a personification of rebirth, floating free of
specific historical or political contexts. We then meet Virbius, for-
merly the Greek Hippolytus, who faces his gruesomely violent death
with the equanimity of a Roman or Stoic hero,[26] to be reborn as
an Italian *vir*, if paradoxically one who lurks in a sacred grove in
the countryside. His rebirth is an act of healing at the hands of
Aesculapius; a beneficiary of the Greek god's arts is thus naturalized

---

[23] Barchiesi (1997a) 187–8.
[24] Wickkiser (1999) 132 n. 56, with other reflections on the connections between
the *Met.* and prose history at 130–2.
[25] Kraus (1994) 14–15.
[26] Gildenhard and Zissos (1999) 176–81.

on Italian soil. Aesculapius himself comes from Greece to heal the literal plague in Rome; the abrupt juxtaposition of the installation of Aesculapius as a god in Rome with the apotheosis of Julius Caesar, consequent on a murder which issues from and ushers in civil strife, activates the common image of civil war as plague.[27] This medico-political imagery in the last book forms a ring with its use by Jupiter in the Council of Gods in the first book, in the context of an attempt on his life that is compared in the poem's first simile to an attack on the person of Caesar, and hence on the cohesion of the Roman world as a whole (1.190−1): *cuncta prius temptata, sed immedicabile corpus | ense recidendum est.* Jupiter's *remedium*, the Flood, is of a kind particularly hard to endure, and we might remember Livy's complaint that he lived in a time when (*praef.* 9) *nec vitia nostra nec remedia pati possumus.*

If Ovid does have in mind Livy's use of the common medical image, in *Metamorphoses* 15 he puts it to an unLivian use. Livy never replaced the pessimism of his preface, itself a reflection of the early years of Augustus' career, with an unqualified panegyric of the regime. Ovid pays lip service, at least, to an alternative way of conceiving history as *Heilsgeschichte*, as Virgil had paid lip service, at least, to this scheme of historical crisis and salvation when the disaster of a universal plague at the end of the third *Georgic* is superseded by the rebirth of the society of bees at the end of the fourth book. Ovid's correction of the Sallustian and Livian trajectory of rise and decline (for Sallust into a bestial enslavement to the passions and appetites) is in keeping with the movement in the last books of the *Metamorphoses* away from a relentless catalogue of descent through metamorphosis into the bestial or worse, to a closing sequence of upward meta-morphoses, as man reveals his capacity to draw close to the divine.

If the ideology is unLivian, the pattern of cross-referencing between the several episodes in *Metamorphoses* 15 is generally comparable to Livy's procedure. For Ovid this is, of course, business as usual: the whole of the *Metamorphoses* works like this, and one reason for this is that the whole of the *Aeneid* works like this. As Kraus notes 'Livy's procedure resembles Virgil's'.[28] One effect *within* the *Metamorphoses* is to further erode any possibility of drawing a sharp distinction between the worlds of *fabula* and *historia*. From this point of view there is no

---

[27] Schmitzer (1990) 276–7.
[28] Kraus (1994) 14 n. 61.

paradox in introducing the reader to Roman history proper with an invocation to the Muses.

Can we find any more specific *points de repère* to Livy in *Metamorphoses* 15? One place to look might be the introduction of Aesculapius in 291 B.C., which as we have seen is a pivotal episode in the structure of Ovid's Roman history. It is intriguing, but perhaps no more, that Livy's account of this episode occupied a marked position within his *History*, straddling the divide between books ten and eleven, between the first and second decades, and between second and third pentads. Stadter argues, against Syme, that Livy's tenth book is built up to a climax to mark the end of a decade, but it must be admitted that the brief account of the plague at the end of the book does not obviously contribute to a climactic structure.[29] We might do better to look at the final episode in *Metamorphoses* 15. Why does the narrative proper stop where it does, some 50 years before the time of writing, in 44 B.C.? On Livy's original plan the 120 books of his *History* came down to 43 B.C. — the year of Ovid's birth.[30] Book 120 included an epitaphion for Cicero, possibly the significant closural moment of the book, of the decade (111–20 then took the reader from Pharsalia to the death of the last fighter for the Republic),[31] and of the *Ab urbe condita*. The Livian epitaphion is preserved by the elder Seneca (*Suasoriae* 6.22), a balanced assessment of Cicero's strengths and weaknesses: it concludes *vir magnus ac memorabilis fuit et in cuius laudes exequendas Cicerone laudatore opus fuerit*, but not before observing of his death that *vere aestimanti minus indigna videri potuit, quod a victore <nihil> crudelius passus erat quam quod eiusdem fortunae compos ipse fecisset*.

---

[29] Stadter (1972) 294. Oakley (1997) 111–12 is sceptical on the structural significance of the end of book 10; 112 'Whether books vi–x should be regarded as a unit is rather doubtful, since the continuation of the Third Samnite War makes no real break in subject matter between books x and xi.' If the introduction of Aesculapius was treated in Ennius *Annales*, it would have fallen at the end of book 5 — evidence for composition of the *Annales* by pentads? A break was marked at the beginning of *Annales* 6 by a proem, whose probable first line (164 Skutsch) *quis potis ingentis oras evolvere belli* will, on the evidence of *Aen.* 9.528, have been followed by a prayer to the Muses (Skutsch (1985) 329).

[30] Note that Varro's *De gente populi Romani* was probably completed in 43 B.C. (Feeney (1999) 14), the date alluded to in fr. 9. Taylor (1934) 221–9 argues that it was a piece of Caesarian propaganda, producing Greek and Roman precedents for the deification of a human being, countering Cicero's objections that the bill adding a day in Caesar's honour to all the festivals of the gods was contrary to Roman precedent (*Phil.* 1.13).

[31] Stadter (1972) 298–9.

But more extravagant versions of Cicero's epitaph are to be found in the rhetorical and historiographical traditions,[32] notably in the considerations urged by Ovid's own rhetorical teacher, Arellius Fuscus, in his *suasoria* to Cicero urging him not to beg for Antony's pardon. Arellius offers Cicero the twofold consolation for physical death that Cicero himself had elaborated at length in book one of the *Tusculan Disputations*, the immortality of fame and the immortality of the soul (Seneca *Suasoriae* 6.5–6):

> immortalis humanorum operum custos memoria, qua magnis viris vita perpetua est, in omnia te saecula sacratum dabit; nihil aliud intercidet quam corpus fragilitatis caducae, morbis obnoxium, casibus expositum, proscriptionibus obiectum; animus vero divina origine haustus, cui nec senectus ulla nec mors, onerosi corporis vinculis exsolutus ad sedes suas et cognata sidera recurret.

> Memory, undying guardian of human works, through which great men attain to eternal life, will hand you down to all future generations, sacrosanct. Nothing will die except the body, frail and fleeting, subject to disease, exposed to chance, open to proscription; the soul, which is drawn from divine origins, and knows neither old age nor death, will be freed from the shackles of the body that burdens it and dart back to its home, the stars to which it is akin.
>
> (Trans. M. Winterbottom)

This double immortality, through personal survival and through fame, is that proclaimed by Ovid for himself in the epilogue to the *Metamorphoses*. His *melior pars*, in contrast to his body, i.e. his soul, will survive, echoing the vigorous expansion of Hercules' *melior pars* after the sloughing off of his body at *Metamorphoses* 9.268–70; and his *nomen* will also be indelible. Compare also the language used by Arellius Fuscus in his second bite at the cherry, in the *suasoria* urging Cicero not to burn his writings in return for Antony's promise of his life (Seneca *Suasoriae* 7.8):

> quoad humanum genus incolume manserit, quamdiu suus litteris honor, suum eloquentiae pretium erit, quamdiu rei publicae nostrae aut fortuna steterit aut memoria duraverit, admirabile posteris vigebit ingenium <tuum> ... crede mihi, **vilissima pars** tui est quae tibi vel eripi vel donari potest; ille verus est Cicero quem proscribi Antonius non putat nisi a Cicerone posse [i.e. Cicero's writings].

---

[32] On the declamation tradition see recently Roller (1997), arguing that declamations on the death of Cicero started early and exercised a decisive influence on the historiographical tradition.

So long as the human race survives, so long as literature has the honour due to it, eloquence its reward, so long as the fortune of our country holds or its memory is preserved, your genius shall flourish in the
admiration of posterity. . . . Believe me, it is the least valuable part of
you that can be taken from you or granted to you. The true Cicero
is the one who Antony thinks can be only be proscribed by Cicero.
                                                    (Trans. M. Winterbottom)

The last word of the *Metamorphoses*, *vivam*, can be paralleled in many
places, including the praise of Scipio Aemilianus that Cicero himself
places in the mouth of Laelius at *De amicitia* 102, *Scipio quamquam est
subito ereptus, vivit tamen semperque vivet*. This is echoed in a slightly later
example of the epitaphion for Cicero, at Velleius Paterculus 2.66.5:

> vivit vivetque per omnem saeculorum memoriam dumque hoc vel forte
> vel providentia vel utcumque constitutum rerum naturae corpus, quod
> ille paene solus Romanorum animo vidit, ingenio complexus est, elo-
> quentia inluminavit, manebit incolume, comitem aevi sui laudem
> Ciceronis trahet omnisque posteritas illius in te scripta mirabitur, tuum
> in eum factum execrabitur citiusque e mundo genus hominum quam
> Ciceronis nomen cedet.

> He lives and will continue to live in the memory of the ages, and so
> long as this universe shall endure — this universe which, whether cre-
> ated by chance, or by divine providence, or by whatever cause, he,
> almost alone of all the Romans, saw with the eye of his mind, grasped
> with his intellect, illumined with his eloquence — so long shall it be
> accompanied throughout the ages by the fame of Cicero. All poster-
> ity will admire the speeches that he wrote against you, while your deed
> to him will call forth their execrations, and the race of man shall
> sooner pass from the world than the name of Cicero be forgotten.
>   (Trans. F. W. Shipley)

Interesting in the Ovidian context is the use here of the 'eyes of the
mind' topos with reference to insight into natural philosophy, which
is also applied to Pythagoras' flight of the mind at *Metamorphoses*
15.62–4. There are close connections between the abilities of Pythagoras
and of the disembodied Ovid to rise above mortal limitations; in
Ovid's time did the Ciceronian epitaphion tradition already include
the image of Cicero as the immortal natural philosopher?
    The Ovidian epilogue is a densely woven tissue of clichés and
commonplaces, with multiple specific allusions. Among everything
else I want to suggest that there is an emphatic Ciceronian resonance. *mea tempora* not only implies a challenge to Augustus (I, Ovid,
dominate this age as much as you, Augustus), but also a comparison with the leading man of letters who died in the year that Ovid

was born — and who among other things had written a hexameter poem with the title *De temporibus suis*.[33] The Ciceronian age of Roman literary culture is replaced by the Ovidian. Livy's Roman history ended with the death of Cicero in 43 B.C. Ovid's narrative of Roman history ends with the events of 44 B.C. the death and reanimation of Julius Caesar — to be followed in 43 by the birth of Ovid. To this, naturally, Ovid does not allude overtly, and instead looks forward to two deaths in prospect, firstly that of Augustus, but in final position that of the poet himself. If the *Metamorphoses* tracks the Livian narrative, the place of the death of Cicero is occupied firstly by the unexpressed event of 43, the birth of Ovid (implying a literary succession — or even rebirth?), and secondly by the expressed death of Ovid at an unspecified future date.

Two further considerations may reinforce the case for excavating a Ciceronian space within the Ovidian epilogue. Firstly, Cicero played a crucial role in asserting 'Der Triumph des Geistes' in Buchheit's phrase, the 'triumph of the intellect' over the achievements of the man of action or politician, the superiority of *animus* over *corpus*.[34] The synkrisis between man of action and man of letters is implied in Ovid's juxtaposition of his prospective apotheosis with that of Augustus. Secondly, Ovid was to appropriate a Ciceronian afterlife for himself in his exile poetry, where Cicero's exile, and other stages in the Ciceronian career, including his death, form an important part of his self-fashioning.[35] There are, of course, those who uphold a post-exilic date for the epilogue of the *Metamorphoses*.

The last historical event to be narrated in *Metamorphoses* 15 took place in 44 B.C. But Ovid's Roman history does continue beyond this — in the future tense, in Jupiter's recitation to Venus of what he has read in the Public Records Office of Fate (15.807–39). Lines

---

[33] There may be further Ciceronian ventriloquism in the catalogue of portents that presage the death of Caesar at *Met.* 15.782–98; the earliest surviving Latin epic catalogue of portents happens to come from Cicero's other poem on his achievements, the *Cons.* (2.1–46 Soubiran). Another specimen of the Ciceronian epitaphion tradition is found in Tullius Laurea's elegy on the hot springs that burst forth at Cicero's villa near Puteoli shortly after its owner's death (Plin. *Nat.* 31.6), appropriately with healing powers for eyes that might read Cicero's works, 9–10 *ut, quoniam totum legitur sine fine per orbem,* | *sint plures oculis quae medeantur aquae*; Ovid anticipates a worldwide readership at *Met.* 15.877–8 (cf. also *Am.* 1.15.8).

[34] Buchheit (1969).

[35] Nagle (1980) 33–5; Fuchs (1969) 159–60. The description of the dismemberment of Absyrtus at *Tr.* 3.9.29–30 *neu pater ignoret, scopulo proponit in alto* | *pallentesque*

822–39 contain the longest and densest historical passage in the whole poem, covering a span of time from the siege of Mutina in 43 B.C. and extending beyond the date of the poem's composition to the apotheosis of Augustus. The immediate model is the consolatory Speech of Jupiter to Venus in Book 1 of the *Aeneid*. In a sense what Jupiter has been reading is not the Three Sisters' imperishable inscriptions on Olympus, but the immortal Roman poet (just as what Mars remembers at the end of the previous book is the Ennian Council of the Gods at which Jupiter promised the apotheosis of Romulus).[36] But the details of the script that Jupiter has been reading are not Virgilian. Jupiter/Ovid here ventriloquises for one very special Roman historian, the emperor himself, the terms of whose *Res Gestae* are echoed at various points, most strikingly at 15.832–4:

> pace data terris animum ad civilia vertet
> iura suum legesque feret iustissimus auctor
> exemploque suo mores reget . . .

> When peace has been bestowed upon the world,
> Turning his thoughts to civil rights, he'll show
> Justice and equity in law-giving
> And by his own example guide men's ways.
> (Trans. A. D. Melville)

Compare *Res Gestae* 8.5:

> legibus novis me auctore latis multa exempla maiorum exolescentia
> iam ex nostro saeculo reduxi et ipse multarum rerum exempla imi
> tanda posteris tradidi.[37]

> By the new laws passed on my proposal I brought back into use many
> exemplary practices of our ancestors which were disappearing in our
> time, and in many ways I myself transmitted exemplary practices to
> posterity for their imitation.
> (Trans. P. A. Brunt and J. M. Moore)

---

manus sanguineumque caput recalls the mutilation of Cicero's corpse, hinting at Augustus playing a persecutory Medea role: Oliensis (1997), drawing on Schubert (1990). Ovid's recurrent protestation that he was undone by an *error*, not a *crimen*, has precedent in Cicero's self-justification to Caesar for having followed the Pompeian cause, *Marc.* 13 *etsi aliqua culpa tenemur erroris humani, ab scelere certe liberati sumus*: Marchetti (1999) 151.

[36] *notavi* is used of the mental note taken both by Mars (14.813) and Jupiter (15.814).

[37] Jupiter's reading of *RG*: Schmitzer (1990) 286–7; see also 183–6 on parallels

This is not the only passage in which Ovid comes strikingly close to the content and language of the *Res Gestae*. Janet Fairweather has pointed to the numerous correspondences between Ovid's autobiographical poem, *Tristia* 4.10, and the biography of Augustus, with detailed parallels in the *Res Gestae*, whether that text itself, or Augustus' lost autobiography, is the actual source for Ovid's words.[38] Incidentally, *Tristia* 4.10 also provides a parallel for allusion to **both** Augustus **and** Cicero at the end of *Metamorphoses* 15, for, as Harold Fuchs shows, the terms in which Ovid gives thanks to the Muse who consoles him in exile, as (118–19) *curae requies, medicina, dux*, echo Ciceronian praises of philosophy.[39]

The extant version of the *Res Gestae* was completed by Augustus in his seventy-sixth year, and scholars differ as to the likely existence and availability of earlier versions.[40] I note only the following: that Ovid's records of fate are inscribed (*incisa*) on adamant in a record office of bronze and iron; the *Res Gestae* were inscribed on two bronze pillars (Preamble, *incisarum in duabus aheneis pilis*), a monumental epitaph. The closing prayer in *Metamorphoses* 15 asks that Augustus' accession to the heavens be long delayed; but Jupiter's prophecy has already reached down to that death, thus making of the whole of his account of the career of Octavian/Augustus a proleptic obituary notice.[41]

Jupiter reads out the *Res Gestae Augusti* in order to dissuade Venus from her attempt to prevent the assassination of Julius by whisking him off in a cloud. The ultimate model for one god warning another not to meddle with fate is Hera's reminder to Zeus that Sarpedon is fated to die (*Iliad* 16.439–57), imitated by Virgil in Jupiter's more kindly words to Hercules on the fated death of Pallas (*Aen.* 10.466–72). But Ovid's version is also the point at which the world of epic *fabula* comes up against the world of *historia*. Venus attempts to follow

---

between the *RG* and Hercules' summary list of his achievements at *Met.* 9.182ff.; Rehork (1965) 454–5, with n. 430 (summary of the correspondences).

[38] Fairweather (1987).

[39] Fuchs (1969).

[40] It is generally agreed that a first draft will have been completed by 2 B.C. at the latest: Brunt and Moore (1967) 6.

[41] Wheeler (1999) 57 on the text that Jupiter has read: 'Like the *RG*, or a funeral monument, it is an elaborate epitaph — a substitute for the absence of the dead or deified'.

her own, Iliadic, examples of whisking off Paris and Aeneas, but the Homeric book has to give place to the Big Book of Augustan history. Is it significant that when Venus takes her stand in the Roman senate house in order to snatch not the living body, as she had done in the case of Paris (805), but the soul of Julius, she is *nulli cernenda* (844)? Because in the world of history we do not see gods descending to earth?[42] If so, Ovid gestures towards the distinction between myth and history that, as we have seen, he elsewhere seeks to efface.

Lucian, at *De historia conscribenda* 49, compares the ideal historian to Zeus, surveying the whole world and looking down impartially on events on earth. In an epic Zeus or Jupiter is also a figure for the epic poet himself, through the inspiration of the Muses omnipresent and omniscient, leading the thread of his narrative down to a satisfying conclusion. But is Ovid's Roman history in *Metamorphoses* 15 as unidirectional and univocal as Jupiter would have us believe? One potential point of fracture is the notion of the *exemplum*. Augustus will rule through example (836 *exemploque suo mores reget*), a conventional topos of imperial panegyric,[43] and another coincidence between the functions of ruler and historian, with the difference that an Augustus offers himself as an *exemplum*, rather than recording *exempla* in the past for imitation. But examples cannot always be followed, as Venus finds out in this episode. One of the ways in which the story of Hippolytus is transferred to Italian soil earlier in the book, as Ingo Gildenhard and Andrew Zissos have pointed out, is by making of the Greek tragic myth a Roman *exemplum*.[44] Virbius offers his own sufferings to Egeria as an *exemplum* that will mitigate her own grief, but this is a spectacular case of failed exemplarity,[45] for Egeria will set no limit to her grief. This does not bode well for the future history of Roman exemplarity. Furthermore *exemplum* may be met by counter-*exemplum*. On one point Ovid begs to differ from Augustus' version of events (the version in which Augustus' own person is the supreme *exemplum*), in the matter of the comparison between the *princeps* and his father. Augustus forbids his own *acta* to be elevated above those of Julius Caesar. The poet counters by using mythical

---

[42] By contrast at *Fast.* 3.701 Vesta claims *ipsa virum rapui*.
[43] Woodman (1977) on Velleius Paterculus 2.126.5.
[44] Gildenhard and Zissos (1999) 182–3.
[45] On the hazards of exemplarity see Goldhill (1991), index s.v. 'exemplification'.

exempla: Augustus is to Julius as Agamemnon to Atreus, Achilles to Peleus, and, the most fully adequate example (*ut exemplis ipsos aequantibus utar*), as Jupiter is to Saturn (*Metamorphoses* 15.852–60).

Predictably, readers of Ovid as anti-Augustan have pointed to the negative elements in the stories of all three of these father-son pairs.[46] One might remember that within the *Metamorphoses* a very different exemplary use of Saturn and Jupiter had been made by Byblis, in her attempt to persuade herself of the legitimacy of her incestuous desire (9.497–9): *di melius! — di nempe suas habuere sorores. | sic Saturnus Opem iunctam sibi sanguine duxit, | Oceanus Tethyn, Iunonem rector Olympi —* before checking herself in horror at 508: *cur haec exempla paravi?* Byblis herself is set up as an example by the poet (9.454): *Byblis in exemplo est, ut ament concessa puellae*. Looking back from book 15 the reader might reflect that in the realm of family and sexual matters the *princeps'* own record was not exactly exemplary.

But I want to dwell not on the possibility of reading subversive undermeanings into the Ovidian text, but rather on the possibility of reading and writing other meanings *tout court*, a possibility that is stated quite unambiguously by Ovid at 15.852–4 *hic sua praeferri quamquam vetat acta paternis, | libera fama tamen nullisque obnoxia iussis | invitum praefert unaque in parte repugnat*. This of course is offered as praise; the panegyrist conventionally struggles with the *modestia* of the *princeps*,[47] it is a sign of the continued survival of Republican *libertas* that a disobedient *libera fama* is not suppressed. Nevertheless the monolithic cohesion of the Jovian/Augustan version of things has been challenged, and the way is open to the more radical division of opinions on the *acta* of the *princeps* that is sketched out by Tacitus at the beginning of the *Annals*, in what Goodyear describes as the 'pro' and 'contra' necrology' of Augustus that 'replaces the conventional *laudatio*'.[48] The uncontrolled and divergent *multus sermo* reported by Tacitus is made more pointed by the unmistakable allusions to the official version of Augustus' reign contained in the *Res Gestae*.[49]

---

[46] See the references at Schmitzer (1990) 293.
[47] Pliny *Pan.* 3.2; 21.1.
[48] Goodyear (1972) 154.
[49] Urban (1979); Goodyear (1972) 159–60, on *Ann.* 1.10.1–3, seeing 'a strong "prima facie" case for deliberate allusion'. See also Woodman and Martin on *Ann.* 3.55.5 ('striking allusion' to *RG* 8.5 in *nostra quoque aetas multa laudis et artium imitanda posteris tulit*).

This is not the only place at which Ovid's Roman history seems to look as much forward to models of imperial, and in particular Tacitean, historiography, as it looks back to Republican and Livian models. I shall conclude with a look at Ovid as an imperial historian.

Pythagoras in his time has been many men (and animals). Virbius has been two men, and is now a god. Cipus is a single individual, whose metamorphosis (sprouting horns) does not deprive him of that human individuality, but does threaten to make of him another kind of *unus homo*, a *rex* (15.594–5). Aesculapius, like his patient Virbius, has 'twice made new his fate' (2.648 *bis tua fata novabis*), a god who became a corpse, that is became a mortal, and was reborn as a god. As a *praesens deus* in Rome, Aesculapius is comparable to Julius Caesar. And so Ovid brings us down to the *unus homo* of his own times, who himself will in due course become a god. Ovid's Roman history is, in its own way, a 'great man' history. Tony Woodman, discussing the biographical and panegyrical tendencies of Velleius Paterculus, traces a development from the corporate history of the Roman people as practised by Fabius Pictor and Cato the Elder, through the increasingly individualistic historiography of Sallust and Livy, until 'The domination of successive individuals during the late republic reached its logical conclusion when Augustus, in his eleventh consulship, established the absolute autocracy of the principate in 23 B.C. The resultant change from the republican ideal could hardly be better illustrated than in these words of Tacitus which, intentionally or not, are a bitter refutation of Cato . . .: *unum esse rei publicae corpus atque unius animo regendum* (*Annals* 1.12.3)'.[50]

Metamorphoses 15 is profoundly engaged with this issue of the *unus homo*. In an earlier work I explored this topic primarily from the point of view of the exploitation by Virgil, Ovid, and later imperial epic poets of the one outstanding individual, the hero.[51] Chris Kraus has demonstrated the importance of the issue in Livy's history of the earlier Republic, where it constantly cross-references the political circumstances of Livy's own times.[52] Thus we have contrasting examples of the one man who saves the state, such as Camillus, or the one man who threatens to destroy the state, such as Manlius Capitolinus. Ovid's Roman history is similarly all geared to the poet's own day;

[50] Woodman (1977) 37.
[51] Hardie (1993) 3–10.
[52] Kraus (1994), index s.v. 'one and only'.

Ulrich Schmitzer goes so far as to claim that all the episodes from
Roman history treated by Ovid are a foil for the rule of Augustus.[53]
The stories in *Metamorphoses* 15 are anticipations of, or *exempla* for, the
one great man Augustus, but the exact relationship between *exemplum*
and that which is exemplified cannot be too hastily pinned down.
'Reading history is as active a process as writing it.'[54] Cipus, hailed
by the haruspex as king if once he enters the city, tells his fellow-
Romans to drive him from the city. The admiring citizens reward
him with a crown and a large grant of land. Is Cipus a pure example of a Republican hero, a counter-example to a Julius or an
Augustus who takes on the *de facto* role of king, or is he a parallel
for Julius' refusal of the royal diadem, and for Augustus' ostenta-
tious return of powers to the Republic? Denis Feeney has brilliantly
drawn out the contrast between the corporate senatorial handling of
the introduction of Aesculapius as a god to Rome, and the 'priva-
tization' of Roman religion within the imperial household hinted at
in the poem's closing prayer to the gods of Rome.[55] But equally one
could read the story of Aesculapius as a comment on the elaborate
charades of senatorial and popular validation of the deifications of
Julius and Augustus. Ovid knew as much about dissimulation as did
either Tiberius or Tacitus.[56]

Ovid's Roman history begins with the kings, the purest type of
the *unus homo*. By Ovid's time there was a long tradition of using
the regal period as a mirror for more recent political and constitu-
tional developments.[57] As we read the first lines of *Metamorphoses* 15
we are at a very early stage of Roman history, but simultaneously
transported to the most burning issue at the time of writing of the
Metamorphoses (15.1–4):

> quaeritur interea, quis tantae pondera molis
> sustineat tantoque queat succedere regi;
> destinat imperio clarum praenuntia veri
> fama Numam.[58]

---

[53] Schmitzer (1990) 279, 285.

[54] Kraus (1994) 14.

[55] Feeney (1991) 208–17.

[56] McKeown on *Am.* 2.2.18 *dissimulare*: 'the verb is inordinately frequent in Ovid';
for Ovid's take on Romulan/Augustan dissimulation see Barchiesi (1997) 161–4.

[57] In general see Fox (1996).

[58] Tony Woodman *per litteras* points out that these lines also seem to contain verbal echoes of Enn. *Ann.* 72–91 Skutsch, the 'search' for the first king of Rome.

> Meanwhile the question is who will sustain
> The burden of so great a charge, who can
> Succeed so great a monarch. For the throne
> Fame, truth's prophetic herald, nominates
> Illustrious Numa.
>
> (Trans. A. D. Melville)

As Augustus grew old the question of the imperial succession, and of whose shoulders might be adequate to the burden of a world-empire, became increasingly urgent.[59] The language in these lines is strikingly close to Tacitean formulations of the same issue: *Annals* 1.4.3 *Agrippam ... non ... tantae moli parem*; 1.11.1 *solam divi Augusti mentem tantae molis capacem*. The power of rumour and gossip is also one of Tacitus' big themes,[60] including the importance of rumour in issues of imperial succession. Already in the *Agricola* Tacitus had noted of an appointment to a provincial governorship (9.7) *haud semper errat fama; aliquando et eligit*. Commenting on history's joke in elevating Claudius to the purple he later notes (*Ann.* 3.18.4) *quippe fama spe veneratione potius omnes destinabantur imperio quam quem futurum principem fortuna in occulto tenebat.*[61] It is indeed possible that Tacitus alludes to the Ovidian passage in his own formulations; if so, eloquent testimony to Ovid's powers as a historian.

---

[59] Hardie (1997) 182–3; Feeney (1999) 28; Goodyear on *Ann.* 1.4.3, 1.11.1; Bruère (1958).

[60] See Gibson (1998).

[61] Other examples of the role of *fama* in narratives of succession: *Hist.* 1.7; 2.1; 4.11.

CHAPTER ELEVEN

THE ALBAN KINGS IN THE *METAMORPHOSES*: AN OVIDIAN CATALOGUE AND ITS HISTORIOGRAPHICAL MODELS

Stratis Kyriakidis

Ovid, *Met.* 14.609–23, 765–76

inde sub *Ascanii* dicione binominis Alba
resque Latina fuit. succedit *Silvius* illi   610
quo satus antiquo tenuit repetita *Latinus*
nomina cum sceptro. clarus subit ***Alba* Latinum.**
***Epytus* ex illo est; post hunc *Capetus*que *Capys*que,**
sed Capys ante fuit; regnum *Tiberinus* ab illis
cepit et in Tusci **demersus** fluminis undis   615
nomina fecit aquae; de quo *Remulus*que feroxque
Acrota sunt geniti: Remulus maturior annis
fulmineo periit, **imitator fulminis**, ictu.
fratre suo sceptrum moderatior Acrota forti
tradit *Aventino*, qui, quo regnarat, eodem   620
monte iacet positus **tribuitque vocabula monti**.
iamque Palatinae summam *Proca* gentis habebat.
rege sub hoc Pomona fuit, . . .
—

haec ubi nequiquam formae deus aptus anili   765
edidit, in iuvenem rediit, et anilia demit
instrumenta sibi talisque apparuit illi,
qualis ubi oppositas nitidissima solis imago
evicit nubes nullaque obstante reluxit,
vimque parat; **sed vi non est opus**, inque figura   770
capta dei nympha est et mutua vulnera sensit.
proximus Ausonias **iniusti miles *Amuli***
rexit opes, *Numitor*que senex **amissa** nepotis
munere **regna** capit, festisque Palilibus urbis
moenia conduntur; Tatiusque patresque Sabini   775
bella gerunt, . . .

Next double-named Ascanius ruled the land
Of Latium and Alba. Silvius
Succeeded him. His son, Latinus, took

The name and sceptre of his ancestor.
After Latinus glorious Alba reigned;
Then Epytus, and next came Capetus
And Capys (Capys first), and following them
The reign of Tiberinus, king from whom
Was named the Tuscan river where he drowned.
Fierce Acrota and Remulus were his sons;
Then Remulus, of riper years, who mimicked
Lightning, was by a lightning-flash destroyed.
Acrota, better balanced than his brother,
Passed on the sceptre to brave Aventine,
Who on the hill where he had reigned was buried
And to that hill bestowed his royal name.
And now King Proca held the sovereignty
And ruled the people of the Palatine.
Pomona lived in good King Procas' reign . . .
—

Thus the god pleaded in the old dame's guise,
But all in vain. Then he resumed his own
Young shape and shed the trappings of old age,
And stood revealed to her as when the sun
Triumphs in glory through the clouds and rain
And bright with beams untrammelled shines again.
No need of force. His beauty wins the day,
As she with answering love is borne away.
Next wicked Amulius by force of arms
Ruled rich Ausonia, till old Numitor
By a grandson's bounty gained the throne he'd lost.
And then on Pales' festal day the walls
Of Rome were founded. Led by Tatius
The Sabine fathers battled . . .

                                        (Trans. A. D. Melville)

Catalogues are a standard feature of Roman literature and of Augustan
poetry in particular. Their study can often disclose poetic intentions,
for quite often they become set-pieces for emulation where poets, by
changing some elements of their models or constructing them in a
certain way, give a new purpose to them. At times, this literary function of a catalogue seems to be served better when its form and
content have as a model a historiographic text rather than a poetic
work. Dynastic or *ktetic* catalogues may be offered as a case study,
since they can be found in epic as well as in historical works of
antiquity, and they are therefore open to comparisons. The order
in which names are listed in a catalogue, the addition or omission
of a name, the qualifying epithets and its structure in general may

be elements which characterise a catalogue, but they can also be used as evidence in an effort to find whether a poet or an author is following a certain tradition. In other words, a catalogue may prove to be a means of studying the relationship between a literary work and its model or cluster of models.

All books of the *Metamorphoses* contain catalogues of proper names, but their frequency, structure and function vary. In Book 14 they occur rather frequently. At line 580 Ovid's *Aeneid* ends,[1] and the death of Turnus is followed by the apotheosis of Aeneas (14.581–608).[2] Then comes the list of the Alban kings, with the names presented in successive order and in an annalistic way (14.609–22). This catalogue thematically brings Ovid back within the contextual bounds of Vergil's *Aeneid*,[3] since Vergil treats the subject of Aeneas' successors within a much broader perspective in the speech of Anchises in the middle of his epic (*Aeneid* 6.756–853).[4]

Before we proceed any further, I think that we should look at the structure of the two catalogues in question. In the Vergilian catalogue, there are four lines (6.756–9) preceding it, starting with the verbal phrase *nunc age* and coming to a close with a verse beginning with the verb *expediam* (6.759), whereas the lines in between, in the form of an indirect question, anticipate its contents.[5] The Vergilian catalogue, therefore, and by extension, the whole prophecy of Anchises, is clearly signalled at its beginning. The list of Alban kings has a *caput* of its own, as the word *primus* (761) shows, referring to Silvius.

---

[1] At 582 according to a different view: see Hinds (1998) 106f.

[2] Some consider that the unit with Ovid's *Aeneid* ends at l. 608 including in it the apotheosis of Aeneas which, although mentioned (*Aen.* 12.794f.), it is not fully treated in Vergil's *Aeneid*; it is, of course, part of the Aeneas legend in the historiographers (Dionysius of Halicarnassus, *R.A.* 60.45, Livy 1.2.6). See e.g. Stitz (1962), which I could not see; Galinsky (1976) 3–18, Bömer (1982) 361, Ellsworth (1986) 27, Baldo (1987) 109–31, esp. 117.

[3] See texts at the end of the paper.

[4] The speech of Anchises is mentioned in the course of Ovid's *Aeneid* but its importance is minimized (14.117–19).

[5] It is interesting to note the structural similarity between these introductory lines and the beginning of the delayed proem in Book 7 of the *Aeneid* (7.37–40). In each case the interest of the poet and the importance he gives to what follows is evident: the prophecy of Anchises is essential to the epic structure of the *Aeneid* and of fundamental importance to the reader; in the delayed proem of Book 7 the importance of what follows is stated by the poet himself (*maius opus moveo*, 7.45). See Hardie (1992) 59–82, esp. 67f. On the delayed proem, see Conte (1992) 152–3, Kyriakidis (1994) 197–206 and now (1998) 161–77.

It is comprised of five names of kings and spreads over thirteen lines
(760–72). The names involved are: *Silvius* (son of Aeneas and Lavinia),
Procas, Capys, Numitor, Silvius Aeneas. The last two lines, *qui iuvenes!*
quantas ostentant, aspice, viris/atque umbrata gerunt civili tempora quercu!
(771–2) mark, in effect, the end of this part of the catalogue before
the next group of place-names (773–6). Then, the list is resumed
with *Mavortius . . . Romulus* (777–8) to be followed by *Caesar* (*Augustus*)
himself. It appears that Vergil does not keep a strict line of succession but his emphasis lies rather with the prominence of persons.[6]

In Ovid now, the corresponding catalogue of the Alban kings runs
for approximately the same length (fourteen lines, 609–22). However,
there are important differences between them. Unlike Vergil's, it has
no frame. Besides, the names of the two catalogues do not match
and in Ovid's list there are more. The increased number of names
within a more or less equal number of lines drastically limits the
space available. The line of succession is different too: *Ascanius, Silvius,*
Latinus, Alba, Epytus, Capys, Capetus, Tiberinus, Remulus, Acrota, Aventinus,
Proca. With the name of Proca, this catalogue is interrupted, like
Vergil's, with the insertion of the story of Pomona and Vertumnus
(623–771); it is taken up again at line 772 by the word *proximus* and
continues with Proca's sons, *Numitor* and *Amulius*. One further difference
between Ovid's and Vergil's catalogues is that the contents of the
Ovidian catalogue are presented as past narrative from the perspective of the poet-narrator whereas in the *Aeneid* the narrator is Anchises
and the time is set well in the future and beyond the time span of
the Roman epic.

The two catalogues, in their first part, however, have another feature in common: they tend to become dense towards their middle.
By 'dense', I mean that the accumulation of names is greater there
than at the beginning or end of the two registers.[7] Vergil lists within
two verses (767–8) three names of kings out of a total of five;[8] Ovid
also lists within three lines (612–14) five names out of a total of

---

[6] Gassner (1972) 67, Austin (1986) *ad* 788ff. with further references. See also
Norden (1899) 467ff. and (1957) *ad* 750–1.

[7] Only proper nouns of the same class are counted on each verse; neither their
attributes, nor any other proper names, related to them, like family names are
included.

[8] Silvius Aeneas, whose name appears in the next line, is given further two whole
lines (769–70), and actually completes this part of the catalogue, leaving out Romulus
who is mentioned at 777.

twelve.[9] Ancient catalogues usually have an internal rhythm; according to one of the rhythmical patterns found, they tend to have an accumulation of names towards or around their middle. This feature can be observed in various lists from as early as Homeric poetry and up to the Augustans. In Homer, at *Iliad* 13.689–93[10] (the battle between the Achaeans and the Trojans) for instance, this pattern takes the form of X[11]–1–3–3–2 within five lines. In Hesiod's *Theogony* 226–32,[12] where the children of Strife are named in a seven-line catalogue, the pattern is followed as 1–3–4–4–2–1–X. In the *Argonautica* of Apollonius of Rhodes in 2.940–5[13] the catalogue of the places the Argonauts sail past through the night on their way to the Assyrian land takes the form of X–2–3–1–X–1. In Vergil's *Aeneid* 3.124–7[14] where the Trojans sail past the Aegean islands, the catalogue has the pattern as 1–2–2–1. Finally, in Ovid, besides the catalogue in question, at *Metamorphoses* 7.228–33,[15] in a six-line catalogue we have the second lot of place-names from which Medea collected the herbs for making her rejuvenating potion; here the pattern is applied as 1–2–2–1–1–X.

The Vergilian and Ovidian catalogues of Alban kings, therefore, are thematically similar, of almost equal length and they are both interrupted; they also seem to share a significant rhythmic characteristic which is also present in other poetic catalogues of antiquity.

---

[9] The name of Capys is not counted twice (613 and 614).

[10] ἐν δ' ἄρα τοῖσιν/ἦρχ' υἱὸς Πετεῶο Μενεσθεύς, οἱ δ' ἅμ' ἕποντο/Φείδας τε Στιχίος τε Βίας τ' ἐΰς· αὐτὰρ Ἐπειῶν/Φυλείδης τε Μέγης Ἀμφίων τε Δρακίος τε/πρὸ Φθίων δὲ Μέδων τε μενεπτόλεμός τε Ποδάρκης.

[11] X represents a line relevant to the clause but containing no name of the same class.

[12] αὐτὰρ Ἔρις στυγερὴ τέκε μὲν Πόνον ἀλγινόεντα/Λήθην τε Λιμόν τε καὶ Ἄλγεα δακρυόεντα/Ὑσμίνας τε Μάχας τε Φόνους τ' Ἀνδροκτασίας τε/Νείκεά τε Ψεύδεά τε Λόγους τε Ἀμφιλλογίας τε/Δυσνομίην τ' Ἄτην τε συνήθεας ἀλλήλησιν,/Ὅρκον θ' ὃς δὴ πλεῖστον ἐπιχθονίους ἀνθρώπους/πημαίνει ὅτε κέν τις ἑκὼν ἐπίορκον ὀμόσσῃ.

[13] νυκτὶ δ' ἔπειτ' ἄλληκτον ἐπιπροτέρωσε θέοντες/Σήσαμον αἰπεινούς τε παρεξενέοντ' Ἐρυθίνους/Κρωβίαλον Κρῶμνάν τε καὶ ὑλήεντα Κύτωρον./ἔνθεν δ' αὖτε Κάραμβιν ἅμ' ἠελίοιο βολῇσιν/γνάμψαντες παρὰ πουλὺν ἔπειτ' ἤλαυνον ἐρετμοῖς/Αἰγιαλὸν πρόπαν ἦμαρ ὁμῶς καὶ ἐπ' ἤματι νύκτα.

[14] linquimus *Ortygiae* portus pelagoque volamus/bacchatamque iugis *Naxon* viridemque *Donusam*,/*Olearon* niveamque *Paron* sparsasque per aequor/*Cycladas*, et crebris legimus freta concita terris.

[15] multa quoque *Apidani* placuerunt gramina ripis,/multa quoque *Amphrysi*, neque eras inmunis, *Enipeu*;/nec non *Peneos* nec non *Spercheides* undae/contribuere aliquid iuncosaque litora *Boebes*;/carpsit et Euboica vivax *Anthedone* gramen,/nondum mutato vulgatum corpore Glauci.

Bearing in mind the above points and the fact that the reader has just concluded the Ovidian *Aeneid*, it is logical to assume that Ovid's succession list invites the reader to recall Vergil's corresponding list. Once this is done, the reader may then easily realise the differences between the two texts. Ovid's catalogue, compared to that of Vergil's with its grandiose style, consciously plays down the grandeur and pride of the latter. Vergil's Alban kings were mentioned within the context of the pride and glory of Anchises' prophecy, whereas Ovid's matter-of-fact list of kings has a more annalistic appearance. It can be said, therefore, that the catalogue in the *Metamorphoses*, while possessing some features in common with that of the *Aeneid* — such as its length — is in reality altered in character and contextual quality.

Similar catalogues of the Alban kings also appear in Livy (1.3.6f.), Dionysius of Halicarnassus (*Antiquitates Romanae* 1.71f.) and in Diodorus Siculus (7.5.6ff.).[16] The names in Dionysius' list almost coincide with those of Livy's and by extension with those of Ovid's. This may be true, but at the same time the focus of Dionysius' list and Diodorus' is on the duration of each king's reign; in the latter's case there are more severe name-discrepancies, though this may be due to the way the text has been transmitted to us.[17]

It seems, however, that Ovid had actually consulted or at least knew all three catalogues. This becomes apparent in lines 613–14 where the poet seems to have used in his own playful and learned way all three catalogues in the space of one and a half lines. Line 613 begins with *Epytus*, a name otherwise present only in Diodorus' list; then, we have *Capetusque Capysque* — the order given by Dionysius — and finally with the first half line at 614 he actually 'corrects',[18] so to speak, his source by reversing the order of names: *sed Capys ante fuit* (614) thus alluding to his third source, the list of Livy.[19] It is

---

[16] See texts at the end of the paper.

[17] The text of Diodorus has been taken from the Loeb edition which in turn used the Latin translation (H. Petermann) of the Armenian edition of Eusebius' *Chronicle*.

[18] But see Gassner (1972) 97–8.

[19] There are a few more discrepancies among the catalogues such as: for instance, the name of *Aeneas* (*Silvius*) which appears in all three historical lists as well as in Vergil's, but is omitted in Ovid's, and *Atys* which is listed in the catalogues of Dionysius and Livy but has been replaced, as we have said, in Ovid's list by *Epytus*. After *Tiberinus*, Ovid does not follow any of the historians when he names *Tiberinus*' successors, *Remulus* and *Acrota* (see also below, note 41) but he agrees with them in the last two names, those of *Aventinus* and *Proca*. All texts seem to be in agreement

interesting that the allusion to all three historiographical accounts is made in the very same lines that the highest accumulation of names occurs. It must be noted here that the names in the middle of the Ovidian list also appear with an increased density in all three historiographical accounts when compared with the rest of the names of each catalogue. It seems that some of them are mere catalogue names without any independent existence outside a list. This thought may then lead us to the assumption of a common source which might very well be poetic.

Looking at the catalogues of these three writers, we see that for reasons of composition, length and diction, the Ovidian catalogue is mainly closer to that of Livy, and to a considerable extent to the list of Dionysius of Halicarnassus. The similarities include various features. We see that the middle of the Ovidian catalogue has the following names in succession: *Alba, Epytus, Capys, Capetus, Tiberinus*; Livy's corresponding part includes: *Alba, Atys, Capys, Capetus, Tiberinus*; and Dionysius' has: Ἄλβας, Κάπετος, Κάπυς, Κάλπετος and Τιβερῖνος. Finally Diodorus has: *Albas Silvius, Epitus Silvas, Apis (= Capys), Kalpet (= Calpetus), Tiberius Sylvius*. In these very lines Ovid particularly stresses his closeness to Livy's list not only by the order of succession but by the way the names are presented. Livy says: *Latino Alba ortus, Alba Atys, Atye Capys, Capye Capetus, Capeto Tiberinus, qui in traiectu Albulae amnis* **submersus** *celebre ad posteros* **nomen** *flumini* **dedit** (1.3.8).

Ovid writes:

> clarus subit Alba Latinum.
> Epytus ex illo est; post hunc Capetusque Capysque,
> sed Capys ante fuit; regnum Tiberinus ab illis
> cepit et in Tusci **demersus** fluminis undis
> **nomina fecit** aquae (612–16)

> After Latinus glorious Alba reigned;
> Then Epytus, and next came Capetus
> And Capys (Capys first), and following them
> The reign of Tiberinus, king from whom
> Was named the Tuscan river where he drowned.
> (Trans. A. D. Melville)

---

in these two names: they all etymologize the Aventine from the name of the king and, unlike Vergil (*Aen.* 6.767: *Troianae gloria gentis*), they all treat Proca as an Alban king.

What we actually have here is a number of names extracted from
a dry and non-poetic list which Ovid accommodates into the middle of his own catalogue, applying the specific rhythmic pattern we
have mentioned above, thus lending to Livy's list poetic qualities
which were already detected in antiquity.[20]

Ovid's approach to the Latin historiographical account seems also
to have been made with a further poetic purpose in mind. To begin
with, an arid catalogue, such as Ovid's, with no stress whatsoever
on personal praise and with minimal additional information given
for the names it contains, tends to be fleshless or 'bony',[21] with no
evidence of glory or *kleos* for those kings who led to the foundation
of Rome.[22] Now, if texts — and especially poetic texts — are responsible for the transmission of that *kleos* to future generations,[23] then
Ovid's text, by adopting a non-heroic approach is being contrasted
with the other great poetic work, the *Aeneid*. Such a treatment on
the part of Ovid seems to reflect his ideology; although he praises
Rome through the prophecy of Helenus, he nonetheless considers it
as only a period of the universal history he is narrating and in which
cuncta fluunt (15.178).[24] This is clearly shown with the catalogue of
cities which had fallen from their glorious existence in the past to
become mere geographical entities: Troy, Sparta, Mycenae, Athens
and Thebes (*Met.* 15.424–30).

nunc humilis veteres tantummodo Troia ruinas
et pro divitiis tumulos ostendit avorum;   425
clara fuit Sparte, magnae viguere Mycenae,
nec non et Cecropis, nec non Amphionis arces.
[vile solum Sparte est, altae cecidere Mycenae,
Oedipodioniae quid sunt, nisi nomina, Thebae?
quid Pandioniae restant, nisi nomen, Athenae?]   430
nunc quoque Dardaniam fama est consurgere Romam.

---

[20] Quintilian *Inst.* 10.1.31: *historia est proxima poetis et quodam modo carmen solutum et scribitur ad narrandum non ad probandum.* In his effort to provide a useful reading list to the orator, Quintilian makes the above remarks about history and continues with some further thoughts on it which end up with his stylistic comments on Sallustius' and Livy's works, where the latter's style is described as *lactea ubertas* (10.1.32).
[21] Little (1972) 398.
[22] E.g. Otis (1970) 295: 'Ovid pays only the scantest attention to the founding of Rome', also Feeney (1991) 208 and (1992) 22.
[23] As Vergil, for instance, seems to believe, *Aen.* 9.446ff.
[24] Barchiesi (1990) 90ff.

> Humbled **now**
> She [sc. Troy] shows her ancient ruins, for her riches
> Only the broken tombs of ancestors.
> Sparta was famous, great Mycenae strong.
> And strong the walls of Cecrops and Amphion.
> Now Sparta lies a waste, Mycenae's towers
> have tumbled down. What but a name is left
> of Oedipus' brave Thebes, or what endures
> of proud Pandion's Athens but a name?
> **Today** from Trojan stock a city arises,
> Rome . . .
>
> (Trans. A. D. Melville)

The reader, after such a catalogue, is expected to reflect on these *exempla* and to anticipate a similar outcome of this poetic contemplation. Contrary to his expectation, however, what he finds is a hymn to the coming glory of Rome in the form of a prophecy. The tension thus created between the reader's expectancy and the text is strong enough to generate the sense that for Rome, for the *urbs mansura*, the danger of following the fate of the other cities is always there.[25] Book 15 closes its first half with the catalogue of the cities which had fallen into oblivion; the second half begins with the theme of the rising Rome. Such a division would be justified if Ovid really meant it. His diction, however, discloses his purpose: the use of *nunc* twice (424, for the cities, 431, for Rome) joined by *quoque* (431)[26] seems to cancel this distinction. In this way, whereas the poet appears to distinguish between the destroyed cities and Rome with its 'promising' future, in actual fact he makes the reader anticipate a similar development. Rome is thus incorporated into the list of cities that are nothing more than mere names.[27]

To return to our catalogue, Ovid in his well-known manner, breaks up the list of the Alban kings and, after the name of Proca, inserts a love story: The love of Vertumnus for Pomona (623–771) which

---

[25] Barchiesi (1990) 86–7, Hardie (1992) 59–61, Tissol (1997) 186–7.

[26] Kenney (1986) xvi; Solodow (1988) 167–8, Barchiesi (1990) 86–7. On *nunc* see Tissol (1997) 195, 197–8.

[27] The lack of a frame on this catalogue may be a further reason for its spreading influence in the narrative. For other instances on the motif of lost cities, see Gow and Page (1968) 428 [ep. ix]. The idea of fate and the future of Rome preoccupied earlier Greek historiography: see Polybius 38.21, Diodorus Siculus 32.42. See also Astin (1967) 282–7, Petrochilos (1974) 116–17, Tissol (1997) 186ff.

is not previously attested in literature as such[28] covers nearly 150 lines; the catalogue is then resumed in a typical fashion with the use of *proximus* at 772 and the names of Amulius and Numitor, the sons of Proca. In three and a half lines, Ovid refers to the unjust nature of Amulius' rule, Numitor's ascent to the throne with the aid of his grand-children, and the construction of Rome's walls (772–5). These references, however, cover the space of only a title-summary.[29] Ovid does not mention what makes Amulius unjust, nor how Numitor lost his kingdom. The poet simply condenses in these few lines whole chapters from the historiographers which are not included in his poem, but their content is presumably known, since they form part of well-known texts, such as Livy's, and besides, they constitute a major part of the foundation myths of Rome. With this omission, however, he hardly distances himself from his historiographical sources; on the contrary, he still alludes to them through the appropriate use of vocabulary. The poet states:

> Proximus Ausonias **iniusti** miles **Amuli**
> rexit opes, Numitorque senex **amissa** nepotis
> munere **regna** capit, festisque Palilibus urbis
> moenia conduntur. (772–75)

> Next wicked Amulius by force of arms
> Ruled rich Ausonia, till old Numitor
> By a grandson's bounty gained the throne he'd lost.
> And then on Pales' festal day the walls
> Of Rome were founded.
>
> (Trans. A. D. Melville)

Amulius is characterised as unjust,[30] ruling by military force. We find the same phrasing in Dionysius' text: he refers to Amulius' unjust rule: ἔπειτα Ἀμόλιος **οὐ σὺν δίκῃ** τὴν βασιλείαν κατασχὼν Νεμέτορι προσήκουσαν (1.71.4), where at least the phrase **οὐ σὺν δίκῃ** equates to the attribute *iniusti* of Amulius in the Ovidian text.[31]

---

[28] Myers (1994a) 225–50, and (1994b) 113f.

[29] Vergil, too, in Anchises' prophecy makes no reference to the foundation myth but considers it known material to his readers. The structure, however, and diction of Vergil's passage clearly show the laudatory style for these kings, without mentioning personal information on any of these characters. See Norden (1957) 773.

[30] A condemnatory epithet for the ancestor of the founder(s) of Rome, as *iustus* is a "distinctively Roman notion": Solodow (1988) 83.

[31] Cf. Diodorus' phrase, as has come down to us: *Amolius **per vim** regnum tenuit* (see, however, next note and note 17 above).

Then, Numitor is introduced as gaining the lost kingdom *amissa* *regna* with the help of his grand-children. The reader then may recall the corresponding phrase in Livy, *ita Numitori Albana re permissa* (1.6.3). The two phrases look at the same event from a different angle.

The whole passage of Livy and Dionysius[32] concerning Amulius' unjust and cruel rule, the growing up of Ilia's twins, the assistance they gave to their grandfather Numitor to overthrow his brother Amulius, and the antagonism of the twins which led to fratricide, has been supplanted in the *Metamorphoses* by just three and a half lines with which the story of the Alban kings and the beginnings of Rome come to an end. In this way, the poet suppresses in his text not only the name of the twins but more importantly, the period of violence and strife that appears in the text of the two historiographers. The reader, however, having detected the close relation of the Ovidian catalogue to the historiographical sources, and in particular to the text of Livy, anticipates the missing part of the story. In its place, however, he finds the love story of Vertumnus and Pomona.

It is important to pause for a while in order to understand the way in which this inserted story operates here. The tale of Vertumnus and Pomona is not functionally connected with the catalogue of the kings. That is, its narrative link is very loose.[33] The only motive the poet gives for telling the story is that Pomona lived during Proca's reign (*rege sub hoc*, 623).[34] One should wonder, therefore, why Ovid

---

[32] I exclude Diodorus' account as too fragmentary and corrupt to allow reliable conclusions to be drawn.

[33] It is a more or less usual practice in the *Metamorphoses*. See e.g. Newlands (1995) 17, who refers to Keith (1992) 150.

[34] Solodow (1988) 15–16 recognises that successive stories are always connected somehow: 'some character or action or place always ties successive stories together, making of the whole an unbroken series'. To this rule he sees an exception: 'the numerous stories which characters within the poem relate to one another, either singly (as when Vertumnus tells Pomona about Iphis and Anaxarete, *Met.* 14.698–771) or in numbers'. He mentions further examples of this type and concludes: 'these exceptions are only apparent, however. Their narration is well motivated within the poem, where story-telling, significantly, is a popular activity'. I do not think, however, that this is the reason for connecting the story of Vertumnus with that of Iphis; a sounder reason could be that they both share the elegiac motif of the *exclusus amator*. Furthermore, none of the cases of narrative link mentioned in his work can satisfactorily justify the connections of this story with the catalogue. It is interesting, however, that the first inset love story in the *Metamorphoses*, that of Apollo and Daphne, is as loosely connected — with a temporal adverb (*nondum laurus erat*, 1.450) — as the last one of the *Metamorphoses*, that of Vertumnus and Pomona, which is also connected temporally (*rege sub hoc Pomona fuit*, 14.623). See also Myers (1994b) 114.

wished to insert his story in a way that would interrupt and indeed undermine a royal register. We should bear in mind that a catalogue of the Alban kings, according to the grand manner in which it was presented in the Vergilian epic, was a poetic piece aspiring to the glory of the community with reference to its ancestors. But, here, this catalogue, as we have seen, has been augmented in names, stripped of its epithets and laudatory phrases and now is being interrupted for a love story to be told. More than that, the royal register becomes the frame of that story, thus losing much of its prestige. P. G. Walsh in his incisive analysis of Livy's work, considers that the magistrate lists at the termination of each year contribute to the *variatio* the Roman historian was preoccupied with. According to him, 'such lists with their details of domestic problems and decisions, provide a respite from the narrative[35] of campaigning in territory often unfamiliar to his readers'.[36] Knowing Livy's preference for annalistic presentation, it is appropriate for one to see the termination of one year's account completed with the elections and the next year's appointments. But when one looks at Livy's work as a literary text, as Ovid presumably did, then the same annalistic feature might be viewed with a reverse function: the recurrence of lists of elected magistrates may not be thought of as closing the year of campaigning, but rather the same lists frame one year's political and military activity. If my suggestion is not fanciful, then we can possibly use it to explain the way in which Ovid has used his list of the Alban kings. Coming from a historiographical source, the list of the Alban kings — like another magistrate list —*frames* instead of *being framed*, as in the case of Vergil, the poetically inspired love-story of Pomona and Vertumnus. It is a tale of the love Vertumnus had for Pomona with another love story within it, that of Iphis for Anaxarete. Comparing both tales with the qualities of their protagonists, as they are depicted in their names, we can detect a subtle irony on the part of the poet as to their outcome.

Pomona was a nymph whose name is etymologised in the text.[37] She is dedicated to gardening and fruits and has no care for love. At the end, however, she will yield to Vertumnus. In spite of his

---

[35] *mora* is the term Ovid used, *Met.* 3.224.

[36] Walsh (1989[2]), 174.

[37] *pomaria*: 635, *poma* 627; 650; 657; 687; 764, and *unde tenet nomen*, 626. Michalopoulos (forthcoming), 284.

ability at disguise, Vertumnus, from *vertere*,[38] does not get very far with Pomona, until he is presented in his very own self to her. Iphis, on the other hand, whose name means 'strong', 'mighty' in Greek, is anything but,[39] as he comes from a humble family (699) and his passion for Anaxarete enfeebles him. Here again, Anaxarete (*generosam sanguine Teucri*, 698), whose name comes from ἀνάσσω (= rule) + ἀρετή (= virtue) and implies her (self?) control, at the end of the story no longer has this power and when she gazes upon the lifeless body of Iphis she is petrified. What we see here is that the *nomen omen* principle operates[40] *e contrario*:[41] Pomona in the end found happiness not in the *poma* she cared for; where the Protean qualities of Vertumnus[42] failed him, he succeeded by being his own self; and in the embedded story of the Cyprean couple, Iphis and Anaxarete, neither benefited from their behaviour. Before going any further, I should perhaps mention that the intertextual dynamics between the Ovidian text and Propertius 4.2 have already been examined effectively;[43] I shall not treat that aspect. But I would like, however, to consider the relation of this particular love-story to its immediate context, which is none other than the list of kings.

---

[38] *versasse*, 646. Maltby (1991) s.v. *Vertumnus*; among others Michalopoulos (forthcoming), 94f.

[39] Note also that in a previous episode (*Met.* 9.668ff.) Iphis was a girl living his life disguised as a boy until she was changed to a man by the grace of Isis. See Wheeler (1997) 190–202 and (1999) 55.

[40] The tension created between context and etymologising of names in Ovid can also be seen e.g. at the case of Astyanax, *Met.* 13.415–6.

[41] The names of *Acrota* and *Remulus* — which, incidentally, appear only in Ovid's list — seem to have a similarly inverted function. *Acrota* is characterised as *ferox* and his name can be thus etymologised from *acer*, but according to context he is *moderatior* (619) than his brother; *Remulus*, on the other hand [etymologised from *remora*(?), as probably *Remus* in *Fasti* (Barchiesi (1994) 146–7 and note 29) and at the same time alluding to the Ennian *Remora*? (*Ann.* fr. 77 and comm. Sk.)] had a behaviour contrary to his name and closer to that implied by the name of his brother. It is perhaps for this reason that Ovid gives these two names a completely different form from that given to the corresponding names of the other registers (see note 19 above).

[42] In *Fast.* 6.409–10 (*nondum conveniens diversis iste figuris/nomen ab averso ceperat amne deus*), Ovid clearly refers to the Propertian text (4.2) without naming him — a common practice among the Augustan poets. Furthermore, Vertumnus does not have his own independent story but is associated with the Velabrum story. See further Newlands (1995) 67–8.

[43] See notes 28, 34 above. See also Hardie's interesting discussion (1992) 74–5. with further references; Marquis (1974) 491–500; Gentilcore (1995) 110–20; Lindheim (1998) 27–38, esp. 34.

Why, then, did Ovid decide to break his list of kings at this specific point, and to continue with an inserted story barely connected with the actual list? Since Ovid's catalogue is close to that of Livy and Dionysius, we see that the story of Vertumnus and Pomona poised between the names of Proca and his sons actually substitutes for the narrative of the two historians concerning the conflict between Numitor and Amulius, the violent behaviour of Amulius to his niece Ilia, and the strife between the twins, Romulus and Remus. In other words, Ovid at this point passes over in silence some crucial episodes from the foundation myth of Rome. In effect, what he has done is to substitute a love-story for a narrative whose keynotes are violence and the struggle for power. And one can go further. The meaning of the catch-phrase with which Ovid almost ends his story, discloses, I think, the poet's political and philosophical message, *sed vi non est opus* (770). Violence has no use; things take their natural course. Livy's comment on the foundation of Rome is also revealing: *Sed **debebatur**, ut opinor, **fatis** tantae origo urbis maximique secundum deorum opes imperii principium* (1.4.1). The natural flow of things functions on its own and there is no need for strife or violence. In this Ovidian phrase *sed vi non est opus* we may have the essence of the inserted story. As a matter of fact, looking at Livy's text, the tincture of violence is spelt out in a variety of expressions. Besides his programmatic comment *plus tamen **vis** potuit quam voluntas patris aut verecundia aetatis* (1.3.10, for Amulius' deeds) which in its reversal, points to Ovid's *sed **vi** non est opus*, violence becomes the motif of the whole passage and it is incorporated at several instances with the appropriate vocabulary:[44] Furthermore, Ovid's learned concealment discloses, I believe, better than a thousand words this conflicting tradition concerning Romulus and Remus and consequently the foundation of the city.[45] Ogilvie states that 'Romulus remained a controversial figure throughout Roman history' and that 'at the back of his career lurked the fratricide and other violent deeds'.[46] It was this violence

---

[44] ***pulso** fratre Amulius regnat. Addit **sceleri scelus;** stirpem fratris virilem **interemit** . . . perpetua virginitate spem partus **adimit*** (1.3.11). At 1.4.3 Livy mentions Amulius' cruelty to the mother and her twins (*a **crudelitate** regia*); at 1.5.7 Romulus' violence is compared: *nec enim erat ad **vim apertam*** *par* before he kills Amulius (= *ita regem **obtruncat***). One could possibly add the phrase *vi compressa Vestalis* (1.4.2) for the way the Vestal virgin was raped by Mars and then conceived Romulus and Remus.
[45] Herbert-Brown (1994) 49–50.
[46] Ogilvie (1970) 85.

and tyrannical rule that was most probably stressed in the 'bad' tradition and of which we get a glimpse in the text of Livy and Dionysius. Knowing this ambiguity in the tradition, and the fact that at this point the poet refers to the foundation of Rome, it is quite possible that Ovid might have preferred to bypass this controversial point in silence. At the same time his concealment seems to be a sort of reaction against the importance the Roman historiography allocated to the foundation myth.

In this catalogue, the one out of two or three in the *Metamorphoses* with Latin names,[47] Ovid discloses his affinity with the historiographical works of the period. The catalogue with this order of names and the form they are given in the hexameter has lost the epic grandeur of its Vergilian counterpart. This catalogue, however, together with the love-story it frames, has its role within the bounds of a different sort of epic.[48]

The epic dimension becomes evident not only in its form but also in its context. The latter is enhanced when contrasted with the similar catalogue of the *Fasti*. There, the list of ancestors beginning with Electra and Jupiter, the parents of Dardanus, proceeds to the Trojan ancestors and the Alban kings and closes with Quirinus and Remus (4.31–56). It is followed by another list of Greeks who had settled in Italy prior to Aeneas' arrival and it is completed with Solymus, a Trojan comrade of Aeneas and founder of the poet's home town Sulmona. At this point where the two lists meet through the name of Aeneas, Ovid takes the opportunity to express his personal grief at being too far away from it. Thus, the whole list closes in a typically elegiac style, as the tenor of the end-piece is the personal grievance of the poet.[49]

> **me miserum**,[50] Scythico quam procul illa solo est!
> ergo ego tam longe — sed supprime, Musa, **querellas**!
> **non tibi sunt maesta sacra canenda lyra**. (4.82–84)

---

[47] The other catalogue is that of the rivers in the same Book (328–30). There is a third list of mixed Greek and Latin names. It describes the places Aesculapius sailed in his voyage to Rome, 15.699–718.

[48] Hinds (1987) 120 and 135.

[49] Feeney (1992) 1–25, Fantham (1998) at 83–4.

[50] For the allusive strength of the phrase in the Ovidian work and in particular its elegiac charge, see Hinds (1987) 29ff. See also Hinds (1992) 106–7 and (1998) 29–34; on this see also Fowler (2000) 122, but for different reasons.

Woe is me, how far is Sulmo from Scythian land! Therefore shall I
so far away — but check, my Muse, your complaints; it is not for you
to sing sacred themes on mournful strings.

(Trans. J.G. Frazer, modified)

Unlike this, the catalogue in the *Metamorphoses* has a more concrete
purpose. It belongs to a *perpetuum carmen*,[51] as the poet himself has
declared from the beginning, where everything is part of a universal history,[52] and in which feelings, situations, natural phenomena,
human actions or whatever else belong. It is a universal history which
begins with the creation of the universe from Chaos and reaches in
time the Rome of Ovid's days.[53] This catalogue of the Alban kings
refers to just a small period of *tempus edax*[54] and — unlike Vergil's — is
stripped of its *kleos*. With its historiographical provenance it declares
itself to be part of a broader and all embracing historical process.
Instead of exalting Rome, therefore, the poet — through his treatment and composition of the catalogue — allows his negative insin-
uations concerning the violence and the struggle for power which
are implicit in the foundation myth of Rome to surface.[55]

---

[51] *Met.* 1.4.

[52] Cf. Tissol (1997) 205; also Wheeler ch. 9 above.

[53] *Met*, 1.4: *ad mea perpetuum deducite tempora carmen:* For the phrase *ad mea . . . tempora*, see Barchiesi (1990) 91, Feeney (1992) 13–14.

[54] Ovid makes his view very clear when he says: *tempus edax rerum, tuque, invidiosa
vetustas,/ omnia destruitis vitiataque dentibus aevi/ paulatim lenta consumitis omnia morte!* (*Met.*
15.234–6).

[55] I thank Mr Corne Janse van Rensburg for his useful suggestions.

Texts

Livy 1.3.6–10.

Silvius deinde regnat, *Ascanii* filius, casu quodam in silvis natus. is *Aeneam Silvium* creat; is deinde *Latinum Silvium*. ab eo coloniae aliquot deductae, Prisci Latini appellati. mansit Silviis postea omnibus cognomen qui Albae regnarunt. **Latino *Alba* ortus, Alba *Atys*, Atye *Capys*, Capye *Capetus*, Capeto *Tiberinus*,** qui in traiectu Albulae amnis **submersus** celebre ad posteros **nomen** flumini **dedit.** *Agrippa* inde Tiberini filius, post Agrippam *Romulus Silvius* a patre accepto imperio regnat. *Aventino **fulmine*** ipse **ictus** regnum per manus tradidit. is sepultus in eo colle, qui nunc pars Romanae est urbis, **cognomen colli fecit.** *Proca* deinde regnat. is *Numitorem* atque *Amulium* procreat; Numitori, qui stirpis maximus erat, regnum vetustum Silviae gentis legat. **plus tamen vis potuit** quam voluntas patris aut verecundia aetatis.

1.4.1. sed debebatur, ut opinor, fatis tantae origo urbis maximique secundum deorum opes imperii principium — — — — — — — — — — — — — — — — —

1.6.3. ita Numitori **Albana re permissa** Romulum Remumque cupido cepit in iis locis . . . urbis condendae.

Vergil *Aeneid* 6.756–776

> **nunc age, Dardaniam prolem quae deinde sequatur**
> **gloria, qui maneant Itala de gente nepotes,**
> **inlustris animas nostrumque in nomen ituras,**
> **expediam dictis, et te tua fata docebo.**
> ille, vides, pura iuvenis qui nititur hasta,   760
> proxima sorte tenet lucis loca, primus ad auras
> aetherias Italo commixtus sanguine surget,
> *Silvius*, Albanum nomen, tua postuma proles,
> quem tibi longaevo serum Lavinia coniunx
> educet silvis regem regumque parentem,   765
> unde genus Longa nostrum dominabitur Alba.
> proximus ille *Procas*, Troianae gloria gentis,
> et *Capys* et *Numitor* et qui te nomine reddet
> *Silvius Aeneas*, pariter pietate vel armis

egregius, si umquam regnandam acceperit Albam.   770
qui iuvenes! quantas ostentant, aspice, viris
atque umbrata gerunt civili tempora quercu!
hi tibi Nomentum et Gabios urbemque Fidenam,
hi Collatinas imponent montibus arces,
Pometios Castrumque Inui Bolamque Coramque;   775
haec tum nomina erunt, nunc sunt sine nomine terrae.

Dionysius of Halicarnassus *Antiquitates Romanae* **1.71**

<u>Σιλουΐου</u> δ᾽ ἑνὸς δέοντα τριάκοντα ἔτη κατασχόντος τὴν ἀρχὴν Αἰνείας
υἱὸς αὐτοῦ διαδεξάμενος τὴν δυναστείαν ἑνὶ πλείω τριάκοντα ἐτῶν
ἐβασίλευσεν. μετὰ δὲ τοῦτον ἓν καὶ πεντήκοντα **Λατῖνος ἦρξεν ἔτη·**
Ἄλβας δὲ μετὰ τοῦτον ἑνὸς δέοντα τετταράκοντα ἔτη. μετὰ δὲ **Ἄλβαν**
Κάπετος ἓξ ἐπὶ τοῖς εἴκοσιν. ἔπειτα **Κάπυς δυεῖν δέοντα τριάκοντα.** μετὰ
δὲ **Κάπυν Κάλπετος** ἄχρι τρισκαίδεκα ἐτῶν κατέσχε τὴν ἀρχήν· ἑξῆς δὲ
Τιβερῖνος ὀκταετῆ χρόνον ἐβασίλευσεν. τελευτῆσαι δ᾽ οὗτος ἐν μάχῃ
παρὰ ποταμῷ γενομένῃ λέγεται· παρενεχθεὶς δὲ ὑπὸ τοῦ ῥεύματος
ἐπώνυμον ἑαυτῷ κατέλιπε τὸν ποταμὸν Ἄλβουλαν καλούμενον πρότερον. Τιβερίνου δὲ διάδοχος Ἀγρίππας ἓν καὶ τετταράκάκοντα ἐβασίλευσεν ἔτη. μετὰ δὲ Ἀγρίππαν Ἀλλώδιος τυραννικόν τι χρῆμα καὶ
θεοῖς ἀπεχθόμενον ἑνὸς δέοντα εἴκοσιν· ᾧπεριφρονοῦντι τὰ δαιμόνια
κατεσκεύαστο **κεραυνῶν τε μιμήματα** καὶ κτύποι βρονταῖς ἐμφερεῖς, οἷς
δεδίττεσθαι τοὺς ἀνθρώπους ὡς θεὸς ἠξίου. ὄμβρων δὲ καὶ κεραυνῶν
εἰς τὸν οἶκον αὐτοῦ κατασκηψάντων τῆς τε λίμνης, παρ᾽ ἣν οἰκῶν
ἐτύγχανε, πλημμύραν οὐκ εἰωθυῖαν λαβούσης **κατακλυσθεὶς** πανοίκιος
ἀπόλλυται· καὶ νῦν ἔτι διαλαμπούσης τῆς λίμνης ἐν μέρει τινί, ὅταν
ὑπονοστήσῃ τὸ νᾶμα καὶ σταθερὸς ὁ βυθὸς γένηται, παστάδων ἐρείπια
καὶ ἄλλα οἰκήσεως ἴχνη φαίνεται. Ἀουεντῖνος δὲ παρὰ τούτου τὴν
δυναστείαν διαδεξάμενος, ἀφ᾽ οὗ τῶν *ἑπτά λόφων* τις ἐπώνυμος ἐγένετο
τῶν συμπεπολισμένων τῇ Ῥώμῃ, τριάκοντα καὶ ἑπτὰ ἔτη τὴν ἀρχὴν
κατέσχεν. *Πρόκας* δὲ μετὰ τοῦτον ἔτη εἴκοσι καὶ τρία. ἔπειτα *Ἀμόλιος*
οὐ σὺν δίκῃ τὴν βασιλείαν κατασχὼν Νεμέτορι προσήκουσαν, ὃς ἦν
αὐτῷ πρεσβύτερος ἀδελφός, δύο καὶ τετταράκοντα ἔτη δυναστεύει.
Ἀμολίου δὲ ἀναιρεθέντος ὑπὸ Ῥωμύλου καὶ Ῥώμου τῶν ἐκ τῆς ἱερᾶς
κόρης γενομένων, ὡς αὐτίκα λεχθήσεται, μετὰ τὸν ἐκείνου θάνατον
ἀπολαμβάνει τὴν κατὰ νόμον δυναστείαν *Νεμέτωρ* ὁ τῶν νεανίσκων
μητροπάτωρ.

Diodorus Siculus 7.5.9ff

7.5.9. *Silvius* nihil dignum memoria in imperio egit et obiit, cum regnasset annis XLIX. Cuius imperium filius eiusdem *Aenias* accepit, qui cognominatus est *Silvius*; dominatusque plus quam triginta annos. Post quem *Latinus* regnavit, qui vocatus est Silvius, annis L. Hic in rebus gerendis et in bello validus repertus finitimam regionem evertit atque urbes antiquas, quae antea Latinorum vocabantur, XVIII condidit: . . . **10**: Defuncto autem Latino rex electus est filius eiusdem *Albas Silvius*, qui annis XXXVIII imperitavit. Post quem *Epitus Silvas* annis XXVI. Quo defuncto in regnum suffectus est *Apis*, qui annis regnavit duodetriginta. Et post eum *Kalpet* eiusdem filius; dominatusque est annis XIII, *Tiberius Sylvius* vero annis VIII. Hic adversus Tyrenos exercitum movens cum per Albam amnem copias traduceret, in gurgitem lapsus obiit, unde et fluvius appellatus est Tiberis. At post eius obitum *Agripas* in Latinos regnavit unum supra quadraginta annos. Postque hunc suscepit (regnum) *Arramulius Silvius* undeviginti annis. 11. . . . 12. Post hunc *Aventius* electus fuit, qui cum VII supra XXX annos potitus esset, in quodam proelio cum suburbanis in angustiam actus iuxta Aventium collem cecidit, unde collis Aventius dicebatur. Demortui in locum suffectus est filius eiusdem *Prokas Silvius* regnavitque annis III supra viginti. Quo mortuo iunior filius Amolius **per vim** regnum tenuit; eo quod in regiones longinquas profectus erat Numitor, eiusdem frater maior natu ac germanus. Amolius paulo plus annis XLIII regnavit atque a Remo et Romilo, qui Romam condiderunt interficitur (Eusebius, *Chronicle*, 1., pp. 284–90, ed. Schöne).

CHAPTER TWELVE

THE FALL OF TROY:
BETWEEN TRADITION AND GENRE

Andreola Rossi

As Aeneas, in book 2, begins his account of the final night of Troy, his recollection of the events follows, at least in its outlines, the path of memory of a rich literary and artistic tradition formed long before Virgil's own time. It is therefore natural that many studies of *Aeneid* 2 analyse Virgil's account in comparison with the intricate labyrinth of versions, literary and other, that the previous tradition had to offer.

Heinze's seminal study[1] had set the standard and many modern scholars have followed along the same path. They have illuminated how Virgil constantly remodels, in his own fashion, the most salient episodes of the last night of Troy inherited from a previous tradition. To cite only some of the material taken into consideration: earlier epics like the *Iliupersis* of Arctinus and the *Little Iliad* of Lesches as we find them in the summaries of Proclus, post-Virgilian Greek epics like the *Posthomerica* of Quintus Smyrnaeus, and the epyllion *The Capture of Troy* ('Ἰλίου ἅλωσις) written by Tryphiodorus.[2] Further, Euripidean dramas of the Trojan cycle,[3] the works of mythographers and, in another genre, historiography, the accounts of Timaeus and Hellanicus, partly preserved in Dionysius of Halicarnassus.

---

[1] Heinze (1993) 3–67.

[2] The relation between the *Aeneid* and these two later works is controversial. Heinze (1993) 37–49, Knight (1932) 178–89, Vian (1959), Campbell (1981), Gerlaud (1982) deny that these Greek authors were influenced by Virgil's *Aeneid*. For an opposite view see Keydell (1954), D'Ippolito (1976). Cf. also D'Ippolito in *E.V. s.v.* Trifiodoro.

[3] On earlier epics on Troy's downfall see Davies (1989) 63–79. See further Anderson (1997) who collects all ancient sources, literary and other, on the topic. More specifically, for scenes of the sack of Troy on vase paintings see Scherer (1963) 96ff., Robert (1923–26), Wiencke (1954), Dugas (1937) 5–26. On the *Tabula Iliaca* see Weitzmann (1959) 34ff., Galinsky (1969) 32ff., Sadurska (1964), Horsfall (1979). On the painting of Polygnotus see Robert (1893), Schefold (1975), Stansbury-O'Donnell (1989). For the relation between Virgil's *Aeneid* and the Cyclic Epics see Kopff (1981) 919–47.

My study of Book 2 of the *Aeneid* analyses the Virgilian account from a different perspective and therefore explores different material. I study how Virgil has described the fall of Troy according to a precise literary *topos* which forms an essential subtext to the entire narration, a *topos* which has been recognized and labeled by ancient rhetoricians as *Urbs Capta*, the *Fall of the City*.

First I outline briefly the origin of the *topos* and its development in various literary genres; then I show how Virgil is able to incorporate in his narration some of its most significant themes. I will conclude by discussing the larger narrative implications of his choice.

It is probably no accident that Polybius' famous criticism of Phylarchus' tragic style (2.56.7–8) focuses on Phylarchus' description and treatment of the capture of Mantinea by Cleomenes. Phylarchus, according to Polybius, "in his eagerness to arouse the pity of his readers (σπουδάζων δ' εἰς ἔλεον), and to enlist their sympathies, treats us to a picture of clinging women with their hair disheveled and their breasts bare, or again of crowds of both sexes together with their children and aged parents weeping and lamenting as they are led away to slavery. This sort of things he keeps up throughout his history always trying to bring horrors vividly before our eyes."[4] Polybius rounds off his criticism of Phylarchus with the charge that the latter is unable to distinguish between history and tragedy, for the object of tragedy is not the same as that of history but quite the opposite. The tragic poet should thrill and charm his audience for the moment by the verisimilitude of the words he puts into his character's mouth, but it is the task of the historian to instruct and convince for all time.[5]

Polybius' criticism has always been interpreted as a more or less justified attack against Phylarchus' pathetic style. Polybius criticizes Phylarchus for the latter fails to distinguish between history and tragedy and regards pleasure, ἡδονή, achieved by an unmediated vividness of dramatic representation, not truth, as the legitimate function of historiography.[6]

---

[4] Polybius 2.56.7–12.

[5] On this passage see, among others, Walbank (1957) *ad loc.* and Wiseman (1993) 134ff.; also Wiseman in ch. 17 below. Other comments throughout his work confirm Polybius' distaste for 'tragic history' although he himself could not escape its influence. Strabo accused him of trying to arouse pity in his readers (8.6.23). On tragic history see also Scheller (1911), Burck (1934) 178–233, Ullman (1942), Walbank (1955), Walbank (1960), Walsh (1961) 23–8, Sacks (1981) 144–70, Feldherr (1998) 7ff.

[6] Other exponents of the so-called 'tragic history' were Duris and Clitarchus.

Though this interpretation is undoubtedly accurate, there are good grounds for assuming that the type of scene described by Phylarchus and so harshly criticized by Polybius was not Phylarchus' own innovation. Diodorus Siculus, especially where his sources are Hellenistic historians, immediately shows the frequency and conventionality of these descriptions. In book 17, probably drawn from Clitarchus, we find the famous description of the capture of Thebes,[7] the description of the Persian camp after the battle of Issus, and the capture of Persepolis.[8] In books 19–20, probably drawn from another major exponent of Hellenistic historiography, Duris of Samos, we have the capture of Syracuse by Agathocles and the capture of Segesta.[9]

In light of the widespread diffusion of this type-scene among Hellenistic historians, we may try to redefine, at least to some extent, the meaning of the Polybian passage. Polybius' criticism is not simply a generic attack against Phylarchus' pathetic style, as is usually suggested; it becomes also a pointed criticism against a tendency common to a certain type of historiography, namely the exploitation of the *topos* of the *Urbs Capta* and of its various components.

The theme itself, to be sure, is not a novelty of Hellenistic historiography. Pseudo-Hermogenes in Περὶ μεθόδου δεινότητος, under the heading περὶ τοῦ τραγικῶς λέγειν (Rabe 439), traces it back to a passage in *Iliad* 9, where, as Phoenix narrates the story of Meleager to Achilles, he has Meleager's wife remind her husband of the many

---

Duris is probably one of the sources for Diodorus Siculus' books 19–21 (Agathocles), Clitarchus for Diodorus' book 17 (Alexander the Great). On the topic see Burck (1934) 195ff. On Duris see also *FGrH* 76 F I Ἔφορος δὲ καὶ Θεόπομπος τῶν γενομένων πλεῖστον ἀπελείφθησαν. οὔτε γὰρ μιμήσεως μετέλαβον οὐδεμιᾶς οὔτε ἡδονῆς ἐν τῷ φράσαι, αὐτοῦ δὲ τοῦ γράφειν μόνον ἐπεμελήθησαν. This brief fragment contains Duris' critique of Ephorus and Theopompus. According to Duris, Ephorus and Theopompus fell far short of the events as they achieved no imitation/representation (μίμησις) or pleasure (ἡδονή) in their presentation, but were concerned merely with writing. Deprived of its original context, the fragment appears quite obscure, but does allow for some speculations about the literary aims of these historians. Duris seems to imply that pleasure is a legitimate function of historiography and that it can be produced by presenting a dramatic re-enactment of events. On the topic see also Kebric (1977) 39ff., Torraca (1988), Gray (1987), Morgan (1993), Feldherr (1998) 8. Cf. also Plutarch (*Per.* 28.1). Plutarch compares Duris' account of the Athenians' capture of Samos with that of Thucydides, Ephorus, and Aristotle and, observing that Duris alone dwelt on the brutal tortures inflicted by Pericles on the Samian captains, condemns him for having turned those events into tragedy (Δοῦρις δ᾽ ὁ Σάμιος τούτοις ἐπιτραγῳδεῖ).

[7] Diodorus Siculus 17.13.
[8] Diodorus Siculus 17.35; 70.
[9] Diodorus Siculus 19.6–8; 20.71.

κήδεα, sorrows, that the inhabitants of a captured city have to endure:[10]

> λίσσετ᾽ ὀδυρομένη, καί οἱ κατέλεξεν ἅπαντα
> κήδε᾽, ὅσ᾽ ἀνθρώποισι πέλει τῶν ἄστυ ἁλώῃ.
> ἄνδρας μὲν κτείνουσι, πόλιν δέ τε πῦρ ἀμαθύνει
> τέκνα δέ τ᾽ ἄλλοι ἄγουσι βαθυζώνους τε γυναῖκας.
> (Homer *Iliad* 9.591–4)

> She supplicated, in tears, and rehearsed in their numbers before him
> all the sorrows that come to men when their city is taken:
> they kill the men, and the fire leaves the city in ashes,
> and strangers lead the children away and the deep-girdled women.[11]

Nevertheless, prior to Hellenistic historiography, it is a different genre that exploited the *topos* to its fullest extent: tragedy. The Euripidean tragedies of the Trojan War and its aftermath, the *Trojan Women*, *Hecuba*, and *Andromache*, are a clear example.[12] But most significantly, Attic tragedy already reveals the potential adaptability of the theme of the *Iliupersis* and transforms it into the *topos* of the *Urbs Capta*. Aeschylus' *Seven against Thebes*, for example, shows how its most important images may be universalized and fruitfully applied to the description of the fate of other cities.

Precisely in its capacity as a *topos* that may move beyond the destiny of a single city, oratory begins to employ it with a certain regularity and for its own purposes. Demosthenes in *De Falsa Legatione* describes the fate of the city of Phocis, reproducing, in his account, its most typical elements:[13]

> **θέαμα δεινόν**, ὦ ἄνδρες Ἀθηναῖοι, καὶ **ἐλεινόν**. ὅτε γὰρ νῦν ἐπορευόμεθ᾽ εἰς Δελφούς, ἐξ ἀνάγκης ἦν ὁρᾶν ἡμῖν πάντα ταῦτα, οἰκίας κατεσκαμμένας, τείχη περιῃρημένα, χώραν ἔρημον τῶν ἐν ἡλικίᾳ, γύναια δὲ καὶ παιδάρι᾽ ὀλίγα καὶ πρεσβύτας ἀνθρώπους οἰκτρούς· οὐδ᾽ ἂν εἷς δύναιτ᾽ ἀφικέσθαι τῷ λόγῳ τῶν ἐκεῖ κακῶν νῦν ὄντων.
> (Demosthenes *De Falsa Legatione* 65)

---

[10] On the topic see Paul (1982).

[11] Cf. also *Il.* 22.60–71 where Priam foretells Hector the destiny of Troy. Here, though, Priam is anticipating specifically the Fall of Troy as there are punctual references to some of its most important episodes.

[12] On the unity of these Euripidean tragedies based on the *Iliupersis* theme see Anderson (1997) 133–73. There were probably also some Sophoclean tragedies that dealt with episodes related to the sack of Troy. On the topic see Anderson (1997) 174–6.

[13] Cf. also Aeschines, *Ctes.* 157.

... the spectacle is horrible and pitiful, men of Athens. For when recently we were on our way to Delphi, we could not help seeing it all — houses razed to the ground, cities stripped of their walls, the land destitute of men in their prime — only a few poor women and little children left, and some old men in misery. Indeed no words can describe the distress now prevailing there.

Interestingly enough, the spectacle of the captured city is introduced by Demosthenes by two significant adjectives which betray its tragic connections: the spectacle is horrible and pitiful (θέαμα δεινόν . . . καὶ ἐλεινόν). The tragic theme of the *Iliupersis* is inherited by a different genre, oratory, and becomes the rhetorical deployment of the *topos* of the *Urbs Capta*.

Despite the decline of Greek tragedy of the classical period, the theme reemerges in Latin literature. Ennius, apart from his tragedies of the Trojan cycle,[14] employs it in the *praetexta* entitled *Ambracia*, the city besieged by Fulvius Nobilior in the Aetolian war. From what we can infer from the title, Ennius here vividly demonstrates how the *topos* functions as a crucial link between two distinct genres: tragedy and historiography. In addition, the theme finds a prominent place in Latin rhetorical theory and Quintilian in the *Institutio* gives us the most detailed account of its major components:[15]

> Sic <et> urbium captarum crescit miseratio. Sine dubio enim, qui dicit expugnatam esse civitatem, complectitur omnia quaecumque talis fortuna recipit, sed in adfectus minus penetrat brevis hic velut nuntius. At si aperias haec, quae verbo uno inclusa erant, apparebunt effusae per domus ac templa flammae et ruentium tectorum fragor et ex diversis clamoribus unus quidam sonus, aliorum fuga incerta, alii extremo complexo suorum cohaerentes et infantium feminarumque ploratus et male usque in illum diem servati fato senes . . .
> (Quintilian *Institutio Oratoria* 8.3.67–68)

---

[14] Besides Ennius, Roman tragedy in the archaic period had an obvious predilection for the Trojan cycle. Livius Andronicus wrote the *Andromeda* and the *Equos Troianus*; Naevius wrote the *Danaë* and the *Equos Troianus*.
[15] Cf. also Aristotle *Rh.* I.7.1365a12; Plutarch *Vit. Hom.* 67; *Rhet. Her.* 4.39. On this last passage see Calboli (1969) *ad loc.*; Marx (1894) *ad loc.* Cf. also Sallust *Cat.* 51.9 *quae belli saevitia esset, quae victis acciderent, enumeravere: rapi virgines, pueros, divelli liberos a parentum complexu; matres familiarum pati quae victoribus conlubuissent; fana atque domos spoliari, caedem, incendia fieri; postremo armis, cadaveribus, cruore atque luctu omnia compleri.* The conventionality of the theme can be best recognized in Latin poets. Cf. Propertius, 4.8.56 *spectaclum capta nec minus urbe fuit*; Ovid, *Met.* 12.225 *captaeque erat urbis imago.*

So too, we may move our hearers to tears by the picture of a captured town. For the mere statement that the town was stormed, while
no doubt it embraces all that such a calamity involves, has all the
curtness of a dispatch and fails to penetrate to the emotions of the
hearer. But if we expand all that the one word 'stormed' includes, we
shall see the flames pouring from house and temple and hear the crash
of falling roofs and one confused clamour made of many cries. We
shall behold some in doubt whither to fly, others clinging to their near-
est and dearest in one last embrace, while the wailing of women and
children and the laments of old men that the cruelty of fate should
have spared them to see that day will strike upon our ears . . .

But it is the last sentence of Quintilian's passage that clearly identifies
the description of an *Urbs Capta* as a *topos* with its own specific conventions: *consequemur autem, ut manifesta sint, si fuerint verisimilia, et licebit
etiam falso adfingere quidquid fieri solet* — and we shall secure the vividness we seek, if only our descriptions give the impression of truth;
indeed, we may even add fictitious incidents of the type which commonly occur.

By Virgil's time, then, the theme of the capture of a city was well
established in at least three different Graeco-Roman literary traditions, tragedy, historiography, and oratory. Tragedy had employed
it in its descriptions of the Fall of Troy, although, as we see in the
case of the *Seven against Thebes* or the *Ambracia* of Ennius, the *topos*
was easily applied and extended to the fate of other cities. Hellenistic
historiography, in turn, derived it directly from tragedy and exploited
it to the full and for obvious reasons: the spectacle of a captured
city was perfectly suited to raising that sense of horror and pity, to
use Demosthenes' words, towards which many Hellenistic historians
were striving, as Polybius constantly reminds us. It comes as no surprise that to achieve those 'tragic' effects historians made use of a
topos that had close connections with the tragic tradition, thus blurring even further the boundary-line between the two genres. Hence
Polybius' criticism of Phylarchus for not recognizing the difference
between history and tragedy.

We may now turn to its employment in epic, and more precisely
in Ennius and Virgil. In his commentary at *Aeneid* 2.313,[16] Servius
makes some very interesting remarks:

---

[16] *exoritur clamorque virum clangorque tubarum.*

> sicut Albam Tullus Hostilius iussit everti.
> (Servius at *Aen.* 2.313)

In the same way Tullus Hostilius ordered Alba to be destroyed.

Soon after, as Pyrrhus is forcing his way into the palace of Priam, a similar observation follows. At *Aeneid* 2.486[17] he, again, mentions Alba Longa in relation to Virgil's description of the sack of Troy:

> de Albano excidio translatus est locus.
> (Servius at *Aen.* 2.486)

This passage is adapted from the sack of Alba.

There can be little doubt, as Norden shows, that Servius is referring to the destruction of Alba as narrated by Ennius in his *Annales*.[18] Nevertheless, the relation of Ennius' text and the Virgilian account remains problematic. For once, it is impossible to establish in what measure and in what manner Virgil draws from the text of Ennius, nor, as Wigodsky showed, do Servian remarks of the kind *translatus est locus*, need to be taken literally.[19] Some speculations may still be allowed. The similarities between Ennius' description of Alba and Virgil's sack of Troy could not have extended, for obvious reasons, to individual episodes. Servius' remarks are therefore most likely meant to indicate the presence, in the two authors, of similar themes.

Livy's account of the capture of Alba further supports this hypothesis. Whether we believe, as Norden does, that Ennius and Livy worked independently, modeling their accounts on similar descriptions of captured cities found in Hellenistic historiography, or that Ennius was Livy's filter,[20] the similarities between Virgil's sack of

---

[17] *at domus interior gemitu miseroque tumultu.*

[18] On the topic see Norden (1915) 154ff. The same opinion is expressed by Skutsch (1985) 279 who also explains possible reasons for the omission of the mention of Ennius in Servius. Cf. also Austin at 313 and Conington at 486.

[19] Cf. also Wigodsky (1972) 70 on Virgil's reasons for employing the Ennian description of Alba Longa: 'Whatever was the nature of the resemblance between Vergil's story of Troy's last night and the earlier descriptions of Rome's first conquest, the echoes may have been meant to lighten the gloom of Troy's fall with a hint of Rome's rise.'

[20] Norden (1915) 158 believes in a common source. More recently Skutsch (1985) 279, although not challenging the thesis that the dramatic elements in Livy's narrative derive from the historical style criticized by Polybius, does not rule out a direct influence of Ennius' account on the Livian description. Livy probably knew Ennius' *Annales* by heart from his school days.

Troy and Livy's description of the capture of Alba give cause for
attention. In addition to some lexical parallels, the similarities appear
in the treatment of similar motifs which form the common repertoire of the *Urbs Capta* theme.[21] These are the features which Virgil,
following a well-trodden path exploited in tragedy and historiography, had probably inherited from Ennius and wanted to reproduce.

Armed with this background we may return to Virgil and reread
the fall of Troy in this new dimension. I will particularly focus on
one theme from this larger movement, which I call the "now and
then" theme. My choice is motivated by two reasons. The presence
of this essential motif has not received recognition commensurate
with its importance from previous commentators. Further it may be
applied fruitfully to the interpretation of another much debated
Virgilian passage, explaining complex temporal/narrative dynamics
operative in the poem.

'Now and Then'

After Aeneas, following the memory of his recollections, has recounted
to Dido all the fatal incidents that led to the capitulation of Troy,
Sinon's deceit, Laocoon's death, and the entering of the Trojan horse
into the city, his story reaches a new climax. He begins to tell the
story of the final night of Troy. To underline the momentum reached
by his narration, a new *exordium* introduces his account of these
events:[22]

> quis cladem illius noctis, quis funera fando
> explicet aut possit lacrimis aequare labores?
> *urbs antiqua ruit multos dominata per annos*;
> (Virgil *Aeneid* 2.361–3)

> Who has the words to tell that night's disaster?
> And who to tell the deaths? What tears could equal
> our agony? *An ancient city falls*
> *that ruled for so many years.*

---

[21] On the relation between Livy and Virgil's *Aeneid* see also Woodman (1989).
[22] Aeneas' new exordium recalls his first one at *Aen.* 2.6–8 *quis talia fando/ Myrmidonum Dolopumve aut duri miles Ulixi/ temperet a lacrimis?*

Ancient Troy which once had ruled for so many years has now fallen. As if to encompass the entire tale of Troy's fatal night in a sort of thematic ring composition, the passage that brings closure to Aeneas' account reiterates a similar idea. This time, though, the subject of the remark is not Troy but its leader Priam. The headless trunk of this once proud ruler of many lands and people of Asia is now lying (*iacet*) on the shore, a nameless body. Like the city of Troy, so also its symbol, the king, has come to a ruinous end:[23]

> haec finis Priami fatorum, hic exitus illum
> sorte tulit Troiam incensam et prolapsa videntem
> *Pergama, tot quondam populis terrisque superbum*
> *regnatorem Asiae. iacet ingens litore truncus,*
> *avulsumque umeris caput et sine nomine corpus.*
>
> (Virgil *Aeneid* 2.554–8)

> This was the end of Priam's destinies,
> the close that fell to him by fate: to see
> his Troy in flames and Pergamum laid low
> *who once was proud king over many nations*
> *and lands of Asia. Now he lies along*
> *the shore, a giant trunk, his head torn from*
> *his shoulders, as a corpse without a name.*[24]

The thematic correspondences shared by the two passages have been noticed by scholars and explained in various ways. Conington in his commentary was the first to link them as sharing a common theme, as both passages compare the past glory of the city to its present nothingness. At verse 557 Conington states: 'Here as elsewhere the extent of Priam's dominion is exaggerated.' Conington therefore interprets the two passages as a hyperbole.

Austin's remark at 2.363 is less concise and proposes an interesting parallel between the Virgilian passage and Livy's epitaph on Alba:[25]

---

[23] Cf. also Aeneas' speech at *Aen.* 2.324–27 *venit summa dies et ineluctabile tempus/ Dardaniae. fuimus Troes, fuit Ilium et ingens/gloria Teucrorum; ferus omnis Iuppiter Argos/ transtulit; incensa Danai dominantur in urbe.*

[24] Quotations from the *Aeneid* are from Mynors (1972). Translations of the *Aeneid* are from Mandelbaum (1981).

[25] Austin at 363. Cf. also Austin's remarks at 554 where he notes that after Priam has been killed, Virgil supplies a coda which is much in the manner of historians, who regularly summarize the life of a dead man with a *formula* such as *hic exitus.* Cf. also Heinze (1993) 59 n. 71. He compares these closing words to those of the *paidagogus* in Sophocles' *Electra* (757), of the messenger in *Andromache* (1161), *Bacchae* (1151), and *Heracles* (1013) where the tone is that of a concluding narrative, suited

unaque hora quadrigentorum annorum opus quibus Alba steterat excidio
ac ruinis dedit

(Livy 1.29.6)

and a single hour gave over to destruction and desolation, the work
of four hundred years during which Alba had stood.

The similarities between the two passages are indeed noteworthy and
Servius' remarks, connecting Virgil's description of the sack of Troy
to the Ennian account, might induce one to see Ennius as a common 'source' for both Virgil and Livy. Yet I believe that we should
move beyond the analysis of specific common sources. We should
recognize the fundamental importance of the idea expressed in the
two passages and its vital role in the *topos* of the *Fall of the City*.

To do this, let us return for a moment to Polybius. In his criticism of Phylarchus, Polybius states that the former, wishing to emphasize Antigonus' cruelty, narrates the terrible suffering to which the
Mantineans had been exposed, adding, at the end of his narration,
as a sort of epitaph that 'such were the misfortunes that overtook
this, the most ancient and greatest city of Arcadia.'[26] The two themes
that we have just analyzed in *Aeneid* 2, antiquity and greatness, are
here linked explicitly.

As Conington at *Aeneid* 557 noted the hyperbole of Aeneas' statement, Walbank, similarly, comments on the Polybian passage: 'But
in any case the present passage is tendentious in Phylarchus and
ironical in Polybius.'[27] This is surely true, but Phylarchus does not
seem to have been the only one inclined to these historical exag-
gerations. A cursory glance at historiographical texts attests to the
extended use of this 'epitaph of closure' in the description of the
topos of the *Urbs Capta*. In Diodorus Siculus, whose source here was
probably Clitarchus, the long description of the downfall of Persepolis
is rounded off in a similar fashion.[28] As Persepolis had exceeded all
other cities in prosperity, so, in the same measure, in the moment

---

to the style of drama. In similar fashion, *Servius Auctus* comments on the dramatic
tone of 363 as he states *sane hoc dolentis est, non narrantis*. At 557 Servius explains the
expression *regnatorem Asiae* in the following way: *quia imperaverat et Phrygiae et Mygdoniae*.

[26] Polybius 2.56.6.
[27] Walbank (1957) *ad loc*.
[28] Diodorus Siculus 17.70.6.

of its downfall, it now exceeded all others in misery. In Livy, a reflective Marcellus, like so many Herodotean characters, contemplates for the last time the city of Syracuse at the moment it is about to fall. In the space of one hour (*momento horae*) the most beautiful city of so ancient glory (*vetusta gloria urbis*) would be reduced to ashes (*arsura omnia et ad cineres reditura . . .*).[29]

Was Polybius then only criticizing Phylarchus for having preferred a *locus communis* to historical accuracy? Although a possibility, we have seen previously that in this entire passage Polybius is concerned mainly with one feature of Phylarchus' writing: Phylarchus is condemned by Polybius for confusing the boundaries between history and tragedy. Set within this larger interpretative frame, Polybius' remark may conceal a more serious criticism. Polybius' 'ironical comment' stresses how Phylarchus is at fault for having applied a tragic narrative pattern to a historical narration. Far from being just a historical slip, or a *locus communis*, the emphasis on the antiquity and vast dominion of the city of Mantinea functions, in Phylarchus' narrative, to exploit the idea of sudden and catastrophic reversal, μεταβολή: the higher the renown the more pitiful the downfall which will eventually follow.

Viewed from this perspective, this reflection moves beyond its function as an inert record of a *topos*. It also becomes functional in the context of a reading of the episode through a tragic frame. This epitaph built on the temporal contrast between the πρότερον and the blessed brilliance of the past, and the present with its dramatic downfall, the μεταβολὴ τῆς τύχης, exemplifies the narrative pattern that constitutes the essence of a tragic narration, and more generally the embodiment of a tragic dialectic. That is the reason for its exploitation by Hellenistic or 'tragic' historiography, and that is probably the reason why Polybius harshly censures the passage in Phylarchus.

Aristotle had already emphasized that this narrative pattern was an essential feature of tragedy. The best tragic action is the one that describes the passage from a state of happiness to a state of unhappiness:

> ἀνάγκη ἄρα τὸν καλῶς ἔχοντα μῦθον . . . καὶ μεταβάλλειν οὐκ εἰς εὐτυχίαν ἐκ δυστυχίας ἀλλὰ τοὐναντίον ἐξ εὐτυχίας εἰς δυστυχίαν.
>
> (Aristotle *Poetics* 13.4)

---

[29] Livy 25.24.11ff. Cf. also Livy 4.59.10 *qui ubi venerunt, oppidum vetere fortuna opulentum tres exercitus diripuere.*

> It is imperative that a fine plot-structure . . . involves a change not from affliction to prosperity but rather the reverse, from prosperity to affliction.

It is Euripides, in Aristotle's opinion, who wins the palm as the most 'tragic' of all poets for his ability to recreate precisely this kind of plot-structure, which 'makes the most tragic impression.'[30] His tragedies from the Trojan cycle are a clear example. Not only does their wider structure imply this pattern; his characters also exploit the theme in an almost obsessive manner. The laments of Hecuba, Andromache, and the choruses are not simply the laments of women in distress. These characters rather embody the essence of tragedy: the falling from a state of blessed happiness, power, and renown, the 'then', to one of unhappiness and ruin, the 'now.'[31] The destiny of Troy is framed by the same tragic dialectic in the laments of Hecuba in the *Trojan Women*:[32]

> ὦ μεγάλα **δή ποτ'** ἀμπνέουσ' ἐν βαρβάροις
> Τροία, τὸ κλεινὸν ὄνομ' ἀφαιρήσῃ **τάχα**
> (Euripides *Troades* 1277–8)

> Troy **once** so proud among the barbarian peoples,
> **soon** you will be deprived of your famous name

We may move beyond the fate of Troy. In the Aeschylean drama of the *Seven against Thebes*, the chorus laments the destiny of Thebes in analogous fashion: 'Pitiful it is to send a city so old to the under-world.' As noted by Hutchinson,[33] the use of ψαφαρᾷ σποδῷ, so concrete an expression, 'powdery ashes' brings out starkly the extremity of the change.[34] To cite one last example, in the *Persians* of Aeschylus, the defeat of the Persian army suggests to the messenger a similar reflection:

> ὦ γῆς ἁπάσης Ἀσιάδος πολίσματα,
> ὦ Περσὶς αἶα καὶ πολὺς πλούτου λιμήν,
> ὡς ἐν μιᾷ πληγῇ κατέφθαρται πολὺς
> ὄλβος . . .
> (Aeschylus *Persae* 249–53)

---

[30] *Po.* 13.5.
[31] Cf. Euripides *Tr.* 194–6 (Hecuba); 506–7 (Hecuba); 614–15 (Andromache); Euripides *Hec.* 619–23. (Hecuba)
[32] Cf. also Euripides *Tr.* 45–7.
[33] Hutchinson (1985) *ad loc.*
[34] Aeschylus *Th* 321–5.

O cities of all the land of Asia, o realm of Persia and boun-
teous haven of wealth, how in a single stroke plenteous wealth
has been shattered.

Let us return to the Virgilian passages. Aeneas' somber reflection on
the μεταβολὴ τῆς τύχης that befell the city of Troy cannot be simply viewed as linked to a specific source model. More fittingly, it
should be interpreted as a re-elaboration of one of the main themes
of the *topos* of the *Urbs Capta* as it is found in tragedy and historiography. Aeneas' use of it as an epitaph of closure, in the fashion
of many historiographical texts, stresses even further the close connection between the Virgilian passage and the historiographical tradition. But more importantly, the vision of the destiny of Troy and
of the destiny of Priam as unfolding within a tragic narrative pattern
of inevitable temporal decline marks his account as a tragic one. In
this capacity, Troy and its downfall become the perfect paradigm
of a tragic vision of history. Through Aeneas' words that downfall
becomes a tragic warning.[35]

Is there a larger function for this warning in the *Aeneid*? After all,
Aeneas moves forward to be the founder of a new city, a new race,

---

[35] A related motif which appears in Aeneas' account may be briefly mentioned
here. As the horse is eventually brought into the city by a jubilant crowd, night
falls and the warriors, hidden inside, are described as getting out while the now
silent city and its inhabitants are deeply buried in sleep and wine (*Aen.* 2.265 *invadunt
urbem somno vinoque sepultam*). Earlier versions of the fall of Troy do not describe the
city and its inhabitants in such a fashion. The image seems again to derive from
the *Annales* of Ennius. Cf. *Ann.* 288 Skutsch *Nunc hostes vino domiti somnoque sepulti;*
366ff. *omnes mortales victores, cordibus vivis/laetantes, vino curatos somnus repente/in campo
passim mollissimus perculit acris.* Cf. also Skutsch (1985) *ad loc.* In the *Aeneid*, though,
the theme is not purely descriptive. It serves a well-defined dramatic function: it
highlights the striking contrast between the former state of foolish happiness and
the catastrophic debacle soon to follow. The same theme, used for a similar purpose, appears in another famous passage of the *Aeneid*, introducing another night
full of reassuring hopes which ends in slaughters. In *Aeneid* 9, as Euryalus and Nisus
are heading towards the camp of the victorious Rutulians, they witness a similar
spectacle (*Aen.* 9.314–19) *egressi superant fossas noctisque per umbram/castra inimica petunt,
multis tamen ante futuri/exitio. passim somno vinoque per herbam/corpora fusa vident, arrectos
litore currus,/inter lora rotasque viros, simul arma iacere,/vina simul.* This image is in stark
contrast with Homer's Thracians, whose sleep is the result only of exhaustion not
inebriation. Like the Trojans, the Rutulians are represented overcome with wine
and sleep to highlight, in dramatic fashion, their state of foolish confidence before
their death, as Nisus points out at 9.188–90 *cernis quae Rutulos habeat fiducia rerum:/lumina
rara micant, somno vinoque soluti/procubuere, silent late loca.*

and a new empire, which in Jupiter's own words to Venus is described as endless. The empire will have limits neither of space nor time:[36]

> his ego nec metas rerum nec tempora pono:
> imperium sine fine dedi.
> (Virgil Aeneid 1.278–9)

> I set no limits to their fortunes and
> no time; I give them empire without end.

No statement could more openly contradict the tragic narrative pattern of Troy's downfall: everything must come to an end, and the higher the entity, the more calamitous its downfall. A fate precisely the opposite of Jupiter's prophecy for Rome's future.

Two competing historical visions emerge and coexist contemporaneously in the poem. The former envisions a development of the history of Rome along a teleological line that spreads from a beginning towards an endless end and that will lead to the formation of Rome's endless empire. The latter is informed by a tragic dialectic, where circularity between rise and fall leads to numberless beginnings and numberless ends. It is precisely, I believe, this duality of visions present throughout the development of the narration that problematizes the reading of the poem.[37] This is especially true where these two visions are present at the same time in the narration. Let us proceed to such a moment.

A passage in the famous parade of heroes in *Aeneid* 6 offers a powerful example. As Anchises begins to reveal the future history of Rome to his son, he shows Aeneas his Alban descendants: Procas, Capys, Numitor, Silvius Aeneas. They will be the founders of new Alban cities, Nomentum, Gabii, Fidena, Collatia, Pometii, Castrum Inui, Bola, and Cora:

> hi tibi Nomentum et Gabios urbemque Fidenam,
> hi Collatinas imponent montibus arces,
> Pometios Castrumque Inui Bolamque Coramque;
> *haec tum nomina erunt, nunc sunt sine nomine terrae.*[38]
> (Virgil Aeneid 6.773–6)

---

[36] As noted by Servius *ad loc.*, *metas* refers to geographical extension, *tempora* to the temporal extension of Roman dominion. On this passage and the employment of *sine fine* in the *Aeneid* see also Mitchell-Boyask (1996).

[37] On this see also Pagán ch. 3 above.

[38] Cf. also *Aen.* 7.411–13, *locus Ardea quondam / dictus avis, et nunc magnum manet Ardea nomen, / sed fortuna fuit.*

For you they will construct
Nomentum, Gabii, Fidena's city,
and with the ramparts of Collatia,
Pometia and Castrum Inui,
and Bola, Cora, they will crown the hills.
These will be names that now are nameless lands.

As the cities of the Alban kingdom are enumerated one by one by
Anchises as necessary steps in the building of the future empire of
Rome, we may detect an inverted role played in this passage by the
'now and then' theme to which there is an allusion by contrast: cities
'now' nameless, will 'then' have a name (*haec tum nomina erunt, nunc
sunt sine nomine terrae*). The allusion by contrast is further emphasized
by an intertextual nexus with Priam's death. As Priam is now in
Aeneas' account a *sine nomine corpus*, so the cities of the Alban kingdom are now (*nunc*) *sine nomine terrae*. Priam's nameless state in his
final stage is that of the Alban cities in their initial condition in
Anchises' pre-history. But the inversion of the motif 'now and then'
is only apparent. Denis Feeney showed that the very Alban towns
which appear in the parade will fade and become ghost towns in
the time of Virgil's reader:[39]

> *haec tum nomina erunt, nunc sunt sine nomine terrae* . . . The tenses are intrigu-
> ingly two-sided, depending on whether one's perspective in time is that
> of Aeneas, or of Vergil's audience. To Aeneas, the words say that
> these will be famous names after his time, whereas now, in his life-
> time, they are areas of land without any title . . . To the contemporary
> audience, the words are saying that the places will be what they are
> in fact — *mere names*; now, for 'us' they are only pieces of land, with-
> out the reputation they once had . . .

To Virgil's reader the *nunc* will therefore have the same application
as that in Priam's death. Like Troy and its leader, these Alban cities
are subjected to a circular and inevitable process of rise and fall.

What will happen to Rome then? Ovid, in the famous speech of
Pythagoras at the end of the *Metamorphoses*, in a passage that is highly
evocative of the Virgilian one, seems to suggest an answer:

---

[39] Feeney (1986) 7. Cf. also Mack (1978) 70: "Already there is a sense of the
evanescent quality of men's achievements. Alba may be replaced by something better, but the city which is (in this account) to be Silvius' contribution to Roman history has already run its course by the time of the third Roman king." Cf. also
O'Hara (1990) 166. On the relation between 'mythological time' and 'Augustan
time' in *Aeneid* 8 see Novara (1986).

sic magna fuit censuque virisque,
perque decem potuit tantum dare sanguinis annos,
nunc humilis veteres tantummodo Troia ruinas
et pro divitiis tumulos ostendit avorum.
clara fuit Sparte, magnae viguere Mycenae,
nec non et Cecropis, nec non Amphionis arces:
vile solum Sparte est, altae cecidere Mycenae;
Oedipodioniae *quid sunt, nisi nomina, Thebae?*
quid Pandioniae restant, *nisi nomen, Athenae?*
nunc quoque Dardaniam fama est consurgere Romam,
Apenninigenae quae proxima Thybridis undis
mole sub ingenti rerum fundamina ponit.
haec igitur formam crescendo mutat et olim
inmensi caput orbis erit.

(Ovid *Metamorphoses* 15.422–35)

Like Troy, magnificent in men and riches,
For ten years lavish with her blood, and now
Displaying only ruins and for wealth
The old ancestral tombs. Sparta, Mycenae,
Athens, and Thebes, *all flourished once, and now*
What are they more than names? I hear that Rome
Is rising, out of Trojan blood, established
On strong and deep foundations, where the Tiber
Comes from the Appenines. Rome's form is changing
Growing to greatness, and she will be, some day,
Head of the boundless world.

This well-known passage works in a curious way. The sage, at the
end of his long speech about endless change and transformation,
predicts the future greatness of the city. Reechoing the prophecy of
Jupiter in *Aeneid* 1,[40] Pythagoras anticipates for Rome an endless
future as head of a boundless world. But his prophecy looks suspicious at best. Rome's close connection with Troy, Sparta, Mycenae,
Thebes, and Athens, which have completed their cycle of rise and
fall and, in an overt allusion to our passage in the *Aeneid*, have now
sunk to be mere names, *nomina*, suggests, as noted by Hardie, something different: 'In the mouth of Pythagoras in *Metamorphoses* 15.431–52
the place of Rome as the final empire in the succession becomes
questionable; when change is king, what guarantee that Rome will
be the exception that proves eternal?'[41]

---

[40] *Aen.* 1.278–9 *his ego nec metas rerum nec tempora pono:/imperium sine fine dedi.*
[41] Hardie (1993) 95. Cf. also, for similar conclusions, Anderson (1963) 27:

But what about Virgil? He, typically is not as straightforward, but maybe the *Aeneid* already suggests which of the two courses Rome will be more likely to follow. In two recent articles Moles[42] and Bowie,[43] following the lead of the famous Servian remark that Priam's death is modeled on Pompey's death, *Pompei tangit historiam*,[44] argue convincingly that in the description of Priam's death we see a sudden irruption of the historical Pompey into the mythical narrative.[45] The notable shift in tense to the present (*iacet*) would serve to accommodate such an intrusion and to erase the temporal gap between narrated events and the audience of the story, which is simultaneously Aeneas' Carthaginian audience and the author's Roman audience.[46]

If this were the case, the headless trunk of Priam, the symbol of the fallen city, who is now lying on the shore, would not only be representative of Troy's downfall. His death would have implications also for Virgil's contemporary reader. From the perspective of Virgil's contemporary audience, Nomentum, Gabii, Fidena, Collatia, Pometii, Castrum Inui, Bola, and Cora are not the only ones to have completed their cycle of rise and fall. By conflating the death of Priam with that of Pompey, Virgil may be implicitly suggesting to that same reader that Rome too has already completed an important cycle of rise and fall.

Now a new cycle awaits Rome, a new cycle indeed, but which carries with it all the uncertainties of new beginnings.

We may return now to Book 2 of the *Aeneid* for some final observations. We have seen how Virgil has intertwined in the narration of the final night of Troy a theme of the *topos* of the *Urbs Capta* that finds its deepest roots in tragedy and historiography. Other motifs and themes should and can be added, motifs which again are part of this literary *topos* and are not present in the earlier or post-Virgilian

---

"Ovid . . . knew (and showed it) that there was no such thing as *Roma aeterna*: his juxtaposition of rising Rome to the fallen cities of the past, nothing but names (15.429ff.) indicates clearly what he foresaw for his city." Cf. also Segal (1969), especially 288 and Solodow (1988) 167–8. On this passage see also Bömer (1986) *ad loc.*

[42] Moles (1983).

[43] Bowie (1990).

[44] Servius at 557.

[45] Moles (1983) argues convincingly that the Virgilian death of Priam is clearly influenced by the description of the death of Pompey the Great, to be found in the *Histories* of his friend and former patron Asinius Pollio.

[46] On this topic see Bowie (1990) 474. Bowie also notices that the intrusion is highlighted by a remarkable example of narrative dislocation. Cf. also Hinds (1998) 9.

epics of the sack of Troy. In light of this assertion we may therefore pose a final question. What does Aeneas stand for, what type of narrator is he?

The obvious answer is hardly surprising. Aeneas is to be compared to Odysseus as the latter recounts his own adventures to the queen of the Phaeacians. From the beginning of *Aeneid* 1 we have grown accustomed to view Aeneas' misfortunes and peregrinations as a reenactment of those of Odysseus. Both heroes, about to reach their destination, are led astray by a new storm provoked by a hostile god. Having landed in a foreign country each is met by a goddess (Venus in the *Aeneid* and Athena in the *Odyssey*) who informs the hero about the country and its rulers, by whom each hero is finally welcomed. Following a banquet, each is requested to tell his own story.[47] Aeneas begins thus:

> sed si tantus amor casus cognoscere nostros
> et *breviter* Troiae supremum audire laborem,
> quamquam animus meminisse horret luctuque refugit,
> incipiam.
>
> (Virgil Aeneid 2.10–13)

> But if you long so much to learn
> our sufferings, to hear *in brief* the final
> calamity of Troy — although my mind,
> remembering, recoils in grief, and trembles,
> I shall try.

Also in his exordium Aeneas seems to reecho the opening words of Odysseus to the queen of the Phaeacians:

> ἀργαλέον βασίλεια **διηνεκέως** ἀγορεῦσαι
> κήδε', ἐπεί μοι πολλὰ δόσαν θεοί Οὐρανίωνες·
> τοῦτο δέ τοι ἐρέω ὅ μ᾽ ἀνείρεαι ἠδὲ μεταλλᾷς.
> (Homer Odyssey 7.241–3)

> Hard it would be my queen to tell **to the end**
> the tale of my woes, since the heavenly ones have given me many.
> But this will I tell you which you ask and inquire.

But, as always, the differences are very significant. As D'Ippolito points out, the Virgilian *breviter* stands in stark contrast and opposi-

---

[47] On the structural and lexical similarities between *Aeneid* 1 and *Odyssey* 5–8 see Williams (1963).

tion to the Homeric διηνεκέως. While Aeneas' story looks back, at least in the first book, to the story of the traveller Odysseus, Aeneas the narrator distances himself from his predecessor.[48] The clear allusion by contrast to the opening statement of Odysseus clarifies Aeneas' rejection of a narrative which is διηνεκέως, as Aeneas, via *oppositio in imitando*, aims at Callimachean *brevitas*. For in Homer's διηνεκέως, Virgil will not have missed the possibility of exploiting the famous Callimachean rejection of ἄεισμα διηνεκές ('continuous song') in the prologue of the *Aitia*.[49] This fundamentally informs Virgil's replacement of διηνεκέως with *breviter*.

There is also another important element of difference between the two accounts, which, as noted by Heinze, seems to distance Aeneas from his Odyssean role:[50]

> Putting the narrative into Aeneas' own mouth seems to us nowadays a straightforward imitation of the technique of the *Odyssey*. But we ought to be aware how new and bold this device must at first have appeared to the poet. The events of Odysseus' homeward journey nearly all involved Odysseus himself, and putting them into the first person instead of the third entailed few changes in the presentation. But for Virgil it was a matter of presenting the ebb and flow of the nocturnal battle through all the streets, palaces and shrines of Troy, and the deeds and sufferings of a whole series of people, as the experience of one single man.

The kind of narration that Aeneas undertakes, so different from that of Odysseus, links him to another model which anticipates the role of Aeneas as narrator and inspires his narrative choices: I have in mind the messenger of a tragedy.[51]

---

[48] D'Ippolito (1976) 26–8 views *breviter* in opposition to the Homeric διηνεκέως as the indication of two juxtaposed narrative modes. Further he notices that the opening lines of Tryphiodorus seems to recall the Virgilian passage (*Il. exc.* 1–5 τέρμα πολυκμήτοιο μεταχρόνιον πολέμοιο/καὶ λόχον, Ἀργείης ἱππήλατον ἔργον Ἀθήνης,/αὐτίκα μοι σπεύδοντι πολὺν διὰ μῦθον ἀνεῖσα/ἔννεπε . . ./κεκριμένου πολέμοιο **ταχείη** λῦσον **ἀοιδῇ**.) Before D'Ippolito, Cartault (1926) 211 had already commented on the importance of this poetic statement: '. . . διηνεκέως est caractéristique de l'ampleur développée de la narration homérique et s'oppose à *breviter* . . . caractéristique de celle bien plus concentrée de Virgile.' For a comparison between the Homeric and the Virgilian passage see also Macrobius (*Sat.* 5.5.2), who already viewed the Virgilian passage as an important programmatic statement.

[49] On Callimachean διηνεκέως see Hunter (1993) 190–95; Cameron (1995) ch. XII with bibliography.

[50] Heinze (1993) 3.

[51] Heinze (1993) 3 does not recognize any connection between the ῥῆσις of the

Many of the narrative affinities of Aeneas' speech with the formal structure of the ῥῆσις of an ἄγγελος have been rightly pointed out by scholars, particularly by Ussani and Austin. I will here confine myself to a brief analysis of the *exordium* of Aeneas' speech.

As for Aeneas it is so painful to remember, *quamquam animus meminisse horret luctuque refugit*, in the same fashion for the messenger of the *Persians* it is painful to recall the memory of the Athenians:

> ὦ πλεῖστον ἔχθος ὄνομα Σαλαμῖνος κλύειν
> φεῦ τῶν Ἀθηνῶν ὡς στένω μεμνημένος
> (Aeschylus *Persae* 284–5)

O name of Salamis most odious to my ears!
Alas, now **I groan when I recall the memory of Athens**

Likewise, Aeneas' emphasis on his role as eyewitness (2.5 *ipse miserrima vidi*), with which he begins his own narration, owes much to the opening statement of messenger's speeches.[52] The messenger of the *Persians* declares in his opening statement that his words are not the result of hearsay. He himself bears witness to the disaster:

> καὶ μὴν παρών γε κοὺ λόγους ἄλλων κλύων,
> Πέρσαι, φράσαιμ᾽ ἄν οἷ᾽ ἐπορσύνθη κακά.
> (Aeschylus *Persae* 266–7)

And in truth, Persians, since *I was present* on the
spot and did not hear the tale from report of others,
I can clearly tell what manner of disaster was wrought.

More importantly, the adverb *breviter* which so clearly marks the contrast between the narrative of Aeneas and Odysseus finds close correspondence in the Persian messenger's claim to brevity:

> πολλῶν παρόντων δ᾽ ὀλίγ᾽ ἀπαγγέλλω κακά.
> (Aeschylus *Persae* 330)

many being the misfortunes, **I announce only a few.**

ἄγγελος and Aeneas' narration. For a different view see Ussani (1950) 237–54 who believes that Aeschylus' messenger in the *Persians* was an important model for Aeneas. Like Aeneas he is the defeated soldier who brings news to the queen Atossa of the Persian defeat, in which he actively participated. See also Austin at 5 for a similar view.

[52] Cf. among others *OT* 1237–40; *Aj.* 748.

A further confirmation may come from another passage in the *Aeneid*. As Aeneas lands on the shores of Carthage and meets his mother Venus disguised as a huntress, it is Venus herself who begins her speech in a similar fashion. Dressed with red boots rather than with the sandals proper to her disguise (*purpureoque alte suras vincire cothurno*),[53] she qualifies herself as a tragic actor, and aptly the exordium of her account of the queen Aeneas is about to meet will recall that of the tragic messenger. Although long is the tale of wrong and long its winding course, she will speak following only the main heads of the story, *summa fastigia rerum*.[54]

Even as Virgil has Aeneas connect Homeric διηνεκέως to Callimachean *brevitas*, he has him simultaneously effecting a genre shift by recreating an affinity with tragedy. It is precisely by recognizing Aeneas' role as a messenger, as an ἄγγελος of tragedy, that Aeneas' narrative choices may be best explained. As a messenger of tragedy, as narrator and focalizer who wishes to inspire in his narratee, Dido, pity and fear, he will exploit the tragic theme of the *Fall of the City* in its most dramatic components as he had inherited them from tragedy and historiography, creating a novel revision and rewriting of the *Iliupersis*. A famous epigram of Callimachus begins: ἐχθαίρω τὸ ποίημα τὸ κυκλικὸν — I hate the cyclic poem.[55] Probably he would not have included Virgil's epic cycle.

---

[53] *Aen.* 1.335. On this passage see Harrison (1973).
[54] *Aen.* 1.342.
[55] *Anth. Pal.* 12.43.1.

CHAPTER THIRTEEN

EPIC ENCOUNTERS? ANCIENT HISTORICAL BATTLE NARRATIVES AND THE EPIC TRADITION

Rhiannon Ash

Introduction

Although the grand genres of epic and historiography certainly embraced many different forms and were never static, perhaps one of the most enduring and potentially fruitful points of interaction between the two modes of writing lies in their representation of battles. Even authors within each genre who stretched audience expectations to the very limit usually included a description of a battle at some point in the narrative. So, although Lucan challenged the expectations of his readers about the nature of epic poetry by infamously dispensing with the divine machinery,[1] (civil) warfare still remains at the heart of the work, whose very first word is *bella*.[2] Similarly, although a writer such as the Hellenistic historian Phylarchus included in his historical narrative material such as miraculous events, love stories and animal tales, nevertheless the scene which prompts Polybius' criticism of his sensational style (*Histories* 2.56) is still a military incident, the fall of Mantinea in 223 B.C.[3] Whether a historical narrative is dominated by the fabulous or by the rational, or whether an epic is located in a historical or mythological period (or both), an interest in warfare tends to prevail, even when the genre is being stretched and modified in other ways.

---

[1] For the disquiet of some ancient readers as to whether Lucan should be considered as a poet at all, see Martial 14.194, Quintilian *Inst.* 10.1.90 and Servius on *Aen.* 1.382. Feeney (1991) 261 proposes: 'The more identity one sees between historical epic and history proper, the more clearly it emerges that the characterful narration of divine action is the irreducible line of demarcation between epic and history — in particular, the more flamboyant species of history'.

[2] Cf. Virgil *Aen.* 1.1 *arma virumque cano*, Silius Italicus 1.1 *ordior arma* and Statius *Theb.* 1.1–3 *fraternas acies alternaque regna profanis/decertata odiis sontisque evolvere Thebas/Pierius menti calor incidit*. Harrison (1988) 49 notes that 'Roman writers tend to define epic subject-matter as "kings and battles"'.

[3] On the theme of the *urbs capta* see Rossi, ch. 12 above.

Fantham refers to a widespread 'transfusion of genres'[4] which distinguished the literature of the first century A.D. This process of transfusion may have taken place even more readily within particular types of scene, such as descriptions of battle, which were common both to historical narratives and to epic. Moreover, since individual writers in the two genres had varying degrees of experience of actual warfare, this must have had some impact both on the level of realism within a battle description and on the level of interaction between genres which took place. At one end of the scale, there is the epic poet Naevius, who, according to Aulus Gellius (*Noctes Atticae* 17.21.45), actively fought in the first Punic war himself and stated this explicitly in the *Bellum Punicum*, presumably in order to add authority to his narrative voice. At the other end of the scale, we can set the Emperor Claudius, who began to write history *in adulescentia* (Suetonius *Divus Claudius* 41.1) before he had had any real experience of warfare, and who continued his narrative after becoming emperor, during which time his direct participation in battle nevertheless remained limited.[5] To put it crudely, some descriptions of 'fictional' battles in epic may have drawn inspiration from the author's actual experience of warfare,[6] while some reports of 'real' battles in historical narratives could have been influenced both by previous accounts in historiography and by epic.[7] This intertextual cross-fertilisation could of course still happen even when an author had himself participated in a particular battle: literature could sometimes offer richer inspiration for an author than real life could, particularly if the audience being addressed itself had rather limited experience of fighting.[8]

---

[4] Fantham (1996) 94.

[5] See Levick (1990) 18–19 for Claudius' historical works.

[6] See Saunders (1999) for a discussion of whether the wounds inflicted by Homer's warriors bear any relation to injuries inflicted in real battles.

[7] For descriptions of military incidents in historical narratives influenced by earlier historical accounts, see Woodman (1979) and Ash (1998). Sabin (2000) 3 makes the following observation about battle-descriptions: 'Some of these, such as Livy's descriptions of fourth century engagements, are of highly dubious provenance, and may simply have been invented for literary or patriotic effect. However, others seem to be based on much more reliable evidence, either tracing back ultimately to eyewitnesses of the battles concerned or else written by an eye-witness, most crucially of course Caesar himself'.

[8] Campbell (1987) 19 observes in the context of a discussion of military handbooks that 'apart from Frontinus and Arrian, the writers of military handbooks, unlike most of the agricultural writers, had no experience of what they wrote about'.

Another point suggests the particularly close intermeshing between historical narratives and epic in the area of warfare, that is the very names by which these works were known. So, we have Caesar's *Bellum Civile, Bellum Gallicum*, (and the continuations *Bellum Alexandrinum, Bellum Africum* and *Bellum Hispaniense*), Sallust's *Bellum Jugurthinum* and *Bellum Catilinae*,[9] all of which are historical works. Some historians explicitly mark off a particular segment of their narrative as being associated with a specific war, as Livy does in the second preface to his work when he says that he is about to describe **bellum** *maxime omnium* **memorabile** *quae umquam gesta sint . . . quod Hannibale duce Carthaginienses cum populo Romano gessere*' (Livy 21.1.1), 'the most memorable of all wars ever waged . . . which the Carthaginians fought with the people of Rome under Hannibal's leadership'. The combination of *bellum* and a modifying adjective can therefore suggest either a particular kind of historical monograph or an account of a specific war embedded in a broader historical narrative. Yet this term can also denote another type of work. We also have Naevius' fragmentary epic, the *Bellum Punicum* and Lucan's epic, the *Bellum Civile*,[10] as well as references to the Augustan poet Cornelius Severus' lost piece about the Sicilian war of 38–36 B.C., the *Bellum Siculum* (Quintilian *Institutio Oratoria* 10.1.89),[11] to Varro Atacinus' *Bellum Sequanicum*, on Caesar's Gallic campaign of 58 B.C., to Archias' epic in Greek on Lucullus' role in the Mithridatic wars (Cicero *Arch.* 21 and *Att.* 1.16.15), to the mysterious *Bellum Actiacum*, an epic by an unknown author about the war between Octavian and Antony and Cleopatra,[12] and to Statius' father's lost epic on the battle between the Vitellians and the Flavians in Rome in A.D. 69 (Statius *Silvae* 5.3.195–204). We also know about an epic written in Greek about Trajan's Dacian wars, since Pliny expresses delight that his friend Caninius is planning to embark on this project:

> optime facis, quod **bellum Dacicum** scribere paras. nam quae tam recens, tam copiosa, tam lata, quae denique tam poetica et quamquam in verissimis rebus tam fabulosa materia?[13]
>
> (*Epistle* 8.4.1)

---

[9] Woodman (1988) 147 n. 1 defends *Bellum Catilinae* as opposed to *De Catilinae Coniuratione* as the title of Sallust's work.

[10] On the title of Lucan's work, see Ahl (1976) 326–32 and Leigh (1997) 74.

[11] On which see further Bramble (1982) 487–8.

[12] See Benario (1983) and Zecchini (1987).

[13] On this letter generally see Sherwin-White (1966) 450–62, who notes (451)

> You are doing an excellent thing in preparing to write a Dacian war. For what subject matter could be so topical, so full of events, so extensive, in short, so poetical and so fabulous, despite taking place amidst events which are most real?

Until Pliny specifically refers to *materia* which is *tam poetica*, it remains unclear whether Caninius' *bellum Dacicum* will be in prose or in verse, and even then, the fact that poetic and fabulous material can still have a place in a historical narrative may leave room for doubt: certainly, the title alone does not clearly denote genre because warfare is such an intrinsic part of both epic and historiography.[14]

Sallust and Virgil

All of these preliminary remarks are meant to suggest that in certain areas the boundary between epic and historiography is not all that clear-cut.[15] Warfare, and in particular battle narrative, constitutes an area where the differences between the two genres often break down most conspicuously and thus provides a relatively narrow area where the cross-fertilisation between the two genres can be usefully examined. In the context of this book, Virgil's *Aeneid* should serve as the Janus-text from which we will look both backwards (to Sallust) and forwards (to Tacitus). In this opening discussion we will examine the grand climax of Sallust's *Bellum Catilinae*, where Catiline finally meets his end in battle. This is a potentially valuable starting-point for a number of reasons. Not only have links between Sallust and Virgil been less well explored than those between Livy and Virgil,[16] but in addition the example of a civil war battle might intersect especially well with the evaluative framework offered by Virgil's decision to let

---

that the 'strangest incident recorded is the message sent to Trajan by the Buri, supposedly inscribed on a giant mushroom, Cassius Dio 68.8.1'. Truth is sometimes stranger than fiction.

[14] Similarly, Ennius' *Annales* happens to be an epic, moving from the fall of Troy until at least 179 B.C., but this was also a label intricately associated with a particular type of history. See Cicero *de Orat.* 2.52, Propertius 3.1.15, Livy 2.54.3 and 43.13.2 (*meos annales*), Juvenal 2.102, Tacitus *Ann.* 4.34.1, 4.43.3 and 4.53.2, and Aulus Gellius 5.18.6. See Wiseman (1979) 9–26.

[15] Cf. Wiseman ch. 17 below.

[16] On the connections between Livy and Virgil, see Walsh (1961) 10–11 and 256–7, Cuénot (1967), Paratore (1971) and Woodman (1989), especially 142 note 17. The question of whether Livy influenced Virgil or *vice versa* has not been resolved.

us see the conflict between the Trojans and Italians as a *civil* war.[17] Moreover, Catiline is clearly a figure who stirred Virgil's interest, as can be seen from the famous apostrophe on the shield of Aeneas where Virgil addresses Catiline and contrasts him with Cato.[18] In addition, there is the intriguing reference in the boat race to the reckless Sergestus (*Aeneid* 5.121), ancestor of the Sergii and therefore of Catiline, who captains a vessel called the Centaur, which runs aground when Sergestus tries to push his way through on the inside: in this context Virgil describes Sergestus as *furens* (*Aeneid* 5.202) and as *infelix* (*Aeneid* 5.204), characteristics which may make us think of Catiline.[19]

Sallust's Catiline memorably meets an honourable death in battle at Pistoria in Etruria in January 62 B.C., after the arrest and execution of his co-conspirators in Rome. The shocking image of Lentulus, strangled with a noose in the filthy and terrifying part of the prison known as the Tullianum (*Bellum Catilinae* 55.2–5),[20] reminds us of the fate which might so easily have awaited Catiline, if he had decided to stay in Rome. Sallust specifically sets up Lentulus' end as *dignum moribus factisque suis* (*Bellum Catilinae* 55.6), thus creating an *exemplum* which gives a clear lead to his readers as to how they should categorise this man in moral terms. Sallust's readers will find that Catiline's end conspicuously lacks this reassuring authorial guidance and that in comparison with this sordid execution, his death is dignified and moving, despite his status as an enemy of Rome. In this context, everything about Sallust's battle-narrative focuses our attention on Catiline. The command-structure is a case in point. The two main commanders in the battle itself are Catiline on the

---

[17] On Virgil's depiction of the war in Italy as a civil war, see Cairns (1989) 92–3 and 96–7 and Harrison (1991) xxv–xxvi, although Fordyce (1977) 122 is more cautious.

[18] Syme (1964) 286, Woodman (1989) 145 note 61 and Harrison (1997) 74 all suggest that these lines indicate that Virgil must have been familiar with Sallust's *Bellum Catilinae*. Feldherr (1995) 254 note 28 observes a parallel between Catiline being punished in Tartarus (*minaci pendentem scopulo*, *Aen.* 8.668–9) and Sergestus' fate in the boat-race (*in scopulo luctantem . . . alto*, *Aen.* 5.220).

[19] Cf. *BC.* 31.9 where Catiline is described as *furibundus* and *Cat.* 24.2 for the *Catilinae furor*. Vretska (1976) 343 observes: '*furor* (bei S. nur trier) und *furibundus* 31.9 . . . sagt S. nur von Catilina'. Cf. Cicero *Catil.* 1.1.1 *quam diu etiam furor iste tuus nos eludet?* and 2.1.1, *L. Catilinam, furentem audacia*.

[20] The Tullianum was the underground execution chamber in the prison at Rome which was supposed to have been built by Servius Tullius (Varro *L.* 5.151).

one side and the legate Marcus Petreius[21] on the other, who is put
in charge by the consul Gaius Antonius, since he himself was *pedibus
aeger* (*Bellum Catilinae* 59.4). Cassius Dio (37.39.4) suggests that Antonius
was in fact malingering in order to avoid an uncomfortable encounter
with Catiline, who earlier on in the narrative had counted him as
a friend (Sallust *Bellum Catilinae* 21.3).[22] However that may be, Antonius
as consul really ought to have been leading the troops into battle,
but he passes the task over to his subordinate. Petreius only appears
in the *Bellum Catilinae* during the battle-narrative, although readers
might well have remembered his dramatic suicide in 46 B.C.[23] This
took place after a fake duel with King Juba designed to create the
impression that both men had died a noble death.[24] We can contrast
such artificially staged grandeur (although it happened much later)
with the genuinely impressive death of Catiline in battle.

Sallust economically depicts Petreius as a *homo militaris* (*Bellum
Catilinae* 59.6) with over thirty years of military service to his credit,
who has an excellent relationship with his soldiers. However, Petreius
is explicitly denied an exhortation in direct speech (*Bellum Catilinae*
59.6) to match Catiline's long address to his soldiers (*Bellum Catilinae*
58).[25] As well as the supreme commanders on both sides, we are
told briefly about some middle ranking officers in Catiline's army.
Catiline is said to have a pair of deputies, Gaius Manlius on the
right wing and an unnamed officer from Fiesole on the left wing
(*Bellum Catilinae* 59.3), but these men are given a very low profile in
the narrative of the battle itself. Their deaths seem to be recorded
mainly as a prelude to Catiline's own death: the generals are killed
in primis pugnantes (*Bellum Catilinae* 60.6) just as Catiline charges into

---

[21] See Wilkins (1994) 103 on Petreius.

[22] Gaius Antonius seems to have been particularly susceptible to the temptations
of a self-indulgent lifestyle. Cicero managed to secure Antonius' neutrality only by
yielding the province of Macedonia to him (*Cat.* 26.4). Antonius was later prose-
cuted on a charge of *repetundae* in connection with his governorship of Macedonia.
There is a memorable description of Antonius' fondness for alcohol and women at
Quintilian *Inst.* 4.2.123–4, which is an extract from Caelius' speech against Antonius.

[23] The *Bellum Catilinae* is usually dated to 42/41 B.C. McKay (1962) suggests that
Sallust published a first draft in the summer of 50 B.C. and a final version in the
late 40's B.C.

[24] See *B.Afr.* 94, Appian *BC.* 2.100, Livy *Per.* 114, Florus *Epit.* 2.13.69.

[25] Syme (1964) 68 calls Catiline's speech a 'fierce and fraudulent oration', but it
is still striking that Petreius is given no words of his own in direct speech. For the
relationship between characterisation and direct/indirect speech, see Scott (1998)
and Laird (1999) 116–52.

the enemy's ranks and dies *pugnans* (*Bellum Catilinae* 60.7).[26] As Woodman notes,[27] Catiline is killed in exactly the way that in his pre-battle harangue he had urged that his men should die, *virorum more pugnantes* (*Bellum Catilinae* 58.21). On the other side, the command-structure is presented even more sketchily, as Sallust omits any mention of Marcus Petreius' military subordinates.[28] Everything is designed to focus attention on Catiline himself at perhaps his greatest moment.

What bearing do these observations about command-structure as presented by Sallust have on Virgil's own strategy in narrating battles? One peculiar aspect of the *Aeneid*, particularly in the eyes of those who read this Augustan epic from the vantage point of the *Iliad*, is that Homer's 'galaxy of rounded personalities'[29] has gone. Willcock observes that instead of a range of heroes such as Odysseus, Ajax, and Diomedes, Virgil presents us with leaders such as Turnus' second-in-command, Messapus, who 'seems to have no personality at all'.[30]

Messapus speaks only once (*Aeneid* 12.296), when he kills Achates in battle, and we certainly never see him conversing with Turnus in direct speech. Instead, Camilla tends to play that role, as we can see when Turnus explains to her his plan to set up an ambush for Aeneas' men (*Aeneid* 11.508–19).[31] Moreover, although Messapus appears in the narrative on numerous occasions, he is almost always described as doing something: only twice does Virgil offer any insight into what Messapus is feeling.[32] Once he is *conterritus* (*Aeneid* 9.123)

---

[26] On the appropriate behaviour of a commander if defeat in battle loomed, see Goldsworthy (1996) 163–5. Vretska (1976) 686 draws parallels with the conduct of Marius (*Jug.* 98.1), and with the deaths of Decius Mus (Livy 10.28.18) and of Hasdrubal (Livy 27.49.3–4).

[27] Woodman in Kraus and Woodman (1997) 20.

[28] Velleius Paterculus 2.25.5 and Florus *Epit.* 2.12.12 both mention Catiline's glorious death, but they do not go into details about the battle. Neither author says anything about Petreius, who does at least appear at Cassius Dio 37.39–40 (although the subordinate officers do not).

[29] Willcock (1983) 95.

[30] Willcock (1983) 95.

[31] On Camilla see Arrigoni (1982). The proposed site of the ambush suggests the genre of history. Gransden (1991) 113 says that 'The narrow pass in which he hopes to ambush Aeneas resembles the Caudine Forks, where a Roman army was trapped by, and surrendered to, the Samnite general Gavius Pontus, 321 B.C.: see Livy 9.2–6'.

[32] For Messapus see *Aen.* 7.691, 8.6, 9.27, 9.124, 9.160, 9.365, 9.458, 9.523, 10.354, 10.749, 11.429, 11.464, 11.518, 11.603, 12.128, 12.289, 12.294, 12.488, 12.550 and 12.661. Horsfall (1999) 451 says of Messapus: 'A major figure in *Aeneid* 7–12, possibly once of greater importance in the Aeneas-legend'.

upon seeing Aeneas' ships turn into sea-goddesses, and once he is
said to be eager to confound the treaty, *avidus confundere foedus* (*Aeneid*
12.290). Messapus' gleaming helmet, which disastrously exposes
Euryalus, almost plays a more emotive role in the epic than its owner
does. Even Aeneas' faithful friend Achates has a greatly diminished
role in the second half of the *Aeneid*, appearing fourteen times in
Aeneid 1–6 and seven times in *Aeneid* 7–12.[33] Perhaps when Numitor
wounds Achates (*Aeneid* 10.344), Virgil is attempting to justify the
small part which Aeneas' subordinate plays subsequently in the war.[34]
Willcock suggests that the low profile of such heroes is achieved
partly by the fact that they do not speak much, whereas Homeric
heroes are always talking to each other and calling on the gods.
Horsfall similarly notes the shortage of what he calls 'major minor
warriors' in the second half of the *Aeneid* and points out that ancient
commentators were also unhappy with the fact that, for example,
the 'heroes' of the Italian catalogue in *Aeneid* 7 largely remain grey
and undeveloped (Macrobius, *Saturnalia* 5.15.6, Servius on 7.647).[35]
The explanation for this phenomenon may lie in the fact that there
was simply a shortage of fighting-age heroes in Virgil's sources, but
surely this is unconvincing. Virgil could easily have invented such
figures and invested them with distinctive personalities, if it had suited
him to do so.

Perhaps there is a more plausible explanation for this phenomenon if we consider that Virgil was writing for an audience steeped
in the traditions of Roman historiography. What strikes someone
reading the *Aeneid* from a Homeric point of view as odd might seem
less unsettling to a reader who was accustomed to enjoying battle
narratives in the historians. Hammond has suggested that the nor-
mal pattern for a battle narrative in ancient historiography tends 'to
offset a simple command structure of one or two men plus subordinates against a serving army in which the only standard differentiation of rank, if it is made at all, is between centurions and *legionarii
milites*'.[36] Sallust's succinct description of the battle at Pistoria with its
simplified command-structure could be said to fit into this pattern.

[33] See *Aen.* 1.120, 1.174, 1.188, 1.312, 1.459, 1.513, 1.579, 1.581, 1.644, 1.656,
1.696, 3.523, 6.34, 6.158, 8.466, 8.521, 8.586, 10.332, 10.344, 12.384 and 12.459.
[34] Harrison (1991) 162 notes this as an example of the Homeric motif of 'war-
rior aims for major hero but strikes his lesser companion'.
[35] Horsfall (1987) 50 note 20.
[36] Hammond (1993) 8.

Hammond has also argued that the historian's most important task in narrating a battle was to reduce a complexity of individual events and motives to manageable proportions.[37] This process of simplification must surely be enhanced by reducing the amount of attention paid to the subordinate commanders in the battle itself. So, for example, Julius Caesar says that on his side at Pharsalus, Antony commanded the left wing, Publius Sulla commanded the right wing, and Gnaeus Domitius took charge of the centre (*Bellum Civile* 3.89.3), while on Pompey's side, Pompey positioned himself on the left wing and Scipio took charge of the right wing (*Bellum Civile* 3.88.2–3).[38] We feel as if we have been given a fair amount of detailed information about the command-structure here, but the striking thing is that none of these subordinate generals is even mentioned in the account of the battle itself, which focuses almost exclusively on the actions of the two armies and the two supreme commanders, apart from praise for the brave veteran centurion Crastinus. Amongst the later accounts, there is some variation in the positions and even in the identities of the generals listed for each side.[39]

Caesar names the intermediate officers in his original eye-witness account, but he allocates them a low profile in the battle narrative, since they neither speak nor do anything particularly conspicuous.[40] For Caesar, this mode of presentation was desirable, in that his subordinates do not thereby take anything away from his own performance in the battle.

We can compare such top-heavy descriptions of the command-structure in historiographical texts with Virgil. For instance, when Turnus leads his army against the Trojans at the start of *Aeneid* 9, we hear:

---

[37] Hammond (1993) 12.

[38] On Caesar's account of this battle, see Lendon (1999). For other ancient accounts, see Lucan's seventh book' Frontinus *Str.* 2.3.22, Plutarch *Pomp.* 68–72, *Caes.* 44–6, Appian *BC.* 2.68–82, Cassius Dio 41.53–60, Eutropius 6.20–1, Orosius 6.15.22–7.

[39] Caesar *Civ.* 3.89: (*Caes.*) Antony (left wing), Domitius Calvinus (centre), Sulla and Caesar (right wing). Caesar *Civ.* 3.88: (*Pomp.*) Pompey (left wing), Scipio (centre), unspecified (right wing). Plutarch *Caes.* 44: (*Caes.*) Antony (left wing), Domitius Calvinus (centre), Caesar (right wing), versus (*Pomp.*) Domitius Ahenobarbus (left wing), Scipio (centre), Pompey (right wing). Plutarch *Pomp.* 69: (*Caes.*) Antony (left wing), Domitius Calvinus (centre), Caesar (right wing) versus (*Pomp.*) Domitius Ahenobarbus (left wing), Scipio (centre), Pompey (right wing). Appian *BC.* 2.76: (*Caes.*) Sulla, Antony, Bomitius Calvinus (positions not given), Caesar (right wing) versus (*Pomp.*), Domitius Ahenobarbus (left wing), Scipio (centre), Lentulus (right wing).

[40] Welch (1998) 90 notes that with a few notable exceptions Caesar's legates are 'names on a page with little or no personality'.

> Messapus primas acies, postrema coercent/Tyrrhidae iuvenes, medio
> dux agmine Turnus.
>
> Messapus is marshalling the advance guard, Tyrrhus' sons the rear,
> while the main body is under the command of Turnus
>
> *(Aeneid* 9.27–28)

However, although Messapus is named as a commander, he plays
a minimal role in the action which follows. We need to consider,
therefore, the possibility that if historians tended to compress the
role played by middle ranking commanders in battle narratives, then
this might have had an impact on Virgil's own techniques in the
second half of the *Aeneid*, as well as on the expectations of the audience. This should not necessarily surprise us. Virgil does after all
signal the historiographical flavour of the second half of the poem
in his invocation to Erato *(Aeneid* 7.37–44),[41] even if at the same time
he calls to mind the start of the second half of Apollonius' *Argonautica*
(3.1–5).[42]

> Nunc age, qui reges, Erato, quae tempora, **rerum**
> quis Latio antiquo fuerit **status,** advena classem
> cum primum Ausoniis exercitus appulit oris,
> **expediam,** et primae revocabo exordia pugnae.
> tu vatem, tu, diva, mone. dicam horrida bella,
> dicam acies actosque animis in funera reges,
> Tyrrhenamque manum totamque sub arma coactam
> Hesperiam. maior rerum mihi nascitur ordo,
> maius **opus moveo**
>
> *(Aeneid* 7.37–44)

> Come now, Erato, I will explain who were the kings, what were
> the phases, what was the state of affairs in ancient Latium when
> the foreign army first beached its fleet on Ausonian shores, and
> I will recall the beginnings of the first battle. You, you, god-
> dess, prompt your bard. I will tell of horrible wars, I will tell
> of battle-lines, of kings bravely rushing to their deaths, of a
> Tyrrhenian band and of all Hesperia mustered under arms. A
> greater succession of events opens before me, and I undertake
> a greater task.

---

[41] Mack (1999) 129 notes the oddity of choosing Erato as a source of inspiration rather than Clio (history), Calliope (epic) or even Melpomene (tragedy), but
suggests that she is appropriate 'to head a book which is infused from beginning
to end with Virgil's love for his native land'.

[42] On the relationship between Virgil and Apollonius Rhodius at this point, see
Hinds (1998) 1, Horsfall (1999) on 7.37, Nelis (2001) 267–8.

The verb *expedio* (*Aeneid* 7.40) certainly sounds more prosaic than the *cano* (*Aeneid* 1.1) with which Virgil opened his epic.[43] We should note that Tacitus uses the same verb to introduce a new section of his historical narrative: *nunc initia causasque motus Vitelliani* **expediam** (*Histories* 1.51.1), 'Now I shall explain the origins and causes of the Vitellian movement'.[44] Likewise, when Virgil undertakes to explain the state of affairs in ancient Latium, we might recall Tacitus' assertion that *repetendum videtur* **qualis status** *urbis, quae mens exercituum, quis habitus prouinciarum, quid in toto terrarum orbe validum, quid aegrum fuit . . .* (*Histories* 1.4.1), 'It seems best to go back and consider what was the state of the city, what was the mood of the armies, what was the condition of the provinces, and what was strong and weak in the whole world. . . .'[45] Even Virgil's famous announcement, *maius opus moveo* (*Aeneid* 7.44) is echoed by Tacitus in his prologue, which is surely intended to whet his audience's appetite: **opus adgredior** *opimum casibus, atrox proeliis, discors seditionibus, ipsa etiam pace saevum* (*Histories* 1.2.1), 'I approach a story that is rich in twists of fortune, fierce in battles, disrupted by rebellions, savage even during peacetime itself. . . .' Even if we think that Tacitus was specifically alluding to Virgil's historiographical invocation in these instances, it would seem difficult to deny that Virgil himself was evoking a historiographical atmosphere in formulating his second evocation.[46]

Yet there may also be a much more specific interaction between Sallust's battle narrative and Virgil's text than has been suggested so far. Sallust shapes his account so that it culminates in the dramatic death of Catiline himself:

> interea Catilina cum expeditis in prima acie vorsari, laborantibus succurrere, integros pro sauciis arcessere, omnia providere, multum ipse pugnare, saepe hostem ferire: strenui militis et boni imperatoris officia simul exequebatur. Petreius, ubi videt Catilinam, contra ac ratus erat, magna vi tendere, cohortem praetoriam in medios hostis inducit eosque perturbatos atque altos alibi resistentis interficit; deinde utrimque ex lateribus ceteros adgreditur. Manlius et Faesulanus in primis pugnantes cadunt. <Catilina>, **postquam** fusas copias **se**que cum paucis reliquom **videt,** memor generis atque pristinae suae dignitatis **in confertissumos hostis** incurrit ibique pugnans **confoditur.**

---

[43] For *expedio*, 'I give an account of, explain, expound', see *OLD expedio* 4 and for *cano* 'I celebrate (in verse), relate, tell of', see *OLD cano* 3.
[44] Cf. Tacitus *Ann.* 4.1.1.
[45] See Goold (1992) 116 with 243 note 24 for further examples, including Tacitus *Hist.* 1.11.3 and *Ann.* 1.2.2.
[46] See Horsfall (1999) 68.

Meanwhile, Catiline went to and fro in the front line with his lightly
armed troops, brought help to those who were struggling, summoned
fresh men to replace the wounded, saw to everything in advance,
fought hard himself and often struck a blow at his enemy: he was performing simultaneously the duties of a hardworking soldier and of a
good general. When Petreius saw that Catiline, contrary to his expectation, was resisting with great vigour, he led the praetorian cohort
against the enemy's centre, and inflicted casualties on them as they
were thrown into confusion by this attack and able to offer only a
sporadic resistance. Then Petreius attacked the others on both sides
from the wings. Manlius and the officer from Fiesole fell fighting in
the front line. Catiline, when he saw that his army was routed and
that he was left with a few men, remembering his noble birth and the
high rank he had once held, plunged into the enemy lines where they
were thickest and fighting there, he was stabbed full of holes.

(*Bellum Catilinae* 60.4–7).

By avoiding capture or flight and by giving himself up to certain
death so memorably, Catiline goes some way to redeeming himself,
even if we can never forget the context in which he dies. Several
points enhance his heroism. The formulation *memor . . . pristinae suae
dignitatis* links him both with his own soldiers whom he urges to fight
memores pristinae virtutis (*Bellum Catilinae* 58.12) and with the veteran
soldiers on the victorious side, who are said to fight *pristinae virtutis
memores* (*Bellum Catilinae* 60.3). The certainty of his death is anticipated
by the superlative as he rushes *in confertissumos hostis*; and the violent
and painful manner of his death is embodied in the verb, *confoditur*,
as he is 'stabbed full of holes'.[47] This is just the right sort of death
for a Roman hero, but one which takes place in the wrong sort of
conflict, a *civil* war.[48] It is this mismatch which encapsualtes the true
tragedy of Catiline's end. This message is only driven home further
by details such as the fact that Catiline and his army went into battle
behind an eagle which had been carried in Marius' army during the
campaign against the Cimbri (*Bellum Catilinae* 59.3), a *foreign* war.[49]
We are left with a sense of wasted potential and misplaced heroism.

---

[47] Ogilvie (1965) 522 says that *confodio* is 'another word avoided by Cicero but
patronized by military historians, e.g. Sallust *Cat.* 60.7, Nepos *Pel.* 5.4, Frontinus
Str. 2.5.33'.

[48] See Leigh (1995) 197 for the 'redeemed Catiline dying amidst the enemy'.

[49] Cf. Tacitus *Hist.* 1.62.2–3 where we can see a mismatch between part of
Vitellius' army, commanded by Fabius Valens, and the real eagle which was leading them into civil war.

This is precisely the sort of message which would have struck a chord with Virgil, and it is perhaps not surprising therefore if we find one death in the epic which offers an intriguing intertext. In *Aeneid 9*, during the siege of the Trojan camp, Virgil relates the death of a minor Trojan hero, Helenor, who conducts himself in his final moments in a manner which may recall Catiline:[50]

> . . . vix unus Helenor
> et Lycus elapsi; quorum primaevus Helenor,
> Maeonio regi quem serva Licymnia furtim
> sustulerat vetitisque ad Troiam miserat armis'
> ense levis nudo parmaque inglorius alba.
> isque **ubi se** Turni media inter milia **vidit**,
> hinc acies atque hinc acies astare Latinas,
> **ut fera**, quae densa venantum saepta corona
> contra tela furit seseque haud nescia morti
> inicit et saltu **supra venabula** fertur—
> haud aliter iuuenis medios moriturus in hostis
> inruit et qua tela videt **densissima** tendit
> *(Aeneid 9.544–55)*

. . . Helenor and Lycus alone escaped with difficulty; of these, Helenor, a man in the prime of youth, whom a slave woman from Licymnia had borne secretly to the Lydian king and sent to Troy in forbidden arms, was lightly armed with a naked sword and a bare shield, with no reputation in war. Helenor, when he saw that he was in the midst of thousands of Turnus' men, and that Latin battle-lines stood around him on this side and that, like some wild beast, who, surrounded by a dense circle of hunters, rages against their weapons, and deliberately throws itself to death and with a leap hurls itself upon the hunting spears, even so did the young man, intent on death, charge right into the middle of the enemy, where he saw their weapons were thickest.

Helenor has not achieved much in life so far: the illegitimate son of a Lydian king, he had been sent to fight at Troy by his mother, but has failed to win much of a reputation. The manner of his death changes all that. Like Catiline, he sees that the situation is hopeless (*ubi se . . . vidit Aeneid 9.549/postquam . . . se . . . videt Bellum Catilinae 60.7*); and where Catiline *in confertissumos hostis incurrit*, Helenor *medios moriturus in hostis inruit*. Virgil, like Sallust, accentuates the certainty of

---

[50] On this passage, see further Raabe (1974) 118–19, 226–27, Hardie (1994) 175–78.

death with a superlative as Helenor heads *qua tela videt densissima* (*Aeneid* 9.555).[51] This superlative only appears once elsewhere in the *Aeneid*, when Pallas stops a rout amongst the Arcadians and urges them to attack *qua globus ille virum densissimus urget* (*Aeneid* 10.373). Amongst other suggestive details, there is Sallust's focus on the *ferocia animi* which was visible on the dead Catiline's face (*Bellum Catilinae* 61.4): Virgil goes one better than this and compares Helenor with a wild-beast (*Aeneid* 9.551), but unusually chooses the generic term *fera*, whereas normally he likes to name creatures in such similes specifically.[52] In addition, although Virgil does not describe Helenor's death directly, there may be something relevant in the simile, where the wild beast is said to hurl herself *supra venabula* (*Aeneid* 9.553), 'onto hunting spears'. Catiline, we remember, is *confoditur*, 'stabbed full of holes', which suggests a similar mode of death.[53] Perhaps Virgil's mysterious reference to *vetitis armis* (*Aeneid* 9.547) also suggests a link with Catiline, who similarly takes up forbidden weapons, but this time in civil war against his country.[54]

Some readers may well question whether we are entitled to detect such intertextuality between the death-scenes of Catiline and Helenor and whether this would in any sense mirror the way in which ancient readers approached Virgil's text. If the echo is there, it is admittedly rather faint. Yet that does not mean that we should not set these two texts side-by-side. As Fowler has observed, 'If intertextuality is a property of the literary system . . . then it is public, not private, and whether we count a particular resemblance between two texts as sufficiently marked to count as an allusion is determined by public competence of readers, not the private thoughts of writers'.[55] Lyne has recently warned against the pitfalls of what he calls the 'fallacy

---

[51] This sort of hopeless death recurs in the *Aen.* at 2.408, *et sese medium iniecit periturus in agmen.*

[52] E.g. *Aen.* 9.339–41, 9.792–6, 10.454–6, 10.723–9, 12.4–8, (*tigris*) 9.730, (*taurus*) 2.223–4, 12.103–6, 12.715–22.

[53] Cf. Silius Italicus 10.2–3, where the *fera* simile is applied to Aemilius Paullus at Cannae, but there are changes as the wild-beast, *telis circumcingentibus, ultro/assilit in ferrum et per vulnera colligit hostem.*

[54] See Hardie (1994) 177–78 for some previous explanations of this phrase: Servius thought that it was a veiled reference to the Roman ban on military service for slaves, while Conington thought that it was a reference to the Homeric parallel of the two sons of the seer Merops, who went to war against their father's wishes (*Il.* 2.832–3).

[55] Fowler (2000) 118.

of audience limitation' and suggests that 'to limit interpretation to aesthetic effects which the imagined audience could supposedly grasp is wrong'.[56] In addition, Farrell makes a number of broad points about Virgilian intertextual practice, specifically that it is pervasive, analytical, thematically motivated and not limited to any single source or model.[57] This should certainly encourage us to compare the texts of Virgil and Sallust.

We should also consider another question, namely what are the implications of reading Helenor through the figure of Catiline in this way. There are various possibilities. At the very least, we could simply see here Virgil redeploying decorative touches from the memorable death-scene of a famous man in order to make Helenor's demise more striking. Allusions to previous texts by Latin authors do not, after all, always have to be laden with special significance.[58] Yet it is possible to read more into the intertextuality if we choose to do so.

There is clearly an element of continuity in the mechanics of the two deaths. In each case, Helenor and Catiline engage in exemplary self-sacrifice, which is highly unexpected in the light of their previous lives, but which nevertheless shows the potential that both men had to achieve better things. However, despite this point of contact between the two men, there is also an important difference: although Helenor was fighting in order to secure a new homeland for the dispossessed Trojan contingent, Catiline is the leader of a group of men whose actions are perceived to threaten the security of that very homeland for which Helenor had sacrificed his life. To win the war in Italy through the bravery of Helenor (and of others like him) is only half of the story: if Rome is to survive, vigilance and self-sacrifice will be needed in the future as well. Although the deaths of Helenor and Catiline each in their own way call to mind the ritual of *devotio*,[59] the parallels bring home the point that there will always be a need for such deaths in the Roman state.

---

[56] Lyne (1994) 198.

[57] Farrell (1997) 228–9.

[58] Thomas (1986) 175–7 refers to the 'casual reference', though he encourages us to treat such references thoughtfully because 'sometimes an apparently casual reference will be far from casual' (177).

[59] Feldherr (1998) 85 defines *devotio* as 'a drastic measure in which a magistrate with *imperium*, consul, dictator, or praetor, to prevent imminent defeat consecrates one individual, who thus takes upon himself the impurities of the entire state'.

Virgil and Tacitus

If there are useful comparisons to be made between Virgil's *Aeneid* and the texts of earlier historians such as Sallust, the intertextuality has proved much less problematic for critics when historiography is perceived to influence epic, rather than *vice versa*. The fact that historians can add colour to their accounts of particular events with phrases and even with whole scenes borrowed from other genres such as epic has always tended to make critics particularly uncomfortable, not least of all because such cross-fertilisation has serious implications for the truth value of a historian's account. I want to turn now to look at a possible example of this filtering of a prose narrative through an epic text to see what implications such intertextuality might have. The first passage is Virgil's account of the Italian assault on the Trojan camp in *Aeneid* 9, while the second is Tacitus' account of the siege of Placentia, where the Othonians are being attacked by some hearty German Vitellians (*Histories* 2.22).[60]

> at tuba terribilem sonitum procul aere canoro
> increpuit, sequitur clamor caelumque remugit.
> accelerant **acta** pariter **testudine** Volsci
> et **fossas implere** parant ac **vellere vallum**;
> quaerunt pars aditum et **scalis ascendere muros**,
> qua rara est acies interlucetque **corona**
> non tam spissa viris. **telorum** effundere contra
> omne genus Teucri ac **duris** detrudere **contis**,
> adsueti longo muros defendere bello.
> saxa quoque infesto volvebant pondere, si qua
> possent tectam aciem perrumpere, cum tamen omnis
> ferre iuvet subter densa **testudine** casus.
> nec iam sufficiunt. nam qua globus imminet ingens,
> immanem Teucri molem volvuntque ruuntque,
> quae stravit Rutulos late armorumque resolvit
> **tegmina**. nec curant caeco contendere Marte
> amplius audaces Rutuli, sed **pellere vallo**
> **missilibus certant**
>
>   (Virgil *Aeneid* 9.503–20)

But the trumpet rang out afar its terrible sound on melodious bronze, a shout followed and the sky re-echoed the noise. The

---

[60] For general discussions of the influence of Virgil on Tacitus see Miller (1961–2) and (1986), Baxter (1971) and (1972), and Bews (1972–3).

Volscians hurried out under a *testudo* that had been driven forwards evenly as they prepared to fill the ditches and to break through the rampart. Some of them tried to get in by climbing the walls with ladders, where the battle-line was thin and light showed through the less dense ring of men. On the other side, the Trojans hurled out all manner of weapons and thrust down with tough pikes, accustomed to defend their walls in the long war. They also began to roll stones of deadly weight, to see if they could break through that armoured column at all, although the Volscians, beneath their thick *testudo*, were nevertheless happy to take whatever blows happened to fall. Yet now they failed. For where a huge throng threatened, the Trojans rolled and hurled down an enormous boulder which scattered the Rutulians far and wide and broke their covering of armour. The Rutulians, brave though they were, did not care to contend any further in blind warfare, but struggled to drive them from the ramparts using missiles.

vixdum orto die plena propugnatoribus moenia, fulgentes **armis virisque** campi: densum legionum agmen, sparsa auxiliorum manus altiora murorum **sagittis aut saxis** incessere, neglecta aut aevo fluxa comminus adgredi. ingerunt desuper Othoniani pila librato magis et certo ictu adversus temere subeuntes cohortes Germanorum, cantu truci et more patrio nudis corporibus super umeros scuta quatientium. legionarius pluteis et cratibus tectus subruit muros, instruit aggerem, molitur portas: contra praetoriani dispositos ad id ipsum **molares ingenti pondere ac fragore provolvunt**. pars subeuntium obruti, pars confixi et exsangues aut laceri: cum augeret stragem trepidatio eoque acrius e moenibus volnerarentur, rediere infracta partium fama.

(Tacitus *Histories* 2.22)

With day having hardly dawned, the walls were full of defenders and the plains glittered with men and with weapons. A dense column of legions and a scattered band of auxiliaries attacked the higher parts of the walls with arrows and with stones, and they assaulted at close quarters the parts of the walls that were in disrepair or crumbling from age. From above, the Othonians, poising and aiming their javelins with surer effect, hurled them at the German cohorts, who came rashly charging underneath, with naked bodies, as is their national custom, chanting fiercely and brandishing their shields over their shoulders. The legionaries covered by their screens and fascines, undermined the walls, built up a mound, and assailed the gates. On the other side, the praetorians rolled forwards with a terrific crash huge millstones, which had been arranged for this very purpose. Some of those beneath were crushed, while others were pierced through

and left mangled and bleeding to death. Panic increased the
slaughter and for that reason wounds were made all the more
eagerly by the assailants on the walls. They retreated, with the
reputation of their side crushed.

Clearly, in both of these scenes, the military situation is broadly similar, with one group of men penned in and defending themselves
from their walls against the attack of a second group, so we should
expect to find some shared terminology. Yet the possibility that
Tacitus might want us to think of Virgilian epic specifically is raised
by his assertion at the opening of the passage that the plains were
gleaming *armis virisque*. This juxtaposition, though natural, calls to
mind the famous opening of the *Aeneid*. If we are meant to think of
Virgil, then the passage in *Aeneid* 9 would be a particularly appropriate one to consider because of its emphasis on the technicalities
of siegecraft. As Hardie observes, 'The Homeric model is the fighting
at the Achaean walls in *Iliad* 12.35–471, but the battle is joined at
the blast of an Ennian trumpet and the siege-craft is Roman rather
than Homeric'.[61] Raabe lists a number of terms in Virgil's passage
which he considers particularly evocative of Roman siege-craft, and
these are emphasized in the text above.[62] It may also be possible
that Tacitus in this passage could have picked up on a particular
narrative trait from Virgil, namely the tendency to use alliterative
pairs of words: Tacitus' *plena propugnatoribus* and *sagittis aut saxis* can
be compared with Virgil's *tuba terribilem* (9.503), *clamor caelumque* (9.504),
accelerant acta (9.505), *vellere vallum* (9.505), *duris detrudere* (9.509), and
amplius audaces (9.519). It also seems likely that Tacitus alludes specifically
to this passage when he says that the Othonian praetorians *molares
ingenti pondere ac fragore provolvunt*, which recalls Virgil's *saxa quoque infesto
volvebant pondere* (*Aeneid* 9.512).[63] This is perhaps the closest point of
contact between the two passages.[64]

---

[61] Hardie (1994) 167.

[62] Raabe (1974) 118–19 and 226–7.

[63] Heubner (1968) 96 suggests as parallels Statius *Theb.* 8.709 *circumque sonori vertice
percusso volvuntur in arma molares* and Curtius Rufus 8.11.13 *ingentia saxa in subeuntes
provolventibus barbaris.*

[64] The only other author who mentions the siege in some detail is Plutarch at
Oth. 6.1–4, but this account focuses largely on the colourful insults which the
Vitellians hurl at the Othonians on the ramparts at Placentia. There is hardly any
description of the technical aspect of the siege and there is no mention of rolling
the stones.

If Tacitus has added some Virgilian epic flavour to his account of the siege, what does he gain from so doing? Above all, he creates an uneasy sense of bathos and decline in various ways. Despite the similarities between the two scenes, it appears that the Othonian defenders are rather less impressive as fighting men than their Trojan counterparts, who were accustomed to siege warfare because of their background. The Othonians choose to attack the easy target first, namely the German cohorts, who are not experienced at conducting this sort of campaign. Momentarily, as the Othonians hurl javelins at the naked wild Germans, we can perhaps forget that this is a civil war, until Tacitus focuses on the Vitellian legionaries, covered by their screens and fascines. There is something particularly jarring about seeing Roman praetorians attacking Roman legionaries using supremely Roman fighting techniques. That sense of bathos also extends to the Vitellian attackers. Although the German Vitellians, as they rashly approach the walls (*temere subeuntes cohortes*), seem to share some superficial characteristics with the primitive Rutulians, whom Virgil wryly calls daring (*audaces*) just as they are retreating, nevertheless their wholesome barbarian qualities will soon be destroyed after their victory by the temptations on offer in Rome.[65] Also, where the Volscians in Virgil had been acting as a unit, the Vitellians are a decidedly more fragmented group, with the German cohorts and Roman legionaries sharply differentiated from one another by their fighting methods.

Finally, we can see that Tacitus adds touches of realism to the Virgilian epic model. So, the ramparts of Placentia bristle with defenders, but as we are brought closer, we see that those walls have been neglected or are crumbling from age. This suggests that the inhabitants have become complacent and may even call to mind the *metus hostilis* theory, that is, the beneficial fear created by the presence of a competent foreign enemy, which forced a nation to put aside internal differences and to unite against a common foe.[66] Placentia, founded in 218 B.C.,[67] had once had to endure frequent attacks from Gauls

---

[65] See Tacitus *Hist.* 2.93–94 with Ash (1999) 45–8.

[66] On *metus hostilis*, see Vretska (1976) 200–6, Conley (1981), Levick (1982) and Paul (1984) 124.

[67] Polybius 3.40.4, Livy 21.25.2, and Velleius Paterculus 1.14.8. Walsh (1992) 174 says of Placentia and Cremona: 'These Latin colonies in the Po valley had been founded in May 23, 218 B.C. with 6,000 settlers each . . . in locations strategically chosen against Gallic incursions'.

(Livy 31.10.2, 33.23.2), Carthaginians (Livy 27.29.11) and Ligurians,
and so would have needed strong walls.[68] Since the dangerous days
of her foundation, however, the town had grown prosperous and
had allowed her defensive walls to fall into disrepair. Tacitus invests
realism not only in the description of Placentia's walls, but also in
the meticulous description of the different types of death caused by
the millstones being rolled down from the walls: some men are
crushed, while others are pierced through and left mangled and
bleeding to death. In contrast, Raabe notes that Virgil's description
of the siege is 'bloodless'. Tacitus certainly did not exclusively see
historical events in terms of decline, but in this scene, the evocation
of Virgilian epic may intensify a sense of disquiet for a Roman reader
who had already been disturbed by the general narrative about the
self-destructive power of civil war.

Conclusion

Even apparently minor moments from descriptions of battles in Latin
historiography and epic can show signs of influence from the other
genre, whether in the phrasing or in the details of a scene. Indeed,
it seems as if battle-scenes in the two genres lent themselves particularly well to this sort of borrowing, especially once Virgil's *Aeneid*
had become a text which readers knew in such detail. Although in
a historical narrative or in an epic cycle, the course of events might
firmly dictate that one side beat another in a particular battle, there
was certainly much scope for a writer with a creative imagination
to draw on other texts to generate exciting details for the narrative.
Not only could writers of epic and history usefully deploy imitation
in certain scenes by borrowing both from elsewhere in their own
texts and from texts by other authors in the same genre, but they
were quite capable of transgressing generic boundaries to add colour
and nuance to their battle-descriptions. The opportunities for doing
this were even higher if the nuts-and-bolts of a particular battle in
a historical narrative were not generally well-known, either because

---

[68] See Brunt (1971) 190–1 for Placentia's early troubles after her foundation. Livy
37.46.9–47.2 explains how Placentia and Cremona were reinforced with further
settlers in 190 B.C.

there were only one or two other accounts of the fighting, or because it was chronologically distant. If we had more texts from both genres, then we would probably be able to trace this sort of cross-generic splicing more extensively. The fact that there are gaps in the historiographical and epic texts which survive should certainly not deter us from exploring the potentially rich and provocative inter-connections between the two genres.[69]

[69] I would like to thank the organisers of the conference, David Levene and Damien Nelis, as well as Tony Woodman, for helpful comments and advice.

CHAPTER FOURTEEN

THE STRUCTURE OF LIVY'S FIRST PENTAD AND
THE AUGUSTAN POETRY BOOK

Ann Vasaly

I

I would like to begin this discussion of Livy's first pentad with an unfashionable foray into authorial intention. Let us say that Livy embarked on his vast history of the Roman people shortly after the battle of Actium in 31 B.C., an event that in retrospect can be seen to signal the end to almost a century of civil wars, but that, at the time, might have seemed but a pause in the long succession of bloody internal struggles that had gripped the body politic since the Gracchi.[1] The first question facing the historian was where to begin. Few would have faulted him if his history had excluded the legends and myths connected with the founding of Rome and had begun with the institution of the Republic or (like that of Claudius Quadrigarius) with the period following the sack of Rome by the Gauls, when traditions and records were somewhat more trustworthy.[2] Attempting to write history with any pretense of accuracy, even starting from the latter event, would have been a daunting task, and Livy knew that the greatest of the Greek historians, Herodotus and Thucydides, had by and large confined themselves to the more recent past, where their own autopsy or that of their informants could serve as the basis for arguing the truth of their accounts. Even Ephoros, who had written a more or less 'universal' history of Greece, had begun with the return of the Heracleidae, an event he evidently believed signaled the dividing line between an age knowable only through myth and

---

[1] For the (much disputed) date of the composition and publication of the first pentad see Luce (1965) with bibliography.

[2] For Quadrigarius' criticism of Roman historical sources before 390 see Plutarch *Num.* 1.2 (if Plutarch's 'Klodius' is Quadrigarius; on which see Frier (1979) 121–6).

one susceptible to the arts of the historian.[3] Livy, however, rejected
these models and arguably with good reason. The subject, after all,
was not just Roman events, but the creation of a people, the 'chief
people on earth', and stories of Rome's foundation expressed, if not
objective, then surely moral and even quasi-religious truths about
that people. So Livy determined to join what he called the 'crowd
of writers' who had written the history of the Roman people *a primordio urbis*.

And yet Livy evidently felt the need to justify and clarify this decision. In the preface, therefore, he states that the facticity of the early
stories was of no real importance to him.[4] He declares that he intends
neither to affirm nor deny these traditions, which he calls more suitable for treatment by poets than historians, and he goes on to assert
that it is appropriate for a great imperial people to consecrate their
origins by attributing them to divine agency. The reader, then, is
led to understand that these stories were important enough to include
in a serious history of Rome, but, unlike the case with recent history, their importance did not depend on their truth content but on
what they had to say about the Roman people and the image they
presented to the world.

This would seem to end the matter. Readers might then expect
that these legends of early Rome would be reproduced without apol-
ogy, and that they would be left to accept or reject them. And more
sophisticated readers would be forewarned by the preface not to
assume that the author was a credulous idiot who was presenting
such stories as literal truth. But Livy is not content to let the matter rest. Instead, he tells these early stories in ways that continually
make clear his unwillingness to attest to their accuracy; for instance,
he gives rationalizing alternatives for the most fabulous of events,

---

[3] See Herodotus 3.122 (separation of the period of myth from that of the 'human
generation'); 1.5 (agnosticism concerning the age of myth). While Thucydides does
not explicitly rule out any period as inappropriate to historical treatment, he does
choose as his subject events that he or his informants knew first-hand. See 1.1.2
(difficulty of accurate assessment of distant past); 1.20.1 (diverse reports of events
of distant past); 1.21.1 (stories of distant past transformed into myth); 1.22.2–3
(autopsy). On Ephoros' history as omitting mythological subjects, see Diodorus Siculus
4.1.3, Barber (1935) 14. On the development of the distinction between the mythic
and 'historical age' see Fornara (1983) 1–12.
[4] A summary of the extensive bibliography on Livy's preface may be found in
Moles (1993) 162 n. 2.

such as Mars' rape of Rhea Silvia or Romulus' apotheosis or Numa's communication with the nymph Egeria.[5]

Given his evident sensitivity to the marginal suitability of this material as history, it is hardly surprising that Livy decided to divide the volumes dealing with the earliest period of Roman history structurally from the rest of the work. Thus the period from the coming of the Trojans to Italy until the sack of Rome by the Gauls is contained in five books, separated from what follows by Camillus' climactic speech at the end of Book 5 affirming the divinely sanctioned destiny of Rome and its people. The objection might be raised that Livy's preface only raises doubts about the veracity of the period, as he says, 'before the city was founded or about to be founded' (*Praef.* 6: *ante conditam condendamve urbem*), a limited part of Book 1. But at the beginning of Book 6, Livy posits the kind of division of material implicit in Ephoros' decision to begin his history with the Return of the Heracleidae. Here Livy writes:

> The deeds that the Romans did from the founding of the city of Rome up until its capture . . . I have set forth in five books. These events are obscure not only by reason of their great antiquity — like places seen from a great distance that are scarcely distinguishable — but also because in those times there was infrequent use of writing, the only faithful guardian of the memory of past deeds; and because even what existed in the commentaries of the pontiffs and in other public and private records to a great extent perished when the city was burned. In what follows, events at home and in the field that are clearer and more certain shall be set forth, starting from the second beginning of the city, which was reborn — so to speak — from the roots, more abundant and more fruitful.[6]

---

[5] Rhea Silvia: 1.4.2; Romulus' apotheosis: 1.16.1–8; Egeria: 1.19.4–5. Livy's treatment of the Romulus legends has been extensively discussed. See e.g. Miles (1995) 7–84 (on Livy's reception of the early tradition); 138–43 (on Romulus). For summary and analysis of Livy's expressed or implied attitude within the first decade to the early traditions, see Forsythe, (1999), esp. ch. 2; also, cf. Wiseman ch. 17 below.

[6] *quae ab condita urbe Roma ad captam eandem Romani . . . gessere . . . quinque libris exposui, res cum vetustate nimia obscuras velut quae magno ex intervallo loci vix cernuntur, tum quod rarae per eadem tempora litterae fuere, una custodia fidelis memoriae rerum gestarum, et quod, etiam si quae in commentariis pontificum aliisque publicis privatisque erant monumentis, incensa urbe pleraeque interiere. clariora deinceps certioraque ab secunda origine velut ab stirpibus laetius feraciusque renatae urbis gesta domi militiaeque exponentur.* Cf. 5.21.9: *sed in rebus tam antiquis si quae similia veri sint pro veris accipiantur, satis habeam. haec . . . neque adfirmare neque refellere est operae pretium.* Kraus (1994) writes that the latter passage '. . . suggests that midway through Book 5 the historian is redrawing the limits of the historically verifiable . . .' (283–4).

II

There can be little doubt, then, that the first five books were viewed by the author as comprising a distinct period, different in fundamental ways from what followed; it is also generally agreed that Livy published these books together as a unit.[7] The subject I want to discuss in this essay concerns *dispositio*, that is, the structure Livy gave to the first pentad. Scholarly discussion of this question has in the past tended to move from small to large. Early in the century Kurt Witte, by means of a close comparison of Livy and Polybius, made a case for Livy's creation of artistic coherence in his treatment of various individual episodes in the third and fourth decades. Burck's 1934 monograph on the first pentad went a good deal beyond this. Relying on his comparison of Livy with Dionysius, he demonstrated the unified structure not only of individual episodes but of entire books, especially Books 3 and 5.[8] Ogilvie's magisterial commentary in 1965 on the first pentad enlarged on Burck's observations at many points, as well as on the work of Walsh and others. Ogilvie saw in each book the working out of a major theme: in Book 1 the overall theme of the pentad, the greatness of Rome, is introduced, and this book serves as well to foreshadow the themes assigned to the other four books — *libertas* in Book 2, *modestia* in Book 3, *moderatio* in Book 3, and *pietas* in Book 5. In his introduction to Book 3 Ogilvie considered briefly the question of structure in the pentad as a whole. Following Burck, he demonstrated how Livy made the Decemvirate of 451–450 the chronological center of Books 2 through 4.[9] Luce,

[7] For the date of publication, see above, note 1. The well known passages concerning Cornelius Cossus (4.20.5–11; 4.32.4), together with Livy's reference to Actium and the second closing of the Temple of Janus by Augustus (1.19.3), suggest 1) that the pentad as originally published predated 29 B.C., and 2) that the pentad as we have it appeared between 27 and 25. The publication of books 1–5 as a unit is widely accepted. (See e.g. Stadter (1972) esp. 289.) On Livy's attitude towards this material Luce (1971) 301 has aptly observed, 'Livy saw nothing wrong with taking a somewhat free hand in narrating the history of early Rome; since it was uncertain and suspect, what else could one do?' Cf. Forsythe (1999) who sees Livy's extreme caution in regards to this early material as extending to the period covered by the entire first decade, although finding it especially evident in Book 1.

[8] See Witte (1910). See also Burck (1934), esp. 8–51, the analysis of Book 3, from which 'der aufbau der ganzen ersten Pentade verständlich wird' (8). For analysis of trends in Livian scholarship, see e.g. Luce (1977) xv–xxvii, Miles (1995) 1–7, Forsythe (1999) 7–11.

[9] On the themes dominating each book, see Ogilvie (1965) 30; for the centrality of the decemvirate, 390.

along with Walsh, Stadter, and a number of other scholars in the 60's and 70's, argued for the pentad or the pentad and the decade as the basic unit not just of the early period but of almost all of the history.[10]

There is an obvious trend here. In the face of claims by Quellenforscher that Livy was almost completely controlled by his sources, that he used these sources haphazardly, and that he was therefore unable to impart structural or notional unity at any level of his history, we have the modest claims, made at the beginning of the century, that individual episodes exhibit an artistic coherence. From such small beginnings we have come a very long way. In recent years, some have argued for the existence of an astonishing level of structural and intellectual complexity in Livy's text. For instance, Gary Miles finds in the first pentad a cycle of rise, decline — reaching its nadir in the avarice associated with the fall of Veii — and refoundation by Camillus, a cycle which he believes Livy suggests might be repeated with the metaphorical refounding of Rome by Augustus. Christina Kraus sees in the first pentad an attempt by Livy to create in his written history a *monumentum* that reflects its subject matter, a narrative of the construction of Rome that itself becomes a parallel construction.[11] While earlier so-called 'literary' analysts of the *Ab urbe condita* tended to base their claims for Livy's excellence on his stylistic merit and did not attempt to rescue him from the prevailing denigration of his methods as an historian, more recent critics have rejected the dichotomy between the literary and the historical. They have tried to show not only that the medium is in many cases the message, but that the message is one of political and historiographical subtlety and perspicuity. Let me say here that I also believe Livy to have been a sophisticated political thinker, no less so because of the fact that his theoretical insights into the nature of political power were most often embodied in the content and form of his narratives, rather than in addresses to his readers *in propria persona*.

---

[10] Most scholars see some unified structure in the following groupings of books: 1–5, 6–15, 16–20, 21–30, 31–40. P. Stadter (1972), supported by Luce (1977) 3–32, argues that grouping by decades continues down to Book 120. See also Walsh (1974) 8–9. *Contra* Syme (1959) esp. 29–32.

[11] See Miles (1995), Kraus (1994), Jaeger (1997), esp. ch. 1, "The History as Monument.

III

Before attempting to describe in more detail the form of the first
pentad, let us consider briefly the means by which structure is created in the *AUC*. First of all we have the form of each book, the
papyrus roll, as a possible determinant of structure.[12] Now Livy was
not obliged to use the form of the papyrus roll in this way; but given
the enormity of his undertaking, which meant that it was surely published in parts over time and that many readers would have been
unlikely to read all of those parts — and certainly not all at once —
it would seem a logical strategy to write books that were unified in
some way, and issue them singly or in a group that was itself thematically or chronologically connected. Livy would have known of
precedents among the Greek historians, at least for creating unified
books within a history[13]

Within each book, Livy might have dealt with the question of
structure in various ways. It should be remembered that there is no
reason a reader would assume in advance that a single volume would
have a particular architecture, other than, perhaps, that the beginning and ending of a book might be marked. After all, a book could
have a dramatic form, in which the high point would be reached,
as in a play, about three-quarters of the way through, followed by
a denouement. Or the entire book could build to a climax at the
end. Or the most vivid and memorable incidents might occur in the
middle of the book. Alternatively, except for the cohesion produced
by treatment of a fixed event like a war or a defined period, the
book *qua* book might have no internal structure at all — as was probably the case with the majority of previous histories.

---

[12] On the book form, see Maehler *OCD*[3] 249–52, Van Sickle (1980) 5–41, Blanck
(1992), Cavallo (1975); Turner (1971, 1987[2]) with bibliography.
[13] See Diodorus Siculus 5.1.4 (Ephoros' division of books '*kata genos*'); Barber
(1935) 13, suggests that 'in Isocrates' recognition of the value of subdivision we may
perhaps find the origin of a later separation into books; and it is just possible that
Ephoros as a student of Isocrates set the fashion of publication volume by volume'.
For interpretation of the meaning of *kata genos*, see Fornara (1983) 43–45, who
writes that Ephorus wrote 'individual books or groups of books, devoted to a unitary concept such as a "topic" or geographical area'. Drews (1963) 252–3, believes
the historian 'restricted each of his books to one of the major fields of history which
were current in his day' such as, e.g., Hellenica, Macedonica, Sicilica, or Persica.
While the passage cited shows that Diodorus intended to structure his own universal history according to a coherent overall plan, the extant books testify to his
failure to achieve this coherence.

It is sufficiently clear, however, that Livy *did* choose to impart structural divisions to many of the extant books of the history, and he used a variety of methods to make the reader aware of these structures. This is a history ultimately derived from annalistic reporting and the basic unit of division, beginning with the post-regal period in Book 2, is the year; but Livy constantly subordinates year by year accounting to coherent narratives that include a beginning, middle, and end extending over a number of years.[14] An obvious strategy he employed, therefore, was to vary the length, vividness, and content of these narrative episodes to create structural patterns. For instance, the most memorable narrative of Book 3 concerns the story of the Decemvirate of 451–450 B.C., describing the rise of the tyrannical Appius Claudius, his attempt to gain power over the plebeian maiden Verginia, the murder of Verginia by her father, the revolt and secession of the plebeian army, and, finally, the overthrow of the decemvirs and re-establishment of Republican magistracies and laws. The story is by far the longest of Book 3, covering some thirty-two and a half of the 90 pages in the OCT edition. It therefore creates formal divisions by being set off through length and content from the shorter episodes around it. It is placed in the middle of the book (and therefore the middle of the pentad) and it also occupies almost exactly the chronological center of Books 2 through 4, which cover the period from 509 to 404 B.C.[15] It thereby creates a structural architecture not only for Book 3 but for the entire pentad.

Livy's use of speeches is another key marker of structural patterns. Unlike Dionysius, in whose history speeches are so frequent as to lose the power to separate large structural units, in the first pentad major speeches, especially in direct discourse, are rare events. To return to Book 3, a speech by T. Quinctius Capitolinus in *oratio recta* forms the climactic end to the book (3.67.1–68.13). This is the first, full-scale speech in the *Ab Urbe Condita*, a harbinger of the great speech of Camillus in Book 5 that ends the pentad as a whole. It is, however, also an echo of a shorter speech at the beginning of

[14] On the annalistic framework, see McDonald (1957) and, most recently, Rich (1997) writes: 'the extreme variety of the year narratives is in fact one of the hallmarks of the first decade. The amount of space accorded to individual years varies hugely . . .' For the 'Aristotelian' construction of episodes with a beginning, middle, and end, see Burck's 1934 study of the early books, and Walsh (1961) 175–90, Luce (1971).
[15] See Ogilvie (1965) 390.

Book 3 by T. Quinctius Cincinnatus, which is partly rendered in
indirect, partly in direct discourse (3.19.4–12).[16] Thus the long central narrative dealing with the decemvirate is bracketed by these
rhetorical interventions, which are made even more striking by the
absence of extended discourse elsewhere in the first three books.

Livy is clearly reserving his rhetorical ammunition in these books.
One might well have expected the first book, covering the monarchy, to end with a speech by Brutus, who leads the revolution against
the Tarquins and ushers in the free Republic. But Livy excuses himself from producing such a composition at this point by telling the
reader that Brutus made a spirited speech to the assembled citizens,
giving a few of the topics he mentioned on the occasion, and then
stating: 'With these and, I suppose, even fiercer remarks, which an
immediate outrage brings to mind but are in no way easy for an
historian to relate, he incensed the people and prevailed on them
to abrogate the king's authority and to order that Lucius Tarquinius
be exiled, along with his wife and children'.[17] This is disingenuous.
Whether or not it would have been easy to create a major speech
at this point, Livy was capable of doing so, but chose not to, apparently for reasons of structure and emphasis within the pentad as a
whole.

Some of my own work in recent years has concerned Livy's use
of stereotypical personae as a structuring device. Few have failed to
notice the crucial placement of similar heroes and anti-heroes within
the first pentad. The Decemvir Appius Claudius of Book 3, who
attempts to enslave Verginia and thereby provokes a revolution
removing him from power, is in many ways a reincarnation of the
tyrannical Tarquinii of Book 1. Nor does it take a great deal of
insight to recognize this since, in the introduction to the story of the
Decemvirate, Livy marks the event as the first great alteration in
governance since the fall of the Tarquins (3.33.1) and later explicitly compares Verginia to Lucretia (3.44.1). It can also be observed
that the character of Camillus, victor over Veii and savior of the
city from the Gauls in Book 5, is connected with that of Romulus

---

[16] Noted by Burck (1934) 49–50.

[17] 1.59.11: *his atrocioribusque, credo, aliis, quae praesens rerum indignitas haudquaquam
relatu scriptoribus facilia subicit, memoratis incensam multitudinem perpulit ut imperium regi abro-
garet exsulesque esse iuberet L. Tarqiuinium cum coniuge ac liberis.* (*subicit* is Walsh's emendation for *subiecit*).

at the beginning of Book 1. Again, little is left to conjecture, since Livy recounts how Camillus was hailed as 'Romulus and father of his country, and a second founder of the city' (5.49.7: *Romulus ac parens patriae conditorque alter urbis*). In this way Book 1 is connected to Book 3 through the figures of the Tarquins and Appius Claudius, and with Book 5 through the paired figures of Romulus and Camillus.

Livy links certain other characters as part of his creation of structural patterns, both within individual books and within the pentad, by means of a sort of familial stereotyping. The Appii Claudii and the Quinctii provide useful examples.[18] In the first pentad Livy characterizes successive Appii Claudii in an identical way, as fierce, arrogant defenders of the patriciate and enemies of the plebeians. Each member of the *gens* in Books 2 and 3 is more extreme, and thus more dangerous to the state then the last, until we reach Appius Claudius the Decemvir, who uses his power to usher in a tyranny and whose attempt upon Verginia is a metaphor for his attempted enslavement of the state as a whole. The appearance of Appius Claudius Crassus, whose speech is followed by concord rather than discord, presents a sort of denoument to this movement.

In contrast, the major Quinctii in Books 2, 3, and 4 are presented as courageous, honest, stern but law-abiding defenders of the state, patricians who put the good of the commonwealth above party politics. I have mentioned above how the speeches of Quinctius Cincinnatus and Quinctius Capitolinus, at the beginning and end of Book 3, frame the narrative of Appius Claudius Decemvir at the center of the volume. But one can go further. Not just the speeches of these two Quinctii, but what we might call the Quinctian persona, revealed in multiple episodes of speech and action, before and after the Decemvirate, is used by Livy within Book 3 as a foil and counterimage to Appius Claudius, who is himself merely a representative of a fixed type which reappears in Books 2 through 4. Within Book 3, therefore, the Quinctian persona functions as the anti-Appius just as Camillus plays this role within the pentad as a whole. What I'm saying here is that the placement of *an* Icilius, *an* Appius Claudius, *a* Valerius, *a* Quinctius, each of which is assigned a stereotypical character, is yet another way in which Livy creates patterns and structures within the pentad.

---

[18] See Vasaly (1987), (1999).

I will not rehearse in detail the many other strategies that create order and symmetry within the individual books of the pentad. Let me simply say that they also include, but are not limited to: formal introductions, such as mark the beginning of some books and all major episodes[19] moralising *sententiae*, emphatic phrases or *Sprichwörter*, battle scenes and urban assembly scenes, notices of foundations, triumphs, prodigies and other material drawn from annalistic records, and repetition of major themes, such as foundation.[20]

Let me set out in brief, then, certain observations about the structure of the pentad. It is clear that two major principals of organization are at work: variation and symmetry. Within each book Livy creates *variatio* in all aspects of the history, but especially through the alternation, on the one hand, of external events — usually wars fought against neighboring communities — and, on the other, of internal affairs — domestic upheavals regularly cast in the form of a *bellum* between classes. These, then are the *foris bella domi seditionis* of which the author speaks in the preface to Book 6 when summarizing the contents of the previous five books. Symmetry is created through the division of most books into two or three major parts, making use of a variety of mutually reinforcing strategies to mark these divisions, some of which have been mentioned above.[21]

The pentad as a whole also exhibits the same features of variation and symmetry found in the individual books. Both are evident in Livy's handling of the theme of *libertas*, a subject which, in its various complex aspects, runs throughout the entire pentad. The most crucial events in Livy's development of this theme, however,

---

[19] Note, especially, the introduction to the Decemvirate in 3.33.1, where the Decemvirate, which in Livy lasts scarcely more than two years, is made the equivalent in historical importance to the monarchy (245 years), and the preceding period of consular government (302 years, according to Livy). Thus the pentad creates a narrative structure with the Decemvirate in Book 3 as its center, surrounded by the earlier and later periods of the Republic in Books 2 and 4, and the monarchy and the sack of Veii/sack of Rome in Books 1 and 5.

[20] On the use of prodigy lists as a structuring device, see Levene (1993) who writes of how, beginning in Book 5, Livy 'binds together great portions of the history with a religious sub-text . . .' (241). On Livy's handling of the themes of foundation and refoundation see Kraus (1994), Miles (1995).

[21] Note, also, that the creation of multiple narrative subdivisions is a distinctive feature of Livian style. See Luce (1971) 285: 'The most characteristic feature of Livy's narrative technique is the division of material into separate units based on groups of people, stages in a developing sequence of events, themes, or differing places'.

are assigned to Books 1, 3, and 5. Book 1 describes the progress of the monarchy, which Livy presents retrospectively as an *educatio* of the Roman people that brings them to a point where they are mature enough to deal responsibly with the blessings of freedom, and culminates in the fall of Tarquinius Superbus and the establishment of the *res publica*.[22] Book 3, as we have seen, revolves around its central narrative, the loss of liberty to a tyrannical power that arises from within, the overthrow of that tyranny, and the recovery of freedom and the Republican state. Book 5 is divided into two major narratives: the first half of the book describes the capture of Veii, which leads, in the second half, to the loss of *libertas* through the Gallic invasion, and ends with its recovery under Camillus. An indication of the crucial nature of these events in Books 1, 3, and 5 can be seen in their connection with the idea of refoundation: in each instance the city is presented by Livy as experiencing, to borrow a phrase, 'a new birth of freedom'. Books 2 and 4, in turn, form the bridges between the critical events found in One, Three, and Five, dealing especially with the deleterious effects of the class struggle on both the internal and external fortunes of the city.

IV

If this assessment of the structure of the pentad is accurate, the next question is why. Why should Livy have chosen to give his history, or rather, the early books of his history, this structure? Some sort of precedent might be argued to exist in Herodotean ring composition, but nothing like the symmetrical construction of the books of the first pentad is to be found in Herodotus. Nor does Hellenistic Greek or earlier Latin historiography, as far as we know, provide a model for anything other than the thematic or chronological unity of individual books and the very general grouping of several books by subject.[23] Livy is an historian well versed in Ciceronian philosophy and rhetoric; perhaps if we had all six books of the *De Re Publica* it would demonstrate that some of the structural strategies used by

---

[22] For the *educatio* theme, see Livy 2.1.1–6.
[23] See above, note 13. We are, of course, hampered in this assessment by the difficulty of reconstructing the earlier histories from existing fragments.

Livy were prefigured in that work of political theory. As it is, however, the closest parallels are to be found not in prose but in poetry.

While the form of Catullus' *monobiblos*, both in terms of the poems
it contained and the order of those poems, is unclear, and the structure of Gallus' four books of elegies must likewise remain a mystery,
a number of the extant poetry books published in the 30's and 20's
show that experiments in book structure are to be identified with
late Republican and Augustan poetic composition.[24] In the early 30's
Vergil published his book of ten *Eclogues*, unified in meter, pastoral
setting, and Theocritean model, but characterized by variation in
subject and tone, and alternation between dialogue and monologue.
It is a work of exquisite balance and symmetry, achieved in part
through the pairing of poems 1 and 9, on the land confiscations, 2
and 8, on passionate love, 3 and 7, the singing matches, and 4 and
6, the so-called Messianic *Eclogue* and the song of Silenus, both of
which are presented as more weighty poems (*paulo maiora canamus*,
says Vergil of 4). The *Eclogue* book also is marked by a beginning,
middle, and end. In One, Tityrus begins his song under a shady
tree, in contrast to his companion who is being forced from what
appears an environment made for ease and poetry. In the middle
of the book, at the beginning of 6, the *Eclogue* poet is identified by
Apollo as Tityrus and is recalled to the genre of pastoral song. The
final lines of 10 are made to culminate both poem and book, recalling the language of 1, but drawing a close to the poet's meditations
in the pastoral mode (*haec sat erit, divae, vestrum cecinisse poetam*). Now
the shade and ease that had inspired the poet at the outset of the
book become 'harmful to singers'.

A few years after the appearance of the *Eclogues* another collection of ten poems was published: the first book of Horace's *Satires*.
While the collection, as befits a work inspired by Lucilius, does not
exhibit the same degree of elaborate book construction as does the
Eclogues, it nevertheless shows careful attention to the structure of the

---

[24] For the hypothesis of Catullus' publication of a symmetrically structured book
of fourteen poems, see Hubbard (1983) with bibliography. Van Sickle (1980) is
devoted to the subject of Augustan poetry books. More generally, see Krevans
(1996). For a survey of approaches to the architecture of the *Eclogues*, see Rudd
(1976) 119–44. Further discussion and bibliography may be found in Leach (1978)
esp. 100–1 n. 3, Santirocco (1986) 5–13, with 179 n. 13 (for bibliography on the
architecture of Vergil's *Eclogues* and on the collections of Tibullus and Propertius),
179 n. 14 (on Horace's *Satires*).

whole. The first nine poems are formally divided into three groups of three. The beginning of the book is marked by the dedicatory vocative to Maecenas in 1.1., the end by the command to the slave-boy at 10.92 to append the verses of the last satire to the *libellum*. Whether the middle of the work is also marked is a difficult question. Some years ago James Zetzel observed that the *Satires*, like the *Eclogues*, and perhaps because of the *Eclogues*, show 'a pattern of responsion around the fifth poem', and he went on to show connections between 4–6, 3–7, 2–8, and 1–9.[25] This would set the fifth *Satire* apart as the central poem in the book, just as the apotheosis of Daphnis is set apart in the *Eclogues* through the pairing of the poems around it. The importance of *Eclogue* 5 is further emphasized by the fact that 6 is treated by Vergil as a new beginning. Similarly, in *Satire* 6, Horace includes a rededication through the mention of Maecenas in the second foot of the first line (just as in the first *Satire*). *Satire* 6 is also a kind of amalgamation of what preceded it, echoing both the diatribe form of 1 through 3 and the autobiographical content of 4 and 5. There is a real problem, however, in attempting to see *Satire* 5, the journey to Brundisium, as central in meaning as well as in structure. Having criticized Lucilius in 4, we see Horace attempting to better his model. But our expectations for the seriousness and importance of the great journey made with the most honoured of his political and literary friends are constantly defeated and deflated; we wait for grand pronouncements and instead hear of stomach aches and eye infections. As if to emphasize precisely this undermining of expectations, the center of the center, 5.52–70, is a verbal confrontation in mock epic style between two buffoons whose jests can only be described as frigid. It might be argued, then, that Horace has assimilated Vergil's structural experimentation so thoroughly as to attempt to undermine the expectations produced by it in order to point the difference between genres.

Rather than deal in detail here with the complex question of the structure of other poetry books in the period, I will simply observe that in the works published not long before and at about the same time Livy was writing his pentad — that is, in the years before and just after Actium — we find in poetry a preoccupation with creating

---

[25] Zetzel (1980). Zetzel rejects many of the more elaborate symmetries suggested by Van Rooy in a series of articles the latter published between 1968 and 1971.

books distinguished by variation between pieces and organized with careful attention to symmetry. Many include programmatic pieces at the beginning and summarizing statements at the end. In a number of cases the pattern created by the books and the use of a 're-introduction' emphasise the central position. The works of which I am speaking include Vergil's *Eclogues*, Horace's second book of *Satires*, Tibullus' book of ten elegies, and the 22 poems of Propertius Book 1 (especially the central group of 6–9 and 10–14), all of which (except the earlier *Eclogues*) were probably published between 30 and 27 B.C.

The Augustan poetry book, however, demonstrates structural experimentation within the scope of the single papyrus roll; a closer connection can be found between Livy's first pentad and multivolume works. Horace's *Odes*, published in 23, should be ruled out of court. Vergil's *Georgics*, probably published in 29 B.C., might well have influenced Livian composition of the final version of the pentad. Here we find the clear division of books by subject, introduction to the work as a whole, and strongly marked beginnings and endings for individual books. Furthermore, the insertion of what amounts to a second proem at the beginning of Book Three creates a special emphasis on the middle of the work.[26]

But the most striking parallels between poet and historian come with Vergil's *Aeneid*. Here any influence between poet and historian would seem to go the opposite way. One of the earliest statement of this thesis came in 1942 with Augusto Rostagni's monograph arguing that Livy's impact on Vergil was profound, most evident in the passages of the *Aeneid* in which Jupiter in Book 1 and Anchises in Book 6 foretell the history of Rome.[27] Rostagni believed that Vergil's debt was signalled at the beginning of the epic by the reference to Antenor's foundation of Padua (1.242–9), a detail concerning the Trojan cycle found conspicuously only in Livy Book 1 and here. Rostagni also saw a debt to Livy in Vergil's articulation of Rome's fated superiority and divine destiny. As P. G. Walsh has written in a similar vein: '. . . there is a remarkable correspondence between

---

[26] On inclusion of a re-introduction in the middle of a poetic work see Conte (1992), who sees the second proem as Alexandrian and programmatic, in contrast to the traditional proem at the beginning of a poem which is expositional and thematic. Oddly, Conte has nothing to say about Apollonius. Thomas (1983) looks to Callimachus' *Aitia* as a model for the *Georgic* passage.

[27] Rostagni (1942).

the spirit animating the first decade of the *Ab urbe condita* and that
of Vergil's *Aeneid*. The same central concept of Rome as *pucherrima
rerum* dominates both works. Both conceive the city as divinely founded
and providentially guided; both emphasise her imperial mission to
establish the *pax Romana* throughout the inhabited world'.[28] My own
view is that, despite these shared sentiments, Livy's view of Roman
history is in many ways different from that of Vergil. Vergil longs
for peace and communicates a profound sadness over the shedding
of civic blood. Livy, of course, regrets the discord between citizens,
and yet he presents the struggle between classes as necessary to the
protection of the rights of each group — a dialectic ultimately responsible for the Republican institutions and laws on which Roman order
and power would rest. Vergil's characters are as much receptacles
of forces beyond their control as they are free actors; for Livy history
is about actions and reactions, by individuals and by groups, who
at every moment make choices to act selfishly or with magnanimity,
out of narrow concerns or on behalf of the good of the whole state,
with violence or in ways that lead to compromise and concord.

In terms of structure, two aspects of the *Aeneid* are particularly
reminiscent of the structural principals underlying the first pentad:
First, just as Livy places the most crucial events in the development
of his major themes in Books 1, 3, and 5, and connects these, in
turn, by books that create a context against which to view these
events, so in the *Aeneid* Vergil alternates between books that are more
important to advancing the line of the narrative (the even numbered
books) and those that create a bridge to these key events (the odd
numbered books). Second, as Livy uses the center of a group of volumes as a crucial moment in the progress of the pentad as a whole,
so one of the most striking aspects of Vergilian construction of the
Aeneid is the focus on the center of the epic, the end of Book 6, in
which the future history of Rome, including the place of Augustus
within that history, is foretold to Aeneas in the Underworld. Does
this mean, then, that Vergil drew on Livy for these structural features of the *Aeneid*? Surely not. Vergil did not need to look to Livy
as an inspiration for the *variatio*, symmetrical balance, and central

---

[28] (1961) 10–11. It should be noted that Walsh also wrote that such sentiments
'were encouraged by Augustus himself', a view much less widely held now, particularly in light of arguments for an early, even pre-Actian, date for the composition of the first pentad. See for instance Woodman (1988) 128–34.

focus found in his poem. All of these are, after all, to be found in miniature in the *Eclogue* book, as well as in the *Georgics*. Or, for that matter, in the experiments within the epic itself in the structure of the single dactyllic line.

To conclude: The form of the first five books of the *AUC*, both in respect to individual books as well as the whole pentad, is unexampled in extant historiography. It is quite possible that Livy was inspired by the experiments in book structure being carried on by Latin poets in the 30's and early 20's — Vergil foremost among them — to use the means of creating form *peculiar to his own genre* to produce the striking innovations we see in the architecture of the early books, where the untrustworthy nature of the historical tradition allowed him to use a particularly 'free hand' in constructing his historical *monumentum*. The application of poetic strategies of construction to the first pentad would hardly be surprising given that Livy declares explicitly the poetic nature of the early stories, that he begins the *AUC* with four feet of dactylic hexameter, and that he goes on to imbue the early books with poetic diction and syntax, no doubt derived in part from Ennius, whom Livy would have known intimately.[29] At the same time, these earlier experiments in poetic book form would reach their culmination in the elegant and complex structure created by Vergil in the *Aeneid*.[30]

---

[29] It is possible that Livy owed some of the structural principals evident in these books to Ennius as well. See Conte (1992) 154–6, for speculation concerning the structure of the *Annales*, including the idea that book 7 opened with a programmatic proem, thus drawing attention to the center (if not the exact center) of the fifteen books.

[30] I would like to thank Professors David Levene and Damien Nelis, who kindly invited me to participate in the Durham University conference at which this paper was originally presented and at which I learned a great deal from the stimulating papers and discussions that followed my paper and those of the other presenters. I am also grateful to my colleagues at Boston University, Professors J. Loren Samons and Pamela Bleisch, for their valuable comments upon a version of this paper.

CHAPTER FIFTEEN

A VARRONIAN VATIC NUMA?: OVID'S *FASTI* AND PLUTARCH'S *LIFE OF NUMA*

Molly Pasco-Pranger

By the early second century B.C.E. Rome's second king, Numa Pompilius, was associated with a nymph or minor goddess named Egeria
who advised him in his administration of the young city; the tradition's earliest extant appearance is in a one-line fragment of Ennius
(fr. 113 Sk.). The relationship between Numa and Egeria, most often
figured as a marriage, finds a place in a wide range of sources and
is clearly a standard piece of the Numan tradition by the Augustan
period.[1] Egeria's close narrative and cultic links to the Camenae[2]
also bring Numa into association with these figures who emerge,
probably in the third century with Livius Andronicus, as the Roman
equivalent of the Muses.[3] When we have, then, a tradition associating
Numa with Egeria and the Camenae, and a reinterpretation of the
Camenae in the third century making them the Italian counterpart
to the Muses, we should not be surprised to find this literary development exerting an influence on the historico-legendary tradition. We
should not be surprised to find authors asking what Numa had to
do with poetry.

A pair of unusual treatments of the life of Numa in Ovid's *Fasti*
and in Plutarch show traces of exactly this inquiry in their association

---

[1] E.g., Cicero *Leg.* 1.1.4; Livy 1.19.5, 1.21.3; Dionysius of Halicarnassus *R.A.*
2.57–76; Ovid *Met.* 15.479–551. On the history of the narrative, see Buchmann
(1912) 38–56; Buchmann argues that the story has a Greek origin and is more a
poetic than a historical tradition.

[2] Egeria shared a grove cult with the Camenae outside the Porta Capena which
both Livy and Juvenal report was founded by Numa (Livy 1.21.3, Juvenal 1.3.11ff.).
The connection between Egeria and the Camenae is not entirely clear, but it seems
sure that both she and they were originally water goddesses and indeed both the
Porta Capena site and Egeria's other major cult site at Lake Nemi are associated
with springs. Dionysius reports that some actually consider Egeria one of the Camenae
(2.60.5).

[3] Ross (1975) 146–69 offers a concise history of the identification of the Camenae
as the Italian Muses.

of Numa with the vatic ideal which rose to such prominence in the Augustan period. I will argue that it is likely that the two share a Varronian source, and consider in particular this theory's implications for the relationship between Varro's antiquarianism and Augustan discourses on the nature of poetry and the role of the poet in the political world. Before turning to the aetiological narratives shared by Plutarch and Ovid, I will briefly examine how each author establishes Numa as a poetic figure upon his introduction into the text and into Roman history.

In a 1992 study of Book 3 of the *Fasti*, Hinds noted the strong poetic overtones of two passages that introduce the poem's most extended set of Numan narratives,[4] overtones which draw connections between Numa and the poet of the *Fasti*. The first passage in question sends out signals for a reader familiar with the language of Roman 'Alexandrianism':

> primus, oliviferis Romam deductus ab arvis,
>   Pompilius menses sensit abesse duos,
> sive hoc a Samio doctus, qui posse renasci
>   nos putat, Egeria sive monente sua.

> Numa Pompilius, led down to Rome from the olive-bearing fields,
> first perceived that the year was missing two months, whether he
> had been taught by the Samian who thinks we can be reborn,
> or whether Egeria advised him about this.
>
>   *Fasti* 3.151–4

In line 151, Numa is 'led down' (*deducere*) to Rome. The *carmen deductum*, widely recognized as the Latin equivalent of Callimachus' Μοῦσαν λεπταλέην (*Aet.* 1 fr. 1.24),[5] would perhaps not necessarily leap to mind were it not for the word *doctus* two lines later: Numa may have been taught by the Greek sage Pythagoras, Ovid tells us.[6] The *doctrina*

---

[4] Hinds (1992) esp. 119–20 and n. 5, and 124 n. 9. My discussion owes much to Hinds's, which seeks to demonstrate an affinity between Numa and the material and genre of the *Fasti*. Barchiesi (1997) 110–12 also treats this episode briefly, emphasizing in particular Numa's composition of the *Carmen Saliare* (*Fast.* 3.388).

[5] For a recent discussion of the programmatic use of *deductum* with thorough bibliography see Myers (1994) 4 n. 13. For further discussion of the primary sources, Hinds (1987) 18–21 and notes.

[6] The word *deductus* is used of Numa in Livy as well (1.18.6) without arousing any suspicion of Alexandrianism. Livy also (quite rightly) rejects Pythagoras as Numa's teacher, primarily on chronological grounds (1.18.2–5); on the history of this tradition and its rejection, see Ogilvie (1965) *ad loc.*

of the poet is also a defining characteristic of Hellenistic poetry, and the placement of the word in the midst of a learned periphrasis typical of the Alexandrians and their followers hammers home the point.[7] Numa is both *doctus* and *deductus*, highly suited to the *Fasti*'s aetiological elegy.

Ovid also offers an alternative possibility to explain Numa's calendrical acumen: perhaps Numa made his calendrical revisions under the advice of his wife (*Egeria . . . monente*, 154). This phrase too points to the king's affinity with the poet of the *Fasti*, whose continual requests for information from the gods are often phrased with the verb *monere*.[8] Especially telling is his request to Egeria herself, just over a hundred lines later: *nympha, mone, . . . nympha, Numae coniunx . . .* (Advise me, nymph . . . nymph, wife of Numa . . .) (3.261–62). Numa and the poet both 'write' their calendars, *Egeria . . . monente*.[9]

This request to Egeria leads off a second passage replete with programmatic language, Ovid's description of the grove at Aricia in which he places the meetings between Numa and the nymph:

> vallis Aricinae silva praecinctus opaca 263
>   est lacus, antiqua religione sacer
>   . . .
> defluit incerto lapidosus murmure rivus:
>   saepe, sed exiguis haustibus, inde bibi.
> Egeria est, quae praebet aquas, dea grata Camenis: 275
>   illa Numae coniunx consiliumque fuit.

> Encircled by the shady woods of the valley of Aricia, there is a lake, sacred in the old religion . . . A rocky stream flows down with a hesitant murmuring: I've drunk from it often, but in little sips. It's Egeria who offers the water, the goddess pleasing to the Camenae: she was wife and councilor to Numa.
>
> *Fasti* 3.263–4, 273–6

---

[7] Granted, this is a glaringly obvious periphrasis compared to the many nearly opaque references made when a demonstration of learning is the issue at hand. Here, however, the point is not the learnedness itself, but an allusion to the *style* of learned periphrases, which is accomplished neatly without introducing unnecessary confusion. On the Pythagorean practice of avoiding naming the master, see Bömer (1986) on *Met.* 15.60.

[8] 1.227, 467; 3.167; 4.247; 5.447. On the didactic and sacral significance of the verb *monere* in the *Fasti*: Merli (2000) 94 n. 38.

[9] Myers (1994) 81–2 notes the similarity of Numa's 'research' in Croton in *Met.* 15.4–11, to the antiquarian search for aetia undertaken by the narrator of the *Fasti*. It seems Ovid found Numa well-suited to this genre.

Here, Ovid sets up Egeria in the *locus amoenus* of a shady grove with running water. This location is an ideal place for poetic inspiration, recalling the literary topos of poetic initiations that goes back to Hesiod's meeting with the Muses on Helicon. As Kambylis demonstrated in his study of post-Hesiodic initiation scenes, water becomes, for the ancient poets, a recurrent and central symbol of poetic initiation.[10] In this particular shady grove, the poet does not claim to have been initiated by the Muses, but does claim to have drunk of Egeria's water, 'in little sips', and calls the goddess 'pleasing to the Camenae'. The manner of the poet's drinking activates the play between 'big' and 'small' so common in discussions of epic and the lesser genres: we might think of Propertius' poetic initiation in poem 3.3.[11] Ovid's 'autobiographical' intrusion into the narrative of an aetion, rare in the *Fasti*, is surely pointed, drawing a parallel between Numa and the poet: just as Numa received inspiration (*consilium*) from the goddess for his establishment of laws and rites, so the poet of the *Fasti* received poetic inspiration in writing his own version of the sacral year. Ovid, then, adduces Numa as a model in his own vatic activity and aligns him, through programmatic language and through the figure of Egeria, with Augustan poetics.

Perhaps we expect this from Ovid, inclined as he is to exploit the poetic potential of traditional narratives; but when we turn to Plutarch's treatment of the relationship between Egeria and Numa we again find implicit connections between Numa and the poetic tradition of inspired poets. In a detail unique to him, Plutarch emphasizes the asceticism of Numa's life prior to his call to Rome, and his solitary, rural existence:[12]

ὁ δὲ Νομᾶς ἐκλείπων τὰς ἐν ἄστει διατριβὰς ἀγραυλεῖν τὰ πολλὰ καὶ πλανᾶσθαι μόνος ἤθελεν ἐν ἄλσεσι θεῶν καὶ λειμῶσιν ἱεροῖς καὶ τόποις ἐρήμοις ποιούμενος τὴν δίαιταν. ὅθεν οὐχ ἥκιστα τὴν ἀρχὴν ὁ περὶ τῆς θεᾶς ἔλαβε λόγος, ὡς ἄρα Νομᾶς ἐκεῖνος οὐκ ἀδημονίᾳ τινὶ ψυχῆς καὶ πλάνῃ τὸν μετὰ ἀνθρώπων ἀπολέλοιπε βίον, ἀλλὰ σεμνοτέρας γεγευμένος ὁμιλίας καὶ γάμων θείων ἠξιωμένος, Ἡγερίᾳ δαίμονι συνὼν ἐρώσῃ καὶ συνδιαιτώμενος, εὐδαίμων ἀνὴρ καὶ τὰ θεῖα πεπνυμένος γέγονεν.

[10] Kambylis (1965) 65–7.
[11] Knox (1985), Conte (1994) 109–11. Cf. Ovid *Am.* 1.15.35–6, *ex Pon.* 4.2.15–20.
[12] A fragment of Cassius Dio mentions that Numa sometimes stayed in the countryside, but apparently leaves it at that (fr. 6.2); Dio, of course, postdates Plutarch.

Numa, leaving behind the pastimes of the city, preferred to live outside for the most part and to wander alone, making a life in the groves of the gods and the sacred meadows and empty places. Not least from this did the story about the goddess arise, that Numa hadn't left behind life among men because of any distress or aberration of the spirit, but because he had had a taste of more august company and had been thought worthy of divine marriage; that Egeria fell in love with him and by being with and living with her, he had become a blessed man and one wise in divine matters.

Numa 4.1–2

Strangely, Plutarch treats the story of Numa's relationship with Egeria as a result of his odd lifestyle. In a subsequent section (*Numa* 4.6), the biographer offers numerous parallels to Numa's relationship with the goddess and, in particular, lists poets who had a special relationship with a god or the Muses: Pindar with Pan, Archilochus and Hesiod with the Muses, and Sophocles with Asclepius. Here again, the Hesiodic parallel is worth noting: Hesiod's encounter with and subsequent instruction by the Muses at the foot of Mount Helicon (*Theogony* 22–34) occurs while the poet is shepherding, and thus alone in the quasi-wilderness of bucolic groves. The verb ἀγραυλεῖν which Plutarch uses of Numa's solitary existence is rare and likely meant to echo the Muses' opening address to Hesiod: ποιμένες ἄγραυλοι . . . (Field-dwelling shepherds . . .) (26); in any case, the verb is regularly associated with shepherding.[13] With the Hesiodic model in mind, the causal connection Plutarch draws between Numa's rural, solitary lifestyle and the story of his relationship with Egeria is more clear: solitary groves and meadows are the sorts of places one meets Muses.[14]

---

[13] In Homeric usage, the adjective occurs only of shepherds (*Il.* 18.162: again, ποιμένες ἄγραυλοι) and of cattle (*Il.* 10.155, *Od.* 12.253). Apollonius uses it in the same way (*Arg.* 1.575: ἀγραύλοιο . . . σημαντῆρος; 4. 317: ποιμένες ἄγραυλοι). Strabo 15. 3. 18. 17 uses the verb with ποιμαίνειν in an almost hendiadic phrase describing the life of the Cappadocians.

[14] One more brief example from those listed by Plutarch shows that even an urban poet must come out of the city for such a meeting. Archilochus' meeting with the Muses is reported in an inscription of the third century B.C.E. from the Archilocheion outside Paros (*Inscr. Mnesiep.* E¹ II 20–57 = Lasserre and Bonnard (1958) fr. A 11a.): as a young man, Archilochus was sent into the country (εἰς ἀγρόν) by his father to drive a cow to market; in the pre-dawn hours he meets a group of women on the road; they greet him with teasing jests, and offer to buy the cow from him at a fair price; the women and the cow disappear, and a lyre is there in their place. The women, of course, are the Muses; their mocking behavior has much in common with that of the Hesiodic initiation (*Th.* 26–29) a characteristic picked up again in Theocritus (7.20, 42 and 128). Though Archilochus is

Both Plutarch and Ovid, then, prepare readers to see Numa in poetic terms, and particularly encourage them to read Numa's relationship with Egeria as akin to the divine inspiration evoked by the Hesiodic model. This aura of divine inspiration is likewise a key element in the *vates* figure which emerges as the ideal poet in the Augustan period. Previously used somewhat derisively of prophets and fortunetellers, the word *vates* was gradually adopted and adapted by Augustan poets to describe their own place in the world. As Newman put it in his 1967 study of the term, '*Vates* were new and yet traditional, Roman, and yet backed by Greek learning, leaders of society and yet religious and mystical leaders with no dangerous political implications.'[15] I will return to the question of the *vates* figure's 'political implications' below. Following from the vatic introductions I have just discussed, Ovid's extended treatment of Numan stories in *Fasti* 3 and Plutarch's *Life of Numa* report a shared set of unusual aetiological narratives concerning Numa that heighten the vatic and poetic associations of the king. The two share three basic narrative segments: in the first, Numa binds the sylvan gods Picus and Faunus in order to find out how to expiate lightning; second, Numa engages in a word-duel with Jupiter Elicius to work out the terms of said expiation; finally, a mystically charged shield falls from the sky, and Numa institutes rites involving it. For convenience, I will concentrate in each case on the Ovidian versions, and point to the significant passages of Plutarch for comparison.

Ovid introduces this set of narratives by asking, 'Now who will tell me why the Salii carry Mars' heavenly arms and sing "Mamurius"?' (3.259–60) The arrival of the March 1 festival of Mars during which the Salian priests made a ritual dance through the city, prompts the inquiry.[16] The twelve priests of Mars carried bronze shields called *ancilia*, eleven of them said to be copies of an original *ancile* which, during the reign of Numa, fell from the sky as a sign of the gods' favor. In order to protect the original shield, Numa had a bronzesmith, Veturius Mamurius, make eleven copies, and entrusted all twelve shields to the Salii. As a reward, Mamurius asked that his

---

not shepherding when the divine encounter takes place, the pretext for his presence in the countryside, driving a cow to market, is surely a close second!

[15] Newman (1967) 16. Of continuing importance to the history of the concept (though overly ambitious in their reconstructions) are Dahlmann (1948) and Bickel (1951). Important recent revisions to the picture are found in Hardie (1986) 16–22.

[16] Scullard (1981) 85–6.

name be included in the Carmen Saliare. This narrative, given by both Plutarch (*Numa* 13) and Verrius Flaccus' epitomizer Festus (117 L), is surely sufficient answer to the question which leads off this aition, and Ovid reports it faithfully in most details (3.367–92).

Varro is recognized as the most likely immediate source for this narrative: Verrius Flaccus often depends heavily on the earlier antiquarian; in addition, Varro's etymology of *ancile* (*De Lingua Latina* 7.43) and his explanation of the Salii's call of *mamuri veturi* as *memoriam veterem* ('ancient memory', *De Lingua Latina* 6.49) are reproduced or alluded to in both Ovid and Plutarch.[17] Barchiesi has observed that Ovid's version of this aetion, like the *Fasti* passages discussed by Hinds, makes Numa a poetic forerunner of Ovid himself: Numa is presented as the composer of the Carmen Saliare, and as the instigator of Veturius' 'artistic' work. There is some evidence that Varro, too, considered the Carmen Saliare Numa's own composition: in the preface to *De lingua Latina* 7, Varro expounds upon the difficulty of explicating obscure poetic words and refers particularly to the opacity of the Song of the Salii; in doing so, he dates the song and thus the Romans' first *verba poetica* to the reign of Numa (*De Lingua Latina* 7.3). In the story of the Salii and the *ancile*, then, we have a Numan narrative with an acknowledged Varronian pedigree which casts Numa in the quite literal role of poet.

Before he arrives at the story of the *ancile*, however, Ovid inserts two other Numan episodes which he shares only with Plutarch and the Sullan annalist Valerias Antias: the binding of Picus and Faunus, and the conjuring of Jupiter Elicius. The connection of these two episodes to the Salii and the *ancile* is Ovid's own innovation:[18] in his version the *ancile* is sent by Jupiter Elicius. This invented connection brings three narratives with poetic associations into contact with one another and thereby reinforces the *Fasti*'s representation of Numa as a quasi-poet.

The first of these episodes belongs to a type first exemplified by

---

[17] Varro explains that the *ancilia* are named *ab ambecisu, quod ea arma ab utraque parte ut Thracum incisa*; cf. *Fast.* 3.377–78; Plutarch gives a variety of Greek etymologies (*Num.* 13.5–6, with a disclaimer at the end) but begins his list with a reference to the Latin etymology from *ambecisus/incisus*: τὴν περιφέρειαν . . . ἔχει ἐκτομήν (*Num.* 13.5). On *mamuri veturi*, see Plutarch *Num.* 13.7, Ovid *Fast.* 3.389–92; Barchiesi (1997) 111–12 makes the argument for Ovid's allusion to Varro in this instance.

[18] Amply demonstrated by Porte (1985) 131–9, and recently given support on more literary gounds by Merli (2000) 118–20. But see below, n. 33 for Wiseman's intriguing suggestion of an earlier connection between these stories.

the binding of Proteus in *Odyssey* 4.395–570, where the sea-god, captured by Menelaus, goes through numerous changes of form in an
effort to escape his captor. When the god returns to his original
shape, he answers Menelaus' questions. The poetic associations in
Homer are weak: Proteus becomes the internal narrator of Menelaus'
nostos, and has mantic/poetic knowledge of events both past and
future. Nonetheless, the scene's potential as an exemplar of poetic
production seems to have struck a chord with Vergil at least, who
twice uses binding scenes in highly programmatic passages: shepherd
boys bind Silenus in *Eclogue* 6, and Aristaeus binds Proteus in *Georgics*
4.[19] These two uses of the topos point to its susceptibility to exploitation for poetic purposes, with both the bound god and the binder
acting in part as stand-ins for the poet; the image of binding, which
forces the gods to deliver meaning, invites its use to explore the
poetic manipulation of language.[20] As an image of magical control
of the natural world, the binding scenes are also closely linked to
what Ross has called 'scientific poetry', poetry about nature sung by
poets with the power to control nature.[21] As Hardie has argued, in
a world where poets are exploring the connection of their art to true
efficacy in the social and political realm, scientific and cosmological
poetry play a key role in the emerging vatic ideal.[22] For Vergil, the
binding image seems to have been a particularly powerful tool for
exploring that ideal.

---

[19] *Eclogue* 6's distinctly Roman *recusatio* (3–8) with its clear echoes of Callimachean
poetics (*Aet.* fr. 1.21–4 Pf.) sets up a programmatic tone continued by the narration of the binding of Silenus and by the god's song itself, which is, in Clausen's
words, 'a neoteric *ars poetica* artfully concealed, with but a single subject: poetry,
poetry as conceived by Callimachus (and poets after Callimachus) and now embodied in Gallus' (Clausen [1994] 177). The closing lines of the god's 'poem' even
include a second programmatic poetic initiation, that of Gallus, to complement
Vergil's own conversation with Apollo in the first lines. Although the motivation
for binding here is only the shepherd boys' light-hearted desire to hear a song from
the god, the result is a quite serious exploration of the bucolic genre's relation to
love elegy and the effectiveness of song as a cure for love. For discussion of the
programmatic and poetic issues of Vergil's later use of the topos (*Geo.* 4.387ff.) see
Thomas (1988) vol. 1, 14–15, vol. 2, 201–39.
[20] The shape-changing nature of Proteus (which I have for the most part ignored
in this brief overview) in the original Odyssean narrative, as well as in the *Georgics*
passage, makes the analogy still more desirable, at least in our age, where the gap
between language and meaning has become a hotly debated and often debilitating
issue. Plutarch has Picus and Faunus change shapes before answering Numa's request
(*Num.* 15.4).
[21] Ross (1975) 28–31.
[22] Hardie (1986) 16–22.

When the topos is reused by Ovid, we should perhaps read carefully, then, for poetic connotations. We have already been put on alert by the clearly programmatic description of Egeria's Arician grove which precedes these lines. The description of the grove on the Aventine where Numa ambushes Picus and Faunus echoes details of Egeria's: clear water flows over rocks in both groves (*defluit incerto lapidosus murmure rivus* (3.273, of Egeria's grove); *manabat saxo vena perennis aquae* (3.298, of Picus and Faunus'); just as the Arician grove is shady (*silva praecinctus opaca*, 3.263), so too is this Aventine grove (*niger Ilicis umbra*, 3.295). In Plutarch's version as well the Aventine grove is equipped with these details, and is separated from the life of the city:

μυθολογοῦσι γὰρ εἰς τὸν Ἀβεντῖνον λόφον οὔπω μέρος ὄντα τῆς πόλεως οὐδὲ συνοικούμενον, ἀλλ᾽ ἔχοντα πηγάς τε δαψιλεῖς ἐν αὐτῷ καὶ νάπας σκειράς, φοιτᾶν δύο δαίμονας, Πῖκον καὶ Φαῦνον· ... τούτους φασί χειρώσασθαι τὸν Νομᾶν. οἴνῳ καὶ μέλιτι κεράσαντα τὴν κρήνην ἀφ᾽ ἧς ἔπινον συνήθως.

For the story goes that two demi-gods, Picus and Faunus, frequented the Aventine hill when it wasn't yet a part of the city or even inhabited, but still had abundant streams and shady groves on it ... They say that Numa caught these two by mixing wine and honey into the spring from which they were accustomed to drink.
Numa 15.3–4

Again, this scene is ideally bucolic, just the place for shepherds to cool off in the heat of the day, water their flocks, nap, and perhaps sing a song or two; the Hesiodic model of the shepherd-poet again lingers in the background.

The setting of the binding of Picus and Faunus and the scene itself as a type, then, have affinities to earlier passages clearly concerned with poetic production, its effectiveness and its style, passages key to the development of the *vates* in Augustan poetics. But what is the information that Picus and Faunus actually deliver to Numa? In Ovid, the king asks the gods how to expiate a recent spate of lightning strikes (*Fasti* 3.311). Their answer, however, does not match his question: Picus and Faunus refuse to speak about the topic requested by Numa, Jupiter's lightning bolts, claiming that it is beyond their power to do so; that is, they deliver a classic *recusatio* of 'big' themes (*magna petis*, 313). Augustan *recusationes*, as a rule, include an offer of an alternative sort of poetry or speech, and this one is no exception: the gods offer *carmina* (3.323) to evoke Jupiter Elicius —

'spells', but also 'songs'. In lines 317ff. the plan is revealed: Numa, with the help of powerful arts (*valida ars*), will bring the sky-god to earth; the verb once again is *deducere*, whose Alexandrian connotations I discussed above. The alternative, then, to the *magna* requested by Numa is not a *carmen deductum*, but a *carmen deducens*! The passage gives Callimachus' refusal of Zeus and his thundering in *Aetia* fr. 1.19–20 a clever twist: this Jupiter, *deductus* and disarmed,[23] can find a place in Ovid's (and Picus and Faunus', and Numa's) song.[24]

Plutarch's articulation of what the bound gods tell Numa hints at what Ovid might have begun with in his source:

ἐπεὶ δὲ ἔγνωσαν ἑαλωκότες ἰσχυράν καὶ ἄφυκτον ἄλλα τε προθεσπίσαι πολλὰ τῶν μελλόντων καὶ τὸν ἐπὶ τοῖς κεραυνοῖς ἐκδιδάξαι καθαρμόν. ὅς ποιεῖται μέχρι νῦν διὰ κρομμύων καὶ τριχῶν καὶ μαινίδων. ἔνιοι δὲ οὐ τοὺς δαίμονάς φασιν ὑποθέσθαι τὸν καθαρμόν, ἀλλ᾿ ἐκείνους μὲν καταγαγεῖν τὸν Δία μαγεύσαντας . . .

But when they recognized that they were inescapably caught, they both made many prophecies about future events and taught him the charm against lightning which is accomplished to this day using onions, hair and sardines. But some say that the demi-gods didn't suggest the charm; rather they drew down Jupiter using magic arts . . .

Numa 15.4–5

Picus and Faunus predict unspecified future events: this already brings us into the world of vaticism, tapping in to the prophetic side of the *vates* concept. More specifically, they offer a solution to Numa's present lightning problem. Plutarch tells two versions of the solution offered: in one, Picus and Faunus themselves give Numa the formula for expiating lightning; in the other, they 'draw down' Jupiter, charming him, and the sky-god negotiates his own terms. Here, one can imagine a Latin source that used the language of incantation; the refrain of Vergil's *Eclogue* 8, in which a woman casts a spell to bring her lover home, provides a good paradigm: *ducite ab urbe domum, mea carmina, ducite Daphnin* (8.68, 72, 76 etc.); the speaker also claims that *carmina* can draw down the moon (again, *deducere*) (8.69). Like Ovid, Vergil is playing with the relationship between the poetic and mag-

---

[23] Cf. Hinds (1992) 120.
[24] The Alexandrian emphasis on τέχνη/*ars* is reflected here as well, as the force and efficacy of the charm is expressed in precisely those terms in line 321: *Iuppiter huc veniet, valida perductus ab arte*. The word *ars* is emphasized again in 324.

ical meanings of the word *carmen*,[25] but a Latin source reporting Picus and Faunus' charming of Jupiter would likely have used similar language, language translated into Plutarch's Greek by καταγαγεῖν and μαγεύσαντας. For an Augustan poet, this language of charming is contiguous with and related to the language of poetry and would have presented a strong temptation to read this scene as Ovid seems to have done, that is, as a contribution to the contemporary discourse on the efficacy of poetry in the world.

One further vatic element informs Ovid's version of the Picus and Faunus narrative: the bound gods share a concern for saying only what is religiously right (*fas*) with both Numa and the poet of the *Fasti*. Faunus' refusal to answer Numa's request for the means of expiating lightning is based expressly on this concern:

> magna petis, nec quae monitu tibi discere nostro
>   fas sit: habent fines numina nostra suos.

> You're asking for big things, and it's not right for us to teach them to you: our divinity has its limits.
>
> Fasti 3.313–14

As Feeney has pointed out, the issue arises often in the calendar poem, in large part because of the nature of the calendrical material:[26] the *fasti* began as a division of days on which certain kinds of speech were permitted (*dies fasti*) and days they were not (*dies nefasti*); cf. *Fasti* 1.47–8. A typical example interrupts Ovid's narrative of this very scene, since it is *nefas* to report the charm itself to his readers:

> emissi laqueis quid agant, quae carmina dicant,
>   quaque trahant superis sedibus arte Iovem
> scire nefas homini. nobis concessa canentur
>   quaeque pio dici vatis ab ore licet.

---

[25] Another indication that this double meaning of *carmen* was easily activated is Horace *Sat.* 2.1.82–5, where the satirist's interlocutor warns him that the sacred laws make the composition of *mala carmina* against someone actionable. The reference is almost certainly to the Twelve Tables' provision against the casting of evil spells partially preserved for us by Pliny in a discussion of the power of incantations: the law provided penalties for those *qui malum carmen incantassit* (*Nat.* 28.18). The satirist nonetheless answers as if *mala carmina* meant 'bad poems'. Another provision of the Twelve Tables against slanderous speech or songs (preserved in Cicero *Rep.* 4.12) likely also enters into the joke. On the Horace passage see Muecke (1993) 113 and bibliography there.

[26] Feeney (1992) esp. 12–13.

What they did when they were released, what charms they spoke,
and by what arts they drew Jupiter from his lofty home, it is
wrong for a man to know. Let me sing only what is allowed to
me and what can be spoken by the pious mouth of a poet.

Fasti 3.323–6

The poet specifically calls himself a *vates* in this instance, associating
this title with concern for the religious propriety of his words. The
positioning of the *vates* figure at the intersection between poet and
priest, and the vatic poet's privileged access to divine truths[27] give
this issue a vatic flavor each time it arises in this scene.

The concern about right speech is reiterated once more in the
next section of the episode, as Ovid turns to the related narrative
of Numa's interview with Jupiter. The king addresses a request for a
means of expiating lightning to the god, but he only wants his request
to be granted if it is asked with a 'pious tongue' (*si pia lingua rogat*
[3.336]). The parallel to *pio . . . ab ore* in 326 is striking, and underlines the similarity between Numa's difficult and (if it turns out that
the material is, in fact, *nefas*) dangerous enterprise and that of the
poet — the articulation of rites through language, and the negotia-
tion of power over those rites with a god. In this narrative, Numa
and Jupiter play a word game whereby the god's request for a human
sacrifice is revised to an expiatory offering of an onion, human hair,
and a sardine. Ovid's version runs as follows:

> adnuit oranti, sed verum ambage remota
>   abdidit et dubio terruit ore virum.
> 'caede caput' dixit; cui rex 'parebimus' inquit;
>   'caedenda est hortis eruta cepa meis'.
> addidit hic 'hominis'; 'sumes' ait ille 'capillos'.
>   postulat hic animam; cui Numa 'piscis' ait.
> risit, et 'his' inquit 'facito mea tela procures,
>   o vir conloquio non abigende deum'.

> [Jupiter] agreed to his prayer, but hid the truth in obscure ambi-
> guity and frightened the man with unclear speech. 'Cut a head',
> he said; to which the king said, 'We will obey: an onion head
> dug from my garden must be cut'. The first added, 'A man's'.
> Said the other, 'You will receive a man's hair'. The first asked
> for a soul, to which Numa answered, 'A fish's'. He laughed and
> said, 'See to it that you ward off my weapons with these items,
> o man not to be put off from conversation with the gods'.

Fasti 3.337–44

---

[27] See Newman (1967) 14–21; Hardie (1986) 16–17.

Dumézil has interpreted the scene as 'a test whereby the god makes sure that the king understands the importance of vocabulary and syntax'.[28] Jupiter's approval of the substitutions indicates not just an admission of defeat, but an expression of admiration for Numa's skillful manipulation of language. Ovid's version in particular lends itself to Dumézil's reading in large part because of the lines that introduce the exchange. Jupiter agrees to Numa's request before the contest begins, but 'hides the truth' by speaking ambiguously. The god *intends* for Numa to re-interpret his words; 'the truth' is that he does not want a human sacrifice at all. So why the word game? Why does Jupiter not simply ask for an onion, human hair, and a fish, if that is what he wants? This indeed seems to be a test of Numa's ability to manipulate language, by sound-play (*caput/ cepa/ capilli*), syntax-play, and even anagrams (the original play with *anima* involved the name of a fish, *maena/ maina*).[29] The parallel to the strategies of poetic production and interpretation, and to the etymologizing approach to religious rites often employed in the *Fasti* is striking.[30] Jupiter's laugh at the end of the game signals his approval of Numa's use of language. Plutarch's version of this narrative (*Num.* 15.5–6) closely parallels Ovid's, though the word-play does not work as well in the Greek; at the end of the game, Plutarch uses an etymology of Elicius from ἵλεω, 'propitious', to express Jupiter's approval.

As noted before the Picus and Faunus and Jupiter Elicius narratives found in Ovid and Plutarch also appear in a fragment of the Sullan annalist Valerius Antias (*HRR* fr. 6). Plutarch clearly knew Valerius' work: he cites him four times, once in the *Numa* itself (22.4). It is thus entirely possible that Plutarch is following Valerius at this point; this is, in fact, the tentative conclusion reached by Peter in his study of the sources of the Roman *Lives*.[31] Otherwise, however, Peter proposes Valerius Antias as a major source for Plutarch only in the life of Valerius Poplicola, to whom the annalist might have given special attention through familial pride. It is difficult to imagine why Valerius would be a particularly attractive source for the

---

[28] Dumézil (1970) 40–1, 123. For other discussions, see Bayet (1969) 142, Ahl (1985) 300–1, Porte (1985) 131–2.

[29] Valerius Antias *HRR* fr. 6.

[30] Cf. Hinds (1992) 120: 'a display of quintessentially *Fasti*-like religious learning, ending with a contest in the art of sacred etymology against the king of the gods himself'.

[31] Peter (1865) 167–8. Plutarch's other citations of Valerius in the *Lives* are *Rom.* 14 and *Flam.* 18.

life of Numa. For Ovid to have used Valerius Antias as a source
for the Numan narratives, would be even odder: as Bömer notes in
his commentary on this passage, we have no evidence of Ovidian
use of the annalist elsewhere.[32] As a source for the vatic/poetic overtones I have noted, Valerius Antias' version comes up short: in the
binding scene, the bound gods neither prophesy, nor deliver a *carmen*;
Jupiter is not *deductus*, nor does he signal approval of Numa's artful
use of language; neither Numa nor the bound gods express concern
for the religious propriety of their speech. In addition, numerous
details in Valerius are entirely absent from Ovid and Plutarch, most
strikingly, a group of twelve young men who actually accomplish the
ambush and binding.[33]

Uneasy with tracing Ovid's narrative to Valerius, Bömer suggests
that Varro may have acted as an intermediate source;[34] Varro and
his follower Verrius Flaccus are Ovid's most used sources of antiquarian information in the *Fasti*. Plutarch too could easily have used
Varro for this story: the antiquarian is frequently cited or readily
identified as Plutarch's source in the *Lives* of Romulus and Numa.[35]
In addition, several lines of interest and inquiry connected to the
Picus and Faunus and Jupiter Elicius episodes may be traced in
Varro. These lines, I will argue, make Varro a likely source for both
authors' versions of the Numan narratives, and also suggest that the
antiquarian was more than a simple conduit from Valerius Antias
to the later authors.

Before I proceed, I should make it clear that neither Ovid nor
Plutarch is likely to have used Varro's extant works as major sources;
other titles in the extensive Varronian corpus would certainly have
organized information in ways more useful to the calendar-poet and
the biographer. Collections of Numan narratives might have been
available in Varro's *Aitia, Antiquitates*, or *De Vita Populi Romani*. I stress
this in part as a forewarning: the argument that follows will, of neces-

---

[32] Bömer (1958) on *Fast.* 3.291.

[33] Wiseman (1998) 21–2 suggests that the twelve young men are in fact present
in Ovid's narrative: they are the twelve Salii who appear in the next section of the
episode (3.387–8). Wiseman uses Ovid's connection between the Elicius episode and
the aetiological story of the *ancile* and the Salii to explain Valerius' mysterious band
of young men. He suggests that the two narratives formed part of a play presenting the aitiologies of both the cult of Jupiter Elicius and the priesthood of the Salii
and their rites. For the argument that the connection of the two narratives is original to Ovid, see above, n. 18.

[34] Bömer (1958) on *Fasti* 3.291.

[35] Peter (1865) 146–72; Valgiglio (1976).

sity, be based on suggestive pieces of the *De Lingua Latina*, always with the understanding that these are being treated as quasi-fragments of Varro's more expansive treatments of Numa.

With that caveat in mind, it must be confessed that neither the Picus and Faunus episode nor the story of Jupiter Elicius is expressly told in any extant piece of Varro. What we do have on the subject of Elicius is, as we might expect, an etymology: *sic Elicii Iovis ara in Aventino, ab eliciendo* (Thus the altar of Jupiter Elicius on the Aventine is named from 'eliciting'.) (Varro *De Lingua Latina* 6.94). No narrative context is given to the etymology, but the semantic context is telling: the words Varro is explicating in this section all have to do with summoning and luring *people*. Varro begins from the word *inlicium* which he has found in old census records, explaining it as a summons of the people prior to the official call to assembly. We might contrast Livy's subtly different explanation of the same epithet. The historian is addressing Numa's creation of the *pontifex* and the new priest's duties. Numa places the *pontifex* in charge of all public and private rites including, among other things, the official reaction to and expiation of prodigies. The altar of Jupiter Elicius is connected to this last duty: *ad ea elicienda ex mentibus divinis Iovi Elicio aram in Aventino dicavit deumque consuluit auguriis, quae suscipienda essent* (In order to elicit these things from divine minds, he dedicated an altar on the Aventine to Jupiter Elicius and, using augury, consulted the god concerning what prodigies should be acknowledged.) (Livy 1.20.7). Here, Numa erected the altar of Jupiter Elicius as a means of eliciting religious *information* from a divine source; nowhere is the narrative familiar from Ovid and Plutarch implied. For Ovid, it is Jupiter himself who is elicited: *eliciunt caelo te Iuppiter; unde minores/ nunc quoque te celebrant Eliciumque vocant* (They 'elicit' you from the sky, Jupiter; from this, posterity even now worships you and calls you 'Elicius'.) (*Fasti* 3.327–8). The context of Varro's etymology implies that the epithet refers to someone, rather than something, 'elicited'; the similarity of the Varronian and Ovidian etymologies almost guarantees that the Varro passage refers to the same narrative found in Ovid. The very brevity of Varro's explication might indicate that he expected the narrative to be familiar to his readers — perhaps he could do so because he had already given it a fuller treatment elsewhere.[36]

---

[36] As I noted above, Plutarch does not follow Varro here, but rather substitutes

This is the extent of our evidence for Varro's likely interest in Jupiter Elicius. However, if Varro told the Jupiter Elicius story, it is highly probable that he told the Picus and Faunus one as well: the two stories are narratively connected in all three of the authors that report them and do not appear separately in other sources. Since no convenient etymological aition is attached to the Picus and Faunus story, we should not be surprised if it leaves no trace in the *De Lingua Latina*. There is, nonetheless, a piece of the etymological work which may indicate familiarity with the tradition. In Book 7, which focuses on words used by poets, Varro explicates a line of Ennius which defines his work against earlier Saturnian epic:

> versibus quo<s> olim Fauni vatesque canebant.

> Fauni dei Latinorum, ita ut et Faunus et Fauna sit; hos versibus quos vocant Saturnios in silvestribus locis traditum est solitos fari <futura, a> quo fando Faunos dictos. antiqui poetas vates appellabant a versibus viendis, ut <de> poematis cum scribam ostendam.

> In verses which *Fauni* and *vates* once sang.

> *Fauni* are gods of the Latins, so that there is both a male *Faunus* and a female *Fauna*; there is a tradition that they used to speak of (*fari*) future events in wooded places using the verses they call 'Saturnians', and thus they were called '*Fauni*' from 'speaking' ('*fando*'). The ancients called poets '*vates*' from 'weaving verses' ('*versibus viendis*'), as I will demonstrate when I write about poetry.
> Varro *De Lingua Latina* 7.36

This passage has received a great deal of attention because of its importance to the history of Latin literature. Carefully avoiding the complications of what Ennius might have meant by this line, let us turn our attention instead to what Varro has to say.

First, we learn of a tradition (*traditum est*) that Fauni used to speak prophecies in Saturnian verses. Can this be read as a reflection of the Picus and Faunus story? Prophetic speech seems to be a central element in the binding motif generally — think of Menelaus and Proteus in the *Odyssey* — and we might recall that Plutarch's Picus and Faunus too, once bound, gave Numa general prophecies (*Numa*

---

an etymology from the Greek adjective ἵλεω for the untranslatable Roman one (*Num.* 15.6).

15.4). The Picus and Faunus story could be at least part of what Varro had in mind when he referred to the prophetic habits of the Fauni.

What of the Saturnian meter of the Fauni's speech? This strange detail is, of course, motivated by Varro's effort to make sense of Ennius' poetic polemic — what do Fauni have in common with Ennius' poetic predecessors (and not with Ennius himself)? If we imagine the Picus and Faunus story in the background of this detail, however, Varro's insistence that the Fauni prophesied in verse is given some substance: Varro may be thinking of a narrative where Faunus both tells the future and delivers a *carmen* to his captor. Ovid's play with the relationship between *carmen* as spell and poem in his version of the Picus and Faunus story, which I discussed above, is intensified if we think of Varro in the background, linking the history of Latin verse to the songs of the Fauni.

Finally, Varro's setting of the Fauni's prophetic versification in a wooded grove (*in silvestribus locis*) makes religious sense — Faunus is, after all, a woodland god. Nonetheless, in this brief exegesis, Varro's inclusion of a particular setting might be more marked than that. Of course, I would like to suggest that Varro has a particular grove in mind, the Aventine one so carefully described in both Ovid and Plutarch as the setting of the binding of Picus and Faunus.

In addition to its importance for the early history of Latin literature, Varro's explication of this Ennian line is a key piece in the history of the *vates* concept. Varro's etymology here *a versibus viendis* emphasizes the poetic/artistic side of the word *vates*. The antiquarian complements this emphasis elsewhere, however, with further etymologies focused on the inspired nature of the *vates*, his special status as a conduit of divine speech: in *De Lingua Latina* 6.52, Varro connects the related term *vaticinari* to prophecy, and gives an etymology from *vesana mente* (crazed mind), again promising to elaborate later in a section or a work on poets; testimonia in Isidorus and Servius report a third Varronian etymology *a vi mentis* — the force or power of the mind.[37] As both Newman and Dahlmann have demonstrated,

---

[37] Servius *Aen.* 3.443, Isidorus *Orig.* 8.7.3. For discussions of the likely shape and contents of Varro's *De poematis* and *De poetis*, see Dahlmann (1953) and (1963).

Varro gives us the first extant uses of *vates* as poet. Dahlmann has, in fact, argued that Varro's promised proof that *vates* was the old word for poet was the starting point for its use by the Augustan poets, and this theory has met with some approval.[38] Whatever the case, it is clear that Varro took a particular interest in the term *vates* and his promise of further discussion likely speaks for the novelty of his explications of the word.

Another suggestion put forth by Dahlmann in the same article has received less attention, but merits addressing here in connection with the Numan narratives we have been tracing. Dahlmann proposed that Varro's extended explication of this Ennian verse, aligning the divinely inspired poetic figure of the *vates* with Faunus, a god of the woodlands and (through his identification with Pan) of shepherds, stands in the background of Vergil's first uses of the word *vates* qua poet, applying it to singing shepherds in *Eclogues* 7.28 and 9.33–4. The proposal bears some consideration — Lycidas and Thyrsis are not the most obvious candidates for the mystical, almost priestly, *vates* label. But these first Vergilian *vates* do sing their songs, like Varro's Fauni, *in silvestribus locis*, in the wooded groves to which they have retired in the heat of the day, well-equipped with cool, clear water for their flocks. The Varronian exploration of the term, in part by means of the Ennian line, may indeed have helped Vergil towards the application of *vates* to his rustic shepherd-poets.[39] By combining Dahlmann's suggestion with my argument that the Picus and Faunus story might have played a role in Varro's explication of Ennius' *Fauni vatesque*, we can go even a bit further. First, we have in the Picus and Faunus story *precisely* the sort of woodland setting we find in the *Eclogues*: a shady grove with fresh water; in all three extant versions of the narrative Picus and Faunus came to this grove particularly to drink (*Fasti* 3.299, *Numa* 15.4; Valerius Antias *HRR* fr. 6). The Aventine grove is the ideal bucolic noon-time watering hole, and thus brings us a great deal closer to Vergil than the simple 'wooded places' we have in our extant Varro.

---

[38] Dahlmann (1948). Dahlmann's basic suggestion is followed, for example, by Newman (1967) 15–17, Wiseman (1994) esp. 57; Jocelyn (1995) esp. 32–3. The most extensive challenges to Dahlmann's argument are offered by Bickel (1951).

[39] Bickel (1951) 303–10 argues instead that Vergil's application of the term *vates* to his shepherd-poets reflects his real experience in the fields and woods of Mantua, i.e., he argues that, outside of the capitol, real pre-literary shepherd-poets were applying the word to themselves in a positive, honorific sense throughout the Republican period. Though intriguing, the theory remains unsubstantiated.

Vergil also gives us a binding scene in the *Eclogues*: as we saw above, a pair of shepherd boys in *Eclogue* 6 bind the satyr Silenus and force him to deliver a song. The cosmologic, theogonic, metamorphic *tour de force* that Silenus sings has long been recognized as an exploration and embodiment of the possibilities of the new Roman poetry; if, as Hardie has argued, cosmological poetry falls squarely in the domain of the Augustan *vates*,[40] Silenus surely qualifies. But why this scene at all? The prototypes generally pointed to offer only a partial explanation. In the *Odyssey* the bound god Proteus delivers a prophecy, which at least brings us into the vatic realm; however, we find none of the same cast of characters, and we have a seaside setting rather than a pastoral one.[41] A number of ancient sources refer to Midas' capture of Silenus, and in some versions, Silenus gives the king moral-philosophical advice;[42] still, he is never compelled to do so by binding, nor is he said to prophesy or sing. Where does Vergil get the vatically charged Silenus he gives us in the *Eclogues*?

Once again, a Varronian telling of the Picus and Faunus story, especially if it were in the context of a discussion of the term *vates* in a work *De Poematis* or *De Poetis*, would provide us with an apt source. The Faunus figure of the Numan narrative, early identified with the Greek goat-god Pan, would easily elide with the satyr Silenus. More importantly, the Picus and Faunus story has the woodland gods delivering a *carmen*, one that specifically has to do with the religious and magical control of the physical world: they either give a Numa a spell against lightning or one to conjure Jupiter out of the sky. For Vergil, Silenus' *carmen* of cosmological poetry likewise has a controlling effect on the physical world: when Silenus sings, fauns and animals dance and oaks nod their heads (*Eclogues* 6.27–8). If a Varronian version of the binding of Picus and Faunus had the sorts of vatic resonances I have noted in Ovid and Plutarch, the antiquarian would have provided an important precedent to Vergil's extraordinary Silenus episode.

I suggest, then, that Varro treated the Picus and Faunus narrative at some length in one or more of his works on poetry in connection

---

[40] Hardie (1986) 16–22.

[41] Homer does, however, liken Proteus among his seals to a shepherd among his sheep in the simile at *Od.* 4.413.

[42] Herodotus 8.138, Xenophon *An.* 1.2.13; Athenaeus 2.45.c (with reference to Theopompus and Bion); Aelian *VH* 3.18 (with reference to Theopompus); Ovid *Met.* 11.90–9; Philostratus *VA* 6.27, *Im.* 1.22.

with a discussion of the term *vates* based in part on explication of
the Ennian line on *Fauni vatesque*. Such a treatment would have been
familiar to and perhaps influential on early Augustan poets like Vergil
as they negotiated their poetic authority in its competition with and
reliance on Augustus' order and authority. Though Varro may have
also treated the Jupiter Elicius narrative in his work on poetic theory,
both narratives together would easily have found a place in sections
on Numa in more historical works. A perceived connection between
these Numan narratives and a developing theory about a poetic
figure called a *vates* might, in fact, have influenced Varro's depiction
of Numa in these more historical sources. If Numa not only receives
inspiration from his nymph/muse wife, but also receives *carmina* from
woodland gods who sing in Saturnians, he is not far removed from
the inspired poet figure Varro seems to have in mind in his etymologies for the word *vates*. This vatically flavored Numa is reflected in
the Ovid and Plutarch treatments we have traced. I am thus suggesting that, in this case, Varro's own works on poetic theory and on leg-
endary/historical/antiquarian topics are cross-pollinating one another.[43]

Finally, to bring us back to the Ovidian narrative, our starting
point in this inquiry, I would like to consider how Ovid (and possibly other Augustan poets) might have read this Varronian vatic
Numa ten, twenty, even forty years after its composition. Whether
or not we accept Dahlmann's claim that Varro originated the Augustan
use of the term, *vates* was not, in the 40s and 30s B.C.E., the full
blown 'concept' it became. It took years of poetic and political developments for the Augustan *vates* to develop into a concept including
(to quote Hardie): 'the belief that the poet has a serious contribution to make to the progress of his society, and that poetry and

---

[43] The relative chronology of the relevant Varronian works (H. Dahlmann, *RE*
suppl. 6, coll. 1172–277, *s.v.* 'M. Terentius Varro') make an absolute argument as
to the direction of influence difficult. The *De Poematis* and *De Poetis* date to sometime after the *De Lingua Latina* (col. 1221) which we only know was begun by 47
B.C.E. (coll. 1203–04). The *Antiquitates Rerum Humanarum* was published before the
Antiquates Rerum Divinarum, which was finished by 47 (col. 1230). The *De Vita Populi
Romani* dates from sometime between 49 and 32, but was most likely begun around
43 (col. 1243). Nothing is known of the date of the *Aitia* (coll. 1246–47). The
chronology then, is both uncertain and close, allowing the possibility that some
Numan narratives in the antiquarian works postdate Varro's publication of his *vates*
theory. In addition, *L.* 7.36 and 6.52 make it quite clear that Varro was working
on this theory well before it was published.

music have a regulatory and civilizing effect; the belief that the poet
has serious things to say about religion and the gods ... [and] the
belief that, through some form of inspiration, the poet has privileged
access to eternal truths'.[44] Whatever connections Varro saw between
Numa and poetry, we must admit that the king fits the bill of the
vates even more closely when the concept is more fully developed.
Numa's dedication to religion and his divinely inspired ordering and
civilizing of the young Roman society are the cornerstones of his
legendary persona. This extraordinary fit between a legendary-his-
torical figure and a poetic ideal, and thus Ovid's attraction to Numa
as a vatic model, may not be entirely accidental. Varro's depiction
of Numa may have in part shaped the formation of the vatic ideal
in the early Augustan period, serving as a model for the learned,
religious, mystical leader of society that J. K. Newman outlined in
his definition of the *vates*.

However, Newman's last qualification in his definition of the *vates*
figure was that it had 'no dangerous political implications'. In more
recent studies of Augustan poetry, most have acknowledged that
poetic claims of this sort are necessarily political, whether dangerous or not: Numa's careful manipulation of language to negotiate
power with a god in the Jupiter Elicius story might stand as a model
for even this side of the *vates* ideal. In a recent study, Wiseman offers
one way of concretizing the political implications of the *vates* figure,
arguing that the *vates* as prophets had a continuous political presence in Republican Rome as a source of power and authority independent of the senate.[45] The public role of these prophets peaked
in the fourth and early-third centuries B.C.E., was subject to intensified
senatorial control in the late-third and second centuries, and experienced a revival in the first century in response to the nearly continuous state of political crisis of those years. Wiseman emphasizes that
vatic power was potentially subversive (as evidenced by Augustus' confiscation and destruction of prophetic writings in 12 B.C.E.), but could
also be, as it is in Lucretius (1.102–11), 'a conservative force, preach-
ing traditional piety enforced by threats of punishment in Hades'
(66). This history of the prophetic side of the *vates* figure militates

---

[44] Hardie (1986) 16.
[45] Wiseman (1994).

against an apolitical reading of the poetic side. The possibility I have raised here that the poetic vatic model was drawn in part from a historiographical exploration of a legendary political figure only underlines the depth of the connections between politics and poetics, history and poetry in the Augustan world.

CHAPTER SIXTEEN

THE EXTINCTION OF THE POTITII AND THE SACRED HISTORY OF AUGUSTAN ROME

Hans-Friedrich Mueller

We begin with myth.[1] After his victory over Geryon (Cacus defeated, cattle recovered) Hercules was hospitably entertained by Evander along with two ancient Roman families, the Pinarii and the Potitii. In recompense for this, their hospitality, Hercules taught these latter families how to worship him. A banquet was prepared. The Pinarii were not yet there. What to do? The entrails were eaten. Only then did the Pinarii finally arrive. Hercules, angry at their tardiness, decreed that the Pinarii should at subsequent repetitions of the ceremony receive no share of the entrails and that they should always in all matters take second place to the Potitii. We move now from myth to (dubious) history: These two families remained the priests of Hercules until 312 B.C. when the censor Appius Claudius, not yet Caecus, for 50,000 pounds of copper purchased Hercules' original instructions from the Potitii, and transferred care of Hercules' sacred rites at the *Ara Maxima* from private control to public slaves. The Pinarii seemed to have missed yet another profitable opportunity until it became clear that Hercules was again displeased. He blinded Appius Claudius, now Caecus, and obliterated the Potitii (12 families and thirty men within the year, or, according to others, within 30 days — our sources do not agree). Only the Pinarii escaped punishment, because they had not colluded in the transfer of jurisdiction over the *sacra*. We

---

[1] For Hercules' treatment of the Potitii: Livy 9.29.9–10, Dionysius of Halicarnassus *A.R.* 1.40.5, Valerius Maximus 1.1.17, Macrobius 3.6.12ff., Servius on *Aen.* 8.179, *Origo gentis Romanae* 8, *Liber de viris illustribus* 34, Lactantius *Inst.* 2.7.15. A most convenient discussion of sources for Hercules in general remains Winter (1910) 193–250. Translations of ancient authors in this paper (except those of Valerius Maximus) derive from the Loeb Classical Library. This paper has benefited from the generous comments and criticisms of Karl Galinsky, David S. Levene, and W. Jeffrey Tatum, in whose debt I stand for guidance towards whatever is cogent in my argument, but who bear no responsibility for infelicities, flaws, and gaps that remain.

have in short an ancient Roman cult whose foundation may be lost
in myth, but which appears to have entered into the light of history
when in 312 B.C. the censor Appius Claudius nationalized a cult
that had previously been a private patrician monopoly.

The last century has seen considerable scholarly acumen and ingenuity devoted to sorting out the establishment of the cult of Hercules
at the *Ara Maxima* and its cultic personnel.[2] Valuable as investigations into ultimate origins have been, this essay will not attempt to
re-evaluate our imperial sources with a view to reconstructing what
may have happened when Hercules sat down to supper with Evander
and the Potitii, but explore rather representations of the Potitii amid
the interstices of history, historiography, and Augustan poetry.

We may begin by placing the re-organization of Hercules' cult in
the context of political events surrounding the year of Appius Claudius'
censorship. Appius Claudius, not the Potitii, stands in the center. The
political aims of the censor have elicited widely divergent scholarly
interpretations. Niebuhr saw a die-hard patrician reactionary; Mommsen, on the other hand, a demagogue and revolutionary (at least
during his censorship).[3] One could even in the 1950s see a third
way, neither a reactionary nor a revolutionary, but instead an entre-
preneur, a man whose primary motivations were to foster continued
economic growth and opportunity for all Rome's citizens.[4] Whence
such disparate interpretation? Our surviving ancient sources, in the
dispassionate listing of Broughton, document the following:

> Claudius paved the Appian way to Capua, built the Claudian aque-
> duct, admitted sons of freedmen to the senate, and gave landless cit-
> izens full citizen rights; also these censors [i.e. Appius and his colleague,
> C. Plautius Venox, who may or may not have abdicated] forbade the
> *tibicines* to hold their festival in the temple of Jupiter, and transferred
> the cult of Hercules at the *Ara Maxima* from the Potitii to public slaves.[5]

---

[2] See especially Peter (1884–1890), Winter (1910), Wissowa (1912) 271–7, Bayet
(1926), Dumézil (1970) 2:432–9, Latte (1960) 213–25, Coarelli (1988), McDonough
(1990), Ritter (1995).

[3] Mommsen (1996 [1894]) I:501–6; cf. I:395–7 and (1962 [1864]) 301ff.

[4] Stavely (1959).

[5] *MRR* I:160 *sub anno* 312 B.C. Sources (after Broughton): Cicero *Cael.* 34–5,
Livy 9.29.5–11 and 33–4 and 46.10–11, Diodorus Siculus 20.36.1–6, Elog. 10, *CIL*
1², p. 192, Ovid *Fast.* 6.654–92, Valerius Maximus 1.1.17, 2.5.4, Frontinus *Aq.* 1.5,
Plutarch *Popl.* 7.5, Suetonius *Cl.* 24, Eutropiua 2.9.3, Pomponius *Dig.* 1.2.2.36,
Servius on *Aen.* 8.179, Lactantius *Inst.* 2.7.15, Jerome *Chr. ad ann.* 325, p. 125 Helm,
Festus 270 L, Macrobius 3.6.13.

Why such disagreement about the import of these actions? Because, as the demolition inaugurated already by Mommsen's and Münzer's analyses of the anti-Claudian historiographical traditions of Augustan Rome,[6] but more recently, and more thoroughly and forcefully argued by T. P. Wiseman, the annalists upon whom our surviving sources depend (namely, Livy, Dionysius, Valerius Maximus, and company), these annalists in general, but, according to Wiseman, one 'hostile source' in particular, simply fabricated stories about Appius Claudius in conformance with an anti-Claudian political agenda.[7]

According to Wiseman, of the events listed by Broughton *mirabili sub anno* 312, we ought to accept the historicity only of Appius' road and his aqueduct; scholars have in general too often failed to recognize the scale of the rhetorical and tendentious fabrications that have been spuriously registered amid the legitimate deeds of the ancient annals.[8] Appius' extended sole censorship (after the abdication of his colleague Plautius), his admission of freedmen to the senate, his extension of citizen rights, and other political manoeuvres, are hallmarks of later fabrication, especially when considered against the practical backdrop of road-building and aqueduct-construction and Appius' later successful conduct of war against the Etruscans in 296 B.C., during which he vowed, and after which he subsequently built, a more historically grounded temple to *Bellona*.[9] The alleged politics of the sources do not match the documented deeds of the man; they are in this reading at best projections of a late republican present upon the events of a much-earlier, and hence to our sources, unimaginable, republican past. In short, our sources' representation of Appius' political schemes are simply 'unhistorical,' and the supposed transfer of Hercules' *sacra* from the care of the Potitii to public slaves an 'equally fictitious legend'.[10]

Historiographical analysis has revealed, then, that, even if we take care to avoid the mythical beginnings of our tale (that is, the supper

---

[6] Cf. Mommsen (1996 [1894]) I:495–508, (1962 [1864]); and e.g. Münzer (1899).

[7] Wiseman (1979) 57–139, esp. 85ff.

[8] Wiseman (1979) 52.

[9] Wiseman (1979) 85–6.

[10] Wiseman (1979) 87. Here Wiseman (1979) 88 n. 88 concurs with Palmer (1965), whose alternative and speculative reconstruction of the events of 312 we cannot recapitulate here. The skepticism of Wiseman and Palmer has not, however, been accepted universally; cf. Cornell (1995) 468 n. 14, Beard, North, and Price (1998) I:68.

Evander shared with Hercules and the initial organization of the cult at the *Ara Maxima*), we are left groping still in historical darkness. If we accept the argument that the story of the transfer of Hercules' *sacra* as well as the subsequent blinding of Appius and the extinction of the Potitii are fabrications invented to slander Appius Claudius in particular and the Claudian *gens* in general, and that once fabricated these spurious anecdotes entered the annalistic tradition to be reproduced uncritically thereafter, have we extracted all the meaning to be had? Wiseman points a way out of this darkness:

> The elaboration of Claudius Pulcher's defeat [at Drepanum in 249 B.C. after drowning the sacred chickens who refused to eat] is, I think, the hostile annalist's masterpiece, approached only by the story of Appius Claudius Caecus and the Potitii, which similarly became a standard historical exemplum as soon as it was written.[11]

Our sources are imperial. The anecdote appears to have resonated with our surviving imperial sources, and thus apparently with their contemporary audiences. T. P. Wiseman has pointed the way, then, and Mary Beard, who argues that, because origins cannot be recovered from our sources, we ought instead to examine the issues to which they do speak,[12] provides a lamp. We must interrogate our surviving sources in order to inquire why the alleged events of 312 B.C. should have maintained their exemplary grip on an early imperial imagination.

We may begin to trace this influence in the eulogy of Tiberius for Augustus. Tiberius was of course neither the first to find comfort in Hercules nor the first to note the similarity of Hercules to Augustus. Cicero, as Galinsky notes, had 'idealized Hercules as the perfect embodiment of Stoic wisdom and virtue.'[13] Hercules, according to Cicero, had paved his own way to immortality through his deeds on earth,[14] and Hercules thus represented, we might add, a suitable comparandum when the bereft Tiberius sought some celestial precedent to make sense of his deceased father's earthly deeds. The words of Tiberius according to Cassius Dio:

---

[11] Wiseman (1979) 91.
[12] Beard (1987).
[13] Galinsky (1972) 128.
[14] Cicero *Tusc.* 1.32; *N.D.* 2.62.

ἐπεὶ δε ἐπιβουλευθέντος αὐτοῦ πάντα τὰ κοινὰ ἐταράχθη. τῷ τε πατρὶ
ἅμα ἱκανῶς ἐτιμώρησε καὶ ὑμῖν ἀναγκαίως ἐπεκούρησε. μήτε τὸ πλῆθος
τῶν ἐχθρῶν φοβηθεὶς μήτε τὸ μέγεθος τῶν πραγμάτων δείσας μήτε τὴν
ὀλιγοετίαν τὴν ἑαυτοῦ ὀκνήσας. καίτοι τί τοιοῦτον ἢ Ἀλέξανδρος ὁ
Μακεδὼν ἢ Ῥωμύλος ὁ ἡμέτερος, οἵπερ που μάλιστα νεαροὶ ὄντες ἐλλόγιμόν
τι ποιῆσαι δοκοῦσιν, ἔπραξαν ἀλλὰ τούτους μὲν ἐάσω, ἵνα μὴ καὶ ἐξ
αὐτοῦ τοῦ παραβάλλειν οἱ καὶ παραδεικνύναι σφᾶς, καὶ ταῦτα ἐν ὑμῖν
μηδὲν ἧττον ἐμοῦ αὐτοὺς εἰδόσι, σμικροτέραν τὴν τοῦ Αὐγούστου ἀρετὴν
ποιεῖν νομισθῶ. πρὸς μόνον δὲ δὴ τὸν Ἡρακλέα καὶ τὰ ἐκείνου ἔργα
παραθεωρῶν αὐτὸν ὀρθῶς μὲν ἂν κατ' αὐτὸ τοῦτο ποιεῖν δόξαιμι. τοσοῦτον
δ' ἂν τῆς προαιρέσεως διαμάρτοιμι, ὅσον ἐκεῖνος μὲν ἔν τε παισὶν ὄφεις
καὶ ἐν ἀνδράσιν ἔλαφόν τέ τινα καὶ κάπρον καὶ νὴ Δία καὶ λέοντα ἄκων
καὶ ἐξ ἐπιτάξεως ἀπέκτεινεν. οὗτος δὲ οὐκ ἐν θηρίοις ἀλλ' ἐν ἀνδράσιν
ἐθελοντὴς καὶ πολεμῶν καὶ νομοθετῶν τό τε κοινὸν ἀκριβῶς ἔσωσε καὶ
αὐτὸς ἐλαμπρύνθη.

(Cassius Dio 56.36.2–5.)

When, after the conspiracy against Caesar, the whole state was thrown
into confusion, Augustus at one and the same time amply avenged his
father and rendered much-needed assistance to you, neither fearing
the multitude of his enemies nor dreading the magnitude of his responsibilities nor hesitating by reason of his immaturity. Yet what deed like
this can be cited of Alexander of Macedon or of our own Romulus,
who perhaps above all others are thought to have performed some
notable exploit in youth? But these men I shall pass over, lest from
merely comparing them with him and using them as examples — and
that among you who know them as well as I — I may be thought to
be detracting from the virtues of Augustus. With Hercules alone and
his exploits I might compare him, and should be thought justified in
so doing, if that were all; but even so I should fall short of my purpose, in so far as Hercules in childhood only dealt with serpents, and
when a man, with a stag or two and a boar which he killed, — oh,
yes, and a lion, to be sure, albeit reluctantly and at somebody's behest;
whereas Augustus, not among beasts, but among men, of his own free
will, by waging war and enacting laws, literally saved the commonwealth and gained splendid renown for himself.

Cassius Dio wrote some two centuries distant from the events of
A.D. 14, but we need not fear spurious anecdotes inserted into the
annals quite so much as we did for the events *sub anno* 312 B.C.[15]

---

[15] Contra: Millar (1964) 101: 'If any authentic record of Tiberius' oration survived
Dio failed to follow it . . ., and it can be assumed that it was a composition by Dio
made up to suit the occasion." The main charge against Dio's account is that he has

Indeed, although contemporary witness was lost to Livy's Appius, Dio's Tiberius enjoys the corroborative testimony of Augustan poetry. Tiberius, it seems, was not the only Augustan to whom the comparison had occurred. Vergil has Aeneas look during his trip to hell upon an unborn but Herculean Augustus:

> hic vir, hic est, tibi quem promitti saepius audis,
> Augustus Caesar, divi genus, aurea condet
> saecula qui rursus Latio regnata per arva
> Saturno quondam, super et Garamantas et Indos
> proferet imperium. . . .
> nec vero Alcides tantum telluris obivit,
> fixerit aeripedem cervam licet, aut Erymanthi
> pacarit nemora et Lernam tremefecerit arcu.
>   (Vergil *Aeneid* 6.791– 803).

> This, this is he, whom thou so oft hearest promised to thee, Augustus Caesar, son of a god, who shall set up the Golden Age amid the fields where Saturn once reigned, and shall spread his empire past Garamant and India. . . . Nor in truth did Alcides range o'er such space of earth, though he pierced the brazen-footed deer, or brought peace to the woods of Erymanthus, and made Lerna tremble with his bow.

Vergil compared the unborn Augustus to Hercules.[16] Norden, in his analysis of the larger passage to which this excerpt belongs, argues that Vergil's composition corresponds point-by-point to the formal requirements of standard Greek and Hellenistic panegyric of kings, especially of Alexander.[17] Is it, in this context, really so unlikely that

---

Tiberius call himself διάδοχος. Do anachronisms and mistakes, however, necessarily spell wholesale invention? Manuwald (1979) 133–40 takes a more nuanced view, arguing that because the speech Dio puts in the mouth of Tiberius differs from Dio's own assessment of Augustus, the speech goes back to another intermediary source, not historical, however, but rhetorical. Both scholars, on the other hand, fail to adduce contemporary comparisons of Octavian/Augustus to Hercules. Even Huttner (1997a), despite his excellent collection of just such evidence, on the authority of Millar and Manuwald likewise dismisses Dio: "Der Vergleich ist hier auf alle Fälle kaum mehr als eine rhetorische Floskel (383)." In short, Dio's representation of Tiberius' rhetoric is condemned on the grounds that it is rhetorical.

[16] The figure of Hercules is, according to Kienast (1982) 236–8, an important element in the equation of Augustus with Alexander. On the importance of Herakles to Alexander's pretensions, see Huttner (1997b) 86–143. For a more ambiguous analysis, compare Putnam (1998) 162ff., who questions the "received critical opinion that Hercules prefigures Aeneas-Augustus'. On Hercules as a paradigmatic model for Augustus see Marinčič, ch. 8 above.

[17] Norden (1899). For a more recent discussion of panegyric in Latin, see Levene (1997) with further literature; on Herakles in Greek panegyric, see Huttner (1997b).

Tiberius, in praising the deceased Augustus, reached for comparisons that already had some currency amongst the finest poets associated with his adoptive father's court? On the other hand, even if Cassius Dio simply invented a speech using a familiar *topos*, it is apposite to note that the ancestry of this *topos* has the highest literary authority.

Horace too had similarly already in B.C. 24 compared Augustus returning from Spain[18] to the return of Hercules from his victory over Geryon:

> Herculis ritu modo dictus, o plebs,
> morte venalem petiisse laurum
> Caesar Hispana repetit penatis
> victor ab ora.
> (Horace *Odes* 3.14.1–4)

> Caesar, O citizens, who but now was said, like Hercules, to be in quest of the laurel purchased at the price of death, rejoins again his household gods, victoriously returning from the Spanish shore.

Hercules was by this post-Actian date '*hoffähig*' (more on pre-Actian considerations below).[19] Syndikus, who puts this ode squarely in the context of the traditions of Greek king-worship and the attendant duties incumbent on the court poet to sing suitably upon the return of his patron, also carefully delineates how the public festivals of the people are linked to the public displays of Augustus' family as well as to the celebrations of a private citizen like the poet, Horace, himself.[20] Finally, we may note here too that the *public* hero, statesman, and incipient god, returns to his own *private* family gods (we shall return to this theme).

These comparisons resonate more significantly when one considers that, prior to Augustus' triple triumph in 29 B.C., Hercules had been, after Dionysus, a most significant element in Antony's propaganda.[21] When, during these early days of struggle, Hercules figured in the literature of the Caesarian faction at all, it seems to have been in representations of Hercules as a willing slave to Omphale.

---

[18] For a full account of Augustus' Spanish campaign, see Schmitthener (1962).

[19] Ritter (1997a) 139.

[20] Syndikus (1973) 142–53. A more barbed reading may be found in Lyne (1995) 169–73. For Hercules and Augustan Rome in general, see Schilling (1942) and Huttner (1997a).

[21] For details and further literature, one may consult Ritter (1995) 70–81.

Propertius recalls the disastrous consequences to a man who allows himself to be ruled by a woman:[22]

> Omphale in tantum formae processit honorem,
>   Lydia Gygaeo tincta puella lacu,
> ut, qui pacato statuisset in orbe columnas,
>   tam dura traheret mollia pensa manu.
> (Propertius 3.11.17–19)

> Omphale, the maid of Lydia, bathed in the Gygian lake, rose to such renown of beauty that he who had set up his pillars in the world he had tamed to peace, with horny hands plucked soft tasks of wool.

The lessons and parallels one might draw apropos Antony and Cleopatra are patent, and have not escaped modern commentators.[23] Plutarch spells them out:

> Ἀντώνιον δ', ὥσπερ ἐν ταῖς γραφαῖς ὁρῶμεν τοῦ Ἡρακλέους τὴν Ὀμφάλην ὑφαιροῦσαν τὸ ῥόπαλον καὶ τὴν λεοντὴν ἀποδύουσαν, οὕτω πολλάκις Κλεοπάτρα παροπλίσασα καὶ καταθέλξασα συνέπεισεν ἀφέντα μεγάλας πράξεις ἐκ τῶν χειρῶν καὶ στρατείας ἀναγκαίας ἐν ταῖς περὶ Κάνωβον καὶ Ταφόσιριν ἀκταῖς ἀλύειν καὶ παίζειν μετ' αὐτῆς.
> (Plutarch Comp. Dem. et Ant. 3.4)

> Antony, on the contrary, like Hercules in paintings where Omphale is seen taking away his club and stripping off his lion skin, was often disarmed by Cleopatra, subdued by her spells, and persuaded to drop from his hands great undertakings and necessary campaigns, only to roam about and play with her on the sea-shores by Canopus and Taphosiris.

The victories celebrated by the triple triumph, however, of 29 B.C. had certainly put an end to all that. On 13 August 29 B.C., the day after the common feast day of both *Hercules Invictus* and *Venus Victrix*, Caesar, son of the divine Julius, began three days of celebration and thanksgiving for his triumph over the Dalmatians, his vic-

---

[22] Richardson (1976) 365 suggests that the poem may have been written for the *Ludi Quinquennales* in 24 B.C., but, despite its post-Actian date, the poem, nevertheless, recalls with vivid horror the types of dangers that had all too recently threatened Rome.

[23] Richardson (1976) 359–68: 'Each of [Propertius'] examples is . . . a facet of the archvillainess, Cleopatra (360).' Cf. Stahl (1985) 234–47.

tory at Actium, his subjugation of Egypt. And the altar to which he went first? The *Ara Maxima*. We have then an historical context, if not for the transfer of Hercules' *sacra* in 312 B.C., at least for the telling of the tale of the alleged transfer in 312 B.C. of Hercules' *sacra*.

We may compare our principal early imperial sources:

eodem Appio auctore Potitia gens, cuius ad Aram Maximam Herculis familiare sacerdotium fuerat, servos publicos ministerii delegandi causa sollemnia eius sacri docuerat. traditur inde, **dictu mirabile et quod dimovendis statu suo sacris religionem facere posset**, cum duodecim familiae ea tempestate Potitiorum essent, puberes ad triginta, omnes intra annum cum stirpe exstinctos; nec nomen tantum Potitiorum interisse sed censorem etiam [Appium] memori deum ira post aliquot annos luminibus captum. (Livy 9.29.9–10)

νῦν μέντοι οὐκέτι τοῖς γένεσι τούτοις ἡ περὶ τὰς ἱερουργίας ἐπιμέλεια ἀνάκειται, ἀλλὰ παῖδες ἐκ τοῦ δημοσίου ὠνητοὶ δρῶσιν αὐτάς. δι' ἅς δὲ αἰτίας τὸ ἔθος μετέπεσε, καὶ **τίς ἡ τοῦ δαίμονος ἐπιφάνεια** περὶ τὴν ἀλλαγὴν τῶν ἱεροποιῶν ἐγένετο, ἐπειδὰν κατὰ τοῦτο γένωμαι τοῦ λόγου τὸ μέρος, διηγήσομαι.

Dionysius of Halicarnassus *Antiquitates Romanae* 1.40.5)

Hercules quoque detractae religionis suae et gravem et manifestam poenam exegisse traditur: nam cum Potitii sacrorum eius ritum, quem pro dono genti eorum ab ipso adsignatum velut hereditarium optinuerant, auctore Appio censore ad humile servorum <publicorum> ministerium transtulissent, omnes, qui erant numero super XXX, puberes intra annum extincti sunt nomenque Potitium in XII familias divisum ~ prope interiit, Appius vero luminibus captus est. (Valerius Maximus 1.1.17 [*de neglecta religione*])

It was Appius too, by whose warranty the Potitian clan, with whom the priesthood of Hercules at the Ara Maxima was hereditary, taught the ritual of that sacrifice to public slaves, in order to devolve that service upon them. Tradition relates that after this a strange thing happened, and one that might well give men pause ere they disturb the established order of religious ceremonies. For whereas at that time there were twelve families of the Potitii, and grown men to the number of thirty, within the year they had perished, every man, and the stock had become extinct; and not only did the name of the Potitii die out, but even the censor, by the unforgetting ire of the gods, was a few years later stricken blind.

To-day, however, the superintendence of the sacrifices no longer devolves on these families, but slaves purchased with the public money perform them. For what reasons this custom was changed and how the god manifested himself concerning the change in his ministers, I shall relate when I come to that part of the history. [The more thorough treatment promised by Dionysius does not survive.]

History teaches us that Hercules also exacted inexorable and manifest vengeance for slights to his religious honors. Indeed, after the Potitii had, at the instigation of the censor Appius, transferred to the care of public slaves the ritual of his worship, which Hercules himself had assigned to their clan as a gift and as a sort of hereditary possession, all of them (and they numbered above thirty grown men) died within the year, and the name Potitius, which was distributed across 12 families, almost perished. Appius, moreover, was deprived of his eyesight.

Comparison of Livy, Dionysius of Halicarnassus, and Valerius Maximus reveals that early imperial sources view (to varying degrees) divinity and divinity's concerns with human behavior as active historical agents. Moreover, what Livy introduces with the disclaimer 'amazing to tell' (*dictu mirabile*)[24] is in Dionysius portrayed as 'a manifestation of divinity' (τίς ἡ τοῦ δαίμονος ἐπιφάνεια). Valerius, however, our Tiberian author, speaks most plainly and without messy historical details:[25]

> Hercules quoque detractae religionis suae et gravem et manifestam poenam exegisse traditur.
>
> (Val. Max. 1.1.7)

> History teaches us that Hercules also exacted inexorable and manifest vengeance for slights to his religious honors.

Valerius' account is especially instructive because we can gauge his tone rather precisely from the context in which he tells the tale. The extinction of the Potitii forms part of a series of anecdotes illustrating the manifest power of gods to punish ritually and morally unacceptable behavior. Just how seriously Valerius takes the powers of the gods to intervene in nature is difficult to assess from just one passage, but, fortunately, Valerius states rather precisely his position vis-à-vis not just gods, but also the miraculous:

> non admiratione ista [= miracula], sed memoria prosequi debemus, cum sciamus recte ab ea [= natura] plurimum licentiae vindicari, penes quam infinitus cuncta gignendi labor consistit.
>
> (Valerius Maximus 1.8.*ext*.18)

> We ought not to be amazed at miracles but rather commit them to memory because we perceive that nature in whose charge the endless task of creating all things resides legitimately claims extensive freedom of action.

Valerius moves well beyond *mirabile dictu*.[26] Wiseman's observation apropos the Potitii is well worth repeating, namely, that this anecdote, which in our surviving sources first surfaces in early imperial authors, continues to be repeated by later authors uncritcally.[27] Consultation of these later authors likewise confirms rather dramatically continuing regard both for Hercules' power and for his interest

---

[24] For literary analysis of Livy's religiosity, see Levene (1993), and, for technical aspects of Roman religion in Livy, compare Linderski (1995), both with further literature.

[25] Valerius ignores details while exalting history in general. Like Livy, Valerius emphasizes the authority of history in the word *traditur*.

[26] For further discussion of religious elements in Valerius Maximus, compare Mueller (1998) with further literature.

[27] Wiseman (1979) 91.

in morality.[28] Whatever, then, our own beliefs regarding the alleged divine interventions of Hercules in Roman history, we must acknowledge that Roman authors seem to have drawn a very serious moral lesson from the manifest power of an angry god.

Historiographical attention to our sources' varying degrees of religiosity lead us in turn to questions that have not hitherto been asked of our sources. If we, for the sake of understanding the ways in which our sources thought about their own religious history, grant that Hercules himself punished the Potitii (and Appius), we may ask why Hercules was angry. Can we begin to sort out the nexus of ritual and moral offenses that surround the extinction of the Potitii? What do the lessons that our imperial authors derive from the events of 312 B.C. tell us about the reinterpretation of religion and republican politics in Augustan Rome in general and perhaps even in Augustan poetry in particular? Such questions bring us back to issues that we initially eschewed, namely, the original establishment of the cult of Hercules at the *Ara Maxima* and the initial instruction of the Pinarii and Potitii.

The eighth book of Vergil's *Aeneid* provides an imperial glimpse of Eden, an idyllic Italy innocent not only of the moribund republic's civil wars, but also of the epic battles that would soon cost both Pallas and Turnus their lives. Evander, the still relatively happy ruler of this idyllic land, tells Aeneas about Hercules' recent and mighty deeds as well as the foundation of the *Ara Maxima* and its organization under the stewardship of Pinarii and Potitii.[29] Aeneas himself worships Hercules along with Evander. A Potitius leads the sacred rites:

> devexo interea propior fit Vesper Olympo.
> iamque sacerdotes primusque Potitius ibant
> pellibus in morem cincti, flammasque ferebant.
> instaurant epulas et mensae grata secundae
> dona ferunt cumulantque oneratis lancibus aras.
> (Vergil *Aeneid* 8.280–84)

---

[28] Later sources for Hercules' anger: Macrobius 3.6.12ff., Servius on *Aen.* 8.179, *Origo gentis Romanae* 8, *Liber de viris illustribus*. 34, Lactantius *Inst.* 2.7.15. One may compare the discussion of Schilling (1942) and Liebeschuetz (1979) 170ff. for the continuing moral significance of Hercules to late imperial Rome.

[29] The place of the Hercules-Cacus episode and its relation to larger interpretative issues in Vergil is beyond the scope of this paper. We look here at the role of the Potitii, so far as possible, in context. For the larger context, see especially, Münzer (1911), Galinsky (1972) 153ff., Galinsky (1966), Lyne (1987) 27–35 and Marincic ch. 8 above. On the role of Hercules as both saviour of the site of Rome and founder of ancestral religion in the *Aeneid*, cf. also Hardie (1986) 213–19.

Meanwhile, evening draws nearer down heaven's slope, and now the priests went forth, Potitius at their head, girt with skins after their fashion bearing torches. They renew the banquet and bring the welcome offerings of a second repast, and heap the altars with laden platters.

Salii appear,[30] the deeds of Hercules are recited, and then:

> exim se cuncti divinis rebus ad urbem
> perfectis referunt. ibat rex obsitus aevo,
> et comitem Aenean iuxta natumque tenebat
> ingrediens varioque viam sermone levabat.
> miratur facilisque oculos fert omnia circum
> Aeneas, capiturque locis et singula laetus
> exquiritque auditque virum monimenta priorum.
> (Vergil *Aeneid* 8.306–12)

The sacred rites discharged, all return to the city. There walked the king, beset with years, and as he moved along kept Aeneas and his son at his side as companions, relieving the way with varied talk. Aeneas marvels as he turns his ready eyes all around, is charmed by the scene, and joyfully seeks and learns, one by one the records of the men of yore.

Aeneas was suspended in a momentary and, granted, fleeting Eden, back, as it were, before the later Roman history (down to Actium, we should note) that closes that same eighth book so vividly on Vulcan's shield, and certainly back before the political and moral corruption of Appius and the Potitii in 312 B.C. Aeneas, in this momentary but poetically timeless paradise of ritual and moral purity,[31] studies (oral) history (*monumenta priorum*),[32] and, if Roman history's exemplary traditions are a useful guide, in order to learn moral lessons for future conduct.[33] This exemplary world, inaugurated by worship of Hercules, was a state of affairs that the military and legislative powers of Augustus aimed to revive.[34] No coincidence, then,

---

[30] As Huttner (1997a) 375 notes, Octavian's name was by decree of the Senate inserted into the song of the Salii; Octavian thus received the same honours as Hercules receives here, and the song of the Salii in Vergil's Aeneid likely includes allusion to this political context. Augustus *R.G.* 2.21 *nomen meum senatus consulto inclusum est in saliare carmen, et sacrosanctus in perpetuum ut essem et, quoad viverem, tribunicia potestas mihi esset, per legem sanctum est.*

[31] On the use of exemplary moments to create illusions of eternal verity, see Mueller (1998) 258.

[32] Cf. Vergil *Aen.* 3.102 and 8.362–5.

[33] Cf. e.g. Livy *praef.*; Valerius Maximus *praef.*

[34] Augustus *R.G.* 2.12 *legibus novis me auctore latis multa exempla maiorum exolescentia iam ex nostro saeculo reduxi et ipse multarum rerum exempla imitanda posteris tradidi.*

perhaps that his first sacrifice on his days of triple triumph occurred at the *Ara Maxima*. And the Potitii? Are they merely a byword for the fate that awaited Italy's native sons if they angered the gods or if they allowed religious scruples to be corrupted for the sake of material gain? What defense was there against extinction?

We may turn again to a keen observer of Augustan Rome for another tentative answer. Tiberius, whose sentiments are here represented by Tacitus, is once more grief-stricken, this time by the death of his adoptive son Germanicus. He admonishes a too demonstrative senate and people,[35] instructing them in their moral duties by appeal to the examples of history, although in point of fact:

> nil opus vetustioribus exemplis, quotiens populus Romanus cladis exercituum, interitum ducum, funditus amissas nobilis familias constanter tulerit. principes mortalis, rem publicam aeternam esse.
>
> (Tacitus *Annals* 3.6)

> There was no need to show by earlier examples how often the Roman people had borne unshaken the slaughter of armies, the death of generals, the complete annihilation of historic houses. Statesmen were mortal, the state eternal.

The *quotiens* in Tiberius' remarks to the senate will perhaps permit us to include the *Potitii* along with both the more worthy *Fabii*[36] and the historically more significant *Julii* and *Claudii*. We might also add that Augustus had taken certain precautions; by appropriating the fairer part of the old republic and its religion, by establishing his house as a cult centre complete with priests and sacred rites, the *domus Caesaris* would outlast both Julians and Claudians, becoming as eternal as the imperial state itself. It is here that we may recall also the celebratory words of Horace *Odes* 3.14 (cited above). Horace celebrated a public statesman who was returning to his family's private gods, thus occasioning public thanksgiving that included public displays by the women of his own household, women belonging ide-

---

[35] As opposed to the doubts cast upon the authenticity of Tiberius' speech in Cassius Dio, Syme (1958) I:319 finds phrases in this speech aphoristic enough to represent Tiberius' very words (cf. 2:700–3). The honours lavished upon Germanicus by the *Tabula Siarensis* do not necessarily contradict the restraint of Tiberius. In fact, we know that the senate expressly approved the moderation of Tiberius' family's display of grief: *dolorem fidelissumum et in dolore moderatione<m> senatum probare* (*s.c. de Cn. Pisone patre* 145–6); the text is taken from Eck, Caballos, and Fernández (1996).

[36] The origins of the Fabii, we may note, were also closely associated both with Hercules as well as with the idyllic Italy of Evander; cf. Holleman (1976).

ologically to the domestic sphere or private realm. The poet himself planned to celebrate these public victories in the privacy of his own home, and thus included instructions to fetch a woman to enliven his own private festivities. Why this emphasis on women? Hercules, although he excluded women from his public worship at the *Ara Maxima*,[37] hardly abstained from intimate relations with women. The Herculean head of the Roman state, sanctioned, as always, by religion, similarly enjoys domestic support in the public display of his household's private religion by the women who belong to his household.[38] Our statesman hero comes back to a pacified state and to the domestic tranquillity of thankful women, and these women, in the context of Augustan moral legislation, surely provide another essential means by which extinction will be prevented. If these imperial women (and the women who follow their divinely sanctioned examples) live in accordance with the will of heaven (the gods demand chastity, which lends fertility) and the precepts of moral legislation on earth,[39] all will be well. The control of women in private constitutes another essential prophylactic element in the Augustan arsenal against public (male) extinction.

In Antony and in Potitius' descendants (and by extension all those like them) lay the threat of corruption and the concomitant horrors of extinction. The victorious leader of Horace *Odes* 3.14 comes back, however, to a state that he has organized against political upstarts. Horace, who shares the general viewpoint of the contemporary regime, prefers this Herculean state-of-affairs to the times of the consulship of Plancus,[40] a time that threatened political extinction through civil war. Plancus (the consul of Horace's ode) brings us, not ironically (upon reflection), to Plancus' brother, who had been adopted into the *gens Plautia*, and who was thus heir to the colleague of the censor, with whom we began when first attempting to place these investigations in some historical context. It is indeed worth noting that

<hr/>

[37] *De Origo gentis Romanae* 6.7; Plutarch *Quaest. Rom.* 60, Macrobius 1.12.28. The Hercules of Propertius 4.9 who unsuccessfully demands water from the spring of the *Bona Dea* (whose rites were forbidden to men) must be left aside here, but may be pursued with further literature in DeBrohun (1994), Janan (1998), and Lindheim (1998).
[38] On the integration of women belonging to the imperial family in public triumphal displays, see Flory (1998).
[39] On the intersections of chastity, religion, and law in early imperial Rome with extensive references to related secondary literature, see Mueller (1998).
[40] *MRR* II:357: L. Munatius L. f. L. n. Plancus (30) Cos. 42.

Horace's consul's brother, L. Plautius Plancus[41] (who was sacrificed to
the triumvirs with his brother's consent during the proscriptions of
43 B.C.),[42] had minted a coin that on its reverse, it is argued, celebrated his adoptive ancestor (the censor, C. Plautius Venox, Appius
Claudius Caecus' colleague in 312 B.C.) with an allusion to the striking *tibicines*, whom the censor Plautius caused to be brought back to
Rome while they were in a drunken stupor.[43] We may recall the
scene with yet another Augustan poet, Ovid:

> iamque per Esquilias Romanam intraverat urbem,
>   et mane in medio plaustra fuere foro
> Plautius, ut possent specie numeroque senatum
>   fallere, personis imperat ora tegi.
>   Ovid *Fasti* 6.683–6

> And now the wain had entered the city of Rome by the Esquiline,
> and at morn it stood in the middle of the Forum. In order to
> deceive the Senate as to their person and their number, Plautius
> commanded that their faces should be covered with masks.

Was this the way censors were to behave? Ovid introduces the events
of 312 B.C. with a comparative look at the censorship of a man
destined (like Hercules) to become a god:

> te quoque magnifica, Concordia, dedicat aede
>   Livia, quam caro praestitit ipsa viro.
> disce tamen, veniens aetas: ubi Livia nunc est
>   porticus, immensae tecta fuere domus;
> urbis opus domus una fuit spatiumque tenebat,
>   quo brevius muris oppida multa tenent.
> haec aequata solo est, nullo sub crimine regni,
>   sed quia luxuria visa nocere sua.
> sustinuit tantas operum subvertere moles
>   totque suas heres perdere Caesar opes:
> sic agitur censura et sic exempla parantur,
>   cum vindex, alios quod monet, ipse facit.
>   Ovid *Fasti* 6.637–48

> To thee, too, Concordia, Livia dedicated a magnificent shrine,
> which she presented to her dear husband. But learn this, thou
> age to come: where Livia's colonnade now stands, there once

[41] *MRR* II:602; cf. II:448: 'L. Plautius (Plotius) Plancus (Munatius 26); cf. Plotius
10 [Praef. or Leg., Lieut., agr. dand. assign. 44, Pr. 43]); Monetal ca. 47'.
[42] The sources are collected by *MRR* II:339.
[43] Grueber (1970 [1910]) I:516ff. n. 2.

> stood a huge palace [belonging Vedius Pollio]. The single house
> was like the fabric of a city; it occupied a space larger than
> that occupied by the walls of many a town. It was leveled with
> the ground, not on a charge of treason, but because its luxury
> was deemed harmful. Caesar brooked to overthrow so vast a
> structure, and to destroy so much wealth, to which he was him-
> self the heir. That is the way to exercise the censorship; that is
> the way to set an example, when an upholder of the law does
> what he himself wants others to do.

Roman historical memory was long indeed, especially in Rome's
poets. Neither Appius nor his colleague Plautius seems to have represented the type of censor admired in Augustus' Rome.

We confront certain ironies. The year 312 B.C., as recorded by
our imperial historians, upon examination by modern historians yields
more myth than history, while the poetic myth of Hercules, Evander,
Potitius, and Aeneas gains in historical resonance through historiographical comparison. The extinction of the Potitii is, if nothing else,
surely exemplary. I have attempted to read the relations of the Potitii
to Hercules through the national grief professed (or represented to
have been professed) by Tiberius and through the identification of
Augustus and Antony with Hercules in his various guises in Augustan
poetry. Historiography, if not history, provides a relatively simple
answer. Because the patrician Potitii sold their religious birthright,
the Potitian *gens* had to die. Fears of patrician extinction, moral legislation promoting the production of children to prevent just that,
fears of divisive politicians and politics all weigh heavily (and anachro-
nistically) in turn upon Vergil's poor (and singular) Potitius. Vergil,
on the other hand, in an admittedly minor example of his proleptic technique (Potitius appears in only one line) transmuted historiography's riches into poetic myth, showing us that what would be
might not have been, and, one surmises, for reasons similar to, but
likely more nuanced than the reason offered by the likes of Valerius
Maximus (or the present author).

CHAPTER SEVENTEEN

HISTORY, POETRY, AND *ANNALES*

T. P. Wiseman

1. *Livy and Varro*

Livy begins his preface with a conspicuous half-hexameter and an allusion to Ennius, and ends it with the wish that he could exploit the prefatory conventions of epic poetry.[1] In the central passage, however, he emphasises the *differences* between what he does and what the poets do:[2]

> quae ante conditam condendamve urbem poeticis magis decora fabu-
> lis quam incorruptis rerum gestarum monumentis tradita, ea nec
> adfirmare nec refellere in animo est.

> I intend neither to endorse nor to refute those traditions of events
> before the city was founded or planned which are more appropriate
> to the stories of poets than to the uncorrupted records of history.

More appropriate in what way? Livy is evidently expressing a generic distinction between poetry and history,[3] but on what criterion?

The temporal phrase *ante conditam condendamve urbem* implies that chronology is what marks off poetic from historical material, and that is perhaps what we should expect. Just a few years earlier, in 43 B.C., Varro had published his major work on history and chronology, the four books *De gente populi Romani*,[4] in which he had carefully distinguished three periods of the past (*discrimina temporum*).[5] The

---

[1] Livy *Praef.* 1, 13. On §1, cf. Quintilian *Inst.* 9.4.74 (*T. Livius hexametri exordio coepit*) and Ennius, *Ann.* fr. 494 Skutsch; Moles (1993) 141–2. On §13, see Moles (1993) 156–8.

[2] Livy *Praef.* 6: this passage and *Praef.* 13 are the only places in the whole of Livy's extant text where the noun *poeta* or the adjective *poeticus* occurs.

[3] Moles (1993) 148: '*decora* is used of what is generically appropriate'.

[4] Fragments in *HRR* II. 10–24 and Fraccaro (1907) 255–86; for the date, see Fraccaro (1907) 77–8, and Horsfall (1972) 124–5.

[5] Fr. 3p (Censorinus 21.1–5); cf. Fraccaro (1907) 255–7.

first, the ἄδηλον or obscure, ran from the creation of mankind to
the first flood (that of Ogyges, not Deucalion), and could not be cal-
culated in years. The second, about 1600 years from the flood to
the first Olympiad, he called μυθικόν because many of the supposed
events of that period were *fabulosa* — and it is clear from the fragments that he attributed the *fabulae* to poets.[6] Only the third period,
from the first Olympiad onwards, could be called ἱστορικόν because
the events that took place in it were recorded in 'true histories'.

Varro's choice of 776 B.C. as the dividing-line between the realms
of poetic fiction and historical truth corresponds quite closely with
Livy's dating, since it just allows the beginning of the foundation
story (*condenda urbs*) to fall within the historical period. The dispute
over the Alban kingship which resulted in Amulius' overthrow of
Numitor and murder of his son, and the consecration of Numitor's
daughter as a Vestal Virgin, took place three years before the conception of Romulus and Remus, and thus, on Varro's chronology,
in 775 B.C.[7]

However, it is not as simple as that. As Livy's next sentence makes
clear, the particular poetic legend he has in mind is the conception
story itself:[8]

> datur haec venia antiquitati ut miscendo humana divinis primordia
> urbium augustiora faciat; et si cui populo licere oportet consecrare
> origines suas et ad deos referre auctores, ea belli gloria est populo
> Romano ut cum suum conditorisque parentem Martem potissimum
> ferat, tam et hoc gentes humanae patiantur aequo animo quam imperium
> patiuntur.

> Antiquity is granted this licence, to make the origins of cities more
> august by mingling the human with the divine; and if any people ought
> to be allowed to sanctify its origins and claim gods as founders, such
> is the martial glory of the Roman people that when it declares Mars
> in particular as its parent and the father of its founder, the nations of
> the world may put up with that too, as readily as they put up with
> our imperial rule.

---

[6] Fr. 6p (Augustine *CD* 18.8), on the birth of Minerva from the head of Jupiter:
poetis et fabulis, non historiae rebusque gestis est adplicandum (the antithesis accepted as
Varronian by Fraccaro [1907] 42). Fr. 13P = 23F (Augustine *CD* 18.12), on Jupiter
and Europa: *quod de Iove poetae cantant*, as opposed to *historica veritas*. Fr. 17P = 29F
(Augustine *CD* 18.16), on the metamorphosis of Diomedes' companions, which Varro
thought was not fictitious: *non fabuloso poeticoque mendacio sed historica adtestatione confirmant*.
[7] Conception on 24 June 772 (Varro ap. Plutarch *Rom.* 12.3–6), τετάρτῳ ἔτει
after Ilia's consecration (Dionysius of Halicarnassus *A.R.* 1.77.1).
[8] Livy *Praef.* 7.

So now it seems that what marks off the poet's territory from the historian's is the participation of gods in human affairs, the 'mingling of human and divine'. And if the poets say that Mars really appeared on earth to father the twins on Rhea Silvia, they must mean that he did so in 772 B.C., four years into Varro's historical period.[9]

Of course it is absurd to be so pedantic. Both Varro and Livy were serious authors dealing with a serious issue, and neither of them was content with a merely mechanical solution.

The way Livy dealt with the problem has been well explored by David Levene.[10] There were plenty of allegedly supernatural events in Roman history, and Livy's consistent technique in dealing with them is to distance himself with an exculpatory formula (*dicitur, ut ferunt, traditur memoriae,* etc), sometimes offering an alternative explanation on the merely human level;[11] but he will often report, as a fact, that contemporaries accepted the event as supernatural, and by narrating the favourable outcome he allows his reader to infer that they were right to do so.[12] Sometimes he leaves out a famous divine — intervention story altogether, but leaves a hint to remind his readers of it, as when he refers to the *caelestia arma* of the Salii, or the dictator's vow to the Dioscuri at the battle of Lake Regillus, or the *insigne nomen* of Claudia Quinta at the reception of the Magna Mater in 204.[13]

One particularly revealing instance of his technique is the narrative of the disappearance of Romulus.[14] After the sudden storm that left the king's throne mysteriously empty, the Romans were prepared

---

[9] Above, n. 7: Plutarch citing the calculations of Varro's friend Tarutius.

[10] Levene (1993), esp. 16–30. See also Feldherr (1998) 64–78 and Forsythe (1999) 87–98.

[11] E.g. 1.4.7 (Acca Larentia as *lupa*), 1.31.4 (either divine voice or response of *haruspices*), 5.22.5 (either divine inspiration or young man's joke). Note also the use of *certe* (e.g. 1.36.6, 2.7.2, 5.22.6) to mark the transition to what Livy *is* prepared to endorse.

[12] E.g. the warning voice at 5.32.6–7: Livy commits himself only to the fact that M. Caedicius reported to the tribunes that he had heard it, but acceptance of its genuineness is part of the *religio* which enables Rome to survive the disaster (5.50.5, 5.52.11).

[13] 1.20.4, 2.20.12 (*nihil nec divinae nec humanae opis dictator praetermittens*), 29.14.12; cf. respectively Ovid *Fast.* 3.259–392, Dionysius of Halicarnassus *A.R.* 6.13 and Ovid *Fast.* 4.291–344. Cicero uses the same technique at *Rep.* 2.13 (*orantibus*), 2.37.4 (*scintilla ingenii*), 2.45.3 (*caede maculatus*): see Zetzel (1995) 170, 192, 201. Otherwise unattested divine-intervention stories may be inferred from Livy 1.12.7 on Romulus and Jupiter Stator (*tamquam caelesti voce iussi*) and 10.19.17 on Ap. Claudius and Bellona (*velut instigante dea*).

[14] Livy 1.16.2–8; Levene (1993) 132–3.

to believe the *patres* who had been standing close to him when they
said he had been snatched up by a whirlwind. On the initiative of
just a few people (presumably the *patres* themselves), the Romans
now hailed Romulus as a god and the son of a god. But then Livy
goes on (1.16.4):

> fuisse credo tum quoque aliquos qui discerptum regem patrum manibus
> taciti arguerent; manavit enim haec quoque sed perobscura fama; illam
> altera admiratio viri et pavor praesens nobilitavit.

> I believe that even then there were some who claimed in secret that
> the king had been torn to pieces at the hands of the *patres*; for this
> tale too has spread, very obscure though it is. Admiration of Romulus
> and the fear felt at the time has made the former version famous [or
> noble].

What made the Romans believe in Romulus the god was the prudent judgement (*consilium*) of one man, Iulius Proculus, who reported
to the people's assembly that Romulus had descended from heaven
and told him to tell the Romans of his deification.

Livy reports as fact Proculus' report, and the belief it created,[15]
but his use of the word *consilium* clearly implies that it was a piece
of deliberate policy to keep the people happy — a 'noble lie' (γεννα῀ιον
ψεῦδος) as in Plato's *Republic*. His use of the ambiguous word *nobil-
itavit* may be an allusion to that famous passage; so too Plutarch
describes as 'not ignoble' (οὐ φαῦλον) the tradition that Numa invented
the story of his divine mistress and adviser Egeria, for the same reason.[16] Livy may not have been as much of a philosopher as Plutarch,
but he was interested in the subject, and wrote philosophical dia-
logues.[17] So an allusion to Plato is not out of the question.

As for Varro, who certainly was a philosopher (among many other
things), his complex argument in *De gente populi Romani* about myth,
history and divine intervention can be reconstructed from Book 18
of Augustine's *De civitate Dei*, which is largely based on it.[18] Varro
ended Book 2 of *De gente* with the Trojan War, which divided his
'mythical' period — from Ogyges' flood to the first Olympiad — into

---

[15] Livy 1.16.5 (*consilium, fides*), 1.16.8 (*fides*, twice).
[16] Livy 1.16.4; Plato *Rep.* 3.414b–415d; Plutarch *Num.* 4.8 (also Lycurgus and his
lawcode 'from Apollo').
[17] Seneca *Ep.* 100.9.
[18] See Fraccaro (1907) 23–67 for an analysis of Augustine's sources in book 18.

two unequal parts, of which the latter was closer to the 'historical' category.[19] But even in the earlier period, as Augustine remarks in a passage which is agreed to be Varronian,[20] there were true histories which were turned into myth by the poets.

Augustine has just given a long list of *fabulae fictae*, all of which involved physical impossibilities: Triptolemus and his winged serpents; the Minotaur; the Centaurs; three-headed Cerberus; Phrixus and Helle on the flying ram; the Gorgon's gaze; Bellerophon on Pegasus; Amphion and his miraculous lyre; Daedalus and Icarus; Oedipus and the Sphinx; Antaeus the son of Earth. Then he comments:[21]

> hae fabulae bellum ad usque Troianum, ubi secundum librum Marcus Varro de populi Romani gente finivit, ex occasione historiarum, quae res veraciter gestas continent, ita sunt ingeniis hominum fictae ut non sunt opprobriis numinum adfixae.

> Down to the time of the Trojan War, which is where Marcus Varro ended the second book of *De gente populi Romani*, these mythical stories were made up by the ingenuity of men, taking the opportunity offered by histories which contain things that truthfully happened, in such a way as not to link them with slanders on the divine powers.

That last phrase alludes to a Varronian obsession, the 'tales unworthy of the gods' which made up the *theologia fabularis* of poets and playwrights,[22] and Augustine goes on to some examples of such stories, such as Jupiter's alleged abduction of Ganymede (not true, it was king Tantalus who did it, just as it was the Cretan king Xanthus who abducted Europa).[23]

But whether slanderous or not, these myths were made up by poets out of true historical records. That is how Varro and Augustine saw it; we of course see it the other way round, as the creation of 'history' by the rationalising of myth. So Erichthonius was not conceived by the earth from Vulcan's ejaculation as he tried to rape

---

[19] Fr. 3P (n. 5 above), fr. 14P = 28F (Augustine *CD* 18.13).

[20] Fr. 14P = 28F (Augustine *CD* 18.13).

[21] Augustine *CD* 18.13.

[22] Varro *Ant. div.* frr. 7 and 10 Cardauns (Augustine *CD* 6.5); see Wiseman (1998) 17–24. Varro *De gente populi Romani* fr. 8P = 18F (Augustine *CD* 18.10): *Marcus Varro non vult fabulosis adversus deos fidem adhibere figmentis, ne de maiestatis eorum dignitate indignum aliquid sentiat.*

[23] Augustine *CD* 18.12 (Europa), 18.13 (Ganymede) — both passages with explicit reference to the stage. Xanthus' abduction of Europa counted as *historica veritas* (cf. n. 6 above).

Minerva: that was an *opinio fabulosa* arising from the 'fact' that the infant was found in the temple of those two gods.[24] And the dispute between Minerva and Neptune over the city of Athens was settled not by a vulgar display of miracle-working, as the myth has it, but by a ballot of the Athenians themselves in which the women defeated the men by one vote; as Augustine observes, for Varro this was *non fabulosa sed historica ratio*.[25]

So the chronological criterion for poetic myth or factual history was by no means hard and fast. Nor, more surprisingly, was that of supernatural intervention in human life.

It may well be that Varro had a strictly natural 'historical' version of all those miraculous stories listed by Augustine. But he certainly did not rule out the supernatural *a priori*. In Book 3 of *De gente* he reported as historical fact the metamorphosis of the companions of Diomedes into birds, citing as support the transformation of Ulysses' men by Circe, and the werewolves of the Arcadian Lycaeus cult.[26] Augustine insists on Varro's judgement — *historica adtestatio*, not *fabulosum poeticumque mendacium* — and it leads him into a long digression on the powers of daemones.[27]

That was a matter of some importance to Augustine, and he returns to it more than once in *De civitate Dei*. In Book 10, discussing the 'miracles of the gods of the gentiles', which resulted from the power of demons, he cites as examples the migration of the Penates from Alba to Lavinium, Attus Navius' cutting of the whetstone, the voyage of Aesculapius' snake from Epidaurus to Rome, Claudia Quinta pulling the ship from the mudbank, and the Vestal who proved her innocence by carrying water in a sieve. When Tertullian had dealt with the same question, he too cited Claudia Quinta and the Vestal with the sieve, but also the epiphany of Castor and Pollux and the reddening of Domitius' beard.[28] Both writers knew Varro's works well and used them extensively, and I think it is likely that all these examples come from him.

---

[24] Fr. 13P = 24F (Augustine *CD* 18.12).
[25] Fr. 7P = 17–18F (Augustine *CD* 18.9–10).
[26] Fr. 17P = 29F (Augustine *CD* 18.16–17). Contrast Pliny *Nat.* 10.127 (on the *fabula* of Diomedes' companions), 8.81–2 (on the Arcadian story as *Graeca credulitas*).
[27] Augustine, *CD* 18.18: he leaves open the possibility that Apuleius' *Golden Ass* was a factual narrative. On *daemones* see Brenk (1986).
[28] Augustine *CD* 10.16 (*illa ... miracula deorum gentilium, quae commendat historia*); Tertullian *Apol.* 22.12. For Domitius see Suetonius *Nero* 1.1 and Plutarch *Aem.* 25.3–4.

One of them certainly did, as is proved by a neglected passage in *De civitate Dei* book 22:[29]

> Nam si ad eorum miracula veniamus, quae facta a dis suis obponunt martyribus nostris, nonne etiam ipsa pro nobis facere et nobis reperientur omnino proficere? nam inter magna miracula deorum suorum profecto magnum illud est quod Varro commemorat, Vestalem virginem, cum periclitaretur falsa suspicione de stupro, cribrum implesse aqua de Tiberi et ad suos iudices nulla eius parte stillante portasse. quis aquae pondus supra cribrum tenuit? quis tot cavernis patentibus nihil inde in terram cadere permisit? responsuri sunt: 'aliquis deus aut aliquis daemon.'

> And now if we turn to examine the miracles of paganism, the achievements of their gods which they oppose to those of our martyrs, we shall find that those achievements support our side, and supply us with invaluable assistance. In fact, among their greater miracles is the one recorded by Varro concerning a Vestal Virgin who had come under suspicion of unchastity and was in danger of her life. The story goes that she filled a sieve with water from the Tiber and carried it to her judges without spilling a drop. Now who was it that kept that weight of water in the sieve? Who was it who prevented the water from pouring out on to the ground from all those gaping holes? The reply will be, 'Some god, or some demon.'

The Vestal's name was Tuccia, and her trial before the *pontifices* took place about 230 B.C.[30] The way Varro dealt with her story is not beyond detection.

At the beginning of the twenty-eighth book of the *Natural History*, for which Varro was one of his named sources, the elder Pliny discusses the power of words, in particular prayers and incantations. One of his prime examples is the *deprecatio* which enabled Tuccia to carry the water in the sieve.[31] When Valerius Maximus tells the Tuccia story, he quotes her rash prayer to Vesta as the cause of the

---

[29] Augustine *CD* 22.11, trans. H. Bettenson (Penguin Classics). The passage escaped the notice of Cichorius (1922) 20–1, Münzer (1939) (see also n. 31 below), and Broughton (1951) 227.

[30] Livy *Per.* 20, mentioned after the subjection of Sardinia and Corsica in 231. The MSS of Pliny *Nat.* 28.12 give *anno urbis* DCVIIII (145 B.C.), to be emended to DXXIIII (230 B.C.): Münzer (1897) 177 n. 1 and (1937) 206.

[31] Pliny *Nat.* 28.12, *qua usa aquam in cribro tulit*; cf. 28.10, *polleantne aliquid verba et incantamenta carminum*. See Münzer (1897) 177–8 for Varro as the source, and (1937) 205: 'Es liegt ohne Zweifel hier überall eine mehr antiquarisch als annalistische Überlieferung zugrunde'. See n. 29 above: Münzer was evidently unaware of the Augustine passage which confirmed his conjecture.

miracle.[32] Dionysius of Halicarnassus, in a part of his *Roman Antiquities* for which he certainly used Varro, inserts into his account of the foundation of the Vesta cult a digression on the manifestations of the goddess: two Vestals, Aemilia and Tuccia, are cited as having prayed to Vesta and been empowered to perform miracles.[33] Aemilia's prayer is quoted verbatim; Tuccia's is only referred to, but is clearly an important part of the story.[34]

From this triangulation of the extant sources, the outline at least is visible of the Varronian treatment of Tuccia's story as evidence of the power of Vesta's *numen*. Perhaps it was one of a series of examples of divine manifestation in Roman history, as in Tertullian and Augustine.[35] It was certainly a question as important to Varro's theology as it was to theirs.

Livy had quite different priorities, either omitting miracle stories altogether or distancing himself from them by the use of *oratio obliqua*.[36] He wanted his readers to draw appropriate moral conclusions from his narrative whether or not they believed in supernatural manifestations. It was a controversial question — and though he may have relegated such stories to the 'appropriate to poetic legends' category, there is no reason to suppose that all Romans would agree with him.

2. *Cicero*

The *locus classicus* for the respective modes of poetry and history is the conversation that opens Cicero's *De legibus*. It takes place by the river Liris, in the grounds of the Cicero house at Arpinum. This

---

[32] Valerius Maximus 8.1.abs.4. For Valerius' use of Varro, see Bloomer (1992) 113–26.

[33] Dionysius of Halicarnassus *A.R.* 2.68–9 (ἐπιφάνεια at 68.1 and 69.3); Varro cited at 2.21.2, 2.47.4 and 2.48.4. For Aemilia (also Valerius Maximus 1.1.7, Prop. 4.11.53–4), see Münzer (1920) 173–7 and (1937) 199–203: the legendary version of a real event in 178 B.C. (Livy *Per.* 41, Obsequens 8).

[34] Dionysius of Halicarnassus *A.R.* 2.68.4 (Aemilia), 2.69.2 (Tuccia, τὴν θεὸν ἐπικαλεσαμένην ἡγεμόνα τῆς ὁδοῦ γενέσθαι).

[35] See n. 28 above. The subject may have been treated in the last book of Varro's *Antiquitates diuinae* (on the *di selecti*, including Vesta: frr. 229 and 281–3 Cardauns), or in *Curio de cultu deorum* (cf. Augustine *CD* 7.34–5), or just possibly in *Gallus de admirandis* (cf. Macrobius 3.15.8).

[36] See n. 10 above. He evidently reported Tuccia's condemnation (Livy *Per.* 20); if he mentioned the miracle as an alternative tradition (as suggested by Münzer [1937] 207), it will have been to reject it.

ancient oak, says Atticus — it must be the very one where Marius saw the eagle in Marcus' epic poem. If you like, says Quintus; but Marius' oak was planted by a poet, and that's the sort of tree that never dies.[37] So Atticus consults the author himself: was it his own verses that planted the tree, or did Cicero have a factual source for what he wrote?[38]

Marcus replies by asking Atticus two questions of his own. Did Romulus really appear to Julius Proculus (on the Quirinal, close to Atticus' house in Rome), and did the north wind really carry off Oreithyia (at the Ilissus, close to Atticus' old house in Athens)?[39] 'Why do you ask?', says Atticus.[40]

> nihil sane, nisi ne nimis diligenter inquiras in ea quae isto modo memo-riae sint prodita.

> No reason — except this, that you shouldn't inquire too carefully into events that are recorded in that manner.

At first sight, it looks straightforward enough: if *isto modo* means 'like a poet', then *modus* should mean something like 'generic convention'. But this *modus* is a means of *memoriae prodere*, which is the historian's job.[41]

In any case, Atticus is still not satisfied:

> atqui multa quaeruntur in Mario fictane an uera sint, et a nonnullis, quod et in recenti memoria et in Arpinati homine uersere, ueritas a te postulatur.

> But people ask about many things in the *Marius*, whether they are true or invented; and since you are dealing with recent events and a man of Arpinum, some people are demanding the truth from you.

Evidently not everyone thought it was enough just to say 'this is poetry, not history'. But Marcus insists that it is:

---

[37] Cicero *Leg.* 1.1–2 (1.14 for the Liris bank). Cicero's *Marius*: Courtney (1993) 174–8.

[38] Cicero *Leg.* 1.3: *tuine versus hanc quercum severint, an ita factum de Mario, ut scribis, acceperis.*

[39] Ibid.: *certen . . . verumne sit . . . sic enim est traditum.* (Plato, *Phdr.* 229b for the Ilissus, surely a deliberate allusion by Cicero.)

[40] Cicero *Leg.* 1.4 (the following three quotations).

[41] *TLL* 8.677.70–78: e.g. Cicero *Diu.* 1.55 (*omnes historici*), Nepos *Them.* 10.5 (Thucydides). The phrase occurs sixteen times in Livy (*memoriae tradere* seven times, *memoriae mandare* twice).

et mehercule ego me cupio non mendacem putari; sed tamen non-
nulli isti, Tite noster, faciunt imperite qui in isto periculo non ut a
poeta sed ut a teste ueritatem exigant; nec dubito quin idem et cum
Egeria conlocutum Numam et ab aquila Tarquinio apicem inpositum
putent.

Well, I certainly don't want to be thought a liar! But my dear Titus,
those 'some people' of yours are naive in demanding the truth in such
a case, not as from a poet, but as from a witness. I've no doubt they
think Numa really talked with Egeria, and the eagle really put the cap
on Tarquin's head!

So, says Quintus, you think that different laws are to be observed
in a history and in a poem? Of course, replies Marcus, for in a history what matters is truth, in a poem it's mostly enjoyment.[42]

That 'mostly' (*pleraque*) is important, as is the concession Marcus
immediately makes, that there are countless *fabulae* in Herodotus and
Theopompus.[43] He knows that his schematic distinction between
poetry and history is not universally valid, and that people like Atticus,
naive or not, are entitled to ask whether a poem on a historical subject is to be believed. So if, as Denis Feeney puts it, the question at
issue in this conversation is 'what you can narrate in a particular
genre', 'the appropriate treatment of the data of received tradition',[44]
it is clear that more than one type of answer could legitimately be
given.

That is spectacularly demonstrated in another dialogue of which
Cicero and his brother were the interlocutors (this time without
Atticus), namely *De divinatione*. Do the gods really communicate their
will to men?[45] In Book 1 Quintus argues that they do: although its
workings are mysterious, genuine divination can and does exist, as
is proved by the overwhelming testimony of past authorities.[46] In
Book 2 Marcus speaks for the sceptics: since divination is inherently

---

[42] Cicero *Leg.* 1.5: *quippe, cum in illa [historia] omnia ad veritatem, Quinte, referatur, in hoc [poemate] ad delectationem pleraque.*

[43] Ibid.; cf. Strabo 1.2.35 (C43). For myths in history see Marincola (1997) 117–27.

[44] Feeney (1991) 259, 260; the whole chapter on 'epic of history' (250–312) is fundamental.

[45] Cicero *Div.* 1.1: *magnifica quaedam res et salutaris, si modo est ulla, quaque proxime ad deorum vim natura mortalis possit accedere.*

[46] E.g. 1.12: *nihil est autem quod non longinquitas temporum excipiente memoria prodendisque monumentis efficere atque assequi possit.*

improbable and cannot be explained, the supposed evidence for it must be either invented or explicable by other means.[47]

Although the negative argument comes second, Cicero as author is careful to keep both possibilities open. The Academic philosopher's purpose is 'to compare arguments, to set out what can be said for any proposition, and without asserting his own authority to leave the audience's judgement free and unimpaired'.[48] Who knows how many of the audience agreed with Quintus?

The distinction between history and *fabula* is central to the whole discussion. Quintus insists on the authority of written records, which may be either poetry or prose.[49] One of his prime exhibits is the whetstone cut in half by Attus Navius:[50]

> negemus omnia, comburamus annales, ficta haec dicamus, quidvis denique potius quam deos res humanas curare fateamur.

> Let's deny it all, let's burn the annals, let's say it's an invention — anything at all rather than admit that the gods care about human affairs!

Which is precisely the answer Marcus gives in Book 2: philosophy should not accept invented stories.[51] Again, such stories may be in poetry or prose. After all, says Marcus, why should I believe Herodotus any more than Ennius?[52] Literary genre seems not to be the main issue here.

However, there is a passage in Book 1 which does address the status of poetic stories. Quintus has been citing examples from Greek historians, including Philistus' report of what the mother of Dionysius of Syracuse dreamed when she was pregnant.[53] That reminds him

---

[47] E.g. 2.27: *hoc ego philosophi non esse arbitror, testibus uti qui aut casu veri aut malitia falsi fictive esse possunt.*

[48] 2.150: . . . *conferre causas et quid in quamque sententiam dici possit expromere, nulla adhibita sua auctoritate iudicium audientium relinquere integrum ac liberum.* See Beard (1986), Schofield (1986).

[49] *scriptores*: 1.31. *scribere*, with named author: poetry 1.22, 87; prose 1.33, 36, 46, 48, 50, 53, 56, 121, 130. *scriptum est* etc, anonymous: 1.31, 39, 52, 89, 101, 121. *historia*: 1.37, 38, 49, 50, 55, 121. *annales*: 1.43, 51, 100. *monumenta*: 1.12, 33, 72, 87.

[50] 1.33; cf. Livy 1.36.4–5, who narrates it with *ut ferunt . . . ferunt . . . memorant. . . .*

[51] 2.80: *contemne cotem Atti Navii; nihil debet esse in philosophia commenticiis fabellis loci.*

[52] 2.115: *Herodotum cur veraciorem ducam Ennio? num minus ille potuit de Croeso quam de Pyrrho fingere Ennius? fingere* also at 2.27, 58, 136; *fabula* and/or *commenticius* at 2.27, 80, 113.

[53] 1.37: *age, barbari vani atque fallaces; num etiam Graiorum historia mentita est?* Chrysippus

of the dreams of Ilia and Priam in Ennius, which he admits are
invented *fabulae*; but he quotes them all the same, because they are
no different from historical examples like the dream of Aeneas in
Fabius Pictor.[54]

All three of those dreams (since Ennius' Ilia was the daughter of
Aeneas) were far back in what Varro called the mythical period. But
now Quintus takes a historical example:[55]

> sed propiora videamus. cuiusnam modi est Superbi Tarquinii som-
> nium, de quo in Bruto Acci loquitur ipse?

> But let us look at something more recent. Of what sort is Tarquinius
> Superbus' dream, which he talks about himself in Accius' *Brutus?*'

What exactly is Quintus asking here? *Cuiusnam modi est?* can hardly
mean 'What genre is it?', because the genre is obvious: it is a play,
a *fabula praetexta*. At this point his concern is not primarily with poetry
or prose,[56] but with fact or fiction in *any* genre. Accius' play was on
a historical subject, so the question 'Did Tarquin really have that
dream?' is a perfectly reasonable one, even though Marcus in Book
2 does not bother to answer it.[57]

What Marcus' answer would have been, we can guess from the
contemptuous reference in *De legibus* to 'events recorded *isto modo*'.
For him, as no doubt for Cicero the author, the only *modus* that
counted as valid history was one where the author guaranteed his
report with evidence and argument; mere narrative had no authority in itself.[58] But not everyone took that view. Cicero is careful to
let us see both sides of the argument, and to give them spokesmen
of equal status. Quintus speaks not only for the naive majority, the
imperiti, but also for thinking people, readers of philosophical dia-
logues, who chose not to be bound by the scepticism of the Academy.

---

on the Delphic oracle (1.37–8), Chrysippus and Philistus on dreams (1.39); the theme
resumes after the digression with Heraclides Ponticus, Dinon, and one of the
Alexander-historians (1.46–7).

[54] 1.40–3 (*fabulae* at 40 and 43, *ficta* and *commenticium* at 42): Ennius *Ann.* 1.34–50
Skutsch and *Scaen.* 50–61 Jocelyn; Fabius Pictor *FGrH* 809 F1.

[55] 1.43: Accius *Brutus* 651–72 Dangel (= 17–38R).

[56] He ends the digression at 1.46 with *age nunc ad externa redeamus*: Greek v. Latin
is as important as prose v. poetry.

[57] Cf. *Div.* 2.136 on *multa . . . a te ex historiis prolata somnia*, not citing the examples from Ennius or Accius and dismissing those from the Greek historians (*quis
enim auctor istorum?*).

[58] Cicero *Leg.* 1.4. For the rival modes of *historia* and *aphegesis* (inquiry and story-
telling), see Wiseman (1993) 135–8.

3. *Dionysius and Plutarch*

Twenty years or so after Livy made his prefatory comment about stories more suitable to poetry, Dionysius of Halicarnassus faced the problem of narrating the conception of Romulus.

He reported as fact the rape of Ilia in the grove sacred to Mars. Someone did it[59] — but who? Some say it was one of the girl's suitors (a version hardly consistent with Ilia being a Vestal); others that it was Amulius himself, dressed in armour to terrify her (a version evidently designed to rationalise the story that Mars was responsible).[60] But those are the exceptions:

> οἱ δὲ πλεῖστοι μυθολογοῦσι τοῦ δαίμονος εἴδωλον, οὗ τὸ χωρίον ἦν, πολλὰ καὶ ἄλλα τῷ πάθει δαιμόνια ἔργα προσάπτοντες ἡλίου τε ἀφανισμὸν αἰφνίδιον καὶ ζόφον ἐν οὐρανῷ κατασχόντα.

> Most authors relate the legend that it was an apparition of the divine power to whom the place was sacred, adding to the incident many supernatural occurrences, including a sudden disappearance of the sun and darkness spread over the sky.

The apparition was bigger and more beautiful than a man; they say that it comforted the girl afterwards (by which it became clear that it was a god), and then disappeared up to the sky wrapped in a cloud.[61]

Dionysius is aware that more is involved here than just a disagreement among authorities. He suggests two possible approaches. One is to reject such stories outright because they attribute to the gods the frailties of humanity; on this view (which is that of Varro), sexual desire is 'unworthy of the incorruptible and blessed nature' of the gods. The other approach is to suppose that the substance of the universe is mixed, and that between human and divine a third category exists, a race of *daimones* who couple sometimes with mortals, sometimes with gods. It is not for a historian to decide:[62]

> ὅπως μὲν οὖν χρὴ περὶ τῶν τοιῶνδε δόξης ἔχειν, . . . οὔτε καιρὸς ἐν τῷ παρόντι διασκοπεῖν ἀρκεῖ τε ὅσα φιλοσόφοις περὶ αὐτῶν ἐλέχθη.

---

[59] Dionysius of Halicarnassus *A.R.* 1.77.1, with βιάζεταί τις τῷ τεμένει delayed for emphasis to the end of the sentence.

[60] Ibid.: τινες μὲν ἀποφαίνουσι . . . οἱ δὲ . . . (cf. Plutarch *Rom.* 4.2 for the second version).

[61] Dionysius of Halicarnassus *A.R.* 1.77.2; *Origo gentis Romanae* 20.1 (from Fabius Pictor book 1).

[62] 1.77.3 (cf. n. 22 above for Varro); *pace* Gabba (1991) 124–5, Dionysius does not endorse the first (or either) of these alternatives.

What view should we take of such matters? This is not the appropriate place to consider it; what the philosophers have said on the subject is sufficient.

The only safe thing to say is 'The Romans believe that the twins were the sons of Mars'.[63]

The next miracle story in the narrative is the suckling of the twins by the she-wolf. Dionysius reports it from Fabius Pictor as an apparently supernatural event,[64] but then offers the rationalised version in which the *lupa* was really Acca Larentia.[65] He attributes the latter to 'those who think that mythical material does not belong in historical writing', but he himself does not privilege that version. Like Livy, no doubt he wanted to satisfy readers of both persuasions.[66]

So too on the disappearance of Romulus, Dionysius juxtaposes the 'more legendary' story, that he was swept up to heaven by his father Mars, and the 'more credible' version, that he was killed by the senators.[67] But this time he adds a comment of his own:

ἔοικε δ᾿ οὐ μικρὰν ἀφορμὴν παρέχειν τοῖς θεοποιοῦσι τὰ θνητὰ καὶ εἰς οὐρανὸν ἀναβιβάζουσι τὰς ψυχὰς τῶν ἐπιφανῶν τὰ συμβάντα ἐκ τοῦ θεοῦ περὶ τὴν σύγκρισιν τοῦ ἀνδρὸς καὶ τὴν διάκρισιν.

But the things that happened by divine agency concerning both the formation and the dissolution of that man seem to provide no little material for those who make mortality divine and take the souls of famous men up to heaven.

He refers to the two mysterious eclipses of the sun that took place at the conception and the death of Romulus, even though the former had been part of his 'mythical' narrative of that event.[68]

The impression that Dionysius' sympathy did not lie with the sceptics is strengthened by his treatment of Numa. He knows, of course, the standard explanation of the Egeria story, that it was Numa's

---

[63] 2.2.3 (Dionysius' summary of book 1).
[64] 1.79.7, δαιμόνιόν τι χρῆμα. 1.83.3 for Fabius *FGrH* 809 F4(b).
[65] 1.84.4; cf. Livy 1.4.7 (*inde locum fabulae ac miraculo datum*), Plutarch *Rom.* 4.3 (ἐπὶ τὸ μυθῶδες ἐκτροπὴν τῇ φήμῃ παρασχεῖν), *Origo gentis Romanae* 21.1 (from Valerius Antias).
[66] 1.84.1. Cf. 1.8.3 for the various categories of his readership, including those who like their enjoyment undisturbed (ἀόχλητος).
[67] 2.56.2–4; for the μυθωδέστερα/πιθανώτερα contrast, cf. 1.39.1 and 41.1 on Hercules (τὰ μὲν μυθικώτερα τὰ δ᾿ ἀληθέστερα).
[68] 2.56.6, cf. 1.77.2.

'noble lie' to impress the people; but he attributes it to 'those who remove all legends from history', and conspicuously fails to endorse it himself, saying that such matters relating to the gods would require too long a discussion.[69]

When he comes to Numa's establishment of the Vesta cult, his digression on the historical evidence for the goddess's miracle-working powers is introduced with a very explicit declaration:[70]

ὅσοι μὲν οὖν τὰς ἀθέους ἀσκοῦσι φιλοσοφίας, εἰ δὴ καὶ φιλοσοφιάς αὐτὰς δεῖ καλεῖν, ἁπάσας διασύροντες τὰς ἐπιφανείας τῶν θεῶν τὰς παρ᾽ Ἕλλησιν ἢ βαρβάροις γενομένας καὶ ταύτας εἰς γέλωτα πολὺν ἄξουσι τὰς ἱστορίας ἀλαζονείαις ἀνθρωπίναις αὐτὰς ἀνατιθέντες, ὡς οὐδενὶ θεῶν μέλον ἀνθρώπων οὐδενός. ὅσοι δ᾽ οὐκ ἀπολύουσι τῆς ἀνθρωπίνης ἐπιμελείας τοὺς θεούς, ἀλλὰ καὶ τοῖς ἀγαθοῖς εὐμενεῖς εἶναι νομίζουσι καὶ τοῖς κακοῖς δυσμενεῖς διὰ πολλῆς ἐληλυθότες ἱστορίας, οὐδὲ ταύτας ὑπολήψονται τὰς ἐπιφανείας εἶναι ἀπίστους.

Those who practise the atheist philosophies (if they deserve to be called philosophies at all), who ridicule all the manifestations of the gods which have taken place among either Greeks or foreigners, will reduce these reports as well to mocking laughter and attribute them to human trickery, on the grounds that none of the gods is concerned with anything human. But those who do not absolve the gods from the care of humanity, but after going deeply into history conclude that they are favourable to the good and hostile to the wicked, will not suppose that even these manifestations are incredible.

'Going deeply into history' is just what Dionysius claimed to be doing, and this sort of subject matter was well worth recording.[71] Indeed, it was an essential part of the usefulness of history for statesmen and politicians, as Dionysius points out when narrating the part played by *daimones* in revealing a conspiracy in the ninth year of the Republic.[72]

That could hardly be further away from our Polybian preconceptions about what is appropriate to history.[73] But perhaps it would not have surprised Varro, or the Q. Cicero of De divinatione. I think

---

[69] 2.60.5–61.3 (quotation from 61.1); see above, n. 16.
[70] 2.68.1–2 (see above, nn. 33–4), citing the reports of οἱ συγγραφεῖς.
[71] 1.5.4, 3.18.1, 7.66.1–3, 11.1.4–5 (*akribeia*); 2.68.1 (πάνυ δ᾽ ἄξιον . . . ἱστορῆσαι).
[72] 5.56.1, cf. 5.54.1–3; not in Livy. (Probably from Tubero: see Wiseman [1994] 54–7.) Dionysius writing for *politikoi*: 1.8.3, 5.75.1, 11.1.1.
[73] Cf. Polybius 3.47.6–9 on the participation of gods and heroes in real events as πάσης ἱστορίας ἀλλοτριώτατον.

Emilio Gabba was mistaken in saying that Dionysius 'sought, as far
as it lay within his power, to leave aside any myth involving divine
intervention in human affairs'.[74] On the contrary, he not only related
such myths but even drew his readers' attention to the philosophical
issues involved in them.

The clearest statement of Dionysius' position comes in Book 8.
Coriolanus has yielded to his mother and withdrawn his army; the
Senate has honoured the women of Rome by the dedication of a
temple to Fortuna Muliebris. There follows an episode which Livy
omits, but which Dionysius expressly describes as 'appropriate to the
form of history'.[75] The *matronae* had had a statue of the goddess made
at their own expense; on the day of the dedication, this statue spoke,
not once but twice (so there could be no mistake), confirming the
propriety of the women's act.[76] The event was recorded in the chronicle of the *pontifices*, and Dionysius reports it for two very specific
reasons:[77]

... ἐπανορθώσεως ἕνεκα τῶν οἰομένων μήτ᾽ ἐπὶ ταῖς τιμαῖς ταῖς παρ᾽
ἀνθρώπων χαίρειν τοὺς θεοὺς μήτ᾽ ἐπὶ ταῖς ἀνοσίοις καὶ ἀδίκοις πρά-
ξεσιν ἀγανακτεῖν... ἵνα τοῖς μὲν εὐλαβεστέροις περὶ τὸ συνέχειν ἃς
παρὰ τῶν προγόνων δόξας ὑπὲρ τοῦ δαιμονίου παρέλαβον ἀμεταμέλητος
ἡ τοιαύτη προαίρεσις καὶ βεβαία διαμένῃ, τοῖς δ᾽ ὑπερορῶσι τῶν πατρίων
ἐθισμῶν καὶ μηθενὸς ποιοῦσι τὸ δαιμόνιον τῶν ἀνθρωπίνων λογισμῶν
κύριον μάλιστα μὲν ἀναθέσθαι ταύτην τὴν δόξαν, εἰ δ᾽ ἀνιάτως ἔχουσιν,
ἔτι μᾶλλον αὐτοῖς ἀπεχθάνεσθαι καὶ κακοδαιμονεστέροις εἶναι.

To correct those who think that the gods are neither pleased by honours received from mortals nor offended at unholy and unjust
acts ... [and] that those who are more scrupulous in preserving the
beliefs about the divine power which they have inherited from their
forefathers may keep their conviction firm and unwavering, while those
who despise ancestral custom and claim that the divine power has no
control over human reason may either abandon that view or, if they
are incorrigible, become even more hateful and god-forsaken.

---

[74] Gabba (1991) 118; but cf. Dionysius of Halicarnassus *A.R.* 1.40.5 (epiphany of
Hercules in 312 B.C., story promised), 2.68.3 (much more to say on Vesta's epiphanies), 6.13 (Castor and Pollux at Lake Regillus), etc. What Dionysius rejected at
2.18.3–19.1 was not myth as such (Gabba [1991] 119–20) but 'tales unworthy of
the gods' (n. 22 above).
[75] 8.56.1 (ἱστορεῖται at 56.2, ἱστορίαν at 56.4). For the ἱστορίας σχῆμα, cf. 1.41.1,
with Fox (1993) 44–5.
[76] 8.56.2–4; cf. Valerius Maximus 1.8.4 and Plutarch *Cor.* 37.3.
[77] 8.56.1 (ὡς αἱ τῶν ἱεροφαντῶν περιέχουσι γραφαί) = *Annales pontificum* fr. 20
Chassignet; cf. Frier (1979) 118.

Yet again we find that the question asked was not so much 'What is appropriate to the genre?' as 'What ought we to believe?'.

That order of priorities is even more evident in Plutarch, whose biographical format allowed him more space than Dionysius had for philosophical reflection. On the disappearance of Romulus: can we really believe that the body of a great man, and not just his soul, might be borne up to heaven? On Numa and Egeria: although the gods must love virtuous mortals, and may instruct wise rulers, surely they cannot take sexual pleasure in a mortal body? On the appearance of Castor and Pollux in the Forum at the time of the battle of Lake Regillus: why should it not be credible, when even in modern times the divine power can bring instant news of battles far away?[78] These are important questions, and Plutarch is not dogmatic about them. 'If anyone says otherwise, "broad is the way", as Bacchylides has it.'[79]

As for the speaking statue, of course it was impossible (statues have no vocal cords), and if the historical evidence forces us to believe it, then we must assume that some dream-like power of the imagination caused people to believe they heard it speak.[80] But as Plutarch knows, there is also quite another way of looking at it:

οὐ μὴν ἀλλὰ τοῖς ὑπ' εὐνοίας καὶ φιλίας πρὸς τὸν θεὸν ἄγαν ἐμπαθῶς ἔχουσι, καὶ μηδὲν ἀθετεῖν μηδ' ἀναίνεσθαι τῶν τοιούτων δυναμένοις, μέγα πρὸς πίστιν ἐστὶ τὸ θαυμάσιον καὶ μὴ καθ' ἡμᾶς τῆς τοῦ θεοῦ δυνάμεως.

Nevertheless, for those who are passionate in their devotion and love for the divine, and incapable of rejecting or denying anything of this kind, the main argument for belief is the wonderful and transcendant nature of the divine power.

On this view, miracles are impossible only in human terms: divine power is beyond our understanding. Plutarch himself urges a cautious middle way, between empty superstition and arrogant contempt for the gods.[81]

---

[78] Plutarch *Rom.* 28, *Numa* 4, *Aem.* 25; Wardman (1974) 163–6.

[79] Plutarch *Numa* 4.8. Other gnomic quotations in the same context: *Rom.* 28.6 (Pindar), *Cor.* 38.4 (Heraclitus), *Cam.* 6.4 (Delphi motto).

[80] Plutarch *Cor.* 38.3, ὅπου δ' ἡμᾶς ἡ ἱστορία πολλοῖς ἀποβιάζεται καὶ πιθανοῖς μάρτυσιν.... For Romans who believed in animate statues, cf. Lucilius 484–9M = 524–9W (on *terriculas Lamias, Fauni quas Pompiliique instituere Numae*).

[81] Plutarch *Cor.* 38.3–4; *Cam.* 6.4 for another talking statue (Juno's, at Veii).

It seems therefore that what we are disposed to think of as a matter of literary decorum was in reality a profound philosophical and theological question. Those who argued that myths had no place in history were not just defining a genre; they were putting into practice a controversial belief about the nature of the gods. Dionysius and Plutarch were both familiar with that school of thought,[82] but neither endorsed it himself, and there is no reason to suppose that they were unusual in that.[83]

4. *Valerius Maximus and Livy*

My final witness is an author whose evidential value has been long neglected because of a misconception about the purpose of his work. It is a widely held view — but one based on no evidence that I know of — that Valerius Maximus' collection of historical *exempla* was written as a handbook 'for students and practitioners of declamation'.[84] The author's own statement of his aim is set out clearly enough in the preface, which deserves quoting in full:[85]

> (1) urbis Romae exterarumque gentium facta simul ac dicta memoratu digna, quae apud alios latius diffusa sunt quam ut breviter cognosci possint, ab inlustribus electa auctoribus digerere constitui, ut documenta sumere volentibus longae inquisitionis labor absit.
> (2) nec mihi cuncta complectendi cupido incessit: quis enim omnis aevi gesta modico voluminum numero comprehenderit, aut quis compos

---

[82] No myths in history: Dionysius of Halicarnassus *A.R.* 1.84.1, 2.61.1. No divine involvement in human affairs: Dionysius of Halicarnassus *A.R.* 1.77.3, 2.56.6, 2.68.2, 8.56.1; Plutarch *Cor.* 38.3, *Cam.* 6.2–4.

[83] Cf. Cassius Dio 55.1.4 on a miraculous apparition in 9 B.C.: θαυμαστόν μὲν οὖν . . . οὐ μέντοι καὶ ἀπιστεῖν ἔχω. Dio became a historian when τὸ δαιμόνιον appeared in his sleep and encouraged him. See n. 160 below, and Millar (1964) 179–81: 'an unquestioning adherent of traditional pagan belief and observance' (179).

[84] Bloomer (1992) 1, cf. Fantham (1996) 133: 'a reference work for orators, or more likely declaimers, needing precedents for the subjects of their speeches'. *Contra* Skidmore (1996) xvi–xvii, 53–4. Wardle (1998) 12–15 hedges his bets: 'I would argue that the serious moral purpose envisaged by Skidmore should be combined with a primary audience of those involved in declamation . . .' (The reference to *declamantes* in the preface to Iulius Paris' *epitome* is evidence only for the fourth or fifth century A.D.)

[85] Text as in J. Briscoe's 1998 Teubner edition and D. R. Shackleton Bailey's Loeb (2000); R. Combès' Budé (1995) reads *alacritatis* (with the best MSS), not *claritatis*, at §4. I have added the section numbers.

mentis domesticae peregrinaeque historiae seriem felici superiorum stilo
conditam vel attentiore cura vel praestantiore facundia traditurum se
speraverit?

(3) te igitur huic coepto, penes quem hominum deorumque consensus
maris ac terrae regimen esse voluit, certissima salus patriae, Caesar,
invoco, cuius caelesti providentia virtutes, de quibus dicturus sum,
benignissime foventur, uitia severissime vindicantur:

(4) nam si prisci oratores ab Iove Optimo Maximo bene orsi sunt, si
excellentissimi vates a numine aliquo principia traxerunt, mea parvitas
eo iustius ad favorem tuum decucurrerit, quo cetera divinitas opinione
colligitur, tua praesenti fide paterno avitoque sideri par videtur, quorum eximio fulgore multum caerimoniis nostris inclutae claritatis acces-
sit: reliquos enim deos accepimus, Caesares dedimus.

(5) et quoniam initium a cultu deorum petere in animo est, de condi-
cione eius summatim disseram.

(1) I have decided to set in order a selection, from distinguished authors,
of the memorable deeds and sayings of Rome and of foreign nations,
which are too widely scattered in other writers for knowledge of them
to be acquired in a short time, in order to save those who wish to
receive the lessons the labour of long research.

(2) I have not been seized by the desire to include everything. For
who could embrace the events of all time in a small number of volumes? Who in his right mind could hope to hand on the whole
sequence of Roman and foreign history, recorded in the happy style
of previous writers, either with more careful accuracy or with more
outstanding eloquence?

(3) You therefore, Caesar, the surest salvation of our country, I invoke
for this enterprise — you whom the consensus of men and gods has
wished to be the ruler of land and sea, you whose heavenly providence most generously favours the virtues, and most strictly punishes
the vices, of which I am about to speak.

(4) For if the orators of old rightly began with Jupiter Best and Greatest,
if the most excellent bards took their beginnings from some divine
power, all the more properly will my humble self have had recourse
to your favour, in that the rest of divinity is inferred from mere opinion, whereas yours is seen by immediate faith as equal to the star of
your father and grandfather, whose exceptional brightness added much
splendid brilliance to our ceremonies; for the other gods we have
received [from the past], the Caesars we have given [to the future].

(5) And since it is my intention to seek my starting point in the worship of the gods, I shall deal briefly with its nature.

Valerius uses the idiom of historiography — not just *omnis aevi gesta*
and *historiae series* (§2), but the title phrase itself, *facta ac dicta memoratu
digna* (§1), which is reminiscent of Cicero's definition of the subject-

matter of history in *De oratore*.[86] His opening phrase, and *cupido inces-sit* in §2, seem to be borrowed from Sallust.[87] But the most striking feature of this passage is its repeated intertextual reference to a famous preface of about sixty years earlier, that of Livy himself.

The first allusion defines Valerius' purpose (§1). Livy had carefully registered the ethical value of history:[88]

> hoc illud est praecipue in cognitione rerum salubre ac frugiferum, omnis te exempli documenta in inlustri posita monumento intueri; inde tibi tuaeque rei publicae quod imitere capias, inde foedum inceptu foe-dum exitu quod vites.

> It is this in particular which is salutary and beneficial in the knowl-edge of history, that you behold lessons of every sort of example set forth in a conspicuous monument. From there you may take, for your-self and your republic, what to imitate and what, corrupt in origin and corrupt in outcome, to avoid.

Valerius repeats the key word *documenta* and applies to it the verb *sumere*, corresponding to Livy's *capias*. Failure to recognise this has resulted in some strange translations of *documenta sumere volentibus*,[89] but the allusion and the meaning are both clear enough: *documenta* is from *docere*, and history teaches.

Livy's conspicuous second-person address to the reader is trans-ferred by Valerius to the emperor (§3) — no longer the citizen of a republic choosing what to imitate or avoid, but a god-like arbiter meting out reward and punishment. Even so, Valerius' *virtutes* and *vitia* are recognisably the *quod imitere* and *quod vites* of Livy's preface. Similarly Livian are the passages where Valerius identifies accuracy

---

[86] Cicero *de Orat.* 2.63: *vult enim, quoniam in rebus magnis **memoriaque dignis** con-silia primum, deinde acta, postea eventus exspectentur, et de consiliis significari quid scriptor pro-bet et in rebus gestis declarari non solum quid **actum aut dictum** sit, sed etiam quo modo....* For *memoratu dignum*, and the more frequent *memoria dignum*, see Oakley (1998) 138–9; the idea goes back at least to Herodotus (1.16.2, 1.117 ἀξιαπηγητότατα). Servius auctus on *Aen.* 1.373 (*digna memoratu*) and Isidore *Etym.* 1.44.3 (*digna memoria*) pre-serve Verrius Flaccus' account of the *annales maximi*: Frier (1979) 27–37, 40–1.

[87] Sallust *Cat.* 6.1 (*urbem Romam*, imitated by Tacitus *Ann.* 1.1.1), 7.3 (*cupido incesserat*); cf. Guerrini (1981) 29–60, *Valerio Massimo e Sallustio*. Tony Woodman reminds me that *omne aevum* (§2) may be an allusion to Catullus 1.6, and thus to Nepos' *Chronica*.

[88] Livy *Praef.* 10; Moles (1993) 152–5.

[89] E.g. 'those who want concrete evidence' (Bloomer [1992] 14); 'those who wish to embrace the examples' (Wardle [1998] 29); 'chi volesse compulsare tali fonti' (Faranda [1971] 65). The key explanatory text is Varro *L.* 6.62, defining *documenta* as *exempla docendi causa*.

and style as the possible ways to surpass one's predecessors (§2),[90] and appeals to the poets' habit of beginning with the gods (§4).[91] Finally, where Livy had referred to the *magnitudo* of his rivals, Valerius speaks of *mea paruitas* (§4).[92]

In view of all this, and of the brute fact that in his time Livy's huge narrative was the classic statement of *domestica historia*, one might expect Valerius to share Livy's attitude to stories of miracles and divine intervention. But no: in his first book alone, he presents gods and goddesses acting as protagonists in one story after another,[93] and his moral lesson on the ubiquity of divine concern for mortals, and divine punishment of wickedness, is spelt out again and again.[94]

The fire burns on Servius Tullius' head;[95] the voice of Silvanus is heard in the wood;[96] Castor and Pollux fight for the Romans at Lake Regillus;[97] T. Latinius reports his vision to the Senate, and is cured;[98] the statue of Fortuna addresses the matrons;[99] queen Juno of Veii says she wants to go to Rome;[100] a divine vision warns Decius Mus and his colleague in a dream;[101] the angry Hercules blinds Appius Claudius and wipes out the Potitii.[102] Miracle stories which Livy either omits altogether or keeps in careful *oratio obliqua* are narrated by Valerius in a confident indicative mode which leaves no room for doubt.[103]

---

[90] Livy *Praef.* 2, *novi semper scriptores aut in rebus certius aliquid allaturos se aut scribendi arte rudem vetustatem superaturos credunt.* Parallel noted by Herkommer (1968) 79 n. 1.

[91] Livy *Praef.* 13, *precationibus deorum dearumque, si ut poetis nobis quoque mos esset . . .*; cf. n. 1 above.

[92] Livy *Praef.* 3, *nobilitate ac magnitudine eorum qui nomini officient meo consoler.* Valerius perhaps alludes to his own *cognomen* Maximus, itself evidently a badge of *nobilitas* (Skidmore [1996] 113–7); but if so, the allusion is modest, not 'ludic' (Wardle [1998] 70).

[93] 1.1.18 (Apollo), 1.1.19 (Aesculapius), 1.1.ext.1 (Juno), 1.6.12 (Jupiter).

[94] 1.1.ext.3, *lento enim gradu ad vindictam sui divina procedit ira*; 1.6.1, *sic humana consilia castigantur ubi se caelestibus praeferunt*; 1.6.12, *quibus apparet caelestium numen . . . voluisse*; 1.7.1, *quid ergo aliud putamus quam divino numine effectum . . .?*; 1.8.2, *numen ipsius dei . . . comprobavit.*

[95] 1.6.1 (Livy 1.39.1, *ferunt*). Also L. Marcius in 211 B.C.: 1.6.2 (Livy 25.39.16, *miracula addunt*).

[96] 1.8.5 (Livy 2.7.2, *adiciunt miracula*).

[97] 1.8.1 (not in Livy: see n. 13 above).

[98] 1.7.4 (Livy 2.36.8, *traditum memoriae est*).

[99] 1.8.4 (not in Livy); see above, nn. 75–7, 80–1.

[100] 1.8.3 (Livy 5.22.6, *fabulae adiectum est*).

[101] 1.7.3 (Livy 8.6.9, *dicitur*).

[102] 1.1.17 (Livy 9.29.10, *traditur*). On this story see Mueller ch. 16 above.

[103] Not only in book 1: see also 5.6.2 on M. Curtius and the chasm (Livy 7.6.1, *dicitur, ferunt*), 5.6.3 on Genucius Cipus (not in Livy: see n. 112 below), 8.1.abs.5 on Tuccia (Livy *Per.* 20, cf. nn. 29–36 above).

Particularly revealing is what he does with the material he takes from Cicero. In Book 2 of Cicero's *De natura deorum*, the Stoic spokesman Lucilius Balbus uses divine epiphanies as part of his argument for the existence of the gods; for instance, on the day of the battle of Pydna in 168 B.C., P. Vatienus of Reate was met by two young men on white horses who told him that king Perses had just been captured. In book 3, however, C. Cotta pours scorn on all such stories as mere unsubstantiated rumour. Valerius ignores the sceptic's point, and reports the epiphany story as simple fact,[104] just as he does with two dream stories adduced by Quintus Cicero in Book 1 of *De divinatione* and refuted by Marcus in Book 2.[105]

Valerius was writing moral protreptic, not philosophical argument. He sets out his position with admirable clarity:[106]

> nec me praeterit de motu et voce deorum immortalium humanis oculis auribusque percepto quam in ancipiti opinione aestimatio versetur, sed quia non nova dicuntur sed tradita repetuntur, fidem auctores vindicent: nostrum sit inclutis litterarum monumentis consecrata perinde ac vana non refugisse.

> I am not unaware how controversial is the question of the perception by human sight and hearing of the movement and voices of the immortal gods. But since what is said is not new, but a repetition of what has been handed down, my authorities may defend their own credibility. Let it be my part not to have avoided, as if they were false, events that have been consecrated in famous literary monuments.

The particular event that gave rise to this declaration was the miraculous double migration of the Penates from Alba Longa back to their home in Lavinium. We know some of the famous literary monuments in which that story was consecrated: the fourth book of the pontiffs' *Annales maximi*,[107] the second book of L. Cincius Alimentus' history,[108] the second book of L. Iulius Caesar's *Pontificalia*,[109] the first

---

[104] Cicero *ND* 2.6 (3.11–13); Valerius Maximus 1.8.1, with close verbal parallels. For the name (not Vatinius) see Taylor (1960) 262–3.

[105] Cicero *Div.* 1.56 and 59 (2.136–41); Valerius Maximus 1.7.5–6, verbal parallels again.

[106] Valerius Maximus 1.8.7. Wardle (1998) 59 unfortunately translates Kempf's 1888 Teubner text, which made nonsense of the passage by printing Novák's conjecture *vera* for *vana* in the final phrase.

[107] *Origo gentis Romanae* 17.3 = *Annales pontificum* fr. 3 Chassignet; Frier (1979) 50–2.

[108] *Origo gentis Romanae* 17.3 = *FGrH* 810 F9 (unnecessarily categorised as doubtful); Richard (1983) 165–6.

[109] *Origo gentis Romanae* 17.3, cf. 9.6, 15.5; Richard (1983) 139.

book of Q. Aelius Tubero's *Historiae*,[110] and the first book of Dionysius of Halicarnassus' *Roman Antiquities*.[111] Not one of them was the work of a poet.

5. *Poetry and Annales*

So Varro, Cicero, Dionysius, Plutarch and Valerius Maximus have brought us to an unexpected conclusion. Livy's comment on what is appropriate to poets' stories, far from being a truism, turns out to be a partisan statement of philosophical scepticism. Other historians took the opposite view, and did accept miracle stories and divine epiphanies as a proper part of their subject matter. The issue was one not of literary convention but of theological belief.

The common ground of prose and poetry is well illustrated by an item in Valerius Maximus' chapter on patriotism. The praetor Genucius Cipus, leaving the city on campaign, finds that he has grown horns; the soothsayers tell him that it signifies he will be king if he returns; he goes into voluntary exile. The same story is told in Ovid's *Metamorphoses*.[112] Valerius' account of the Penates' migration offers a similar parallel. He introduces it as something 'recognised in its own time [which] has come down to later generations' — just what Virgil puts more succinctly when he has a miracle to report: *prisca fides facto, sed fama perennis*.[113]

It was a way of thinking very familiar to the Romans. To believe in miracles and divine intervention is to believe that the gods are concerned with the world of humans, that they take note of moral excellence and its opposite, and reward or punish it accordingly. Cicero, in his guise as legislator, made it the programme of his law-code to secure that belief in the minds of the citizens, and we

---

[110] *Origo gentis Romanae* 17.3, not in Peter's *HRR* fragments. Preliminary material on Tubero in Wiseman (1979) 135–9.

[111] Dionysius of Halicarnassus *A.R.* 1.67.2 (θαῦμα μέγιστον λέγεται γενέσθαι). Possibly from Timaeus (cf. *FGrH* 566 F59); but Dionysius used authors who used the pontifical chronicle (*A.R.* 1.73.1, 1.74.3, 4.2.1, 7.1.6, 8.56.1), and Tubero was one of his Roman patrons (Dionysius of Halicarnassus *Thuc.* 1).

[112] Valerius Maximus 5.6.3, *novi atque inauditi generis prodigium*; Ovid *Met.* 15.565–621. Pliny (*Nat.* 11.123) calls Cipus *fabulosus*, like Actaeon.

[113] Valerius Maximus 1.8.7, *quod suo saeculo cognitum manavit ad posteros* (trans. Wardle [1998] 59); Virgil *Aen.* 9.79. Cf. Ovid *Met.* 1.400 (*quis hoc credat, nisi sit pro teste vetustas?*), *Fast.* 4.203–4 (*pro magno teste vetustas creditur: acceptam parce movere fidem*).

have seen both Dionysius and Valerius Maximus deliberately select-
ing their material to do the same.[114]

So it should not be a surprise to find that the *pontifices* — whose
duty it was to instruct the people,[115] and whose chronicle was consulted as a repertory of precedent and example[116] — included in that
chronicle such exemplary paradigms of divine power as the migrat-
ing Penates and the speaking statue of Fortuna Muliebris.[117] They
also included one of the weirdest of all such manifestations, the phan-
tom phallus that appeared in the royal hearth and fathered a miraculous child on queen Tanaquil's maidservant. Dionysius, Pliny and
Plutarch all have that story, and so does Ovid, in a poem about
'sacred matters drawn from the old *annales*'.[118] We may as well burn
the *annales*, says Quintus Cicero, if we are not going to believe in
the gods' concern for mortals. He was talking about the story of
Attus Navius and the whetstone, which no doubt also featured in
the pontiffs' chronicle.[119]

Modern historians treasure the idea of the *annales pontificum* as an
ancient archive, guaranteeing at least the framework of early Roman
history.[120] In my view that is a somewhat sanguine idea. It was certainly an archive, but what the pontiffs chose to record for the good
of the citizens was not necessarily what the historian of *res gestae*
would like to know. It is ironic that the very item which is supposed
to show how far the chronicle went back — the report in the *annales
maximi* of an eclipse on 21 June 'about 350 years after the foundation of the city' — is cited by Cicero not from a historian but from
Ennius' epic poem.[121] Indeed, Ennius evidently took the title, and

[114] Cicero *Leg.* 2.15–16; see above, nn. 70, 77 (Dionysius), 94 (Valerius).

[115] Livy 1.20.6–7, on Numa's appointment of the first *pontifex*: . . . *ut esset quo consultum plebes veniret . . . ut idem pontifex edoceret . . .* Cicero *de Orat.* 2.52, on the notice-
board put up in the house of the *pontifex maximus: potestas ut esset populo cognoscendi.*

[116] Livy 8.18.11–12, 27.8.8–9; Frier (1979) 98–100.

[117] See above, nn. 77, 107.

[118] Dionysius of Halicarnassus *A.R.* 4.2.1–3 = *Annales pontificum* fr. 13 Chassignet;
Pliny *Nat.* 36.204, Plutarch *Mor.* 323b–c (*De fortuna Romanorum* 10); Ovid *Fast.*
6.625–36; also Arnobius *Adv. nat.* 5.18. *sacra . . . annalibus eruta priscis:* Ovid *Fast.* 1.7,
cf. 4.11.

[119] Cicero *Div.* 1.33 (n. 50 above); cf. Frier (1979) 222.

[120] See most recently Cornell (1995) 13–15 and Oakley (1997) 24–7. Servius auctus (on *Aen.* 1.373) says the *pontifex maximus* recorded *digna memoratu . . . domi militiaeque terra marique gesta;* but that evidently reflects the eighty-book edition described
by Verrius Flaccus (Frier [1979] 27–37).

[121] Cicero *Rep.* 1.25 = *Annales pontificum* fr. 8 Chassignet = Ennius *Ann.* fr. 153

perhaps the concept, of his *Annales* from the pontiffs' chronicle, long before any prose writer ever used that title for a historical work.[122]

The word *annales* occurs in the first book of the *Aeneid*, where the shipwrecked hero introduces himself to his disguised mother:[123]

> o dea, si prima repetens ab origine pergam
> et vacet annalis nostrorum audire laborum,
> ante diem clauso componet Vesper Olympo.
> nos Troia antiqua, si vestras forte per auris
> Troiae nomen iit, diversa per aequora vectos
> forte sua Libycis tempestas appulit oris.
> sum pius Aeneas, raptos qui ex hoste penatis
> classe veho mecum, fama super aethera notus;
> Italiam quaero patriam, et genus ab Iove summo.

> O goddess, if I were to start at the beginning and retrace our whole story, and if you had the time to listen to the annals of our suffering, before I finish the doors of Olympus would close and the Evening Star would lay the day to rest. We come from the ancient city of Troy, if the name of Troy has ever reached your ears. We have sailed many seas and by the chance of the winds we have been driven ashore here in Libya. I am Aeneas, known for my devotion. I carry with me on my ships the gods of my house, the Penates, wrested from my enemies, and my fame has reached beyond the skies. I am searching for my fatherland in Italy. My descent is from highest Jupiter.'

By *annales* in line 373 Aeneas refers to the long story he will eventually tell in Books 2–3, a narrative full of miracles and divine interventions. But the ancient commentators took the word to be a specific allusion to the pontiffs' chronicle; indeed, it is from their commentary on that line that much of our information about the chronicle derives.[124] They inferred that Aeneas is to be thought of as a *pontifex*, which seems reasonable enough given his self-definition as *pius Aeneas* and the carrier of the Penates.

Sk (*ex hoc die quem apud Ennium et in annalibus maximis consignatum videmus*); Skutsch (1985) 311–13. The year date is very uncertain: see most recently Humm (2000) 106–9.

[122] Skutsch (1985) 6–7; Frier (1979) 216–19. The first certain use of *Annales* as the title of a prose history was evidently by L. Piso *censorius* after 120 B.C.: Wiseman (1979) 12–16, Forsythe (1994) 42 ('Piso's work is the earliest Roman history for which a strictly annalistic treatment of the early and middle republic is attested').

[123] Virgil *Aen.* 1.372–80, trans. D. West (Penguin Classics).

[124] Macrobius 3.2.17; Servius auctus on *Aen.* 1.373.

The *Aeneid* was being composed at the time of Augustus' restoration of the 82 temples, when the people wanted him to be *pontifex maximus*.[125] Horace in the last of his 'Roman Odes' was repeating the traditional lesson that the gods control everything, and success depends on their goodwill.[126] Aeneas the pious *pontifex*, ancestor of Augustus, fits well into that context.

On 6 March 12 B.C., Augustus finally did become *pontifex maximus*, to the huge enthusiasm of the Roman people;[127] and at some point not far distant from that date (between Cicero and Verrius Flaccus), a vast new eighty-book edition of the *annales pontificum* was produced.[128] It seems to have been a characteristically Augustan project. Just like the great lists of consuls and *triumphatores* that decorated his triumphal arch, or the annotated statues of the heroes of the Roman past that thronged his new Forum, so too the accumulated (and no doubt expanded) documentation of all past *pontifices maximi* would encompass the whole of Roman history in a teleological sequence culminating in Augustus himself.[129]

If we are right to see miracle stories and reports of divine intervention as part of the pontiffs' traditional material — and two of the four certain fragments of the eighty-book edition are clear examples of that[130] — it is worth remembering that Augustus' own memoirs were full of such stories,[131] and according to Suetonius one of his

---

[125] Augustus *RG* 10.2 (*populo id sacerdotium deferente mihi*), 20.4 (temples, begun in 28 B.C.).

[126] Horace *Odes* 3.6, esp. 5–6: *dis te minorem quod geris, imperas: hinc omne principium, huc refer exitum*. Compare Cicero *Leg.* 2.15: *sit igitur hoc iam a principio persuasum civibus, dominos esse omnium ac moderatores deos, eaque quae gerantur eorum geri iudicio ac numine*.

[127] Augustus *RG* 10.2, cf. Ovid *Fast.* 3.415–28. For the importance of the pontificate in Augustus' self-presentation, see Bowersock (1990).

[128] Frier (1979) 193–200; Chassignet (1996) xxxvi–xl refuses to accept Frier's conclusion, but nowhere engages with his arguments.

[129] For learning and scholarship as tools of Augustan authority, cf. Wallace-Hadrill (1997) 11–22; the eighty books were 'a great collection of aitiological explanations of Roman rites and institutions' (Rawson [1991] 15).

[130] *Annales pontificum* frr. 3 and 5 Chassignet (*Origo gentis Romanae* 17.3, 18.3); the others are frr. 4 and 7 (ibid. 17.5 and Aulus Gellius 4.5.1–6).

[131] Augustus *De vita sua* frr. 4, 6, 7, 12 Malcovati (Tertullian *De anim.* 46; Pliny *Nat.* 2.93; Servius auctus on *Ecl.* 9.46; Plutarch *Brut.* 41.5): prophetic visions seen by Cicero and M. Artorius, the comet signifying *Caesaris animam inter deorum immortalium numina receptam*, and the instant punishment of a *haruspex* who revealed the secrets of the gods. For the autobiography and its context, see Ando (2000) 139–43: 'to remind people of the reasons for their gratitude and their loyalty'. Sulla's memoirs were similarly full of divine interventions (frr. 6, 8, 9, 15, 16, 18, 21 P); and a later imperial author, Marcus Aurelius in his *Meditations* (2.11, 9.27, 12.28), was

favourite entertainments was listening to *aretalogi*, story-tellers who specialised in tales of the deeds and power of the gods.[132] Yet that was the type of story that Livy in his preface saw as appropriate to poetry.

Perhaps this is the place to bring in something Livy says in book 5, where the phraseology, clearly reminiscent of the passage in the preface, may cast some light on what sort of poetry he had in mind.[133]

> sed in rebus tam antiquis si quae similia veris sint pro veris accipiantur, satis habeam; haec ad ostentationem scenae gaudentis miraculis aptiora quam ad fidem neque adfirmare neque refellere est operae pretium.

> But in matters so ancient let me be content if some things like the truth are accepted as true. It is not worth the trouble either to endorse or to refute these things: they are more appropriate to the ostentation of the stage, which delights in miracles, than to credibility.

This refers to an episode which Livy carefully introduces as a *fabula*, the next act of which was the speech of Juno Regina, signifying her willingness to go to Rome.[134] Since *fabula* can also mean the plot of a play, perhaps, as in Varro,[135] the *poetae* Livy was thinking of were dramatists.

The stage that delighted in miracles was among other things a vehicle for the moral and political education of the Roman people,[136] and that included instruction about the gods — how they helped Rome,[137] how they championed virtue,[138] how they punished sinners.[139] That is something not often mentioned in histories of Roman

---

quite sure that the gods exist, care about human affairs, and communicate their will through dreams and oracles.

[132] Suetonius *Aug.* 74. Examples of aretalogy are listed, with bibliography, in Engelmann (1975) 37, 55–6.

[133] Livy 5.21.9. The echo of *Praef.* 6 is noted by (e.g.) Moles (1993) 148–9, Kraus (1994) 283–4, Forsythe (1999) 43.

[134] Livy 5.21.8 (*inseritur huic loco fabula*), 5.22.6 (*inde fabulae adiectum est vocem quoque dicentis velle auditam*). *Fabula praetexta* inferred by Ribbeck (1881).

[135] Augustine *CD* 6.5 (= Varro, *Ant. div.* frr. 7–10 Cardauns), cf. 6.6 (on *di poetici theatrici ludicri scaenici*).

[136] Moral: full documentation and discussion in Rawson (1991) 570–81. Political: Polybius 6.56.8 and 11, with Zorzetti (1980) 64–5; Cicero *Rab. Post.* 29, with Leigh (1996) 186–8.

[137] Plautus *Am.* 41–5 (gods in tragedies reporting their benefactions).

[138] Ovid *Fast.* 4.326 (the miracle of Magna Mater and Q. Claudia).

[139] Cicero *S. Rosc.* 66–7, *Pis.* 46, *Leg.* 1.40, *Ac.* 2.89, *Har.* 39 (the Furies and their blazing torches as a commonplace of tragedy).

drama, but the evidence for it is clear enough. Nor is it often mentioned in accounts of the pontiffs' chronicle that those responsible for the eighty-book edition saw fit to include (at Book 11) a learned explanation for an iambic *senarius* line, *malum consilium consultori pessimum est*, allegedly sung by children round the city when the wicked machinations of Etruscan *haruspices* were foiled.[140] Perhaps it was a catch-phrase from a popular play on the subject; at any rate, it suggests common ground in the preoccupations of the pontiffs and the stage.

What I think may have happened is this.

First, it was an ancient custom (though we do not know how ancient) for the *pontifex maximus* to put up in the public part of his house a notice-board listing events for the information of the Roman people. According to Cato, crop failures and eclipses were characteristic items; no doubt the main purpose was to make known items that might reveal the gods' attitude towards Rome, and thus to encourage the citizens in pious and god–fearing behaviour.[141]

This material was also accumulated into a chronicle, variously known as *annales publici*,[142] *annales populi Romani*,[143] *annales pontificum*,[144] or *annales maximi*.[145] Presumably the chronicle consisted of a series of volumes,[146] added to by successive *pontifices maximi*, and kept in a place where they could be consulted by the learned and literate.[147]

I imagine the ordinary people had little use for the chronicle. A bulletin board was one thing (Roman citizens were used to reading notices, or having notices read to them),[148] but they needed no consolidated archive to discover how the immortal gods had manifested

---

[140] *Annales pontificum* fr. 8 Chassignet (Aulus Gellius 4.5.5). Pliny *Nat.* 28.15 (citing *annales*) for a similar story.

[141] Cicero *de Orat.* 2.52, Servius auctus on *Aen.* 1.373, Dionysius of Halicarnassus *A.R.* 1.74.3; Cato *Origines* fr. 77P = *Annales pontificum* fr. 2 Chassignet (Aulus Gellius 2.28.6). Cf. Livy 1.20.6 on the *pontifices'* responsibility for *omnia publica privataque sacra*.

[142] Cicero *Rep.* 2.28; Seneca *Cons. Pol.* 14.2; Diomedes *Gramm. Lat.* 1.484K.

[143] Cicero *Dom.* 86.

[144] Cicero *Leg.* 1.2.6; *Origo gentis Romanae* preface, 17.3, 17.5, 18.3.

[145] Cicero *de Orat.* 2.52, *Rep.* 1.25; Aulus Gellius 4.5.6; Festus (Paulus) 113L; Macrobius 3.2.17; Servius auctus on *Aen.* 1.373.

[146] Cf. Horace *Ep.* 2.1.26 (*pontificum libros*), which could be a reference to the chronicle. Its original form may be inferred by comparison with the evidence for Etruscan 'linen books' in the fourth century B.C.: see most recently Torelli (1996) 13–22, esp. 19–20, figs. 2–3.

[147] E.g. by Ennius, and probably by L. Cincius Alimentus about 200 B.C.: see above, nn. 121 and 108.

[148] Public notices: e.g. Cicero *Agr.* 2.13 (text of law), *Att.* 2.20.4, 4.3.3 (edicts, speeches); cf. Millar (1998) 45, 103. Private notices (lost property, debts, etc): e.g. Plautus *Rud.* 1294; Cicero *Quinct.* 50, *Att.* 1.18.8; Prop. 3.23.23; Seneca *Ben.* 4.12.2.

their power and majesty in times past. They had prophets (*uates*) to tell them that, and to keep the fear of divine punishment firmly before their eyes.[149] And those who were too sophisticated to 'listen to a prophet' (one of the signs of superstition, according to Cicero) would get the same message from the performances at the *ludi scaenici*.[150]

Part of the prophets' task was taken over by the poets of early Roman literature (which is why in post-Varronian Latin *uates* can also mean a poet).[151] In the preface to Book 7 of his *Annales*, a famous passage, Ennius carefully distanced himself from the Saturnian metre of 'the Fauns and the *vates*', but his subject-matter, especially in the early books, must have substantially overlapped with theirs.[152] About seventy years later, L. Piso the ex-censor published a dry historical chronicle in prose — a very different author and a very different work, but he evidently called it *Annales*, and what it had in common with Ennius' epic poem may be seen from how they dealt with the Trojan pre-history of their subject. Ennius' Anchises foretells the future, Venus having given her lover the power of prophecy; Piso's Aeneas passes through the victorious Greek forces at Troy by a miracle, thanks to his piety.[153] Either of those items could have come from the pontiffs' chronicle, which indeed both authors evidently used.[154]

It is difficult for moderns to imagine a world in which prophecy, poetry, history and moral exhortation were not always thought of as separate conceptual categories. The best evidence is provided not by the great thinkers but by the commonplace minds of antiquity. Here is Diodorus Siculus in the preface to his *Universal History*:[155]

---

[149] Lucretius 1.102–9 and Dionysius of Halicarnassus *A.R.* 5.54.3, with Wiseman (1994) 49–67. Cf. Livy 25.1.7–10 (*vates* in the Forum, 213 B.C.); Isidore *Orig.* 6.8.12 (*praecepta* of the *vates* Marcius).

[150] See above, nn. 137–9. Cicero *Diu.* 2.149 on *superstitio*: *instat enim et urget et quo te cumque verteris persequitur, sive tu vatem sive tu omen audieris . . .*

[151] See also Pasco-Pranger ch. 15 above.

[152] Ennius *Ann.* frr. 206–7 Skutsch (quoted by Varro *L.* 7.36; Cicero *Brut.* 71, 75–6, *Orat.* 157, 171, *Diu.* 1.114; Quintilian *Inst.* 9.4.115; *Origo gentis Romanae* 4.5); cf. frr. 54–5 and 110–11 Sk (Romulus' deification), 113 Sk (Egeria), 139 Sk (Lucumo and the eagle), etc.

[153] Ennius *Ann.* fr. 15–16 Skutsch; Piso fr. 3 Forsythe (= 2P). Forsythe (1994) 96–7 wrongly translates *miraculo* as 'by way of inspiring awe and amazement': awe and amazement are the result, not the cause, of the *miraculum*, as is clear from Livy (5.46.3) on the similar story of Fabius Dorsuo.

[154] Ennius: n. 121 above. Piso fr. 33 Forsythe = *Annales pontificum* fr. 5 Chassignet (*Origo gentis Romanae* 18.3), a story of divine punishment.

[155] Diodorus Siculus 1.2.2, cf. Polybius 6.56.12; Polybius, not a commonplace mind, treats it as a means of social control.

εἰ γὰρ ἡ τῶν ἐν ᾅδου μυθολογία τὴν ὑπόθεσιν πεπλασμένην ἔχουσα πολλὰ
συμβάλλεται τοῖς ἀνθρώποις πρὸς εὐσέβειαν καὶ δικαιοσύνην, πόσῳ
μᾶλλον ὑποληπτέον τὴν προφῆτιν τῆς ἀληθείας ἱστορίαν, τῆς ὅλη φιλοσοφίας οἱονεὶ μητρόπολιν οὖσαν, ἐπισκευάσθαι τὰ ἤθη μᾶλλον πρὸς καλοά-
γαθίαν;

If the [poets'] mythology of Hades, fictitious though its subject-matter
is, makes a great contribution to piety and justice among men, how
much more must we assume that the prophetess of truth, history, which
is as it were the mother-city of philosophy in general, is even more
able to equip men's characters for a noble way of life?

Narrative set in the underworld was reserved to the poets. So too
was narrative set in heaven, as Servius remarks about the *Aeneid*:[156]

... constat ex divinis humanisque personis, continens vera cum fictis;
nam Aeneam ad Italiam venisse manifestum est, Venerem vero locu-
tam cum Iove missumve Mercurium constat esse compositum.

It is made up of divine and human characters, and contains both truth
and fiction; for Aeneas' journey to Italy is plain fact, whereas Venus'
conversation with Jupiter and the mission of Mercury are agreed to
be invented.

Virgil himself marks the transition from the underworld back to the
historical mode by the passage of Aeneas through the ivory gate.[157]
Everything that happens on earth, including divine manifestations
and even Jupiter brought down to earth to bargain with Numa, could
appear equally in a historian, and for the same hortatory purpose.[158]

P. Mucius Scaevola, who was *pontifex maximus* from 130 to about
115 B.C., ended the practice of putting up the notice-board in his
house. Presumably, though we cannot be sure, that means that under
the next seven *pontifices maximi* there were no further additions to the

---

[156] Servius on *Aen.* 1 preface. The clearest statement is by an anonymous poet
of the first century A.D. (*Aetna* 74–91), inveighing against the stage (*plurima pars
scaenae rerum est fallacia*, 75) and the *mentiti vates* (79): his examples of their *mendosae
vulgata licentia famae* (74, cf. *libertas* at 91) are the sinners and law-givers in the underworld, the wars of the gods, and Jupiter's adulterous disguises.

[157] Virgil, *Aen.* 6.893–9. Cf. Donatus *vita Verg.* 38 and ps.Probus, *vita Verg. ad fin.*,
quoting a poem on Augustus' refusal to allow the *Aeneid* to be burned: *tu, maxime
Caesar, non sinis et Latiae consulis historiae.* According to Servius (on *Aen.* 1.382), Lucan's
epic was a *historia*, not a *poema*; it is noteworthy that the underworld narrative is
not in the poet's voice but at third hand, as the revived corpse tells what he says
the ghosts told him (Lucan 6.776–9).

[158] Valerius Antias fr. 6P (Arnobius *Adv. nat.* 5.1); cf. Wiseman (1998) 21–3.

pontiffs' chronicle.[159] But during those hundred years there was plenty
of material to be recorded, as the disasters of the dying Republic
offered evidence of the gods' anger. We see the late Republic through
the rational eyes of Cicero, but other sources can give us a different
angle: Dio, for instance, reveals the anxiety of the people in 55–54
B.C. when Gabinius restored the king of Egypt against the express
instructions of the Sibyl.[160]

The prophets were busy throughout that time.[161] So too were the
historians, the poets and the playwrights, recording and dramatising
the catastrophes.[162] When the crisis was eventually over, the charis-
matic son of Divus Iulius would find no shortage of pious examples
and moral paradigms to present to the grateful people, whether in
his own memoirs or in a great new edition of the pontiffs' chronicle.[163] What I think we have to infer is a complex process of mutual
borrowing and mutual influence among the poets, the prose-writers
and the *pontifices*, lasting from at least the third century B.C. to the
time of Augustus. The eighty books of the new pontiffs' chronicle
will have contained a vast amount of stuff taken from literary sources,
but those sources themselves may well have been influenced by the
chronicle in its earlier manifestations. And the whole enterprise would
have been meaningless without the fundamental motivation that we
have found in one ancient source after another — the need to understand the true relationship between gods and men.

If this is a credible reconstruction, then Livy's position becomes
a little clearer. I take it that when he wrote his preface, at a time
when guilt and anxiety were still prevalent, the old pontiffs' chronicle was largely forgotten and the new one not yet created. What
we see in him is not so much Augustan piety as a tolerant and patriotic form of Ciceronian scepticism.

---

[159] L. Metellus Delmaticus, ?115–103 B.C.; Cn. Domitius Ahenobarbus, 103–?89;
Q. Mucius Scaevola, ?89–82; Q. Metellus Pius, 82–63; C. Iulius Caesar, 63–44;
M. Aemilius Lepidus, 44–12.

[160] Cassius Dio 39.15.1–4, 55.3, 56.4, 59.3, 60.4–61.4 (esp. 61.1 on the Tiber
flood, 61.3 on the anger of τὸ δαιμόνιον); cf. n. 83 above.

[161] E.g. Cicero *Div.* 1.4 and Plutarch *Mar.* 42.4 (87 B.C.); Sallust *Hist.* 1.67.3M
(78 B.C.); Cicero *Cons.* ap. *Div.* 1.18 (63 B.C.).

[162] Playwrights: no fragments or titles known, but lost plays — on the death of
C. Gracchus, the crossing of the Rubicon, the Ides of March — are inferred by
Wiseman (1998) 52–63 and Weinstock (1971) 353–4.

[163] See above, nn. 125–31.

For Livy, divine intervention was not appropriate to 'uncorrupted' history — but we know that other historians thought it was. For Cicero, different rules applied when history was written in prose or in verse — but Quintus had had to ask him whether that was his view, which shows that not everybody thought so.[164] The very fact that purists tried to insist on rational criteria entitles us to infer that the general attitude was different from theirs. Even in the sophisticated Rome of the first century B.C., for many readers the distinction between the proper pursuits of poets and historians was far from clear-cut, and certainly not a simple matter of literary genre.

---

[164] Livy, *Praef.* 6; Cicero *Leg.* 1.5.

BIBLIOGRAPHY

Ahl, F. M. 1976. *Lucan: an Introduction*. Ithaca.
—— 1985. *Metaformations: Soundplay and Wordplay in Ovid and Other Classical Poets*. Ithaca.
Alonso-Núñez, J. M. 1987. 'An Augustan World History: The *Historiae Philippicae* of Pompeius Trogus', *G&R* 24, 56–72.
—— 1990. 'The Emergence of Universal History from the 4th to the 2nd Centuries B.C.', in Verdin, Schepens and De Keyser 1990, 174–92.
—— 1992. *La Historia Universal de Pompeyo Trogo*. Madrid.
Altheim, F. 1951–3. *Römische Religionsgeschichte*. 2nd edition. 2 vols. Baden-Baden.
Altheim F. and Stiehl, R. (eds.) 1965. *Die Araber in der alten Welt* ii. *Bis zur Reichstrennung*. Berlin.
Alton, E. H., Wormell, D. E., Courtney, E. (eds.) 1997. *P. Ovidi Nasonis Fastorum libri sex*. 4th edition. Leipzig.
Ancona, R. 1994. *Time and the Erotic in Horace's Odes*. Durham, NC.
Anderson, A. R. 1928. 'Heracles and his Successors', *HSCPh* 39, 7–58.
Anderson, J. C. 1984. *The Historical Topography of the Imperial Fora*. Brussels.
Anderson, M. J. 1997. *The Fall of Troy in Early Greek Poetry and Art*. Oxford.
Anderson, W. S. 1963. 'Multiple Change in the *Metamorphoses*', *TAPhA* 94, 1–27.
—— (ed.) 1977. *P. Ovidi Nasonis Metamorphoses*, Leipzig.
Ando, C. 1999. 'Was Rome a polis?', *ClAnt* 18, 5–34.
—— 2000. *Imperial Ideology and Provincial Loyalty in the Roman Empire*. Berkeley.
Arnold, B. 1994. 'The Literary Experience of Vergil's Fourth Eclogue', *CJ* 90, 143–60.
Arrigoni, G. 1982. *Camilla, amazzone e sacerdotessa di Diana*. Milan.
Ash, R. 1998. 'Waving the White Flag: Surrender Scenes at Livy 9.5–6 and Tacitus, *Histories* 3.31 and 4.62', *G&R* 45, 27–44.
—— 1999. *Ordering Anarchy: Armies and Leaders in Tacitus' Histories*. London.
Astin, A. E. 1967. *Scipio Aemilianus*. Oxford.
—— 1978. *Cato the Censor*. Oxford.
Austin, R. G. 1964. *P.Vergili Maronis Aeneidos: Liber Secundus*. Oxford.
—— 1977. *P.Vergili Maronis Aeneidos: Liber Sextus*. Oxford.
Badian, E. 1966. 'The Early Historians', in Dorey 1966, 1–38.
Bakhtin, M. 1981. *The Dialogic Imagination: Four Essays*, tr. C. Emerson and M. Holquist. Austin.
Baldo, G. 1987. 'Il codice epico nelle Metamorfosi di Ovidio', *MD* 16, 109–31.
Bandera, C. 1981. 'Sacrificial Levels in Virgil's *Aeneid*', *Arethusa* 14, 217–39.
Barber, G. L. 1935. *The Historian Ephorus*. Cambridge.
Barchiesi, A. 1990. 'Voci e istanze narrative nelle Metamorfosi di Ovidio', *MD* 23, 55–96.
—— 1994. *Il poeta e il principe: Ovidio e il discorso augusteo*. Rome.
—— 1996. 'Poetry, Praise, and Patronage: Simonides in Book 4 of Horace's *Odes*', *ClAnt* 15, 5–47.
—— 1997. *The Poet and the Prince: Ovid and Augustan Discourse* (translation of Barchiesi 1994). Berkeley.
—— 1997a. 'Virgilian Narrative: Ecphrasis', in Martindale 1997, 271–81.
—— 1997b. 'Endgames: Ovid's *Metamorphoses* 15 and *Fasti* 6', in Roberts, Dunn and Fowler 1997, 181–208.

—— 1998. 'The Statue of Athena at Troy and Carthage', in Knox and Foss 1998, 130–40.

Bardon, H. and Verdière, R. (eds.) 1971. *Vergiliana. Recherches sur Virgile.* Leiden.

Barker, D. 1996. '"The Golden Age Is Proclaimed"? The *Carmen Saeculare* and the Renascence of the Golden Race', *CQ* 46, 434–46.

Barthes, R. 1975. *The Pleasure of the Text*, tr. R. Miller. New York.

—— 1986. *The Rustle of Language*, tr. R. Howard. Berkeley.

Baxter, R. T. S. 1971. 'Virgil's Influence on Tacitus in Book 3 of the *Histories*,' *CPh* 66, 93–107.

—— 1972. 'Virgil's Influence on Tacitus in Books 1 and 2 of the *Annals*,' *CPh* 67, 246–69.

Bayet, J. 1920. 'Les origines de l'arcadisme romain', *Mélanges de l'École française de Rome* 38, 62–143.

—— 1926. *Les origines de l'Hercule romain.* Paris.

—— 1969. *Histoire politique et psychologique de la religion romaine.* 2nd edition. Paris.

Beard, M. 1986. 'Cicero and Divination: The Formation of a Latin Discourse', *JRS* 76, 33–46.

—— 1987. 'A Complex of Times: No More Sheep on Romulus' Birthday', *PCPhS* 23, 1–15.

Beard, M., North, J. A. and Price, S. R. F. 1998. *Religions of Rome.* 2 vols. Cambridge.

Bellen, H. 1963. 'Adventus Dei. Der Gegenwartsbezug in Vergils Darstellung der Geschichte von Cacus und Hercules (Aen. VIII 184–275)', *RhM* 106, 23–30.

Belloni, L., Milanese, G. and Porro, A. (eds.) 1995. *Studia classica Iohanni Tarditi oblata.* Volume 1. Milan.

Benario, H. W. 1983. 'The *Carmen de Bello Actiaco* and Early Imperial Epic', *ANRW* II 30.3, 1656–62.

Bernstein, M. 1994. *Foregone Conclusions: Against Apocalyptic History.* Berkeley.

Bettini, M. 1991. *Anthropology and Roman Culture: Kinship, Time, Images of the Soul*, tr. J. Van Sickle. Baltimore.

Bews, J. 1972–3. 'Virgil, Tacitus, Tiberius and Germanicus', *PVS* 12, 35–48.

Bickel, E. 1951. 'Vates bei Varro und Vergil,' *RhM* 94, 257–314.

Bienkowski, P. I. L. 1900. *De simulacris barbararum gentium apud Romanos.* Kraków.

Binder, G. 1971. *Aeneas und Augustus. Interpretationen zum 8. Buch der Aeneis.* Meisenheim am Glan.

—— 1983. 'Lied der Parzen zur Geburt Octavians. Vergils vierte Ekloge', *Gymnasium* 90, 102–22.

Blagg, T. and Millett, M. (eds.) 1990. *The Early Roman Empire in the West.* Oxford.

Blanck, H. 1992. *Das Buch in der Antike.* Munich.

Bleicken, J. 1998. *Augustus. Eine Biographie.* Berlin.

Bloomer, W. M. 1992. *Valerius Maximus and the Rhetoric of the New Nobility.* London.

Bol, R. 1998. *Amazones Volneratae: Untersuchungen zu den ephesischen Amazonenstatuen.* Mainz.

Bollack, M. 1967. 'Le retour de Saturne', *REL* 45, 304–24.

Bömer F. 1957–8. *P. Ovidius Naso. Die Fasten.* 2 vols. Heidelberg.

—— 1969–86. *P. Ovidius Naso. Metamorphosen: Kommentar.* 7 vols. Heidelberg.

Bonjour, M. 1975. *Terre natale. Études sur une composante affective du patriotisme romain.* Paris.

Bosworth, B. 1999. 'Augustus, the *Res Gestae* and Hellenistic Theories of Apotheosis', *JRS* 89, 1–18.

Bowie, A. M. 1990. 'The Death of Priam: Allegory and History in the *Aeneid*', *CQ* 40, 470–81.

Boyle, A. J. (ed.) 1993. *Roman Epic.* London.

Bramble, J. C. 1970. 'Structure and Ambiguity in Catullus LXIV', *PCPhS* 16, 22–41.

—— 1982. 'Minor Figures' in Kenney and Clausen 1982, 467–94.

Brenk, F. E. 1986. 'In the Light of the Moon: Demonology in the Early Imperial Period', *ANRW* II 16.3, 2068–145.

Brink, C. O. 1971. *Horace on Poetry II: The 'Ars Poetica'*. Cambridge.

Brooks, P. 1984. *Reading for the Plot: Design and Intention in Narrative*. Oxford.

Bruère, R. T. 1958. 'Ovid *Met.* 15.1–5 and Tacitus *Ann.* 1.11.1', *CPh* 53, 34.

Brunt, P. A. 1982. 'The Legal Issue in Cicero, *Pro Balbo*', *CQ* 32, 136–47.

—— 1987. *Italian Manpower 225 B.C.–A.D. 14*. 2nd edition. Oxford

—— 1988. *The Fall of the Roman Republic and Related Essays*. Oxford.

Brunt, P. A. and Moore, J. M. 1967. *Res Gestae Divi Augusti. The Achievements of the Divine Augustus*. Oxford.

Bruun, C. (ed.) 2000. *The Roman Middle Republic: Politics, Religion, and Historiography c. 400–133 B.C.* Rome.

Buchheit, V. 1963. *Vergil über die Sendung Roms. Untersuchungen zum Bellum Poenicum und zur Aeneis*. Heidelberg.

—— 1969. 'Ciceros Triumph des Geistes', *Gymnasium* 76, 232–53.

—— 1973. 'Vergilische Geschichtsdeutung', *GB* 1, 23–50.

Buchmann, W. 1912. *De Numae regis Romanorum fabula*. Dissertatio Inauguralis, Leipzig.

Burck. E. 1934. *Die Erzählungkunst des T. Livius*. Berlin.

Burde, P. 1974. *Untersuchungen zur antiken Universalgeschichte*. Diss. Erlangen-Nürnberg.

Burkert, W. 1979. *Structure and History in Greek Mythology and Ritual*. Berkeley.

Burrow, C. 1989. 'Original Fictions: Metamorphoses in *The Faerie Queene*,' in Martindale 1989, 99–119.

—— 1999. Review of D. K. Money, *The English Horace: Anthony Alsop and the Traditions of British Latin Verse*, *London Review of Books* 21.16, 3–4.

Butler, H. E. and Barber, E. A. 1933. *The Elegies of Propertius: Edited with an Introduction and Commentary*. Oxford.

Butrica, J. L. 1983. 'Propertius 3,3,7–12 and Ennius', *CQ* 33, 464–8.

—— 1996. 'The *Amores* of Propertius: Unity and Structure in Books 2–4', *ICS* 21, 85–158.

Cairns, F. 1972. *Generic Composition in Greek and Roman Poetry*. Edinburgh.

—— 1979. *Tibullus: A Hellenistic Poet at Rome*. Cambridge.

—— 1983. 'Horace *Epode* 9: Some New Interpretations', *ICS* 8, 80–93.

—— 1984. 'Propertius and the Battle of Actium (4.6)', in Woodman and West 1984, 129–68 and 229–36.

—— 1989. *Virgil's Augustan Epic*. Cambridge.

Calame, C. (ed.). 1988. *Métamorphoses du mythe en Grèce antique*. Geneva.

Calboli, G. 1969. *Rhetorica ad C. Herennium*. Bologna.

Cameron, A. 1995. *Callimachus and his Critics*. Princeton.

Campbell, B. 1987. 'Teach Yourself How to Be a General', *JRS* 77, 13–29.

Campbell, M. 1981. *A Commentary on Quintus Smyrnaeus Posthomerica XII*. Leiden.

Camps, W. A. 1961. *Propertius Elegies Book I*. Cambridge.

—— 1965. *Propertius Elegies Book IV*. Cambridge.

—— 1966. *Propertius Elegies Book III*. Cambridge.

—— 1967. *Propertius Elegies Book II*. Cambridge.

Cartault, A. 1926. *L'art de Virgile dans L'Énéide I*. Paris.

Carter, J. M. 1997. *Caesar: The Civil War*. Oxford.

Cavallo, G. 1975. *Libri, editori e publico nel mondo antico: guida storica e critica*. Rome.

Cavarzere, A. 1992. *Orazio. Il libro degli epodi*. Venezia.

Chassignet, M. 1996. *L'Annalistique romaine*. Tome 1. Paris.

Christ, W. von, Schmidt, W. and Stählin, O. 1920. *Geschichte der griechischen Litteratur*, 2. Teil, 1. Hälfte. 6th edition. Munich.

Cichorius, C. 1922. *Römische Studien*. Leipzig.

Clarke, K. 1999. 'Universal Perspectives in Historiography', in Kraus 1999, 249–79.
Classen, C. J. 1993. *Die Welt der Römer. Studien zu ihrer Literatur, Geschichte und Religion.* Berlin.
—— 1998. *Zur Literatur und Gesellschaft der Römer.* Stuttgart.
Clausen, W. 1994. *Vergil's Eclogues.* Oxford.
Coarelli, F. 1988. *Il foro boario dalle origini alle fine della repubblica.* Rome.
Conington, J. and Nettleship, H. 1858–83. *The Works of Virgil.* London.
Conley, D. F. 1981. 'The Stages of Rome's Decline in Sallust's Historical Theory', *Hermes* 109, 379–82.
Conte, G. B. 1992. 'Proems in the Middle', *YClS* 29, 149–59.
—— 1994. *Genres and Readers: Lucretius, Love Elegy, Pliny's Encyclopedia,* tr. G. W. Most. Baltimore.
Cornell, T. J. 1995. *The Beginnings of Rome: Italy and Rome from the Bronze Age to the Punic Wars (c. 1000–264 B.C.).* London.
Courtney, E. 1988. 'Propertius 3.3.7', *Acta Classica* 31, 95–105.
—— 1993. *The Fragmentary Latin Poets.* Oxford.
—— 1995. *Musa Lapidaria: A Selection of Latin Verse Inscriptions.* Atlanta, Ga.
Crawford, M. 1996. 'Italy and Rome from Sulla to Augustus' and 'Appendices', in *CAH* vol. 10, 2nd edition, 414–33 and 979–89.
Creighton, J. D. and Wilson, R. J. A. (eds.) 1999. *Roman Germany: Studies in Cultural Interaction.* Portsmouth, RI.
Crump, M. M. 1931. *The Epyllion from Theocritus to Ovid.* Oxford.
Cuénot, C. 1967. 'Une Comparison littéraire. L'épisode d'Hercule et de Cacus chez Tite-Live et chez Virgile', *L'information littéraire* 19, 230–4.
Curran, L. C. 1969. 'Catullus 64 and the Heroic Age', *YClS* 21, 169–92.
D'Alessio, G. B. 1996. *Callimaco: Aitia, Giambi, Frammenti elegiaci minori, Frammenti di sede incerta.* Milan.
D'Ippolito, G. 1976. *Trifiodoro e Vergilio: il proemio della "Presa di Ilio" e l'esordio del libro secondo dell'Eneide.* Palermo.
Dahlmann, H. 1948. 'Vates', *Philologus* 97, 337–53.
—— 1953. *Varro's Schrift 'de poematis' und die hellenistisch-römische Poetik.* Wiesbaden.
—— 1963. *Studien zu Varro 'de poetis'.* Wiesbaden.
David, J.-M. 1996. *The Roman conquest of Italy.* Oxford.
Davies, M. 1989. *The Epic Cycle.* Bristol.
De Man, P. 1971. *Blindness and Insight: Essays in the Rhetoric of Contemporary Criticism.* Oxford.
DeBrohun, J. B. 1994. 'Redressing Elegy's Puella: Propertius IV and the Rhetoric of Fashion', *JRS* 84, 41–63.
Decker, K.-V. and Selzer, W. 1976. 'Moguntiacum: Mainz von der Zeit des Augustus bis zum Ende der römischen Herrschaft', *ANRW* II 5.1, 476–77.
Della Corte, F. 1985. *Le bucoliche di Virgilio: commentate e tradotte.* Genova.
Deroux, C. (ed.) 1998. *Studies in Latin Literature and Roman History.* Vol. 9. Brussels.
Diggle, J., Hall, J. B. and Jocelyn, H. D. (eds.) 1989. *Studies in Latin Literature and its Tradition in Honour of C. O. Brink.* Cambridge.
Doblhofer, E. 1992. *Horaz in der Forschung nach 1957.* Darmstadt.
Dorey, T. A. (ed.) 1966. *Latin Historians.* London.
Dowden, K. 1997. 'The Amazons: Development and Functions', *RhM* 140, 97–128.
Drews, R. 1963. 'Ephoros and History Written *kata genos*', *AJPh* 84, 244–55.
Du Quesnay, I. M. Le M. 1977. 'Vergil's Fourth Eclogue', *PLLS* 2, 25–99.
Du Quesnay, I. M. Le M. 1995. 'Horace, *Odes* 4.5: *Pro Reditu Imperatoris Caesaris Divi Filii Augusti*', in Harrison 1995, 128–87.
Due, O. S. 1974. *Changing Forms: Studies in the Metamorphoses of Ovid.* Copenhagen.
Dugas, Ch. 1937. 'Tradition littéraire et tradition graphique dans l'antiquité grecque', *AC* 6, 1–26.

Dumézil, G. 1970. *Archaic Roman Religion*, tr. P. Krapp. 2 vols. Chicago.

Dunston, A. J. 1973. 'Horace, *Odes* i 12 yet again', *Antichthon* 7, 54–9.

Eck, W., Caballos, A. and Fernández, F. 1996. *Das senatus consultum de Cn. Pisone patre*. Munich.

Ellsworth, J. D. 1986. 'Ovid's *"Aeneid"* Reconsidered (*Met.* 13.623–14.608)', *Vergilius* 32, 27–32.

Elsner, J. 1991. 'Cult and Sculpture: Sacrifice in the Ara Pacis Augustae', *JRS* 81, 50–61.

Engelmann, H. 1975. *The Delian Aretalogy of Sarapis*. Leiden.

Errington, R. M. 1998. 'Aspects of Roman Acculturation in the East under the Republic', in Kneissl and Losemann 1998, 140–157.

Étienne, R. and Le Dinahet, M. Th. (eds.). 1991. *L'Espace sacrificiel dans les civilisations méditerranéennes de l'antiquité*. Paris.

Fairweather, J. 1987. 'Ovid's Autobiographical Poem, *Tristia* 4.10', *CQ* 37, 181–96.

Fantham, E. 1996. *Roman Literary Culture: From Cicero to Apuleius*. Baltimore.

—— 1998. *Ovid: Fasti Book IV*. Cambridge.

Faranda, R. (tr.) 1971. *Detti e fatti memorabili di Valerio Massimo*. Turin.

Farrell, J. 1997. 'The Virgilian Intertext', in Martindale 1997, 222–38.

Fedeli P. 1985. *Properzio: il libro terzo delle elegie: introduzione testo e commento*. Bari.

—— (ed.) 1994. *Sex. Properti elegiarum libri IV*. 2nd edition. Stuttgart.

Feeney, D. C. 1984. 'The Reconciliations of Juno', *CQ* 34, 179– 94.

—— 1986. 'History and Revelation in Vergil's Underworld', *PCPhS* 32, 1–24.

—— 1991. *The Gods in Epic: Poets and Critics of the Classical Tradition*. Oxford.

—— 1992. '*Si licet et fas est*: Ovid's *Fasti* and the Problem of Free Speech under the Principate', in Powell 1992, 1–25.

—— 1993. 'Horace and the Greek Lyric Poets', in Rudd 1993, 41–63.

—— 1999. '*Mea tempora*: Patterning of Time in the *Metamorphoses*', in Hardie, Barchiesi and Hinds 1999, 13–30.

Feldherr, A. 1995. 'Ships of State: *Aeneid* V and Augustan Circus Spectacle', *ClAnt* 14, 245–65.

—— 1997. 'Livy's Revolution: Civic Identity and the Creation of the *res publica*', in Habinek and Schiesaro 1997, 136–157.

—— 1998. *Spectacle and Society in Livy's History*. Berkeley.

—— forthcoming. 'Metamorphosis in the *Metamorphoses*', in P. Hardie (ed.) *The Cambridge Companion to Ovid*, Cambridge.

Fitzgerald, W. 1984. 'Aeneas, Daedalus, and the Labyrinth', *Arethusa* 17, 51–65.

Flory, M. B. 1998. 'The Integration of Women into the Roman Triumph', *Historia* 47, 489–94.

Flower, H. I. 1996. *Ancestor Masks and Aristocratic Power in Roman Culture*. Oxford.

Fontenrose, J. E. 1959. *Python: a study of Delphic myth and its origins*. Berkeley.

Fordyce, C. J. 1977. *P. Vergili Maronis Aeneidos Libri VII–VIII*. Oxford.

Fornara, C. W. 1983. *The Nature of History in Ancient Greece and Rome*. Berkeley.

Fornaro, S. 1997. *Dionisio di Alicarnasso, Epistola a Pompeo Gemino*. Stuttgart.

Forsythe, G. 1994. *The Historian L. Calpurnius Piso Frugi and the Roman Annalistic Tradition*. Lanham Md.

—— 1999. *Livy and Early Rome: A Study in Historical Method and Judgment*. Stuttgart.

Fowler, D. P. 1990. 'Deviant Focalisation in Virgil's Aeneid', *PCPhS* 36, 42–63.

—— 1991. 'Narrate and Describe: The Problem of Ekphrasis', *JRS* 81, 25–35.

—— 1995. 'Horace and the Aesthetics of Politics', in Harrison 1995, 248–66.

—— 2000. *Roman Constructions. Readings in Postmodern Latin*. Oxford.

Fox, M. 1993. 'History and Rhetoric in Dionysius of Halicarnassus', *JRS* 83, 31–47.

—— 1996. *Roman Historical Myths. The Regal Period in Augustan Literature*. Oxford.

Fraccaro, P. 1907. *Studi Varroniani: De gente populi Romani libri IV*. Padova.

Fraenkel, E. 1957. *Horace*. Oxford.

Frier, B. W. 1979. *Libri Annales Pontificum Maximorum: The Origins of the Annalistic Tradition*. Rome.

Fuchs, H. 1969. 'Ovid in der Besinnung auf Cicero', *MH* 26, 159–60.

Gabba, E. 1991. *Dionysius and the History of Archaic Rome*. Berkeley.

Gagé, J. 1930. 'La *Victoria Augusti* et les auspices de Tibère', *Revue archéologique*, 5e ser., 32, 1–35.

—— 1932. 'Un thème de l'art imperial romain: La victoire d'Auguste,' *Mélanges d'archéologie et d'histoire* 49, 61–92.

Galinsky, G. K. 1966. 'The Hercules-Cacus episode in *Aeneid* VIII', *AJPh* 87, 18–51.

—— 1968. '*Aeneid* V and the *Aeneid*', *AJPh* 89, 157–85.

—— 1969. *Aeneas, Sicily, and Rome*. Princeton.

—— 1972. 'Hercules Ovidianus', *WS* 6, 93–116.

—— 1972a. *The Herakles Theme. The Adaptions of the Hero in Literature from Homer to the Twentieth Century*. Oxford.

—— 1975. *Ovid's Metamorphoses: An Introduction to the Basic Aspects*. Berkeley.

—— 1976. 'L'"*Eneide*" di Ovidio (*met.* XIII 623–XIV 608) ed il carattere delle *Metomorfosi*', *Maia* 28, 3–18.

—— 1996. *Augustan Culture: An Interpretative Introduction*. Princeton.

Gassner, J. 1972. *Katalog im römischen Epos: Vergil—Ovid—Lucan*. Munich.

Gatz. B. 1967. *Weltalter, goldene Zeit und sinnverwandte Vorstellungen*, Hildesheim.

Gentilcore, R. 1995. 'The Landscape of Desire: The Tale of Pomona and Vertumnus in Ovid's *Metamorphoses*', *Phoenix* 49, 110–20.

George, E. V. 1974. *Aeneid VIII and the Aitia of Callimachus*. Leiden.

Gerlaud, B. 1982. *Triphiodore. La prise d'Ilion*. Paris.

Gibson, B. J. 1998. 'Rumours as Causes of Events in Tacitus', *MD* 40, 111–29.

Gildenhard, I. and Zissos, A. 1999. '"Somatic Economies": Tragic Bodies and Poetic Design in Ovid's *Metamorphoses*', in Hardie, Barchiesi and Hinds 1999, 163–82.

Gill, C. and Wiseman, T. P. (eds.) 1993. *Lies and Fiction in the Ancient World*. Exeter.

Girard, R. 1977. *Violence and the Sacred* (trans. P. Gregory). Baltimore.

Glei, R. F. 1991. *Der Vater der Dinge. Interpretationen zur politischen, literarischen und kulturellen Dimension des Krieges bei Vergil*. Trier.

Goldhill, S. 1991. *The Poet's Voice. Essays on Poetics and Greek Literature*. Cambridge.

Goldsworthy, A. K. 1996. *The Roman Army at War 100 B.C.–A.D. 200*. Oxford.

Goodyear, F. R. D. 1972. *The Annals of Tacitus*. Volume 1: *Annals 1.1–54*. Cambridge.

—— 1981. *The Annals of Tacitus*. Volume 2: *Annals 1.55–81 and Annals 2*. Cambridge.

Goold, G. P. (ed.) 1990. *Propertius: Elegies*. Cambridge Mass.

—— 1992. 'The Voice of Virgil: The Pageant of Rome in *Aeneid* 6', in Woodman and Powell 1992, 110–23.

Gottlieb, G. 1998. 'Religion in the Politics of Augustus (*Aen.* 1.278–291; 8.714–723; 12.791–842)', in Stahl 1998, 21–36.

Gow, A. S. F. 1952. *Theocritus*. 2 vols. Cambridge.

Gow, A. S. F. and Page, D. L. 1968. *The Greek Anthology: The Garland of Philip*. 2 vols. Cambridge.

Graf, F. 1988. 'Ovide, les *Métamorphoses* et la véracité du mythe', in Calame 1988, 57–70.

Gransden, K. W. 1976. *Virgil: Aeneid Book VIII*. Cambridge.

—— 1991. *Virgil: Aeneid Book XI*. Cambridge.

Gray, V. 1987. 'Mimesis in Greek Historical Theory', *AJPh* 108, 467–86.

Grimal, P. 1958. 'La chronologie légendaire des *Métamorphoses*,' in Herescu 1958, 245–57.

Grueber, H. A. 1910. *Coins of the Roman Republic in the British Museum*. 3 vols. Oxford.

Günther, H.-C. 1997. *Quaestiones Propertianae*. Leiden.

Guerrini, R. 1981. *Studi su Valerio Massimo*. Pisa.

Gurval, R. A. 1995. *Actium and Augustus: The Politics and Emotions of Civil War*. Ann Arbor.

Habinek, T. N. 1998. *The Politics of Latin Literature: Writing, Identity, and Empire in Ancient Rome.* Princeton.

Habinek, T. N. and Schiesaro, A. (eds.) 1997. *The Roman Cultural Revolution.* Cambridge.

Häussler, R. 1976. *Das historische Epos der Griechen und Römer bis Vergil. Studien zum historischen Epos der Antike I: Von Homer zu Vergil.* Heidelberg.

Hall, L. G. H. 1996. 'Hirtius and the *Bellum Alexandrinum*', *CQ* 46, 411–15.

Hamilton, P. 1995. *Historicism.* London.

Hammond, C. 1993. *Narrative Explanation and the Roman Military Character.* Oxford D. Phil. thesis.

Hanslik, R. (ed.) 1979. *Sex. Propertii elegiarum libri IV.* Leipzig.

Hardie, P. 1986. *Virgil's Aeneid: Cosmos and Imperium.* Oxford.

—— 1987. 'Ships and Ship-Names in the *Aeneid*', in Whitby, Hardie and Whitby 1987, 163–71.

—— 1992. 'Augustan Poets and the Mutability of Rome', in Powell 1992, 59–82.

—— 1993. *The Epic Successors of Virgil: Studies in the Dynamics of a Tradition.* Cambridge.

—— 1993a. 'The Mirror of Man', review of E. A. Schmidt, *Ovids poetische Menschenwelt*, *CR* 43, 264–5.

—— 1994. *Virgil: Aeneid Book IX.* Cambridge.

—— 1997. 'Questions of authority: the invention of tradition in Ovid *Metamorphoses* 15', in Habinek and Schiesaro 1997, 182–98.

—— 1999 (ed.). *Virgil: Critical Assessments of Classical Authors.* London.

Hardie, P. R., Barchiesi, A. and Hinds, S. (eds.) 1999. *Ovidian Transformations. Essays on the Metamorphoses and its Reception.* Cambridge.

Harrison, E. L. 1973. 'Why did Venus wear Boots?—Some Reflections on *Aeneid* 1.314 ff.', *PVS* 12, 10–25.

Harrison, S. J. 1988. 'Vergil as a Poet of War', *PVS* 19, 48–68.

—— 1991. *Vergil: Aeneid 10.* Oxford.

—— (ed.) 1995. *Homage to Horace: A Bimillenary Celebration.* Oxford.

—— 1997. 'The Survival and Supremacy of Rome: The Unity of the Shield of Aeneas', *JRS* 87, 70–6.

—— 1998. 'The Sword-belt of Pallas: Moral Symbolism and Political Ideology', in Stahl 1998, 243–42.

Heath, M. 1989. *Unity in Greek Poetics.* Oxford.

Heckel, W. 1997. 'Introduction', in *Marcus Junius Justinus, Epitome of the Philippic History of Pompeius Trogus. Books 11–12: Alexander the Great.* Translation and appendices by J. C. Yardley; introduction and commentary by W. Heckel. Oxford.

Heinze, R. 1993. *Virgil's Epic Technique*, tr. H. and D. Harvey and F. Robertson. Berkeley.

Henderson, J. 1997. *Figuring out Roman Nobility: Juvenal's Eighth Satire.* Exeter.

Herbert-Brown, G. 1994. *Ovid and the Fasti. A Historical Study.* Oxford.

Herescu, N. I. (ed.) 1958. *Ovidiana.* Paris.

Herkommer, E. 1968. *Die Topoi in den Proömien der römischen Geschichtswerke.* Diss. Tübingen.

Herter, H. 1948. 'Ovids Kunstprinzip in den Metamorphosen', *AJPh* 69, 129–48.

Heubner, H. 1968. *P. Cornelius Tacitus. Die Historien. Band II: Zweites Buch.* Heidelberg.

Heyworth, S. J. 1986. 'Notes on Propertius, Books III and IV', *CQ* 36, 199–211.

Hinds, S. 1987. *The Metamorphosis of Persephone: Ovid and the Self-conscious Muse.* Cambridge.

—— 1992. '*Arma* in Ovid's *Fasti*', *Arethusa* 25, 81–154.

—— 1998. *Allusion and Intertext: Dynamics of Appropriation in Roman Poetry.* Cambridge.

—— 1999. 'Time and Teleology from *Metamorphoses* to *Ibis*', in Hardie, Barchiesi and Hinds 1999, 48–67.

Hofmann, H. 1985. 'Ovid's *Metamorphoses*: carmen perpetuum, carmen deductum,' *PLLS* 5, 223–41.

Holleman, A. W. J. 1976. 'Larentia, Hercules, and Mater Matuta (Tib. II 5)', *AC* 45, 197–207.

Horsfall, N. 1972. 'Varro and Caesar: Three Chronological Problems', *BICS* 19, 120–8.

—— 1976. 'Virgil, history, and the Roman tradition', *Prudentia* 8, 73–89.

—— 1979. 'Stesichorus at Bovillae', *JHS* 99, 26–48.

—— 1985. 'Illusion and Reality in Latin Topographical Writing', *G&R* 32, 197–208.

—— 1987. '*Non viribus aequis*: Some Problems in Virgil's Battle Scenes', *G&R* 34, 48–55.

—— 1991. *Virgilio: l'epopea in alambicco*. Naples.

—— 1999. *Virgil Aeneid 7: A Commentary*. Leiden.

Hubbard, T. K. 1983. 'The Catullan Libellus', *Philologus* 127, 118–37.

Humm, M. 2000. 'Spazio e tempo civici: riforma della tribù e riforma del calendario alla fine del IV secolo a.C.', in Bruun 2000, 91–119.

Hunter, R. L. 1993. *The Argonautica of Apollonius: Literary Studies*. Cambridge.

Hutchinson, G. O. 1985. *Septem contra Thebas*. Oxford.

Huttner, U. 1997. *Die politische Rolle der Heraklesgestalt im griechischen Herrschertum*, Stuttgart.

—— 1997a. 'Hercules und Augustus', *Chiron* 27, 369–91.

Jachmann, G. 1952. 'L'Arcadia come paesaggio bucolico', *Maia* 5, 161–74.

Jacoby, F. 1909. 'Über die Entwicklung der griechischen Historiographie und der Plan einer neuen Sammlung der griechischen Historikerfragmente', *Klio* 9, 80–123.

Jaeger, M. 1997. *Livy's Written Rome*. Ann Arbor.

Janan, M. 1998. 'Refashioning Hercules: Propertius 4.9', *Helios*, 65–78.

Jenkyns, R. 1989. 'Virgil and Arcadia', *JRS* 79, 26–39.

Jocelyn, H. D. 1971. 'Horace, *Odes* i 12. 33–6', *Antichthon* 5, 68–76.

—— 1973. 'Horace, *Odes* i 12.33–6: Some Final Remarks', *Antichthon* 7, 62–4.

—— 1995. '"Poeta" and "Vates": Concerning the Nomenclature of the Composer of Verses in Republican and Early Imperial Rome', in Belloni, Milanese and Porro 1995, 19–50

Johnson, W. R. 1969. 'Tact in the Drusus Ode: Horace, *Odes* 4.4', *CSCA* 2, 171–81.

—— 1973. 'The Emotions of Patriotism: Propertius 4.6', *CSCA* 6, 151–80.

Jones, C. P. 1986. *Culture and Society in Lucian*. Cambridge, Ma.

Jonkers, E. J. 1963. *Social and Economic Commentary on Cicero's De Lege Agraria Orationes Tres*. Leiden.

Kambylis, A. 1965. *Die Dichterweihe und ihre Symbolik. Untersuchungen zu Hesiodos, Kallimachos, Properz und Ennius*. Heidelberg.

Kebric, R. 1977. *In the Shadow of Macedon: Duris of Samos*. Wiesbaden.

Keil, H. (ed.) 1857–1880. *Grammatici Latini*. 7 vols. Leipzig.

Kennedy, D. 1992. '"Augustan" and "Anti-Augustan": Reflection of Terms of Reference', in Powell 1992, 26–58.

Kenney, E. J. 1976. '*Ovidius prooemians*', *PCPhS* 22, 46–53.

—— 1986. Introduction to *Ovid: Metamorphoses* (tr. A. D. Melville). Oxford.

Kenney, E. J. and Clausen, W. V. (eds.) 1982. *The Cambridge History of Classical Literature*, volume 2. Cambridge.

Keydell, R. 1954. 'Quintus von Smyrna und Vergil', *Hermes* 82, 254–6.

Kienast, D. 1982. *Augustus: Prinzeps und Monarch*. Darmstadt.

Kierdorf, W. 1994. '*CECINIT* ODER *CECINI*. Neue Überlegungen zum Text von Properz 3.3.7', *Hermes* 122, 368–72.

Kinsey, T. E. 1965. 'Irony and Structure in Catullus 64', *Latomus* 24, 911–31.

Klingner, F. (ed.) 1959. *Q. Horati Flacci Opera*. 3rd edition. Leipzig.

—— 1965. *Römische Geisteswelt*. Stuttgart.

Kneissl, P. and Losemann, V. (eds.) 1998. *Imperium Romanum: Studien zur Geschichte und Rezeption. Festschrift für Karl Christ zum 75. Geburtstag*. Stuttgart.

Knight, J. 1932. 'Iliupersides', *CQ* 26, 178–89.
Knox, P. E. 1985. 'Wine, Water and Callimachean Poetics,' *HSCPh* 89, 107–19.
—— 1986. *Ovid's Metamorphoses and the Traditions of Augustan Poetry*. Cambridge.
Knox, P. E. and Foss, C. (eds.) 1998. *Style and Tradition: Studies in Honor of Wendell Clausen*. Stuttgart.
Koestermann, E. 1963. *Cornelius Tacitus: Annalen*. Volume 1: Books 1–3. Heidelberg.
Konstan, D. 1977. *Catullus' Indictment of Rome: The Meaning of Catullus 64*. Amsterdam.
—— 1993. 'Neoteric Epic: Catullus 64', in Boyle 1993, 59–78.
Kopff, C. 1981. 'Virgil and the Cyclic Epics', *ANRW* II 31.2, 919–47.
Kraggerud, E. 1960. 'Einige Namen in der Aeneis', *SO* 36, 30–39.
—— 1968. *Aeneisstudien*. Oslo.
Kraus, C. S. 1994. *Livy Ab Urbe Condita Book VI*. Cambridge.
—— 1994a. '"No Second Troy": Topoi and Refoundation in Livy, Book V', *TAPhA* 124, 267–89.
—— 1998. 'Repetition and Empire in the *Ab Urbe Condita*', in Knox and Foss, 1998, 264–83.
—— (ed.) 1999. *The Limits of Historiography: Genre and Narrative in Ancient Historical Texts*. Leiden.
Kraus, C. S. and Woodman, A. J. 1997. *Latin Historians*. Oxford.
Krevans, N. 1996. *The Poet as Editor: The Poetic Collection from Callimachus to Ovid*. Ann Arbor.
Kukula, R. C. W. 1911. *Römische Säkularpoesie*. Leipzig.
Kuttner, A. 1995. *Dynasty and Empire in the Age of Augustus: The Case of the Boscoreale Cups*. Berkeley.
Kyriakidis, S. 1994. 'Invocatio ad Musam (*Aen.* 7.37)', *MD* 33, 197–206.
—— 1998. *Narrative Structure and Poetics in the Aeneid: The Frame of Book 6*. Bari.
Labate, M. 1987. 'Poesia cortigiana, poesia civile, scrittura epica (a proposito di Verg. Aen.1,257ss e Theocr. 24,73ss)', *MD* 18, 69–81.
Laird, A. 1999. *Powers of Expression, Expressions of Power: Speech Presentation in Latin Literature*. Oxford.
Lasserre F. and Bonnard, A. 1958. *Archiloques fragments*. Paris.
Latacz, J. 1994. *Erschließung der Antike. Kleine Schriften zur Literatur der Griechen und Römer*. Stuttgart.
Latte, K. 1960. *Römische Religionsgeschichte*. Munich.
Leach, E. W. 1971. 'Eclogue 4: Symbolism and Sources', *Arethusa* 4, 167–84.
—— 1978. 'Three Collections of Ten: Vergil, Horace, Tibullus', *Ramus* 7, 79–105.
Lee, G. (ed.) 1982. *Tibullus: Elegies*. 2nd edition. Liverpool.
Leigh, M. 1995. 'Wounding and Popular Rhetoric at Rome', *BICS* 40, 195–212.
—— 1996. 'Varius Rufus, Thyestes and the Appetites of Antony', *PCPhS* 42, 171–97.
—— 1997. *Lucan: Spectacle and Engagement*. Oxford.
Lendon, J. E. 1999. 'The Rhetoric of Combat: Greek Military Theory and Roman Culture in Julius Caesar's Battle Descriptions', *ClAnt* 18, 273–329.
Lepelley, C. (ed.), 1998. *Rome et l'intégration de l'Empire, 44 av. J.-C.—260 ap. J.-C. Tome 2, Approches régionales du Haut-Empire romain*. Paris.
Levene, D. S. 1993. *Religion in Livy*. Leiden.
—— 1997. 'God and Man in the Classical Latin Panegyric', *PCPhS* 43, 66–103.
Levick, B. M. 1982. 'Morals, Politics and the Fall of the Roman Republic', *G&R* 29, 53–62.
—— 1990. *Claudius*. London.
Liebeschuetz, J. W. H. G. 1979. *Continuity and Change in Roman Religion*. Oxford.
Linderski, J. 1993. 'Roman Religion in Livy', in Schüller 1993, 53–70.
Lindheim, S. H. 1998. 'I am Dressed, Therefore I Am? Vertumnus in Propertius 4.2 and in *Metamorphoses* 14.622–771', *Ramus* 27, 27–38.

—— 1998a. 'Hercules Cross-Dressed, Hercules Undressed: Unmasking the Construction of the Propertian *Amator* in Elegy 4.9', *AJPh* 119, 43–66.

Little, D. 1972. 'The Non-Augustanism of Ovid's *Metamorphoses*', *Mnemosyne* series 4.25, 389–401.

Livrea, E. 1979. 'Der Liller Kallimachos und die Mäusefallen', *ZPE* 34, 37–42.

Lloyd-Jones, H. 1967. 'Hercules at Eleusis: P. Oxy. 2622 and P.S.I 1391', *Maia* 19, 221–9.

Lowenthal, D. 1985. *The Past is a Foreign Country*. Cambridge

Lowrie, M. 1997. *Horace's Narrative Odes*. Oxford.

Luce, T. J. 1965. 'The Dating of Livy's First Decade', *TAPhA* 96, 209–40.

—— 1971. 'Design and Structure in Livy: 5.32–55', *TAPhA* 102, 265–302.

—— 1977. *Livy: The Composition of His History*. Princeton.

Luck, G. (ed.) 1988. *Albii Tibulli aliorumque carmina*. Stuttgart.

Ludwig, W. 1965. *Struktur und Einheit der Metamorphosen Ovids*. Berlin.

Lyne, R. O. A. M. 1987. *Further Voices in Vergil's Aeneid*. Oxford.

—— 1994. 'Vergil's *Aeneid*: Subversion by Intertextuality: Catullus 66.39–40 and Other Examples', *G&R* 41, 187–204.

—— 1995. *Horace: Behind the Public Poetry*. New Haven.

—— 1999. 'Drayton's Chorographical Ovid', in Hardie, Barchiesi and Hinds 1999, 85–102.

McDonald, A. H. 1957. 'The Style of Livy', *JRS* 47, 155–72.

McDonough, C. M. 1990. *Hercules of the Ara Maxima: A Study in Roman Religion and Cult*. MA thesis, University of North Carolina (Chapel Hill).

McGushin, P. 1992. *Sallust: The Histories. Volume 1: Books i–ii*. Oxford.

Macherey, P. 1978. *A Theory of Literary Production*, tr. G. Wall. London.

Mack, S. 1978. *Patterns of Time in Vergil*. Hamden. Ct.

—— 1999. 'The Birth of War. A Reading of *Aeneid* 7', in Perkell 1999, 128–47.

MacKay, L. A. 1962. 'Sallust's *Catiline*: Date and Purpose', *Phoenix* 16, 181–94.

McKeown, J. C. 1998. *Ovid Amores: Text, Prolegomena and Commentary in four volumes: III A Commentary on Book Two*. Leeds.

McLennan, G. R. 1976. 'Arcadia before Vergil' *LCM* 1, 135–7.

Maehler, H. 1996. 'Books, Greek and Roman', in *OCD³*, 249–52.

Maltby, R. 1991. *A Lexicon of Ancient Latin Etymologies*. Leeds.

Mandelbaum, A. 1972. *The Aeneid of Virgil*. Toronto.

Mankin, D. 1995. *Horace: Epodes*. Cambridge.

Manuwald, B. 1979. *Cassius Dio und Augustus*. Wiesbaden.

Marchetti, S. C. 1999. 'Il potere e la giustizia. Presenze della tragedia greca nelle elegie ovidiane dell'esilio', *MD* 43, 111–56.

Marincola, J. 1997. *Authority and Tradition in Ancient Historiography*. Cambridge.

—— 1999. 'Genre, Convention, and Innovation in Greco-Roman Historiography', in Kraus 1999, 281–324.

Marquis, E. E. 1974. 'Vertumnus in Prop. 4.2', *Hermes* 102, 491–500.

Martin, P. M. 1971. 'Les 'Antiquités Romaines' de Denys d'Halicarnasse', *REL* 49, 162–79.

—— 1972. 'Heraclès en Italie, d'après Denys d'Halicarnasse (A. R., I, 34–44),' *Athenaeum* 50, 252–75.

Martina, M. 1979. 'Ennio «poeta cliens.»', *Quaderni di filologia classica* 2, 13–74.

Martindale, C. (ed.) 1989. *Ovid Renewed*. Cambridge.

—— 1993. *Redeeming the Text*. Cambridge.

—— (ed.) 1997. *The Cambridge Companion to Virgil*. Cambridge.

Marx, F. 1894. *Incerti auctoris. De ratione dicendi ad C. Herennium libri IV*. Leipzig.

Merkelbach, R. 1961. 'Aeneas in Cumae', *MH* 18, 83–99.

Merli, E. 2000. *Arma canant alii: materia epica e narrazione elegiaca nei fasti di Ovidio*. Florence.

Michaelopoulos, A. (forthcoming). *Etymological Wordplay in Ovid's Metamorphoses*. Leeds.
Miles, G. B. 1995. *Livy: Reconstructing Early Rome*. Ithaca.
Millar, F. 1964. *A Study of Cassius Dio*. Oxford.
—— 1998. *The Crowd in Rome in the Late Republic*. Ann Arbor.
Miller, N. P. 1961–2. 'Vergil and Tacitus', *PVS* 1, 25–34.
—— 1986. 'Virgil and Tacitus Again', *PVS* 18, 87–106.
Miller, P. A. 1994. *Lyric Texts and Lyric Consciousness: The Birth of a Genre from Archaic Greece to Augustan Rome*. London.
Mitchell-Boyask, R. N. 1996. 'Sine Fine: Vergil's Masterplot', *AJPh* 117, 289–307.
Moles, J. L. 1983. 'Virgil, Pompey, and the *Histories* of Asinius Pollio: *Aen.* 2.554–58', *CW* 76, 287–8.
—— 1993. 'Livy's Preface', *PCPhS* 39, 141–68.
Momigliano, A. 1977. 'Time in Ancient Historiography', in *Essays in Ancient and Modern Historiography*. Oxford. 179–204.
—— 1987. 'The Origins of Universal History', in *On Pagans, Jews, and Christians*. Middletown, Ct. 31–57.
Mommsen, Th. 1864. 'Die patricischen Claudier', *Römische Forschungen*. Hildesheim. Volume 1, 285–325.
—— 1894. *The History of Rome*, tr. W. P. Dickson. 4 vols. London.
Morgan, J. R. 1993. 'Make-believe and Make Believe: The Fictionality of Greek Novels', in Gill and Wiseman 1993, 175–229.
Morgan, L. 1998. 'Assimilation and Civil War: Hercules and Cacus', in Stahl 1998, 175–97.
Morson, G. S. 1994. *Narrative and Freedom: The Shadows of Time*. New Haven.
Mosshammer, A. A. 1979. *The Chronicle of Eusebius and the Greek Chronographic Tradition*. Lewisburg, Pa.
Muecke, F. 1993. *Horace Satires II*. Warminster.
Mueller, H.-F. 1998. '*Vita, Pudicitia, Libertas*: Juno, Gender, and Religious Politics in Valerius Maximus', *TAPhA* 128, 221–63.
Münzer, F. 1897. *Beiträge zur Quellenkritik der Naturgeschichte des Plinius*. Berlin.
—— 1899. 'Ap. Claudius Caecus', *RE* 3.2, 2681–5.
—— 1911. *Cacus der Rinderdieb*. Basel.
—— 1920. *Römische Adelsparteien und Adelsfamilien*. Stuttgart.
—— 1937. 'Die römischen Vestalinnen bis zur Kaiserzeit', *Philologus* 92, 47–67 and 199–222.
—— 1939. 'Tuccia (12)', *RE* 7A.1, 768–70.
Myers, K. S. 1994. *Ovid's Causes: Cosmogony and Aetiology in the Metamorphoses*. Ann Arbor.
—— 1994a. 'Ultimus ardor: Pomona and Vertumnus in Ovid's *Met.* 14.623–771', *CJ* 89, 225–50.
Mynors, R. A. B. (ed.) 1972. *P. Vergili Maronis Opera*. Oxford.
Nagle, B. R. 1980. *The Poetics of Exile: Program and Polemic in the Tristia and Epistulae ex Ponto of Ovid*. Brussels.
Nelis, D. P. 2001. *Vergil and Apollonius: The Aeneid and the Argonautica*. Leeds.
Newlands, C. E. 1995. *Playing with Time. Ovid and the Fasti*. Ithaca.
Newman, J. K. 1967. *The Concept of Vates in Augustan Poetry*. Brussels.
Nicolet, C. 1991. *Space, Geography and Politics in the Early Roman Empire*. Ann Arbor.
Nisbet, R. G. M. 1999. 'Roman Generalship in an Epic Context', in Hardie 1999, 254–64.
Nisbet, R. G. M. and Hubbard, M. 1970. *A Commentary on Horace, Odes, Book 1*. Oxford.
—— 1978. *A Commentary on Horace, Odes, Book II*. Oxford.
Norden, E. 1899. 'Ein Panegyrikus auf Augustus in Vergils *Aeneis*', *RhM* 54, 466–82.
—— 1915. *Ennius und Vergilius. Kriegsbilder aus Roms grosser Zeit*. Leipzig.

——— 1957. *P. Vergilius Maro: Aeneis Buch VI*. 4th ed. Stuttgart.
——— 1959. *Die germanische Urgeschichte in Tacitus Germania*. 4th ed. Stuttgart.
Novara, A. 1986. *Poésie virgilienne de la mémoire. questions sur l'histoire dans l'Énéide 8*. Clermond-Ferrand.
Nugent, S. G. 1992. 'Vergil's "Voice of the Women" in *Aeneid* V', *Arethusa* 25, 255–92.
O'Hara, J. J. 1990. *Death and the Optimistic Prophecy in Vergil's Aeneid*. Princeton.
Oakley, S. P. 1997. *A Commentary on Livy Books VI–X*. Volume 1. Oxford.
——— 1998. *A Commentary on Livy Books VI–X*. Volume 2. Oxford.
Ogilvie, R. M. 1965. *A Commentary on Livy Books 1–5*. Oxford.
Oliensis, E. 1997. 'Return to sender: the rhetoric of *nomina* in Ovid's *Tristia*', *Ramus* 26, 172–93.
——— 1998. *Horace and the Rhetoric of Authority*. Cambridge.
Ostrowski, J. A. 1996. 'Personifications of Countries and Cities as a Symbol of Victory in Greek and Roman Art', in Schmidt 1996, 264–71.
Otis, B. 1970. *Ovid as an Epic Poet*. Cambridge.
Pagán, V. 1999. 'Beyond Teutoburg: Transgression and Transformation in Tacitus, *Annales* 1.61–62', *CPh* 94, 302–20.
Palmer, R. E. A. 1965. 'The Censors of 312 B.C. and the State Religion', *Historia* 14, 293–324.
Paratore, E. 1971. 'Hercules et Cacus chez Virgile et Tite-Live,' in Bardon and Verdière 1971, 260–82.
Pasquali, G. 1920. *Orazio lirico*. Florence.
Paul, G. M. 1982. '*Urbs Capta*: Sketch of an Ancient Literary Motif', *Phoenix* 36, 143–55.
——— 1984. *A Historical Commentary on Sallust's Bellum Jugurthinum*. Liverpool.
Peek, W. 1955. *Griechische Vers-Inschriften*. Band I, *Grab-Epigramme*. Berlin.
Perkell, C. (ed.) 1999. *Reading Vergil's Aeneid*. Norman, Ok.
Peter, H. 1865. *Die Quellen Plutarchs in die Biographieen der Römer*. Halle.
——— 1902. 'Die Epochen in Varros Werk *De gente populi romani*', *RhM* 57, 231–51.
Peter, R. 1884–90. 'Hercules', in W. H. Roscher (ed.), *Ausführliches Lexikon der griechischen und römischen Mythologie*, vol. 1, 2901–3023. Leipzig.
Petrochilos, N. 1974. *Roman Attitudes to the Greeks*. Athens.
Pfeiffer, R. 1968. *History of Classical Scholarship: From the Beginning to the End of the Hellenistic Age*. Oxford.
Porte, D. 1985. *L'Étiologie religieuse dans les Fastes d'Ovide*. Paris.
Powell, A. (ed.) 1992. *Roman Poetry and Propaganda in the Age of Augustus*. London.
Purcell, N. 1990. 'The Creation of Provincial Landscape: the Roman impact on Cisalpine Gaul', in Blagg and Millett 1990, 5–29.
Putnam, M. C. J. 1961. 'The Art of Catullus 64', *HSCPh* 65, 165–205.
——— 1970. *Virgil's Pastoral Art. Studies in the Eclogues*. Princeton.
——— 1986. *Artifices of Eternity: Horace's Fourth Book of Odes*. Ithaca.
——— 1988. *The Poetry of the Aeneid*. 2nd edition. Ithaca.
——— 1989. 'Virgil and Tacitus, *Ann.* 1.10', *CQ* 39, 563–4.
——— 1998. *Virgil's Epic Designs: Ekphrasis in the Aeneid*. New Haven.
Quint, D. 1993. *Epic and Empire*. Princeton.
Raabe, H. 1974. *Plurima mortis imago: Vergleichende Interpretationen zur Bildersprache Vergils*. Munich.
Rawson, E. 1985. *Intellectual Life in the Late Roman Republic*. London.
——— 1985a. 'Cicero and the Areopagus', *Athenaeum* 63, 44–6.
——— 1991. *Roman Culture and Society: Collected Papers*. Oxford.
Reckford, K. J. 1960. 'The Eagle and the Tree (Horace, *Odes* 4.4)', *CJ* 56, 23–8.
Rehork, J. 1965. 'Tatenbericht und dichterisches Herrscher-Enkomion in augusteischer Zeit,' in Altheim and Stiehl 1965, 379–491.

Reynolds, L. D. (ed.) 1983. *Texts and Transmission: A Survey of the Latin Classics.* Oxford.
Ribbeck, O. 1881. 'Ein historisches Drama', *RhM* 36, 321–2.
Rich, J. 1997. 'Structuring Roman History: The Consular Year and the Roman Historical Tradition', *Histos* 1 (http://www.dur.ac.uk/Classics/histos/1997/rich1.html).
Richard, J.-C. 1983. *Pseudo-Aurélius Victor, Les origines du peuple romain.* Paris.
Richardson, L., Jr. 1976. *Propertius: Elegies I–IV.* Norman, Ok.
Ricoeur, P. 1988. *Time and Narrative.* Vol. 3. Chicago.
Ritter, S. 1995. *Hercules in der römischen Kunst von den Anfängen bis Augustus.* Heidelberg.
Robert, C. 1893. *Die Iliupersis des Polygnot.* Halle.
—— 1923–26. *Die griechische Heldensage, III.2.* Berlin.
Roberts, D. H., Dunn, F. M. and Fowler, D. P. (eds.) 1997. *Classical Closure. Reading the End in Greek and Latin Literature.* Princeton.
Rohde, E. 1891. 'Studien zur Chronologie der griechischen Literaturgeschichte', *RhM* 36, 524–75.
Roller, M. B. 1997. '*Color*-blindness: Cicero's death, declamation, and the production of history', *CPh* 92, 109–30.
Rosati, G. 1999. 'Form in Motion: Weaving the Text in the *Metamorphoses*', in Hardie, Barchiesi and Hinds 1999, 240–53.
Ross, D. O. 1975. *Backgrounds to Augustan Poetry: Gallus, Elegy and Rome.* Cambridge.
—— 1987. *Virgil's Elements. Physics and Poetry in the Georgics.* Princeton.
Rostagni, A. 1942. *Da Livio a Virgilio e da Virgilio a Livio.* Padua.
Rothstein, M. (ed.) 1920–4. *Die Elegien des Sextus Propertius I–II.* Berlin.
Rudd, N. 1976. *Lines of Enquiry.* Cambridge.
—— (ed.) 1993. *Horace 2000: a Celebration: Essays for the Bimillennium.* Bristol.
Sabin, P. 2000. 'The Face of Roman Battle', *JRS* 90, 1–17.
Sacks, K. S. 1981. *Polybius on the Writing of History.* Berkeley.
—— 1990. *Diodorus Siculus and the First Century.* Princeton.
Sadurska, A. 1964. *Les Tables Iliaques.* Warsaw.
Santirocco, M. 1986. *Unity and Design in Horace's Odes.* Chapel Hill.
Saunders, K. B. 1999. 'The Wounds in *Iliad* 13–16', *CQ* 49, 345–63.
Sauron, G. 1991. 'Les autels néo-attiques du théâtre d'Arles', in Étienne and Le Dinahet 1991, 205–16.
Scanlon, T. F. 1998. 'Reflexivity and Irony in the Proem of Sallust's *Histories*', in Deroux 1998, 186–224.
Schefold, K. 1975. *Wort und Bild: Studien zur Gegenwart der Antike.* Basel.
Scheid, J. and Svenbro, J. 1996. *The Craft of Zeus: Myths of Weaving and Fabric,* tr. C. Volk. Cambridge, Ma.
Scheller, P. 1911. *De hellenistica historiae conscribendae arte.* Diss. Leipzig.
Scherer, M. R. 1963. *The Legends of Troy in Art and Literature.* New York.
Schilling, R. 1942. 'L'Hercule romain en face de la réforme religieuse d'Auguste', *RPh* 16, 31–57.
Schlüter, W. 1999. 'The Battle of the Teutoburg Forest: Archaeological Research at Kalkriese near Osnabrück', in Creighton and Wilson 1999, 125–59.
Schmidt, E. A. 1972. *Poetische Reflexion. Vergils Bukolik.* Munich.
—— 1985. *Catull.* Heidelberg.
—— 1991. *Ovids Poetische Menschenwelt: Die Metamorphosen als Metapher und Symphonie.* Heidelberg.
Schmidt, E. G. (ed.) 1996. *Griechenland und Rom.* Tbilisi.
Schmidt, V. 1972. *Redeunt Saturnia Regna. Studien zu Vergils vierter Ecloga.* Delft.
Schmitthener, W. 1962. 'Augustus' Spanischer Feldzug und der Kampf um den Prinzipat', *Historia* 11, 29–85.
Schmitzer, U. 1990. *Zeitgeschichte in Ovids Metamorphosen. Mythologische Dichtung unter politischem Anspruch.* Stuttgart.
Schofield, M. 1986. 'Cicero For and Against Divination', *JRS* 76, 47–65.

Schubert, W. 1990. 'Zu Ovid, Trist. 3.9', *Gymnasium* 97, 154–64.
Schüller, W. (ed.) 1993. *Livius: Aspekte seines Werke*. Konstanz.
Scott, J. M. 1998. 'The Rhetoric of Suppressed Speech: Tacitus' Omission of Direct Discourse in his *Annals* as a Technique of Character Denigration', *AHB* 12, 8–18.
Scullard, H. H. 1981. *Festivals and Ceremonies of the Roman Republic*. London.
Seel, O. 1955. *Die Praefatio des Pompeius Trogus*. Erlangen.
Segal, C. 1969. 'Myth and Philosophy in the *Metamorphoses*: Ovid's Augustanism and the Augustan Conclusion of Book XV', *AJPh* 90, 257–92.
Shackleton Bailey, D.R. 1956. *Propertiana*. Cambridge.
—— (ed.) 1985. *Q. Horati Flacci Opera*. Stuttgart.
—— 1989 [1998]. 'Two Passages in Cicero's Letters,' *AJAH* 14, 70–2.
Sherwin-White, A. N. 1966. *The Letters of Pliny*. Oxford.
—— 1973. *The Roman Citizenship*. 2nd edition. Oxford.
Sinclair, P. 1995. *Tacitus the Sententious Historian: A Sociology of Rhetoric in Annales 1–6*. University Park, Pa.
Sirago, V. 1958. 'Lucanus an Apulus?' *AC* 27, 13–20.
Skidmore, C. 1996. *Practical Ethics for Roman Gentlemen: the Work of Valerius Maximus*. Exeter.
Skutsch, O. 1985. *The Annals of Quintus Ennius*. Oxford.
Small, J. P. 1982. *Cacus and Marsyas in Etrusco-Roman Legend*. Princeton.
Smith, R. R. R. 1988. '*Simulacra gentium*: the *ethne* from the Sebasteion at Aphrodisias', *JRS* 78, 50–77.
Smyth, W. R. 1970. *Thesaurus Criticus ad Sexti Properti Textum*. Leiden.
Snell, B. 1953. *The Discovery of the Mind*. tr. T. G. Rosenmeyer Oxford.
Solmsen, F. 1968–82. *Kleine Schriften*. 3 vols. Hildesheim.
Solodow, J. B. 1988. *The World of Ovid's Metamorphoses*. Chapel Hill.
Soubiran, J. 1964. 'Thèmes et rythmes d'Epopée dans les *Annales* de Tacite', *Pallas* 12, 55–79.
Spoerri, W. 1959. *Späthellenistische Berichte über Welt, Kultur und Götter*. Basel.
Stadter, P. 1972. 'The Structure of Livy's History', *Historia* 21, 287–307.
Stahl, H.-P. 1985. *Propertius: 'Love' and 'War': Individual and State under Augustus*. Berkeley.
—— (ed.) 1998. *Vergil's Aeneid: Augustan Epic and Political Context*. London.
Stanford, W. B. 1980. *Enemies of Poetry*. London.
Stansbury-O'Donnell, M. D. 1989. 'Polygnotos's *Iliupersis*: A New Reconstruction', *AJA* 93, 203–15.
Starr, R. J. 1981. 'The Scope and Genre of Velleius's History', *CQ* 31, 162–74.
Stavely, E. S. 1959. 'The Political Aims of Appius Claudius Caecus', *Historia* 8, 410–33.
Steinby, E. M. 1993–9. *Lexicon Topographicum urbis Romae*. 6 vols. Rome.
Stitz, M. 1962. *Ovid und Vergils Aeneis: Interpretation Met. 13.623–14.608*. Diss. Freiburg im Breisgau.
Syme, R. 1939. *The Roman Revolution*. Oxford.
—— 1958. *Tacitus*. 2 vols. Oxford.
—— 1959. 'Livy and Augustus', *HSCPh* 64, 27–87.
—— 1964. *Sallust*. Berkeley.
—— 1978. *History in Ovid*. Oxford.
—— 1979–91. *Roman Papers*, eds. E. Badian and A. R. Birley. 7 vols. Oxford.
—— 1986. *The Augustan Aristocracy*. Oxford.
Syndikus, H. P. 1972–3. *Die Lyrik des Horaz. Eine Interpretation der Oden*. 2 vols. Darmstadt.
Tarpin, M. 1998. 'L'Italie, la Sicile, and le Sardaigne', in Lepelley 1998, 1–70.
Tarrant, R. J. 1983. 'Horace', in Reynolds 1983, 182–6.
—— 1997. 'Aspects of Virgil's Reception in Antiquity', in Martindale 1997, 56–72.
—— 1998. 'Parenthetically Speaking (in Virgil and other Poets)', in Knox and Foss 1998, 141–57.

Taylor, L. R. 1934. 'Varro's *De Gente Populi Romani*', *CPh* 29, 221–9.
—— 1960. *The Voting Districts of the Roman Republic*. Rome.
Thomas, R. F. 1982. *Lands and Peoples in Roman Poetry: the Ethnographical Tradition.* Cambridge.
—— 1983. 'Callimachus, the Victoria Berenices, and Roman Poetry', *CQ* 33, 92–113.
—— 1986. 'Virgil's *Georgics* and the Art of Reference', *HSCPh* 90, 171–98.
—— 1988. *Virgil: Georgics*. Cambridge.
Thomas, Y. 1996. *'Origine' et 'commune patrie.' Étude de droit public romain (89 av. J.-C.–212 ap. J.C.)*. Rome.
Tissol, G. 1997. *The Face of Nature: Wit, Narrative and Cosmic Origins in Ovid's Metamorphoses.* Princeton.
Toll, K. 1991. 'The *Aeneid* as an Epic of National Identity: *Italiam laeto socii clamore salutant*', *Helios* 18, 3–14.
—— 1997. 'Making Roman-ness and the *Aeneid*', *ClAnt* 16, 34–56.
Torelli, M. 1995. *Studies in the Romanization of Italy.* Edmonton.
—— 1996. 'Riflessioni sulle registrazioni storiche in Etruria', *Eutopia* 5.1–2, 13–22.
—— 1999. *Tota Italia*. Oxford.
Torraca, L. 1988. *Duride di Samo: la maschera scenica nella storiografia ellenistica.* Salerno.
Tränkle, H. 1960. *Die Sprachkunst des Properz und die Tradition der lateinischen Dichtersprache.* Wiesbaden.
Treloar, A. 1969. 'Horace, *Odes* i 12.35', *Antichthon* 3, 48–51.
—— 1972. 'Horace, *Odes* i 12. 33–6: A Reply', *Antichthon* 6, 60–2.
—— 1973. 'Horace, *Odes* i 12 yet again: A Rejoinder', *Antichthon* 7, 60–1.
Turner, E. G. 1987. *Greek Manuscripts of the Ancient World*. 2nd edition, rev. P. J. Parsons. Oxford.
Ullman, B. L. 1942. 'History and tragedy', *TAPhA* 73, 25–53.
Urban, R. 1979. 'Tacitus und die Res Gestae divi Augusti. Die Auseinandersetzung des Historikers mit der offiziellen Darstellung,' *Gymnasium* 86, 59–74.
Ussani, V. 1950. 'Eschilo e il libro II dell' *Eneide*', *Maia* 3, 237–54.
Valgiglio, E. 1976. 'Varrone in Plutarco', in *Atti del congresso internazionale di studi varroniani*, volume 2, 571–95. Rieti.
Van Sickle, J. 1980. 'The Book-Roll and Some Conventions of the Poetic Book', *Arethusa* 13, 5–41.
—— 1992. *A Reading of Virgil's Messianic Eclogue*. New York.
Vasaly, A. 1987. 'Personality and Power: Livy's Depiction of the Appii Claudii in the First Pentad', *TAPhA* 117, 203–26.
—— 1993. *Representations. Images of the World in Ciceronian Oratory*. Berkeley.
—— 1999. 'The Quinctii in Livy's First Pentad: The Rhetoric of Anti-Rhetoric', *CW* 92, 513–30.
Verdin, H., Schepens, G. and De Keyser, E. (eds.) 1990. *Purposes of History: Studies in Greek Historiography from the 4th to the 2nd Centuries B.C.* Leuven.
Vian, F. 1959. *Recherches sur les Posthomerica de Quintus de Smyrne*. Paris.
Vretska, K. 1976. *Sallust: De Catilinae Coniuratione*. Heidelberg.
Walbank, F. W. 1955. 'Tragic History: a reconsideration', *BICS* 2, 4–14.
—— 1957. *A Historical Commentary on Polybius*. Volume 1. Oxford.
—— 1960. 'History and Tragedy', *Historia* 9, 216–34.
—— 1974. '*Symploke*: Its Role in Polybius' *Histories*', *YClS* 24, 197–212.
Walker, B. 1952. *The Annals of Tacitus: A Study in the Writing of History*. Manchester.
—— 1991. 'Virgilian Elements in Tacitus' Historical Imagination', *ANRW* II 33.4, 2987–3004.
Walker, S. and A. Burnett. 1981. 'Augustus and Tiberius on the "Sword of Tiberius"', in *Augustus: Handlist of the Exhibition and Supplementary Studies*. London.
Wallace-Hadrill, A. 1987. 'Time for Augustus: Ovid, Augustus and the *Fasti*,' in Whitby, Hardie and Whitby 1987, 221–30.

—— 1997. '*Mutatio morum*: The Idea of a Cultural Revolution', in Habinek and Schiesaro 1997, 3–22.

Walsh, P. G. 1961. *Livy. His Historical Aims and Methods*. Cambridge.

—— 1974. *Livy*. Oxford.

—— 1992. *Livy: Book XXXVII (191–189 B.C.)*. Warminster.

Wardle, D. 1998. *Valerius Maximus: Memorable Deeds and Sayings Book 1*. Oxford.

Wardman, A. 1974. *Plutarch's Lives*. London.

Waszink, J. H. 1948. 'Vergil and the Sibyl of Cumae', *Mnemosyne* series 4.1, 43–58.

Weinreich, O. 1948. Epigrammstudien I: *Epigramm und Pantomimus*. Heidelberg.

Weinstock, S. 1971. *Divus Julius*. Oxford.

Weitzmann, K. 1959. *Ancient Book Illumination*. Cambridge, Ma.

Welch, K. 1998. 'Caesar and his Officers in the Gallic War Commentaries', in Welch and Powell 1998, 85–110.

Welch, K. and Powell, A. (eds.) 1998. *Julius Caesar as Artful Reporter: The War Commentaries as Political Instruments*. London.

West, D. 1975–76. '*Cernere erat*: the Shield of Aeneas', *PVS* 15, 1–6.

—— 1998. *Horace Odes II: Vatis Amici*. Cambridge.

—— 1998a. 'The end and the meaning. *Aeneid* 12.791–842', in Stahl 1998, 303–18.

West, D. and Woodman, A. J. (eds.) 1979. *Creative Imitation in Latin Literature*. Cambridge.

Wheeler, S. M. 1993. 'Changing Names: The Miracle of Iphis in Ovid, *Metamorphoses* 9', *Phoenix* 51, 190–202.

—— 1999. *A Discourse of Wonders: Audience and Performance in Ovid's Metamorphoses*. Philadelphia.

—— 2000. *Narrative Dynamics in Ovid's Metamorphoses*. Tübingen.

Whitby, M., Hardie, P. R. and Whitby M. (eds.) 1987. *Homo Viator*. Bristol.

White, H. 1987. *The Content of the Form: Narrative Discourse and Historical Representation*. Baltimore.

White, P. 1993. *Promised Verse: Poets in the Society of Augustan Rome*. Cambridge, Ma.

Wickkiser, B. L. 1999. 'Famous Last Words: Putting Ovid's Sphragis back into the *Metamorphoses*', *MD* 42, 113–42.

Wiedemann, T. 1979. '*Nunc ad inceptum redeo*: Sallust, *Jugurtha* 4.9 and Cato', *LCM* 4, 13–16.

Wiencke, M. 1954. 'An Epic Theme in Greek Art', *AJA* 58, 285–306.

Wifstrand Schiebe, M. 1981. *Das ideale Dasein bei Tibull und die Goldzeitkonzeption Vergils*. Uppsala.

—— 1997. *Vergil und die Tradition von den römischen Urkönigen*. Stuttgart.

Wigodsky, M. 1972. *Vergil and Early Latin Poetry*. Wiesbaden.

Wilamowitz-Moellendorff, U. von 1906. *Die Textgeschichte der griechischen Bukoliker*. Berlin.

—— 1924. *Hellenistische Dichtung in der Zeit des Kallimachos*. 2 vols. Berlin.

Wilkins, A. T. 1994. *Villain or Hero: Sallust's Portrayal of Catiline*. New York.

Wilkinson, L. P. 1951. *Horace and his Lyric Poetry*. 2nd edition. Cambridge.

—— 1958. 'The World of Ovid's *Metamorphoses*,' in Herescu 1958, 231–44.

Williams, G. 1974. 'A Version of Pastoral: Virgil, *Eclogue* 4', in Woodman and West 1974, 31–46.

Williams, R. D. 1960. *Virgil: Aeneid V*. Oxford.

—— 1963. 'Virgil and the *Odyssey*', *Phoenix* 17, 266–74.

Willcock, M. 1983. 'Battle Scenes in the *Aeneid*', *PCPhS* 29, 87–99.

Wimmel, W. 1973. '*Hirtenkrieg*' und arkadisches Rom. Reduktionsmedien in Vergils Aeneis*. Munich.

Winter, J. G. 1910. *The Myth of Hercules at Rome*. New York.

Wiseman, T. P. 1979. *Clio's Cosmetics: Three Studies in Greco-Roman Literature*. Leicester.

—— 1987. *Roman Studies: Literary and Historical*. Liverpool.

—— 1993. 'Lying Historians: Seven Types of Mendacity', in Gill and Wiseman 1993, 122–46.

—— 1994. *Historiography and Imagination: Eight Essays on Roman Culture*. Exeter.

—— 1998. *Roman Drama and Roman History*. Exeter.

Wissowa, G. 1912. *Religion und Kultus der Römer*. 2nd edition. Munich.

Witte, K. 1910. 'Über die Form der Darstellung in Livius' Geschichtswerk', *RhM* 65, 270–305, 359–419.

Woodman, A. J. 1975. 'Questions of Date, Genre and Style in Velleius: Some Literary Answers', *CQ* 25, 272–306.

—— 1977. *Velleius Paterculus. The Tiberian Narrative (2.94–131)*. Cambridge

—— 1979. 'Self-Imitation and the Substance of History: Tacitus, *Annals* 1.61–5 and *Histories* 2.70, 5.14–15,' in West and Woodman 1979, 143–55.

—— 1983. *Velleius Paterculus: The Caesarian and Augustan Narrative (2.41–93)*. Cambridge.

—— 1988. *Rhetoric in Classical Historiography: Four Studies*. London.

—— 1989. 'Virgil the Historian: *Aeneid* 8.626–62 and Livy', in Diggle, Hall and Jocelyn 1989, 132–45.

—— 1998. 'Propertius and Livy,' *CQ* 48, 568–9.

Woodman, A. J. and Powell, J. G. F. (eds.) 1992. *Author and Audience in Latin Literature*. Cambridge.

Woodman, A. J. and West, D. (eds.) 1974. *Quality and Pleasure in Latin Poetry*. Cambridge.

—— (eds.) 1984. *Poetry and Politics in the Age of Augustus*. Cambridge.

Zanker, P. 1968. *Forum Augustum. Das Bildprogramm*. Tübingen.

—— 1987 *Augustus und die Macht der Bilder*. Munich.

—— 1988. *The Power of Images in the Age of Augustus* (Translation of Zanker 1987). Ann Arbor.

Zecchini, G. 1987. *Il Carmen de Bello Actiaco: storiographica e lotta politica in età augustea*. Stuttgart.

Zetzel, J. E. G. 1980. 'Horace's *Liber Sermonum*: The Structure of Ambiguity', *Arethusa* 13, 59–77.

—— 1989. 'Romane Memento: Justice and Judgment in *Aeneid* 6', *TAPhA* 119, 263–84.

—— 1995. *Cicero De re publica: Selections*. Cambridge.

—— 1997. 'Rome and its Traditions', in Martindale 1997, 188–203.

Zorzetti, N. 1980. *La pretesta e il teatro latino arcaico*. Naples.

INDEX OF PASSAGES DISCUSSED

GENERAL INDEX

LIST OF CONTRIBUTORS

Clifford Ando, Assistant Professor of Classics, University of Southern California.

Rhiannon Ash, Lecturer in Greek and Latin, University College London.

Francis Cairns, Professor of Classical Languages, Florida State University.

C. J. Classen, Emeritus Professor of Classical Philology, Georg-August-Universität, Göttingen.

Cynthia Damon, Assistant Professor of Classics, Amherst College.

Andrew Feldherr, Assistant Professor of Classics, Princeton University.

Philip Hardie, Reader in Latin Literature and Fellow of New Hall, Cambridge.

Stratis Kyriakidis, Associate Professor of Latin, Aristotle University of Thessaloniki.

D. S. Levene, Professor of Latin Language and Literature, University of Leeds.

Marko Marinčič, Lecturer in Latin, University of Ljubljana.

Hans-Friedrich Mueller, Assistant Professor of Classics, University of Florida.

D. P. Nelis, Professor of Latin, Trinity College Dublin.

Ellen O'Gorman, Lecturer in Classics, University of Bristol.

V. E. Pagán, Assistant Professor of Classics, University of Wisconsin-Madison.

Molly Pasco-Pranger, Assistant Professor of Classics, University of Puget Sound.

Andreola Rossi, Assistant Professor of the Classics, Harvard University.

Ann Vasaly, Associate Professor of Classical Studies, Boston University.

Stephen M. Wheeler, Associate Professor of Classics, Pennsylvania State University.

T. P. Wiseman, Professor of Classics, University of Exeter.

SUPPLEMENTS TO MNEMOSYNE

EDITED BY H. PINKSTER, H.S. VERSNEL,

D.M. SCHENKEVELD, P. H. SCHRIJVERS and S.R. SLINGS

Recent volumes in the series

171. BAKKER, E.J. (ed.). *Grammar as Interpretation*. Greek Literature in its Linguistic Contexts. 1997. ISBN 90 04 10730 4
172. GRAINGER, J.D. *A Seleukid Prosopography and Gazetteer*. 1997. ISBN 90 04 10799 1
173. GERBER, D.E. (ed.). *A Companion to the Greek Lyric Poets*. 1997. ISBN 90 04 09944 1
174. SANDY, G. *The Greek World of Apuleius*. Apuleius and the Second Sophistic. 1997. ISBN 90 04 10821 1
175. ROSSUM-STEENBEEK, M. VAN. *Greek Readers' Digests?* Studies on a Selection of Sub-literary Papyri. 1998. ISBN 90 04 10953 6
176. McMAHON, J.M. *Paralysin Cave*. Impotence, Perception, and Text in the *Satyrica* of Petronius. 1998. ISBN 90 04 10825 4
177. ISAAC, B. *The Near East under Roman Rule*. Selected Papers. 1998. ISBN 90 04 10736 3
178. KEEN, A.G. *Dynastic Lycia*. A Political History of the Lycians and Their Relations with Foreign Powers, c. 545-362 B.C. 1998. ISBN 90 04 10956 0
179. GEORGIADOU, A. & D.H.J. LARMOUR. *Lucian's Science Fiction Novel* True Histories. Interpretation and Commentary. 1998. ISBN 90 04 10667 7
180. GÜNTHER, H.-C. *Ein neuer metrischer Traktat und das Studium der pindarischen Metrik in der Philologie der Paläologenzeit*. 1998. ISBN 90 04 11008 9
181. HUNT, T.J. *A Textual History of Cicero's* Academici Libri. 1998. ISBN 90 04 10970 6
182. HAMEL, D. *Athenian Generals*. Military Authority in the Classical Period. 1998. ISBN 90 04 10900 5
183. WHITBY, M. (ed.). *The Propaganda of Power*. The Role of Panegyric in Late Antiquity. 1998. ISBN 90 04 10571 9
184. SCHRIER, O.J. *The* Poetics *of Aristotle and the* Tractatus Coislinianus. A Bibliography from about 900 till 1996. 1998. ISBN 90 04 11132 8
185. SICKING, C.M.J. *Distant Companions*. Selected Papers. 1998. ISBN 90 04 11054 2
186. P.H. SCHRIJVERS. *Lucrèce et les Sciences de la Vie*. 1999. ISBN 90 04 10230 2
187. BILLERBECK M. (Hrsg.). *Seneca*. Hercules Furens. Einleitung, Text, Übersetzung und Kommentar. 1999. ISBN 90 04 11245 6
188. MACKAY, E.A. (ed.). *Signs of Orality*. The Oral Tradition and Its Influence in the Greek and Roman World. 1999. ISBN 90 04 11273 1
189. ALBRECHT, M. VON. *Roman Epic*. An Interpretative Introduction. 1999. ISBN 90 04 11292 8
190. Hout, M.P.J. van den. *A Commentary on the Letters of M. Cornelius Fronto*. 1999. ISBN 90 04 10957 9
191. Kraus, C. Shuttleworth (ed.). *The Limits of Historiography*. Genre and Narrative in Ancient Historical Texts. 1999. ISBN 90 04 10670 7
192. Lomas, K. & T. Cornell. *Cities and Urbanisation in Ancient Italy*. ISBN 90 04 10808 4 *In preparation*
193. Tsetskhladze, G.R. (ed). *History of Greek Colonisation and Settlement Overseas*. 2 vols. ISBN 90 04 09843 7 *In preparation*
194. Wood, S.E. *Imperial Women*. A Study in Public Images, 40 B.C. - A.D. 68. 1999. ISBN 90 04 11281 2
195. Ophuijsen, J.M. van & P. Stork. *Linguistics into Interpretation*. Speeches of War in Herodotus VII 5 & 8-18. 1999. ISBN 90 04 11455 6
196. Tsetskhladze, G.R. (ed.). *Ancient Greeks West and East*. 1999. ISBN 90 04 11190 5
197. Pfeijffer, I.L. *Three Aeginetan Odes of Pindar*. A Commentary on *Nemean* V, *Nemean* III, & *Pythian* VIII. 1999. ISBN 90 04 11381 9
198. Horsfall, N. *Virgil*, Aeneid 7. A Commentary. 2000. ISBN 90 04 10842 4
199. Irby-Massie, G.L. *Military Religion in Roman Britain*. 1999. ISBN 90 04 10848 3
200. Grainger, J.D. *The League of the Aitolians*. 1999. ISBN 90 04 10911 0
201. Adrados, F.R. *History of the Graeco-Roman Fable*. I: Introduction and from the Origins to the Hellenistic Age. Translated by L.A. Ray. Revised and Updated by the Author and Gert-Jan van Dijk. 1999. ISBN 90 04 11454 8
202. Grainger, J.D. *Aitolian Prosopographical Studies*. 2000. ISBN 90 04 11350 9
203. Solomon, J. *Ptolemy* Harmonics. Translation and Commentary. 2000. ISBN 90 04 115919

204. WIJSMAN, H.J.W. *Valerius Flaccus,* Argonautica, *Book VI.* A Commentary. 2000. ISBN 90 04 11718 0

205. Mader, G. *Josephus and the Politics of Historiography.* Apologetic and Impression Management in the *Bellum Judaicum.* 2000. ISBN 90 04 11446 7

206. Nauta, R.R. *Poetry for Patrons.* Literary Communication in the Age of Domitian. 2001. ISBN 90 04 10885 8

207. Adrados, F.R. *History of the Graeco-Roman Fable.* II: The Fable during the Roman Empire and in the Middle Ages. Translated by L.A. Ray. Revised and Updated by the Author and Gert-Jan van Dijk. 2000. ISBN 90 04 11583 8

208. James, A. & K. Lee. *A Commentary on Quintus of Smyrna,* Posthomerica V. 2000. ISBN 90 04 11594 3

209. Derderian, K. *Leaving Words to Remember.* Greek Mourning and the Advent of Literacy. 2001. ISBN 90 04 11750 4

210. Shorrock, R. *The Challenge of Epic.* Allusive Engagement in the *Dionysiaca* of Nonnus. 2001. ISBN 90 04 11795 4

211. Scheidel, W. (ed.). *Debating Roman Demography.* 2001. ISBN 90 04 11525 0

212. Keulen, A.J. *L. Annaeus Seneca* Troades. Introduction, Text and Commentary. 2001. ISBN 90 04 12004 1

213. Morton, J. *The Role of the Physical Environment in Ancient Greek Seafaring.* 2001. ISBN 90 04 11717 2

214. Graham, A.J. *Collected Papers on Greek Colonization.* 2001. ISBN 90 04 11634 6

215. Grossardt, P. *Die Erzählung von Meleagros.* Zur literarischen Entwicklung der kalydonischen Kultlegende 2001. ISBN 90 04 11952 3

216. Zafiropoulos, C.A. *Ethics in Aesop's Fables: The* Augustana *Collection.* 2001. ISBN 90 04 11867 5

217. Rengakos, A. & T.D. Papanghelis (eds.). *A Companion to Apollonius Rhodius.* 2001. ISBN 90 04 11752 0

218. Watson, J. *Speaking Volumes.* Orality and Literacy in the Greek and Roman World. 2001. ISBN 90 04 12049 1

219. MacLeod, L. *Dolos and Dike in Sophokles' Elektra.* 2001. ISBN 90 04 11898 5

220. McKinley, K.L. *Reading the Ovidian Heroine.* "Metamorphoses" Commentaries 1100-1618. 2001. ISBN 90 04 11796 2

221. Reeson, J. *Ovid* Heroides *11, 13 and 14.* A Commentary. 2001. ISBN 90 04 12140 4

222. Fried, M.N. & S. Unguru. *Apollonius of Perga's Conica:* Text, Context, Subtext. 2001. ISBN 90 04 11977 9

223. Livingstone, N. *A Commentary on Isocrates' Busiris.* 2001. ISBN 90 04 12143 9

224. Levene, D.S. & D.P. Nelis (eds.). *Clio and the Poets.* Augustan Poetry and the Traditions of Ancient Historiography. 2002. ISBN 90 04 11782 2

225. Wooten, C.W. *The Orator in Action and Theory in Greece and Rome.* 2001. ISBN 90 04 12213 3

226. Galán Vioque, G. *Martial, Book VII. A Commentary.* 2001. ISBN 90 04 12338 5

227. Lefèvre, E. *Die Unfähigkeit, sich zu erkennen: Sophokles' Tragödien.* 2001. ISBN 90 04 12322 9

228. Scheidel, W. *Death on the Nile.* Disease and the Demography of Roman Egypt. 2001. ISBN 90 04 12323 7